Think Rest & Pray

Daily readings that will build your faith all year round

Think Rest & Pray

GEOFF FEASEY

New Life Publishing Co

New Life Publishing Co

Nottingham, England

First published in the UK, 2003

ISBN 0-953610-08-X

Printed by Cox & Wyman Ltd, Reading, Berks.

Geoff Feasey's first book 'Putting Things Into Perspective' has sold right across the UK and in several other countries too. It is available from Christian bookshops and also during his seminars and conferences. The book was also published in Italian in 2002.

Dedication

This book is dedicated to three people
and their husbands.

Firstly, it is dedicated to my sister, Marjorie, and
her husband, Richard.
Secondly, it is dedicated to my two sisters-in-law, Doreena
and Media, and their husbands, Winslow and Bob.

These three people and their husbands have been a great
help and support to my wife, Carole, and me
during the past few difficult years.

Thanks so much for all your help.

Acknowledgements

My grateful thanks go to those who have helped me in the preparation of this daily devotional book. Help has been given in the form of proof reading, positive critical comment, and instructional insight.

My thanks must also go to Dr R T Kendall for his reading and analysis of my work and his very kind Foreword.

Many thanks also to John Glass, Paul C Weaver and Bobby Ball, for their comments that are recorded on the back cover.

My thanks especially must be recorded to the 'one' who has had endless patience with me during the writing of this work – which has been fitted in during very odd hours of the day and night. Carole has put up with me disappearing into the world of the computer for hours on end.

My very grateful thanks to you all.

Geoff Feasey

FOREWORD

This is an unusual devotional book. It is not every day that one comes across an opportunity to draw close to God by heart-felt praying and also stretching of the mind. Usually it is one or the other that is available. To mix resting in God with a helpful word study is a welcome discipline that every Christian should embrace, every day. This book indeed presents a wonderful combination.

I was not prepared for how much I would enjoy and admire this book. The Rev Geoff Feasey has performed a valuable service for the Church generally that can, therefore, make not only those in his own denomination proud, but those outside of his denomination appreciative as well. This book should cross all theological and ecclesiastical lines; the reader will profit, no matter what one's theology or Church background. What is more, the youngest Christian could use this as an introduction to his or her new faith, and yet the most seasoned believer will be amazed, day after day, by how much there is to learn.

Geoff Feasey is a highly respected minister in the Elim Pentecostal Church. He is the regional superintendent of the North East Region of Great Britain. My own association with Elim goes back over 25 years, when I first began preaching among their churches with a great sense of being loved and accepted. I myself have been described as a 'closet Pentecostal' and I plead guilty!

I pray that this devotional book will not only have widespread acceptance but that everyone who uses it will be continually blessed and drawn closer to the Lord. Geoff shows that, when used simply (as he consistently does), the ancient Greek language of the New Testament is neither boring, nor tedious, but exciting. It is a privilege to write the Foreword for this lovely devotional book.

Dr R T Kendall
Key Largo, Florida

Introduction

Several years ago, a well-known chocolate company wanted to re-invent their product and ultimately produced a new slogan. The slogan became so well known that as soon as the words were heard, the brand, the colour and the taste came quickly to mind. The product is now so widely embraced that even in Third World countries the confectionary is loved and consumed.

The slogan consisted of an all-embracing message that sought to cover every aspect of our lives, stating that this chocolate bar would help us to 'work, rest and play'. We believed it and we bought it and then we consumed it, and the rest, as they say, is history.

I have borrowed from the slogan and adapted it so that this book of daily meditations seeks to:

Stimulate the mind to ***think****,*

Cause you to ***rest*** *in the Word and,*

Finally bring you to a place where you can ***pray*** *and praise.*

In other words, it is meant to help you to 'Think, Rest and Pray'.

The New Testament was written in Greek, and during its translation into English some of the true meaning of the words has been lost. And in some cases where there was no direct translation for a particular word the translators settled for the nearest equivalent. There were also occasions when the writers brought two or more different Greek words together to emphasise a certain truth; it was as if they 'invented' new words to convey fresh truth.

For each day of the year, I have sought to bring a word that will help the full meaning of certain words and Scriptures to 'flow through' and bring fresh insight into our everyday world. At times I have used one text and sought to search its meaning, which has taken several days, or sometimes a whole week, to study and consider. This fresh approach and insight should stimulate our 'pure minds by way of remembrance', causing us to think, rest and pray, and then to seek the Lord while He is near. I trust that new Christians will find help and encouragement from these thoughts and I trust too, that preachers and teachers will find inspiration and help from the fresh insight into New Testament Greek words.

There are many and varied daily devotional books on the shelves of Christian bookshops, however, I commend these daily pages to you with the prayer that each day will be fresh, new and inspiring. May God bless you greatly as you 'Think, Rest and Pray'.

January 1st

KEY WORD: **Key**

KEY VERSE: **Luke 11 : 52**

"Woe to you experts in the law, because you have taken away the 'key of knowledge'. You yourselves have not entered, and you have hindered those who were entering."

Jesus used words that were very strong and very confrontational when He approached the whole subject of truth and the way that the experts and teachers in the law had hidden truth from the ordinary people. He was scathing in His condemnation of the fact that they had hidden from the people the 'key of knowledge'. God wants His people to know truth as the truth always sets you free and brings you into liberty. No one should hide truth and everyone ought to help each other in the discovery of truth. This is why God has placed in the Church all the ministry gifts necessary to bring truth into light and to bring hidden truth to discovery.

This new daily devotional book seeks each day to reveal truth that might be hidden due to the changes in the meanings of words over the centuries of use. It also seeks to bring the original Greek language, which is a difficult language but a very creative and inventive one, into everyday use.

Each day we shall consider a Greek word which will be a *'key word'* and it will have its context in the Scriptures as a *'key verse'*. Following the *'key verse'* of Scripture there will be a daily aspect of teaching which will seek to uncover the truth of the *'key word'* and bring its relevance to our everyday lives.

Following this daily devotional teaching there will be a *'key prayer'* and a place for a *'key thought'* for your own journal and daily notes. In this way daily Bible study will be consistent and systematic and ought to produce thinking that is clear and profitable for each one of us. The whole concept of this new daily devotional is to reveal hidden keys of truth.

The Greek word for 'key' is the word '*kleis*' which literally means 'a key', and its New Testament use is mainly metaphorical, which means that it is used for the description of 'a key' rather than an 'actual key'. We find in New Testament writings the 'keys of the kingdom' which is a metaphorical picture of authority and power. We also find the 'the keys of death and hell' which again is a picture of the authority of Jesus over life and death.

In the key verse today, Jesus was talking about the 'key of knowledge', which again is not a literal key but a symbolical key of God's revealed knowledge to His people.

As we study each day my prayer is that you will discover more and more truth and that in the discovering of the keys of truth you will also discover more of God's will for your life and ministry. This discovery is vital as it will bring you to a place of fulfilment and confidence in God and will be a spiritual satisfaction to your life and service.

May God bless you as you 'Think, Rest and Pray' throughout this whole year.

My Journal

KEY PRAYER

Heavenly Father, I thank you today for truth and for the way that it brings hidden things into light. Help me to learn more and more of you throughout this year and help me to discover more and more about myself. As I read these pages each day I pledge to seek your face and I promise to bring my life under your Lordship and control.

January 2nd

KEY WORD: **Potter**

KEY VERSE: **Romans 9 : 21**

Does not the potter have the right to make out of the same lump of clay some pottery for noble purposes and some for common use?

The whole nature of the potter and the clay is a very descriptive one in the Bible. How many times have sermons been preached on this subject with great blessing? It serves to show just who God really is and just how weak and feeble we are without Him. It also serves to show us just how little we can do without Him too. On this second day of the new year this lesson is one that we need to re-learn again and again.

In the New Testament however the emphasis in the Greek word for 'potter' is not just that of a worker in clay or a worker of art, as it is in the Hebrew Old Testament. The word used is the word *'kerameus'*, which is a word that is derived from two words meaning 'to mix' or to 'use clay'. The emphasis being on the act of the potter rather than the potter himself. This use is deliberate as it seeks to bring the emphasis upon what the potter achieves, it seeks to illustrate the potter's power and authority over a piece of clay. This is what Paul was stating in this key verse in Romans 9, the potter has the right to do whatever he likes when he is casting clay on to the wheel. He can make a worthy vessel or an unworthy vessel, he can use the clay for good purposes or for common purposes. It is quite up to him.

Paul was seeking to show that God – the master potter – has complete and utter sovereignty over us and that He can do just whatever He wants with us. It is vital that we remember this when we pray and when we worship.

The word is used very sparingly in the New Testament, just three times in this form, and its little use gives it an even greater power as in its limited use it gives no occasion for doubt or interpretation. When you have words being used over and over again there is the opportunity for interpretation and opposing views. However, when there is such limitation upon use it serves to allow no such luxury.

What we have then is a situation where the potter – God in this reference – has absolute and total power over the clay, and His right was being declared by Paul to do whatever He requires with the mix of the clay and with its use. We need to understand however that in New Testament terms God is a God of love, a God of infinite patience and a God of eternal grace. Whatever He does with His vessels, it is done out of a desire to see us prosper and a desire to see us grow into the image of His Son. Therefore, all that takes place during the mixing and the moulding is to allow His grace to be applied to our lives, and, remember, during the mixing, the moulding and the shaping, the clay never leaves the potter's hands. He is always at work within our lives.

My Journal

KEY PRAYER

Heavenly Father, I pause today to thank you for the way in which you, as the heavenly potter, keep working within my life. All my problems are when I assert my own will and seek to follow the dictates of my own heart. My best days are when I allow you your way in my life and when I follow your will for my life. Help me to keep learning this lesson over and over again during this new year.

January 3rd

KEY WORD: **Fellowship**

KEY VERSE: **Acts 2 : 42**

They devoted themselves to the apostles' teaching and to the fellowship, to the breaking of bread and to prayer.

The Greek word *'koinonia'* has become a very fashionable word in recent years. It has been preached and practised - in a measure - by many churches and by many groups. The word translated means 'fellowship' or 'communion' and 'sharing in common', and it has become the 'in word' in many church circles. It appears in this key verse today because it was a foundational part of the New Testament life style.

The reason for the increase in the use of this word today is the rising need to find a deeper level of fellowship by many churches. We have 'cell churches', we have 'house groups' and we have 'home fellowships' all striving to break out of the routine of church life into a new function of fellowship. The structure of some churches has changed, in order to facilitate meetings of smaller groups in homes that foster fellowship and impact people's lives in a greater way than the usual traditional structure of mid-week meetings.

I well remember my early days in one of my pastorates. The church was a 'down town', city-centre church, and one member asked me if I had been to visit another member yet. I could not bring to mind the person that was being talked about and the description did not help very much. The person being described rejoiced under the all-embracing term of 'her with the red hat who sits on the left'. It transpired that both these people had been in church for many years. Both were members who had broken bread, worshipped and prayed in the same building, yet names were not known and probably no conversation had ever taken place, as the one who was questioning me normally sat on the right-hand side of the building. In church, but not in relationship.

'Koinonia' carries with it the impact of mutual contribution and all things in common. It appears in Romans 15 : 26 when the Macedonian Church made a contribution to the poor saints in Jerusalem. It carries the impact of caring for others, reaching out to those in need and giving beyond yourself. However, *'koinonia'* also means communion in the sense of bonding with one another and trust in relationship. Normally our understanding of fellowship is fairly superficial. It is quite possible to be in worship, in prayer and even in church without really developing any bond of trust. Smaller groups can help in the development of relationships, but there has to be a personal decision to enter into relationships with others.

Fellowship and relationship are both costly in terms of trust and giving. At the beginning of another year it would be good to set out on a course of action that brings you into a relationship with others and which will produce fellowship that is deep and pure and more meaningful.

My Journal

KEY PRAYER

Heavenly Father, please help me to cultivate a depth of fellowship with others that goes beyond the normal understanding of friendship. Help me when this course of action leaves me vulnerable, and please help me to understand that 'we all need each other' and that 'church' means people not just activities. I give thanks now for all who have been instrumental in bringing me to the place where I am today, and I rejoice in my friends who care for me.

January 4th

KEY WORD: **Restoring**

KEY VERSE: **1 Peter 5 : 10**

The God of all grace, who called you to His eternal glory..., after you have suffered a little while, will Himself restore you and make you strong, firm and steadfast.

One of the most beautiful words in the whole of the New Testament is found in today's key verse, 1 Peter 5, when Peter was teaching the Church on the whole problem of suffering. In verse 10 he stated that suffering is only for a while and that when the pain and anguish have passed we will be restored, strong and firm.

In Peter's teaching - quite late in life - he brought back to his remembrance a scene that took place in his very early development as a disciple. Peter, James and John were mending their fishing nets when Jesus passed by. Turning to them He called them to a far higher occupation: that of fishing for men. They then 'forsook all to follow Him'.

When dealing with the whole aspect of prayer, Peter returned to that scene in an effort to convey just what is taking place when we travel through a period of suffering. He used the Greek word '*katartizo*' which is the same word that was used for the mending of nets by the shores of Galilee. So from this teaching on suffering we learn that while we are going through pain, uncertainty or sorrow, using the basis of this word, we see that the God of all grace is mending our nets.

In order to fully understand what Peter was seeking to say, we would have to understand fishing during the time of Jesus. Net mending was a major exercise first thing in the morning following a night of fishing, especially if the catch was large. Nets would be torn and tangled, twisted and knotted, and it was a major undertaking to 'put the nets back into effective order'.

The exercise would involve a measure of pulling, stretching, tying and untying, sewing and mending, and as Peter sought to convey what God did during a period of suffering he could explain it no better than 'net mending'. God sometimes stretches us, unties knots and pulls our lives back into shape, which eventually produces a far more effective Christian life. Suffering, in other words, is good for us. I remember spending time with an elderly man during a time of tremendous suffering in which there was pain and, at times, total disillusionment in what was happening to him. He could not understand why he was suffering this way – a common problem to us all during times of distress. Yet I can recall that there were times of great fellowship when I sat beside his bed and he was a blessing to me as we talked of the goodness of the Lord. It reminded me of the life of Job when he stated, in spite of total loss, 'I know that my redeemer lives'.

This elderly man knew the stretching of God through his suffering. '*Katartizo*' is a most beautiful word to describe what is happening when God take us through the 'valleys of shadow'. During it all, the God of all grace is mending our nets.

My Journal

KEY PRAYER

Heavenly Father, please help me to understand the process of pain and suffering so that through it all I can understand what goes on in my life. Please help me, too, to surrender afresh to the 'ways of the Lord' and allow my nets to be mended.

January 5th

KEY WORD: ***Be still***

KEY VERSE: ***Mark 4 : 39***

He (Jesus) got up... and said to the waves, "Quiet! Be still!" Then the wind died down and it was completely calm.

Those of us who have been brought up in Sunday school from an early age will no doubt have heard several times over the story of Jesus and the storm. The picture was formed in early years of a fearsome storm with brave, hardy mariners beside themselves with fear, and professional fishermen wishing that they had never set sail. The picture continues with Jesus, having awoken from sleep, standing in the front of the vessel speaking directly to the winds and waves and stilling the storm.

The formed picture is one of several New Testament stories that do not do justice at all to what was actually happening. Yes, there was a fearsome storm, a storm so great that it made the fishermen wish for the day. Yes, Jesus did stand and still the storm. But the actual events record a far more sinister plot and a far more active confrontation.

Jesus did not speak to the winds and the waves as it seems to suggest at first reading, He actually confronted the authorship of the storm. Apart from His time in the desert, this was the first time that Jesus was vulnerable, asleep in the back of the boat. Here was an opportunity for Satan to halt the march of man's salvation, and he took it, producing a storm so violent and so satanic that it caused professional men to panic. Jesus, sensing the authorship of this storm, defies the elements and attacks the one behind the storm and cries to the wind and waves to cease their activities. He uses a word that in Greek conveys a majestic message. He commands 'Peace be still'. The word used is '*phimoo*', which is the term used by an animal trainer, who, in the process of taming the beast, produces a muzzle. The farmer would also use this word as he muzzled an ox in order to keep the animal on course and working.

This was no ordinary storm and this was no ordinary confrontation. Jesus rebuked the elements and the author of the storm.

This is not just a Sunday school story, or just a word picture for the church. It is far more than that, the prophetic picture of Jesus in the boat is a reminder of the fact that all storms have been stilled and all satanic attacks can be quelled when we remember how to stand against them. Satan's power against us is only temporary and has no effect. We have been saved from the power and penalty of sin and one glorious day we shall also be saved from the presence of sin. As Jesus overcame this fierce storm, so can the church overcome and so can all believers overcome their storms. The winds and waves may blow and the storm might be as fearsome as ever, but the author has no power against us at all, as we can muzzle the enemy every day.

My Journal

KEY PRAYER

Heavenly Father, thank you for the victory that you have given to us. Help us to appreciate the fact that day by day all is well. Even when the winds blow, you are in the boat, and you bring our storm to peace. Give me constantly the assurance of victory and help me to understand just how great you are, so that even the winds and the waves obey your voice.

January 6th

KEY WORD: ***Refreshment***

KEY VERSE: **1 Corinthians 16 : 18**

For they refreshed my spirit and yours also. Such men deserve recognition.

In 1 Corinthians 16 : 18, Paul talked about three people who are fairly unknown in New Testament terms. They are not apostles or prophets nor do they have a major ministry, but their arrival in Paul's life at that moment in time was one of tremendous blessing.

Stephanas, Fortunatus and Achaicus were people who had devoted themselves to ministry, and their arrival on the scene of Paul's life brought to him a wonderful sense of refreshment. His words were literal and far reaching, he spoke of them as 'having refreshed my spirit'. The Greek word used in this key verse is the word '*anapauo*' which translated means, 'to rest from labour'. It is actually two words in one: '*ana*' meaning 'back' and '*pauo*' meaning 'to cease'. So literally Paul was saying these people caused him to cease doing what he was doing for awhile, and they caused him to go back to a basic position.

Paul's life was a very hectic one. There were so many cities, towns and villages to visit, so many churches to plant, so many people to instruct, and every day the care of oversight ministry within the churches was upon him. He obviously had a great need at this time as he states that these three people supplied what was lacking: a period of rest and reflection.

In some manuscripts the word seems to have been derived from an agricultural term, which was used when a field was allowed to lie fallow for a season in order for it to recuperate from loss. Constant tilling, sowing and reaping would cause the field to become drained of its nutrients and goodness, and a period of rest would allow the soil to recover. It is this kind of rest that Paul needed at this time, and it was this kind of rest that Stephanas, Fortunatus and Achaicus brought.

We are not talking here about an earthly kind of break, when a holiday revitalises your body and your tiredness drains away to be replaced with a kind of renewed energy. This is not what Paul needed. Paul required a period of spiritual renewal when his spirit as well as his body would be refreshed: the kind of rest that Jesus said He would give to those who were burdened and heavy laden. He would grant spiritual rest to body, soul and spirit. Paul received this kind of rest and greatly enjoyed the experience, and it would have refreshed him for the next phase of ministry.

According to the historians, Moulton and Milligan, early Christians used to use the word *'anapauo'* on their gravestones, followed by the date of their death. This signified that upon their death they had gone to a better place of permanent rest, which was a wonderful thought.

I have sat at the bedside of many saints who were about to end their work here on earth and who were about to enter their rest. I can testify to seeing the 'face of peace' as they concluded their work and received their call to rest.

We would do well to remember during our work and activity to draw apart, cease from labour and rest in the Lord.

My Journal

KEY PRAYER

Heavenly Father, cause me to know rest and reflection during my time here on earth so that I can renew my spirit and be refreshed. Cause me also to be a blessing of refreshment to others so that they too might learn to rest in you.

January 7th

KEY WORD: **Magnify**

KEY VERSE: **Luke 1 : 46-47**

"My soul glorifies the Lord and my spirit rejoices in God my Saviour."

In this wonderful verse of Scripture, Mary cried from the depths of her being a song of joy. A better translation of this song, however, would be 'my soul magnifies the Lord', because this song has been called by many people over the years 'the Magnificat'. It has been the source of inspiration for countless songs of praise by a myriad number of composers. It was Mary's song to her Lord and Saviour.

The Greek word used in this passage of Scripture is the word '*megaluno*' which means to 'make great'. From this Greek word we derive the English word 'mega' and from this word the term megastar has been created. In the world of sport, screen and television anyone who excels in their field is labelled as being a megastar. It is interesting that the word was first used of the Lord in order to convey His greatness.

It is an interesting thought however, that in her song Mary was seeking to 'make great' her God, as if she could actually make God greater than He is. This is the concept of the word. We can make things appear to be greater by magnifying them under a microscope. We don't actually make them greater, but they appear to become greater due to the optical enlargement. We can not make God greater than He is, He is great. We can not make Him to appear greater than He is, there is nothing in this world or the next world that can magnify God to a greater extent. There is an absolute to His greatness. He does not get greater as the years go by, He does not change, He has not changed and He never will change. He remains always the same, He is great! So how does Mary's song relate to us and Him? What Mary was trying to convey in her song was the amazing fact that she was becoming more aware of God's greatness. It was not that God was getting greater, but that her awareness of Him was growing. She was conveying that as she got to know Him and as her awareness of Him was developing, He was becoming greater in her understanding.

As we walk with God and as we grow in Him, He remains the same but our awareness of His presence, His grace, His peace, His love, in fact everything about Him becomes greater in our understanding. I remember an eminent preacher once stating that the more he knew about God the less he really understood. We haven't yet plumbed the depths of the unsearchable riches of God and, even when we get to the place where we think that we have finally grasped a measure of truth, we uncover a further, deeper level. He is growing in greatness all the time in our understanding yet He remains exactly the same. This is the mystery of '*megaluno*', every time we praise Him, He becomes greater, yet He remains the same. Every time we discover more truth, He grows greater in our awareness, yet He never varies. This is the mystery of magnifying Him.

My Journal

KEY PRAYER

Heavenly Father, like Mary, I magnify you today. My soul reaches out to you and seeks to make you greater. Help me to understand this mystery that although I make you greater in my mind and spirit, you never change. Help me to grasp this vital aspect of truth so that I might worship you more. With Mary today, my soul glorifies the Lord.

January 8th

KEY WORD: **Abba**

KEY VERSE: **Romans 8 : 15**

For you did not receive a spirit that makes you a slave again to fear, but you received the Spirit of sonship. And by Him we cry, "Abba, Father."

This beautiful word *'Abba'* is actually an Aramaic word and translates to itself. It is used in the book of Romans as *'Abba'*, with the following word 'father', which is the nearest equivalent. However, 'father' is a little too impersonal to be completely accurate. The actual translation is much nearer to that of the English word 'daddy'.

Old Testament and New Testament slaves were not allowed to use the word *'Abba'* when they were addressing the head of the household as it signifies a very close relationship. In fact it is such a close relationship word that it is used entirely within the family relationship setting. *'Abba'* is the word that is first used on the lips of infants and it denotes the feeling of unreasoning trust of a child to its parent. Therefore slaves were not allowed this kind of privilege.

Paul took this word to convey the wonderful relationship that we now have with Almighty God through the aspect of grace. He was now no longer just Father, and certainly no longer a God that was far removed from us and unapproachable, He had drawn nigh to us and had allowed Himself to be addressed by us as *'Abba'*. A relationship that is as close as a child to his father. Paul was seeking to convey that we have entered into something that is very precious. We do not just have a 'Heavenly Father', an expression in itself that is close and precious, after being slaves of sin and the devil; but we have a much closer relationship than even this. He has become 'daddy' to us and we have become His children.

The word was also used by Jesus Himself when He addressed His own Father in heaven at the time of Gethsemane. He was at the time being crushed by the weight of sin and suffering. All earthly help had been removed from Him and He cried out to God, not in the sense of God being removed from Him but in the sense of being so close. "*Abba* Father, let this cup pass from me". The words and passion used denote a very real and close relationship, there was nothing that He could not say, there was nothing that was hid and there was nothing that His Father would withhold from Him. This same relationship is now ours. We are not impoverished saints begging God to do something for us, we are His children, so close that by the spirit of adoption we can use the word that no slave was ever allowed to utter, 'my father' or in fact, 'my dad'.

Galations 4 : 6, even takes it a step further when Paul stated that not only are we sons through this relationship but we are heirs of God. '*Abba*' does not just denote a close relationship but also denotes the fact that we inherit all things through this relationship. Like a child we belong to Him and like a child we inherit the Father's love, blessing and destiny. The two words '*Abba,* Father' expressed together denote the love and intelligent confidence of the child-like faith that has been bequeathed to us through grace.

My Journal

KEY PRAYER

Heavenly Father, I thank you that I can address you in such a way that brings me so close to you. You have allowed me to draw near to you and as I do so, you draw near to me. Help me to understand just how real this is and help me to continually appreciate just how wonderful my relationship is with you. Thank you for this child-like faith that has been borne in my heart.

January 9th

KEY WORD: ***Say***

KEY VERSE: **John 12 : 49**

"For I did not speak of my own accord, but the Father who sent me commanded me what to say and how to say it."

This is a very interesting word, but firstly let me deal with the English word before I attempt to deal with the correct Greek word. Jesus was speaking to a crowd of people and He commenced to say that He was not speaking on His own behalf but He was speaking as from the Father. The Father commanded Him what to say and even how to say it.

The word therefore is not just a simple word conveying a form of speech but a word that conveys the whole impact of commandment, of authority and of pronouncement. It appears in this form many times in the New Testament, especially when Jesus was conveying truth. In one of the gospels it says of Jesus, 'that no man ever spoke like Him'. The word denotes 'impact'.

However, it becomes even more striking when the Greek word used for 'say' is translated, the word used is '*lego*.' which translated means 'to affirm' or to 'pick out choice words'. It refers especially to the substance of what is being said, which is why Jesus used this word to convey the thought that 'God told Him what to say and how to say it'. The connection of choice words is the theme behind the word '*lego*'. It is not just what was said, nor is it just the way that the words of conversation were used, but the way in which choice words were picked out, uttered with authority and used in a skilful way.

It is an interesting fact that when a toy company was issuing a new form of plastic building bricks that would inter-connect and that would place brick upon brick to form buildings and other objects, they used a Greek word to convey the message of connection, and '*lego*' was born and the result is now history.

Jesus spoke the words of His Father. He came to speak authoratively to a world that was steeped in religious messages, filled with wandering preachers and totally lacking in a real 'word from God'. The world was destitute of a word of authority and when Jesus came the people followed Him, not just for the miracles but for 'what He said'. They came from the cities, the towns and the villages and they followed Him day and night. Peter said, "where else can we go, you have the words of life". When the chief priests sent men to capture Him they came back empty handed stating that, 'never had a man spoken like this man'.

When God communicates with us, it is with authority and power. When we are searching for His will or plan of direction for our lives, His words bring light, guidance and direction into our darkened situation. I have often heard the phrase used that 'I think that God is trying to tell me something', and I understand that image behind the words, but God does not 'try' to say something. God speaks clearly, He speaks with authority and He speaks with direction. The only 'trying' that goes on is when we try to hear Him. There is no problem with the communicator, but there is at times a problem with the listener.

His words are life, His words are power and His words are clear in direction. The word '*lego*' can also be translated as, 'telling', 'uttering', and 'pronouncing', giving the whole impact of powerful words of life. As we start the day it is good to know that He has spoken and even better that He has spoken to us.

KEY PRAYER

Heavenly Father, thank you today for your words of life, beautiful words, wonderful words, words of power and direction. Thank you too, that you have chosen to speak to me and I rejoice in the fact that the God of the universe has spoken directly with me. Help me to understand this awesome fact and help me to be ever listening for your voice.

January 10th

KEY WORD: **Revelation**

KEY VERSE: **Luke 2 : 32**

"A light for revelation to the Gentiles and for glory to your people Israel."

Over the next few days we shall be looking at one of the most unique words in the entire Scriptures, a word that has several meanings yet all stemming from the same original word. In English the word revelation can have several meanings and the richness of the meanings delights our minds. However, in Greek the word for revelation is the word *'apokalupsis'* and its translation is quite fascinating. It has a richness that quite defies the mind. For instance, the meaning that we look at today in this key verse, is where it is used very early on in the New Testament when Simeon took Jesus in his arms and praised God at the dedication of Jesus and proclaimed Him to be a light for revelation to the Gentile world.

It was as if the old priest drew back a veil and uncovered a startling fact that this little child in his arms was the answer to all Hebrew prayers, that the Messiah had come and with Him a new day for the whole world.

'Apokalupsis' can mean 'an uncovering', as if a curtain or a veil was drawn back and light was allowed to come into a darkened room. The priest was completely right in his assessment. Here was a world lying in darkness, and here was God's answer for all mankind. God allowed a moment in time to be the uncovering of His only begotten Son, and a light to lighten the darkness of a sick and dying world.

When anyone accepts Jesus as Lord and Saviour the same uncovering takes place each and every time. Light shines into darkened lives and as revelation takes place, a sinful soul commences its journey into light and the uncovering of a new future and an eternal destiny begins to form in the new believer's mind.

When I think of this aspect of 'uncovering' I remember a young man in London, many years ago, who received Jesus as Lord and Saviour. His life was a mess and his countenance was a 'dark' and bleak one. He prayed the sinner's prayer and walked off into the night – a new creation. There was no immediate change externally as he disappeared, but on a subsequent meeting just two days later he was unrecognisable, in fact he had to introduce himself due to the incredible external change that had taken place. Light was present where only darkness had been, bleakness had been transformed into hope. If ever a revelation had taken place it was here. The '*apokalupsis*' of God had been delivered into a new child of God, revelation of a hope, a future and a peace. The veil had been drawn back and the life flooded with light

My Journal ______________________________

KEY PRAYER

Heavenly Father, I rejoice today in sins forgiven and peace with God. Thank you for the revelation of your goodness and I praise you for the time when you drew back the veil of my eyes and the veil of my soul to the wonderful glories of your presence. Help me each day to keep sensing this gift of revelation, so that I might uncover more of your glory and grace.

January 11th

KEY WORD: **Revelation**

KEY VERSE: **Romans 16 : 25-26**

Now to Him who is able to establish you by my gospel and the proclamation of Jesus Christ, according to the revelation of the mystery hidden for long ages past, but now revealed and made known...

Paul wrote to the Roman Church in today's key verse, and stated that now revelation has come and mysteries are now revealed. The same word '*apokalupsis*' is used in this Scripture but this time the meaning is not just an uncovering of truth, but a revealing of a mystery - as if clues had been laid down for a detective to follow. And by careful analysis and a strict code of deduction, the problem had been solved and the mystery had been revealed. Of course this is just what Paul was alluding to. God had allowed a succession of prophets to glimpse a little of truth and what they had been allowed to 'see', they spoke out. The Old Testament is full of prophecies concerning the first appearance of Jesus, the age of the Church, the age of grace and the Second Coming of Jesus. All, however, were either misunderstood or rejected by a disbelieving world. They were words of mystery.

Yet Jesus came and fulfilled all that was said of Him. He had returned to Heaven as it had been prophesied and the Church had commenced its ministry. And Paul, having received revelation from God, was now writing and confirming that the age of mysteries was over and that revelation was now clear.

This kind of 'revealing' takes place as we grow in God – we are constantly seeing new things. The fact is that these new things were there all the time, we just did not 'see them'. I am constantly amazed at the glorious fact that Bible reading can become a revelation, as verses that are well known, even well 'preached' can suddenly spring into life, and fresh understanding can dawn upon your mind. It is as if a mystery is suddenly cleared up and truth dawns in its fullness.

Paul talked of the mystery being hidden for ages. In fact during the whole age of the Old Testament, men and women died longing for truth to be revealed, but they all died under law and under the shadowed mysteries of hidden truth. Abraham, for instance, was looking for a city whose builder and maker was God but he died in the shadows of Old Testament truth. All the Old Testament saints died 'not having received the promise', but Paul however, rejoiced in the fact that he was living in the age of clear revelation, when truth was being revealed, and his obvious joy was communicated to the Roman Church.

Revelation is not just an uncovering of darkness, it is also the whole aspect of mysteries being revealed and God's purposes being fulfilled.

My Journal ______________________________

KEY PRAYER

Thank you, Heavenly Father, for your constant love which is no longer a mystery but a revelation. Thank you too, for showing me your goodness. Help me each day to find new truth and to live in a constant sense of expectancy as you speak to me through your Word.

January 12th

KEY WORD: **Revelation**

KEY VERSE: **1 Corinthians 14 : 6**

Now, brethren, if I come to you and speak in tongues, what good will I be to you, unless I bring you some revelation or knowledge or prophecy or word of instruction?

In this passage of Scripture, Paul wrote to the church at Corinth stating that he must bring some revelation in order for them to know the mind of God. The same Greek word is used – '*apokalupsis*', yet it carries now a slightly different meaning than uncovering or the revealing of mystery.

This use of the word carries with it the sense of the expressing of God's mind and has the impact of a sudden understanding of what God is saying. It is not that we have stumbled across a hidden mystery or that we have suddenly had darkness removed from our minds. It is the amazing fact that God has seen fit to bring a word of revelation from His mind to ours so that we might have instruction, guidance, help or knowledge. The main aspect of this meaning is in the whole area of prophecy, when a prophetic message is brought to a church, a group of people or even to someone in an individual way. Prophecy can be both corporate and personal, God speaking to His Church or to one of His children.

In the New Testament both kinds of prophecy were seen. At the church in Antioch, God spoke to a group of praying leaders and said 'Paul and Barnabus were to be separated to the work of missions'. A sudden word of revelation and a little of God's mind to the church.

Earlier in the book of Acts, Paul received a 'word from God' when Agabus stated that he would be 'bound and taken prisoner' if he went to a certain city. A sudden word of revelation concerning his personal future.

It is not that God shares everything all at once with His Church. It is, however, a glimpse of the 'mind of God', an insight into one aspect of truth. He gives a small portion of revelation granted to our minds in order for us to know what to do at a certain time, or a small portion of revelation granting us insight into the future. I well remember as a very small boy hearing about a prophecy that was given in my home church. It concerned a future event that was going to take place that would amaze us and bring us great joy. No one at that time knew what this prophecy meant. It caught the church unawares and was the object of much discussion for several weeks until it was finally revealed that Billy Graham was coming to the Harringay Arena for a major crusade. In fact, it was his first crusade outside the USA. Harringay was only a 'stones throw' from our church and subsequently the whole of London was impacted by a crusade that did not just last for its designated time of a few weeks, but ran over into months of blessing, joy and growth to the church. God supernaturally revealed it to us, weeks and weeks before it was finally revealed in a natural way to the local churches in the area.

Revelation is the mind of God being communicated to the natural mind of man, in a supernatural way that brings guidance, instruction and direction.

My Journal

KEY PRAYER

Heavenly Father, thank you for speaking to the church and thank you too, that you speak to me. I praise you today for your willingness to communicate and your longing to give us guidance. Help me today to live in a constant sense of your presence, so that I might be ready to listen when you speak, and then ready to obey your voice.

January 13th

KEY WORD: ***Revelation***

KEY VERSE: **1 Peter 1 : 7**

These have come so that your faith – of greater worth than gold, which perishes even though refined by fire – may be proved genuine and may result in praise, glory and honour when Jesus Christ is revealed.

In today's key verse the apostle, Peter, used the Greek word '*apokalupsis*' and he used this word to convey another shade of meaning, other than the ones that we have looked at already – namely the uncovering of mysteries, the light penetrating darkness and the knowledge of God's mind – in a sudden way to His Church.

This fourth aspect of revelation is the great impact of the Second Coming of Jesus, when He comes for His Church in the Rapture. Peter sought to instil in his writings to the Church, that the Coming of the Lord would be a great revelation to the world, to the Church and to all believers world wide.

This Second Coming of the Lord will be the greatest revelation yet of God's only begotten Son. His first coming was as a baby, His Second Coming will be as a king. His first coming was to a limited geographical place. His Second Coming will be to the whole world and every eye will see Him. His first coming only attracted a handful of people, however, His Second Coming will attract His whole Church of all ages and of all peoples. Simply a great revelation. However, this is not the uncovering of a mystery, or the light penetrating the darkness, or even the knowledge of God communicated to us, this is the fullness of revelation which has been prophesied throughout all ages. In other words, the complete revelation, the culmination of all things.

When Peter commenced upon this theme he was stating that the Coming of the Lord will be the fulfilment of all prophecies, but also the commencement of the End Times, when all things will be completed and when Jesus becomes Lord of all and the age of grace comes to an end. We shall be looking at the End Time revelation tomorrow; however, Peter said this great revelation of the Coming of the Lord will be with great praise, glory and honour. Therefore Peter is addressing the Church, a Church that has waited with patience for this moment of history. The Church has looked for this moment, it has longed for this moment and it has been declaring this moment throughout its history on this planet. So, when the time is fully come the Church will rejoice with joy unspeakable. However, the world will face a moment in time that will be both salutary and devastating. There will be no rejoicing and certainly no joy for a world that will come under the judgement of a righteous God, a God who was not willing that any should perish and that all might come to know Him. He gave ample time for this to be achieved, and now time will be no more.

What a revelation for the Church and what joy shall we behold.

My Journal

KEY PRAYER

Heavenly Father, thank you for your eternal salvation and thank you for the Church. Thank you that I am part of the Bride of Christ, your Church, and that you are returning for me. I bless you today for all your promises and I await the fullness of time and the final great revelation of your Coming to this world to receive your Church. Help me to proclaim your arrival and help me to constantly look up as your redemption draws near.

January 14th

KEY WORD: ***Revelation***

KEY VERSE: ***Revelation 1 : 1***

The revelation of Jesus Christ, which God gave Him to show His servants what must soon take place.

This final aspect of revelation is very different to all the others that we have looked at these past few days. On each occasion when the English word revelation has been used it has been a shade of meaning from the multifaceted Greek word '*apokalupsis*'. We have seen four or five shades of meaning from the discovery of a mystery, to the final full revelation of all time, when Jesus returns. However, here is another shade of meaning that the apostle John uses when he closes the New Testament with a final book of judgements.

The book of Revelation is not just a book that uncovers mysteries, although it does do that, and it is not just a book that gives God's Word to man, although it does that too. It is the final and complete picture of a world, and a Church and a people. The actual Greek title for this book is 'Apocalypse', a word that has been taken by film makers and authors and used for the description of final acts or final conflicts and even dramatic events that defy the imagination. Apocalyptic events!

That is exactly what John was seeking to convey when he wrote this final book of the New Testament. He was under no illusion – this was the final act of a dying world and the final act of a living God. For following the Rapture of the Church, God was going to bring His wrath upon sin, suffering and Satan, and He was going to see that His Son would be enthroned in final glory, and be Lord of all.

As the 22 chapters of this final book unfold, it is an obvious fact that this world will have never seen such devastating acts as the ones that will overtake it. Final judgements and final conflicts, the conclusion of time and the entrance of eternity, the fall of Satan and the rise of world peace, and the emptiness of sin and the fullness of God's blessing. What a finish, and what an apocalyptic conclusion. The Church will receive the revelation of the Coming of the Lord with great joy and will be received home, to be forever with the Lord. However, the Coming of the Lord will be received by the world with great despair as final judgements are dispensed. He came once as a baby to Bethlehem, He will come again as King of kings and as Lord of lords, and He will reign forever and forever, and of His kingdom there shall be no bounds.

My Journal

KEY PRAYER

Heavenly Father, I bless you today that your Second Coming holds no terror for me, for you have removed the guilt and penalty of sin from my life and I rejoice in peace with God and sins forgiven. Help me today to live my life as witness to your glory and help me to ever watch for your Coming. I pray for those who are not yet in the kingdom of God and I ask you to forgive those of my friends and family who do not yet know you. I ask for opportunities to speak of your love before it is too late.

January 15th

KEY WORD: ***Hallelujah***

KEY VERSE: ***Revelation 19 : 1***

After this I heard what sounded like the roar of a great multitude in heaven shouting: "Hallelujah! Salvation and glory and power... to our God."

Here is a wonderful word that is used virtually in every language. I have ministered in churches all over the world where the natural language is a major barrier both for them and for me, yet one common word overcomes the barrier: 'hallelujah'. It is used in both the Old Testament and the New Testament and literally means, 'praise ye the Lord'. In the Old Testament the translation was, 'praise ye Jah', or 'praise ye Jehovah'.

The Greek word, *'hallelouia'*, was the song of heaven and it appears several times in the book of Revelation denoting the song of the great multitude. It was the keynote song of praise and will ring through heaven throughout the ages. It is also the song of the Church, as it conveys greatness, power, majesty and glory to God.

The word is sometimes found written as 'alleluia' which is a misspelling and does not convey at all the greatness of the song of praise, nor does it convey the correct sentiment of a great and mighty God. Hallelujah is both our song of praise and majesty and at the same time it is the description of God in His glory.

In the book of Revelation, in chapter 19, it is used four times in six verses and it is not just used as a song but as a shout. Three out of the four times that the word appears it is preceded by 'they shouted' and the only time that they did not shout it states that 'they cried'. So you have the very creative and very dramatic descriptions of the host of heaven not just singing and certainly not simply breathing out the phrase, but shouting glory to God with hallelujah coming from the very depths of their being.

In the western world we have become very staid in our forms of worship. Even in the most flamboyant of churches we would hardly shout out loud – we might raise our voices but it would come nowhere near the shout of heaven. It would not even be close to the Old Testament saints who used this expression in their singing of psalms when they would also 'shout unto the Lord'. It might be a good thing to practise shouting praise unto the Lord in your private devotions. Revelation 19 calls this act of worship the sound of a roar, in other places in the same book the sound of heaven is likened unto the 'sound of many waters' and the 'loud pealing of thunders'. It might be difficult to practise this aspect of praise in a church service, but within your own home, or even alone on a beach or on a high hill, to shout unto the Lord would be a very releasing aspect of praise. We will be doing this throughout eternity, so it might be good to start now!

My Journal ________________________________

____

____

____

____

____

____

____

____

____

____

KEY PRAYER

Heavenly Father, forgive me for only praising you in one fashion and for allowing my western culture to overtake my mode of prayer. Please help me to give you praise in other ways and fashions and help me to be released in my worship. I bring you my hallelujahs and I praise your glory and majesty.

January 16th

KEY WORD: **Maran - atha**

KEY VERSE: **1 Corinthians 16 : 22**

*If anyone does not love the Lord – a curse be on him.
Come, O Lord!*

'*Maran – atha*' is the Greek spelling for two Aramic words that found their way into Paul's writings when he was seeking to convey a strong message of truth. In 1 Corinthians 16, he was closing his writings to the church in Corinth with the words that, should someone reject the Lord, then he is also rejected. Then in order to strengthen the statement he used the two Aramic words in Greek text. He literally said, 'The Lord is Coming', making therefore imperative that we should all seek to 'know the Lord' before it is too late.

'The Lord is Coming' was a statement of truth not just the expression of a desire. To desire the Lord to come would be a good desire and would of course be truth, however, the extent of the form of these two words shows that this was not a desire but an ejaculation of a statement of fact. 'The Lord is Coming' formed the basis of prayers, worship and the foundation of all New Testament truth. The New Testament saints lived in a constant state of readiness, expecting the Lord at any time to re-appear from heaven; their worship stated it, their prayers expected it and their teaching endorsed it.

Two millennia have passed and the Church still awaits the Coming of the Lord, however, this ancient word has not just one fulfilment but is a continuing statement of truth. Whenever we 'gather ourselves together', the Lord Comes. Whenever we seek His face in prayer, the Lord Comes in a spiritual way. Whenever we have a need requiring ministry, the Lord Comes in a spiritual way ,however, we still await the glorious fact that the Lord will come personally and physically from heaven.

As we approach today with all its expectancies and pressures, we can expect the Lord to come into our day and walk with us. Whatever today brings forth we can still expect the Lord to come and bear our pressures with us, for He comes when we breathe *'Maran – atha'*.

When the Church met in the 1st century there was a prayer that was used quite often. It found its way into history by being printed in the 2nd century within the 'Apostolic Constitutions'. We will use this 1st century prayer together as we commence our day and we will say together *'Maran – atha'*.

My Journal

KEY PRAYER

Gather us all together into thy kingdom which thou hast prepared. Maran - atha, Hosanna to the Son of David, blessed is He who comes in the name of the Lord. (1st century Christians' prayer)

January 17th

KEY WORD: **Righteous**

KEY VERSE: **James 5 : 16**

The prayer of a righteous man is powerful and effective.

Within this key verse from James there are several words that require examination, because they bring forth teaching that at first glance is not always apparent. Over the next few days we will seek to uncover truth by looking at this text and examining its teaching.

James said that the prayer of a righteous man was powerful and effective, suggesting therefore that there were times when prayers might not be as powerful and effective if the praying person was not righteous. James was not seeking to elevate one person above another, nor was he suggesting that a level of righteousness is needed before a prayer will be answered.

The Greek word for 'righteous' gives us the clear answer to this dilemma when it reveals that the one who is praying is 'without prejudice or partiality'. The Greek word is '*dikaios*', and its meaning is one who is 'just'. It is not that God prefers one above another or that our righteousness counts before God, rather it is God who has made us 'just' and He treats us without prejudice. Our sin stood before God and us and all our righteousness was as filthy rags before a holy and pure God. Yet God, through Jesus at Calvary, made us without blame, He washed our filthy rags and made us clean. When we therefore come before God to pray it is not our goodness, righteousness or position that gives us the right to come before Him, rather it is His blood that made the way. It is His grace that gives us an entrance and it is His righteousness that affords us the right of being just and holy. We can come before Him with all our needs and He makes us acceptable in the Beloved.

It is this kind of righteousness that gives us power before God, not that our prayers are more powerful than anyone else's, but that our position before God is strengthened by our acceptance through His grace.

James was seeking to convey to the Church that everyone who has tasted of the goodness of God and who has found peace through His blood can have access to the very throne of God when they come before the Lord in prayer. In the context of this Scripture, sins can be forgiven, sickness can be healed and prayers can be answered, when the one who is praying has found their righteousness in God's righteousness.

'*Dikaios*' is a 'God-type word' – it stands for God's right and rule, it is His justice and right to do whatever He wants to do. In this context He wants to place His righteousness upon us and He wills to accept us through the blood of His cross. It is His decision to accept us when we pray through grace. Grace and only grace.

My Journal

KEY PRAYER

Heavenly Father, thank you for the amazing fact that I am now accepted in the Beloved. Thank you that my sins have been forgiven and thank you that when I pray, you hear and answer my prayers. I come before you today as an example of your righteousness and I stand before you as a testimony of your goodness.

January 18th

KEY WORD: ***Powerful***

KEY VERSE: ***James 5 : 16***

The prayer of a righteous man is powerful and effective.

Yesterday we saw that God's plan for us is that we become righteous through His righteousness and that when we pray, our prayers are therefore powerful. However, the word powerful conjures up the thought that our prayers are stronger than someone else's and, therefore, that our prayers can attain more than someone else who comes before the Lord.

However, understanding the Greek word here puts things into perspective. The word used is the word *'energeo'*, from which we derive our word energy. This word is more correctly translated 'to work' or to 'be effectual'. The Old King James Bible translates this word as the 'effectual fervent' prayer denoting a measure of heat, fervency and power.

It is not that God is moved by powerful utterances, nor is it that God is affected by noise, loud voices, energetic actions or powerful aerobics. The fact is, however, when a righteous man commences to pray he rises to a level that is above the norm. He begins to see things that he had not seen before and he begins to hear things that he had not heard before. He enters a realm where he begins to participate with God in an area of His divine will in such a way that he actually comes into line with God's will for his life. It is this kind of working that he begins to understand.

It is not that God jumps into action when they pray, nor is He affected by any actions on their behalf, however, when a righteous prayer commences action before God it is they who move, not God. They move towards His will when *'energeo'* takes place, the working of God's plan becomes their plan, the centre of God's will comes into sharper focus and they move towards the will of God.

James used the illustration of Elijah to help us understand this key word. Elijah was a man like unto us, he had the same passions as us, yet he prayed an effectual, powerful prayer and the heavens withheld their rains. He prayed again and the earth saw rain and it produced its crops. It was the time of great sin on the earth and God used Elijah as the means of famine and the means of plenty. He was righteous through God's righteousness and he was so powerful in prayer that heaven obeyed. Actually it was Elijah who moved into the orbit of God's will when he bowed his knees in prayer and sought the face of God. God's ways then became Elijah's way and God's plan became the focus of Elijah's petitions. He prayed with a power that 'made things work' and '*energeo*' was seen by the nations when rain was held back and then later when rain fell from heaven. When we pray it is not our will that should be done but we should pray 'Lord let your will be done on earth as it is in heaven', this is true, powerful praying.

My Journal ______________________________

KEY PRAYER

Heavenly Father, I do recognise that there are times when I seek to impose my will on yours and I ask for things that are not right for me. Help me to constantly be powerful in prayer so that I only hear what you want me to hear and that I only do what you want me to do.

January 19th

KEY WORD: ***Effective***

KEY VERSE: ***James 5 : 16***

The prayer of a righteous man is powerful and effective.

Having read and thought and prayed over this key verse in the past two days, the closing word of this text – effective – is an interesting one. God honours the prayers of the righteous man who prays with a desire to work with the will of God. When our will bends to God's will and when we come into line in our prayer life with God's plan for our lives, we can expect our prayers to be effective.

However, effectiveness does not necessarily mean that each and every prayer will be answered in the ways that we desire. The Greek word for effectiveness is the word *'ischuo'* and it is translated in three different ways. It can mean to be strong in body, in the sense of being robust. It can mean to have a sense of overwhelming power and it can mean to be of great force. It is the third meaning that is used in this key verse of James 5 : 16. James was stating that the one who prays with a powerful understanding of God's will is one who will have great force in the area of prevailing prayer. Great force in prayer therefore is not just answers to prayer, nor is it the length of sustained prayer, it is however, force that is capable of producing results.

Once again Elijah was the illustration of prevailing prayer that was capable of producing results. He prayed that it would not rain and it did not rain. He prayed again that it would rain and heaven sent forth its rain upon the earth. His prevailing forceful prayers produced results that changed his nation and brought about a spiritual revival.

Church history is full of illustrations of men and women of prayer, people who changed lives, people who changed churches, people who changed countries and nations. A young girl prayed and the Welsh revival was born. A man cried out to God and China was opened to the Lord and the China Inland Mission was born. Prayer that is sustained and powerful in its understanding of God's will, is capable of producing results. It is a sad fact that some of our churches find that the regular weekly prayer meeting is the lowest attended meeting of the church's weekly programme. This is a very sad thing when sustained powerful prayer is capable of producing results. It could be that the weekly prayer meeting has lost its way and lost its momentum due to some people's long and highly involved prayers. It could have lost its way due to the fact that often there are too many unspecific prayers being prayed and it could also be that people have lost the desire to pray because not much has been seen to take place recently.

Some prayer meetings need to undergo a radical rethink in order that they might regain their effectiveness, and a few lessons learned from James 5 : 16, just might help.

My Journal

KEY PRAYER

Heavenly Father, please help me to learn the lessons that the book of James is seeking to teach. Help me to learn how to pray, when to pray and what to pray for. Help me learn too, that you delight to bless those who pray along with your will and that you are a rewarder of those who diligently seek you. You are a giving God and I bless you today for your constant goodness.

January 20th

KEY WORD: ***Prayer***

KEY VERSE: ***James 5 : 16***

The prayer of a righteous man is powerful and effective.

Having looked at the effectiveness of powerful, sustained prayer it is only right that we take a look at the whole concept of what prayer really is. The Greek word used for 'prayer' in James 5 : 16 is the word *'euchomai'*, which is the word that is used for a desire or a wish and it carries with it the concept of a very strong expression of longing. The word was used by Paul quite often and was stated by him when he was before King Agrippa, when he said "I pray... that you all would become like me except for my chains." Acts 26 : 29. He was expressing the strong desire that the king would become a Christian and it became his prayer.

We have always taught and believed that prayer is a two-way matter – us talking to God and God talking with us. However, we have not placed great emphasis in our teaching on the fact that prayer is a sustained desire and longing. It is possible that in our fast changing world with its instant activities that we have relegated prayer to a kind of quick fix. If it works instantly then praise God, if it doesn't work instantly then we move on rather than holding on, and we give up rather than prevailing.

God longs to speak with us and longs for us to spend time with Him. If only we could cultivate the same kind of longing that the word *'euchomai'* brings to us, our prayer life might become strong and more effective. I often wonder just how God feels when our ten minutes of prayer contains a list of our needs and a one way discourse of us telling God how, when, and why He should be doing certain things. Sadly, many church prayer meetings use this model. However, James used Elijah as his model when addressing the subject of prayer and it is interesting to read the full account in the book of Kings. When Elijah was praying he remained in the position of prayer in order to hear God's voice and he stayed there until a cloud the size of a man's hand was seen on the horizon.

There is nothing wrong in us addressing God concerning our needs – even though before we speak He knows our needs. There is nothing wrong in us telling God just how we feel, but there is everything wrong in racing away from prayer in order to get on with the day, before we have allowed God to address us. Just staying in prayer allows the quietness of His presence to overwhelm us and allows the deep sense of peace to engulf us. If we do not have this strong sense of desire and wish to remain in God's presence there is something very wrong about the way that we have cultivated our prayer life.

It has often been said that if we treated our friends in the same way that we treat God, we would not have many friends. Our friends would not put up with us dominating the conversation for ten minutes and then moving on before they were allowed to enter the conversation.

When Elijah's cloud appeared on the horizon it was time to begin to move from prayer to action. We should learn this and allow time for God to move on to the contours of our own horizons before we conclude what we call 'our time of prayer'.

My Journal ______________________________

____

____

____

____

____

KEY PRAYER

Heavenly Father, please forgive me for neglecting the place of communion with you and forgive me for my excessive speaking, when all the time you long to speak to me. Help me to learn to listen and help me to learn to stay still and cultivate a listening ear. Help me too, to enjoy my times before you so that I can start my day with a different perspective.

January 21st

KEY WORD: **Praise**

KEY VERSE: **Luke 1 : 64**

Immediately his mouth was opened and his tongue was loosed, and he began to speak, praising God.

Having spent several days looking at the aspect of prayer it is now time to concentrate on the wonderful world of praise. There are several words in the New Testament that are translated into the one English word 'praise'. Many times different aspects of praise were drawn together in order for us to understand what praise really is, however, the English language is not as rich as the Greek language and so all the shades of meaning become lost in one word, praise. Over the next few days we shall seek to uncover these shades of meaning in order to allow the fullness of praise to overwhelm us.

In Luke 1 : 64, this key verse outlines the emotion of Zechariah, the priest who had become dumb following the visit of the angel of the Lord and the prophecy concerning the birth of his son, John the baptist. Once the time of birth drew near he was released from his dumbness and his first and immediate desire was to praise God. The Greek word used here is '*eulogeo*', which is translated more correctly as 'to speak in high praise of '. It is the word that is most used when addressing God. When we raise our voices in praise we are addressing God and speaking in praise of Him. It is most used when angels give thanks to God and it is also used of men when we come before Him in thanksgiving. The wonderful thought of angels and men speaking in high praise of the most high God is the concept that this word seeks to convey.

The word does not just mean that every time we sing or speak words of praise we are actually speaking in praise of God. Much of our worship can be very subjective and addresses our own emotions, whether we feel good at the time or whether we feel down. Much of what we call praise is self orientated and addresses our emotions of happiness, gladness and freedom. All of this is of course not wrong, there is a place for singing or speaking about how we feel, but it is not *'eulogeo'*. *'Eulogeo'* is a greater dimension of reality, it is the realisation that God is in control of all things, both the good that affects us and the bad that overwhelms us at times. But in spite of it all we address God and speak in praise of Him. It is the dimension of reaching beyond ourselves and touching heaven, something that we need to cultivate in what we call our 'praise time'. It is interesting to note that our English word 'eulogise' is derived from the Greek word, when we speak highly of someone or something we are eulogising them, in other words we are speaking in high praise of them.

My Journal

KEY PRAYER

Heavenly Father, I long to praise you correctly and I long to address your majesty and glory. Help me to keep in perspective how I feel and teach me to address you as King. I long for my voice to join with the angels in a mighty chorus of praise and I commence today with a note of thanksgiving and I praise you as King of kings and as Lord of lords. I eulogise before you today and I speak highly of you.

January 22nd

KEY WORD: ***Praise***

KEY VERSE: **Acts 16 : 25**

About midnight Paul and Silas were praying and singing hymns to God...

This very well known account of the prison in Philippi and Paul and Silas's midnight experiences brings us to a very important aspect of praise. The New International Version of the Bible quite rightly states that the two mission travellers sang hymns to God at the midnight hour. However, the King James Version and the Revised Version wrongly state that 'Paul and Silas prayed and praised' at midnight. The Greek word used is the word *'humneo'* and it is from this Greek word that the English concept of hymn is derived. The word literally translated means 'to hymn God' and it is taken from the paschal hymns contained in the book of Psalms, Psalm 113 through to Psalm 118 and also includes Psalm 136. The Jews called these psalms 'the great hallel'.

Paul and Silas were drawing from their memories these Old Testament songs and they began to sing out loud the songs of the great hallel to God. *'Humneo'* means to sing a song of greatness extolling God for His greatness, and it appears in several places within the New Testament. It appears at the final passover meal that Jesus was eating with His disciples just before His betrayal in Gethsemane. After they had eaten the meal, they sang a hymn and left for the garden. The hymn that they sang was one of the great hallels – it was a song of praise to the greatness of God.

It appears again in the book of Hebrews, when the writer was seeking to convey just how great Jesus is, and that although He was made a little lower than the angels, He is now crowned with glory and honour. In verse 12, the writer then stated that 'in the presence of the congregation I will sing praises'. It is the concept of the singing of great hymns, or I will 'hymn God'.

When we stand in the company of others and turn to a song book or even sing the words that appear on a screen above our heads, we are joining with an angelic host who are 'hymning God'. It is more than songs on a sheet or a screen and it is certainly more than just the reciting of words penned from history. It is the expression of worshippers who are seeking to fill their minds with something greater than they can understand and who seek to worship the one who is above all and through all.

It is the kind of praise that heaven rejoices in and the kind of praise that heaven is well used to. In the book of Revelation, we gain a very slight glimpse into the world beyond, when we are taken in the spirit by John before the throne of God. Chapters 4 and 5 draw back the veil and we see living creatures singing a new song. We see 24 elders also singing a new song and we see angelic beings singing with loud voices. We also see creatures that are in heaven and in the earth and creatures that are under the earth, all singing with one voice. And what is the song that they all sing? It is the extension of the great hallel, the chorus of majestic praise to the most high God.

As we commence a new day let us join our voice with this great company and bless the Lord.

My Journal

KEY PRAYER

Heavenly Father, enthroned in splendour, I bless you today, I raise my voice with this great heavenly choir and I honour you for all that you have done. Help me each day to continue this anthem of praise so that my praising is without end. Help me too, to rise above my circumstances so that in all things and through all things I might praise you.

January 23rd

KEY WORD: **Praise**

KEY VERSE: **James 5 : 13**

Is any one of you in trouble? He should pray. Is anyone happy? Let him sing songs of praise.

Here is a very interesting word that is used by James to convey a point of truth. The word used is usually translated into English as praise, which is not wrong, however within the translation something precious has been lost. The more correct translation should be, 'Is anyone happy? Let him twitch or twang!'

The Greek word used by James in this key verse is the word '*psallo*' and it is the word that is used for the playing of a stringed instrument with the fingers. In using this word in particular, James was calling for those who are happy to go beyond the simple rhetoric of a song and to stretch themselves, like a harp or a stringed instrument, and to produce sounds of praise that are costly and which take a period of time to produce. Most of what we call praise takes no time at all. We borrow someone's words and sing them and we use someone else's songs and call them our own. James was asking for far more than this when used the 'stretching word' of twitching and twanging, he was asking for something that is costly and which takes time for us to learn and time for us to produce.

This word used by James is more of a ' life time' concept of praise. It is relatively easy to praise when you are happy and it very easy to praise when God has answered prayer. However, it is much more difficult to continue to praise God when there has been no answer from heaven and when there have been periods of difficulty. The word is not just used of praise but it is used within the whole framework of the surrounding verses when James talked about 'those who are in trouble', and in the following verses when he asked if there are 'those who are sick'. During times of trouble and during times of sickness we should still practise the art of producing praise. As the skilful fingers of the harpist have practised until perfect the art of harp playing, producing sounds that are melodious, so should we practise the art of praise that produces the sounds of thanksgiving.

The writer in the book of Hebrews spoke of bringing the sacrifice of praise which is the fruit of our lips in Hebrews 13 : 15. The sacrifice of praise is praise that has been produced through sacrificial offerings, and everyone knows that sacrifices are costly events. Only praise that is continual through the good times and the bad times is real praise, therefore let us twitch and twang our instruments of thanksgiving so that God receives the praise and that we learn to trust through all things.

My Journal ___

KEY PRAYER

Heavenly Father, forgive me when I have only praised you for what I have received and forgive me for only praising you when I felt like it. Help me to learn lifestyle praise, which is praise through all things, both good and bad. Help me today to praise you even when it is costly and help my life to bring forth sweet sounds of thanksgiving like those who play upon the harp.

January 24th

KEY WORD: **Happy**

KEY VERSE: **Acts 26 : 2**

"King Agrippa, I count myself happy (fortunate) to stand before you today..."

Paul's words to King Agrippa reveal something of the heart of the apostle. He was delighted to be able to stand before kings and governors – even though he might be in chains, as he was able to minister to them and proclaim the gospel.

His words 'happy' or 'fortunate' carry with them a thrust of joy – he was overjoyed at the opportunities that were being afforded him. The Greek word used in this key verse today is the word '*makarios*', which is a word that is better translated as 'blessed'. He counted it a blessing to stand in a courtroom before the law makers, even kings, as it meant further opportunities to reach the world. From the Greek word '*makarios*', the Greek Orthodox Church has an Arch-bishop who rejoices in the name of Arch-bishop Makarios, who is the virtual head of this church. It is he who leads this branch of the Eastern Church and it is he who receives much publicity.

However, the photographs that appear in public show a man who is dressed entirely in black and who has a fairly sad demeanour. This is a far cry from the meaning of his name 'Makarios', which means blessed, happy or overjoyed. It is an adjective which denotes a state of uncontainable happiness and it has its origins in 'that which is the highest good'. It is used in several places in the New Testament, especially in the gospel of Luke, where it appears frequently in Luke's version of the 'sermon on the mount'. Jesus stated over and over again: blessed or happy are those who are within His kingdom and who obey His laws. It is used seven times in the book of Revelation where John stated that those who read the Revelation and those who remain pure until the end, are those who will be the most happy, blessed and complete. They will inherit the kingdom.

It is a word that describes not just how we feel, but it goes beyond that to describe the state of those who will endure unto the end. In other words, we are blessed and happy even when we do not feel blessed and happy, it is a word that does not just describe feelings but makes a statement about our nature in Christ. We are a happy people even when we are sad.

It is even used twice of God Himself, when Paul wrote to Timothy and said, 'God who is blessed, God, who knows no changes and who is always constant, is a happy God'. We can rest in the glorious fact that we are happy and we will always be happy in spite of anything that we may go through on our journey to heaven. Because the God who decreed our forgiveness and who Himself rests in a state of happiness has also decreed our position of blessedness.

My Journal ____

____

____

____

____

____

____

____

____

KEY PRAYER

Heavenly Father, thank you for making me a happy and a blessed child of God, I rejoice in my position today. Help me to understand that this position of happiness and blessedness does not depend on my circumstances, nor does it depend on what is going on around me and it certainly does not depend upon how I feel. Thank you that I am happy all the time and please help me to understand this glorious truth and help me to live in it.

January 25th

KEY WORD: **Cheerful**

KEY VERSE: **2 Corinthians 9 : 7**

Each man should give what he has decided in his heart to give, not reluctantly or under compulsion, for God loves a cheerful giver.

Having looked yesterday at the state of happiness and blessedness, the next step is an obvious one, that of being cheerful. Our state of happiness does not rest upon how we feel, but cheerfulness does. We can choose to be cheerful or we can choose to be the opposite.

Only once in the New Testament does the word cheerful appear in the way that it does in 2 Corinthians 9. In this context Paul was teaching about giving, and within this context he was talking primarily about the giving of finances. The Greek word used is the word *'hilaros'*, which is more correctly translated as 'a state of joyousness bordering on a sense of overwhelming glee', and this state is induced by our willingness to obey God in every area, especially in the whole area of the giving of our finances.

God loves a cheerful giver, or, more correctly, God loves a giver of overwhelming joy. It is from this root word that we derive our English word hilarious, a word that has come to be used when someone is in the state of advanced happiness brought on by an act or by our actions. I will leave you to draw the picture on whether or not your giving borders on a hilarious act! At times our giving is a reluctant act and at times our giving is almost that of a grudging action, when all the time God is looking for those who give with a hilarious spirit. We can either choose to be cheerful or we can choose to be a reluctant participator.

Paul was setting before the Church the two factors upon which our state of joy will depend, it is up to us whether we choose the state of generous joy or the state of a grudging spirit. Paul reminded us, too, in the preceding verse, 'that we will reap what we sow'.

The Greek root of this word '*hilaros*' can be traced back to that of a Hebrew word which is found in the book of Psalms. In Psalm 104 : 15 the writer spoke of 'wine that gladdens the heart... and oil that makes the face to shine'. It is the word 'shine' that is the root for the word '*hilaros*', which places another dimension upon the way that we behave as children of God. We can choose to be in a place of cheerfulness which can border on the way that oil makes our faces shine when we are anointed. Or we can choose not to be cheerful and not to shine and remain in a place where we reap what we sow.

I have met a lot of people who shine with an anointing and who have chosen the lifestyle of giving, they are hilarious. I have also met a lot of people who have chosen not to be cheerful. I know who I like to be around the most!

My Journal

KEY PRAYER

Heavenly Father, teach me over and over again that I will reap what I sow and help me to learn the lesson. Help me to be a cheerful giver so that my life is one of hilarity. I choose this life style rather than that of a grudging giver, so help my life to shine with your glory so that I might be an attractive child of God.

January 26th

KEY WORD: ***Anointing***

KEY VERSE: ***James 5 : 14***

Is any one of you sick? He should call the elders of the church to pray over him and anoint him with oil in the name of the Lord.

Having looked yesterday at the 'oil that makes the face to shine', the obvious next step would be to look at the oil itself as a token or symbol of the Holy Spirit. Throughout the New Testament and in fact throughout the Old Testament too, oil was used as a symbol of the work of the Holy Spirit , the anointing of the Holy Spirit and in fact any function of the Holy Spirit's ministry. We also find water as a symbol, as too are the symbols of fire and wind, but over and above all, oil is the greatest symbol.

There are several words in the Greek for the word 'anointing'. The main one and the one most generally used is '*aleipho*', which means to 'refresh'. This word is used in three different ways. Firstly, to give physical refreshment following washing, secondly, to place a measure of oil upon a sick body and thirdly, to embalm a dead body. In all three cases the whole procedure was one of refreshment.

In the aspect of washing, the refreshment was obviously one of pure cleansing. You were made clean by water and then you were kept clean by the anointing of yourself by oil, much in the same way that today we would place a perfume or an aftershave lotion upon ourselves.

In the second case, placing a measure of oil upon a sick person was very much a symbol of the ministry of the Holy Spirit touching a person in need and identifying with the need. The small portion of oil was an indication that the Holy Spirit was drawing near to heal.

In the third case, that of the anointing of a dead body, this was a clear sign of preparation for the future. It was a sign that an embalming had taken place and that in the future life a fragrance would be appreciated and would be a preparation of an entrance into heaven.

In each case there is a clear sign to us of our lives under the ministry of the Holy Spirit. We need to be refreshed, we need to know the touch of the Spirit upon us and we also need the fragrance of His person in preparation for our acts of service.

In the Old Testament all acts of anointing carried with them the sense of sacredness, as in the anointing of a priest. In the New Testament the oil is much more of a symbol of the spirit and should be treated as such. There is no special anointing oil and there is nothing sacred about the small drop placed upon one's body – we should always take care to remember that. However, we should not allow the symbolism to blind us to the fact that we still need God's anointing each and every day in order to minister for Him.

We should also remember too, that a small drop is not enough for ministry, it is enough as a symbol but it is not enough for our lives, our ministries and our daily growth in God.

My Journal ______________________________

KEY PRAYER

Heavenly Father, thank you for the daily outpouring of your Spirit upon our lives. Thank you too, that with each and every infilling there is power for service, freedom for worship and refreshment in our daily lives. Please fill me again and again with your Spirit so that I might be more and more effective for you.

January 27th

KEY WORD: **Oil**

KEY VERSE: **Mark 6 : 13**

They drove out many demons and anointed many sick people with oil and healed them.

When we looked at the anointing yesterday, we saw that there were several symbols for the anointing, namely oil, water, fire and wind. However, oil was the most frequently used symbol. The Greek word for 'oil' is a very interesting one, it is the word *'elaion'*, and the reason that it is an interesting word is that there were pure oils and inferior oils. Only pure oil was allowed to be used for priestly anointing.

This oil was called pure because it was extracted by great pressure and without any heat being used within the process. It could be known as 'beaten oil' or golden oil and is better known today as virgin oil or olive oil. The word *'elaion'* is used over 200 times throughout the Bible and is closely associated with all anointing of a priestly function.

Other uses for oil, particularly in the New Testament, were for the lamps within the temple, for medicinal uses, for anointing purposes such as feasts and dead bodies, and lastly, for the whole purpose of declaring a sense of miraculous power, as in today's key verse of Mark 6 : 13.

Jesus gave His disciples power over demons and sickness and the world. He sent them out to change the world and the symbolism of the oil was a declaration that they had been anointed with power.

The whole dimension of this anointing of power was to show to them and to the world that they were more than just mere travelling preachers and more than just the normal type of itinerant teachers, who travelled constantly the length and breadth of the land. These were men and women of the Spirit who had received an endowment of power from on high and the outward showing of this was not just the miracles and the healings but the flowing of oil upon them. Oil that would remind them of priestly functions and of refreshing cleansing and of purity for service.

Golden oil and pure oil that flowed upon them would be the symbol of an anointing that would abide upon them. They would smell its fragrance for days and they would never forget the moment that Jesus poured oil upon them. The anointing oil that came upon them still comes upon us today and its fragrance dwells with us constantly.

My Journal

KEY PRAYER

Heavenly Father, thank you today for your anointing upon my life and thank you for the fragrant sense of your presence that rests upon me right now. I glorify you for the fact that you have chosen me and anointed me to serve you in my generation. Help me every day to appreciate this anointing and help me 'to live and move and have my being' under a daily fresh touch of your oil.

January 28th

KEY WORD: **Fish**

KEY VERSE: **1 Corinthians 15 : 39**

All flesh is not the same: Men have one kind of flesh, animals have another, birds another and fish another.

It is an interesting thought to know that the word fish or fishes is only used 26 times in the whole of the New Testament and 25 of them are in the gospels. In other words it only appears once in the New Testament outside of the life and ministry of Jesus as portrayed by Matthew, Mark, Luke and John. This is a surprising fact given that fish played such an important part in the whole aspect of ministry by the disciples, by the apostles and by the Church.

The Greek word for fish is *'ichthus'*, and it was the word that was used by the Church as a sign of a meeting place when persecution came upon the Church; it was used as the symbol of the fact that believers were present. Later the actual word was replaced by the sign of a fish, which is still in use today. In actual fact, I find it interesting that when the Church was birthed, the sign of a fish was seen in great numbers. As we get nearer and nearer to the end of the Church Age it seems to me that there has been a very strong revival of the sign of the fish. In fact, world wide, more fish are seen today on cars, in homes and in some shops, than ever before. Was the Church born on earth with the sign of the fish, and is the Church closing its work on earth with a revival of the sign of the fish?

'Ichthus' denotes a fish and 25 times it is used in the gospels when Jesus and His disciples caught fish, ate fish and left the fish in order to catch men. The catching of men rather than fish is the very reason why the word and then the sign was used by the Church to denote its actions. The new Church was a 'fishing catching' Church, but it caught men and women, and boys and girls rather than fish. Jesus sought to teach His disciples this 'catching' lesson

when He commanded them to lower their nets on the other side after they had toiled all night and had caught nothing. The result was a huge catch of fish. This lesson was not just that they might learn to trust and obey Him, nor was it just a matter of a miracle feeding, following a tiring night's labour. This was in fact a prophetic picture showing the disciples that there would be a time when a fish-catching church would receive great shoals of fish that would be added to the church daily as people were saved.

This '*ichthus*' fellowship would be founded upon one great fact, that it would see tremendous growth and blessing but that it would be 'not by might, nor by power', nor would it be by great strength, or by toiling all night and catching nothing. It would be by the direct command of a Lord and Saviour, who would give direction to His Church, and would in fact be Lord of the Church.

The fish found its way into every level of society and was the sign of a great ingathering of souls – so much so, that the fish is very much alive and well today.

My Journal ____

KEY PRAYER

Heavenly Father, thank you for the great fact that the Church is alive and well today, you have preserved the Church through great persecution and threat, and yet it is stronger now than 2000 years ago. I rejoice today in being part of your great Church, help me to become an active fisher of men so that the kingdom might be extended and that I might be blessed. Help me to rejoice whenever I see a 'fish', as it is a sign, even today, of someone who is a part of a world wide, God-glorifying, earth-changing Church: the Church of the Lord Jesus Christ.

January 29th

KEY WORD: **Scattered**

KEY VERSE: **Acts 8 : 1**

Saul (Paul) was there, giving approval to Stephen's death. On that day a great persecution broke out against the church at Jerusalem, and all except the apostles were scattered throughout Judea and Samaria.

Acts chapters 7 and 8 are a turning point in the life and work of the New Testament Church. They mark the occasion of the first Christian martyr – Stephen. They record the entrance of Saul (Paul) into Church history. They also reveal the first occasions of persecution against this new Church and they also mark the time when the first scattering of believers commenced. Believers left Jerusalem and fled to other cities, towns and areas in order to escape what was happening to the Church. This was in fact the first of many scatterings that would take place, as this initial persecution was quickly followed by other times and seasons of hurt and disorder upon the Church.

There are several epistles written in the New Testament to those who were scattered abroad as more and more people fled into the far reaches of the Middle East in order to escape. As they went they planted churches, and as they went the Church became more and more widespread. What was planned as the destroying of the Church actually became its salvation, as the plan of God to reach the uttermost parts of the earth took place.

The Greek word for scatter is the beautifully descriptive word '*diaspeiro*', which literally translated means 'to scatter abroad'. However, this simple translation does not do the word its full justice. A deeper look at the word brings forth something far more penetrating. The '*diaspeiro*' is actually formed by taking two separate words and making them one. The first part of the word is formed by using the word *'dia'* which means 'throughout'. The second part of the word is formed by using the word *'speiro'* which means 'to sow seed'.

So instead of a simple translation meaning 'to scatter abroad', we now have the fuller and deeper meaning of the Church being 'sown as seed throughout the world'. The picture is an obvious one of a farmer who walks the length and breadth of his fields scattering grain to the four corners of his fertile soil. You could not get a greater picture or understanding of what God was doing at this time than that. God was seeking to reach the uttermost parts of the earth – which was what the Great Commission called for in the first place: 'go and make disciples of all nations', Matthew 28 : 19. Having seen the Church confine themselves mainly to Jerusalem, God allowed the suffering of persecution to drive the Church 'into all the world'. This was a divine scattering of holy seed into a fertile and longing world – the exact conditions for a vast harvest of divine proportions.

Suffering has always produced pain, but along with pain there has always been growth, blessing and a fuller picture of God building His Church, and of God building His people. The words of James – who wrote one of the epistles that was addressed to those who were scattered abroad – are quite apt in gaining a fuller understanding of the bigger picture taking place. He wrote in his first chapter, verses 3 and 4, 'Consider it joy my brothers, when you face trials of many kinds, because you know that the testing of your faith develops perseverance. Perseverance must finish its work so that you may be mature and complete, not lacking in anything.'

The Church was bigger, stronger and far more mature as the result of 'the scattering' as the Church became a world wide church and the people became a universal people.

KEY PRAYER

Heavenly Father, I rejoice and count it joy when I face trials as I have come to learn that I shall be bigger and stronger as a result of them than I would have been if I remain settled and secure. Help me to continue to learn this lesson each and every day, and help me to praise you through pain, and help me to understand your ways within my life.

January 30th

KEY WORD: **Witness**

KEY VERSE: **Acts 1 : 8**

You will receive power when the Holy Spirit comes on you; and you will be my witnesses in Jerusalem, and in all Judea and Samaria, and to the ends of the earth.

Jesus commanded His Church to be a witness throughout the world and yesterday we saw just how this process took place, with the scattering of the Church into all the earth. God was sowing His seeds into fertile soil.

The command to be a witness has several meanings. Obviously anyone who gives testimony to the saving grace of the Lord Jesus Christ is giving a witness or bearing a witness. Anyone who shares news of a healing or a miracle is also bearing a testimony of God's goodness. However, that is not the full meaning of the word, nor is it the complete picture of what Jesus was seeking to convey when He commanded His disciples to be His witnesses.

The Greek word used in the key verse of Acts 1 : 8, is the word '*martus*'. It is from this Greek word that we derive our English word 'martyr', which places a whole new impact on the words of Jesus. He was actually calling them to 'lay down their lives' as they receive power to become the leaders of the new Church and as they would travel to the ends of the earth. The interesting fact is that almost all who heard His words that day would actually face a martyr's death later in Church history.

So the fuller impact of the command of Jesus is to bear witness by death. Yesterday we noticed that in Acts chapters 7 and 8, that Stephen's death produced the first Christian martyr. As he died, the Church was scattered, but as he died the penetrating impact of God's command rocked the new Early Church to its very foundations. The fuller impact of what it meant to be a disciple began to filter deep into the minds of those who had joined the Church. It is an interesting fact of Church history that when persecution breaks out upon the Church, the Church has always become stronger. When martyrdom has been seen there has always been a surge forward in those who apply for mission work.

The word obviously carries with it the very real sense of laying down your life for that of the Church and its witness. Throughout Church history there have been intense times of persecution when millions have lost their lives in the cause of the gospel. However, the word also carries with it the sense of one who 'bears the cost of giving a testimony', which can and has meant the loss of life. However, it also means the cost of giving a testimony in the sense of being ridiculed by those who refuse to hear. It can mean the shame of isolation when one who has become a Christian is removed from the family or from friends. It also means in a very real way the loss of your own ambition, desires and will, in that when you follow Jesus you take up the cross and follow Him, leaving your own plans in the dust of the past to rise to the atmosphere of His plan and destiny for your life.

My Journal

KEY PRAYER

Heavenly Father, I may never feel the full impact of being a martyr but help me to still become a strong witness for you even when it may mean the loss of friends and family and the loss of status within the world in which I live. Help me to live and move and have my being in you, so that the world might see that I belong to you and you live within me. Help me to always bear witness of your love and grace.

January 31st

KEY WORD: **Marks**

KEY VERSE: **Galatians 6 : 17**

Finally, let no-one cause me trouble, for I bear on my body the marks of Jesus.

In this Scripture, Paul pleaded for understanding in the fact that no-one can stand against him or speak against him as he has carried his cross and borne his sufferings as an apostle. He was speaking of the fact that as an apostle, he passed the test of his faithfulness and has fought a good fight. He was actually making a defence of his suffering.

As you read the book of Acts you begin to realise just what this man suffered for the sake of the gospel. There were beatings, shipwrecks, ridicule, lashes of the whip on numerous occasions, not to mention the constant travelling and care of the churches. The physical marks borne by the apostle were grievous indeed and he bore them with a sense of fulfilment in that he had run the race and fought the fight.

As we saw yesterday when we reviewed the word 'martyr', Paul suffered the loss of his own ambitions and plans for his life when he laid down his life for the Lord, and he suffered the loss of a comfortable life for that of the life of an apostle. Yet he knew that this was no loss at all because he received a hundredfold of blessing and joy and he counted it all but loss for the glory of the cross. He would eventually literally lose his life in Rome as a martyr and would pass through the veil into eternity, having laid down his life in the fullest sense. He would finish the course with great faithfulness.

However, the marks that he spoke of carry a deep sense of feeling. The Greek word used is the word *'stigma'*, which literally translated means a 'brand' or a 'prick in the skin'. It was used by masters when they branded their slaves when the body mark was a symbol or a sign that they were belonging to another. It denoted the fact that they no longer belonged to themselves, but they were branded as belonging to a master who had paid a price for their slavery.

However, Paul's words to the Galatian Church do not just carry this kind of understanding, as if he was literally saying that no one could speak against him as he bore on his body the marks of the ownership of a master. What Paul was saying however, was much deeper than this – he was saying that he was bearing the marks or the *'stigma'* of his devotion to the Lord. Paul was probably not a pleasant person to look at, which was a *'stigma'* in itself, yet he bore the burden with a sense of pride in the fact that he belonged to the Lord, and he counted it joy. Marks like this were forbidden under the law of Moses, however, Paul had not inflicted them upon himself, these marks were inflicted by others who had sought to hinder the spread of the gospel and who had sought to harm Paul's work.

My Journal

KEY PRAYER

Heavenly Father, help me to understand the pain of suffering and the cost of following you, as at times I feel that I have given nothing in return for your loss. I pledge allegiance to the Lamb and I will seek to follow you all the days of my life, even when it might mean bearing in my body the marks of this cost. I praise you today for your willingness to lay down the life of your Son that I might be saved.

February 1st

KEY WORD: **Cross**

KEY VERSE: **Philippians 3 : 18**

For, as I have often told you before and now say again even with tears, many live as enemies of the cross of Christ.

As we commence a new month of daily meditations, what better way of starting than to remember the cross of Jesus. We do this each time when we break bread in the communion service. We also remember the cross each time that our thoughts stray to the fact that 'it was for me' that Jesus died.

We all have a picture in our minds of the crucifixion scene. This picture is of course entirely subjective, it is made up of our own understanding of the writings within the gospels and it is drawn from reminiscences of sermons heard over the years and it is also drawn from our memories of paintings and other descriptions of the cross. However, our understanding may be faulty due to the fact that 2,000 years have passed and we are drawing thoughts from history and other people's understandings.

The Greek word for cross is '*stauros*'. This word primarily denotes an upright stake of wood, or in our western understanding a 'pole'. This is to be distinguished from the normally understood 'T' shape of the Church's perceived cross. It is quite clear that the 'T' shape cross came from a pagan sign and symbol, and by the 3rd century the Christian Church had moved away from some of the doctrines of faith and with the increase of pagans and heathens joining the Church, several of the most commonly held beliefs were being changed or adapted.

Constantine had a major effect upon the Church when he declared that he had received a vision which had 'brought him to faith' and that Jesus had died upon an X-shaped cross, but this was never really accepted by the Church.

The Roman method of execution was borrowed from the Phoenicians and the Greek word *'stauros'* denotes a stake, so it could have been a straight pole, which was the most commonly held theory of the time. However, pagan or not as a symbol, the 'T' shape has come to be held as the Church's natural understanding of the form of death that Jesus had to endure. However, it is not the shape of the cross that matters nor is it the wood that has an effect, it is the man on the cross that makes the difference. There is no discussion concerning His death, although there could be much discussion about the manner and nature of His death. Whether it was a 'T' shape or a straight pole matters not one bit, the fact that He died for our sins is the central fact of our faith and our future.

It is an interesting fact that the same word *'stauros'* is used within the epistles when the writers declared the fact that we must be identified with 'the cross'. In the verse that we read this morning Paul declared that some people have become enemies of the 'cross', but went on to say that our destiny and citizenship is in heaven, Philippians 3 : 20. In other parts of the epistles we are urged to take up our cross and identify with the sufferings of Jesus which are our glory. It is not the shape of the cross but the glorious fact that He died for our sins and that He rose again. We therefore glory in the cross gladly for it is our only hope, both now and forever.

My Journal ______________________________

____

____

____

KEY PRAYER

Heavenly Father, thank you for the cross, thank you for the glorious fact that Jesus died for me. Today I give you thanks for this central fact of history, that changed our daily calendars from BC to AD, and that changed the course of human history and even more than that, for the fact that it has changed my life. Help me to live within the shadow of the cross and help me to constantly give thanks for the fact that 'it was for me' that Jesus died.

February 2nd

KEY WORD: **Sorcerer**

KEY VERSE: **Revelation 21 : 8**

The cowardly, the unbelieving, the vile, the murderers, the sexually immoral, those who practise magic arts, the idolaters and liars - their place will be in the fiery lake of burning sulphur. This is the second death.

This verse in the book of Revelation is one of the most challenging and graphic verses in the entire Bible. It describes the final end of those who are 'outside of the kingdom' and this final end is most horrific and sad. Those who face a final end within this lake of burning sulphur are those who have set their face against the Lord and who have consistently turned aside to their own ways. The word that we are considering today is translated two ways, in the NIV the word is translated 'magic arts' and in the KJV it is translated as 'sorcerer'. In both of these versions of the Bible the translation is really not complete. The Greek word is *'pharmakos'* and this is the word that is used for 'one who is involved with drugs'. We derive our English word pharmacy from this Greek word and of course from the word pharmacy we derive the word chemist.

In order to describe the lifestyle of some of the people who are outside of the kingdom of God, established words are used that are in keeping with time and history. However, times move on and of course, times are changing. It is only within our brief lifetime that this word has sadly become all too familiar. The drug scene and the drug cartels are now quite commonplace and young people particularly have become addicted to a lifestyle that other generations have not known.

As this word found its way into the text within the book of Revelation it is therefore quite obvious that one of the signs of the End Times is a rise in what was translated as sorcery and magic arts, but which really has an even more tragic meaning, that of mass drug use and abuse. The word '*pharmakos*' however, does not mean one who uses drugs but it has an even more pointed meaning, that of dependency. The word has an imperative use within it which is more correctly translated as 'devoted to' or 'dependent upon'. This imperative sense implies not just a casual usage but a lifestyle that has become 'dependent upon', or 'devoted to' and even the sharper sense of 'plying trade'.

The word that is used in this text is also used within other texts that imply that along with drug usage is the form of witchcraft and occult powers. I would take this to mean, therefore, that the pliers of the drug trade, the pushers and the dealers and the cartels are the ones that the book of Revelation describes. Those who use this devilish trade for their own financial gain are the propagators of intense evil and they will find their final end not in profit but in loss, not in success but in total and abject failure.

We often see evil going unpunished and the workers of evil growing proud and arrogant. However, the Bible makes it quite clear that there will be a final punishment for evil and evil-doers and that pure justice will be seen.

Even though this verse in the book of Revelation is a negative verse, it is quite clear that there is still a way of escape from sin, even gross sin, before the great and terrible day when the Lord comes upon the earth. We are still in the age of grace and God is still a God of all grace, not willing that any should perish but that all might be saved.

KEY PRAYER

Heavenly Father, I thank you today for the amazing fact that grace has touched my life and that I am saved from destruction. I rejoice today in sins forgiven and peace with God. However, I pray today for those who are still outside of the kingdom, those who work the acts of darkness and I pray that there might be a mighty harvest of those who practise such arts. I thank you that heaven will be full of people who once walked in darkness but who found perfect light.

February 3rd

KEY WORD: **Fasting**

KEY VERSE: **Matthew 4 : 2**

After fasting for forty days and forty nights, Jesus was hungry.

Having considered gross acts of sin in yesterday's meditation the correct thing to do is to look at ways of bringing a remedy to situations that are beyond our control. The New Testament is quite clear that there are times when prayer alone is not sufficient to bring about a remedy, therefore Jesus taught and introduced the subject of prayer and fasting. His apostles also continued this teaching and practice within their times of intercession.

Fasting was not just a New Testament practice; however, the Jews within their acts of worship practised fasting as part of their devotion to the Lord. The Greek word that is used for fasting has a very rich meaning that is often overlooked in the English translations. The word used is the word '*nesteia*', and it literally means to 'abstain voluntarily from food'. It is the act of voluntary abstinence that gives this word its impact. The act of fasting is not an imposed act nor should it be a forced act from outside of your situation. '*Nesteia*' means to feel the need to abstain from food on a purely voluntary basis, the need comes from within you.

There are times when we are faced with situations that are greater than we can cope with and situations that require more of an urgent need than simply that of prayer. When times like this are upon us we have an extra weapon within our armoury, that of prayer coupled with times and seasons of fasting. However, it is we who have to make the choice to take part in an act of abstinence from food, or favourite pastimes, or acts of leisure. The act of fasting is a purely personal one and focuses upon your own need and your own remedy to solve it. It is also quite clear that we should not discuss this matter openly and we are also to take steps to hide the fact that we have chosen this method of spiritual warfare. This does not mean that we keep this act as a totally private matter, there are times when sharing the need and allowing others to fast with you can be greatly beneficial. However, fasting is not to be paraded as something that is far more spiritual than it is, and it certainly is something that should never be used as a lesson to prove that you are more spiritual because you fast, than those who have chosen not to fast.

The Old Testament use of fasting was often a national thing which goes beyond the Greek meaning of the word. The Jews would use fasting as a means of conveying great repentance and it would also be used as a means of showing God just how motivated they were in certain situations of great need. However, it could be abused, as in the cases where the Pharisees would openly display their piety by boasting of acts of fasting. This is why Jesus told His disciples to anoint their faces and to hide the fact that they were conducting periods of prayer and fasting.

Days of prayer and fasting and indeed seasons of prayer and fasting can be a stronger method than that of simply praying about a need. In the text today we read that Jesus fasted for forty days and forty nights in order to overcome temptation. He chose to go into the wilderness following His baptism and He chose the path of separation and abstinence for a season in order to develop a stronger relationship with His Father. 'Nesteia' has the imperative form to its meaning which allows us the choice to include fasting along with our times and seasons of prayer. Those who have used this method know just how beneficial it can be.

KEY PRAYER

Heavenly Father, thank you for reminding me today just how helpful and beneficial fasting can be within my times and seasons of prayer. I thank you that this weapon is available for my use, however, I pray that I shall never become boastful or spiritually proud as a result of using this method of spiritual warfare. Help me always to remember that 'the Father who sees in secret rewards in the open', and help me always to understand that fasting is part of my relationship with you and not for public display.

February 4th

KEY WORD: **Miracle**

KEY VERSE: **Acts 19 : 11**

God did extraordinary miracles through Paul.

Having looked yesterday at the concept of prayer and fasting and having seen that fasting is a personal weapon in the believer's armoury that can produce beneficial results, it is only right that we consider today the results of what we have come to know as miracles. The New Testament is full of miraculous acts that are very obviously the acts of God. There were times when having seen great acts the disciples came to Jesus to ask how these things might be accomplished and Jesus referred them to prayer and fasting.

When we face a situation that is beyond our human resources to remedy we have a weapon that is able to produce results and to bring about a miracle. It is just this thought that the New Testament writers had in mind when they wrote about miracles and they used a word that conveys just the meaning. The Greek word for miracle is the word *'dunamis'*, which literally means 'power of a supernatural ability producing works that can not be produced by natural means'. It is a little word that has a massive meaning, and I often feel that we have not yet grasped the full impact of this word. When there are no other means of obtaining a required result with our natural abilities, and then God comes to produce a result for us, it can quite rightly be classified as a miracle. Whether it is a healing, or a deliverance or a provision, or is quite simply an answer that came beyond the natural way, God has performed a miracle.

We derive our English word 'dynamite' from the root of this Greek word *'dunamis'*, which conveys the picture of a massive explosion of power, and this is exactly what the New Testament is trying to convey. When God comes in an extraordinary way to bring us an answer to our prayers which is beyond any natural means to achieve, we see an explosion of God's almighty power. However, it is an interesting fact that the word *'dunamis'* is only used eight times in the New Testament. Obviously there are more than eight miracles with the 27 books of the New Testament, yet the use of this word is confined to only eight references. The probable reason for its limited use is the fact that God requires us to use the concept of this word carefully.

It is so easy to consider any and every answer to be a miracle. However, the word *'dunamis'* does convey the very strong thought that only an answer that is beyond the natural means to achieve can be called a miracle. Maybe the limited use of the word should teach us to give careful analysis to those things that happen in order that all the praise and all the glory might go to the One who produces explosive acts of a supernatural kind.

Our very breath each day is a miracle, the fact that we are saved and on our way to heaven is a miracle. These things are beyond our natural ability to achieve and we thank God each and every day for His miracle intervention within our lives.

My Journal ________________________________

____

____

____

____

____

____

____

KEY PRAYER

Heavenly Father, thank you today for miracles within my life, and thank you for your explosive acts of supernatural power. Help me never to forget and never to take for granted that all that I have and ever will be is only because of your intervention within my life. I bless you today for the time when you came and exploded into my life, for this was the greatest miracle of all.

February 5th

KEY WORD: **Forgive**

KEY VERSE: **Matthew 9 : 2**

Some men brought to Jesus a paralytic, lying on a mat. When Jesus saw their faith, He said to the paralytic, " ...son, your sins are forgiven."

The word 'forgive' is a most wonderful word, it conjures up the feelings of release and peace, and it displays the feelings of emotion and reunion. The whole word seems to ring with emotion and feeling as forgiveness brings with it the atmosphere of the fact that, following an act of wrong, you now have been released from any penalty of guilt, and that nothing is being held against you any longer. You are forgiven.

Of course these feelings of emotion are quite right as forgiveness is just that kind of act, no longer are we guilty and no longer are we made to pay – the act of forgiveness is given. Yet this is only part of the meaning of this very rich word.

The Greek word used for our English word 'forgive' is the word '*aphiemi*' and it is more correctly translated as 'to be sent away with all things being cancelled'. It has its root meaning within the whole area of the financial world, where at times debts would be cancelled and you would be sent away free from any debts. The crippling effects of debts now cancelled would bring an immediate change of circumstances and a feeling of great release.

Is it any wonder therefore, that the New Testament writers chose this word to convey the thought of forgiveness of sin, when the cancellation of sin and its debt would bring the truth of real forgiveness. Not only are we forgiven of our sins but we are released from all debt; debt that is past and debt that is present. It is no wonder that the writers rejoiced in this word as it correctly displayed the full impact of forgiveness. However, we must remember that this act of divine forgiveness is quite different to that of human forgiveness, because we often forgive but we do not often forget. We will forgive acts against us but we retain the ability to remember, and quite often these remembrances will surface if we are ever wronged again. In the case of the word '*aphiemi*' the debt is not only cancelled and forgiven, it is also forgotten in the sense that the cause of the offence is removed. God not only forgives us, He not only cancels the debt, He completely removes the cause of the offence – sin, and He wills to forget what we owe. There is no more debt and we are sent away free from the past accumulations of sin and wrongdoing. We are forgiven by a God who wills never to remember things against us again.

This is the true meaning of forgiveness, as in the text that we read today, Jesus, having seen the faith of the men who brought a sick man on a bed to be healed, did not just heal the man but brought him the greatest act of release, He forgave his sins. The man went away released from sickness, with all that this meant to him, but he also was sent away with his sin and guilt cancelled. Jesus drew attention to this when He later said to the crowd, who had watched this great event: "Which is easier: to say, 'Your sins are forgiven,' or to say, 'Get up and walk'?" He drew attention to the greater of the miracles, that of forgiveness.

My Journal

KEY PRAYER

Heavenly Father, I have seen today the real meaning of forgiveness, thank you that you have forgiven me. I have been sent away with not just my sins forgiven but with my whole debt cancelled and I praise you for this wonderful fact. Help me to learn to forgive those who trespass against me and help me each day to learn to practise true forgiveness, not just forgiving but forgetting all things that have ever been done against me.

February 6th

KEY WORD: **Masterbuilder**

KEY VERSE: **1 Corinthians 3 : 10**

By the grace God has given me, I laid a foundation as an expert builder (masterbuilder), and someone else is building on it. But each one should be careful how he builds.

Paul introduced us to quite an interesting subject when he wrote about the building of the local church. He called himself a masterbuilder, or as the NIV translates it, an expert builder. He was seeking to convey the fact that every ministry is unique within the Church and all ministries are needed so that the Church might function correctly. He sought to draw the distinction between different ministries and different men in order that the Church might understand that one sows and one reaps, but it is God who gives the increase.

However, he did describe himself as a masterbuilder in the sense that he laid a foundation for others to build upon, and that he laid it wisely and carefully in order that the Church might have a foundation that was strong and spiritual and that would allow growth and development in the future.

The word used was translated differently in the KJV and in the NIV. The KJV used the word masterbuilder and the NIV used the words expert builder; both are right to a point. However, the Greek word that was used places a slightly different emphasis upon the fuller meaning that Paul was seeking to convey.

The Greek word used is *'architekton'*, and it would be obvious that from this word we have derived our English word 'architect'. The word architect in our understanding means one who designs or draws the plans for a building, however, *'architekton'* goes further than this and introduces a different aspect of truth. The word used conveys the meaning of 'rule' or 'beginning' and it was used of those who 'had the inception of an idea'. It did not mean just those who drew up a plan or those who had designed something, it was deeper than that. The word brought about the understanding that someone had received an initial idea and had set out to convey this idea – probably in written form – to others.

When Paul said that he had been the architect of the Corinthian Church he was talking about the whole concept of planting this church, directing this church and setting its course for the future. This is why he deliberately stressed the fact that those who followed him should be careful how they built upon his foundation. This was stated because he had not just commenced this church in the sense of planting or pioneering, but he had designed this church and brought about its course of destiny.

We could of course use this word in the sense of God's great design within our lives, He is the great masterbuilder who has fashioned our lives and He has set our lives on a course according to His great plan, to bring us to an eternal destiny.

The word is a word of action and a word of peaceful exercise, Paul was in control of the Church, having laid its foundation, and it was to be a church that, in spite of its problems and carnality, was to be a beacon of light within a pagan city. It was to this church that Paul gave the clearest instructions regarding the use of the gifts of the Spirit and the practice of the communion service, among other great teachings. All this came about because He was the great expert builder. Our Heavenly Father knows our needs and builds accordingly as our masterbuilder.

KEY PRAYER

Heavenly Father, you know all things, you have planned all things and you are building within my life. Thank you today that you are not just leaving me to work things out as I go along, but you have designed my life to function, as you are the great divine architect of all things. I praise you today for your goodness and I ask you to help me to understand this plan each day so that I might submit to you constantly. Thank you too, for all those who have built good things into my life since the day that I came to know you.

February 7th

KEY WORD: **Songs**

KEY VERSE: **Ephesians 5 : 19**

Speak to one another with psalms, hymns and spiritual songs. Sing and make music in your heart to the Lord.

Here is a lovely word that produces a lovely thought and brings us to a lovely concept. Paul urged the Ephesian believers to sing and he suggested that there are three forms of singing. They could sing firstly, with psalms – beautiful Old Testament songs of praise. They could sing secondly, with hymns – once again taken from the songs of the Old Testament and songs that were being created within the New Testament Church. He also urged them to sing thirdly, with spiritual songs.

The fact that he added the word 'spiritual' to the songs that he was suggesting they sing brings a whole new, fresh meaning to worship. He could have meant 'spiritual' songs that would be the opposite to songs of the world, or he could also have meant 'spiritual' in terms of singing in the Spirit or singing in tongues.

The Greek word for song or songs is '*ode*', and we derive our English word 'ode' from this word which literally translated means 'song' or 'expressive poetry'.

In New Testament terms there are many types of new songs. There are the new songs of heaven, there is the song of the Lamb and there are also these spiritual songs – and these songs are quite different. These spiritual songs are very much part of church life in the early church and they carry with them a different expression of praise. The way that Paul taught them to the Ephesian Church, places quite a strong emphasis on the way that they are to be sung.

Firstly, they are to be sung to one another. In most churches today people are encouraged to 'sing unto the Lord' and this of course is quite right, however, Paul placed strong emphasis upon the fact that the singers were to encourage one another with songs. They were expressly told to build each other up with music as it was beneficial to all. In some ways we have lost this emphasis and we should seek to get back to the way in which this aspect of worship builds faith in each other.

Secondly, they were encouraged to sing to themselves and make music in their own hearts. This is another aspect of praise that we should seek to cultivate, we should be often singing to ourselves. If singing to each other builds each other up, how much more singing to ourselves should help to keep us buoyant in faith, especially in times of adversity.

Thirdly, the Ephesian believers were encouraged to sing unto the Lord. There is nothing greater than to bless God with music and singing, in fact the whole of heaven is filled with wonderful music for the whole of eternity. It is the sound of many waters and it is the sound of mighty thunders. It is the new song of expressive praise.

As the New Testament Church, the first church, was encouraged to sing and as the Early Church was instructed in the ways of song, we too should seek to sing in our day and generation as we are the Church at the close of the age of grace.

My Journal ______________________________

____

____

____

____

KEY PRAYER

Heavenly Father, thank you for music, thank you for singing and thank you too, for spiritual songs. Help me each day to sing to others so that they might be built up in holy faith. Help me to sing to myself by way of exhortation, and help me, too, to make melody to you at all times. I bless you for creative songs that have lasted the whole Church age. Help me to keep singing so that my songs can be blended with the new songs of heaven.

February 8th

KEY WORD: ***Justification***

KEY VERSE: **Romans 4 : 25**

He was delivered over to death for our sins and was raised to life for our justification.

This word justification is a very heavy, theological sounding word, and as with other theological sounding words we often neglect them and avoid them because they sound too hard to understand. Yet with a little perseverance and understanding these words can become very real. We have often sung about this word and its concepts in song without possibly understanding the full meaning or grasping the full truth.

Someone once said that understanding 'justification', or its kin word 'justify', is really quite simple, it means you have been forgiven and that it is 'just-as-if-I' had not sinned at all. God sees me clean and righteous, through His precious blood and He has willed to forget my sin, and it is as if I had never sinned at all.

The Greek word for justification is the word '*dikaiosis*' and the amazing fact is that this great central doctrine of justification is only mentioned twice in the entire New Testament. Both of these references are found in the book of Romans, and the whole truth is based upon these two verses. It is true to say of course that the word justify is found many times in the Scriptures, but the theme of justification and its truth is only mentioned twice in this form.

I believe the reason for this limited use of this word in this form, is that it is such a revelationary truth that it is protected from over-use and the reason that the word '*dikaiosis*' is limited to two verses is to keep the whole truth precious. The Greek word means to pronounce righteous, as it happens in law. It is not just a matter of being forgiven nor is it a matter of simply being made clean – God through His Son on Calvary acquitted us from sin. As a judge in law would send a man on his way, absolutely free, following the judgement from a jury of being found not guilty, so God has allowed His Son to bear our punishment, and therefore sees us as free men and women; we are no longer guilty of sin or of punishment. Therefore He acquits us and allows us to go free.

This amazing truth is therefore protected from overuse and is limited to just two verses so as to highlight the discovery of the truth of acquittal and freedom.

How good God is to free us from the penalty of sin and how gracious He is to allow His Son to take our punishment, the just for the unjust. How even greater is God to pronounce the matter closed by our acquittal from the court of justice to allow us to walk free. Not guilty any longer!

The second reference to this truth is found in the very next chapter, chapter 5 : 18, where Paul spoke of justification bringing life to all men. Therefore, not only are we acquitted, not only are we freed from guilt and punishment, we all are the recipients of a gift, the gift of life. Life that is not only temporal but eternal. What a truth to discover and what a truth to receive.

My Journal

KEY PRAYER

Heavenly Father, help me to understand this wonderful truth, help me to sit just a little while longer to think on this gift and to embrace its truth. Help me to live within the truth, that I am justified in the sight of God. I bless you today for this wonderful truth.

February 9th

KEY WORD: **Eternal**

KEY VERSE: **Titus 1 : 2**

A faith and knowledge resting on the hope of eternal life, which God, who does not lie, promised before the beginning of time.

Here is a marvellous word that even in English sounds a wonderful concept – 'eternal'. A concept however, that sounds wonderful but is hard to grasp. We live of course in time, which is a realm of minutes and days, a realm of months and years. Living in such a realm it is so hard to grapple with unlimited space and eternal concepts. Yet the marvellous fact is that our eternal life has already commenced, eternity is not something that begins when we die but has already started. The moment that we accepted Jesus as Lord and Saviour, eternity began for us.

However, the word improves both in depth and understanding when the fullness of the Greek word is translated. The word used is '*aionios*', which translated means 'endless', and it is used to convey the thought that a period, normally known as time, will change to that of an endless nature and that this period is of an undefined nature. All this is impossible for us to grasp as we struggle with our limitations of time and space, yet there is coming an undefined, endless concept, a concept that has no ending. We can not even call this concept a 'period' of 'time', because it is not a period neither is it time. We can not call it an 'age' because even that word suggests an ending or a conclusion, because all ages have a start and an end.

This '*aionios*' word however brings us an improvement and a deeper understanding when it is seen within the context of its use when it describes people and things. For instance it is used of God. God is eternal; He was, He is and He ever shall be. He was in the beginning and He was the beginning.

It is also used of the Holy Spirit in the sense that God is a trinity and that the Spirit of God dwelt with the Father from before the foundations of the earth.

It is also used of the salvation of the saints and of the future rule and role of heaven and of the nature of the resurrected body. All these references and descriptions provide a slightly better understanding of the whole concept of things that are eternal. However, we will never really understand until time gives way to eternity and this body of death is changed into a glorious body. Only then will we really appreciate the concept of no time, no ending, no finish and no conclusion. Eternity will have commenced and it will never end.

My Journal

KEY PRAYER

Heavenly Father, it is so hard for me to understand the concept of eternity. I struggle to understand because my world is so limited and my grasp of eternal things is so shallow. Please help me today to dwell on those things that are beyond time and space and help me to lift my eyes higher than the things that I can touch, see and know. Help me to see eternal things as very real. I praise you for the fact that my communion with you will one day never end.

February 10th

KEY WORD: **Evil**

KEY VERSE: **Philippians 3 : 2**

Watch out for those dogs, those men who do evil, those mutilators of the flesh.

Having considered yesterday the glorious fact that one day we shall leave behind this scene of time and we shall enter the nature of eternity, with all its glories, it is now important to consider another aspect of eternal things, that of the removal of evil. When eternity commences evil will be concluded as heaven will not tolerate anything that is impure. Sin with its evil and its wickedness will be removed to the lake of fire and will no longer play a part within what we know as life.

The word evil is a very interesting word. Our first thought concerning evil and evil works is utter wickedness, however, the Greek word throws a different slant upon what we call evil. The word used is *'kakos'*, and it literally means 'anything that is the opposite to things beneficial, pure, good and useful'. This is an interesting concept, because our first understanding would be that evil is the work of those who are wicked, and that evil is the nature of those who are bad. Yet the word *'kakos'* suggests that anything that is the antithesis of purity should be regarded as essentially evil.

The word is used for evil thoughts and imaginations. It is also used for the evil nature of speech and actions and it is used when moral and ethical boundaries are crossed. So it is a word that is far more than just a simple understanding of wrongdoing.

Whatever is evil in character and base in its influence and effect is indicated within the word *'kakos'* and the whole nature of the word is the opposite of things that are good. Which brings us to a very interesting thought – God is good – so anything that is the opposite of good is therefore evil. God's nature is essentially good, righteous and pure, so in the sight of God anything that stands against Him and is the antithesis of Him, is rightly called evil and is within itself, evil and base.

The word also has a stronger edge to it than just the concept of being the opposite of purity, it is also used in an active sense when things are destructive. It is used in the story of Paul's rescue from the shipwreck only to be bitten by a snake, but no 'harm' came to him and the people were astonished, Acts 28 : 5. No evil befell Paul, the snakebite could have produced harm and been essentially destructive, it was an evil attack, yet God was with him and brought deliverance and healing.

Anything that causes danger and destruction is an evil thing and the verse that we read today has the same kind of thought behind it. Paul called those who propagate evil, 'dogs' and 'mutilators of the flesh'. How lovely to know that one day all this comes to an end and eternity begins with its God-like nature of purity and peace.

My Journal

KEY PRAYER

Heavenly Father, I live in a world of noise, destruction and evil and it is so easy to be drawn into actions and desires that are not godly. I long to be removed from such a world as this, and I thank you that one day I shall be removed from evil. Help me each day and especially today to live righteously and pure and to become more like Jesus.

February 11th

KEY WORD: **Word**

KEY VERSE: **John 1 : 1**

In the beginning was the Word, and the Word was with God, and the Word was God.

I suppose that almost everyone knows the fact that the Word is the '*logos*'. This great fact has been taught in church life throughout the generations and is a wonderful truth. The Greek word '*logos*' has been used by Christian bodies and Christian organisations as a way of expressing truth within the concept of the organisation's ministry. However, although the word is known and used, it is not always appreciated.

'*Logos*' does not mean the mere name of an object or an idea, it is far more than that. '*Logos*' has two main meanings. Firstly, it means 'an expression or thought' – this is the concept behind the thought of a revelation from God or the concept of 'words from God'. The idea that a revelation or an expression from God can be delivered is the whole essence of this word. In the book of Acts this type of theory is detailed time after time, when men spoke a word as from God. It is seen in its fullest sense when Paul and Barnabas stayed in Antioch and preached the Word of the Lord, Acts 15 : 35. They were not just preaching in the sense of a declaration or sermon, they were in fact delivering the expression of God to the Antioch Church. This 'Word' was not just messages of healing and hope to a church meeting. Paul and Barnabas were delivering something far more than that, they were bringing to a new church the revelation of God. It came with authority and power and it was the revealed will of God, the expression of God's heart to His people.

The second meaning of the word '*logos*' is far more personal and intimate, it is the name or the title of 'the Son of God'. In John's gospel we have, right at the very beginning, the statement clearly made that God was in the beginning and that the Word – the *'logos'* was with God and was God. This amazing statement produced by John showed right at the commencement of his gospel, that Jesus was in fact God and that He was the expression of God to man and that this expression was in the beginning. This spoke of Jesus and His creative power, it spoke of His divinity and His distinct personality, and it also spoke of His right to be called God.

Wherever Jesus went, He was God revealing Himself to men. Every time He uttered truth, it was God speaking to men and every time He healed, it was God reaching out and touching mankind.

The statement that 'the Word became flesh and lived among us', was God reaching out to us in love through His Son, who was the Word - the *'logos'* on earth and caring for us.

My Journal

KEY PRAYER

Heavenly Father, thank you for sending Jesus and thank you Jesus that you came, as our Lord and Saviour. Thank you that today I can have a relationship with you and that you are the direct expression of God the Father to my heart. I bless you today for your goodness and I pray that you will help me to appreciate more and more your glory and grace.

February 12th

KEY WORD: **Word**

KEY VERSE: **John 8 : 20**

He spoke these words while teaching in the temple area near the place where the offerings were put.

Having considered yesterday the penetrating fact that the Greek word *'logos'* stood for the name and personal title of the Lord Jesus Christ, we will now consider another Greek word that has its translation into English as 'word'. However, to translate this second Greek word into just the English word 'word,' does not do it justice nor does it fully complete the understanding.

The word we are thinking about today is the word *'rhema'* and it is the Greek word used in the text above but is an entirely different word to that of *'logos'* which is also translated 'word' or 'words'.

The word *'rhema'* is the Greek word that denotes 'that which is spoken', and it is used of an individual word and not the 'words of the whole Bible'. In other words, the Bible is the *'logos'*, the Word of God, and *'rhema'* is the singular word of a Scripture that the Holy Spirit brings to us at any time of need. To convey this truth accurately, the apostle John used his thoughts in chapter 8 : 20 very carefully. He stated that Jesus was teaching, this is the Word of God. Jesus always used Scripture when He preached, this was not open to question. However, while He was preaching and teaching, John said that He 'spoke these words'. These words were the *'rhema'* of God – words that came fresh and new. God inspired words just for that moment and just for that need.

One of the most important ways that God brings us a *'rhema'* word is when we have stored the Word of God - the *'logos'* word in our hearts. Having God's Word in our minds and hearts allows God to bring any word to life, whenever He wants to speak. So our first thought when we consider the Scriptures is to ask the question,

'Am I hiding God's Word in my heart?'

Whenever God wants to speak, either through prophecy or through revelation, if we have hidden the Word in our hearts we will be able to be used by Him at any moment in time to allow Him to bring thoughts to our remembrance. We should be actively reading the Word with the intention of memorising the Scriptures. There are many verses in the Bible that teach the need to retain the Word of God, therefore we are being obedient when we search the Scriptures and when we seek to remember them.

Hiding the Word of God in our hearts allows the Holy Spirit to bring to our remembrance the Word that is hidden and each time that it is spoken out it becomes a '*rhema*' word from the '*logos*' word.

My Journal

KEY PRAYER

Heavenly Father, as I read the Scriptures today please help me to retain the words in my mind and in my spirit, so that, when needed, 'rhema' words can be brought back to my remembrance. I long to be used by you in ways that I have not yet seen so I offer myself afresh today as an instrument of use. Help my mind to be clear so that you can flow through me.

February 13th

KEY WORD: ***Joy***

KEY VERSE: **Philippians 4 : 1**

Therefore, my brothers, you whom I love and long for, my joy and crown, that is how you should stand firm in the Lord, dear friends!

As we commence a new day there is no better way than to be reminded of a great fact, and this word today is a great word. As you read the apostle Paul's words in this key verse in Philippians 4 you can feel the impact of what he himself was feeling. He was expressing his feelings for the church at Philippi and he stated that these people were his joy and crown. You can feel the heartbeat of his love for these people.

These people in Philippi were his 'joy', even in the English language there is no mistaking his passion, yet his passion becomes even stronger when the Greek word is understood. The word for joy is the word '*chara*' which should be translated as 'greater joy' or 'stronger joy' and can also be translated as 'pure delight'. So the feeling of his passion receives an even stronger impact than that of just joy. Paul was expressing pure delight in his church in Philippi.

The word '*chara*' is a very interesting one. It is used sparingly within the New Testament and is only found when intense pleasure is being expressed. For instance, when the angels announced to the shepherds that the Saviour had been born, they expressed their feelings by saying that they were bringing 'Good news of great joy', Luke 2 : 10. Not just that a baby had been born but that the Saviour of the world had been born.

The word is used in Matthew's and Luke's gospels several times, but only once in Mark's gospel, however, John used this word more than all the others in his gospel. It is not mentioned in Paul's first letter to the church in Corinth at all, but is found frequently in his second letter. This kind of use suggests that the New Testament writers only used the word when no other passionate expression could be justified. They did not want to express a simple kind of happiness, other words would do for that kind of feeling, but when no other word could convey just how deeply they felt in their passion, '*chara*' was the word that they chose.

James in his epistle used this word when he was seeking to convey just how we should feel when we fall into trials and temptations. We should count the testing times as ones of pure delight as we are being drawn closer to the Lord through the pain of testing and trial. Sometimes we feel a sense of anger that we should be suffering at all, sometimes we feel a sense of isolation and unfairness when testing times come. However, James said that we should count it all joy. There should be therefore, in James' understanding, a sense of great delight when we face trials and testing times, as the whole process draws us nearer to the Lord and produces within us a greater amount of faith. This whole process is one of pure delight.

Joy is associated with life and living, and all experiences are capable of bringing us an enlarged capacity for growth, blessing and gladness. Persecution also increases the possibility of joy, as does sorrow and sadness. This action of course is the opposite experience to that of the world. In the world, sadness leads to a greater degree of sadness and sorrow leads to depression. However, in God's kingdom the reverse should take place, which is why James said, 'count it all joy', as the testing and trials commenced.

KEY PRAYER

Heavenly Father, teach me each day to experience real joy as I long to know pure delight in trial. I acknowledge that you are the source of all joy and I bow before you to worship today. Help me when I pass through trials to see beyond the experience that is immediately before me and allow me to see your plan and purpose. I rejoice today in your goodness.

February 14th

KEY WORD: **Love**

KEY VERSE: **John 13 : 34-35**

"A new command I give you: Love one another. As I have loved you, so you must love one another. By this all men will know that you are my disciples, if you love one another."

February 14th is normally, in most parts of the western world, regarded as the day of love. This day is the day when expressions of love are shown to those around us. Therefore, it is the right day to consider how the Bible treats love and how we should love one another.

There are two main words for Christian love within the New Testament, we will consider one today and then the second one tomorrow.

The main word for the expression of God's love toward us is the Greek word *'agapao'*, which correctly translated means 'God's love'. However, it is a very hard word to fully understand as it is a new word expressing a new truth. This word expresses things that were previously unknown and it has an entirely distinctive meaning with the New Testament. It seeks to convey the main characteristic of God, that of full, divine and constant love.

It was used of God's love towards His Son Jesus. It was also used of God's love towards us and then it produces its greatest challenge when it is used of the way that we should love each other. *'Agapao'* love, is love that is revealed without an impulse of feelings. Most human love is prompted by an action, for instance if someone loves us and shows this love by actions, then we return that expression by our outward showing of love. However, this kind of impulsive love is stirred by feelings and is quite changeable by actions. Passions can change, affections can be limited and our natural ability to love can be turned into the opposite of feelings very quickly. '*Agapao*' love however, is quite different in its nature. It is the expression of God's love.

God's love is unchangeable and God's love is constant. It does not matter what happens, God loves us and God is love. No circumstances can change or diminish His love toward us and no circumstances can alter the fact that God is love. We who are the most unworthy of all, are the objects of God's constant attention and '*agapao*' love.

Therefore when John seeks to convey just how we should love one another he uses the greatest and most challenging word of all. We are to love each other in the same way that God loves us. No circumstances should alter our love for each other, no actions against us should diminish our love for those around us. This kind of love is not a natural love, it can only be expressed by receiving love from God and sharing it with others. This is such a high challenge that it demands actions of obedience from us. We will never fulfil the criterion of love unless we learn to live close to the Lord and unless we learn to receive His love toward us.

The challenge is quite simple, the only way that the world will know that we are His disciples is by the expression of love that we have for one another. It will not be our good works that count and it will not be our gifts that are measured. The only thing that counts in the measurement of our treatment of one another, is the perfect and the pure expression of God's love to others.

KEY PRAYER

Heavenly Father, thank you for your constant and steadfast love towards me, I rejoice in your love because it does not change or alter by circumstances. I thank you for your love and rest in the fact that I am the object of your divine passion. Help me each day to appropriate your love and help me too, to love others with the same degree of passion and care that you express towards me. By this will all men know that I am your disciple.

February 15th

KEY WORD: **Love**

KEY VERSE: **John 21 : 17**

The third time Jesus said to him, "Simon son of John, do you love me?" Peter was hurt because Jesus asked him the third time, "Do you love me?" He said, "Lord you know all things, you know that I love you." Jesus said, "Feed my sheep."

The second word for love within the New Testament reveals a different kind of love. Where *'agapao'* reveals God's love and is a constant and unchanging love, this second word reveals a different level of passion. The Greek word used is the word *'phileo'* and is the word for love between friends. Our term 'brotherly love' stems from the root meaning of this word and is seen in the expression of kind acts and warm friendship.

This word is never used in a command for us to love God. God does not require us to love Him as a friend, He requires *'agapao'* love from us. The 'love' word between friends can mean the tenderest of affections and is seen in the unselfish desire to serve one another within church life. Kind acts and charitable deeds come under the heading of this word and it is very much a 'church' word as it carries with it the kind of Christian virtue of ministry to one another.

In the context of today's key verse , the interesting dialogue between Jesus and Peter reveals the different dimensions between the two 'love' words *'agapao'* and *'phileo'*. There have been enough sermons preached on these verses to last a lifetime but the comparison is important to understand. Jesus asked Peter twice if 'he loved Him', and Jesus used the *'agapao'* word. In other words Jesus asked Peter 'do you love me with the distinctive love of God', Peter replied twice, 'yes Lord, you know I love you', and Peter used the *'phileo'* word. Literally Peter was responding, 'yes, you know I have affection for you as a friend.' Peter finally got the right answer when later in life he wrote his first epistle and having been fully restored to faith and ministry and having seen wonderful acts of God's almighty power and having been used of God greatly, he stated that 'having not seen Jesus we love Him', 1 Peter 1 : 8. In this text he used the '*agapao*' word, simply saying we may not have seen Him, but our love for Him is more than friendship and affection, it is love like that of God's love to us.

The challenge then is to love God and each other with a love akin to God's love, and then to do kindly acts of friendship and affection to each other.

My Journal

KEY PRAYER

Heavenly Father, thank you for Calvary's love, the greatest expression of love ever given. Because of Calvary my love for you grows each day. Help me to love you constantly with the same kind of love that you love me with, and help me each day to do acts of affection and kindness to those who are around me.

February 16th

KEY WORD: **Wonders**

KEY VERSE: **Acts 2 : 22**

Men of Israel, listen to this: Jesus of Nazareth was a man accredited by God to you by miracles, wonders and signs, which God did among you through Him, as you yourselves know.

Here is a very descriptive word indeed, it is a word that stretches the imagination and creates a thirst for the things of God. The Greek word used is the word '*teras*' which translated means 'a strange thing'. Wonders as expressed in the New Testament are therefore strange acts from God, they are not necessarily explainable nor are they things that can be analysed. By their very nature they are things that caused you to 'wonder'.

In New Testament terms wonders are usually connected to signs, so the phrase 'signs and wonders' is normally linked together. John Wimber used to say that 'a sign is something that points you in a certain direction and a wonder is something that you wonder about,' that statement is of course not very theological but it is correct.

The Greek word '*teras*' is used 16 times in the New Testament and is found always in the plural form, so we are not talking about a singular wonder but many wonders linked with signs. Out of the 16 times that '*teras*' is mentioned, nine of them are in the Acts of Apostles – where we find miracles abounding, along with signs and wonders. Three times the word is linked with false agents such as the works of Satan through human flesh.

Of the 13 times when the word is used in the sense of wonderful things taking place, the whole impact is one of great blessing. If we take John Wimber's statement and accept that a sign gives you direction and a wonder causes you to wonder, then a sign would appeal to the mind. A sign would touch the intellect and would seek to cause us to think, giving our thought processes a richer understanding and a time of development and process. However, a 'wonder' would appeal to our sense of imagination and to our sense of creativity.

A 'wonder' is hard to analyse and is also hard to explain, but that is the whole purpose and nature of God expressing Himself. We can not analyse God and He is certainly not explainable. He is divine and we are very human and the two are not compatible. We have to accept that God can do anything that He wants to, because He is God. To have any measure of faith we have to believe that God is; no explanations and no analysing – God is God. When He wants to express Himself through signs and wonders He is perfectly allowed to do so, He does not have to explain Himself. I think that at times God likes to surprise us and performs a 'wonder' just to get our attention and cause us to wonder.

In all wonders, as in all signs, we ascribe praise and glory to Him and we thank Him for His wonderful unexplainable works.

My Journal

KEY PRAYER

Heavenly Father, thank you today for signs and wonders that you perform. They are things that caused us to marvel at your wonderful works. Please help me always to approach these things with a child-like spirit and help me to understand that these things are far beyond my ability to analyse. I thank you for your glory and I thank you for signs and wonders and I ask you to express yourself within my life in any way that you want to.

February 17th

KEY WORD: ***World***

KEY VERSE: **Matthew 13 : 35**

So was fulfilled what was spoken through the prophet: "I will open my mouth in parables, I will utter things hidden since the creation of the world."

There are two words that are used within the New Testament for the English word 'world'. They are used interchangeably and appear simply in English as 'world'. However they are very different and unless we understand them we do not always appreciate just what the New Testament writers were seeking to convey.

Today we will consider one of them and then tomorrow we will take time to think on the second word.

The word most commonly used for 'world' is the Greek word '*kosmos*' and it is from this word that we derive our English word 'cosmos', which means to us the 'world in which we live'. However, '*kosmos*' speaks of many things such as the order and arrangement of the planets and the adornment of nature and the order of the universe. It is therefore a very big word. It is found 187 times in the New Testament and speaks of the beauty of creation and the spectacle of God's ordered world.

It is used by the writers when they speak of the earth and its beauty and the Greeks used this word when they were considering the order and pattern of things associated with the earth.

It was also used to contrast the difference between heaven and earth; earth may be beautiful in its order and creation but heaven is even more wonderful and glorious.

It is used when the writers were seeking to convey the colour and the wonders of a world in splendour – this would normally be used in the sense of adornment. You only have to see the glory of a sunset or the colours of autumn to know that God displays Himself in nature. This sense of adornment creates within us a breath of amazement as the world in which we live and move sparkles with God's creative power. It is a wonderful world, in some ways spoilt and polluted by man's hand, but nevertheless it still radiates with God's colours, glory and spectacle of creative power.

My Journal

KEY PRAYER

Heavenly Father, I only have to see a sunset or a sunrise to know that you are behind all things and in all things. I only have to see the colours of autumn or the buds of springtime to know that your glory is expressed in our world. Thank you that you gave your Son for this world and that His blood is sufficient to reach this world and all that is within it. As in the book of Revelation, this world and all its beings cry 'Holy, Holy, Holy'. Help me today to glorify you for a wonderful, wonderful world.

February 18th

KEY WORD: **World**

KEY VERSE: **1 Corinthians 1 : 21**

For since in the wisdom of God the world through its wisdom did not know Him, God was pleased through the foolishness of what was preached to save those who believed.

In yesterday's reading we considered the word *'kosmos'* which means the 'world in which we live and move' and we saw that this is one of the meanings of our English word 'world'. However, there is a second word used for the word 'world' which has an entirely different meaning.

There are times when the English word 'world' stands to mean something completely different to that of the world in which we live. But both are translated the same and unless we grasp the difference we do not understand the New Testament writers' teaching.

The second Greek word that is used for our word 'world' is the word *'aion'*. Translating it to our word 'world' is completely right but it does not convey its true meaning. The word *'aion'* means two things: firstly, the system and order of the world structure and secondly, the period of time that we would call the ages of time.

This word is commonly used when the writers were seeking to convey the spiritual and moral characteristics of our world. They were not talking about the wonder and beauty of the world – *'kosmos'* – in which we live when they used this word, but they were conveying the thought that there is a system and order that is contrary to that of God's system and order, the world of the *'aion'*. This is a worldly order that sets itself against the things of God, this is the system that the New Testament states we should not belong to as we are 'not of this world'.

We are very much part of the *'kosmos'*, with its beauty and its creative wonder, but we are not part of the *'aion'*, the system and order of this present world.

I sometimes wonder, looking at the way that we often live, if we really understand the difference between these two words for 'world'. God made the *'kosmos'* with its colours, fragrances, beauty and wonder. When He made it all, He said that it was good. Every part of God's creative work was seen to be good and wholesome for us to enjoy. However, when man imposed his system and structure upon God's creative work, spiritual and moral decay set in immediately. And now we have decline and sin rampant all around us. This decline and the resultant sin is the *'aion'* of our present world. What God created is very, very good; what man created is very, very bad.

My Journal ________________________________

KEY PRAYER

Heavenly Father, thank you for this wonderful world that you have created and provided for my pleasure. I thank you that you order and sustain it all the time. I pray however that you would keep me from the system and order of this world so that I might be pure and holy before you at all times. I pray that there might be those I meet who will be delivered from the system of this world through my life and service before them.

February 19th

KEY WORD: **Apostles**

KEY VERSE: **Ephesians 4 : 11**

It was (God) who gave some to be apostles, some to be prophets, some to be evangelists, and some to be pastors and teachers.

God has set in the Church five ministry gifts which we commonly call the 'ascension gifts' – they are listed in Ephesians 4. They are apostle, prophet, evangelist, pastor and teacher, and in our western culture and our church traditions, we are very comfortable with three out of these five gifts. We enjoy the ministry of the pastor, the teacher and the evangelist, we are getting a little more used to the ministry of the prophet but we have great difficulty in recognising and releasing the ministry of the apostle.

God has set these five ministry gifts as a foundation for the Church and as an ascension gift to us for the preparing of God's people for works of service. These ministry gifts are therefore absolutely vital in the whole plan and scope of the Church. Over the next few days we will consider each one of the five ministry gifts and seek to uncover the meaning of each one.

God has given to the Church the ministry of the apostle. The Greek word used for apostle is the word '*apostolos*', which means 'one sent out', and conveys the thought of someone who is released into a gift rather than one who is sent out to preach. We are all sent out to preach but we are not all released to the gifting of apostleship.

The first twelve disciples, who had received special training and who had a special relationship with Jesus, were naturally released into this ministry and were called apostles. However, with the loss of Judas the gap was filled not by the one who was voted on by 'lot', as the church in Acts chapter 1 tried to do, but by Paul. Paul was called and released by a risen Lord who chose him and added him into the first apostolic band. It naturally appeared that the first apostles were witnesses of the resurrection as a qualification of their apostleship, and Paul would therefore fit this qualification as he saw the Lord on the road to Damascus.

However, it is quite clear that the calling and gifting and therefore the releasing into ministry of apostles was not confined to just those who had seen the Lord. There are several people whom the New Testament writers recognised as apostles, who were not part of the original band and who had not seen the Lord, nor were they witnesses of His resurrection. People such as Barnabas who is called an apostle in Acts 14 : 4. In Romans 16 : 7 it is stated that Andronicus and Junias were apostles. It is clear from other references such as Philippians 2 : 25 and 1 Thessalonians 2 : 6 that Epaphroditus, Silas and also Timothy received the designation of apostle, too.

My Journal

KEY PRAYER

Heavenly Father, I thank you for the wonderful and supernatural ministry of the apostle, and I pray that more and more apostles will be revealed to the Church in these last days of ministry, as this gift to the Church is vital.

February 20th

KEY WORD: **Apostles**

KEY VERSE: **Ephesians 4 : 11**

It was (God) who gave some to be apostles, some to be prophets, some to be evangelists, and some to be pastors and teachers.

God has set in the Church five ministry gifts which we commonly call the 'ascension gifts' – they are listed in Ephesians 4. They are apostle, prophet, evangelist, pastor and teacher, and in our western culture and our church traditions, we are very comfortable with three out of these five gifts. We enjoy the ministry of the pastor, the teacher and the evangelist, we are getting a little more used to the ministry of the prophet but we have great difficulty in recognising and releasing the ministry of the apostle.

As we saw yesterday, the '*apostolos*' were those who were 'sent out' by the Lord, it is therefore understood that the ministry of apostleship was not just designated to those who saw the Lord, nor was this ministry confined to those who were at the beginning – although the twelve apostles of the Lamb do hold a very special place. It is clear too, that the ministry of the apostle was not concluded when the first apostles concluded their ministry. Apostolic ministry continued on and continues unto this day within the Church.

The question then is quite obvious, what makes a person an apostle and what sets them apart within this ministry? It is clear in my mind that the word '*apostolos*' carries with it the concept not just of one who is sent or released but also two other concepts. Firstly, there is the concept of the supernatural. When Jesus sent out His apostles it was with authority to do supernatural things, this is mentioned several times in the gospels and in the epistles. Especially in 2 Corinthians 12 : 12, where Paul stated that the marks of an apostle, namely 'signs, wonders and miracles' were clearly seen.

Secondly, there is the concept of the bigger picture. Paul was sent to the whole gentile world, he was not just sent out. Those mentioned in 2 Corinthians 8 : 23, were called 'apostles of the churches' and when Jesus sent out His apostles He gave them authority over spiritual forces. So if we take these two concepts today, those who could be designated as apostles would be, firstly, those who have spiritual authority and who do supernatural things and secondly, those who see the bigger picture within the Church.

It is possible that we have more apostles than we realise, it could be that we just do not recognise them and that we may not have the courage to release them to this ministry. Something to consider!

My Journal

KEY PRAYER

Heavenly Father, I thank you today for all the ministry gifts within the Church; thank you for the ministry of the apostle. Help me to see with new eyes those who might be manifesting this kind of ministry and help me to understand this gift. Help me too, to seek my own gift and calling that I might be a blessing to those around me.

February 21st

KEY WORD: **Prophet**

KEY VERSE: **Ephesians 4 : 11**

It was (God) who gave some to be apostles, some to be prophets, some to be evangelists, and some to be pastors and teachers.

God has set in the Church five ministry gifts which we commonly call the 'ascension gifts' – they are listed in Ephesians 4. They are apostle, prophet, evangelist, pastor and teacher, and in our western culture and our church traditions, we are very comfortable with three out of these five gifts. We enjoy the ministry of the pastor, the teacher and the evangelist, we are getting a little more used to the ministry of the prophet but we have great difficulty in recognising and releasing the ministry of the apostle.

The second ministry gift that Jesus gave to His Church is the gift of the prophet. If we accept that apostles are still within the Church today then the obvious fact would also be, that prophets are still within the church today. We can not say – as some do – that three gifts remain, pastors, teachers and evangelists but apostles and prophets were superseded. Either all the gifts remain or all the gifts are concluded, and we know that the ministry of the pastor and the teacher and the evangelist are still in operation within the Church, therefore it holds that all the ministries would therefore still function.

The Greek word for prophet is '*prophetes*' meaning one who 'speaks forth openly'. Within Greek culture one who spoke openly and one who spoke forth was normally one who interpreted the things of the gods. However, the New Testament takes a different line, it is not simply one who speaks or even speaks forth openly, it was one who brought revelation from God to man.

In the Old Testament the picture of the prophet is drawn for us of one who knew God intimately and who was called to prophesy the things of God. This could involve the telling of the future or the call to repentance. It describes the feature of the prophet as one upon whom the Spirit of God rested and the hallmark of this anointing was the ability to 'know things'.

The New Testament concept of the prophet is slightly different in that within the Church, prophecy firstly has its emphasis within the areas of comfort, edification and exhortation, 1 Corinthians 14 : 3, as well as the possibility of knowing the future. The ministry of the prophet is therefore within New Testament terms, one who brings God's Word. This can be in part a form of preaching, and there are many of us who have sat under the ministry of God's Word, and we knew we were not just listening to a sermon. We knew that we were hearing more than just a message, we were hearing a prophetic word.

However, there is much more to prophecy than preaching a prophetic word, the whole concept of the word '*prophetes*' is one who 'speaks out' or one who 'speaks forth'. This speaking out, carries with it the concept of divine revelation of God's will to the Church and it carries with it the concept of the counsels of God to the world. In the Acts of Apostles there were several occasions when the prophet brought a word from God to His people and there were times within the epistles when it is obvious that God was speaking concerning future events and times and seasons.

The voice of the prophet still echoes within the Church today and we need their messages to be received. However, the message should be tempered with judgement and thought, as Paul stated in 1 Corinthians 14, so that the voice of the prophet and their messages might be pure.

KEY PRAYER

Heavenly Father, thank you for gifts and ministries and I bless you especially today for the gift of the prophet. I pray that more and more we shall hear the voice of the prophet within our worship times so that we become more and more a prophetic people of revelation. I offer my life afresh to you so that my giftings and callings might be at your disposal.

February 22nd

KEY WORD: **Evangelist**

KEY VERSE: **Ephesians 4 : 11**

It was (God) who gave some to be apostles, some to be prophets, some to be evangelists, and some to be pastors and teachers.

God has set in the Church five ministry gifts which we commonly call the 'ascension gifts' – they are listed in Ephesians 4. They are apostle, prophet, evangelist, pastor and teacher, and in our western culture and our church traditions, we are very comfortable with three out of these five gifts. We enjoy the ministry of the pastor, the teacher and the evangelist, we are getting a little more used to the ministry of the prophet but we have great difficulty in recognising and releasing the ministry of the apostle.

The concept of the gift of an evangelist is very well known to us and very well accepted. Whether it is the 'mass multitude evangelist' that holds sway over thousands in a crusade or whether it is a 'one to one' evangelist, we are very happy with the gift and very comfortable with the concept.

We have been considering over the past few days the areas of gifting that include the apostle and the prophet and we have noticed just how few there are who function within these gifts, and we have noticed just how difficult it is to embrace these gifts. However, with the gift of the evangelist we have no such problems or difficulties.

The concept is acceptable and the gift is released and it functions on the 'one to one' level or the 'mass multitude' level and of course at every level in between. The Greek word for evangelist is an interesting one, it is the word '*euangelistes*' and of course it translates well into English, as the word appears to be spelt very similar in both Greek and English. However, it is a word that was cultivated from two Greek words, '*eu*' which means 'well', and '*angelos*' which means 'messenger'. So correctly translated the word simply means, 'a well messenger', which places the emphasis on the gift rather than the message. The message is good news, but the giver of the message is 'one who is well', a 'good messenger', or a 'messenger of good'.

The gospel is always featured in the New Testament as good news. Jesus came to preach good news and was always to be found declaring this good news wherever He went. The New Testament concept of evangelist is not just the bringer of good news, he is also a good vessel. God's gift to the Church in this respect was simply that a vessel of goodness was placed on earth in the Church to provide the world with hope. The fact that the message and the messenger were declared to be good was a vital fact in understanding this role. The New Testament declared that even the feet of those who brought good news 'were blessed'.

Any one who proclaims the good news can quite rightly be called an evangelist. Missionaries who cross oceans to overseas fields are certainly evangelists, as too are those who just cross the street to proclaim the message to their neighbours.

We, in our organised world, designate certain people to wider functions, and we recognise the fact that some are called to a major platform of evangelism. Billy Graham is world-renowned as an evangelist and was released and recognised by the worldwide Church in this gifting. However great the function or however small the function, those who proclaim the good news are good messengers.

My Journal ______________________________

____

____

____

KEY PRAYER

Heavenly Father, thank you for those who proclaim your Word to men, thank you that I was born into the family of God because someone proclaimed the good news to me. I bless you for every one of these gifts in the Church and I ask you today to help me become an active messenger of good in my day and generation.

February 23rd

KEY WORD: **Pastor**

KEY VERSE: **Ephesians 4 : 11**

It was (God) who gave some to be apostles, some to be prophets, some to be evangelists, and some to be pastors and teachers.

God has set in the Church five ministry gifts which we commonly call the 'ascension gifts' – they are listed in Ephesians 4. They are apostle, prophet, evangelist, pastor and teacher, and in our western culture and our church traditions, we are very comfortable with three out of these five gifts. We enjoy the ministry of the pastor, the teacher and the evangelist, we are getting a little more used to the ministry of the prophet but we have great difficulty in recognising and releasing the ministry of the apostle.

However, even with our acceptance of three of the ascension gifts we still fail to understand the form of the gift of pastor. For example, if someone is a teacher we still call them pastor. If someone is an evangelist, we still grant them the designation of pastor. This at times of course is a form of endearment, however, it can and in fact does produce a fracturing of our understanding concerning the function and form of the ministry of the pastor.

For instance, the Greek word for pastor is '*poimen*', which translated means 'one who tends sheep'. It carries with it the thought of tending in the sense of feeding, guiding, caring and overseeing their needs. It is therefore rightly used in Ephesians 4 as the word for 'pastoring'. The pastor is a gift ministry that was bequeathed to the Church by a risen and ascended Lord, who required His sheep to be superintended by one who was a pastor, not just in name but in function of ministry.

I remember hearing the story of an aged and very well-known Christian leader who was visited in his last hours on earth by a colleague who spent some time with him before he was called home to his reward. The aged leader spent most of his last hours enquiring about people that he knew, churches that he had pastored and other leaders that he had served with. His final earthly communication to his friend was the same as Paul's in Acts 20, when he was about to leave Ephesus, ' keep watch over the flock'. A true pastor went home to his reward exercising his gift right unto the end.

A pastor is more than a 'sheep feeder' and the gift is more than just simply a 'shepherd of the flock'. We often confuse the ministry of eldership with that of 'pastoring' – all pastors are elders but not all elders are pastors. The true pastoral gift is one of oversight ministry within the Church and should be treated as such. It could be time to give thanks for all the shepherds who have fed you, guided you and cared for you during your earthly walk with God. It is a good time too, to seek out the shepherds who care for you and to honour them with your love, submission and thanks.

My Journal

KEY PRAYER

Heavenly Father, please help me to give thanks for all those who have guided me during my Christian walk. I give praise for their faithfulness and kindness manifested through their loving gift. Please help me to appreciate those who exercise this gift and cause me to honour them with thanksgiving.

February 24th

KEY WORD: **Teachers**

KEY VERSE: **Ephesians 4 : 11**

It was (God) who gave some to be apostles, some to be prophets, some to be evangelists, and some to be pastors and teachers.

God has set in the Church five ministry gifts which we commonly call the 'ascension gifts' – they are listed in Ephesians 4. They are apostle, prophet, evangelist, pastor and teacher, and in our western culture and our church traditions, we are very comfortable with three out of these five gifts. We enjoy the ministry of the pastor, the teacher and the evangelist, we are getting a little more used to the ministry of the prophet but we have great difficulty in recognising and releasing the ministry of the apostle.

The gift of the teacher within the New Testament is similar to that of evangelist but different within its area of function. Where the evangelist proclaims the good news of the gospel, the teacher proclaims the structure of truth and foundations of righteousness. The Greek word used is the word '*didaskalos*' which translated means quite simply 'teacher'. There is no hidden meaning and no hidden truth, it is a very open word.

The word was used of Jesus, who taught the kingdom of God, the word is used of all teachers of truth within the churches. It was used of Paul within his teachings and within his writings and it was used of all teachers of God's news. It was coupled with another word when false teachers were seeking to destroy the Church, they were called '*pseudodidaskalos*'. We derive our English word 'pseudo' from the first part of this Greek word, when we are seeking to convey the fact that someone looks right but is not the real thing, they are pseudo.

This gift and function of ministry was placed within the Church in order that new converts and adherents would be structured into truth and receive a foundation of learning. This gift is of course, still within the Church, anyone who teaches in any form can rightly be designated 'a teacher'. This gift is found in the Sunday School and it is found in 'one to one' teaching and it is found in the Bible study class.

As with the gift of evangelist there are, however, those who are called on to a more public platform as expounders of the Word. There are those who can teach the Word so expertly that we are enthralled by the deep things of God explained so simply by those who exercise this kind of ministry. This kind of function is so essential within the Church so that we are not swayed by false teaching and false teachers, who preach something that looks right but is not the real thing. Pseudo-teachers and pseudo-truths.

The word '*didaskalos*' is also interchangeable with the word '*rabbi*' which also means teacher and it is used in either form in several places. Jesus was called '*rabbi*' on several occasions which gave Him the title effectively of 'teacher'. In Jesus' time there were hundreds of wandering '*rabbis*', both good and bad, and both true and false, who gained the title 'teacher'. They taught from the laws of Moses and the teachings of the Pharisees, from town to town. All these people could quite rightly be called '*didaskalos*' or '*pseudodidaskalos*'. However, when speaking of Jesus, the men who were sent to capture Him stated that they could not imprison Him due to the fact that 'no man spoke like this man'. Jesus was a true teacher and was therefore recognised as such even by ungodly men. Those who teach within the Church, whether it be by written form, by 'one to one ministry' or by the major platform function of teaching, should all seek to reach the stage where it could be said that 'no one spoke like this'.

KEY PRAYER

Heavenly Father, thank you today for those who took the time to take me on to one side in order that I might be taught the ways of The Lord. Thank you for structured teaching and guidance that was given to me over the years. Help me I pray to become one who instructs both by words and lifestyle. Help me too, to give a reasoned answer for the hope that lies within me so that others might grow into truth.

February 25th

KEY WORD: **Appoint**

KEY VERSE: **1 Timothy 1 : 12**

I thank Christ Jesus our Lord, who has given me strength, that He considered me faithful, appointing me to His Service.

Having considered over the past few days the whole spectrum of ministry from Ephesians 4 concerning apostles, prophets, evangelists, pastors and teachers, it is now time to look at the whole question of how these ministries find their way to appointment. It is interesting that at local church level there are a multitude of ways that these ministries come into being. Some churches have a voting system and some churches have an appointment system, some churches have a nomination system by those in office while other churches have a nomination system from members of the congregation.

Some churches would not vote at all upon the offices of ministries while other churches have a percentage vote that is needed in order to reach an office. The New Testament does not seem to indicate which method is right or wrong, it seems to leave the matter up to the local situation and as the years have passed by, the systems that churches operate by have become very different and varied.

An interesting point to note is that the very first New Testament procedure for the appointment of the apostle to replace Judas – a ballot – was not accepted, as God had already replaced Judas with Paul, who at that time was not even saved!

Paul himself appointed elders and leaders and also gave instructions to others to appoint local leaders, which seems to indicate that there was a system of appointment that was without reference to the local body or a voting system. However, it would be hard to argue that case as there may well have been a confirmation system to the appointment.

There are fifteen Greek words that are used for our English word 'appoint' and they range from a word that indicated 'an appointed time' to a word that was used for 'an arrangement'. Other words included the sense of being 'reserved for a situation' and there is the word that was used for 'the seasons of the year' that were 'appointed seasons'. However, the main word used in the New Testament for appointment to offices of ministry is the word '*tithemi*'; this word is used 90 times. This is the main word used that conveys the whole concept of an appointment to a form of service, a better translation than that of 'appointment to service' would be 'one who is set into service'. It was used by Jesus of His disciples when He said in John 15 : 16, 'I chose you and appointed you to bear fruit'. It was used of Paul when he described the method of his calling and stated that he was appointed to God's service in the key verse today.

It is also used of Jesus when the writer in the book of Hebrews, chapter 1 : 2, stated that 'God has now spoken through His Son, whom He has appointed as heir of all things'.

The whole concept of this word is that those in offices of ministry are not there because of man, even though there may be a human form of appointment or vote or nomination. They have been appointed by God and set in this ministry for God's glory and for the Church's benefit and for the believers' growth and equipping. It is God who calls and sets forth into ministry and we should seek to honour those who fulfil ministries, as they are there due to the hand of God being extended and due to the fact that they have been set into this ministry.

KEY PRAYER

Heavenly Father, I thank you today for the tremendous fact that those in ministry are in their positions, not because a congregation voted them there, or because someone in a due season appointed them there, but because you ordained them to ministry and set them in the Church. Help me each day to honour those who are ministering to me and help me too, to find ways of blessing them. Thank you that you care for your Church by releasing people into ministry and I praise you for the glorious fact that the Church prospers because of godly men and women who are available as gifts for your use.

February 26th

KEY WORD: **Free**

KEY VERSE: **John 8 : 32 & 8 : 36**

"Then you will know the truth, and the truth will set you free."

"So if the Son sets you free, you will be free indeed."

The word 'free' and the word 'freedom' are words that convey a most beautiful feeling, the words conjure up in our minds the sense of release and escape. To be set free is to be brought into a place of total and complete liberty, a place where there are no longer any restrictions. This thought is brought to us by our understanding of the simple concept of freedom. This is of course completely right and is also the Bible concept of true freedom.

The Greek word used in the New Testament for being made free is the word *'eleutheros'* and this word translated literally means 'free of restraint'. It is a word that had its origins in the whole concept of slavery, when a slave was finally set free from his master to pursue his own way in the world. At this time the former slave was no longer under the restraints of his master but was now a free man. The overwhelming emotion of that moment is hard for us to grasp but for the man at that moment the emotion must have been indescribable. From being enslaved with no rights and no future to that of being absolutely free with no restrictions, just liberty.

The word is used of those who find the truth of the Lord as Saviour, they are free from sin and they are free indeed!

The word is also used in connection with the Law, having found Jesus as Lord and Saviour, we are now free from the constraints of the Law and we have entered into grace. The word is also used in a general sense in that having found grace and having been made free, we are now in a place where nothing can have dominion over us. We may still face temptation but we are free from its power if we follow the Lord, the New Testament teaches that we are free from the dominion of sin, we do not have to give in to sin and temptation, we are free.

This tremendous truth needs to be learned over and over again as we often fail and fall into sin because our understanding of New Testament truth is weak. God has given us the ability to overcome in every sense of the word. We can overcome temptation, not in our own strength but in His. We can have dominion over fleshly habits, we can have dominion over compulsive actions and we can certainly live in a place where the slavery of constant sinful compulsion loses its power. The whole concept of New Testament freedom however, goes even further than forgiveness of sin and freedom from its power, the New Testament writers understood the concept of freedom to include everything that touches our lives. Freedom from compulsive actions of any kind and nature, freedom from past memories and accusations and freedom from future fears and worries. New Testament teaching is that when the Son sets you free you are free indeed.

'*Eleutheros*' is the word that produces a new start with the past blotted out, the present free from restraints and the future, clear of all that would seek to dominate our lives. We are free indeed.

My Journal ______________________________

KEY PRAYER

Heavenly Father, thank you for the freedom that you have granted to me through the gift of your Son Jesus. Thank you that sin can no longer have dominion over me and that I am now released from its guilt, its power and its effects. I rejoice today in the freedom of restraint that tells me that I am His and He is mine. Help me to continuously live in this truth, that I am free indeed.

February 27th

KEY WORD: **Slaves**

KEY VERSE: **Romans 6 : 18**

You have been set free from sin and have become slaves to righteousness.

Yesterday we studied together the wonderful truth of freedom from sin, where we no longer are restrained by temptation or the forces of evil. However, once we are free from sin we become slaves to another master, not the mastery of sin but the mastery of righteousness and the bond-slave of God. This type of bond-slavery seems to contradict the fact that we are free, so we must really understand what this means.

This concept was of tremendous blessing to Paul as he returned to this theme time after time in his epistles. He revelled in the thought that having been released from sin and its power he was now enslaved to another master, the Lord Jesus Christ. He taught this over and over again to the churches of the New Testament.

The truth that he sought to bring was one of willing servanthood which was not controlled by finance or by legal documents or by a master who controlled a man's destiny through the act of slavery. His teaching of being bond-slaves or servants was that now through Christ we are willingly tied to our new master, not by another's constraints but by our own will that allowed us to exercise the right to belong to another.

The Greek word used for this concept is a wonderful word, it is the word '*doulos*' which translated correctly means 'to bind', and it conveys the thought of 'one who gives himself up to the will of another'. In other words, once we had no options and we were bound to sin and Satan, and as such we were enslaved to their power. Now through Grace we are free to belong to another master who has treated us kindly and saved us from sin, so we willingly give up the rights of our lives in order to belong to Him.

This word is borrowed from the world of slavery and it was used as the lowest form of servitude. The weakest slave and the lowest of creatures was given the designation of *'doulos'*. The whole word conjured up the harshest form of slavery where the worst practices were seen, and this word taken from this world was the word that Paul used when he described his relationship to God. It just seems that Paul was looking for the worst word to convey the best of feelings. It is just like God to take the lowest form of slave treatment to convey the highest form of relationship in the kingdom of God.

However, in Paul's use of the word within the New Testament there is no sense of bondage conveyed, he did not feel that there was a restraint upon him in the sense of wanting to 'get away from a master' but being tied there without a remedy. His understanding of being a bond-slave and a servant was one of freedom to willingly belong to his master. This to him was the highest form of a love relationship. He was bound unto the Lord not by the cords of restraint but by the cords of Calvary's love and grace.

My Journal ______________________________

KEY PRAYER

Heavenly Father, in the words of an old hymn I come before you today, 'I love, I love my master, I can not go out free'. I rejoice today in the glorious fact that I am free to belong to you, thank you for this privileged position of grace, that I am bound to you. Help me to appreciate every day the wonder of my place in your kingdom and help me each day to live in the freedom of being your bond-slave.

February 28th

KEY WORD: **Good**

KEY VERSE: **Mark 10 : 18**

"Why do you call me good?" Jesus answered. "No-one is good – except God alone."

The words of a praise song say: 'God is good, all the time', and 'all the time, God is good'. This theme is quite obviously taken from the words of Jesus when He was confronted by the rich young ruler and in His answer, He stated that 'only God is good.'

The concept of goodness is of course applied to God who is at all times and in all ways, good! To believe anything else concerning God would be false and a heresy. God is good all the time and all the time, God is good.

The word used to introduce this truth to us within the New Testament is the Greek word *'agathos'* and its meaning is quite unique. It is the word used to convey the thought of 'that which is truly good in its character and beneficial in its effect'. There are some things that might be called 'good', but do not do you good, for instance 'a good night out' might not be a good night when it comes to the effects that are felt the very next morning! However, the word *'agathos'* conveys the thought that goodness is pure and its effects are beneficial to all.

It was used of certain objects, Jesus called a tree 'good' and its fruit 'good', in Matthew 7 : 17, when He was talking in His sermon on the mount.

In Luke 8 : 8, Jesus called certain ground 'good ground' in the parable of the sower. In these references what was being called 'good', was essentially good and produced good things that were beneficial.

People were called 'good' at certain times. Barnabas was called a 'good man' in Acts 11 : 24, and so was Joseph of Arimathea in

Luke 23 : 50. Both Barnabas and Joseph were good men and did good deeds that were beneficial to others.

Slaves were instructed by Peter to be good slaves in submission to their masters, 1 Peter 2 : 18, and in Romans 5 : 7, we are told that in some circumstances a good man might die for others.

All these references point to a form of goodness that is deeper than the usual understanding of 'that which is just good.' These references rightly show that real goodness is 'that which is in its character and beneficial effect 'good'.

God is good, everything about Him is good. From His being to His works, everything is good. His character is good, His effect upon us is good and His desires for us are good. We receive good things from His hands and our future is laced with acts of goodness that go far beyond anything that anyone else could offer us. In Old Testament terms, Psalm 23 offers us the prospect of 'goodness and mercy following us all the days of our lives'. This kind of goodness can only come from a good God, who can only do good things, because His character is essentially good.

My Journal

KEY PRAYER

Heavenly Father, I pause to thank you today for your goodness, I never cease to be amazed at the goodness of my Father who cares for me at all times. Help me to understand even more fully just how good you are and help me to proclaim at every point of my life, that God is good all the time and that all the time, God is good.

February 29th

KEY WORD: **Doubt**

KEY VERSE: **John 20 : 27**

Then Jesus said to Thomas, "Put your finger here; see my hands. Reach out your hand and put it into my side. Stop doubting and believe."

Doubt and unbelief are the two instruments that the enemy uses to rob God's people of their rightful blessings. To doubt God or to doubt His Word is to lose the whole effect of spiritual growth, spiritual passion and joy. There is nothing worse to the believer than doubt and unbelief.

The Bible is littered with people who lost out in God because they did not believe and the New Testament teaches us to stop doubting and just believe God, because it is the pathway to blessing and wholeness. The words of Jesus to Thomas in the upper room have an urgency about them; it was time to stop doubting and it was time to simply believe.

The Greek word used to convey this truth is the word '*diaporeo*' and its meaning is quite significant. The word was used for someone who had 'lost their way' or who had 'no way out', and its impact was very striking in its forcefulness. It was a word that was used to convey 'utter despair'. So here is a picture drawn for us of a man who was on a journey who had somehow lost his way and, having sought direction, could no longer understand any commands that were being given. Now, near to despair, he is totally perplexed at his situation and now totally lost finds that he is in a maze-like experience and has no way forward and no way back; he is in a place of no way out. That picture of despair is conjured up by the word '*diaporeo*'.

This must have been how Thomas felt when his whole world came crashing down around him. He had left all to follow Jesus and now He was dead and buried in a tomb and his whole future was one of despair. Even the words of the other disciples who had already seen Jesus could not lift this feeling of hopelessness. Thomas was in a place of no hope and no way out. Then Jesus came and said, "Stop doubting and believe."

In our walk with God the same stinging rebuke with its edge of grace and comfort needs to be spoken over lives. How many of us have missed God because we simply did not believe? I wonder just how much blessing has been lost to us because we placed ourselves in a 'maze' with no way out, and in our perplexity became utterly overwhelmed with despair. The words of Jesus need to come again and again to us. Now is the time to put away doubt and now is the time to believe.

My Journal

KEY PRAYER

Heavenly Father, I receive the words today concerning my doubts and fears and I seek to do what Thomas did when you entered his experience, he cried out 'My Lord and my God'. I seek you today in order that my fears and doubts might be dispelled and I come before you seeking forgiveness for my lack of trust and belief. Help me today to rise above my feelings and to learn to trust you more.

March 1st

KEY WORD: **Appearance**

KEY VERSE: **Luke 9 : 29**

As Jesus was praying, the appearance of His face changed, and His clothes became as bright as a flash of lightning.

Appearance is a good word to start a new month with. Luke in his writings records the fact that when Jesus was praying on the mount of transfiguration, His face was changed and the glory of His appearance was likened by Luke to that of a flash of lightning. Luke used a very special word when he sought to describe this moment.

The Greek word used, which is translated 'appearance' in this key verse, is the word *'eidos'* which more correctly should be translated as 'that which strikes the eye'. In actual fact it has two forms of meaning as it can also be used when seeking to describe something that is 'seen by the eye', and it can also be translated as 'being exposed'. This meaning is used when something comes into view that was previously hidden.

So we have the thought here that as Jesus was praying, Luke's eye was drawn to the changes that were taking place within the bodily form of Jesus, and as He was transfigured the change 'struck Luke's eye' and the concept of something previously hidden came into full view. It is a wonderful word that Luke used as it conveys more than just a change of features or a change of emphasis, it conveys exactly what happened to Jesus; He was completely changed. The human form was transfigured into His divine form and glory and it 'struck Luke's eye' as nothing had done previously.

This word is also used when the Holy Spirit, like a dove, appeared on the head of Jesus during His water baptism. There had not been an appearance of a dove before and it once again caught the eye of Luke when he described this in Luke 3 : 22.

This word only appears five times within the New Testament and is therefore a rare feature and, as with the rare usage of a word, each and every time it is used, it is important that every meaning is gleaned. It appears when Paul was seeking to convey the importance of abstaining from all appearance of evil. Paul was actually saying that if we indulge ourselves in temptation and we allow the very appearance of evil within our lives, we are exposing ourselves to something that will catch the eye of others. Therefore abstain from all appearance of evil, as we do not want any striking act of sin to be seen.

It was also used when Paul was conveying to the Corinthian Church the vital teaching that we walk by faith and not by sight. In using this word *'eidos'*, Paul is seeking to bring the truth of the fact that we do not seek to live by the form of appearances, we do not need striking acts to increase our faith, our trust and faith is based upon what we do 'not see'. Our whole experience is based upon the fact that we live and walk by faith, trusting God through our experiences, even when we cannot see and even when we cannot understand.

As we start a new month, it is a good time to remind ourselves of this walk of faith and it is a good time to tell the Lord that we trust Him fully even when the times are hard.

My Journal ____

____

____

____

KEY PRAYER

Heavenly Father, I bless you on this first day of a new month and I pledge before you that I will seek to constantly build up my faith so that I learn every day to trust you more. I will not live by things that can be seen but I will trust you through the hard times and I will live by your Word and your Word alone. Thank you that you never leave me nor forsake me.

March 2nd

KEY WORD: ***Angels***

KEY VERSE: ***Matthew 4 : 11***

Then the devil left Jesus, and angels came and attended Him.

Throughout the entire Bible we are left with no doubt whatsoever that angels are very real beings. In the Old Testament their appearances are very frequent and even in the New Testament, where the Holy Spirit takes a more centre stage, angels are still to be found manifested throughout the pages.

Angels are God's messengers and agents to a fallen world, they are given powers of authority and are mighty beings whose appearances often caused great fear. The actual Greek word for angel is '*angelos*' and the English name is therefore derived quite simply from the Greek word. '*Angelos*' translated means a messenger or a guardian and can even mean a representative, and it can also mean an agent. These translations therefore mean that at any one time an angel can be involved in numerous activities. For instance, an angel could be delivering a message from God, he could be giving guardianship to someone in need and he could also be representing God to man at a time appointed.

In Matthew 4 : 11, following the temptations of Jesus, angels came and cared for Him. At this moment in time the '*angelos*' were guardians of the Saviour at a moment of human weakness. It is also a well known fact that angels have been designated as guardians of each one of us 'less we strike our foot against a stone', so their ministry unto us is that they have been commanded to care for us. In Psalm 91 : 11-12, angels are created beings who are greater and more powerful than man, they hold an order that is superior to created mankind and they belong to a different world, but they frequent this world as they perform their unique ministry. Hebrews 1 : 14 states that they are sent forth to serve those who inherit salvation.

The Bible makes it very clear that angels are spirits and not human, although they can assume human form when needed, and the Bible also makes it clear that their sole purpose is to do the will of God at His direction. They are called holy beings and they have an awesome power that is always directed towards the safety of God's chosen people. Throughout Church history there have been occurrences when angels have appeared unto men and their appearances have always been to do the will of God. It is also quite possible that we have entertained angels unaware of exactly who we were giving hospitality to, Hebrews 13 : 2.

The possibility that each one of us has been ministered to by Angels without knowing it is absolutely certain and we can thank God for all the times that He sent an angel on a mission of care and comfort to us even if we did not know it. We should all be praying that God will give us eyes to see what we can not see naturally, as the possibility is that there are Angels all around us, as they were for Elisha's servant, in 2 Kings 6 : 17.

My Journal

KEY PRAYER

Heavenly Father, please forgive me today for my 'natural' approach to all things, I live in a natural world and often only see with natural eyes. Give me eyes to see what I can not see and help me to understand that you have given the command that angels should watch over my life, and I bless you today for the care that has been manifested towards me.

March 3rd

KEY WORD: ***Archangel***

KEY VERSE: ***Jude 9***

But even the archangel Michael, when he was disputing with the devil about the body of Moses, did not dare to bring a slanderous accusation against him, but said, "The Lord rebuke you!"

As we saw yesterday, the angels have a powerful and very effective ministry and they conduct this ministry at the direction of God and towards God's people.

Within the multitude of the angels of heaven however, it is quite clear that there are designations of greater power and greater strength and it seems that there are designated ranks. The Bible speaks of archangels and it also speaks of cherubim and seraphim. In the key verse today an angel is given a name, that of Michael, and he is also given the rank of archangel. The interesting fact however, is that there are only two references to archangels in the entire Bible and they are both within the New Testament. The one in Jude verse 9 and the other in 1 Thessalonians 4 : 16, where the archangel comes down from heaven at the Second Coming of Jesus and shouts with a great command.

The only archangel to bear a name in the Bible is Michael, this could mean that there is only one archangel or it could mean that there are many archangels but only one is given a name. As we only have two verses to draw truth from, it is hard to know exactly. However, what we do know is that Michael serves within a superior rank to that of an angel and as we saw yesterday, angels have great and awesome power. Therefore if an archangel stands above the other angels then how great is Michael's power and authority?

In the two verses that have been allotted to this ministry we can partly answer the question of 'how great is an archangel's power and authority?' Firstly, we note that at the Second Coming of Jesus it is the archangel that is given the authority to proclaim the advent of the Son of God. His voice proclaims this event with such magnitude that those who are dead in Christ are quickened and those who are live and remain are caught up in this great rapture of the Church.

Secondly, in Jude, it was the archangel who was given the authority to denounce the devil when there was a dispute over the body of Moses. Great and awesome power is given unto these beings within heaven and within earth. The Greek word for archangel is quite simply *'archangelos'* and the English name is derived naturally from the Greek. The translation is also very easy to understand as it simply means 'chief prince' or 'chief agent'. God has at His disposal ranks of angels who display their power towards the people of God. We should take comfort today in that God has set these mighty beings in place to guard us and to care for us, and there is at least one archangel who is even greater in his ministry than that of an angel. Why then should we fear when these beings are set in their authority over our lives.

My Journal ____________________________________

____

____

____

KEY PRAYER

Heavenly Father, I bless you today for the revelation that in heaven and on earth you have designated angelic beings to care for us. I thank you for your great love towards us in that not only do we have a Son who died for us and a Holy Spirit who comforts us but we also have ranks of great beings who ever watch over our lives. I rest more securely today in the knowledge that around and about me are the agencies of greatness.

March 4th

KEY WORD: **Faith**

KEY VERSE: **1 Corinthians 2 : 4-5**

My message and my preaching were not with wise and persuasive words, but with demonstration of the Spirit's power, so that your faith might not rest on men's wisdom, but on God's power.

Faith – what an amazing word and what an amazing world it opens up to us when it is exercised. Faith brings us to God and faith keeps us true each and every day of our lives.

Faith is the substance that pleases God, and according to Hebrews 11, faith is being sure of a world that we do not see, and faith brings us the evidence and certainty of what we hope for. Without faith we can not please God; and how hard it is at times to manifest faith. Certain believing people had to ask Jesus to help them manifest more faith.

To understand this substance called faith we have to analyse its very nature. The word used for our English term faith, is the Greek word *'pistis'*, which should more correctly be translated as a 'certain and firm persuasion' or even more pointedly, 'a conviction based upon hearing'. This second form of translation is taken from the world of public debate where men would be only persuaded by clear and concise argument and their trust and faith would only be activated when they were convinced of the matter. All this is vital in the world of trust and conviction, however, we trust God through the evidence of things unseen and we approach God, not on an argument basis of being convinced but through simple trust in a living God and His living Word. This is why Peter would write to the church in commendation, praising them that they trusted in Jesus when they had never seen

Him. Their trust was not in an argument but in an invisible world.

The word *'pistis'* is used in two different ways. It can mean trust – trust that is made known when all things are against us. Paul said "I believe God", when the boat was sinking and all seemed lost. His trust was in the fact that God had called him to Rome therefore the boat could not sink and therefore they would not be lost. This was faith in something unseen.

It can also mean trustworthiness, as in the case when Paul was setting out a case for trusting God in Romans 3 : 3, when he said to the Roman Church that 'God is faithful'. The situation was that God was trustworthy and man was not!

'Pistis' also has an element attached to it of a stronger nature. It is quite possible to put faith in a man or in a woman, and you can also put faith in an object, in the sense that you can trust a rope to haul you to the top of a cliff – you just believe that the rope will take the strain. This was the thought that Paul was arguing against when he was setting out the fact that he came to Corinth, in the key verse today, without seeking to gather men together with persuasive words of men's wisdom. He did not want his converts putting their trust in a man or an argument.

However, *'pistis'* is a word of a stronger nature than trusting man or objects. This word carries with it the sense of trusting in an invisible, unseen world and it is this kind of trust that pleases God. We have put our trust and faith in a fact of truth that, having not seen God, we believe, and that even when He fails to answer prayer in the way that we expected, we still trust Him. It is this kind of faith that the world calls foolish and that God calls commendable.

KEY PRAYER

Heavenly Father, like one of old I say today that 'I believe, but please help my unbelief''. I affirm before you today that I trust and believe and I declare that my faith is in the world of the invisible and unseen blessing of God. Yet I acknowledge that my faith level is not always what it should be. Help me to exercise my faith more so that I grow in trust and belief.

March 5th

KEY WORD: ***Faithfulness***

KEY VERSE: **2 Thessalonians 3 : 3**

But the Lord is faithful, and He will strengthen and protect you from the evil one.

We have faith in God and in the unseen things of an eternal world, and as we saw yesterday this kind of faith receives God's commendation. If faith is the word that manifests conviction and trust as the Greek word *'pistis'* conveys, then faithfulness goes even further.

The word used for faithfulness is the word that is a kin word to *'pistis'*. It is the word *'pistos'* and it conveys two senses, one that is active and one that is passive. In the passive sense it is reliability, and in the active sense its meaning is the term that speaks of a believer. If we take the passive sense first it will help us to understand just where this word fits in the whole spectrum of faith in an unseen world and faith in God.

'Pistos' means reliability. In the key verse today, Paul set out to the Church in Thessalonica that tremendous fact that God is faithful and that He would never let them down. He would protect them from the evil one and He would always give them strength. Paul is stating the clear fact that we have come to embrace – that God is faithful, He is utterly reliable and that His Word is to be trusted. This passive sense of the word brings us to a place where we can submit totally to Him, the One who never fails, and that we enter a state of rest when we know that He is faithful.

The active sense of this word is in the meaning of our participation in God's faithfulness. Abraham was commended for his trust in a faithful God, in Galations 3 : 9, when Paul states that Abraham was blessed and was called a man of faith.

Abraham in this instance placed an active trust in God and the word *'pistos'* conveyed this trust and lays stress upon the active nature of Abraham's faith.

We have learned in our walk with God thus far that when we are active in our demonstration of faith, God, who is faithful, never lets us down. These two senses of this lovely word come together in agreement and they produce for us a dimension of trust that goes far beyond anything that we can actually describe, because faith is a substance that is unseen.

My Journal

KEY PRAYER

I praise you today for your faithfulness through all generations and I bless you for your faithfulness to me. Help me to understand more and more your faithfulness towards me and help me to walk worthy of this faithfulness throughout the day.

March 6th

KEY WORD: ***Little faith***

KEY VERSE: ***Matthew 6 : 30-31***

"If that is how God clothes the grass of the field, which is here today and tomorrow is thrown into the fire, will He not much more clothe you, O you of little faith. So do not worry."

Before we leave the subject of faith which has been the theme of the past two days, we need to look at the reverse of the situation, or the negative aspect of faith. God commends faith, even a little faith as small as a grain of mustard seed, however there is a rebuke against those who manifest unbelief or little faith.

The word used for the English equivalent of 'little faith' is the Greek word *'oligopistos'* and it is the opposite of the word that we studied together yesterday. Yesterday we saw that *'pistos'* was reliability in a God who never fails, and as a God who never fails He expects us to trust Him. *'Oligopistos'* means quite simply 'little faith'. It is a combination of two words, *'oligos'* meaning 'little' and *'pistos'* meaning 'faith'.

This word is used only five times in the entire Bible, they are all in the New Testament and they are all from the lips of Jesus. It seems that it was a word reserved for only His use, no apostle or prophet ever used this term, it was a word combination that was used by Jesus and Jesus alone.

He used it five times to convey two truths. In the first instance He used this word in the context of anxiety. In the key verse today, Jesus asked 'why do we worry?' when God who clothes even the grass of the field, will take even more care of our clothing and needs. He was seeking to address the fact that our little faith needs strengthening and that the strength could be drawn from the fact that God takes care of all things, even grass, so why should anxiousness be a part of our life style. Jesus actually used this word twice in the context of worry and anxiety and therefore we should take careful note. The God who is faithful will take care of us.

The second instance where this word appears is when Jesus brought a gentle rebuke concerning fear. He actually uses the word in the context of fear three times, and they are all in the gospel of Matthew. When a fierce storm gathered around the boat on Galilee and the disciples were about to lose their minds with fear, Jesus rebuked them and said, "You of little faith," Matthew 8 : 26.

When Peter was about to sink, having manifested faith in the first instance and actually got out of the boat, but now seeing the waves, he was about to go under, Jesus caught him by the hand and said, "You of little faith, why did you doubt?" Matthew 14 : 31. It is an interesting fact that in the same context and at almost the very same moment, Peter manifests both '*pistos*' and '*oligopistos*', faith and little faith.

The third instance of this word being used in the context of fear is when Jesus rebuked the Pharisees and Sadducees, when they were asking for a sign, and Jesus said again, "You of little faith," Matthew 16 : 8. In these three instances against fear and the two instances against worry, Jesus showed that there is a sense of rebuke when we do not trust God in the way that we should. '*Oligopistos*' is not a hard word of censure, it is in fact a soft word of sadness. Jesus did not show anger against those who failed to believe, but He was saddened in the sense that there was evidence all around them but people failed to believe God.

KEY PRAYER

Heavenly Father, I seek today to place my trust in you totally. I affirm my allegiance to the One who never fails, and I ask for an increase in my level of trust and obedience. I praise you today that even though at times my faith is small, your love and grace overwhelm me and I reach out to you again and find you ever faithful.

March 7th

KEY WORD: **Peace**

KEY VERSE: **Romans 15 : 33**

The God of peace be with you all. Amen.

Today we will seek to evaluate and assess a really wonderful word, a word that conveys something that is hard to explain and hard to fully understand – Peace.

It has been said that real peace is not the absence of war but the presence of God, because even in the midst of war and tension, and even trouble and affliction, you can still retain a measure of peace, if you know the Lord.

There are several words in the New Testament that can be translated as peace, but the overwhelming one that is used is the Greek word *'eirene'*. This word appears in every New Testament book except one, that book is the first epistle of John. Even in its absence from this book the nature of peace remains, as John uses several other words such as love, joy, comfort and completeness so that you know that John has a peace in his heart that the world could not possibly give him.

'Eirene' is the word that is used for harmony, freedom, friendliness and quietness, and it conveys something of the nature of God. The statement, the 'God of peace' appears quite often within the New Testament which in itself conveys the glorious fact that God is peace and that peace is God. The Greek word is derived from its corresponding Hebrew equivalent, 'shalom', which means wholeness and completeness, and again this speaks of God's peace upon us.

The word is used in several instances within the New Testament and can be found in various ways. It is used of relationships between people who have found peace with one another. It used when nations are no longer at war and have entered into a relationship of peace as told by Jesus in Luke 14 : 32. It is used for acts of kindness between churches as reported by Luke in Acts 15 : 33.

It is used by Paul in 1 Corinthians 14 : 33 when he was giving instructions in the use of spiritual gifts and he chose this word to convey the fact that God does not bring disorder but peace. All these uses are perfectly correct, however, the word comes into its own when it is coupled with the fact that God gives peace and brings peace upon us when we trust Him. He is the God of all peace, as the key verse states today. To couple the word with the name of God is absolutely perfect as He is perfect peace. The same kind of feeling is described in 2 Thessalonians 3 : 16, when Paul again is seeking to convey the truth of a wonderful peaceful God, when he uses the expression of the Lord of peace.

'Eirene' is perfect peace, and it is right that today we seek to honour and praise Him who is peace and who gives peace to those who trust in Him.

My Journal

KEY PRAYER

Heavenly Father, thank you for the wonderful fact that you are real peace. I recognise the fact that without you there would be such disharmony in our world and such disorder within our lives. I bless you today for the fact that I live in peace due to your presence and I glorify you. Help me to retain this sense of peace throughout the day and help me to keep close to you so that perfect peace might be my portion.

March 8th

KEY WORD: **Peacemakers**

KEY VERSE: **Matthew 5 : 9**

Blessed are the peacemakers, for they will be called sons of God.

If, as we saw yesterday, God is Peace and Peace is God, then when He manifests Himself to us He will bring to us a measure of quietness and completeness and deep peace. And if the word *'eirene'* means God's perfect peace, then 'peacemakers' is a word that needs to be examined.

It is a word that appears in the English form only once in the New Testament and it also appears only once in its Greek form. The word used for peacemakers is the word *'eirenopoios'*. Its correct translation should be 'one who is the bringer of peacefulness'.

It is a word that is derived from two Greek words and it had its composition in the teaching of Jesus when He addressed His disciples in what has now come to be known as the sermon on the mount. Jesus was seeking to convey a brand new form of truth, therefore a new word needed to be invented. So two Greek words were combined in order to convey the fullest truth concerning those who brought peace. The two words used by Matthew to convey the teaching of Jesus are *'eirene'* which of course means 'peace' and *'poieo'* which means 'to bring'. Therefore the word now used within this composition meant 'bringer of peace' or 'peacemaker'.

Jesus no doubt had in mind the future days when His Church would speak into a world of noise and confusion, when His Church would plant new congregations in towns and cities where there was no word of peace. He therefore chose His audience carefully when He used this word and He also chose the situation very carefully. He was actually stating that when the Church brought good news of hope and peace, the bringers of this news would be called 'bringers of peace' and they could quite rightly be designated 'sons of God'.

There is also another aspect of 'peace bringing' that can be associated with this word in its form of 'peacemakers'. It would be quite right to allow the word *'eirenopoios'* to be used in the context of those who would bring wise words of counsel and direction into situations that could be fraught with difficulty. The ministry of bringing peace into times and seasons of disorder is a valued ministry and allows the pouring of oil onto troubled waters, thus soothing and calming troubled seas. This ministry could also receive the designation 'peacemakers' and 'bringers of peace'.

There is also a kin word in the New Testament that has a bearing upon the ministry of a peacemaker, it is the Greek word *'Eirenikos'* . This is a similar word but has a slightly deeper meaning, its translation means peaceful or peaceable. This word conveys the nature of God and the nature of those who are peacemakers. They themselves are peaceful people and they display a sense of peace when you are in their presence. It would be right today to pray for a sense of peace and a sense of peacefulness, so that those around us might sense real peace and the presence of the Lord.

My Journal ________________________________

____

____

____

____

KEY PRAYER

Heavenly Father, I pray today for a sense of calm and all prevailing peace, I long to be a peacemaker and I long to glorify your name with a serenity and a calmness that only comes from you. I give my life to you afresh so that you might use me to bring peace to others. I pray that my life might be peaceful in every respect.

March 9th

KEY WORD: **Man**

KEY VERSE: **Matthew 4 : 4**

Jesus answered, "It is written: 'Man does not live on bread alone, but on every word that comes from the mouth of God'."

The Bible and especially the New Testament, has a lot to say about 'man'. The Bible paints the very clear picture of 'man' as a fallen creature that needs salvation, it also portrays just how much 'man' is loved by an eternal, loving Heavenly Father, who sent His Son to redeem 'man' from sin. It also portrays just what salvation can do in restoring 'man' to a position of blessing and peace.

When the Bible uses the word 'man' it is not speaking of just the masculine form of human beings, but it is using the Greek word *'anthropos'* as the form of word that embraces both masculine and feminine. The word actually describes 'mankind'. We derive our English word anthropology from the Greek word *'anthropos'* and we have come to know that anthropology speaks of the study of man, both in the male and female gender.

God loves 'man', both male and female and He gave His Son to save the whole race. *'Anthropos'* is used to describe the human being and it is used of one person, or a race of people; it is even used to describe the frailty of man and his sin.

The New Testament teaches that when 'man' accepts Jesus as Saviour he becomes a new man, not in the sense of a change of bodily form but in the sense of a change of spiritual nature. Paul loved to play with words and he uses the terms 'old man' and 'new man' to describe the fallen nature and the renewed nature of man. These terms are unique to Paul, no one else in the New Testament uses these terms. It seems that he found them to be very helpful in the understanding of the nature of man's spiritual change and in the presentation of this change to the churches. He also uses two other terms to convey truth. He sought to understand and teach that man had an external nature and an internal nature and he produced the theme of the 'outward man' and the 'inward man', to convey the thought of the external frame of flesh and the internal spiritual nature of a changed man of God.

These expressions brought the truth to the churches that man was fallen and sinful, but that through the blood of Jesus, man could find forgiveness and redemption so that the 'old man' might become a 'new man'. There were also other words concerning 'man' that were used by Paul to convey truth.

This designation: 'man of God', which Paul used quite often was not used as a title nor an office, but as a simple description of the 'new man' in Christ whose nature has been changed and whose will has been subordinated to the will of God. This is the 'new man' of the New Testament whose heart is right with God and who only seeks to glorify God in all that he does. We can thank God today for redemption and for the fact that a change of heart and a change of nature is possible. We thank God too for the fact that having been an 'old man' with an old nature, we are now made into 'new men' with a brand new nature.

Old things are passed away and all things have become new and fresh.

My Journal

KEY PRAYER

Heavenly Father, thank you today for my brand new nature and my brand new future, I bless you for sending your Son into a world of sin that was full of the old sinful nature of man. Cause me each day to rejoice in my new nature and keep me close to you at all times.

March 10th

KEY WORD: **Woman**

KEY VERSE: **Galations 4 : 4-5**

But when the time had fully come, God sent His Son, born of a woman, born under law, to redeem those under law, that we might receive the full rights of sons.

In yesterday's study we saw that there was a word used that was all embracive of mankind, it was the Greek word *'anthropos'*. This word is used throughout the New Testament, hundreds of times, for both the male and female gender. There is however, a specific word used that can only be translated into our English word 'woman'. This word is used 192 times in specific cases where the writers wanted to convey the fact that the person in question was not a man or mankind, it was in fact a female person, a woman.

The Greek word that is used for the word 'woman' is the word *'gune'* and it is used whether the woman was a single person or a married person, and it is a term of endearment or a term of respect. I believe that the New Testament writers were seeking to establish the fact that now in the age of grace, women were being elevated into a higher status than they had enjoyed previously and this term of endearment was used to enhance this status and to improve their position in life.

You only have to study how Jesus talked about women and treated women, to know that 'things were different now'. To give the female gender their own special word when the word *'anthropos'* covered both male and female, is to highlight the fact that women were special.

Jesus used this term in contrasting situations, it was used when He addressed His own mother and He also used it when He confronted the adulterous woman of Samaria at Jacob's Well.

When the English word 'woman' was first heard, the term seems to be a little harsh and one of rebuke or even of censure and rebuff, however, the term used by Jesus and by New Testament writers is a special term of greatest respect. The account of Jesus at Galilee, when He turned water into wine illustrates this fact perfectly. His mother came to Him stating the fact that the wedding had run out of wine, and Jesus turned to His mother and said, "Dear woman, why do you involve me?" At first sight, a rebuff and rebuke of the hardest nature, until the word 'woman' is analysed. Jesus used the Greek word '*gune*' which almost elevated Mary to the highest place in a love relationship. What actually passed between them was a conversation of great intimacy, Mary was confiding in Jesus as a mother would to a loving son, and Jesus responded with great care and feeling, saying literally, there is no obligation upon either of us to help in the matter, but love is the key. This is why Mary responded as she did, in John 2 : 5, "Do whatever He tells you."

Mary would not have responded in this way if she had been negatively rebuked or censured, the reason for her positive response was the fact that Jesus had treated her so kindly and with great affection in a public place.

From this moment on, the place of every woman in the New Testament took on an increased stature and the role of the woman was elevated. Even our key verse today goes at length to state that Jesus was born of a woman. It could have been left at the fact that Jesus was born, but Paul wants to underline the fact that God chose to use a female vessel to bring His Son to birth. Church history has gone on to prove the valued role of women in church life and the Church is blessed to have a place of dignity for them.

KEY PRAYER

Heavenly Father, thank you for the way that you brought about a change in status for women and I bless you for their role and place within the Church as well as within the home. I pray today for all those who have blessed the Church in times past, and for those that you are still using today.

March 11th

KEY WORD: **Brothers**

KEY VERSE: **Romans 1 : 13**

I do not want you to be unaware, brothers, that I planned many times to come to you (but have been prevented from doing so until now) in order that I might have a harvest among you, just as I have had among the other Gentiles.

Over the past few days we have been looking at both the human genders of male and female and we have seen that the Bible uses the word 'man' to mean both male and female persons. But we have also seen that the Bible uses a word that is especially for women and that Jesus sought to provide a special place for women within His ministry and within the Church. However, before we leave the subject of the human gender another New Testament word demands our attention. The New Testament speaks much about 'brothers' and 'brethren' in the church sense of a corporate body, it seems to be an embracive word concerning the body of believers.

As with the fact that the word for 'man' is also an all embracive word for both male and female persons, this word 'brother' is also a genderless word. The Greek word used for the term 'brother' is the word *'adelphos'*, which translated means 'near kinsman' if it is used in a singular way. It can also mean 'community' when it is used in a plural form in the meaning of 'brethren'.

The word *'adelphos'* was a word that was used in a wide way by cultural understanding, it could be used in a family setting when talking about male children of the same father and mother, a brother, as it still is today. It could be used in the setting of national identity in the sense of a race of people being a family and being called brethren. It could be used in the context of a neighbour, or a group of people with a common aim. It was also used in quite a strange way of all mankind. This meaning is still used today when people speak of the 'brotherhood of man'.

It found its way into New Testament Church life very early on when Jesus introduced the word concerning His disciples, when He said to the women who had gone to His tomb following His death, "Go and tell my brothers to go to Galilee, there they will see me." Matthew 28 : 10. The word found its way into full use in the book of Acts where it became a common term for those who were 'within the church'. It came to denote those who were on a common journey and a corporate mission and was used to convey the message that these people were 'one in spirit' and 'one in family'. It was used of this family in a corporate sense whether they were male or female.

As time went by the term 'brother' became used in a way that was an endearment, and its use brought the believers closer together and bonded them into a greater understanding of togetherness, especially when they were faced with persecution. This is why James uses the word *'adelphos'* when he writes to those who are scattered among the nations, when he says, "Consider it pure joy, my brothers, whenever you face trials of many kinds." James 1 : 2.

The use of the word to those who were scattered sent the message that they might not be together but they were still brothers in the Lord and part of the family of God.

This family is still alive and well today and we are all brothers in the Lord and brethren together. As we pray today we should thank God for His goodness and for the fact that we belong to a great family and that we have brothers throughout the world through Christ.

KEY PRAYER

Heavenly Father, I thank you today for my brothers in the church, millions of whom I have never met and will not meet until we all get to heaven. I thank you for each one and praise you for the fact that we belong together. Thank you for placing me in a great family and help me each day to appreciate my brothers in the Lord.

March 12th

KEY WORD: **Almighty**

KEY VERSE: **Revelation 19 : 6**

Then I heard what sounded like a great multitude, like the roar of rushing waters, and like loud peals of thunder, shouting: "Hallelujah, for our Lord God Almighty reigns."

When words are used within the New Testament we often take them quite for granted, and our minds accept the fact that they are there and that they exist. What we do not often do is take time to think about them and to study them. Today, here is just such a word, 'almighty'. We know that God is Almighty and we know that the Bible addresses Him as such and that hymns and spiritual songs have expressed this great fact over the years. It is so well known and so well used that we just take it for granted.

However, this word 'almighty,' is only used in a very limited way within the New Testament, in fact it is only mentioned once in the epistles, and this was a direct quote from the Old Testament, and it is only used nine other times, and all of these are in the book of Revelation. This word that is so well known and so often used by hymn writers is only mentioned ten times in the entire New Testament.

The Greek word used for the English word 'almighty' is the word '*pantokrator*', which means 'ruler of all' or another translation might be 'holder of all things'.

This word is only used of God and is only used in a very limited way. Paul uses this word just once in all his writings, which is quite strange seeing that he often thought of the magnitude of God and His glory. As he used this word only once, in 2 Corinthians 6 : 18, we ought to study the verse closely. Paul is setting out in this chapter the difference between light and darkness, and righteousness and unrighteousness. He attempts to explain that we can not be yoked together with unbelievers and the only way that he can make this contrast clear and concise is to quote from the Old Testament. So he uses the Old Testament truth that God is so great and so holy that nothing unclean can stand before His presence. He speaks of God as being 'Almighty', 'the ruler and holder of all things'.

The apostle, John, uses the word only nine times in his book of Revelation and all the references are descriptions of God in His glory, in His majesty and in His 'Almighty power'. John is seeking to establish the fact that God is awesome and that He is the centre of heaven and that nothing now or nothing that is to come, will be able to stand before Him.

God holds all things and rules all things in such a way that He is totally and absolutely 'Almighty'. The next time that you sing this word on numerous occasions within a worship time, remember it was only used in a limited way by New Testament writers, as the fact of God's 'Almighty power' was such a holy and awesome thing. Breathe this fact with great care.

My Journal ______________________________

KEY PRAYER

Heavenly Father, I acknowledge before you that I often treated you and your power with such casualness and lightness. Forgive me today for not appreciating just how great and Almighty you are. Help me to live in the knowledge of your greatness and help me to always treat you with great reverence and godly fear.

March 13th

KEY WORD: **Chosen**

KEY VERSE: **Colossians 3 : 12**

Therefore, as God's chosen people, holy and dearly loved, clothe yourselves with compassion, kindness, humility, gentleness and patience.

In this text there are several words that need to be understood in order that the truth being conveyed is received in its fullness. Over the next few days we will look at the words individually, so that the full impact of the Scripture is revealed.

As God's chosen people, Paul encourages us to clothe ourselves with several virtues, so that we might fulfil the full meaning of 'God's chosen people'. It is this word 'chosen' that is the key word within the text, so it is with this word that we commence to understand the teaching of the apostle.

The truth that we have been chosen by the Lord is a problem for many people, the tension between the free will of man and the sovereignty of God has always been an issue. However, the Bible clearly teaches that 'we did not choose Him but that He chose us.' The glorious fact that God saw us before the world was created and chose us to be predestined to the image of His Son, is an awesome fact. The Greek word for the English word 'chosen', brings this truth into even greater focus when it is understood. The Greek word used is '*eklego*' and it is used to describe the process of selection, or the process of 'picking out' individuals. It does not convey that some are rejected or declined, nor does it convey a kind of partiality, in that God chooses some and leaves out others. It is a word that combines the truth of kindness and favour mixed with God's grace and His will.

God does not choose some to be lost, because all are lost, the fact is, that He has chosen by His grace and favour to select those whom He knew would come to Him and He predestined them to be 'made like His Son'.

The fact that we have been chosen by the Lord should increase our feeling of trust and humility, there was nothing in us that deserved His favour and there is nothing in us that deserves His forgiveness. Yet He sought us, and found us, and as the word *'eklego'* states, He selected us to be with Him.

The same process was used when Jesus strode along the beach at Galilee and 'chose' Peter, James and John to join Him in His crusade to save the world. There would have been scores of fisherman mending their nets at that time, but He chose three to join Him. There were dozens of tax collectors in Jerusalem but He walked up to Matthew's tax table and chose Him to be included within the growing band of disciples.

The same could be said of Zacchaeus and many, many others who were conducting themselves in the normal way, when Jesus passed by and changed their lives and their destiny with His words, "Come and follow me". He chose them, not against their will, because He knew that they would follow Him, He knew that Zacchaeus would come down from the tree to follow Him. Therefore He chose them before they knew Him and selected them to become the people of God. If we were to review our personal history for a moment we would find that there were several instances taking place before we 'knew the Lord', that were drawing us to Him. On the day of our salvation we would say that 'we found the Lord' however, the word *'eklego'* reveals that there was an altogether different process going on. Before the world was created, He saw us, and the process of leading us to Him was set in motion before we were born.

KEY PRAYER

Heavenly Father, it is hard for me to understand the truth that I did not choose you but that you have chosen me. It is hard for me to understand that you found me before I knew you and it is even harder to understand that grace was at work, drawing me to you before I knew about the process. But I thank you for the truth and I lift up your name today and I bless you for your wonderful favour, and I will seek to walk worthy of my high calling in Christ Jesus.

March 14th

KEY WORD: **Holy**

KEY VERSE: **Colossians 3 : 12**

Therefore, as God's chosen people, holy and dearly loved, clothe yourselves with compassion, kindness, humility, gentleness and patience.

Having been called by God to follow Him and appreciating the impact of the fact that He has chosen us, we therefore have to understand who we are in Christ. Paul writes that we are 'holy' people and a people who are dearly loved. It is easy to understand that we are dearly loved, because we also love people dearly; however, our love, even a love that is 'dear', pales into shadow when God's perfect love shines into our hearts. Yet we can understand the fact of 'dear love'.

It is harder to understand and harder to express just what being 'holy' means. For some, 'holy' means a dark expression, or a vow of poverty. It is expressed in a drab way as if a lifestyle that manifests a kind of separation from anything that is light and brightness is being holy and being religious.

We talk about 'holy' people who have joined the seclusion of a monastic style of living, or we talk of 'holy' people who have long since died and who have been canonised by the Church for their endeavours. All this talk and all this understanding is a very long way from the reality of the Bible way of holiness. Holiness is not separation from the world, it is separation unto the Lord. It is not 'thou shalt not' but it is very much 'thou shalt'. In other words it is positive and not negative. It is a shame that the Church has dwelt for years on the negative side of holiness and has preached a lifestyle of not doing this and not doing that, and not going here and not going there and not being involved with this and not being involved with this or that. This kind of holiness is a negative understanding of the Bible's teaching on holiness.

The Greek word used for holiness and holy living is '*hagiasmos*' and it refers to two main features. Firstly, it is the word that is used for bringing 'something towards something else'. In other words in this context, it is the 'bringing of someone to the Lord.' It is not used as a kind of separating 'away' from something, but rather a separating 'unto' something. So in this context holiness is not coming away from the world but rather coming to the Lord.

Secondly, the word refers to the state of holiness or the results of coming to the Lord. We receive something when we draw near to the Lord. Something of His likeness is reflected in us, which actually places a deeper emphasis on the fact that holiness is not dark or secluded, it is a bright and open experience of growth and glory. The results of drawing nearer to the Lord also have the extra blessing of the fact that once you have tasted the blessing of God and are more aware of Him then the world loses its values and attraction.

Therefore holiness is not withdrawing from the world, it is much more the fact that once drawing near to Him the world loses its drawing power. '*Hagiasmos*' is the word that provides us with the insight of attraction and its results. If the church could understand this, the preaching of holiness would take on a greater revelation.

KEY PRAYER

Heavenly Father, thank you for drawing me to you and thank you for the results of this. I bless you today for the fact that my understanding of holy living and the state of holiness has been enhanced by the truth of this revelation. Help me each day to remember that I am not saved from anything but that I am saved unto the Lord, and help me too, to remember that my state of holiness does not depend upon what I do or what I do not do, but it depends upon my closeness to you.

March 15th

KEY WORD: **Compassion**

KEY VERSE: **Colossians 3 : 12**

Therefore, as God's chosen people, holy and dearly loved, clothe yourselves with compassion, kindness, humility, gentleness and patience.

If we now understand the impact of being called and chosen by the Lord and we also understand that our state of holiness does not depend upon what we do, or what we do not do, but on the closeness of our relationship to the Lord, then we can move on to the place where the 'outworking' of this can be achieved. Paul states that we must clothe ourselves with several attributes in order to see the fulfilment of Colossians 3 : 12. He emphasises five attributes that are vital if we are to see the completed picture of our position as chosen people that are holy and loved.

The first attribute – the one that we shall study today is 'compassion'. Compassion is a Bible word that occurs over and over again – it is an active word rather than a passive word. Sympathy is passive; it feels and it hurts with great pain, but it does not do very much other than feel. However, compassion is the active ingredient that actually does something. Jesus was moved with compassion when He saw the widow of Nain, He did not just have sympathy and stand by the side of the road feeling and caring. He crossed the road and took an active part in the funeral procession because He had compassion.

The Greek word for compassion in this Scripture is *'oiktirmos'* and it is the word that is used for the 'seat of emotion' or the depths of emotions. It is often used with another word attached to it, and we find the expression of 'bowels of compassion' or 'bowels of mercies' It is also the word that is often used of God who is moved with compassion when we are in distress and He has to act on our behalf. The word *'oiktirmos'* is the word that actively demonstrates the love of God and the love that we ought to have for one another, so that when one suffers we are moved with compassion to act on their behalf.

The word used however, conveys even more than the act of being moved, it reaches inward parts deeper than words or ordinary feelings can reach. It would not be unusual for this word to be used when someone is feeling deeply touched with another person's pain. The seat of emotion is affected, the heart of compassion is aroused and the inward parts of deep affection are stirred. This is why Paul uses such a word. If we are God's chosen and holy, dearly loved people, we must react to those in need with more than a simple caring attitude of fellowship or friendship. God reached out to us because He cared, He reached out to us because of an inward desire to touch us at the point of our pain. If He did that for us, we must, as the people of God, reach out to others in a likewise fashion.

Compassion cares and acts, just like God did for you and me.

My Journal ______________________________

KEY PRAYER

Heavenly Father, I thank you today for your compassion that reached down to me when I was not even aware of you or your presence. I bless you for the way that you came into my life in such a powerful way. Help me to constantly be aware of those around me who may suffer and hurt, so that I might fully demonstrate the power of compassion.

March 16th

KEY WORD: **Kindness**

KEY VERSE: **Colossians 3 : 12**

Therefore, as God's chosen people, holy and dearly loved, clothe yourselves with compassion, kindness, humility, gentleness and patience.

As God's chosen and beloved people we now seek to be more holy and to clothe ourselves with the attributes of godliness. Compassion is the first attribute required by Paul in the key verse, and we studied this together yesterday, the second attribute is kindness. The first thought that springs into mind when the word kindness is expressed is acts of kindness shown to others or good deeds expressed to those around us, and of course this is quite right.

However, Paul is not talking simply about acts or deeds but a lifestyle change. It could be quite easy for a selfish person to do one or two good deeds before slipping back into the selfish lifestyle of the normal pattern. Paul is stating a major fact here, in that God's chosen and dearly loved people operate under a different code of conduct, the code of conduct that puts other people first and themselves second.

The Greek word used is '*chrestotes*', which translated means 'goodness of heart' or 'pleasant and gracious'. It is the word that is used for a lifestyle of imparting goodness to others. I have known people throughout my ministry who have manifested a 'good heart', their lifestyle is giving and caring and it is a joy to be in their presence. Sadly, I have also known people in the church, whose selfish attitudes and non-caring lifestyle are plain to see and very visible to others. Even in a simple analysis of the two differing lifestyles it is very plain to see which one of them has friends around them and which one people seek to avoid.

Paul is actually stating in this text that the lifestyle of believers should be a dimension above that of the world and also above that of ordinary living. The people of God are different to those who populate this planet; their attitudes and lifestyles are contrary to those of the normal system, light can not dwell with darkness and spirit can not dwell with flesh. So the important question then arises, if the style of those in the Church does not differ from those outside of the Church, where did it all go wrong?

I am convinced that there are people who are members of churches who do not have an experience of regeneration, in other words, they are not born again. Their whole lifestyle is selfish, their conduct is worldly and carnal and their attitude towards others is secondary to their attitude to themselves. Paul goes on to say in the first book of Corinthians that 'tongues without love is like a resounding gong or a clanging cymbal' and that 'prophecy without love' is like 'having nothing'.

Jesus also said that 'many will come in that day saying that they have done mighty deeds' and that the Heavenly Father will say in that day 'depart from me for I never knew you', Matthew 7.

The lifestyle of the people of God is different to that of any other person or any other lifestyle, the word '*chrestotes*' makes the difference. The goodness of heart and an attitude of pleasant caring and sharing set the believers apart, it should be obvious to those around that the people of God have a different set of values and a different code of conduct. Jesus said 'you will know my disciples by their love', John 13 : 35. If love and compassion are absent, there is a very big problem and if deeds of kindness are not visible, the problem is immense!

KEY PRAYER

Heavenly Father, I recognise today that sometimes my lifestyle is not what it ought to be and I come before you with repentance, I seek to do what is right and I confess my sin of selfishness. Help me each day to live as you require me to live and help me each day to conduct myself as a true child of God. Thank you for the lifestyle of Jesus who is our true example.

March 17th

KEY WORD: **Humility**

KEY VERSE: **Colossians 3 : 12**

Therefore, as God's chosen people, holy and dearly loved, clothe yourselves with compassion, kindness, humility, gentleness and patience.

If God is searching for the lifestyle within His children of love and compassion and kindness and caring, then according to Paul in this key verse, He also searches for humility. The apostle, Peter, also states in his first epistle, in chapter 5 : 5-6, that we are to clothe ourselves with humility, but he also says that this action is our action because he quite rightly says, "Humble yourselves".

It is not God's duty to humble us, it is our duty to humble ourselves. I might add, that God will humble us if we do not take the action required in bringing ourselves to a state of humility. If we are to be humble and to clothe ourselves with humility, we ought to know what this means and what we have to do.

The Greek word used by Paul in this verse for humility is the word '*tapeinophrosune*', which is a difficult word to say and an even more difficult word to understand. The word is taken from two different Greek words and they are joined together to form a word that means 'to be low of spirit'. The two words are '*tapeinos*' meaning 'low-lying,' as in being 'brought down', and '*phren*', which means 'the mind'. The two words joined together therefore combine to produce a very clear picture of humility. Paul is actually stating that to clothe ourselves with humility means to 'bring our minds to a low-lying position'.

If a lifestyle of compassion and kindness are required by God for His children, it goes without saying that humility is also a very strong requirement. We are required as a personal action to take the responsibility to bring our minds into a place of low degree, and we must understand what this means in order to co-operate with God's requirements. The word *'tapeinos'* is always used in the New Testament in a good sense, it is the word that denotes lowliness and a humble spirit. When it is joined with *'phren'* it denotes an act of will in the bringing of our minds into a place of lowliness. Satan did the opposite when he exalted himself above God and suffered the consequence. God's desire for us is that we live in a place where we do not think of ourselves more highly than we ought to think but that we dress ourselves with a cloak of lowliness of spirit. This action of bringing ourselves down is the one action that will determine the fact that, in due season, God will raise us up and exalt us.

The picture comes into sharp focus in the story of the Pharisee and the publican. The publican takes his place at the back of the temple and quietly confesses his sin, while the Pharisee parades himself before men stating that he was glad that he was not like the publican. However, God stated that the publican went away justified. The act of clothing ourselves with humility is the act that pleases God. It is our action and responsibility to please Him and it is our duty to bring ourselves low before Him and before all men.

My Journal ______________________________

____

____

____

KEY PRAYER

Heavenly Father, as I come before you today I present myself in the right way and with the right spirit. I bring myself before you with humility and I clothe myself in the right mind. Forgive me for not always recognising this spirit and forgive me for my attitude of pride. Help me each day to remember to humble myself so that I dress in the right way to please you, help me to clothe myself in the correct way before you.

March 18th

KEY WORD: **Gentleness**

KEY VERSE: **Colossians 3 : 12**

Therefore, as God's chosen people, holy and dearly loved, clothe yourselves with compassion, kindness, humility, gentleness and patience.

The chosen and beloved people of God have a different attitude and lifestyle to those of the family of this world and they therefore should clothe themselves with the attributes of godliness. Compassion, kindness and humility are the hallmarks of this lifestyle and they fit the wearers with great distinction.

In this text, Paul paints a beautiful picture of a tender child of God who is seeking to clothe themself with the right garments. As he develops his theme of godly living, Paul goes on to speak about gentleness as another of the hallmarks of this lifestyle. Gentleness is often mistaken for weakness and a cowardly sense of withdrawal. Quite often in church life the gentle, caring child of God seeks to distant themself from quarrels and divisions. They do not want to be involved with the actions of disagreement and strife and their withdrawal from such things can be interpreted as weakness and an inability to stand up for themselves. However, their withdrawal from this kind of action should not be interpreted as weakness, this withdrawal from actions of division is more often the desire to pray and not to fight because their lifestyle imposes a different course of action than that of contention.

The Greek word used by Paul in this text for the word gentleness is a most descriptive and beautiful word, it is the word '*praotes*' and its meaning is very deep. It is not a word that has an outward effect that can be easily seen by others. Kindness is an action word that is revealed by good deeds, but gentleness or meekness as it is sometimes translated has to do with the inner workings of man's soul. During these inner workings of the soul it is God who sees the outworking of gentleness rather than man, for the gentleness of spirit is what responds to the touch of God's Spirit. It is this attitude of spirit that seeks to run to God in conflict rather than to respond in a defensive way. The gentle heart seeks not to gain revenge or rightness in a conflict but seeks rather to submit to God and His ways. It is this kind of action that leads to the wrong kind of interpretation, as we see gentleness and meekness as weakness and an inability to withstand pressure.

The word *'praotes'* is a hard word to understand because it comes from a different perspective of spirit. Everything within the natural spirit seeks to justify itself and stand up for itself and even seeks to gain revenge and justice for itself, whereas gentleness runs to God and hides itself in Him and allows His ways to be proved. However, Jesus was called 'gentle, meek and mild' yet He righteously cleansed the temple, and He set Himself against the Pharisees and the stinking religious nature that blinded the eyes of His people. Gentleness and meekness are not to be interpreted as weakness and cowardice.

It is far better to have an attitude of gentleness and allow God to have His way within your life than to have a spirit that seeks revenge and justice. Paul called for a clothing of our mind and will when he sought to teach that the chosen and dearly loved people of God were a different breed of people altogether.

KEY PRAYER

Heavenly Father, I am learning all the time that my life should reflect your nature and not the old nature, help me to grasp these truths so that I might walk worthy of your high calling in Christ Jesus. Teach me to lean upon you and not upon the ways of the flesh so that I might be clothed in the right fashion during my earthly journey.

March 19th

KEY WORD: **Patience**

KEY VERSE: **Colossians 3 : 12**

Therefore, as God's chosen people, holy and dearly loved, clothe yourselves with compassion, kindness, humility, gentleness and patience.

We have all heard the prayer 'Lord give me patience and give it to me quickly'! We have all also heard the motto that 'patience is a virtue,' suggesting that patience can be naturally gained or learned. However, this motto is incorrect. Paul is not talking about anything that is natural or gained by experience. He is talking about a new kind of lifestyle. The lifestyle of the chosen and dearly loved people of God is radically different to that of the world, and the attributes are quite different too. Paul sought to teach that there were five attributes within this context that needed to be worn so that the people of God were correctly clothed.

Compassion, kindness, humility and gentleness are the attributes of those who walk worthy of their high calling in Christ Jesus. The concluding attribute in this key verse is the testing attribute of patience, and anyone who has sought to develop patience knows just how hard it is to practise. The knowledge of the root meaning of the word patience however, might help in the outworking of this precious and rare gift. Paul uses the Greek word '*makrothumia*' which is often translated as long suffering in some versions of the Bible. The word means 'to forbear' and it is taken from the joining of two separate words, '*makros*' which means 'long' and the word '*thumos*' which means 'temper'. Understanding this train of thought used by Paul helps in the grasping of the attribute that he seeks to convey as part of the new lifestyle of God's people.

The people of God are to have a long temper and not a short fuse! I have noticed at times just how short some people's temper really is, they 'fly off the handle' at the least thing and quite often it is the simplest thing and the merest thing that causes this rush of blood to the head and the 'flying off' of the handle.

Paul says that this is not the lifestyle of the new kingdom, it is a quite different way of life with a quite different attitude of mind and spirit. Longsuffering and patience is a kind of self-restraint that is practised even under extreme provocation and which does not react or retaliate. It is used of God's ways under provocation and it is associated with His mercy. It is a great comfort that He did not react with provocation when we were outside of His kingdom, but with patience and longsuffering He sought us and found us.

Two theologians, Hog and Vine, state that 'patience is the quality that does not surrender to circumstances or succumb under trial, it is the opposite of despondency and it is associated with hope'. '*Makrothumia*' is easily explained but hard to fulfil, it is not 'Lord give me patience and give it to me quickly', it is rather 'Lord teach me to trust you in all circumstances and help me to allow the outworkings of trust to be my teacher, leading me to react in a different way'. Paul said that we were to clothe ourselves with all the attributes of a new spirit, and patience is the greatest test of them all.

KEY PRAYER

Heavenly Father, as I come to the end of this text and the last of the five attributes of grace, help me to learn the lessons quickly so that I might be clothed in the right fashion at the right time. I thank you for the way that Paul conveys these lessons to the Church and I seek today to submit myself to his teaching so that my lifestyle might be compatible with your desire for your chosen and dearly loved people.

KEY WORD: **One**

KEY VERSE: **Philippians 1 : 27**

Whatever happens, conduct yourselves in a manner worthy of the gospel of Christ. Then, whether I come and see you or only hear about you in my absence, I will know that you stand firm in one spirit, contending as one man for the faith of the gospel.

Paul wrote to the church at Philippi with a main message of hope and thanksgiving and in this particular text, he wrote concerning the unity of 'one spirit' and of 'one man'.

Numbers in the Bible have a great significance far above that of just keeping numeracy correct. Numbers spoke symbolically of certain things and, in the New Testament, numbers were often a feature of truth and teaching. In the next twelve days we will study together the numbers one to twelve, and seek to understand the truth that they convey.

'One' in the Bible speaks symbolically of unity, which is Paul's main message within this text. He states that the Philippian Church ought to stand firm in 'one spirit' and that having stood firm they would then contend for the faith as 'one man'. He was expressing the major truth that 'oneness' stands for unity and that anything else was division and disunity. Jesus prayed for His Church in the gospel of John, 'that they might be one'. This was a prayer of unity based upon the fact that 'He was one with His Father'.

The Greek word for our English word 'one' is '*heis*' and its use is varied and widespread; it is used to signify the fact that at times there are many and at times there is just 'one'. It is used often to teach that 'God is one', as in Romans 3 : 30, where Paul states that ' there is only one God'. The word also appears when the Scripture seeks to place emphasis upon the fact that a certain 'one' came to Jesus. This is used to signify that a particular person had presented himself before Jesus as opposed to a multitude.

The word 'one' also is used to convey 'one day' or 'one week' or even 'one of the Sabbaths'. Each time that it appears it seeks to convey the normality of a simple figure. However, *'heis'* is more than a mere number and more than a designation of numeracy, it conveys a spiritual dimension too, as *'heis'* is also used when unity needs to be expressed. For example, it appears when the apostles were finally of 'one mind' and 'one accord' in 'one place.' The use of the word does not just mean that finally the apostles were found together physically in the same geographical location, they were of course in the same place, it was the upper room. However, the use of the word 'one' in this particular dimension conveyed the fact that they were finally in unity. The outcome of this unity was the glorious fact that now, having arrived at a unified position, the Holy Spirit could be poured out upon them all.

It is this dimension of 'oneness' that Paul is seeking to convey when he urges the Philippian Church to stand as 'one'. He was not speaking to only one person in the church, but a band of people that would be in a position of unity in order that they might convey to earth and heaven the powerful truth that being 'one with each other' would further the prospect of the increase of the gospel. Unity always prospers; division and disunity always harms the Church and the proclamation of the truth.

My Journal ______________________________

____

____

____

KEY PRAYER

Heavenly Father, you prayed that the Church would be one. Help me at all times to seek unity and oneness with those around me so that no harm or division comes to your body, the Church. Thank you too, that I am 'at one' with you and that there is nothing in-between.

March 21st

KEY WORD: **Two**

KEY VERSE: **Ephesians 5 : 31**

"For this reason a man will leave his father and mother and be united to his wife, and the two will become one flesh."

When Paul wrote these words to the Ephesian Church he was bringing together two important facets of truth. Firstly he was addressing the fact that in the union of marriage, a man and a woman become, in God's eyes, one flesh. This is the mystic and spiritual union of 'oneness' that is created when a man leaves his father and mother and joins himself to his wife. Paul writing about this union speaks of it as 'being one flesh' and in this union 'two' become 'one'.

However, in this key verse Paul is also stating something that is more than just a numerical fact, he is uttering something that has spiritual dimensions too. One is unity, as we saw yesterday, and two can be symbolically compared with division. Two separate people, who possibly did not know each other up until a few weeks or months ago and who were two totally separated people, yet in a mystic and spiritual way were brought together, and the two separate people now become one. Division is moved to one side and unity takes place.

The Greek word for our English word 'two' is '*duo*' and this word can mean 'twain' or 'two' and it has a kin word which is '*dis*', which translated means 'twice'. The word '*duo*' can mean a figurative number as in 'two men' or ' two days' and it can be used together as '*duo duo*' which means the 'two by two', the way that the disciples were sent out together.

The word also conveys the fact that at times 'two' is not the will of God, as in 1 Corinthians 6 : 16-17, where Paul speaks of sexual perversion. He says, 'Do you not know that he who unites himself with a prostitute is one with her in body? For it is said, "The two will become one flesh." But he who unites himself with the Lord is one with him in spirit.' Paul states that sin degrades to the place where division is seen. This Scripture teaches that oneness with God is only maintained when we are united with the Lord.

We are told to flee away from sin because sin divides us from God and we lose the closeness of a spiritual union that was God's first desire for us all.

The word *'duo'* however, also appears in the Gospels at the point of the crucifixion, when the veil in the temple was torn into two separate pieces and brought about a turning point in God's relationship with mankind. In this case one piece of cloth became divided to allow an entrance for man to reach God and to allow God to reach man. This is the only time where division was acceptable because in God's eyes division is something to be totally avoided at all costs. We are to pray for unity and to seek unity as it is God's will for His Church and it is God's will for our lives.

My Journal

KEY PRAYER

Heavenly Father, you came into this world that I might be saved and you came into this world that division might be swept away by the current of your love and grace. I praise you today that I am no longer divided from you by sin and despair, but that you and I are one, through the precious blood of Jesus.

March 22nd

KEY WORD: **Three**

KEY VERSE: **Mark 9 : 31**

"The Son of Man is going to be betrayed into the hands of men. They will kill Him, and after three days He will rise."

The number 'three' in the Scripture always symbolically speaks of the Godhead, God the Father, God the Son, and God, the Holy Ghost. The number three is always associated with the Trinity and is normally accepted as the 'God number'.

The number 'three' is also associated with testimony or confirmation as in Paul's teaching concerning the gifts of the Spirit, where he stresses the need for prophecy to be 'judged in twos or threes', 1 Corinthians 14 : 29, and tongues to be used by 'two, or at the most by three', 1 Corinthians 14 : 27. The use of the term 'three' also confirms the fact that there was a group of 'three' that were chosen as closer companions to Jesus. Peter, James and John, saw things that the others did not see and they were party to teaching and miracles that the others did not enjoy. The basis of three seems to be a kind of confirmation or testimony that goes beyond a simple agreement and into the realm of godly decision making.

The Greek word for 'three' is the word '*treis*' and it is used in the simple way of numerical counting, as in 'three days' or 'three people' and it is also used in the symbolical sense of three being the testimony of heaven, as in the Trinity.

It is an interesting fact that this symbol of testimony and confirmation is corrupted and counterfeited by the enemy of God, Satan. Satan himself leads the way and has with him the Antichrist or the beast and the false prophet. A confederacy of three that seeks to lead astray the Church, the world and the nation of Israel. There is of course another evil confederacy ranged against the Church, and again it is a corrupted and counterfeited 'trinity'. Our enemy is the world, the flesh and the devil.

The number three is therefore woven into the fabric of the Scriptures and is more than a simple numerical base, it is the symbol of God and His Glory and is therefore, of course, a target for Satan and his actions.

Revelation 21 however, points to a new beginning when three new agencies combine together to produce a magnificent end to all things, when a new heaven and a new earth and a new Jerusalem are formed. This will be the end of all things that we know and the beginning of all things that we do not know as yet.

My Journal

KEY PRAYER

Heavenly Father, I come before you today to thank you for the fact that I am in the kingdom of God and that I am saved from the awful end of the wicked confederacy that rages against us. Help me to live my life today so others might see and know that I have met the Master. Help me always to give clear testimony by my manner of life, by my actions and deeds and by my desire to serve you.

March 23rd

KEY WORD: **Four**

KEY VERSE: **John 11 : 17**

On His arrival, Jesus found that Lazarus had already been in the tomb for four days.

The number 'four' is only found in the New Testament in three different places, it occurs in the gospels, it is found in the Acts of the Apostles and it is also found in the book of Revelation. Its most frequent occurrence is in this last book of the Bible.

'Four' generally speaks symbolically of completeness in the Bible, as we have four complete seasons and we find four gospels and a four-square city; we also find four beasts that complete the picture of God's throne in heaven. We also find an enlargement of four, as in the 40 days and 40 nights of Jesus' temptations. God seems to hide truth within numbers and the number 'four' is no exception.

In the key verse today we find a period of suffering about to be relieved – by the time that Jesus arrived in Bethany, Lazarus had been dead and buried for four days. These four days would have been filled with sadness and grief, misunderstanding and doubt and above all they would have been filled with a kind of resentment that Jesus did not come on time.

In our walk with God we often find that what appears to be a late arrival of a miracle or a deliverance is in fact a completed picture. God is never late and God is never early, but He is always complete, He is always right on time. However, we ought to note that it is not our time schedule that He works to but His own time schedule.

The Greek word for 'four' is the word '*tessares*' and this word can be joined with others to produce other words such as 'four and 20' for the elders around God's throne. Other numbers such as 'fourteen' are made up from this word so that ten and four combine to produce the number and it is expressed as '*dekatessares*' – ten and four. Four hundred is expressed in the same way, '*tetrakossia*' – four and a hundred. In other words '*tessares*' is a foundational number from which other numbers are produced, this does not seem to be a great fact until you realise that 'four' stands for completeness. It is from this number that many others are produced.

Our completeness in God is a foundational fact, it is upon this foundation that everything else is built – we can not go to heaven unless we are saved, this is a basic foundational fact. We can not find God the Father unless we come through Jesus the Son, we can not receive salvation through any other means than Calvary, these are all complete and facts of theology and Christian truth.

God has declared that our salvation and destiny are all completed in Him and without Him we have nothing. 'Four' therefore speaks of completed ways and foundational truth. It took four gospels writers, Matthew, Mark, Luke and John, to bring the truth of the life and ministry of Jesus to the Church, and it is upon this basis that we teach that there is no other way to God and through no other method can we find salvation. The truth is complete in Him.

KEY PRAYER

Heavenly Father, thank you for my completeness in you; I rejoice today that there is no other name and no other way to you but through Jesus. Truth stands complete in Him and my destiny is complete in Him and I bless you for this great foundational fact that I am saved. Help me always to trust you and always to expect you to deliver me when I call upon you, but help me too, to understand that your times and seasons are not necessarily my times and seasons, but that you are always there, right on time.

March 24th

KEY WORD: **Five**

KEY VERSE: **2 Corinthians 11 : 24**

Five times I received from the Jews the forty lashes minus one.

Five appears in the New Testament fairly often and is associated with feasts and festivals and is also symbolic of both smallness and powerfulness, which seems to be a contradiction in terms.

Some Bible commentators have suggested that the Greek word that is used for 'five' which is '*pente*' is derived from the fingers of the hand or the nature of a fist, which would account for the seeming contradiction of smallness yet power. The fist or the hand is relatively small yet it can become a powerful weapon.

The word '*pente*' is a foundational word in the Bible and it is combined with others to produce the word '*Pentateuch*', which of course are the first five books of the Bible. A small start to the whole Bible but a powerful combination of books.

The word is also combined with another word to produce '*pentekostos*' which is the fiftieth day after the passover feast – a combination of five days multiplied by ten – to produce the powerful feast of the Old Testament and the coming of the Holy Spirit in the New Testament.

There are other various combinations of the word all of which produce a powerful picture of the number five. Five, of course, has also been taken as a symbol of power by various agencies around the world today. In the United States of America they have the Pentagon, a smallish building from which emanates the most powerful of systems that flows around the world. Other nations also use the word '*pente*' to form their own principalities and powers.

In the text today Paul is reminding the Church that he received an official Roman lashing of whips on five occasions and he is testifying to the fact that suffering has occurred in the work of the gospel being spread around the nations. However, his list of sufferings in 2 Corinthians 11, is not a catalogue of disasters but a declaration of the fact that in spite of grievous pain and anguish, God stood by him and brought him through what would normally have defeated most men. The fact that God stands by us at all times is a great reminder of His faithfulness and of our dependency upon Him. We can bless God today for the fact that He is in control of our lives and even when seemingly things go wrong, God is in all and through all and around and above all.

So, as with Paul, we can testify to His faithfulness at all times.

My Journal

KEY PRAYER

Heavenly Father, we testify today to your great faithfulness and we bless you for your goodness, and we declare that we trust you to bring us though whatever might befall our pathway. Help us each to keep our eyes upon you so that we might walk by faith in constant victory, even when things go wrong.

March 25th

KEY WORD: ***Six***

KEY VERSE: **Luke 13 : 14**

Indignant because Jesus had healed on the Sabbath, the synagogue ruler said to the people, "There are six days for work. So come and be healed on those days, not on the Sabbath."

The number six holds a place of significant symbolism as it is one less than seven, and seven stands for perfection. So in Bible terms six stands for incompleteness or imperfection. This was the thinking behind the ruler of the synagogue's words when he sought to undermine Jesus in the key verse today. He was not just thinking about the 'desecration of the Sabbath', that was bad enough in his terms, but he was also thinking of the fact that in his mind the Sabbath was a perfect day. The other six days would therefore have been imperfect days, so why not heal on those days.

The Greek word used for our word 'six' is *'hex'*, a word which has come to be known in our world today as a kind of spell or magic art, this would be bad enough if it stood alone. However, the word *'hex'* has a deeper and darker meaning than just that of a form of spell making.

The word is combined symbolically into a man-made trinity in the book of Revelation and is formed as three sixes, or *'hex, hex, hex'* and features as the title of the 'man of Sin' or the 'Beast'.

This three-fold number suggests the pride of man which became fully developed under Satanic control. Man is one step from perfection and a little lower than the angels. When Satan brings his final plan to bear he controls and influences one man who rises as a beast to confront the things of God and the people of God. His number in the Scripture is six, six, six. Or *'hex, hex, hex'*.

This man who is imperfect, believes that he has become perfect like unto God and commences a reign of power and terror within the world. His final overthrow and that of his creator, the devil or Satan, is found in the book of Revelation, but while he reigns there is utter darkness. To understand these things is the beginning of wisdom and we are urged to read the book of Revelation, even if we do not fully understand it. As John the apostle states, we will be blessed by its reading and 'blessed are those who hear it and take to heart what is written in it, because the time is near', Revelation 1 : 3.

However, like all corruptions of truth, the real truth shines through – six is the word that stands for imperfection but it also has a place of its own. For the sixth precious stone in the foundations of the wall of the heavenly Jerusalem in Revelation 21 : 20, is the stone called sardius or the sardine stone. The beauty of this stone is its transparent brilliance and of the high polish that it can bring, and it was a favourite of the ancients of Scripture. Its bright transparent redness was a symbol of the blood of Jesus and it was placed within the walls of the heavenly Jerusalem as a sign of victory. Satan may seek to inflict the world with evil, but great is the Lord and great is His victory.

My Journal

KEY PRAYER

Heavenly Father, I thank you today for victory in the blood of Jesus and I praise you for the fact that I overcome through the blood of the Lamb and through the word of my testimony. Help me each day as it grows darker to remember that God is on the throne and that all is well.

March 26th

KEY WORD: ***Seven***

KEY VERSE: **Hebrews 11 : 30**

By faith the walls of Jericho fell, after the people had marched around them for seven days.

The number seven in the Bible speaks of perfection or wholeness and this is generally derived from the fact that God created the world in six days and on the seventh day He rested from His labours. This seventh day became very sacred and very holy and many extreme laws and regulations were created to protect it from 'misuse'.

The word seven appears many times throughout the Bible and particularly in the New Testament and many, many times in the book of Revelation. The number seven appeared to have a kind of fascination for the Jewish people as it often found its way into their thinking. Many of their sacred rituals involved the number seven.

When people look to the heavens, it is generally regarded that there are seven major planets in our system and ancient peoples have often been guided by stars and signs that included the number seven. Seven was a special number not just to the Jewish peoples but to several other groups of people in olden times.

In Hebrews 11 : 30, the key verse for today, the writer reminds the Hebrew Church that the Israelites marched around the walls of Jericho for seven days, again a symbol of perfection and wholeness. This march brought them victory and deliverance.

Jesus used the number seven as a symbol of forgiveness when He was asked the question, "How many times shall I forgive...? Up to seven times?" Seven being the perfect number to forgive. The answer was a symbolical, "seventy times seven!"

Matthew 18 : 22, KJV. This answer was a not a kind of mathematical formula for forgiveness but an added degree of perfection and wholeness – seventy times seven – in other words God's forgiveness was limitless therefore our forgiveness should reflect this.

The Greek word for seven is *'hepta'*, which can be translated as fullness or abundance. Any words that begin with *'hepta'* or its close kin word *'hebdo'*, reflect the kind of full abundance and perfection of the Bible standard. So you can find *'heptakis'* which means 'seven times', and many others such as, *'hebdomos ouranos'* which means 'seventh heaven'.

The theme of the word seven is in its completeness and its perfection and it is a good thing to remember that in the whole area of forgiveness, Jesus used it to convey the truth that our lifestyle should be one of unlimited forgiving toward those who would seek us harm. God forgave us for all our wrongdoing, this kind of attitude should be manifested by us at all times, even to as many as seventy times seven.

My Journal ______________________________

KEY PRAYER

Heavenly Father, thank you for your complete and perfect forgiveness; without your forgiveness I would be far from you today. Help me at all times to remember this constant act of perfection and give me the grace to continue to forgive those who would seek to do me harm.

March 27th

KEY WORD: **Eight**

KEY VERSE: **Luke 2 : 21**

On the eighth day, when it was time to circumcise Him, He was named Jesus.

Eight in the Bible is symbolically the number of salvation and this symbol is generally thought to have been derived, in the first instance, by the number of people that were saved in Noah's Ark. From that time on the Jewish people have always held to its symbolism as a mark of saving or salvation.

In the key verse today Jesus was circumcised on the eighth day, the eighth day being the day of the law when male children should be brought before the Lord for their circumcising. There were two symbols involved in this act, firstly, there was the act itself and secondly, there was the timing of the act. The act of circumcision itself was a type or picture of salvation, the cutting of the flesh was a symbol of the cutting of the heart of flesh at the time of salvation and produced a spiritual picture of saving grace.

The timing of the act of circumcision was again a type of salvation, it was the eighth day, an important day in Jewish minds as the day of salvation. Paul uses this kind of analogy when he gives his testimony to the Philippian Church in Philippians 3 : 5, when he speaks of being 'circumcised on the eighth day'. In this context he was saying, I may have been saved by the old covenant of circumcision and I may have been true to the Law, but I now 'count all things as rubbish, that I may gain Christ'. Philippians 3 : 8.

The Greek word for 'eight' is the word *'okto'* which means octave or octagon, there are eight notes in an octave and an eight-sided building or shape is an octagon.

The act of salvation and its gift of eternal life has been granted not through the works of the law or through a procedure of fleshly symbolism but through the grace of God who gave His Son as an offering for all. As Paul says, all other things and all other ways are 'but loss' in the light and glory of Christ. It is not a symbol of salvation that we have been given but the full and glorious gift from an eternally giving God.

My Journal

KEY PRAYER

Heavenly Father, thank you for saving me, thank you for your gift of eternal life and thank you, too, for the wonderful way in which I have passed from death unto life. Help me each day to keep the freshness of this truth ever in my mind so that I never treat this wonderful gift with contempt.

March 28th

KEY WORD: **Nine**

KEY VERSE: **Luke 17 : 17**

Jesus asked, "Were not all ten cleansed? Where are the other nine?"

In the Scriptures it is hard to prove that the number nine has an important symbolical meaning, in fact the word 'nine' only appears once in the New Testament on its own. The only appearance of the word comes in the key verse for today where Jesus asks the question of the thankful and returning leper, when ten lepers were cleansed and healed, "Where are the other nine?"

There are many references to the word 'ninth' in the New Testament. We have the 'ninth hour' mentioned many times, we find that topaz was the ninth precious stone in the heavenly Jerusalem. The word nine does appear several times connected to other words – we find 90 and nine sheep in the sheepfold and the shepherd searching for one lost sheep. However, on its own the word 'nine' appears just once.

There is one Bible commentator who feels that 'nine' speaks of unthankfulness, which is probably drawn from the story of the nine lepers who did not return to give thanks for their healing, but it is hard to prove that symbolism.

The Greek word for 'nine' is *'ennea'* which is translated as the simple figure 'nine'. It has no hidden meaning and no symbolic meaning that we can find. However, it does seem that there is a special unknown aspect to the ninth hour of the day. It was at the ninth hour or three in the afternoon, that Jesus cried out on the cross, and it was the ninth hour, again three in the afternoon, that the apostles were going to prayer in Acts 3 : 1 and it was the ninth hour when Cornelius was praying in Acts 10 : 3. There could be something significant about this hour as the New Testament Church had obviously established a practice of prayer at this hour and Cornelius, who was then an unsaved man, was also praying at that time.

Whatever truth there may be in all of this the main thought as we pray today is that unthankfulness is a sin and that prayerfulness must be a major factor in our lives. It is not particularly important to pray at the ninth hour but it is vital that we pray without ceasing.

My Journal ______________________________

KEY PRAYER

Heavenly Father, as I come before you today I seek to root out of my life any form of unthankfulness and any form of disobedience. Help me to be continually thankful for the many blessings that you grant to me and help me to return thanks to you at all times for all things.

March 29th

KEY WORD: **Ten**

KEY VERSE: **Luke 17 : 17**

Jesus asked, "Were not all ten cleansed? Where are the other nine?"

The number 'ten' in the Bible is a symbolic number thought to mean the number of human responsibility. It occurs several times when there was a need for people to become responsible for their actions. In the text today, ten lepers should have given thanks for their cleansing and their healing, and only one returned.

In the story of the ten virgins and the marriage supper, the virgins were responsible for the filling of their lamps with oil and caring of the lamps ready for supper to begin. Ten virgins should have been ready for the supper but only five were wise in their responsibilities.

In the Old Testament ten occurs quite frequently and in many cases there is a measure of human responsibility involved. Sodom and Gomorrah would not have been destroyed if ten righteous people could have been found. Daniel and his friends did not partake of the Babylonian fare and they spent ten days seeking God and were found to be ten times better than the others.

In the Jewish sense, ten was the number of people that were required in order that the synagogue could function – it was felt that ten was the number for a congregation to call itself a 'meeting'.

Ten of course appears in the teaching of giving – ten, or a tenth, is the amount that was required as a tithe, the tenth part of all income.

Ten features throughout the Bible therefore as a number that seems to symbolise responsibility and rightness. The Greek word used for 'ten' is '*deka*' and this number is still in use today as we call ten years a 'decade' and a ten-sided building is a 'decagon'.

It is in the whole area of giving however, that this word finds its fullest use. Abraham taught us to tithe when he gave Melchizedek a tenth of all the proceeds of battle, in Genesis 14 : 18. From that moment the Jewish people set aside the tenth of all substance as 'unto the Lord'. In the New Testament however, the tenth is superseded as everything belongs unto the Lord, yet if the Old Testament saints had to give a tenth of their substance, how much should we tithe unto the Lord? If the legal requirement under the law was a tenth our requirement should be even greater.

As we give and as we thank Him, we should always remember that it is our responsibility to make sure that our giving is right and that our praising is continuous. This is our responsibility.

My Journal ______________________________

KEY PRAYER

Heavenly Father, I have learnt today that my responsibility is to give thanks, with my time, my talent and my tithe. I would want to be right about everything that I do before you, so I ask for your help in all my actions, so that your blessing might fall upon me.

KEY WORD: **Eleven**

KEY VERSE: **Acts 1 : 26**

Then they cast lots, and the lot fell to Matthias; so he was added to the eleven apostles.

Eleven is a very strange number and in fact a very strange thing happens to this number in the New Testament. The only point that the number eleven appears in the New Testament – six times – is when Judas removed himself at the time of the betrayal of Jesus. From this moment on, until the key verse that we are looking at today in the book if Acts, the disciple band are called 'the eleven'. It seems that it was almost a matter that was taken for granted, that the twelve became the eleven. The six occasions of the use of 'eleven' all refer to the same matter.

In Acts 1 : 26, the apostles decided to cast lots to add another one to the eleven, in order that the twelve might be completed. Matthias was the one who received the vote or 'the lot', and he was added to the twelve. However, this was not what God had in mind. God had already chosen Saul (or Paul) to be the added 'one' in the number. The fact that Saul (or Paul) was not even saved at this time was immaterial, God had chosen and God would have His way. The strange thing about all this is the fact that 'the eleven' were almost taken for granted in the gospel accounts, as was the fact that Matthias would vanish from Church History following his elevation to apostleship. In fact, there are only two verses concerning him in the entire New Testament, both in Acts chapter 1. Following this vote or casting of lots, Matthias receives attention for just two verses and then disappears, although it is obvious that he was still involved with the twelve up to and including the appearance of Saul or Paul. Acts 6 : 2 states that the twelve were making decisions and functioning in the Church during this time.

This strange event in the Early Church caused one commentator to state that the number eleven is therefore symbolic of 'confusion'. However, it must be said that only one person makes this assumption, and there are no other confirmations of this anywhere else in the Bible.

The Greek word for 'eleven' is *'hendeka'*, which means literally 'one and ten'. There are no other places where the word appears and there are no other references to check for meanings.

There is however, the word 'eleventh' which is *'hendekatos'*. This word is used only three times and refers to the eleventh hour on two occasions and the eleventh stone on the other occasion of its use. The eleventh stone in the heavenly city of God is a jacinth stone.

These limited references to the word eleven cause us no major problems of interpretation and pose no difficulties to overcome. If the one commentator is right, and the word is symbolic of 'confusion', we can quite clearly state that this causes us no difficulties whatsoever, as God is the God of peace and not the author of confusion or disorder, 1 Corinthians 14 : 33.

My Journal ______________________________

____

____

____

____

____

KEY PRAYER

Heavenly Father, I thank you today for your infinite wisdom, patience and grace, even when a church gets things wrong, as in the voting procedure for Matthias, you have a plan and purpose that is not destroyed by man's assumptions and you have your way among us. Thank you that you do not rule and reign in disorder or confusion but you guide us with peace and you bring us to the place of perfect understanding.

March 31st

KEY WORD: ***Twelve***

KEY VERSE: **1 Corinthians 15 : 5**

Jesus appeared to Peter, and then to the twelve.

The word 'twelve' is a very interesting number in the Bible and especially in the New Testament. The word seems to be symbolic of two things, firstly it symbolises 'the Church' and secondly it symbolises 'God's order' or 'God's divine administration'.

The number 'twelve' appears over and over again in the Bible, we find twelve patriarchs in the Old Testament and the twelve tribes of Israel. There are Twelve disciples in the New Testament and twelve apostles of the Lamb. There are twelve foundations and twelve precious stones in the heavenly city of God in the book of Revelation. All these occurrences ensure the fact that the number twelve is noticed as a very symbolical number in the Bible.

If these symbolic references are correct as proof of 'God's perfect order' and 'God's divine administration' then we can take great encouragement because it shows yet again that God is in control of all things. It can at times seem as if things are going wrong and things are out of control, yet these numbers prove that God works to a plan, and even when it seems to be wrong, God has His way. The twelve tribes of Israel had, at several times during their history, moments of great failure and agony, yet God was in control and brought them through, and, even when division and sadness came, there were still twelve tribes numbered.

When Judas removed himself from the band of disciples and the number dwindled to eleven, God had a plan that would restore the twelve to a place of effectiveness. God always has a

'Paul' waiting in the wings ready to be released just when it seems that everything has gone wrong. God has His plan and is always right on time.

The Greek word for 'twelve' is '*dodeka*' and it literally means 'two and ten'. It appears scores of times in both Old and New Testaments and, throughout its appearances, God shows Himself to be Lord of all. Lord of all, in the sense of having a divine plan and purpose and completing this plan and purpose, come what may.

The numbers that we have studied these past twelve days all combine to prove that we serve a great God and that He is still on the throne.

My Journal

KEY PRAYER

Heavenly Father, thank you today for the perfect order and symbolism of your might and glory. I bless you for your goodness and I praise you for your faithfulness to all generations. Help me to always remember that you are in total and absolute control and that all is well.

April 1st

KEY WORD: ***Foundations***

KEY VERSE: ***Hebrews 1 : 10-12***

"In the beginning, O Lord, you laid the foundations of the earth, and the heavens are the work of your hands. They will perish, but you remain; they will all wear out like a garment. You will roll them up like a robe; like a garment they will be changed. But you remain the same, and your years will never end."

On this first day of a new month the concept of change is one that we shall consider and we shall do so for the next few days. The writer to the Hebrews introduced a major thought for us when he wrote about change. Most of us hope that a new month will bring about changes in circumstances or health, we also hope that a new month might bring with it a change in fortunes within our families and friends. However, not many days go by in a new month before we realise that most things stay the same. The dates might change but often the circumstances remain the same.

However, the writer to the Hebrews talked about a day when radical change would take place on planet Earth. God would bring about a major change within the circumstances of this world that would alter things forever and for eternity. It is these concepts that we will consider for a few days at the beginning of this new month.

The first consideration in the concept of change that the writer to the Hebrews introduced was the fact that the foundations of the earth and heavens were the works of the hand of God. He expressed quite clearly the concept that it was God and not evolution that brought about the earth and heavens. He stated quite forcefully that God is, that God was, and that God created all things.

The word for foundations is a very interesting word, the Greek word used in this text is the word '*themelioo*' and it was used to convey the thought of 'someone who placed a stone'. However, this concept is not simply just one of placing a stone upon the ground, it is far more than that. The Greek word conveys the thought that when you are seeking to build a pillar or a column you have to have a sound base. It is with this thought in mind that the writer used the word '*themelioo*'. The word is taken from two words, '*tithemi*' which is 'to place' and '*lithos*' which means a 'stone'. Placing a stone in the right place and in the right way will allow you to build a structure that will be solid. The story of the wise man and the foolish man comes to mind!

The same word appears when New Testament writers talked about the foundation of the Church being Jesus, it also appears when Paul particularly talked about the ministry of the gospel and the doctrines of the Church. Both the gospel and the Church are built upon a solid foundation which can not be moved. In verse 10 of Hebrews chapter 1, the writer introduced an interesting use of this word when he sought to show just what would happen to planet Earth in the future. He talked of an amazing change that would take place when even the earth, with its solid foundations built upon a sound rock base, would undergo a transformation. The writer was conveying the fact that the earth would change and decay but that the Lord who created all things would remain as true and as firm as He has ever been.

It is with this thought in mind that we can commence another month. Heaven and earth may change and our planet may decay but the Lord will never change. His faithfulness is from everlasting to everlasting and we can trust Him because He always remains the same. What a good thought as we commence a new month, the calendar may have changed but God has not!

KEY PRAYER

Heavenly Father, I bless you today for the wonderful fact of your unchanging nature; this world is changing fast and everything around me is decaying but you remain the same. Help me to understand this concept and help me to rest in the fact that you were there before all things, you are still the same and that you will always be the same.

April 2nd

KEY WORD: **Perish and wear out**

KEY VERSE: **Hebrews 1 : 10-12**

"In the beginning, O Lord, you laid the foundations of the earth, and the heavens are the work of your hands. They will perish, but you remain; they will all wear out like a garment. You will roll them up like a robe; like a garment they will be changed. But you remain the same, and your years will never end."

In our thoughts yesterday we considered the fact that even though the foundations of the earth are decaying all around us, God never changes. The Hebrew writer in bringing this thought to us talked about the foundations of earth perishing and wearing out like a garment. This thought of decaying and perishing is a very interesting one as it introduces a very special theme.

The writer used two Greek words to describe this process of decay, he first talked of the earth perishing and he introduced the thought of wearing out. The first word that he used is '*apollumi*' which means to 'be destroyed' or to 'suffer destruction' and the second word that is used is '*palaioo*' which means to 'make old' or 'to decay'. In using these two words together the writer was seeking to convey the fact that the earth was not just ageing in the sense of growing older, nor was it merely facing the problems of an ageing experience. In using these two words together the writer was portraying the fact that something far more serious was happening to the world in which we live.

He spoke of a destructive force at work within the world that was causing the earth to decay, the word '*palaioo*' is used of a fabric that has become so aged that it is beyond its usefulness and that it has begun to fall apart at the seams. This decaying process is now beyond any remedy and '*apollumi*' has set in, which is utter destruction. The picture is drawn of a world that is dying without a hope and without a remedy. We only have to look around us to see that this graphic picture, painted 2,000 years ago by a writer that was viewing the world in a prophetic sense, is taking place before our eyes.

There are now six billion people crowded onto this planet, and the number is increasing rapidly. The world can not sustain this kind of overcrowding with its demand for food, water and space. It also seems that the natural resources of this planet are under threat and are decaying so fast that fuel and energy are in rapid decline. If we add to this the fact that the high demand for life and living has seriously damaged the ozone layer which in turn allows the penetrating rays of the sun to burn their way into human skin and the very fabric of life. We can only agree that this world is in serious decline and is decaying at a rate that means that there is no human remedy.

This is the picture that was presented to us by the Hebrew writer. However, he went on to say that the picture was not as bleak as it appeared to be because the God who created all things is still in total control, because He would 'roll up this world like a garment'. God is still on the throne and He will never allow what He has created to destroy itself totally without stepping into the picture and taking control. He has never taken His hands off this world and He never will. At the final end of all things a new heaven and a new earth will be created and this old decaying world will find itself the subject of God's eternal care, as He lovingly caresses the fabric of decay and rolls it up like an old garment and brings the picture to an end.

KEY PRAYER

Heavenly Father, thank you for your kindness and love towards this rebellious planet; you still have a love affair with planet earth. This earth is a world that you gave your only Son for and a world that you will never allow to perish without your care and attention. Help me to constantly praise you for your kindness and love.

April 3rd

KEY WORD: ***Same***

KEY VERSE: **Hebrews 1 : 10-12**

"In the beginning, O Lord, you laid the foundations of the earth, and the heavens are the work of your hands. They will perish, but you remain; they will all wear out like a garment. You will roll them up like a robe; like a garment they will be changed. But you remain the same, and your years will never end."

This world is decaying and destroying itself, even though its foundations were laid with care by a loving and creative God. God made this planet and He still cares for this planet and His final goal for this planet is peace and safety. Everything will perish but God will remain, because He is always the same.

For us to understand this concept is very hard because the world in which we live and move and the body in which we dwell is constantly changing. We only have to take a look in a mirror to see the changes taking place before our eyes. Yet the Scripture states that 'God remains the same'.

The word 'same' is an interesting word even in English, yet in Greek it has as an even greater dimension. In English it means 'similar' or 'identical' and it can even mean 'equal', and of course it means ' unchanging', which is the concept here. However, in the Greek use of this word the Hebrew writer conveyed something stronger. The Greek word is *'autos'* which means 'the same' or 'unchanging' just as it does in English, however, the word also denotes a stronger sense of 'itself'. In other words, two things can indeed be the same, which is where the English translation can mean 'identical', but both identical things will still change at the same rate. But *'autos'* means 'of itself there will be no change'.

God can not and will not change. Everything around God will change but He, of Himself, will remain the same.

It is the same concept that the angel stated to the apostles in Acts chapter 1: when Jesus ascended into heaven, the angel said 'this same Jesus will return again'. Not another Jesus, nor a changed Jesus, but the self same Jesus, who could not change even if His Second Coming were to take thousands of years. We know now that at least two thousand years would pass before the Second Coming would take place, but even though this time period would elapse, Jesus would stay exactly the same.

In a fast changing world and a decaying situation which is slowly but surely destroying itself we can rejoice that our salvation is sure because He remains the same yesterday, today and forever.

My Journal

KEY PRAYER

Heavenly Father, I do rejoice in you today for my salvation is complete and assured in you. Thank you for your unchanging love and your everlasting ability to remain the same. Everything around me is changing and it is hard to understand the concept of an unchanging God. But even though I can not fully understand, I rejoice in the truth that you remain forever the same.

April 4th

KEY WORD: **Roll**

KEY VERSE: **Hebrews 1 : 10-12**

"In the beginning, O Lord, you laid the foundations of the earth, and the heavens are the work of your hands. They will perish, but you remain; they will all wear out like a garment. You will roll them up like a robe; like a garment they will be changed. But you remain the same, and your years will never end."

In our thoughts concerning this verse, I have left the best word until the last. We have seen that the world in which we live is destroying itself and that it will finally tear itself apart at the seams. Yet God, who remains the same and who will never change will finally have the last word. He will roll up this world like a garment and things will change forever, there will be a new heaven and a new earth and we shall be with the Lord forever.

The Hebrew writer was quite descriptive of this final event concerning planet Earth – it will be rolled up like a garment. The Greek word used here is *'heilisso'* which conveys two things. Firstly, it denotes the fact that something has been simply 'rolled up' like that of a scroll or a piece of paper. The process of rolling up is quite simple and takes very little time. Secondly, and more importantly it means 'the action' of rolling up which is far more important than the actual piece of paper or a scroll. When someone has finished with the scroll the action of rolling up symbolises completeness or finality, it is often undertaken with a flourish.

The picture of a scroll or a manuscript is in mind when *'heilisso'* is used here and the truth being conveyed is one of the world being finally and completely finished with for all time, and with a great eternal flourish, God completes His purposes with this planet and He rolls it up.

The same thought is in mind when the apostle, John, wrote in the book of Revelation when God allowed the heavens to be rolled back at the end of all things in chapter 6 and verse 14. The rolling back of the earth and the heavens signals that God has completed His purposes and that it is time to introduce the concept of eternity.

Our lives were very much like this, in that God took us from a pit of sin and clothed us in His righteousness and set our feet upon a rock and put a new song in our mouths. When this process took place our sin and our guilt was rolled up and removed from us, never to be remembered again. With a great loving flourish, God took away our sin forever.

This verse in the book of Hebrews is a great verse to study and as we have taken time to look at several key words we have discovered the truth of God's unchanging love and the truth of His purpose and His completion of all things. As we pray today we will thank Him for the fact that we are in His hands forever.

My Journal ______________________________

KEY PRAYER

Heavenly Father, it is with great joy that I have studied your word and it is with great joy that I have discovered your purposes for this world. I have rejoiced in the fact these past few days, that although everything may decay you remain the same and that all is well. Help me to remember these truths day after day and help me to trust you forever.

April 5th

KEY WORD: **Seasons**

KEY VERSE: **2 Timothy 4 : 2**

Preach the Word; be prepared in season and out of season; correct, rebuke, and encourage – with great patience and careful instruction.

Over the past few days we have been considering the purposes of God for this world in which we live and we have noticed that God has a plan that will bring all things to a conclusion. We have noticed too, that God will have His way and that all things are on His agenda. This agenda has a time span and God is always on time.

There are many Scriptures that reveal the times and seasons of God's plan and purposes, and it will be very helpful for us to study together these times and seasons so that we understand a little more about God's agenda. The Bible reveals a lot about seasons, there are seasons of growth and seasons of blessings, there are also seasons of judgement and seasons of famine. In order for us to really understand what God means about the times and seasons we have to go back to the Scriptures for truth.

The Greek language has two words for our English word 'seasons', they are *'kairos'* and *'chronos'*. *'Kairos'* means 'to measure' or 'proportion' and *'chronos'* means 'a space of time'. It is from this word that we derive our English word chronology, which means the sequence of time.

'Kairos' denotes the season of harvest and spring time, it is the word most used when the New Testament writers were seeking to convey the truth of 'opportunity'. This is the word used by Paul to Timothy in the key verse today when he said that Timothy should be ready to preach and minister in whatever season he found himself.

It is an important fact that we should be prepared to pray and to worship, to preach and to witness at all times. It is not a question of whether we actually 'feel like it' or not, our duty is to be ready, in each and every season, to minister. This was the key message that Paul was seeking to convey to Timothy.

However, '*chronos*' denotes the actual period of time. This word was used for the occasions when the writers were seeking to convey the thought of a time span, and it was the word that was most used when the writers were talking about the Coming of the Lord. For instance it was used when Paul was preaching to the Thessalonians in his first book to them when he stated that there was a 'time when Jesus would return', chapter 5 verse 1. We know that the time draws nearer for His return and we are constantly on guard so that we are ready to greet Him.

Basically speaking, '*kairos*' is the word that speaks of special features and it marks the quality of time, and '*chronos*' is the word that speaks of the quantity of time and it marks the duration of periods.

In our terms the quantity of time, '*chronos*,' is nearing the end of all things, and while this duration is passing we are enjoying the special features of '*kairos*' that this season brings, such as seasons of blessing and grace. As we pray today we will thank God that He is working to His plan, and that while this plan is being completed we are experiencing His blessing and grace.

My Journal ______________________________

____

____

____

KEY PRAYER

Heavenly Father, thank you for your mercy and grace that is granted to us every day. While this season of grace is here we pledge our allegiance to you and we will seek to do all that we can to reach others while this season lasts. For we know that the night is coming when no man can work so we will be ready in season and out of season to work and witness, and worship and wonder.

April 6th

KEY WORD: **Spring**

KEY VERSE: **Mark 4 : 27**

Night and day, whether he sleeps or gets up, the seed sprouts and grows, though he does not know how.

Having considered yesterday the concept of the natural seasons of the year it would be good to consider now the four seasons of spring, summer, autumn and winter individually, as God has something to say about all four of them. The natural place to start would be with the first season of year, that of springtime.

However, we have an immediate problem in that the New Testament has ten different words for the English word 'spring' and not one of them refers to the natural season of springtime. The words that are used are words that mainly deal with 'the springing up of seed' or the 'spring of water' that bubbles to the surface of the earth. There are words that deal with crops that grow together and 'spring up' into flower, and there are words that are used for the action of 'springing' into battle. Springtime in the New Testament is not directly referred to, but however, our season of springtime is alluded to in the parable of the sower and reaper, told by Jesus and written into the gospels by Matthew, Mark and Luke.

The sower sowed his seed at the right time so that he might reap the benefit of good crops. He would have sowed during the season of early spring so that the seed might germinate and finally produce. The Scripture that is used today in Mark 4, is the very one that spoke of the seed springing forth from the soil and giving the sower his crops. The Greek word used is the word '*blastano*' which means to 'spring up and bud'. The sower would not have sown his seed in the winter or at any other season as the action of early spring time is the very atmosphere that the seed needs in order to develop and grow and to spring up and bud.

God has a season of springtime in His plan and purpose for our lives. We often live our lives in a period of winter where it seems dark and cold and the blessing of God seems to be absent, we will deal with the aspect of winter in a few days time. There are times when we do not see what God is doing and we fail to understand His ways in our lives, yet springtime is always 'just around the corner'. There comes a day when God draws near and the warmth of sunshine fills our lives and the sky appears bright and fresh and we feel 'good' about ourselves and good about God.

This is the freshness of springtime and it is God's way of reminding us that He is still there and still in control of our lives. Springtime always follows winter, like daytime always follows night-time. God allows the wintertime in order that we fully appreciate springtime.

Spring is the season of joy and fullness, it is the season when life begins again and the buds appear. The sun begins to arise a little earlier and the warmth of sunshine fills our lives. It is the season of fresh growth and new beginnings and the trees and the grass; the plants and soil all begin to look fertile again. It is a lovely season and as the sower went forth to sow, in readiness for his harvest, we can renew our vows before the Lord and enjoy the surge of fresh blessing and vibrancy.

If you are just coming into the spiritual season of springtime, enjoy the fresh season of blessing. If you are still in a period of winter, rejoice because spring always follows the darkness of wintertime.

KEY PRAYER

Heavenly Father, thank you for the season of hope, the springtime season. I bless you today for the wonderful blessing of new life, new joy and the warm sunshine of your love. Help me to appreciate that you are always there even when I do not feel your presence and help me to appreciate even more the season when you appear to draw a little near. Thank you for your goodness and thank you for the springing up of life and joy.

KEY WORD: **Summer**

KEY VERSE: **Luke 21 : 29-30**

"Look at the fig tree and all the trees. When they sprout leaves, you... know that summer is near."

Summer in the New Testament is an interesting season as there are many references that allude to its presence but only on three specific occasions is it actually mentioned as a season of the year. It is also an interesting fact that all three references in the New Testament that refer to the summer season actually refer to the very same event. Jesus drew the attention of His disciples to a fig tree and made the statement that when the leaves appear, everyone knows that summertime draws near. He used this word picture to talk about the end of the ages and the nation of Israel in particular.

In using the picture of summertime as a reference point to the culmination of all things Jesus was actually stating that summertime is a picture of completion and a full destiny. It is as if summer was regarded as the complete season as the winter rains produced the moisture for the spring sowing of grain and the summer sunshine and the warmth of the soil was the last and most important action of all, as it completed the picture and cycle of atmosphere that the seeds needed in order to fulfil their destiny, as it is with seeds, so it is with the world.

The Greek word for 'summer' is the word '*theros*' and it denotes 'heat' or 'fullness'. It was this word that Matthew, Mark and Luke used in order to convey the truth of completion or fullness of all things. The fact that each writer only used this word once is interesting and it suggests that God wanted summer to be the focal point of heat and completion but that He did not want our attention to be so focussed upon summertime that we lose the perspective of everything else. We can not live in summertime all the time, sunshine and beauty, heat and radiance are not the only things that matter. We all enjoy a 'summer' holiday, but we can not stay on holiday, we have to come home and continue with everything else around us. It is as if Jesus is saying look at the summertime and be glad of its presence, enjoy its fullness but be ready to move on as the night comes when no man can work.

Summertime is a wonderful time and we need the heat and light that it gives, however, we need to remember to keep summer as a season to enjoy and always be ready to move into the next period of growth that God has for us all.

In summer we rest and play but we must not linger there as the fields are white unto harvest and the labourers are few.

My Journal

KEY PRAYER

Heavenly Father, help me to fully enjoy the blessing of a good and wonderful summer, help me to appreciate its splendour and wonder but help me to always understand that there is work for me to do and that I must move into the next season of harvesting and gathering. Thank you for the rest that summertime can bring and I bless you today for your goodness in supplying a time of heat and fullness, and of rest and relaxation.

April 8th

KEY WORD: ***Autumn***

KEY VERSE: ***Jude 12***

They are clouds without rain, blown along by the wind; autumn trees, without fruit and uprooted – twice dead.

Only once in the New Testament is the season of autumn mentioned, however, there is no greater sight than the harvesting of grain and the abundance of ingathering. We watch farmers bringing the grain with great pleasure and we acknowledge the fact that this season above all other seasons really expresses God's heart. The winter rains produce moisture that softens the soil allowing the fertile earth to germinate seed. The summer sunshine heats the soil allowing the grain to grow and mature and the autumn harvest completes a picture of seeds and soil. As with the natural picture so it is with God and His love towards us.

Jude, when writing his epistle to the Church, used autumn in a negative way however, when he used word pictures to state that ungodly men become like clouds blown around by the wind and like autumn trees who appear as if dead and have no fruit upon them. The wording within this key verse states these trees were 'twice dead', this refers to a lifeless tree and the absence of fruit. Therefore, no life and no fruit equalled 'twice dead'. This negative context is quite acceptable as the word used here is the complex Greek word *'phthinoporinos'*. This almost unpronounceable word is used just once in the New Testament and its meaning is quite clear, it is the word that is used when describing something that is 'wasting away' or 'worthless'. The word is made up from two separate words *'phthino'* which means 'to waste away' and *'opora'* which means our 'autumn' period or season. The combining of the two words by Jude conveys the very strong word picture of a season coming to the end of its life and wasting away and becoming worthless.

The joyful picture of a wonderful harvest with its ingathering and plenty is soon replaced by the knowledge that winter is approaching when darkness and emptiness will appear. It is this truth that Jude was seeking to convey when he used the two words in a combined form to portray the fact that the ungodly are wasting away even though they might appear to prosper. Their end is worthlessness and their harvesting will produce for them a sad and final end of judgement.

It is a good thing to keep in mind when watching a farmer harvest his grain, that winter approaches with its coldness and darkness. This thought conveys exactly what Jude was trying to convey when he used the 'autumn' word to describe the state of the ungodly. The picture of dead trees without fruit is a very clear picture of those without God. It would be good today to remind ourselves of our previous state and now our present state. Once we were without God and without hope, but now we have been brought into a relationship with God the Father and we are His sons. As we pray today it would be good to thank Him that He ever sought us and found us and brought us into this wonderful relationship.

My Journal ________________________________

____

____

____

____

KEY PRAYER

Heavenly Father, you sought us and found us, and then you brought us into a wonderful relationship as your sons and daughters, thank you that this took place for us. No longer are we like dead trees without fruit but now we are part of the vine which is producing fruit and tended by your loving hands. I rejoice today in the truth of this fact and I praise you.

April 9th

KEY WORD: **Winter**

KEY VERSE: **Titus 3 : 12**

Do your best to come to me at Nicopolis, because I have decided to winter there.

The word 'winter' appears nine times in the New Testament and it is always used in the most simple of ways, it simply means the 'season of winter' and the conveying of this thought is usually associated with a spell of inclement weather. Paul used the word 'winter' several times when he was on his way to Rome and found the journey to be difficult. He said that he was staying in certain places during the winter in order to travel onward in better circumstances.

In Titus chapter 3, it is obvious that he was staying in Nicopolis due to bad weather and that the arrival of Titus would be a comfort to him during the winter period.

There are two different Greek words that are used for our English word 'winter' they are the words '*cheimon*' and '*paracheimazo*'. The two words are generally regarded as meaning 'a winter season' and a 'place to stay' in during the season of winter. Our understanding of winter in the western world is one of cold dark nights and periods of rain and snow and it is this atmosphere that Paul and other New Testament writers were seeking to convey when they wrote.

The cold and darkness of winter, however, have another emphasis that God would have us to understand, it is the emphasis of the purpose of winter. Most of us would long for and wish for the end of winter as we crave the sunshine of the spring and summer seasons. However, without winter there would be no spring crops and no summer fruits, and certainly no autumn harvests. It is during the wintertime that the ground rests from its labours and regains the nutrients that are necessary for the spring seeds to germinate. The winter rain and snow provide the soil with its vital ingredients of moisture, and moisture produces the softening of clay and the provision of energy.

We often feel that in a wintertime period nothing much is taking place because the soil lies empty and the ground is cold, yet beneath the surface untold features are replenishing the soil with nutrients ready for springtime. We often feel that in our spiritual periods of winter that God has deserted us and that nothing is taking place and we long for the energy and vitality of springtime, yet without the resting and the replenishing period of winter our lives would be of less value. Like Paul, we should learn to rest awhile during a wintertime period so that we rise to new heights during the fresh seasons of spring and summer.

God is always doing something in our lives, even when we feel that it is a winter period of deadness. As we pray today let us remember that even winter is good for us.

My Journal

KEY PRAYER

Heavenly Father, thank you for wintertime, even though at times we do not appreciate what you are doing within our lives. We need this period of rest and reflection and I praise you today for providing this period for me. Help me to appreciate all that you are doing for me, even during the seeming emptiness of a wintertime experience.

April 10th

KEY WORD: ***Prepared***

KEY VERSE: ***2 Timothy 4 : 2***

Preach the Word; be prepared in season and out of season; correct, rebuke, and encourage – with great patience and careful instruction.

Several days ago we studied this text together and considered each word in turn, we then went on to consider the seasons of the natural world and God's thoughts about them.

Having looked at the natural seasons and learned some spiritual lessons it would be a good thing to turn our attention to the command of Paul to Timothy. Paul told this young and inexperienced pastor to be prepared in all seasons to conduct himself wisely before his congregation and to continue to exercise his ministry among the people.

It is the call to be 'prepared' that we will consider today. Timothy was often quite afraid of ministry and felt at times quite inadequate. Paul, who was his mentor, charged him to always be ready and prepared in spite of the season, to fulfil his ministry. The Greek word used for the word 'prepared' is the word '*hetoimazo*' and this is the word that is used when someone was getting 'ready for a function'. It is used by Jesus when He was asking His disciples to go ahead to the upper room in Mark 14 : 15. Jesus said go and 'make ready' or prepare the room. It is this truth that Paul was seeking to convey to Timothy when he charges him to make himself prepared or to make himself ready for use.

We are often called to be ready in Christian service and our state of preparedness and readiness should depend upon the circumstances that are around us. We often do not feel like doing certain things, but we are called to serve like Timothy, in season and out of season. The Greek word *'hetoimazo'* carries with it a form of directness, in other words the word has a force to it. It is not an optional word but a direct word, Paul was not saying to Timothy 'if you like you can prepare yourself', or 'if you like you can get ready', but he was stating the fact that as a Christian and as a pastor there was a duty to make himself ready for service.

In our daily walk with God it is our duty, too, to be prepared. God wants His servants and expects His servants to be ready for action, it is not a question of option nor is it a question of choice. God commands us to be ready and prepared. The word also carries with it a sense of personal endeavour, in other words it is not God who prepares us, it is we who must prepare ourselves. God of course does refine us constantly and He does mature us through circumstances, but the charge here is not one of God doing the work but we ourselves doing the work

We are to set ourselves the task of continual preparation, so that when we are called upon to serve, we are in a permanent state of readiness for action. Whatever the season and however we feel, God expects His servants to be prepared.

My Journal ______________________________

____

____

____

____

____

____

____

KEY PRAYER

Heavenly Father, as I read your Word today I am reminded of my duty to be ready for your use, so I seek today to prepare myself for action. Help me each day to remember that I am bought with a great price and that my life belongs to you and that you expect me to serve you with a willing and a prepared heart.

April 11th

KEY WORD: **Fight**

KEY VERSE: **2 Timothy 4 : 7**

I have fought a good fight, I have finished the race, I have kept the faith.

This was one of the apostle Paul's final words to Timothy and of course through Timothy to the Church world wide. He was stating a very vital fact that having completed his life and having prepared himself for heaven, he was now ready to depart. This departure caused him to review his life and ministry and he stated that he had run well, fought well and kept the faith. The descriptions that he used are quite graphic, he compared his life and his ministry to that of a fight and that of a race, and the words that he used are very picturesque.

The word 'fight' is the Greek word *'agonizomai'* and from this word we derive our English word 'agony'. It is the word that conveys a struggle and the agony of striving for a result. Paul used this kind of word picture to convey just how he felt about his life and ministry, it had been a fight. However, the word *'agonizomai'* is not a negative word in the sense of the fight being utterly painful and hurtful, it is a positive word that was used for the concept of reward. Paul was not saying that he wished that he had not been involved in this fight, he was actually stating the opposite. Paul was saying to Timothy and to the Church, that he had fought a good fight. His concept of this battle was that it was rewarding and greatly fulfilling down here and that he was now going to his eternal reward, which was heaven.

The word also denotes the fact that, in Roman games, a fight would cause each contestant to strive unto the end in order to gain the prize. Each contestant would strain at every nerve and summon every effort to win the prize. No contestant would enter the battle hoping to lose, but each one would do all that they could to win. Paul said, "I have won". His concept of victory was an eternal reward for having fought the fight and finished the race. You can almost hear the victory in his voice as he proclaimed to Timothy the fact that it was almost over and the battle was won.

We can rejoice today in the glorious fact that, having served thus far and having been at times in the thickest of battles, we can rest in the truth that one day, at the end of the battle, there will be a positive result. We have an eternal reward that has been prepared for us and having fought well and finished the race, God has a heaven and a home just waiting for us. Therefore, we fight on and we battle well and we will hear the words spoken over our lives one day, 'well done, good and faithful servant.'

My Journal

KEY PRAYER

Heavenly Father, at times I have found the battle so hard, but I have kept the faith and I have run the race; help me therefore to keep on fighting. Help me to understand that each and every battle has a purpose and that each and every fight is one battle less before I get home. Help me, like Paul, to keep on going and to enjoy the fact that we wrestle on a victorious side.

April 12th

KEY WORD: **Rabbi**

KEY VERSE: **Mark 9 : 5**

Peter said to Jesus, "Rabbi, it is good for us to be here. Let us put up three shelters – one for you, one for Moses and one for Elijah."

We turn today to a very interesting and a very absorbing word, the word *'Rabbi'*. This word appears in the same form both in English and in Greek and its spelling is exactly the same. Occasionally we find the word spelt *'Rabbei'* but it is usually in the form of *'Rabbi'*.

The word means 'master' and can also be used quite rightly as 'teacher'. The root of the word is found in the slave trade where *'rab'* was used for the master in contrast to the slave and it meant a title of respect. It was then passed down through the generations and it came to be used as a title of respect for teachers particularly. In the New Testament the word was used quite often as a mark of respect for all teachers of the law as they preached from city to city.

It became a tremendous word of respect when it was addressed to Jesus, and He was often referred to as *'Rabbi'*. This term became almost His own as His disciples and His followers addressed Him as Master, or Teacher which was *'Rabbi'*.

As this title grew in its use concerning Jesus, the word became expanded and developed into the word *'Rabboni'*. This word was an Aramaic word that was the title of a great master, or could even be used for 'master of masters'. It was a term of great respect; anyone who was addressed in this form was dignified by its use. It was a greater term than just *'Rabbi'*, there were many *'Rabbis'* but there were not many *'Rabbonis'*.

Is it any wonder that when Jesus walked upon the earth

His followers would see in Him a greater sense of destiny, and that in hearing Him they would sense that a greater teacher was among them. '*Rabboni*' became His title and He was addressed as such by people of varying positions in life, such as Mary Magdalene and Blind Bartimaeus.

Many of us have known the Lord for many years and we have come to know Him as the 'Master of masters' and 'the Lord of lords.' Is it any wonder that our worship increases with each revelation of Him. The more we get to know Him the more we love Him and the more that we love Him, the more there is to know about Him. In the words of an old song, 'The longer we serve Him the sweeter He grows'.

As His followers watched and observed Him, they came to the conclusion that there was no one like Him. The countryside was filled with '*rabbis*' who were teaching and preaching, but no man spoke like Jesus. The synagogues were filled with great teachers of the law and many commanded great respect, but Jesus was the 'Master of masters', He alone deserved the title '*Rabboni*', my great Master.

My Journal

KEY PRAYER

Heavenly Father, it is with a sense of wonder that I enter your presence today, because the more that I get to know Jesus the more I realise just who He is. To all of us, and to me especially today, He is the Lord of lords and the King of kings. I worship Him today because He is my Master of masters.

April 13th

KEY WORD: ***Sweet***

KEY VERSE: **Revelation 10 : 9-10**

So I went to the angel and asked him to give me the little scroll. He said to me, "Take it and eat it. It will turn your stomach sour, but in your mouth it will be as sweet as honey." I took the little scroll from the angel's hand and ate it. It tasted as sweet as honey in my mouth, but when I had eaten it, my stomach turned sour.

Yesterday in our study together I referred to the old song, 'The longer I serve Him the sweeter He grows'. This of course is more than the poetic licence of an old song, it is pure truth. However, Jesus can not become sweeter, He is absolute, which means that He is always consistently the same. He is sweet, He can not get sweeter. What the old song was seeking to teach was the fact that it is our perception of Him that gets greater, which makes Him appear sweeter. In actual fact it is our understanding of Him and our awareness of Him that produces the sweetness.

The word 'sweet' appears in the New Testament just a few times, in fact it only appears six times and two of these are the occasions when it appears in the key verse today. There are two Greek words for our English word 'sweet', they are *'glukus'* from which we derive our words glucose and glycerine, and *'euodia'* from which we derive our word odour or sweet smell.

Using these two words that appear in the New Testament as 'sweet' we find a measure of teaching and truth.

'Glukus' is the word that was used when someone was seeking to convey the fact of taste. This is the reason that John used this word in Revelation 10, when he was seeking to understand the revelation of the angel's scroll. In his stomach the scroll

was bitter and turned his stomach into sourness, but in his mouth the scroll tasted sweet.

As we taste of the Lord's goodness and as we worship Him, the taste is sweetness to our lips, which is why the psalmist sang, 'taste and see that the Lord is good'. His taste to some may be bitterness, but to those of us who love Him, He tastes as sweet as honey.

'Euodia' is the word that is used when someone is trying to convey the concept of a sweet smell, an odour that fills the house with sweetness. This is not the same as a taste of sweetness but goes beyond that to one of sense and smell. This is the reason that Paul stated in Ephesians 5 : 2, that Jesus was for us 'a fragrant and sweet offering'. At His death Jesus gave His life as an offering that was acceptable to His Father and was for us a sweet fragrance of life. This was more than a simple taste of sweetness, it became for us a sweet smelling offering, like the offerings of the Old Testament, acceptable to God.

We rejoice today that in Jesus we have a taste that is sweeter than honey and an offering of acceptable sweetness that produces a fragrance that fills our house – the Church.

My Journal ______________________________

KEY PRAYER

Heavenly Father, thank you today for Jesus, who is for us an offering of acceptance and a wonderful savour of sweetness. We have tasted and seen that the Lord is good. Help me each day to continue to taste of Him so that my mouth might be filled with good things.

April 14th

KEY WORD: **Scripture**

KEY VERSE: **2 Timothy 3 : 16-17**

All Scripture is God-breathed and is useful for teaching, rebuking, correcting and training in righteousness, so that the man of God may be thoroughly equipped for every good work.

Over the next few days we shall be studying together these two key verses. Paul's sense of mentoring Timothy is obvious as we read the two epistles, he felt the need to give clear instruction to this young and inexperienced pastor and his wisdom and fatherly approach shines through each verse.

In these two texts we are introduced to the concept of the ministry of God's Word and its effect, and we shall begin with the word 'scripture'. The Greek word used is the word '*graphe*' and this was the word that was used for writings or for drawings and paintings. Our English word graphic is derived from this Greek word. In using this particular word, Paul set out to Timothy the fact that holy writings were God's way of communicating to us and that His Word, in both the Old Testament writings and the New Testament Gospels and epistles that were circulating around the churches, were truth. Paul conveyed to young Timothy that not all writings were God's Word, but that 'Holy Scriptures' were tested and found true, they were those that were God-breathed to us.

In using this word '*graphe*' Paul distinguished between ordinary writings such as historical books and geographical books that were in abundance and the 'set apart books' of the prophets and the law. These books had been judged to be God-inspired, they had been quoted from by Jesus Himself and they had been accepted by the Early Church as 'God's Word'. Paul said these books are 'useful for all teaching.'

In the previous verse, 2 Timothy 3 : 15, Paul said to Timothy, 'you have known the Holy Scriptures from your infancy.' In this verse Paul used a different Greek word which has been translated as our word 'scriptures'. In this verse Paul used the word '*gramma*' which means 'a letter' or 'a single word'. Our word 'grammar' is also derived from this word. In using this word to teach Timothy that he had known the Scriptures from a child, Paul states that Timothy had been aware all his life, that a single word from God could make him wise unto salvation. In linking the two words together, Paul went on to say that, having known that a single word from God can save you, the collective Word of God can instruct you while you are working out your salvation.

The Word of God, the Scriptures, can bring light in darkness and truth in place of error. We know that God has spoken to us through His Word and that the collective Scriptures are the living voice of God to this world. At any time God can take one word from His Word and it can be life to a sinful soul. In other words, one '*gramma*' from the '*Graphe*' can save.

Paul enjoyed using words to convey truth and his use of two Greek words conveyed to Timothy just how important his ministry of the Word could be. As we pray today, we should thank God for His Word and thank Him too, for the fact that 'one word' was enough to save us.

My Journal ______________________________

____

____

____

KEY PRAYER

Heavenly Father, as I approach you today I stand in awe of your Word, it is light and life to my soul. I bless you today for the wonderful moment when your Word brought light and life to me and I thank you that your Word is still the living voice of God to this world. Help me to always bring your Word into every situation of my life.

April 15th

KEY WORD: **God-breathed**

KEY VERSE: **2 Timothy 3 : 16-17**

All Scripture is God-breathed and is useful for teaching, rebuking, correcting and training in righteousness, so that the man of God may be thoroughly equipped for every good work.

Paul's charge to Timothy in these two key verses included the fact that the Scriptures were 'God's breathed' word to the Church. The King James version of the Bible used the statement that all Scripture was 'inspired' by God. The actual Greek word that Paul used was '*theopneustos*'. This word is a combination of two words, '*theos*' which means 'God', and '*pneo*' which means 'to breathe'. This combining of two words brought the truth that God breathed His Word to man, this is why the New International Version of the Bible differs from the King James. The NIV got a little closer to the truth, God's Word is not just inspired it is God-breathed. Many writings can claim to be the work of inspiration, but there is only one God-breathed Word.

Other Bible translators have tried to gain more insight into the word '*theopneustos*' and their studies have led them to the conclusion that they could not just say that the Word of God is inspired, as I said before, many writers could claim that their work was an inspired piece of writing. Therefore, translators like Wycliffe, Tyndale, and Coverdale translate this Greek word into the same meaning that the Scripture is 'inspired of God'. However, not even this translation really does the word justice. The concept of this Greek word is that God was in full action when His Word was being written and that He breathed upon the writers in such a way that they wrote under a mighty anointing. Their writings were therefore breathed by God Himself in such a way that they became the breath of God in written form.

No translation actually does justice to the word as it was a fresh word and a fresh concept. Most writers and translators accepted the nearest and easiest understanding, but the nearest and easiest translation does not bring to light the concept that Paul was thinking of when he wrote to Timothy. What Paul wanted to convey was the amazing fact that God, over thousands of years, breathed divine life into men and women in such a way that they brought, not just an inspired word to man, but that they brought a God-breathed Word that was His breath in written form.

This is why the Word of God is so vital and amazing. This breathed Word from God is life and light to all men and has been planted within the Church for usefulness and profit throughout all ages. We will look at the word 'useful' tomorrow in our study together

As we pray today we should remember to thank God not only for His Word to us but that He oversaw this Word throughout thousands of years and that He breathed upon the pages of parchment in such way that the Word became a living Word and was God's breathed Word to all mankind.

My Journal

KEY PRAYER

Heavenly Father, I stand amazed today as I think of the miracle of your Word. A Word so blessed and inspired that it gives life and light to all mankind. Thank you for breathing your Word on to the pages of parchment but even greater than that, thank you for breathing your Word into my heart. I rejoice that your Word brought salvation and is my meat and drink today.

April 16th

KEY WORD: **Useful**

KEY VERSE: **2 Timothy 3 : 16-17**

All Scripture is God-breathed and is useful for teaching, rebuking, correcting and training in righteousness, so that the man of God may be thoroughly equipped for every good work.

As we have seen, God's Word is not just a powerfully inspired piece of writing, it is His breathed Word into our lives. Paul went on to say that this God-breathed Word is useful for all forms of ministry within the Church. At first sight to use the word 'useful' seems a very casual way of setting out the kind of impact that God's Word can have.

A hammer is a useful instrument, a comb is a useful implement and a light is useful in a dark room. There are lots of very useful objects in day-to-day use, however, it seems very light and casual to say that the Word of God is useful in the same way as a comb is a useful and helpful addition to life. Surely Paul could have found a far more 'impacting' word than useful, to describe the nature of God's Word to us. However, it is not the word that lacks impact, it is the translation of the word that needs attention.

Paul used the Greek word '*ophelimos*' to describe the impact of God's Word upon us, it was translated as being useful in all forms of ministry. However, the word '*ophelimos*' does not merely mean useful or profitable, it has a far deeper aspect of meaning to it and it is a very 'impacting' word.

This Greek word should be translated as 'that which gives assistance towards progress'. This word was used in the realm of physical exercise and featured at a time when someone was making progress and was achieving a goal. It was a provoking word in the sense of pushing you onwards and upwards to achieve something better. Paul chose this very word to convey the thought that, as God's breathed Word came into contact with man and the Church, it had the potential to provoke us to greater heights than we ever dreamed possible. Therefore, it is not just useful, it is vital in our growth and development towards spiritual goals.

The word *'ophelimos'* found its way into other New Testament books and was used when writers were seeking to convey the thought of getting better and growing stronger. It was also used when the writers were seeking to convey the urgency of prayer and prevailing in prayer. The use of this word in our key verse today was one of Paul's greatest moments of creativity. He was not saying that if we applied God's Word we would find it useful, what he was conveying was that, if we apply God's Word to our lives, it will provoke us forward and upward to greater heights than we thought possible. Therefore, God's Word is vital within the Church and will produce good aspects of ministry whatever may be taking place around us and whatever others may be doing.

My Journal

KEY PRAYER

Heavenly Father, I pause today to reflect upon the fact that God's Word is useful to me. Help me as I read your Word to follow its guidance and goals so that I might grow beyond anything that I ever dreamed. Thank you for your Word and thank you for its stimulating and inspired message that blesses and saves.

April 17th

KEY WORD: **Teaching**

KEY VERSE: **2 Timothy 3 : 16-17**

All Scripture is God-breathed and is useful for teaching, rebuking, correcting and training in righteousness, so that the man of God may be thoroughly equipped for every good work.

As we have seen, all Scripture is breathed by God for our use and it provokes us to good works and greater heights. Paul now in the key verse set out four areas where the outworking of 'usefulness' actually touches our lives. Paul said that the God-breathed Word is 'useful for teaching, rebuking, correcting and training'. We will look at each word separately.

The first aspect of the 'usefulness' of God's Word is in the area of training and most of us will understand this word and the concept that Paul was seeking to convey. Every church will have a training programme for new converts and every denomination has a training college for its ministers and leaders. We are very familiar with the aspect of training and teaching. However, the word that Paul used is not so familiar and it is a very creative word within this key verse.

Paul used the Greek word '*didaskalia*' when he sought to convey the aspect of teaching being useful. The word translated means 'the act of teaching' not just what is being taught. There were two words in the Greek language for our English word 'teaching' and it is important that we understand both of them so that this key verse today is fully understood. The first word is '*didache*' which is the word that denotes 'the substance of teaching,' or that which is taught. This is a passive word and conveys the authority of the substance being taught, so in this sense the Word of God has an authority and a very deep message that requires us to think about it and follow its message. The second word, the one that Paul used here, is *'didaskalia'* which means 'that which is actively taught'. This word conveys the action of teaching and is therefore an active word.

The concept then that Paul was seeking to bring to us is that although the Word of God is a powerful substance, the actual action of the teaching of the Word is even more powerful. He commanded Timothy, the young and inexperienced pastor, to teach the substance of God's Word because the action of his teaching would bring growth and maturity to those who heard the Word. This word *'didaskalia'* appears in the New Testament 19 times and is used when the practical act of teaching is being conveyed. The root of this word is to be found in the concept of a 'doctor' with reference to the teachers of the law and the Jewish religion.

Therefore, this concept is one of more creativity than the fact of just teaching and training, every church and every Bible teacher does this. However, this word places emphasis on the powerful authority that is engendered when someone teaches the Word of God. This is why, following a deep and profound Bible study, you feel as if you have received a good meal. It is not just that you have been listening to the Word of God, but that the one who taught brought an authority that conveyed the Word with skill, like a doctor. Paul said to Timothy, 'the usefulness of the Word that is preached is like a skilful doctor, therefore preach the Word of God at all times.'

KEY PRAYER

Heavenly Father, I bless you today for all those who teach your Word, thank you for those who have been instrumental in my growth as a Christian, for those who have skilfully taught me over the years. Thank you that you gave teachers to the Church as a gift. Please help me to bless those who bring your Word into my life every week.

April 18th

KEY WORD: **Rebuking**

KEY VERSE: **2 Timothy 3 : 16-17**

All Scripture is God-breathed and is useful for teaching, rebuking, correcting and training in righteousness, so that the man of God may be thoroughly equipped for every good work.

As we develop the theme of the usefulness of God's Word we come to a word that appears to be, at first sight, a negative word. The Word of God is useful for 'rebuking' as well as teaching and building up.

Paul used a word here that is an interesting word and he commanded Timothy not just to teach and preach but also to bring the action of rebuking to those within his church. The word that Paul chose to use here is the Greek word '*elegmos*'; this word can mean 'rebuke' or 'reprove', and it is the word 'reprove' that finds its way into the Old King James Bible. The New International Version uses the term 'rebuke'. The word can mean both these translations as it carries with it not only the thought of putting things right and telling people off, but also the thought of putting things to the test. The English word rebuke has the connotation of putting things right and bringing a sense of scolding to someone, in other words it has the aspect of being a negative word. However, '*elegmos*' is not a negative word, it is the word that is used when someone is trying to prove a theory. It is used in Hebrews chapter 1 and verse 1, when the writer was seeking to set out what faith really is, and he stated that 'faith is being sure of what we hope for and certain of what we do not see'. Faith is like a test and we prove God by exercising faith and we prove that God's Word is true by testing it.

This aspect of testing and proving is what Paul was seeking to convey within this key verse, he wanted Timothy to be faithful in preaching and teaching and he knew that as Timothy was faithful in this, the Word of God would act in two different ways. It would act as a proving ground for those who heard him and it would also act as a testing ground for him personally as he grew into ministry.

When anyone sets out to prove or test the Word of God the word '*elegmos*' takes place and the Word is found to be true and proven, however, something else also happens when the test is applied. Whenever the Word of God is found to be true and found to pass the test, a sense of conviction takes place that brings us to a place of greater trust. In other words once we have proved the smaller things, it takes us to a place where we can believe for greater things. Faith acts as a spur and takes us onwards and upwards in our trust. Paul said to Timothy that this is what would happen when you bring God's Word into every situation, it would be a testing ground and a spur to those who receive the Word.

As we pray today we shall thank God for the way that we have grown and proved all things through the Word of God, it was good to have been rebuked by the Word as it has acted as a spur to our faith.

My Journal ______________________________

KEY PRAYER

Heavenly Father, today I recognise my need of being rebuked by the Word of God and I thank you for each and every time that the Word has done this to me, even when it has been a painful experience of reproof and rebuke. I bless you today for your Word and I ask for it to be a continual action of proving and testing so that I might grow stronger and better for you.

April 19th

KEY WORD: **Correcting**

KEY VERSE: **2 Timothy 3 : 16-17**

All Scripture is God-breathed and is useful for teaching, rebuking, correcting and training in righteousness, so that the man of God may be thoroughly equipped for every good work.

Yesterday we sought to understand what at first sight seems to be a negative word, that of rebuking. Today we face another such word that at first reading appears to suggest a negative action. Paul said to Timothy that the Word of God can bring correction. The English word 'correction' suggests the action of 'setting something right' and of course the Word of God does this each time that we read it. Doctrine acts as a plumb line of truth and as we read the Word of God, truth is revealed and it keeps us on the right path.

However, the word that Paul used is the Greek word '*epanorthosis*' and of all the words in this key verse this word is the most creative word and the most instructive word. It is a Greek word that is made up of three different words and the joining of them together produces a very memorable word and a very memorable truth.

The three words that are joined together are firstly, '*epi*' which means 'to', secondly, '*ana*' which means 'up' and lastly, '*orthoo*' which means 'to make straight'. So you have a word that literally means 'to bring up and straighten'. In Paul's terms then, he was seeking to convey the thought that as the Word of God is applied to our lives it has the dimension of bringing us to a place where we stand up straight. So the word is a positive one and not a negative one. To be corrected in the English form is to be 'set right' and it suggests a negative action of correcting us and 'setting things right'.

However, the Greek form brings a different light to the meaning of correction. At times the word might bring you to a place where you are 'put right' and it might seem to be a negative action, if you have been doing something wrong. However, the Greek word conveys a stronger meaning than that of simply correcting you, it conveys the wonderful thought of setting you up on a straight course.

This action of setting you up on a straight course is the action of improvement within your life. When we are not straight, we face the problem of deviation, it is very easy to deviate from the correct path and we can easily be led into error. Paul constantly warned the Church about wolves that would enter the Church and cause havoc among the flock with false teaching and error. The act of the Word of God being a correction was the act of keeping the Church on the right straight path. Should a member of the Church fall into error the Word of God, applied through teaching, would act as the remedy. It would pick them up and set them straight.

This is the very reason why Paul said that the Word of God was useful.

My Journal ______________________________

____

____

____

____

____

____

KEY PRAYER

Heavenly Father, thank you for the times when I have needed to be straightened out and the Word of God has done that. Thank you for the times when I have applied your Word to situations in my life and it has been a rock of foundation and correction for me. I praise you for your Word and I will always seek to guide my life by its precepts.

April 20th

KEY WORD: **Training**

KEY VERSE: **2 Timothy 3 : 16-17**

All Scripture is God-breathed and is useful for teaching, rebuking, correcting and training in righteousness, so that the man of God may be thoroughly equipped for every good work.

The last word in this key verse that we shall study together is the word 'training'. This word is an obvious word to all of us as it conjures up the thoughts of preparation for a race or a fitness programme that precedes a certain task that needs a period of training. Paul said to Timothy that the Word of God is useful for the preparation of ministry and that all aspects of usefulness bring us to a state of readiness for action.

The Greek word for our English word 'training' is '*paideia*' which literally translated means the 'training of a child' or the 'chastening of a child'. Paul's use of this word is to bring the concept of continual preparation like the nurturing of a child. A child is not trained just once in its life, its training and nurturing is a continual process. If we look at this concept for a moment the truth begins to be revealed.

A child is taught the basic idea of cleanliness and hygiene from the beginning of its life, it may not even realise that this is being taught but from its earliest moments it is being shown that the act of cleaning and hygiene is vital. This act is not shown to the child just once but it takes place several times a day and the regular act of hygiene is continually ministered until the concept is understood and practised by the child on its own.

The child is taught to speak by the continual and constant introduction of words by both father and mother, this is not a one time act but a process of education over a period of years. Even when the child is able to talk the process of education goes on so that the child becomes proficient in a language. This is the concept of *'paideia'*, the training for life of a child.

Paul used this word to convey the aspect of growth and development, and nurture and progress. He urged Timothy to preach the Word of God as the continual teaching would bring maturity to those who heard and would produce within them the aspect of training and preparation for their own ministry.

The word *'paideia'* however, also carries with it the concept of 'good' training in the sense of the moulding of character and the building of correct disciplines. It is quite possible for a child to be trained in bad habits and practices – this could also be called educating and preparing. A child could be educated in wrong-doing and prepared for life in an incorrect way. The Greek word here, however, does not convey the concept of just any or all forms of training, it conveys the thought of 'good' training. This is why the King James Version of the Bible translates the word into the English word 'instruction' with the thought of Christian doctrine attached to it. Paul required Timothy to prepare people in a 'good' way so that their character and disciplines were moulded into the right fashion.

As we bring to an end the words of this verse we should thank God today for all the preparation that has gone into our lives over the years which has produced the person that we are today.

My Journal ______________________________

____

____

____

KEY PRAYER

Heavenly Father, I do thank you today for all that has been done in my life over the years that has brought me to the place that I am at today. Thank you for your Word that has trained me and equipped me to serve you. Help me to constantly apply your Word to my life so that I might be further prepared for all that you have for me in the future.

KEY WORD: **Every good work**

KEY VERSE: **2 Timothy 3 : 16-17**

All Scripture is God-breathed and is useful for teaching, rebuking, correcting and training in righteousness, so that the man of God may be thoroughly equipped for every good work.

We have concluded the seven words of this key verse and we have looked closely at all of them over the past week. However, we can not leave this Scripture without considering its conclusion. The seven words that we have been considering include the concepts of training and equipping, and correcting and rebuking, bringing us to a conclusion. They are not concepts that merely bring us good thoughts, they bring us to a place of effectiveness. Paul said to Timothy that when he had ministered the seven concepts of preparation the man of God would be ready for every good work. The question is therefore, what are good works?

We would all have a list of what we would consider to be 'good works' and the list would be varied and long. However, it is not what we consider to be 'good works' but what God considers to be 'good works' that matters. Paul joined together two Greek words to convey the thought of a 'good work'. The first word that he used is the word *'agathos'* which means 'that which is good in its beneficial effect' and the second word that he used is the word *'ergon'* which means 'employment' or 'tasks'. So the thought behind Paul's words is the concept of beneficial employment and good tasks.

Many people in church life are employed in doing the very opposite of Paul's concept of good works, they employ themselves quite often in tasks that are not God-glorifying. We often take part in things that are very secondary to the vital tasks of work, worship and witness. Paul sought to raise our awareness of those things which really do matter in the whole aspect of Christian growth.

'Good works' are those things that result from the ministry of God's Word, as the Word of God is preached to us and brings its stimulus to spiritual desire and growth, the aspects of correction and rebuke, and training and equipping, provoke within us the desire to do something more for God. These desires coupled with direction of ministry produce the concept of what Paul was seeking to convey, that of beneficial tasks of goodness.

We can all remember those in our personal histories who did not do 'good works', and how it grieves us to remember. However, we can all remember those who came across our paths and who manifested such a breath of fresh air as they conducted themselves in such a beneficial way that their works brought much blessing. When we finally arrive in heaven all that we shall hear will be 'well done, good and faithful servant'. It will not be 'well done good singer', or 'well done good preacher', we are only servants and our works do follow us. It is a sobering thought that our works will be remembered.

My Journal

KEY PRAYER

Heavenly Father, as we come to an end of our studies within this key verse help me to always remember the fact that all that I do will be remembered and that all that I have ever done has been recorded. Help me to act as one who is beneficial in each and every action and help me too, to constantly bring glory to your name.

April 22nd

KEY WORD: **Bearing fruit**

KEY VERSE: **Colossians 1 : 6**

All over the world this gospel is bearing fruit and growing, just as it has been doing among you since you heard it and understood God's grace in all its truth.

During the past week or so we have been looking at the concepts of growth and good works through the teaching and training of God's Word. We saw too, that God requires good works as a result of our preparation as a servant of the Lord.

Good works are the outcome of good teaching and ministry and they are also the outcome of the grace of God in our lives. Paul wrote to the Colossian Church and urged them to bear fruit just as the gospel was bearing fruit all over the world. Jesus also spoke at length about good fruit in the gospel of John when He sought to convey the truth about the vine in Chapter 15. Jesus said that 'if we remain in the vine we will produce fruit, more fruit and much fruit.'

Bearing fruit has been the anthem of the Church throughout the last 2,000 years, it is the very aspect of the Christian life that is shown to a watching world. Good fruit brings glory to God and bad fruit brings dishonour upon the Church. In order to emphasise the importance of fruit bearing, Paul uses a very powerful Greek word to the Colossian Church. The word he chose to use is the word *'karpophoreo'*. Once again Paul uses two words joined together to convey important truth. The first word is the word *'karpos'* which means 'fruit' and the second word used is *'phero'* which translated means 'to bear'. The translation carries with it the thought of 'fruitful bearing' and was used metaphorically of conduct or activities that produced a good effect and were fruitful in themselves. For instance it was used by Paul again in Romans chapter 7 when he described what used to happen when we were in sin and under the law. He said that 'we bore fruit for death' in verse 5, but that now we belong to Christ, we bring forth different fruit. This was 'fruitful bearing' towards God.

Paul was seeking to convey the thought of bearing good fruit now that we belonged to Christ, as up until then our lives were continually bringing forth fruit that was unto death. This abundance of bad fruit was bad conduct and brought death, God now requires good fruit as we are now no longer under the curse of the law but we are under grace. Grace has changed us to the extent that now our lives bring forth a glory and a grace that produces 'fruitful bearing' and a better conduct and a beneficial effect to those around us.

Paul urged the church in Colosse in the key verse, to continue to be fruitful in their ministries just as they had been since they heard and understood the word of truth. If Paul had to urge this church to continue to bear fruit, it is vital that we also heed the warning and continue to be fruitful in all that we seek to do.

My Journal ______________________________

KEY PRAYER

Heavenly Father, I pause today to bring my life before your searching gaze and I ask you to test my fruitfulness. I realise just how easy it is to allow my fruit to become poor and weak and my testimony to become of no effect. Help me each day to produce fruit that lasts and fruit that is beneficial in its effect.

April 23rd

KEY WORD: **Havoc**

KEY VERSE: **Acts 9 : 21**

All those who heard him were astonished and asked, "Isn't he the man who caused havoc in Jerusalem among those who call on this (Jesus') name?"

Over recent days we have been looking at the whole concept of growth and fruit and we have studied Paul's words very carefully. The apostle, Paul, was a very great man and a man who received very penetrating revelations from God. Most of the New Testament is the work of his pen through which God breathed His Word.

His life was one of utter devotion to the Lord as his journeys and escapades are breathtaking and inspiring. His outlook on life was one of continual searching and striving for God's best and God's perfect will. So the testimony of others about him is to be viewed with great respect. In the key verse today the testimony was one of great perplexity, the men of Damascus said of Paul, "Isn't he the one who caused havoc in Jerusalem?"

Paul's actions up until the day that he was saved are recorded in the Acts of the Apostles, he sought to destroy the Church and all believers and his salvation was one of tremendous, dramatic and total change. Having been the destroyer of the Church he became its greatest advocate, and having sought to bring down Christianity, he now sought to build a greater kingdom. The testimony of the men of Damascus included a word that brought the picture of the tremendous harm and danger that Paul was to the Church before his salvation. They used the word 'havoc,' in the Greek translations the word that was used was *'portheo'*. If you think that the word 'havoc' was a dramatic word then *'portheo'* will fill you with a sense of destruction, as the word literally translated means 'to ravage' or to 'lay waste'. It was Paul's desire, driven by an inner feeling of certainty, to totally destroy the new Church. His own testimony was one of total commitment to the Jewish religion and anything that sought to threaten or harm this religion had to be destroyed.

The picture of him 'breathing out murderous threats' against the Church in Acts chapter 9 and verse 1, is a very graphic picture of a dragon-like creature totally possessed by rage and fear against God and the Church. His war against righteousness was one of total ravage and laying waste to the people of God. To use the word 'destroyer' is quite acceptable in this context as that is the meaning behind the concept of Paul's judgement concerning his task. He sought to bring the Church to the place where it would never become a threat again.

For a short period of time the Church suffered its first major attack of persecution and it came through the hand of Paul, until God saved him, called him to become the apostle of the Gentiles and gave him the task of reaching Rome with the gospel. His intense passion against the Church was now harnessed for the Church and towards his spiritual goals. His teaching, through revelation, brought insight and truth and his passion to reach the world and his passion to build the Church brought inspiration to all who followed him. From havoc to harmony and from despair to delight.

My Journal ____

____

____

____

KEY PRAYER

Heavenly Father, thank you for Paul and men like him who gave their all to the work of the gospel and the building of the Church. Help me not to simply become like them but to become like you. Help me too, to have the passion and zeal that men like Paul manifested. Guide me in my spiritual journey so that I might always be ready to serve those of my generation, as Paul did for his generation.

April 24th

KEY WORD: **Sheep**

KEY VERSE: **John 10 : 11**

"I am the good shepherd. The good shepherd lays down his life for the sheep."

Yesterday we saw Paul portrayed like a dragon seeking to devour the Church, a picture that is a very graphic one and one of total destruction. We thank God that Paul was saved and that he turned his passions towards the Church instead of against the Church.

The picture of destruction however becomes even more dramatic when the Church is presented as the 'sheep' of His pasture. The word 'sheep' was applied to the Church by Jesus and was a very descriptive title that stayed with the Church right the way through the New Testament and in fact still applies today, 2,000 years after Jesus first used the term to describe His followers.

'Sheep' was a word that in some ways was not a very endearing term for those that Jesus loved, but it conveyed a picture of helplessness and total dependence. It would have been nice if another animal had been chosen to represent those who would follow Jesus, but 'sheep' it was and 'sheep' it has remained until this day. The Greek word used for 'sheep' was the word '*probton*', and was the word that the Greek used for all small, four-legged creatures. It was only applied to actual sheep in the New Testament, so it was as if Jesus took this word and moved it away from all types of animals and gave it specifically to 'sheep'.

The word means 'to go forward' and it was applied to all small creatures as they moved, so it was a word that did not actually describe the animal but its movement. Small animals, especially sheep, tend to wander; if one sheep runs then the whole flock tends to run. If one sheep wanders to a place of danger the flock will in turn also move to the place of danger, as if they are incapable of sensing the risk. Jesus took this term and used it to describe His Church. Not a very pleasing thought!

Jesus said that 'like sheep we have all gone astray', depicting the very thought of sheep and danger. Jesus also said that, like sheep, the flock are endangered by beasts like wolves and lions. Again a very clear picture of the danger that lurks from our enemy.

However, having given the uncomplimentary term of sheep, Jesus goes on to say that He Himself is the good shepherd. In other words He was saying that we might be helpless creatures devoid of any true understanding and incapable of helping ourselves, but that He was the good shepherd who would care for us and lead us into green pastures. As a good shepherd, He has never failed us, He has always cared for us and He will always lay down His life for His sheep.

Persecution, like that of a dragon in the shape of a 'Paul' might come, but the good shepherd will always protect His sheep.

My Journal

KEY PRAYER

Heavenly Father, you came to be my shepherd and you came to lead me by still waters and green pastures and I praise you today for your goodness. You are my good shepherd and I am simply one of your sheep, help me to rest in the truth that you will never fail me and that you will always protect me.

April 25th

KEY WORD: **Sheep pen**

KEY VERSE: **John 10 : 1**

"I tell you the truth, the man who does not enter the sheep pen by the gate, but climbs in by some other way, is a thief and a robber."

Yesterday we took a close look at the word 'sheep' and we understood that it was a graphic picture of those who are under the good shepherd's care. In other words we are His 'sheep,' and He constantly cares for us.

The word used for 'sheep pen' or 'sheepfold' is the Greek word *'aule'* and its meaning is very picturesque. The word *'aule'* is only used once in the New Testament and it was Jesus who used it. The word means two things, firstly it means 'an open courtyard' and secondly it means 'an enclosure'. At first sight the two meanings seem to contradict themselves, 'an enclosure' and 'an open courtyard'. However, according to two great theologians, Moulton and Milligan, the actual sheep pen had no real translation yet the word was in very common use. The word denoted a place that was an open courtyard attached to a house, yet was an enclosed area within this courtyard.

This was where sheep were kept for safety as the place of dwelling was attached to the house and covered within the courtyard. The two theologians go on to state that this *'aule'* was often situated by a well, protected by a wall and a covering and often had a tower nearby.

Jesus must have seen many *'aules'* during His time on earth and when seeking to convey the place of safety for sheep could think of no better word than this to describe this haven. If this was the place of safety and if Jesus, who was the good shepherd, used it to describe the place where sheep could dwell, then we have a perfect illustration of the Church.

The Church is a place where, as sheep, we should be safe. A wall was built around the sheep pen indicating protection, God has placed a wall of grace and mercy around us so that we are protected from all alarm.

The sheep pen had a well nearby, and God has planned a deep well of living water for us to drink from so that we will never thirst again.

The sheep pen was protected by a tower, and God has provided us with a strong tower to run to whenever we feel unprotected and afraid. He is the good shepherd and has provided us with all that is necessary for our protection.

When Jesus saw the *'aule'* He could think of no better description of His Church and He used it as the illustration of perfect safety, of a place of grace and of a place where there is always pure refreshment. As we pray today we should thank God for the sheep pen where He has placed us and where we always find rest.

My Journal ____

KEY PRAYER

Heavenly Father, as I think about my church I thank you that you have placed me in a sheepfold where I am loved and cared for. Thank you for being my good shepherd and thank you for bringing me to a place of sanctuary.

April 26th

KEY WORD: **Crown**

KEY VERSE: **Revelation 19 : 12**

His eyes are like blazing fire, and on His head are many crowns.

The feature of the word 'crowns' in the Bible is very significant and very symbolic and usually has obviously to do with 'kingship'. In the key verse today it very much has to do with a vision of Jesus, who, riding a white horse, leads the armies of heaven. He is called 'Faithful and True' and He wears many crowns, which speak of His authority to rule and reign.

The word 'crown' or 'crowns' appears 24 times in the New Testament, three times it appears as '*diadema*' and 21 times it appears as '*stephanos*'. We will look at both of these words, one today and one tomorrow.

'*Diadema*' is the Greek word for a kingly ornament and from this word we derive our English word 'diadem', which is usually the word used for a small crown or ornament worn by royalty. The ornament featured in the Bible was usually a blue band marked with white and it was often worn by Persian kings, with a turban or tiara. The word literally translated means 'to bind around' and it was adopted by Alexander the Great, who bound a '*diadema*' around his head. Among Romans and Greeks it was worn with great distinction, and this headwear featured as a regal badge of great royalty.

The use of the word '*diadema*' in the three appearances in the book of Revelation denoted the symbol of power and authority, it was worn by the dragon in chapter 12 verse 3, where he had 'seven' crowns. It was worn by the beast in chapter 13 verse 1, where he wore 'ten' crowns and it was worn by Jesus in the key verse, where He had 'many' crowns. The symbol of 'seven' crowns and then 'ten' crowns and then 'many' crowns denoted the fact that although the dragon and the beast thought themselves powerful, there was only one who was all powerful, Jesus Himself. He had many crowns. His diadem was such that He was above all and over all things and all things finally would submit to Him. This word is always associated with kingly and imperial dignity and it is the highest honour to be given a diadem. Is it any wonder then, that Jesus had many crowns, as He is the King of kings and the Lord of lords?

There was one Roman emperor who wore a '*diadema*' all the time, his name was Diocletian and he brought the diadem into great fashion as total royal headwear. The fact is that this emperor has long since died, but Jesus lives and His diadem will be seen for ever.

Hymn-writers have used the symbol of the diadem on many occasions during their poetic writings. One hymn-writer recorded that each believer receives a diadem on their entrance into heaven and that they in turn remove their diadem and then cast it at the feet of Jesus. This could just be a feature of hymns, however, the word diadem does not refer to the crown that we shall wear, it only refers to the crown that Jesus wears. The type of crown that we shall wear is a different crown altogether, and we shall study this type of crown tomorrow. However, it does go to show that when all things are completed, Jesus will reign and the only crown that will be featured will be His.

My Journal

KEY PRAYER

Heavenly Father, I thank you today that you are the King of kings and the Lord of lords, and whether or not I cast my crown at your feet, I will always exalt you as my Lord and my God. Your throne will last forever and of your kingdom, there will be no end.

April 27th

KEY WORD: ***Crown***

KEY VERSE: **Revelation 14 : 14**

I looked, and there before me was a white cloud, and seated on the cloud was one 'like a son of man' with crown of gold on his head and a sharp sickle in his hand.

Yesterday we saw that the English word 'crown' was featured 24 times in the New Testament and that three appearances referred to the Greek word *'diadema'*, meaning 'to bind around', and we saw that it had close associations with a tiara or turban. In the other 21 references the word 'crown' is translated as *'stephanos'* and this word translated from the Greek means 'that which surrounds' and it was used to describe a wall or a fence that encircled a piece of ground.

The word was taken from this context and used for a kind of woven garland, normally made of oak, ivy, myrtle or olive wood. Twigs and small branches were taken from these trees and woven into a small circle and then presented as a symbol of triumph. They were used for public honour or for triumph in some race or games. They were also used as a reward for distinguished service or military prowess. Sometimes they were also used at weddings and festivals.

The word was used when Jesus received a 'crown of thorns' at His death on the cross at Calvary's mountain – this was a reverse use of the word as this crown was an attempt at humiliation.

The word *'stephanos'* is not the word to be used as a sign of kingly and imperial dignity, that honour goes to the word *'diadema'*; this is a different form of crown. There is nothing kingly about *'stephanos'*, this is the word that is generally used in the New Testament for the type of crown that a believer will be given, and it appears in this form several times.

Peter referred to a crown of glory in 1 Peter 5 : 4, and James talked about a crown of life in James 1 : 12, and Paul spoke of a crown of righteousness in 2 Timothy 4 : 8. In most of the references within the New Testament this word *'stephanos'* is featured as referring to life, joy, reward and glory, and it is this theme that the hymn-writers should have used and not the form of a crown like that of a diadem.

Should we receive a reward and finally a crown, it will not be the crown of kingly exaltation – that alone belongs to Jesus. However, should we receive a crown of reward similar to those who had run a race or fared well in some form of games, then we shall cast this crown before the feet of the one who wears the greatest crown. Diadems are for Him, we only receive a pale shadow.

My Journal

KEY PRAYER

Heavenly Father, today I come before you recognising that I am only a servant and that I deserve no reward, all I have is grace and all I have received is mercy. Should there ever be a time when I receive a reward I will immediately cast it at your feet, as all that I am and all I ever shall be is due to your glory and grace.

April 28th

KEY WORD: **Throne**

KEY VERSE: **Hebrews 4 : 16**

Let us then approach the throne of grace with confidence, so that we may receive mercy and find grace to help us in our time of need.

Jesus receives the royal diadem and is enthroned in regal splendour. Should we ever receive a reward it will be the pale shadow of the crown that He will wear, and our studies of the past two days reveal this clearly.

Having looked at New Testament crowns it would be a good thing to look at New Testament 'thrones' and seek to understand the teaching concerning the throne of God. The word used for throne in the Greek is the word *'thronos'* and it is obvious that we derive our English word 'throne' from this word. It is the word that is always used for throne except for a few occasions when a different type of throne is mentioned and we shall consider this throne tomorrow.

The throne of God is mentioned many times within the New Testament although it appears in different forms. In the key verse today the writer to the Hebrews spoke of a throne of grace and yet John in his writings within the book of Revelation spoke of a great white throne of judgement, Revelation 20 : 11. It is the same throne but it has a different appearance. For those of us who have accepted Jesus as Lord and Saviour, this throne is one of grace and mercy, our sinful guilt has passed and the throne of judgement has been replaced by a throne of grace. God sees us as having no sin through justification so therefore this throne is one of peace and acceptance. However, for those who have rejected the offer of salvation this throne is still the great white throne of justice and God will judge the small and the great when they finally present themselves before Him.

'Thronos' is depicted in the New Testament as a throne or seat of authority and it is upon this throne that God sits and it is this throne that is referred to at the times of judgement. It is also the same throne that is referred to at the time of the millennium and as the everlasting throne of David. God sits in regal splendour and is worshipped by the hosts of heaven and His throne is set at the focal point of heaven and eternity. It is a great throne that produces fear in those who have rejected Jesus and it is a throne that produces grace and mercy for those who have accepted Him. As the key verse today said, 'therefore we can come before this throne with confidence', as it is the throne where we find help in our time of need.

My Journal ______________________________

KEY PRAYER

Heavenly Father, thank you for this throne of grace and thank you too for the welcome that I receive when I come before you. Thank you that I am accepted in the beloved and that from this throne you bless me and grant access to me. Help me to treat this throne with reverence and help me to understand that this throne holds no fear for me now.

April 29th

KEY WORD: ***Throne***

KEY VERSE: **Acts 12 : 21**

On the appointed day Herod, wearing his royal robes, sat on his throne and delivered a public address to the people.

I mentioned yesterday when speaking about thrones within the New Testament, that except for a few occasions the Greek word '*thronos*' was used to describe a throne. The few exceptions are when the Greek word '*bema*' is used. Both words are translated as throne but the two words have totally different meanings.

In our key verse today King Herod sat down upon a throne that was a different throne to that of a majestic and regal throne. This throne was one that was raised on a platform or a plinth and was mounted by steps, it was from this type of throne that speeches were made. It was also the throne that was used when public orations were needed and when a tribunal was set in motion. King Herod, on this occasion, was due to give a speech, so he mounted the steps and sat upon a '*bema*' seat.

It is this word that was used on the occasions when New Testament writers wanted to convey a different form of judgement to that of God's judgment from His great white throne. Paul spoke of the judgement seat of Christ in 2 Corinthians 5 : 10, where he said that all believers would appear. There is a misconception that, having escaped the penalty and power of sin, all believers are free from judgement. The introduction of the '*bema*' seat within New Testament writings deals with this misconception. All believers will be judged and all believers will face a judgement seat, however, it is not the terrifying great white throne that the unbelievers, both small and great, will have to face. This judgement seat of Christ is a different throne altogether. Paul said that everything that we have done in the body subsequent to our salvation will have to face the test of a *'bema'* seat judgement. This throne is the throne of reward not punishment, although there will be some things that will be tested by the fire of judgement that will not pass the test. These things will perish in the fire but we shall be saved through the flames, 1 Corinthians 13 : 15. Believers receive rewards for their faithfulness to the Lord, but anything that was contrary in their lives to His will and His Word will suffer loss.

We can only thank God today that we have escaped the judgement of the great white throne, however, we will not and can not escape the judgement seat of Christ. Therefore we should examine our lives and seek to put right those things that are wrong and contrary to His will and His Word, so that on that day of judgement we shall hear 'well done, good and faithful servant'. Only those things that are deemed to be gold, silver and costly stones will be saved, and all wood, hay and straw will be consumed, 1 Corinthians 13 : 12.

My Journal

KEY PRAYER

Heavenly Father, thank you for saving me and removing from me the judgements of sin, yet I see today that my life must be pure and free from all sin. Help me to walk worthy of my salvation so that when I stand before you at the judgement seat of Christ, I shall be considered worthy of such rewards and welcomes.

April 30th

KEY WORD: ***Lie***

KEY VERSE: **Colossians 3 : 9**

Do not lie to each other, since you have taken off your old self with its practices.

Today the key verse speaks of a 'lie' which it says should not be practised, we will all probably react to the verse and say that we do not 'tell lies'. Which is probably quite right, however, Paul in this letter to the Colossians was not talking about telling lies, or untruths, or falsehoods, he was dealing with something much more sinister than the telling of 'mere' lies. While we seek to walk worthy of our salvation in the hope that the judgement seat of Christ will find us acceptable, we may not fully appreciate just what the word 'lie' really means in this context.

The Greek word used in this verse is the word '*pseudo*' and we obviously derive our English word 'pseudo' from this word. This word does not just mean simply the act of telling or living a lie, it goes far further than this. The word translated means ' to deceive' and has its roots in the actions of deception, falsehood and idol worship. Paul commanded the Colossians therefore to put aside the actions of deception towards each other. The word was used in the context of Paul speaking about the previous life of sinful immorality and greed and actually went on to speak about idolatry. Paul was seeking to guide the Colossians away from the old life by reminding them that they have put on a new life with new practices.

We can lie to each other and we can lie to ourselves and we can also seek to lie before God in our practices and actions. These are not the deliberate actions of falsehood and the telling of lies but the lifestyle of deception and idolatry. For instance, if we say that we love God and yet have hatred in our hearts towards someone, we are deceived according to the apostle, John. If we live one kind of life in public and another kind of life in private we are operating within deception, and if we glory in another person's failures we are practising a lifestyle of deception.

This is why the word *'pseudo'* is a far more sinister word than that of simply telling lies. In the context that Paul used this word within the key verse, he was talking about the actions of those within the church at Colosse and he warned of deception between each believer. He commanded that they do not lie to each other. The actions of deception are such that we can actually deceive ourselves in the sense of thinking that we are pure and holy. Our outward actions may fool others into thinking that all is well with us, and these false actions can almost lead us to think that we are actually alright. However, if we have anything between us and God and this idol remains in our lives we are committing deception, and although it may appear that all is well within our lives God, who sees all and knows all, will bring judgement upon us. Deception can be one of the vilest sins and it can be within the Church and within our lives. Paul's command should be heard and obeyed.

My Journal

KEY PRAYER

Heavenly Father, I hear your Word to my heart today and I pause to allow it to rest within my spirit. I seek today to put things right before you, before man and within my life. Help me to live according to your Word and to put aside anything that is pseudo and false, so that my life might be pure and honest and true before you.

May 1st

KEY WORD: **Triumph**

KEY VERSE: **Colossians 2 : 15**

Having disarmed the powers and authorities, He made a public spectacle of them, triumphing over them by the cross.

It is good to commence a new month on a high note of victory, even if you do not feel that you are experiencing victory at the present moment. It is always a good thing to praise the Lord and it is always important to believe God even when things are going against you. If you do not feel like being triumphant at present, I trust that you will by the time that we have studied this key word.

The word 'triumph' only appears twice in the New Testament, which is a very strange thing seeing as triumph is very much a part of the Christian message. The two occasions of its use are firstly in 2 Corinthians 2 : 14, and secondly within the key verse today. On both occasions the same Greek word is used, it is the word '*thriambeuo*' and this word translated means 'to lead a procession in triumph'. On both occasions when it is used in the New Testament, the same writer, Paul, had in mind exactly the same theme, that of total and outright victory. In 2 Corinthians 2 : 14, Paul explained about the way that the Lord leads His Church throughout the ages. He speaks of a procession of victory that spreads a fragrance wherever it goes. Paul was setting out the concept of a victorious and overcoming Church that was touching and changing a world through each and every believer.

In the second reference, our key verse today, Paul was also setting forth a concept of victory although this use of the word differs slightly. In this reference Paul was speaking of the fact that God had triumphed over all powers and authorities and that, through the cross, God had made a public spectacle of them. The picture here is one of God leading forth, not His Church on this occasion, but all powers and authorities and all principalities and kingdoms.

The word *'thriambeuo'* is a Greek word that was used by all nations and the Romans in particular, and it was used at the time when a victorious army would lead back the vanquished foes. There would be a procession of the victorious soldiers leading the humiliated prisoners of war back to their nation and home to a victor's welcome. The vanquished army would trail behind with utter defeat written all over their faces and would be a public spectacle of humiliation. Paul said, this is what God had done at the cross, when He triumphed over all kings and kingdoms and brought about a total victory and a humiliation of the enemy. He now leads a triumphant procession with His Son, Jesus, leading the way.

In the first use of the word in 2 Corinthians 2 : 14, God led forth His Church in victory and spread a fragrant aroma throughout the world. In the second use of this verse in Colossians 2 : 15, God led forth His enemies showing to the world a wonderful cross and a wonderful Saviour. The two uses of the same word bring a differing feature but the same kind of victory. Even when we feel defeated, God has brought us victory and even when we feel overcome by the situation around and about us, remember that God has triumphed and the Church is victorious and the enemy has been defeated. God is marching through the land leading a triumphant Church and displaying the fact that His enemies are vanquished, we can praise Him today for the fact that all is well.

KEY PRAYER

Heavenly Father, thank you for your victorious, all-conquering Son, Jesus. Thank you that the powers of darkness have been overcome and that we have victory in Him. Thank you too, that God is leading His Church and that the gates of hell can not prevail against it.

May 2nd

KEY WORD: **Victory**

KEY VERSE: **1 John 5 : 4**

This is the victory that has overcome the world, even our faith.

We saw yesterday that the word triumph only appears twice within the entire New Testament, which is a strange thing seeing that triumph is very much part of the message of the Church. So the fact that the word 'victory' only appears six times in the New Testament is also a very strange thing. It is even stranger when we find out that of the six times that the word 'victory' appears, three of the times are within three verses in 1 Corinthians 15. So the word only appears three times outside of 1 Corinthians, which means that this great word along with the word 'triumph' have very little mention within New Testament terms.

I said several weeks ago when we were studying another key verse and another Greek word, that when there is little reference in the New Testament to what we would feel is a major word, it is obvious that God is projecting truth within the limited references. Victory is very much part of our lifestyle and our message and as the key verse today states, this victory, which we greatly enjoy, 'has overcome the world'. If the word 'victory' brings us a sense of joy and anticipation in the English language it ought to bring even more joy when we discover the truth behind the word. The Greek word used for victory is the word '*nike*', which literally translated means 'gaining victory' or 'has victory' and its major use was in the sense of the end of a battle and the conclusion of a fight when the victors realised that victory was theirs and that 'it was all over'. The greatest and fittest warriors had overcome and the battle was over.

This Greek word '*nike*' is quite well known to us in the western world, as a sports shoe company has borrowed the word in order to proclaim that the 'battle is over and the victory is won', when their shoes are worn. Quite a statement to make!

The apostle, John, used this Greek word to emphasise the fact that our victory is total even though we, as yet, do not see the final battle completed. We walk by faith in every aspect of our lives and with this aspect we at times can struggle. We know that our faith will finally overcome and we also know that all things will culminate in God's triumph over sin and suffering and sickness and over Satan himself. However, we still do not see these things with the natural eye, we still have to combat sin, we still have to wrestle with suffering and we certainly have to trust God through times of sickness and pain. The battle is not over, even though John used the word *'nike'*. The use of such a word was really a faith statement and we have to accept it as such, even though we still struggle with the concept of total victory. Our victory is assured and we shall overcome, this is the promise of faith, and faith according to Hebrews 11 : 1, is 'being sure of what we hope for and certain of what we do not see'. As we pray today we will ask God to increase the substance of our faith so that we can see and understand that victory is ours now, even though we often do not see the finished product.

My Journal ______________________________

KEY PRAYER

Heavenly Father, I come before you today with an urgent request that you would help me to see what I often do not see. I pray that Hebrews 11 : 1, would become a reality for me rather than just a verse of Scripture, help me to receive my victory and to believe for greater things than I see around me. I give you thanks for the fact that my ultimate victory is assured and that I will overcome the world.

May 3rd

KEY WORD: **Mystery**

KEY VERSE: **Ephesians 3 : 8-9**

Although I am less than the least of all God's people, this grace was given me: to preach to the Gentiles the unsearchable riches of Christ, and to make plain to everyone the administration of this mystery, which for ages past was kept hidden in God, who created all things.

Having studied together over the past two days the words 'triumph' and 'victory', and having appreciated that these two words can often cause us problems of understanding, in that we often do not see triumph and victory within our lives, we have to say that there are areas of mystery that we find hard to fathom and difficult to grasp. These areas of mystery have always been there. Paul often spoke of mysteries to the Church when he wrote his epistles. The Church has always grappled with things that it often did not fully understand or fully appreciate. There are times when God has hidden truth, awaiting a season and a time when He could reveal truth and bring revelation to His people.

In the key verse today, Paul spoke of the mysteries of grace, that God chose to hide for 'ages past' in order that a proper season might come when He could reveal the secrets of grace and the secrets of His will. Paul stated that God was now 'making plain' the fact that the Gentile world was now able to partake of grace, and that he, Paul, was a messenger to them. This revelation had been kept hidden until God saw the right time and the right moment to make it plain and to reveal the mystery.

The Greek word for mystery is '*musterion*' which is a major word in New Testament senses. Correctly translated it means 'that which is known to the initiated' and this meaning differs entirely from the normal understanding of the English word 'mystery'. The English word deals with the matter that has been revealed, for instance, if a murder has been committed and the murderer is unknown, it can take years for the mystery to be solved. In other words the mystery lies in the matter that needs revealing. Whereas the correct translation of *'musterion'* lies with the receiver of the mystery. Paul correctly said that he had received an answer to a mystery or a revealing of what was previously hidden.

In New Testament senses the mysteries of truth are outside of natural understanding, we can not fathom some areas of truth because we seek to understand them with our natural minds. We have to understand that truth can only be received by divine revelation and that truth will only be revealed when God makes it known at an appointed time. He also will only make it known to those who are illuminated by His Spirit.

So, New Testament mysteries depend upon the fact that we are in the right place with God, and that we are in the right place at the right time in order to receive.

This revealing of a mystery can happen in two ways. Firstly, God chooses to reveal a major shift in His purposes and plans. God does not change His mind and make a shift in His thinking, but the time to reveal His plans to a watching world has arrived.

The second area of revelation where a mystery is uncovered is in the area of our personal discovery of truth, where suddenly a measure of truth is revealed and you are aware of God's plan for your own life or where you become aware of the reasons for 'what is going on around you'.

In order to fully comprehend this word 'mystery', a quote from Vine's Expository Dictionary of New Testament Words will help us. W E Vine states that 'in the ordinary sense a mystery implies knowledge withheld, however, in Scriptural significance, it is truth revealed.'

KEY PRAYER

Heavenly Father, thank you for the times when you have revealed to a watching world your plans and purposes and I bless you for the uncovering of truth. However, I thank you even more today for the times when you have revealed your plan and purpose for my life and when I have been the recipient of revelation.

May 4th

KEY WORD: **Fall**

KEY VERSE: **Matthew 7 : 27**

"The rain came down, the streams rose, and the wind blew and beat against that house, and it fell with a great crash."

Over the next week I want to introduce to you a word that occurs many times within the New Testament and that at first glance is a very obvious word with a very obvious translation. The key word is the English word 'fall' and its translation is a very obvious one of 'falling down', as it is within the key verse today.

However, the word 'fall' is used in at least 19 different ways within the New Testament and on many of these occasions the Greek word used differs in each case. The only way that the translators could bring the truth to our understanding was to translate on each occasion to the English word 'fall', however, to do this has not allowed the full truth to come through to our understanding. We will seek to put this right over several days.

In the first use of the word fall, we turn to the words of Jesus and His story of the wise man and the foolish man. The wise man built his house upon the rock and it withstood the buffeting of the winds and the waves and it stood firm. The foolish man built his house upon sand and the same elements ravaged the house and its foundation, and in the words of the Kings James Version of the Bible, 'great was the fall of it'. Which is a little more graphic than the NIV translation 'it fell with a great crash.'

The Greek word used in this instance is the word *'ptosis'* which translated means 'to overthrow', and it was used in the New Testament in two references in the same way. It was used in Luke 2 : 34, when Simeon said to Mary concerning Jesus, that

'He is destined to cause the falling and rising of many in Israel'. The use of the word *'ptosis'* meant that there would be those in Israel who would fall into rejection and be overthrown, because they would reject and crucify the Lord and Saviour.

The word has its roots in the concept of final and complete defeat and its use in the key verse today shows its devastating nature. The foolish man built his house upon a foundation that was certain to erode with the onslaught of inclement weather. As soon as the waters rose and the winds came, the house with its unsure foundations fell down with a great crash. The house perished and was overthrown with great devastation.

The word only appears twice in the New Testament and its use shows the overthrow of poor foundations and the final destruction of those in Israel who reject the Saviour. The message is, however, the same: build your life upon a firm foundation and your future is assured.

My Journal ____

KEY PRAYER

Heavenly Father, in my life and in my future I declare today that I long that my spiritual foundations are firm and sound. I therefore seek your will for my life and I ask that you would help me to follow you all the days of my life.

May 5th

KEY WORD: **Fall**

KEY VERSE: **Romans 11 : 11**

Again I ask: Did they stumble so as to fall beyond recovery? ...because of their transgression, salvation has come to the Gentiles to make Israel envious.

In this key verse today Paul used another Greek word that has found its translation as simply 'fall', however it is not as simple as that, as Paul was seeking to convey a truth that is more than a simple fall or falling down.

Paul was speaking of the fact that Israel had rejected their Messiah and was therefore in a place where God had allowed the Gentile world to partake of grace and mercy. He went on to say that having allowed the Gentile population of the world to enter into grace, Israel was therefore in the position of stumbling and falling. The Greek word used in this instance is a different one to that of the word that we studied yesterday. Paul in this verse uses the word *'paraptoma'*, which translated means ' a blunder' or a 'false step'. The concept that Paul was using here was that Israel had made a major blunder in its rejection of Jesus as the Messiah and had therefore taken a false step.

The word has its roots in the whole area of falling into unrighteousness and moral trespass, and is translated this way in only two occasions in the New Testament and both of these occasions are in the same chapter of Romans – chapter 11. On both of these occasions they refer to the major blunder that Israel had made in the rejection of Jesus.

However, the word *'paraptoma'* is used on 21 occasions within the New Testament and it is quite clear that New Testament writers understood this word to be fact, that any rejection of Jesus is a false step away from truth. The translators have taken this word and translated it as 'fault' or 'offence' and on a couple of occasions they have translated it as the word 'trespass' itself. Yet its real meaning comes shining through in the book of Romans, when Paul used it to convey the truth that Israel blundered in its rejection of Jesus, the Lord and Saviour and their own Messiah.

Because of Israel's blunder, God has now allowed the Gentile world to receive the message of grace and mercy and that Paul himself would be the apostle and messenger of this message to the races outside of Israel.

We can thank God today that He allowed the Gentiles to receive grace, or else we would not be saved and we would never have heard the message of salvation. Israel's blunder was our salvation.

My Journal ______________________________

KEY PRAYER

Heavenly Father, thank you for mercy and grace and thank you that you allowed us Gentiles to receive your Word. I praise you today for the wonderful grace of God that even has mercy upon Israel to this day – a nation that refused your Son and who crucified the Lord of glory. Your grace has no limits and your mercy has no boundaries.

May 6th

KEY WORD: **Fall**

KEY VERSE: **Matthew 17 : 6-7**

When the disciples heard this, they fell face down to the ground, terrified. But Jesus came and touched them. "Get up," He said. "Don't be afraid."

In the key verse today we find the use of the word 'fall' or 'fell' in the context of the mount of transfiguration and the fact that Peter, James and John fell on their faces when they saw Jesus in His glorified body. Standing around Jesus at the time were Moses and Elijah and the whole scene terrified the three disciples in such a way that they could do nothing else but fall before Jesus.

When Matthew in his gospel sought to convey the picture that was taking place on this mountain he used a word that was simply translated as 'fall', however, his understanding and his interpretation of the event was such that it was not just the simple matter of three disciples falling down that occurred. Matthew used the Greek word *'pipto'* to convey the scene and his use of this word produced a very graphic understanding. The word means 'to fall' but not in the same way that our understanding would see it. We would see someone who tripped over a hidden branch in a forest as a simple fall or the simple act of falling down, but this word is not a simple fall nor a simple act of falling over. The word has its roots in the act of descending or the act of deliberate prostration. The disciples did not simply fall over when confronted by a supernatural event, they deliberately fell before Jesus in an act of prostration before Him.

This deliberate act of falling down before Jesus conveyed the fact that they were in awe of Him and in awe of what they were seeing. Their only way of facing this event and the only way of responding to a glorified Jesus, was to bow in adoration before Him and to seek to get as low as they could before Him. The word *'pipto'* has its roots in worship and homage and it is used on several occasions in the New Testament in this respect. The apostle, John, fell before Jesus again in the book of Revelation, when he saw Him, in Chapter 1 verse 17, and he said that when he saw Jesus, 'he fell before Him as though dead.'

Jairus fell down before Jesus when he came to plead on behalf of his daughter in Mark 5 : 22. The living creatures and the elders in heaven fell down before the throne of God, in Revelation 5 : 14. Over and over again those who saw Jesus could not do more than fall before Him in an act of homage and worship.

It would be a good thing to fall down and worship the Lord at times; we take Him for granted so often when we pray and we forget His majesty and kingship. Instead of simply praying today why don't you fall before Him in an act of deliberate worship and homage and give Him all the glory.

My Journal

KEY PRAYER

Heavenly Father, I come before you today recognising that I often take you for granted and that I often rush into your presence. I bow down and worship you and I give you all the glory. Help me to remember just how great you really are and help me to come before you each day in the right way and in the right posture.

May 7th

KEY WORD: **Fall**

KEY VERSE: **James 1 : 11**

For the sun rises with scorching heat and withers the plant; its blossom falls and its beauty is destroyed. In the same way, the rich man will fade away even while he goes about his business.

We studied yesterday a Greek word for 'fall' and we saw that '*pipto*' meant to fall before God in a deliberate act of homage and prostration. Today in the key verse, James used the word 'fall' in the context of flowers and blossom, and the rich man's end of fading away even while he goes about his business.

Obviously in this context James is not talking about falling down in an act of worship, he is talking about something far more acute and penetrating than that. The translators have simply used the word 'fall' because it is hard to use other words because the English language at times is quite weak. The Greek word that James used was '*ekpipto*' which is a word that is close to '*pipto*' but not at all the same.

The word '*ekpipto*' means 'to fall out of something' whereas '*pipto*' means to fall down in homage. James used this different word to convey a far different thought, he was seeking to show that when we walk according to our own ways we are in great danger. He used the illustration of a rich man, and it is only right to state right now that riches are not the problem. Many rich people have blessed the kingdom of God and many rich people are greatly blessed by the Lord, however, it is the whole concept of this rich man going about his business, that is the key. Here was a man that was walking in his own ways and not walking with the Lord; riches were his god and he spent his whole time in pursuit of more and more. James said that he will fade away even while he pursues his own ends, and that this fading away is compared to that of flowers dying in the heat of the scorching sunshine.

Flowers in scorching sunshine wither very easily and their blossom falls away and is destroyed. The very graphic picture is portrayed for us of a beautiful flower fading and dying before our very eyes. James used this word picture to describe the end of the selfish rich man pursuing his own destiny.

This same Greek word is also used to describe the falling of Paul's ship as it was buffeted by the waves in Acts 27. The same word is used several times in this chapter although it is translated 'lowered' and 'driven along'. This graphic picture is vivid – a huge ocean-going vessel is hidden beneath the waves during a storm at sea. The graphic nature of a ship striving against the elements possibly on its way to the bottom of the ocean is a terrible scene. The falling into the waves of such a massive vessel is a disaster when it should be floating gracefully and majestically upon the waves.

To fall down and worship is a wonderful thing, however, to fall away and wither and die is a matter that is a tragic disaster. To be buffeted by storms that have the effect of drowning us is a matter that is too graphic to contemplate. As we pray today we can all remember those who are outside of the kingdom of God and unless they are rescued there is nothing but sadness and tragedy.

My Journal ______________________________

KEY PRAYER

Heavenly Father, I come before you today with a heart that is heavy for those that I know who are outside of the kingdom of God. I seek your face for them and I pray that grace and mercy might be shown towards them and I pray that they might be saved. Help me to do all that I can to rescue them before it is too late.

May 8th

KEY WORD: **Fall**

KEY VERSE: **Acts 8 : 15-16**

When they arrived, they prayed for them that they might receive the Holy Spirit, because the Holy Spirit had not yet come upon (fallen upon) any of them.

Here is one of the most interesting and far reaching words in the whole of the New Testament. In the NIV it is translated as 'come upon'; in the Old King James Bible it is translated as 'fall upon'. This act of falling upon, is not in any way like the other words that we have been considering that have been translated as 'fall'. We have seen that we can fall deliberately before God in an act of worship and that people can fall into a false step and blunder themselves away from God. We have also seen that those outside of the kingdom of God will fall away just as a flower's blossom falls and dies.

The word used by Luke in Acts 8 : 15 and 16, our key verse today, is the Greek word '*epipipto*' and it is the word that was most used when the writers described the work of the Holy Spirit. The only way that most writers could demonstrate the work of the Holy Spirit's actions of 'coming upon us', was to use this word, and we find it appearing on many occasions.

The word literally means 'to fall upon' or to 'press upon' and it can even mean to 'embrace'. If we think for a moment about the Holy Spirit's work in our lives, all these translations have wonderful meanings. The Holy Spirit at times 'falls upon us' and at times He 'embraces us' in a wonderful and loving moment. It is used on many occasions when the writers want to convey the action of one being caring and considerate. It was used in Acts 20 : 10, when Paul rushed out of a long and very late meeting to embrace Eutychus when he had fallen from a window. On finding him dead Paul fell upon him in an act of total care and consideration and Eutychus's life returned to him.

It was used when Peter was preaching in Cornelius's house in Acts 10 : 44, when the Holy Spirit suddenly came upon all who were within the house. When Peter later defended what had happened when he spoke to the apostles, he said in Acts 11 : 15, 'The Holy Spirit came upon them as He did upon us at the beginning.'

The picture being created is one of a loving God who reaches out to all mankind, people of all colour, race and creed, and He falls upon them in such a tender and loving way.

God does not want us just to fall before Him in an act of homage and worship, He also wants to fall upon us so that we might feel His embrace and know His mighty power. As we pray today we should allow Him to fall upon us right now and allow Him to have His way within our lives.

My Journal

KEY PRAYER

Heavenly Father, I pause today as I pray in order to allow you to come upon me. I long for your embrace and I long for your touch of power. Help me to grow in my awareness of you and help me too, to linger in your presence.

May 9th

KEY WORD: **Fall**

KEY VERSE: **1 Timothy 3 : 6-7**

He must not be a recent convert, or he may become conceited and fall under the same judgement as the devil. He must also have a good reputation with outsiders, so that he will not fall into disgrace and into the devil's trap.

In this key verse today we discover another Greek word that has simply found its way into the Scriptures as the English word 'fall', however its meaning and its use is entirely different to the other words that we have studied. Yesterday we considered together the Greek word *'epipipto'* and we discovered that it means 'to fall upon.' The word used by Paul in the key verse today is a close kin word to this but is substantially different. It is the word *'empipto'* which translated means 'to fall into'. Because there are no real close translations to these seemingly same words, the translators can only use the English word 'fall,' yet as we are about to see, the close *'pipto'* words that can mean 'fall' are really quite different.

Paul wrote to Timothy regarding the appointment of church leaders and he urged Timothy to be careful about these appointments as the wrong people in the wrong place could do great harm. He laid down certain parameters for Christian leadership and two of them are found within this verse. Paul said that leaders, firstly, should not be recent converts and, secondly, they should have a good reputation with those outside of the church. The reason for these qualifications being set out for leadership is that new converts and those with poor relationships outside of the church are easy prey for the enemy. Paul also stated that those who are easy prey for the enemy could fall into a trap. Therefore he used the word that in the Greek means 'to fall into'.

The word has its origins in the whole area of 'tripping up' or 'landing into something', and it is this thought that is in Paul's mind when he writes to young Timothy, an inexperienced pastor. He was anxious that Timothy should not put people into the place of being vulnerable to the devil's tricks and schemes and therefore tripping themselves and falling into a trap.

This word is used several times within the New Testament and it is always found in the context of a slip up or a trip. For instance, it is found again in 1 Timothy 6 : 9, when Paul was talking about rich people who might fall into a trap concerning their riches. It is found again at the time when Jesus was preaching in Matthew 12 : 11, Jesus was talking about the sheep and their tendency to wander around and that their wandering could cause them to fall into a pit. Jesus was seeking to show that shepherds, even on the Sabbath, would rescue their sheep who had fallen into this kind of trap.

As we pray today it would be a good thing to remember your local church leaders in prayer and pray that they might be on their guard so that they do not fall into any traps that the devil might lay for them. Leaders, by virtue of their position, are out in front and very vulnerable to traps laid by the enemy, therefore they should be on your prayer list constantly. If Paul found it right to warn Timothy to be on his guard, we should find it right to pray on a regular basis for those who have the charge, spiritually, over us.

Tomorrow we shall conclude our studies in this important word 'fall'.

KEY PRAYER

Heavenly Father, I pray today for those who have a spiritual charge over me, I pray that they will be kept from any snare laid by the enemy, so that they do not fall into the trap that is laid. I thank you for them and I pray that you would bless them mightily as they seek to lead me.

May 10th

KEY WORD: **Fall**

KEY VERSE: **Romans 3 : 23**

For all have sinned and fall short of the glory of God.

For the past week we have spent time considering the word 'fall'. We have seen six different Greek words translated into the one English word 'fall' and we have taken the time to review them all. I said at the commencement of our studies in this word, that there were at least 19 different words that find their translation into our word 'fall' we have looked at just a few. The last word that we shall consider is possibly the most serious one of all.

Paul wrote to the Roman Church and used a word that in our key verse today is simply translated as 'fall', however it does not convey at all what Paul was seeking to say. He used the word '*hustereo*' to convey the fact that 'all have sinned and fall short of God's glory'. It is right to translate it as 'fall' but it is not the 'fallen upon' that we have seen before nor is it the 'falling into a trap'. It is not even the 'falling upon' that the Holy Spirit does when He comes upon us, it is a far, far different word from that.

The word '*hustereo*' means to 'come late' or to 'come behind' and it can even mean to 'be inferior'. Paul used this word to convey the fact that we are all inferior when it comes to God's glory and that we have fallen short, in the sense of being behind, when it comes to being part of His glory. The word has its roots in the context of being destitute and failing and was used by the Greeks to convey the sense of being poverty-stricken. When Paul was seeking to convey just how far we are behind God's glory, he could think of no better concept to describe our position than destitute.

This word appears a few times within the New Testament. It appears when the writer to the Hebrews, in chapter 12 verse 15, was seeking to convey the warning of missing out on God's grace. The translators missed the point a little bit and said that 'no one must miss out on the grace of God'. However, the point is not the fact that we can miss out on God's grace but that we miss His grace because we are so far behind His glory and grace that we miss it by light years. It is only the fact that His grace comes to us that actually redeems us. We can never reach Him, the truth of grace is that He reached us.

Paul again used this word when he was making his defence of being an apostle. He stated in 2 Corinthians 11 : 5, that he was not 'inferior to those who called themselves super-apostles'. In other words he was saying that he did not fall behind anyone in gifts and graces because God had called him and commissioned him.

This word is one aspect of the translated word 'fall' that has a negative connotation to it. We could not reach God and we were missing out on His grace, but God took positive action, in that He came to seek and to save those that were lost, so that we might not fall short of His glory, but that we might become His sons and daughters in grace.

My Journal

KEY PRAYER

Heavenly Father, I rejoice today in the fact that you took the initiative and came to save me and I praise you for your grace. Thank you for the truth that you have hidden in simple words like 'fall'. I bless you for uncovering truth to me this past week and I seek to follow all that I have learned.

May 11th

KEY WORD: **Odour**

KEY VERSE: **Philippians 4 : 18**

They are a fragrant offering (odour), an acceptable sacrifice, pleasing to God.

We are going to look at a very precious word today that finds itself translated into many varying English words within the differing translations that we have. The NIV translates this word as 'fragrant' and the Old Kings James Bible translates it as 'odour'; the Revised Version records that this word is translated as 'sweet smell'. Other translations use words that are similar, however, although the word is translated in different ways its truth should not be lost. The Greek word is *'osme'* and its true meaning is 'to smell'. I believe that the Revised Version in this particular case gets nearest to the true meaning of this word.

The word means 'to smell' and it is a positive word and not a negative word. The negative connotation of the word 'smell' is that the smell might be a bad one, but the Greek word *'osme'* is one of the most positive words that you will find. It had its roots in the concept of incense and fragrance and was used to convey the thoughts of a smell that was beautiful and acceptable to those who were around it.

The fact that this word was a positive word and that it conveyed the thought of sweetness and acceptance is the very reason why Paul used it on a couple of occasions to convey the thought that we, as the Children of God, are a sweet odour and an acceptable fragrance to Him.

He used it in the key verse today when he wrote about the actions of Epaphroditus, who brought Paul a gift from the church in Philippi, and his actions in bringing the gift and the church's action in preparing the gift, Paul said was a 'fragrant offering'.

Paul used it again in Ephesians 5 : 2, when he was seeking to describe the actions of Jesus, who gave himself as an offering for the sin of the world. Paul said that this offering was also a very pleasing fragrance to God.

The word also occurs in the gospel of John when he was describing the actions of Mary, who took a pint of pure nard, an expensive and costly perfume, and anointed the feet of Jesus, and it was said 'that the fragrance filled the house'. This offering, said John, 'was acceptable' to Jesus although it was unacceptable to some, who had watched the event take place.

The whole concept of this word is twofold. Firstly, that everything that we do towards God and each other, in charitable Christian acts of kindness, is an offering to God and very acceptable, in the sense of being a sweet smell or odour. Secondly, the concept of this word is also within us, for we ourselves, having been redeemed, are now acceptable to God and an offering that is sweet. You could say that once we were unacceptable but that now we are acceptable; once we were a bad odour to Him but that now, through grace, we are a sweet offering that fills God with delight.

My Journal

KEY PRAYER

Heavenly Father, I take great delight in praising you as I know that as this offering rises to you, it becomes a sweet and fragrant offering. I also know that this offering is acceptable to you because you are pleased with my praise. Help me each day to be a sweet smell before you and help me too, to be an acceptable gift to others.

May 12th

KEY WORD: **Morning star**

KEY VERSE: **2 Peter 1 : 19**

We have the word of the prophets made more certain, and you will do well to pay attention to it, as to a light shining in a dark place, until the day dawns and the morning star rises in your hearts.

For a few days we are going to commence a series of studies on some of the more unusual names that have been ascribed to the Lord Jesus. There are some very well known names that have been used as a description of Jesus in the Scriptures and they are very graphic names like 'the Lion of Judah' and 'the Good Shepherd' and 'the Lamb of God'. These descriptive names of Him are known by all of us, however, some New Testament writers have used names that are not so well known but yet are immensely beautiful. Over the next few days we will study some of them which I am sure will be a great blessing to each one of us.

Peter wrote to the Church in the first chapter of his second epistle concerning prophecy and the Second Coming of the Lord Jesus Christ, and, in the key verse today from this chapter, he alluded to the fact that we have a 'certain hope' that he said 'needs to be given our attention'. He described the Coming of Jesus as being like a light shining in a dark place and the 'morning star' rising in our hearts.

To describe Jesus as the 'morning star' is wonderfully descriptive and sets our minds ringing with all sorts of remembrances. We will remember a dawn breaking on one occasion when we saw the stars light up with the early sunshine's rays breaking across them. We will recall an early scene when just before the dawn the sky in brilliant colours revealed a bright star shining in vivid splendour, bringing beams of light cascading through the morning colours. Peter used this very unique description to bring home with great force just what the Coming of the Lord would be like.

He actually created a kind of new word to describe this scene and used two Greek words to build the picture. The word used in the key verse is *'phosphoros'* from which we gain a word in English that is used in laboratories for a form of metal that when used in chemical ways burns with brilliance. The word means 'light-bearing' and it is formed by using the Greek words *'phos'* meaning 'light' and *'phero'* which means 'to bear'. By joining these two words together Peter has cleverly and wisely brought about a wonderful description of Jesus. He is the 'light-bearer' that lights up our lives when He becomes Lord of all.

The word is used only once in the entire New Testament and it brings us a marvellous insight into just what Jesus really is and just who He really is. It has its fulfilment in two ways. Firstly, Jesus lights up our lives when He becomes Lord at the moment of our salvation. We accept Him and we repent and turn from sin and Jesus comes with a flooding stream of light and our journey of life begins as we are changed from one degree of glory to another. Secondly, this word has its fulfilment at the Second Coming when Jesus takes His rightful place within this world as Lord of all. His Second Coming will see Him lightening up the entire world with great glory.

The brightest star in the heavens is the morning star and it appears at its brightest just before the dawn; what better and greater way could there be to describe just what Jesus has done and just what Jesus will do as He comes to gather His Church.

KEY PRAYER

Heavenly Father, thank you for this wonderful revelation of Jesus as the bright morning star, who shines with clarity and brilliance in a dark sky. Thank you that you have lit up my life already when you found me and saved me. Thank you too, that you are going to light up my life once again when you return to save your Church.

May 13th

KEY WORD: **Light to the Gentiles**

KEY VERSE: **Luke 2 : 32**

A light for revelation to the Gentiles, and for glory to your people Israel.

Here is a wonderfully unusual description of Jesus that was used by the priest who dedicated Him on the eighth day of His birth. Simeon was moved by the Holy Spirit to actually go into the temple that day and he took Jesus in his arms and blessed Him. Then, by revelation, he made this prophetic announcement that Jesus would be 'light' to the 'Gentiles' and 'glory' to 'Israel'.

Over the next couple of days we shall study these four prophetic words that were given and we shall see the significance of each word that Simeon pronounced.

Firstly, the priest said that Jesus was a 'light' to the Gentile world. When Luke was recording this event in his gospel, he used the first part of the Greek word that we studied yesterday, '*phos*', and used it in the way that conveyed the force of the word as 'extreme light'. '*Phos*' means, as we saw yesterday, 'light' and its main use in Scripture was to convey the thought of 'seeing with the eye'. W E Vine says that this word 'enables the eye to discern form and colour, because of the force of luminous emanation'. What he means is that when a striking light reaches the eye, the force of this light forms itself into shape, colour and attractiveness. The eye receives all sorts of pictures and forms but this kind of striking light '*phos*' produces something that no other light produces. Luke could have used other Greek words for light, there are about fourteen words that can be translated as 'light', but none of them conveys the force of a striking form of light that '*phos*' does. This is because Jesus is not just 'a light' or even an 'important light,' He is 'the' light, a light that lights up the world with striking force.

Luke used this word because he wanted to convey just how mighty and magnificent Jesus really is. John also used this word in his gospel, when he was seeking to show that Jesus was the 'light of the world' and that He lights up everyone within the world. John was seeking to prove that as the 'sons of light' we shine with His reflected glory and that we illuminate every place that we inhabit. This force of light must be understood if we are to really comprehend what Simeon was saying at the dedication of Jesus. Simeon prophetically stated that Jesus, this striking force of light, would illuminate the Gentile world in such a way that those who received Him would be become sons of God and that they in turn would radiate light wherever they went.

What an incredible concept, we actually reflect the light of God as we walk around, as we travel about and as we live our lives before others. As we pray today we should ask God to allow this light to burn even brighter as the darkness of this world descends upon us, so that we might illuminate every place that we inhabit.

My Journal

KEY PRAYER

Heavenly Father, thank you for your marvellous light that has lit up my life and all those who have accepted you as Lord and Saviour. Please help me to reflect your glory at all times. Please forgive me for the times when my light may not have shined so brightly and please help me to walk with you and talk with you, so that I might become more and more a mirror image of light and love.

May 14th

KEY WORD: **Light to the Gentiles**

KEY VERSE: **Luke 2 : 32**

A light for revelation to the Gentiles, and for glory to your people Israel.

Yesterday we saw that the priest, Simeon, took the eight-day-old Jesus in his arms and pronounced that He would be a 'light to the Gentiles and glory to Israel'. We also saw that the word 'light' translated in this key verse is the word for striking and forceful light. This striking new light that had appeared on earth was no other than the long awaited Messiah, the Messiah that the whole nation of Israel had prayed for and had longed for over generations. However, Simeon's first thought was not that of his nation Israel, but that of the entire Gentile world, as he speaks about Jesus as being a light to this 'outside world' and this most pagan of people.

The Greek word used for Gentiles in this key verse is '*ethnos*' and of course from this word we derive our English word 'ethnic', which means to us the thought of 'pertaining to races or people groups.' The Greek word used here literally translated means 'heathen peoples' or even 'a multitude of people.' Simeon could not have been more right when he spoke this prophetic word over Jesus, as Jesus was about to light up, not just Israel, God's chosen people, but the entire world of all people groups, and all heathen races.

The Jews had no dealings with what they called the 'Gentile dogs', these 'heathen people' were an abomination to those who felt that they were, in some way very special, as 'God's chosen people'. True Jews would spit on the floor when a 'heathen' Gentile passed by, they would wash themselves if they were even touched by someone that they considered 'unclean'. No Gentiles were allowed near the inner courts of the temple, they were allowed to venture no closer than the outer courts. So, the picture is quite clear the Jews had no dealings with these uncircumcised peoples of the heathen races. So, when Simeon raised his voice to prophesy that Jesus would be the 'Gentiles' light', he was going against the whole concept of Jewish traditions and he was assaulting the whole Jewish basis of life and culture.

It is hard for us to fully understand the total break with tradition and reversal of culture that this prophecy would have had to those who heard his words. His words however, echoed the words of the angels who testified that Jesus would be born to bring new hope and fresh peace to a planet in turmoil.

This striking and forceful light would shine throughout the world and the followers of this light would for generations to come, seek to bring this light to the ends of the earth. We can thank God today for the fact that Jesus came and that His light brought hope and peace to an entire world. We sit today in heavenly places because God sent His Son and because Jesus was willing to bear our sin in His body. This true light has penetrated the Gentile world and has reached all nations.

My Journal

KEY PRAYER

Heavenly Father, thank you that Jesus came, thank you that He was willing to bear my sin and thank you too, that the whole world has been touched by a light that was striking and strong.
I bless you today for your goodness and I seek to be a reflector of your light to those who are round and about me.

May 15th

KEY WORD: **Light to the Gentiles**

KEY VERSE: **Luke 2 : 32**

A light for revelation to the Gentiles, and for glory to your people Israel.

The third part of Simeon's unusual description of Jesus was that He would be 'glory to Israel'. The prophecy decreed that He would light up the Gentile world and that heathen people would be reached for the first time with a salvation message, however, Israel would still be God's first thought, as 'glory' would come to this nation in rebellion.

Luke used a most beautiful word to describe this coming of glory to a nation that longed for a Messiah, and although the nation would not know Him and would even reject Him and crucify Him, glory would still be Israel's blessing.

The Greek word used in this key verse today for 'glory', is the word '*doxa*' which translated has several meanings. It can mean 'a good opinion' (the word's primary meaning), it can mean 'honour' and it can also be translated as 'brightness and splendour'. If we were to bring all these meanings together into one phrase, which is quite acceptable in the Greek translation, we have the most wonderful description of this long awaited and long desired Messiah. The translation could be 'the one in whom there is brightness and splendour that brings Him to a place of honour and high esteem'. We know that this translation is acceptable because New Testament writers used this word '*doxa*' on many occasions and it is translated using these very words and this very theme in varying places within the Gospels and the epistles.

The root of this word can be traced back to the Hebrew word '*skekinah*' which was the word that was used by Old Testament writers when they wanted to convey the awesomeness of God's greatness and glory. When we actually praise God we are giving Him praise which is a form of doxology, a sense of majestic and high esteem conveying the highest and greatest form of glory and praise.

The root of this word comes from a word that was used by people when they wanted to convey the thought of 'impression' or a description of an 'estimation'. We would say of someone that 'they give a good impression' and our estimation of them is therefore quite high. This is what Simeon wanted to convey at the time of the dedication of Jesus. This old priest, who had long waited for the Messiah and who probably had held many male babies throughout his ministry and who would have longed to see the Messiah resting in his arms, now had his dreams come true. He lifted Jesus up before God and said, 'I have the highest opinion of this child and I bring Him before God with honour and praise and I set Him before the nation as the one who will bring brightness and splendour.'

Jesus not only brought light to the Gentile world but He also brought glory and honour to a nation in rebellion and to a people that would ultimately reject Him and crucify Him. Thank God today that we have received Him and that we have also set Him in His rightful place as Lord of all.

My Journal ______________________________

KEY PRAYER

Heavenly Father, you are the Lord of glory and as I pray today I seek to bring my praise and estimation of you into sharp focus. Although there are those who reject you and spurn your ways I want to affirm my love for you today and bring you the praise of my heart.

KEY WORD: **Light to the Gentiles**

KEY VERSE: **Luke 2 : 32**

A light for revelation to the Gentiles, and for glory to your people Israel.

Jesus was, as we have seen over the past few days, the 'light' of the 'Gentiles' and the 'glory' for 'Israel', and the old priest's words set a pattern for His life that would bless multitudes.

This 'light' was a striking light to the eye and the Gentile world of heathens would receive this light in a brand new way. The 'glory' to Israel would be one of highest honour and praise, bringing brightness and splendour. However, this highest honour and praise that would result in brightness and splendour, was to the ancient peoples of the ancient nation of Israel. This coming glory was not to be seen by just any nation or even a major nation, it would only be given to Israel.

The name of Israel first appears in the 32nd chapter of the first book of the Bible, Genesis. It was the name that was given to Jacob at the time of his encounter with God when Jacob wrestled with God throughout the night and finally received his blessing. The name of Jacob meant 'supplanter' or 'cheat' and the new name of Israel meant 'ruling with God' or 'prince'. The cheating Jacob, having found peace with God and a new destiny and a new name, was now to be called Israel, one who 'ruled with God'. This change of nature and its resulting destiny was not just to be the new name of one person however, it was also the name of a new nation and a new people. God always had a place in His heart for the children of Abraham and He had blessed them and nurtured them even when they had rebelled and sinned. But now, they were no longer just a group of 'children' wandering in the desert, they were now God's own people, a mighty nation and a people that were to become God's own property, the nation of Israel.

It was to this nation that God showed His mighty acts and it was to this nation that God showed His covenant of mercy throughout the generations. It was to this nation that God would finally send His Son, and it was this nation that would reject the Lord of glory and would finally crucify Him.

However, God would still love this nation and God would still involve Himself with this ancient people through the two millennia that have passed since Calvary. God will still keep His covenant with Israel even though they have at present rejected Him. We can see just how good God is towards this nation when, even in their total blindness towards Him, He blesses them, fights for them and will still be faithful to all His promises, when the final battle of Armageddon takes place.

Until then, God has chosen to bring the Church, which is at present the spiritual 'Israel,' into His covenant relationship. Although the Gentile world has seen His light, and although the glory has yet to fall upon Israel in their final destiny, the Church has seen His glory and expresses His glory to a dying world.

Israel may have rejected God, but God has not rejected Israel, at present His greatest blessing falls upon the Church, but Israel, the nation that 'rules with God,' is still the apple of His eye and will hold a special place at the Coming of the Lord.

My Journal ______________________________

____

____

____

KEY PRAYER

Heavenly Father, thank you for blessing Israel and for being their Lord. At present they reject you but you still require us to pray for the peace of Jerusalem. I bless Israel today and I pray for its peace and I ask you to have mercy on a blinded people, a people that you still love greatly.

May 17th

KEY WORD: **Son of David**

KEY VERSE: **Mark 10 : 47**

When he heard that it was Jesus of Nazareth, he began to shout, "Jesus, Son of David, have mercy on me!"

In our studies of the more unusual names that were given to Jesus we come to one that has echoes of Old Testament prophecies and blessings. This name, 'Son of David', was only used a few times within the New Testament and it conveyed something very precious to those who used it and to those who heard it.

In the key verse today the name was used by a man who has come to be known as 'Blind Bartimaeus'. This blind beggar was sitting by the roadside in his usual place at the usual time, when a most unusual thing took place. A commotion began to take place in the distance and as it grew louder, people were jostling for position and shouting praises. The beggar asked those around him what was happening and he discovered that Jesus of Nazareth was drawing near. Maybe he had heard the stories of healing or maybe it was just a leap of blind faith, but he cried out 'have mercy upon me.' When those around him asked him to keep silent, he cried out even more, until Jesus heard him and then healed him and then called him to follow.

The name that this blind beggar used was the name that linked Jesus with Israel's greatest and mightiest of kings, that of David. David was a man after God's own heart and was a man that was used and blessed more than any other king. David was also one of the links in the Messianic line to Jesus. In fact Jesus was born in David's royal city, Bethlehem, and He allowed Himself to be called the 'seed of David' in Romans 1 : 3, and He also allowed the writer in the book of Revelation to call Him the 'Root of David' and the 'offspring of David.' In linking Himself so closely to David and allowing the association to be quoted and spoken of, Jesus was confirming the Old Testament and He was confirming the ancient prophecies.

David was Israel's greatest king, and yet here in the New Testament was another King that was even greater, as Peter would preach on the first day of Pentecost, in Acts chapter 2, 'David is dead and buried, but Jesus is alive.'

God blessed David and used him greatly, but God sent His Son Jesus, a greater David and through His seed all men shall live.

My Journal ____

KEY PRAYER

Heavenly Father, thank you for all the Old Testament giants of faith who blessed many and carried with them the nation of blessing. However, I thank you today for Jesus, who is greater than the greatest and King of kings and Lord of lords.

May 18th

KEY WORD: ***Jesus of Nazareth***

KEY VERSE: **Mark 10 : 47**

When he heard that it was Jesus of Nazareth, he began to shout, "Jesus, Son of David, have mercy on me!"

Yesterday we studied together one of the more unusual names of Jesus that was bestowed upon Him by Blind Bartimaeus. Bartimaeus used this name for Jesus when he heard a commotion in the streets and was told that it was 'Jesus of Nazareth'. When the title 'Jesus of Nazareth' was used the name obviously conveyed something of importance to Bartimaeus as he cried out even louder.

'Jesus of Nazareth' is another one of the usual names of Jesus and it is worth studying this name as it brings with it a very rich truth indeed. We all know that 'Jesus' means 'Saviour', this was the name that was given to Him by the angelic messenger at His birth. The angel said 'that He would be called Jesus, for He would save His people from their sins'. However, Jesus was born in Bethlehem and yet He was called 'Jesus of Nazareth'.

This title originated in a very strange way. Following the birth of Jesus and His escape from Herod into Egypt, Joseph and Mary brought Jesus to Nazareth and He spent His childhood years within this town. Nazareth was a town set high in the hills surrounding the lake of Galilee and it had a very bad reputation. The town was synonymous with a crude kind of dialect that was different to any other form of speech in the surrounding area. It was also a town that had a reputation for sin and crime and a very heavy form of religious practice. Because of this bad reputation a common form of statement concerning the town was used. People would say 'can anything good come out of Nazareth'. Nathanael reacted this way when he heard about

'Jesus of Nazareth', in John 1 : 46.

However, in spite of the reputation and the very bad connotation of being linked with such a place, Jesus rejoiced in this title. The town had never really been prominent as it was quite 'out of the way' as a main town or city and it had never really featured much in people's thinking. Yet it was in this town that Jesus grew up, and it was in this town that He prospered as a young boy, and it was in this town that He commenced His ministry. There is another reason however, why Jesus allowed Himself to be closely associated with this town. There was a prophetic element to the title 'Jesus of Nazareth'. Matthew in his gospel recorded the fact that prophets had spoken about this and he said, 'He went and lived in a town called Nazareth, and so it was fulfilled through the prophets that He was a Nazarene,' Matthew 2 : 23.

This obscure town, with its poor reputation, became the home and the title of God's only begotten Son, and it was said of this Son that He would be despised and rejected and that He would be, according to Old Testament prophecies, 'a root out of dry ground'. To answer Nathanael's question, 'can any good thing come of out of Nazareth', we would have to loudly answer, "Yes!" Jesus, the perfect Son of God, allowed Himself to have no reputation in order to give us the greatest reputation as children of God.

KEY PRAYER

Heavenly Father, often we can not understand your ways and we fail to appreciate your plans and purposes, yet we marvel at the way that you 'do all things well'. As an old worship song said, 'we fell in love with the Nazarene, that beautiful Nazarene'. That the most precious and beautiful name of Jesus was linked with the worst town in Israel amazes us, yet we see a prophetic element in this, because Jesus was associated with us. We who were the worst became the target of the best.

KEY WORD: **Alpha and Omega**

KEY VERSE: **Revelation 22 : 13**

"I am the Alpha and the Omega, the First and the Last, the Beginning and the End."

As we conclude our studies in the more unusual names of Jesus we will close with one of the last names to be designated to Him in the New Testament. The apostle, John, when seeking to convey the vital truth that Jesus was before all things and that He concludes all things, could think of no better way than to describe Jesus as the 'Alpha and the Omega'.

In the Greek alphabet the first letter is *'alpha'* and the last letter is *'omega'*, in other words the two letters open and close the language of the New Testament. John was seeking to convey the thought that Jesus 'opens' everything and He 'closes' everything and that He is everything in-between and all in all. The Greek language is like no other language in that it is rich and pictorial and vivid in its concepts. John could think of no better way than to state that *'alpha'* with its rich under tones of 'inception' and 'initiation', is a picture of Jesus commencing all things with a mighty anthem of triumph. Then his use of the word *'omega'* with its depth of meaning as the conclusion of language and letters and its undertones of 'finality' and 'completion', is a picture of Jesus bringing all things to an end with a mighty anthem of triumph.

We have great difficulty in understanding the whole matter and concept of eternity – to think of something that 'was before all things' and then to try and understand the concept that 'things will never end' is quite beyond us. So John, under divine inspiration, put it quite clearly. Jesus is the first and the last, He is the beginning and the end and He is all things, at all times, to all people.

We have a commencement to our lives and we have a conclusion, but we are not the beginning and we are not the end. The 'beginning' was before us, and the 'end' is after us, and we will not grasp the greatness of this until we reach heaven. Until then, John had been quite helpful in describing Jesus as the 'Alpha and the Omega', it helps to put things into perspective.

My Journal

KEY PRAYER

Heavenly Father, thank you for the glorious fact that all things are in your hands and that all things have their commencement and conclusion in you. Nothing in heaven or earth was before you and nothing in heaven and earth is after you. You are the First and Last, the Alpha and Omega.

May 20th

KEY WORD: **Chance**

KEY VERSE: **Luke 10 : 31**

A priest happened to be going down the same road, and when he saw the man, he passed by on the other side.

Yesterday in our last study concerning the unusual and lesser-known names of Jesus, we considered the name that the apostle, John, gave to Him, that of Alpha and Omega. We learned that this name means the first and the last, and we also learned that Jesus is all in all and commences all things and concludes all things. This literally means that if Jesus is the beginning and the end, then everything that happens to us is governed by His will and that there is nothing to fear. If we are in His will, then nothing is left to chance.

The word that we are considering today is a very special word. In the NIV, the word that is used is the word 'happened' but in the King James Bible the word that is used for the same meaning is 'chance'. We are considering this word as it appears in Luke 10 : 31. In this chapter Jesus was recounting the story of the Good Samaritan to those who were expert in the law and who were seeking to test Him according to the law.

As He told the story He stated that a priest was on his way from Jerusalem to Jericho when he saw the man who was beaten and robbed and left for dead. Jesus said that a priest 'happened' to be passing by, the King James Bible used the words 'by chance' a priest passed by. The Greek word used here is '*sunkuria*' which translated means 'a coincidence of circumstances'. However the Greek use is quite different to the English meaning of the word coincidence. The Greek word places emphasis upon the events rather than the 'chance', in other words, in English we would say that something happened by chance, meaning that something took place outside of our control. But the Greek word, placing emphasis upon the events rather than the chance, means that there was control of the events as they transpired as God was behind all things. This meaning delivers to us the truth of God being in total control of our lives and that nothing can happen by chance. The difficulties that we often face are not by chance but by design, God knows all things and controls all things. So this means that when everything seems to go wrong, there is a design and a pattern to the difficulty that God is working out for our good.

The priest was in the right place at the right time although he responded badly to the event by passing by on the other side of the road. Jesus was showing in this story that even when events go wrong, He is in total control and that every part of His plan will be worked out fully according to His design.

Jesus is the Alpha and the Omega, the beginning and the end; this great eternal thought will bring us comfort and rest as we learn daily that He is in full control of our circumstances.

My Journal

KEY PRAYER

Heavenly Father, thank you that nothing happens by chance but that everything happens by divine design. I therefore rest in you today as you work out your plan and purpose in my life. I bless you for your goodness and I thank you for all that happens in my life, both good and bad, and I pray that I will constantly learn to trust you more.

May 21st

KEY WORD: **Foreknowledge**

KEY VERSE: **1 Peter 1 : 2**

(Those) who have been chosen according to the foreknowledge of God the Father, through the sanctifying work of the Spirit.

Today we are going to wrestle with a problem that has concerned the Church throughout the ages. Does man have a free will or does God just choose and predestine people without reference to anyone? This problem has caused much confusion and much discussion throughout the age of the Church, and Bible verses can be quoted by those who take up opposing sides of the argument quite easily. In order to understand the seemingly opposing truths of free will and predestination you have to understand the concepts of the Greek words that are used.

When Peter was seeking to teach the subject of the foreknowledge of God he used a word that appears in the key verse today. The Greek word for 'foreknowledge' is the word '*prognosis*' and it is from this word that we derive our English word for the medical term that is used when a doctor seeks to convey the future outcome of an illness or a disease.

It is this concept concerning the knowledge of the future that Peter used when he sought to convey the truth that God knows all things. The word '*prognosis*' is made up by combining two Greek words together to form one word. The first word used is '*pro*' which means 'before' and the second word used is '*ginosko*' which means 'to know'. Therefore Peter was saying that 'God knows everything before it happens'. When we grasp this truth the whole confusion of free will and predestination begins to be understood.

Man has a free will that allows him to accept or reject the message of the gospel. However, because God knows all things before they ever happen or take place, He knows who will accept Him and who will reject Him, and He therefore predestines those who come to Him. God is not willing that any should perish but He knows that many will perish and He has sought to prevent this by providing them with an escape route anyway.

God knows the act of saving faith which brings salvation, He knows the moment of the acceptance of grace and He knows the moment when many will reject Him. As He knows all things before they take place He makes provision for those who accept Him by electing them to heaven. As both sides of the argument are true and as both sides of the truth are only really eternally understood, the Bible therefore teaches both sides of these truths. In teaching these truths with emphasis upon both of the aspects we therefore fully understand that man has a will that can be exercised freely but that God knows exactly what will happen anyway.

I once heard this truth described in a very clear way. There is a doorway and over the door there is a sign that states that 'anyone can enter'. However, once you pass through the doorway, there is another sign which states 'predestined'. God knows who will pass through the doorway and according to His foreknowledge, He therefore elects them to heaven.

My Journal

KEY PRAYER

Heavenly Father, thank you for the awesome fact that you know all things. I can rest in this knowledge that behind me and before me are paths that you have already seen and have prepared a way for me. I bless you today for the fact that you have predestined me for heaven because I chose to come to you.

KEY WORD: **Fear**

KEY VERSE: **Acts 19 : 17**

When this became known to the Jews and Greeks living in Ephesus, they were all seized with fear, and the name of the Lord Jesus was held in high honour.

If we believe that we are predestined for heaven by a God who knows all things before they ever happen, as we saw yesterday, then we should be able to rest in a secure and peaceful state of blessing. There should be no fear of the future and no fear of what may happen round and about us. Yet 366 times in the Bible we are urged to 'fear not' and someone once said that is one 'fear not' for each day of the year and an extra one for each leap year.

In the New Testament there are at least ten Greek words for our English word 'fear' and because their meanings are quite varied it is important that we understand at least some of them so that we can combat any fears that might arise. Over the next few days we shall seek to understand some of them so that we might 'fear not'.

In the key verse today we find a shocking event, Paul had been preaching in Ephesus when seven sons of a priest called Sceva began to do what Paul was doing. Paul was commanding demons to leave those who were demon possessed and when these sons tried to do the same thing an evil spirit manifested itself and the outcome was indeed shocking. A man with an evil spirit jumped on one of the sons of Sceva and beat him badly leaving him naked and bleeding. When the Jews and Greeks heard this they were all filled with fear.

The Greek word for fear in this verse is the word *'phobos'* and from this word we derive our English word phobia. The normal understanding of phobia is 'a persistent dread or fear of something', however, the Greek translation of '*phobos*' is a little different to this. The meaning of this Greek word is 'that which may cause flight' and it has the connotation of fleeing from something or causing you to run away.

This word appears in the New Testament many times and it is mostly used in a negative way when it is connected to something taking place that causes fear to arise. This is what took place in Ephesus when one of the sons of Sceva was so badly beaten during a demonic manifestation. This word, when it is used in this negative way, is best understood when a kind of fearful intimidation takes place, like that of the Ephesian scenario.

The word occurs too, in a positive way when it is linked with God. For instance, the phrase 'fear of God' occurs quite often, however, this is not the dreaded fear that causes us to run, but it is a wholesome fear of displeasing Him or a fear of not doing His will. When it is used in the positive way, it is best understood when the Church was growing and being greatly blessed in Acts 9 : 31, where it states that 'it was strengthened by the Holy Spirit, it grew in numbers, living in the fear of the Lord'.

The reverential fear of God inspires a constant carefulness in dealing with spiritual matters and the things of God, as we do not want to do anything but serve Him and love Him in the right way.

My Journal ______________________________

KEY PRAYER

Heavenly Father, I thank you today for the fact that my dreaded fear of the unknown and the fear of what Satan can do, has been replaced by a godly and wholesome fear of God. I simply want to serve you and love you in the right way and I want to live my life in a godly, reverent fear. Help me to walk with you and help me to live my life in a way that pleases you at all times.

May 23rd

KEY WORD: ***Fear***

KEY VERSE: **2 Timothy 1 : 7**

For God did not give us a spirit of timidity, but a spirit of power, of love and of self-discipline.

Today we shall study another aspect of fear which is very different to the one that we considered yesterday. The fear that we are looking at today is the fear that brings a sense of fright and a sense of cowardice in the face of danger. This sense of fear is always used in a negative way within the New Testament and it is interesting that the NIV uses the translation 'timidity' whereas the Old King James version used the word 'fear'.

The Greek word used in the key word today for timidity is the word '*deilia*' which translated means 'fright' or 'fearfulness' and it is a word that is only used once in the New Testament and it was used in the most negative of ways.

Paul said to the young and inexperienced Pastor, Timothy, that God has not given us the spirit of fear or timidity, but that He has given us the spirit of power, love and self-discipline. In using the word '*deilia*' Paul was seeking to convey the fact that God has given to us the tools that are necessary to overcome the cowardice and fearfulness of terror. In other words, when we are afraid and when we fear the onslaught of something, it is not of God but its roots and origins are in our enemy. God does not cause fear nor does He use fear as a weapon, anything that causes us fear is a direct attack from the enemy of our souls.

Although this word for fear is only used once, Jesus actually used a root word associated with '*deilia*' in order to convey a similar truth. In John 14 : 27, when Jesus is talking to His disciples about the future, He sought to make them aware of the fact that once He had left them they would have another Comforter who would minister to them constantly. This Comforter would bring peace and strength to them at all times, therefore He said, 'Do not be troubled and do not be afraid'. Jesus was bringing the same concept to His disciples that Paul would later bring to Timothy, in that God ministers to us at all times and that His ministry is of such a nature that peace and safety are the outcome, not fear and timidity. Jesus knew that His disciples would have a natural fear about being left on their own so He brought this root word to them in order to convey the fact that they would never be on their own entirely. There would be no need for them to act in a cowardly manner as the comforter would come.

Fear drives us into a feeling of cowardice and retreat, God's ministry toward us always has the opposite effect, that of bringing us nearer to Him and bestowing upon us the feeling of calmness and strength.

Another associated root of this word appears at the time of the great storm when Jesus rebuked the winds and the waves and told His disciples not to fear. The early disciples, who were still very much fisherman, reeled in fear at the ferocious storm that attacked them on the lake of Galilee. They were very much afraid and the words of Jesus brought comfort and strength and turned their eyes away from the storm and unto Him.

My Journal ______________________________________

____

____

____

____

____

KEY PRAYER

Heavenly Father, as I pray today I take great comfort and strength from your words that I am not to fear because you have brought peace and stability upon me. I praise you that I do not have a spirit of cowardice but that I have a spirit of love and of power and of self-discipline. I praise you for your word to me today.

May 24th

KEY WORD: **Fear**

KEY VERSE: **Hebrews 12 : 28**

Therefore, since we are receiving a kingdom that can not be shaken, let us be thankful, and so worship God acceptably with reverence and awe.

As we are considering at present the several words in the New Testament that are translated as our English word 'fear' we need to turn to a very positive aspect of fear, that of the awesomeness of God. There are about ten Greek words for our English word 'fear' and they are all very different. Over the past few days we have seen the fear of '*phobos*' which is the fear of running away from something that causes us fright. Then we considered the fear of '*deilia*' which is the fear of cowardice and timidity; however, today, we shall consider a kind of fear that is very positive and very much 'of God'.

The writer to the Hebrews used the Greek word '*eulabeia*' which is the word that is used when a Greek person was seeking to convey the fact of reverence and godly fear. The NIV actually translates it as 'reverence,' the Old King James Bible actually uses the words 'godly fear'. This reverential fear is the fear of the awesomeness of God, it is not a fear of cowardice or timidity but a wholesome fear of the greatness and majesty of a God enthroned in purity and splendour. It is not a fear that drives us away from God but it is a fear that drives us towards Him.

In the Old Testament God was treated with a reverential fear that bordered upon caution and deep respect, He accepted worship this way and He blessed those who came before Him in such a manner. However, in the New Testament there was a dramatic change in that the awesomeness of God's presence was treated in a manner that was not so much caution but a godly sense of acceptance. We are welcomed at His throne and we can boldly come before Him because grace has been applied, and therefore, we have an acceptable entrance into His presence.

The same concept appears in Hebrews 5 : 7, when it is said of Jesus at His death that He was willing to obey God's will with 'reverent submission'.

It is not a fear of God that is placed upon us, as His children, but it is a sense of willing reverence that draws us into His presence and inspires us to serve to Him.

My Journal

KEY PRAYER

Heavenly Father, it is with great joy that I come before you today as my fear of the unknown, with its weapons of timidity and cowardice, has been replaced by a godly fear of reverence and worship. I can approach you with grace and I find help from you at my time of need.

May 25th

KEY WORD: ***Fear***

KEY VERSE: **Acts 7 : 32**

Moses trembled with fear and did not dare to look.

Today we conclude our few short studies considering the words that are used in the New Testament for 'fear'; as we have seen, they are varied and many. Most of the words that are used seem to deal with spiritual aspects that are either linked towards God or linked towards our enemy. Today our key verse deals with a very natural form of fear, that of simply being afraid.

When Jesus said, 'do not fear', He was dealing with the outcome of a spiritual fear that dominates and which causes us to shrink back from serving God. This kind of fear should be set aside as we do not live under this kind of fear any more. Yet there is still the natural fear of life and living, and it is this kind of fear that the key verse addresses today.

Luke was the author of the Acts of the Apostles and in chapter 7 he deals with Stephen's speech before the Sanhedrin. Stephen quoted from the Old Testament in his speech and he reminded those who heard him, that God was with the nation Israel from the beginning. He reminded them that God spoke to Moses at Mount Sinai and that when God appeared Moses was afraid. Luke used the Greek word '*entromos*' for the word fear, in this aspect, which literally translated means 'to quake'. This Greek word is a very interesting word, it is made up from the combination of two words, '*en*' which means 'inward' and '*tremo*' which means to 'tremble' or to 'quake. It is from the word '*tremo*' that we derive our English word 'tremor'.

The kind of fear that '*entromos*' brings to us is not a spiritual fear but a natural fear. When Moses saw the presence of God, he naturally feared the outcome of such a visitation and he trembled with fear. The same kind of fear came upon those who experienced the earthquake in Philippi, when Paul and Silas were imprisoned and when God shook the prison house that eventually brought their release. The prisoners, who saw the effects of the earthquake and who had first hand evidence of its destructive force, were afraid and they trembled at the result.

This kind of fear is not a form of sin and it is not condemned in the New Testament. This kind of fear is simply a natural kind of fear that we all have from time to time. There are no rebukes for feeling this kind of fear, however, there are verses of Scripture that speak into this situation. Jesus said that he would never leave us nor forsake us, so we know that when any natural fears arise, the presence of Jesus should be enough to carry us through each and every situation. Having said this, we should also be on our guard as our enemy will seek to use every opportunity to bring us down and bring us into bondage. If there is a natural circumstance that causes us to constantly fear, we should bring it to the Lord in order to gain victory over it, so that the enemy of our souls can not use an opportunity to gain a foothold within our lives.

My Journal

KEY PRAYER

Heavenly Father, thank you for the way that you help me to overcome my fears and my worries, thank you too, that you have promised to never leave me on my own. I praise you today for the fact that I can rest in you and that my fears can be removed as I learn to lean on you and trust you each day.

KEY WORD: **Greeting**

KEY VERSE: **Philippians 4 : 21**

Greet all the saints in Christ Jesus. The brothers who are with me send greetings.

Paul closed most of his epistles with a greeting or a form of salutation and the word that he used is a most interesting word. In the key verse today he was closing off his teaching and ministry to the church at Philippi and he stated that all the brothers that were with him send their greetings. He also stated that he wanted all the saints in Christ Jesus, who were worshipping in the Philippian Church, to be greeted also.

Paul uses the Greek word *'aspazomai'* as his word of greeting and salutation and this word literally translated means 'to greet' or 'to welcome' or even 'to salute'. The word was used by the Greeks as a technical term for the conveying of a greeting at the close of a letter. In the western world our greetings are usually given at the beginning of a letter, as we like to greet people at the commencement of our words. So our letters would normally start with 'Dear' or 'Dearest', this is our form of greeting and it is fairly bland, as we would commence writing in this form to loved ones and strangers alike.

In the eastern world however, and especially in New Testament times, the greeting came at the conclusion of the letters. The commencement of New Testament letters would normally be a kind of statement from Paul particularly concerning his apostleship. Out of the 13 epistles that were written by Paul, nine times he commences in a similar way by stating that he was 'an apostle by the will of God'.

The greeting, therefore, came at the conclusion of his letters and was a kind of technical farewell and a powerful salute to those who would hear or read his words.

'*Aspazomai*' is not just a closing form of words that conveyed a simple 'goodbye' or 'farewell' it is a powerful symbol of love and fellowship. It was received with great blessing by those who were actually mentioned by name, and its use would greatly encourage those who were named within the greeting. The continued use of this kind of greeting by Paul conveyed the full impact of just how much he loved the churches, and just how much he loved the saints of God. We see him on the beach in Ephesus in Acts 20, embracing the Elders of the church at his farewell, and the scene is one of great emotion as he literally 'dragged' himself away from them. The same concept is used in this chapter as the words 'embrace' and 'greeting' have the same root connections.

As Paul closed each epistle, his love and feeling for the churches shone through, and he sought to bless them and encourage them by greeting them in the name of the Lord. When we greet one another we should seek to raise the emotion of our greeting from the western world's more bland and formal approach, to that of the eastern greeting, with its powerful and dramatic sense of love and encouragement. We are all on the same journey and we need each other and we should love each other very much.

My Journal ______________________________

____

____

____

KEY PRAYER

Heavenly Father, thank you that you have placed me in a family during my earthly journey and that my fellow travellers are very important to me. I bless you for the fact that I have loved ones around and about me, and I pray that you will help me to appreciate them more and more, and I pray that I shall be able to encourage them every day in love.

KEY WORD: **Empty**

KEY VERSE: **Philippians 2 : 7**

But (He) made Himself nothing, taking the very nature of a servant being made in human likeness.

The words of Paul in this key verse are words that have a very powerful impact upon us. They come in the middle of a passage that sets out the amazing humiliation of Jesus in that He became a man and that He allowed Himself to become our sacrifice for sin.

The way that Paul describes the humiliation of Jesus has become a very important aspect of doctrine as it conveys the vital fact that Jesus actually became a human being. Some people teach that Jesus was not a man in the fullest sense of the word, and some even teach that He was not even God in the fullest sense. However, this Scriptural passage reveals the awesome twin facts that Jesus was God, and that He was also a man.

The truth lies in the word that was used by Paul to show the fact that Jesus 'became nothing'. The Old King James Bible uses the words that He 'emptied Himself', whereas, the NIV uses the words 'He made Himself nothing'. In this particular Scripture the Old King James version actually gets closer to the truth of Paul's teaching. Paul uses the word *'kenoo'* which translated means 'to empty out,' and the word was used deliberately to convey the thought of Jesus emptying Himself of all His reputation and of all His heavenly position in order to become a man. The word does not mean that He emptied Himself of godhood or that He emptied Himself of His divinity. Jesus was at the same time the Son of God and the Son of man.

In order to give fuller impact to this word, Paul continued the theme of emptying, by writing that Jesus took 'the very nature of a man' and that He was 'made in human likeness'. The amazing fact is that Jesus, the mighty Son of God, who was God and who is God, poured out His reputation in such a way that He took upon Himself the form of human flesh and was subject in every way to the limitations that we all suffer. Not only this, but He allowed Himself to be beaten, abused and crucified so that we might live.

How great was this humiliation and how great was His suffering. As we pray today, we can thank God that Jesus poured Himself out for us, as an offering for sin.

My Journal

KEY PRAYER

Heavenly Father, thank you for the amazing fact that Jesus became the Son of man so that I might become a son of God. Thank you for the wonderful truth that Jesus poured Himself out so that I might be brought into a relationship with you. I bless you today for the fact that I am in Christ because you sent your Son to die for me. How wonderful and how marvellous is this amazing love.

May 28th

KEY WORD: **Recent convert**

KEY VERSE: **1 Timothy 3 : 6**

He must not be a recent convert, or he may become conceited, and fall under the same judgement as the devil.

Today we shall seek to understand an important truth that is contained within the structure of Christian leadership. Paul was writing to Timothy setting out the procedures and requirements for those who would seek to lead the Church of God. There are several chapters that deal with aspects of leadership but there are none better that 1Timothy 3.

The aspect of leadership that Paul was addressing was that of eldership, in his terms he called it 'overseeing'. The requirements for an overseer are very important as this kind of ministry is very much in the public eye and therefore it is very much a ministry of example to the people of God. Paul set out in this chapter the strong guidelines for leadership ministry. In the key verse today, Paul required the leaders of the Church to be men and women of spiritual maturity, and he stated that no one should be offered the role of leadership when they have just recently been converted. Paul also gives reasons for this requirement as he stated that immature Christians leave themselves open to a form of conceit if they assume the role of leadership too early.

The Greek word that is used for the term 'recent convert' in this passage is the word *'neophutos'* which translated means 'newly planted'. It is a word that was formed by the combining of two Greek words in order to give it maximum strength. The two words are *'neos'* which means 'new' and *'phuo'* which means to 'bring forth' or to 'produce'.

The reason that Paul used these two words to convey the

truth that spiritual maturity was needed in Christian leadership was because a 'newly planted' convert did not have the strength that was needed to produce mature fruit. Only a strong fruit tree with a stable root system can produce the best quality fruit, and Paul was afraid that if immature converts were thrust into leadership too quickly they would be placed in a position of vulnerability causing them to become spiritually conceited and open to the attack of the enemy.

We often make the mistake of thrusting a new convert into ministry far too early and usually the mistake occurs in three areas. Firstly, in our desire to see God use them we promote them to use within the Church. Secondly, in our desire to see dramatic testimonies used for God's glory we seek to use them, and thirdly, it is often the good desire of recognising that God's hand might be upon them that causes us to be over zealous in our promotion of them. But as Paul stated, this kind of activity usually only abuses someone as it is far too early for them to cope with the pressure of being in the 'limelight' and being in the glare of an early opportunity of Christian service. We should all pray for wisdom and discernment as we seek to lead the Church and as we bring people into leadership ministry.

My Journal

KEY PRAYER

Heavenly Father, I praise you today for those who have been recently saved and brought into your kingdom, I pray that we shall be able to handle these new gifts wisely and carefully. I take heed today to Paul's words and I shall seek to pray for and guard those who have only recently joined the Church. Help us to care for their souls as well as our own.

May 29th

KEY WORD: **Time of peace**

KEY VERSE: **Acts 9 : 31**

Then the Church throughout Judea, Galilee and Samaria enjoyed a time of peace. It was strengthened; and encouraged by the Holy Spirit, it grew in numbers, living in the fear of the Lord.

In the last three days of this month we shall consider an aspect of the Church that we often neglect and that we often fail to appreciate. In the key verse today there are several vital components that are needed in order for the Church to prosper and be effective, and over the final days of this month we shall seek to understand them.

It was Luke who wrote the book of Acts and in this key verse he places emphasis upon the fact that the Church had entered into a time of peace. The previous chapters had recorded the fact that persecution had broken out within the Church, especially at the hands of a man called Saul, whose name would soon be changed to that of Paul. This man had brought tremendous damage to the new Church and was travelling around bringing persecution upon all who named the name of Jesus. However, in Acts 9, his conversion is recorded and his change of nature was instantly dramatic. Following his conversion, the Church entered into a 'time of peace'.

The word that is used for 'time of peace' is the Greek word '*eirene*' which translated means peace in the sense of 'concord' or 'agreement'. The Old King James Bible translates the word as 'rest' which is also quite acceptable as it conveys the thought of a period of stillness and quietness following a storm. Paul did bring a storm of persecution to the Church but, following his conversion and change of nature, the Church was blessed with a period of stillness and calm.

The word *'eirene'* also carries with it the sense of freedom and it was used when someone, who had been molested and greatly affected by something, now received a period of rest and freedom from this particular experience. The Church had been buffeted by Paul's violent and destructive outburst of persecution and had seen nothing but harm and danger for quite some time. However, now that Paul had 'joined' the Church, the period of rest and peace was being greatly enjoyed by those who had faced the danger.

Luke rejoiced in the fact that now, during this period of peace, progress was being made and that the Church was growing in numbers and that it was walking in the fear of the Lord. His use of the words 'time of peace' also speaks of a kind of period of peace. To him it felt as if an age had passed by and that now an umbrella of calmness had fallen upon the Church and that rest had come.

My Journal

KEY PRAYER

Heavenly Father, thank you for peace and calmness that we feel when we rest in you. I pray today for those in different countries who are experiencing the effects of persecution. I pray that they might experience a time of peace and I pray too, that they might know a wonderful sense of your presence at this time.

May 30th

KEY WORD: **Strengthened**

KEY VERSE: **Acts 9 : 31**

Then the Church throughout Judea, Galilee and Samaria enjoyed a time of peace. It was strengthened; and encouraged by the Holy Spirit, it grew in numbers, living in the fear of the Lord.

Yesterday we saw that the Church received a time of peace from persecution, and that during this time it grew in numbers and in spiritual blessing and had a sense of rapid and accelerating development. Luke also recorded the fact that the Church was strengthened and encouraged by the Holy Spirit during this phase of its development.

The word 'strengthened' that is used here is the Greek word '*oikodomeo*'. This word means 'to build a house' and it was the word that was used when someone was literally seeking to become a builder of a building. The NIV translates the word as 'strengthened' and because of this we miss the point of Luke's understanding concerning this period of Church history. The Old King James Bible uses the word 'edified' in this verse and sadly the use of this word 'edified' still does not fully convey the truth of Luke's use of the Greek word, '*oikodomeo*'.

What Luke was seeking to convey was that, following Paul's conversion and the cessation of persecution, the Church did not just have a time of peace in the sense of stillness and quietness but that a strengthening was taking place in that the building of the Church was taking a giant step forward. What was taking place at this time was the amazing acceleration of spiritual and physical growth within a church that had seen nothing but trouble and affliction for several years. Now, following Paul's conversion and the time of peace, the building of the Church was undertaken without hindrance.

The Greek word used here usually has the thought not just of building but also of the progress of the building. It is not just the fact that a building is in the process of being built but that rapid and effective progress is being seen in its development and growth. God was blessing His Church throughout the world and the Church was being treated to such a wonderful time of peace that the progress of this Church was rapid and strategic.

My Journal ______________________________

KEY PRAYER

Heavenly Father, thank you for your Church and thank you for its progress within the world. I pray today that in countries where there is persecution that you would give your Church a time of peace so that it might prosper. I pray too, that the Church might prosper and grow throughout the world so that many might come to know you as Lord and Saviour. Strengthen your Church today I pray.

May 31st

KEY WORD: **Grew in numbers**

KEY VERSE: **Acts 9 : 31**

Then the Church throughout Judea, Galilee and Samaria enjoyed a time of peace. It was strengthened; and encouraged by the Holy Spirit, it grew in numbers, living in the fear of the Lord.

As we have seen over the past few days the Church, in Acts 9, was undergoing a period of peace and rest from persecution, and during this time of peace the Church was being strengthened by the Holy Spirit. The strengthening took the form of rapid growth and development and this was seen in the way that the Church was being constructed.

Luke placed quite an emphasis upon the fact that the Church was growing numerically at this time, which is an interesting fact that we often miss. In an effort to be seen as not dwelling too much on numbers, we tend to talk about growth as being firstly, and most importantly, spiritual; and then, secondly, as being physical, as if dwelling upon numbers reveals a certain amount of pride. We also feel today that, if we talk about numbers, people will think that we are unspiritual and only concerned about statistics. However, Luke places great emphasis upon the fact that, during this time of peace and during the strengthening of the Church, numbers were important and they were noticed. We only have to understand the Greek word that was used here to see just how important numbers were to the Early Church.

The Greek word that is used in this key verse for 'growing in numbers' is the word *'plethuno'* which translated means 'caused to increase' and it can also mean 'multiply'. Because it can mean 'to multiply', the Old King James version actually uses the word 'multiply,' however, the NIV uses the phrase 'grew in numbers'. The word *'plethuno'* places great emphasis upon the increase of the numbers rather than simply on the fact that something is actually growing, which is why the King James Version uses the word 'multiply'. The use of the word 'multiply' actually informs us that the Church was increasing at a staggering rate, it was not just growing in numbers, it was a rapid and accelerating growth rate.

Unlike us today, the Acts of the Apostles places great store upon the fact that that the Church had a growth rate that could not be effectively measured. In Acts 2, at the day of Pentecost visitation, following Peter's message, it recorded the fact that 3,000 people were added to the Church. In Acts 4, following another message preached by Peter, it recorded that 5,000 'men' were now within the Church. By Acts 9, we are being told that, daily, the Church was growing and that, daily, believers were being added to this rapidly growing and developing Church.

The increase was not just growth but a sense of multiplication that was hard to keep track of and very difficult to keep in the sense of clear records. The word *'plethuno'* is the root word from which we derive our English word 'plethora' which means superabundance or a state of excessive fullness. Without wishing to be seen as unspiritual or dwelling only upon statistics, we ought to pray today that God would give us in the western world a plethora of growth as well as a mighty sense of His presence and fullness in the Spirit.

My Journal ____

____

____

____

KEY PRAYER

Heavenly Father, as we come to the end of another month, we seek your face for a mighty sense of growth within the western church. We long for multiplication and rapid growth, so we pray today that you would give to us the sense of a New Testament plethora that your Church might be strong and greatly blessed.

June 1st

KEY WORD: **Vision**

KEY VERSE: **Acts 9 : 10**

In Damascus there was a disciple named Ananias. The Lord called to him in a vision, "Ananias!"

On this first day of a brand new month we will commence our studies in New Testament words by looking at one of the most important words that you will ever find in the whole of the Bible, the word 'vision'.

Every church needs and longs for a vision of God in order to find direction and guidance for its programme and ministry. We are told that God often speaks through visions and dreams, therefore, we all need to seek God regularly for a vision so that we might know what God wants us to do. Vision and visions dominate the New Testament and the ministry of the apostles and prophets and the Early Church, and through them all, to the people within the churches. We all long that God might speak through the medium of a vision.

The Greek word that is used for the word 'vision' is the word '*horama*', which means 'that which is seen' and it generally denotes two particular things that bring to us the thought and concept of a vision.

Firstly, the word means a 'spectacle that is seen' and the word appears in this form when a major 'happening' takes place such as what took place on the mount of transfiguration. Peter, James and John saw the amazing sight of Moses and Elijah, standing with a transfigured Jesus. Jesus actually said in Matthew 17 : 9, concerning this event, 'tell no one what you have seen'. It was the seeing of spectacle that Jesus said they were not to talk about. The word used for 'seen' was '*horama*' and it was used in the context of an amazing sight that blessed those that saw it, and yet at the same time caused them to fall to the ground with great terror.

Secondly, the word is used when a kind of dream-like state is granted to someone who, although definitely not asleep, sees within this state a vision or a pictorial understanding that is beyond their comprehension. The word appears in this form within the key verse today, when Ananias was called by the Lord to minister to the newly-saved Saul, who would later become Paul. Ananias was praying and within his prayer time a state of spiritual understanding fell upon him in such a way that he understood that he was to minister to Saul. Several visions came in this way within the New Testament, and although they were not strikingly spectacular events they were still classified as *'horama'* as they were beyond the realm of the natural.

Although much emphasis is given to visions and spiritual pictures, it is interesting to note that this word *'horama'* only appears eleven times in this form within the entire New Testament. It was a word that was used sparingly within the Early Church for what was an amazing activity. May God grant to us some amazing activities within this realm, as we need to know what He wants us to do.

My Journal ______________________________

____

____

____

____

____

KEY PRAYER

Heavenly Father, as I commence a new month I do so with the desire to be used of you greatly. I seek your face and I ask that I might find more and more supernatural events taking place around me. It says in your Word, that young men shall see visions and that old men shall dream dreams, and I therefore ask that within my life you would move in supernatural ways.

June 2nd

KEY WORD: **Dream**

KEY VERSE: **Matthew 2 : 13**

When they had gone, an angel of the Lord appeared to Joseph in a dream.

Having considered the word 'vision' in yesterday's study, it would only be natural to continue with another word that is closely associated with the concept of visions, that of 'dreams'. Within the New Testament there are several occasions when God chose to use the night-time activity of sleep to speak to people through the medium of a dream.. A study of this activity is very interesting as it shows the difference quite clearly between a dream and vision.

A vision only happens when someone is awake and is conscious of what is taking place around them. The Greek word used for dream is the word '*onar*' and it is only used when the subject concerned is fully asleep. This dream like impartation of knowledge and guidance, is only granted when sleep has come, unlike a vision, which is imparted when someone is fully awake.

At the birth of Jesus there seems to be a 'flurry' of spiritual dreams granted to various people, particularly Joseph. It seems that Joseph probably had at least four different dreams bringing to him guidance and revelation about the situation surrounding Jesus and His immediate future.

Why God should use visions in some cases and dreams in others is not really understood, and there are certainly no answers within the New Testament. Although it could have something to do with those who were the recipients of the dreams and visions. Some people could be more susceptible to receiving a vision, their spiritual awareness could be tuned to a greater sensitivity than others, which gives them a greater capacity for receiving things from God in this area. Others, maybe, are more tuned-in towards God when they are asleep; it could be that when they are awake they are so busy doing things or so active in their lifestyle that God can not break into their world. However, when they are asleep God is more able to minister to them within this realm.

Whatever God's purposes are within dreams and visions, it is vital that we are prepared to receive and prepared to see what God wants us to see, so that He might speak to us whenever and wherever He wants to.

My Journal

KEY PRAYER

Heavenly Father, I pray today that I might develop more of an awareness of your presence so that, whenever you want my attention, I am ready to receive. I pray that my awareness of you might undergo a dramatic transformation so that I might learn how to receive from you anything that you might to want to give me, whether it is in the night or in the day.

KEY WORD: **Voice**

KEY VERSE: **Matthew 3 : 17**

And a voice from heaven said, "This is my Son, whom I love; with Him I am well pleased."

Having studied together over the past two days the thoughts concerning dreams and visions, it naturally brings us to a place where we have to consider the whole concept of God speaking to us. God is always speaking to us, He is always longing to speak to His Church, and He is always seeking ways to share things with us. Sometimes He speaks in the most natural of ways through circumstances, and He can, of course, speak to us through the gifts of the Spirit. He can also speak through the preaching of His Word and through divine revelation in the outcome of the ministry of others.

However, in spite of these wonderful ways of communication, the fact is that He can still speak to us directly through the inner still voice of our spirit, and through the audible voice of communication from heaven. The Greek word used for God's voice in the New Testament is a powerful word and a very interesting word. The word used is *'phone'* which is of course a very well known word as it has found its way into most languages in the world today, and it still means what it meant to the Greeks. The word means 'the sound that is made with the voice', and our use links it with 'telephone' and 'phonograph' among many. However, this word *'phone'* does not just mean the human voice making sounds, its main use above all other uses in the New Testament, was the use associated with God speaking.

When God spoke to the world at the baptism of Jesus in Jordan's river in our key verse today, it was dramatically *'phone'*, God directly and audibly speaking to all mankind. The word had an edge that was far more than just a voice speaking, although the Scripture does use the same word for an ordinary man speaking with an ordinary voice, however, the 'edge' of the word is far more applicable to divine use than human use.

God still speaks both silently and audibly to man and His voice is still heard today amongst His people. Yet this word directly means that God is speaking, and that Jesus is speaking. It was used when a voice came from heaven and when Jesus spoke from the cross. The word was a special word that meant divine communication was in action, and the New Testament is filled with such instances of blessing.

Church history is also full of times when God clearly spoke to His Church and to His people, and we need to constantly remember that God stills wants to communicate to us today. We often feel that the New Testament is long ago and far away, and that God dealt differently with His Church then, than He does today. However, it must be remembered that God has not changed. We might be more sophisticated today than in New Testament times, and we might be more organised and structured, but we still need God's voice and He still requires us to listen, because God still wants to speak to us. We, therefore, should pray that prophecy, and words of knowledge and words of wisdom might still flow among us. We should also pray that dreams and visions might be seen and that the voice of God might be heard.

My Journal

KEY PRAYER

Heavenly Father, I pray today for more of the supernatural to be revealed within your Church. I long to see dreams and visions and I long to hear your voice. Please help me to be ever sensitive to your voice and help me to retain a greater degree of sensitivity at all times within my prayer times and my worship life.

KEY WORD: **Extraordinary**

KEY VERSE: **Acts 19 : 11-12**

God did extraordinary miracles through Paul, so that even handkerchiefs and aprons that had touched him were taken to the sick, and their illnesses were cured and the evil spirits left them.

The New Testament as we know, is full of acts of power and acts of miracles. These supernatural events were associated with, firstly, the ministry of Jesus and then, secondly, the ministry of the early Church. Signs and wonders dominate the whole of the New Testament pages and in the Acts of the Apostles especially, the miracles are most amazing.

We have studied together over the past few days the whole concept of God speaking supernaturally through dreams and visions. We now naturally turn to the next phase of the supernatural, that of miracles. There are several words in the New Testament that are used for the English word 'miracle' and over the next few days we shall seek to understand them. However, we shall commence with a most startling word that is translated in different ways within different Bible versions.

In the key verse today it states that God did extraordinary miracles through Paul. These 'happenings' were not just miracles but extraordinary happenings that could not be explained by just using the word 'miracle', these were a different kind of divine activity. The Greek word used in this verse is the word '*tunchanos*' and it is translated in different ways. For instance, in the King James Bible the word is translated as 'special', and in the NIV it is translated as 'extraordinary'. Other versions also use different words like 'unusual' to describe these 'happenings'. The word '*tunchanos*' actually means in the Greek 'not common or ordinary', and it was a word that was associated with a strange happening that had no natural or logical explanation.

So we have here a very interesting scenario within the Church, it seems that miracles were accepted as a kind of 'ordinary' event within the life of the Church. These 'ordinary' miracles were accepted as part of the Church's natural ministry and they caused no special excitement and no special demonstration. They were regarded as the most natural of situations within a powerful and God-glorifying church. However, at times it seems that there were things that happened that were very different indeed. These events carried with them a different degree of understanding and a different word was used to convey the 'specialness' of them. The word '*tunchanos*' is only used on two occasions in the New Testament, and both appearances are in the Acts of the Apostles. Firstly, it appears in the key verse today, when God moved in Ephesus in a very different and striking manner, and it also appears, secondly, in chapter 28 verse 2, when Paul was shipwrecked on the island of Malta, where it states that the islanders showed 'unusual' kindness.

In the first instance, in Ephesus, God did very strange and extraordinary things. The miracles were of such a nature that they were special even in New Testament terms. In the second instance, on Malta, the kindness that was shown went further than natural hospitality and further than Paul had ever seen expressed before. So the use of this word seems to demonstrate that there are times when even the word 'miracle' can not fully convey just what is happening when the wonder and glory of God can be seen. We need this kind of supernatural visitation again today.

KEY PRAYER

Heavenly Father, I seek your face today for another visitation of your power and glory within the church. I long to see special things happening, and I long for an extraordinary display of your power. Help me to be ready for use at any time so that you might use me for your purposes.

KEY WORD: **Miracle**

KEY VERSE: **Acts 8 : 13**

Simon himself believed and was baptised. And he followed Philip everywhere, astonished by the great signs and miracles he saw.

In our study yesterday, I made the comment that it seemed that miracles were the most natural of events within the New Testament Church. It seems that miracles were the daily outcome of God moving by His power within the Church and within the world.

In the key verse today, Philip the evangelist is ministering in Samaria and a well known sorcerer called Simon was greatly affected by what he saw going on in and around Philip's ministry. What was taking place was the usual outcome of New Testament ministry in that signs and wonders, and miracles of power were being seen.

In the New Testament there are two words that are used for the English word 'miracle' and they are both used in this key verse. We shall consider one of them today and the second one tomorrow. The main word that is used for the word 'miracle' is the Greek word '*dunamis*', from this word we derive our English word 'dynamite'. The meaning of this Greek word is quite simple. It means 'power' and it is always associated with the works of a supernatural origin. In other words, whenever God moved in a sovereign way to perform healings and deliverances, the word 'power' was attached to these events.

This word was attached to these miracle events because, to the believers and to the watching world, there was no other explanation. Miracles were not natural events, although the New Testament Church came to accept them as the most 'natural' of all events. These miracles were beyond the natural agents and origins and they always produced a sense of God, and they brought people to the place where their minds and senses were challenged to accept the gospel message. Miracles were never acts within themselves. They always confirmed what was being preached, and they always brought people to Jesus. True miracles never brought glory to those who performed them.

My Journal

KEY PRAYER

Heavenly Father, as we have been considering miracles of power, a great longing has been created in my spirit for more of your mighty power. I seek you today and offer my life as an instrument for your use. Please use me so that I might glorify your name.

June 6th

KEY WORD: **Sign**

KEY VERSE: **Acts 8 : 13**

Simon himself believed and was baptised. And he followed Philip everywhere, astonished by the great signs and miracles he saw.

Within this key verse there are two words that are used to describe the outworking of what we call miracles. They are often translated differently into English because our language is not as rich as the Greek language, and we have difficulty at times in translating correctly. The NIV quite rightly uses the word 'miracle' when it translates *'dunamis'* but it gets the next word slightly wrong. Luke wrote the book of Acts, and he was seeking to convey that there was more than just miracles taking place in Samaria under the hand of Philip.

In the key verse the English word 'signs' also appears because there was no other word to describe just what was taking place. *'Dunamis'*, which means 'power', was happening, but so also was *'semeion'*; this word also means miracle but a miracle of a different kind. *'Semeion'* means 'a token giving a sign'. However, the NIV places emphasis upon the sign when really the word *'semeion'* means a powerful miraculous token or sign. The word is used in different ways within the differing Bible versions – sometimes it appears as 'miracle' and at times it appears as the word 'sign'. Another version translates it as 'wonders.' However it is used, the word conveys something that is a little different from just a 'miracle'.

The object of a sign is to point to something or to show the direction of something, like a sign post!

What Luke was seeking to convey was the fact that Philip was instrumental in producing miracles in Samaria that greatly affected those who were watching, and that these miracles were also miraculous signs that brought glory and praise unto the Lord. These signs and wonders also brought direction to the New Testament Church and its ministry in that the signs pointed people not to the evangelist, but they pointed people in the direction of Jesus Himself.

It is vital today that we understand this as we seek for more of God's power. It is not power for the sake of power, but it is power so that God will receive all the glory, and that Jesus will be seen as the only true way and means of salvation.

My Journal

KEY PRAYER

Heavenly Father, I do seek you today for more power and more authority. This has been the theme of my prayers over the past few days. Yet Lord, I seek this power so that you might receive glory, and that people will know that Jesus is the way, the truth, and the life.

June 7th

KEY WORD: **Baptism**

KEY VERSE: **Acts 8 : 13**

Simon himself believed and was baptised. And he followed Philip everywhere, astonished by the great signs and miracles he saw.

As we conclude our studies in this key verse concerning miracles and signs, it is important that we consider one last matter. The outcome of the signs and wonders and the miracles of Philip was that Simon the sorcerer believed and was baptised. Whether he was actually born again is open to question as he was rebuked by Peter a little later on in the same chapter, when he sought the anointing of God through the offering of money. However, the Scripture clearly states that he believed and that he was subsequently baptised.

The general word for baptism in the New Testament is the Greek word *'baptisma'* which means 'the process of immersion or submersion,' and it was attached to all the acts of baptism, including the baptism of John the Baptist and the normal acts of Christian baptism in the Acts of the Apostles. However, in this key verse today, another Greek word is used to describe the baptism of Simon, it is the Greek word *'baptizo.'* This Greek word is a kin word of *'baptisma'* which describes the act of baptism, but *'baptizo'* actually describes the process and form of baptism.

There is much discussion in church life concerning baptism and it ranges from 'how' you actually baptise, to 'who' actually gets baptised. Some churches will baptise very young children, even babies, and some churches will only use 'adult baptism'. Some churches sprinkle water and call it baptism whereas other churches will only immerse people for their act of baptism. However, in this verse the Greek word is quite clear, *'baptizo'* can only mean 'to dip'. The word was used by the Greeks to describe the process of the dyeing of a garment. The garment in question would be dipped into the dyeing solution in order that it might change colour. Water was not sprinkled onto the garment because that would not complete the process of changing one colour to another. The garment had to be immersed into the coloured water in order for the process to be complete

Simon was therefore completely immersed in water in order for his baptism to be complete. Baptism was a sign that someone had repented of their sins and had commenced a new life in Jesus. Water baptism was an outward sign of the inner cleansing, and it was used by the New Testament Church as a clear public witness that believers had turned away from sin to follow the Lord. If you have not yet been baptised in water, there is no better time than now!

My Journal ____________________________________

KEY PRAYER

Heavenly Father, I thank you today for truth and for the fact that I can find truth within your Word. I praise you for the day that I received the Lord as my Saviour, and I praise you for the day of my baptism. Thank you for new life, and for the clear testimony that was given when I was baptised in water.

June 8th

KEY WORD: ***Effort***

KEY VERSE: **Ephesians 4 : 3**

Make every effort to keep the unity of the Spirit through the bond of peace.

We commence today a series of studies within this key verse, and if we take one word each day, it will cover almost a week.

The first word to consider within this text is the word 'effort,' and, as we shall see, this word is an extremely interesting word indeed. The English word 'effort' conveys a sense of 'task' and even a sense of urgency, which is of course quite right. However, the Greek word is even stronger and far more urgent than the English word suggests. The Greek word used here is the word '*spoudazo*' which translated means to 'make haste' and it can even mean 'to be zealous'. If we thought that the English word 'effort' was an urgent kind of word, then how much more urgent is the Greek word.

The word was used when diligence was required in any field of activity, and it has its roots in the concept of exertion for a major task. A task that required you to give more than just a simple courtesy of attention. The word appears several times within the New Testament and was used by several writers when they wanted to convey the thought of hard effort and extreme exertion. The King James Bible translates the word as 'endeavour' and other versions have kin words such as 'giving diligence' and 'desire'.

When Paul was writing to the church at Ephesus he was seeking to convey the fact that the believers in Ephesus should work hard and give great diligence to the concept of working for each other. He insisted that this work for each other should have the outcome of maintaining the spirit of unity. He was well aware of the fact that unity is easily lost and hard to maintain, so his insistence comes shining through as he used the word that speaks of hard work and great diligence.

In Church life today as in the Early Church, unity is still easily lost and hard to maintain. If we neglect to work hard at maintaining unity we shall find that division and strife will quickly abound. As the Ephesian church was urged to work hard, we too should learn the lesson of hard work and great effort in maintaining unity, and we should also learn the lesson of being diligent in service to one another.

My Journal

KEY PRAYER

Heavenly Father, as I pray today I take heed of your words through Paul, that I should work hard at maintaining the unity of the spirit. Please forgive me when I have allowed division to rise and not sought to do anything about it. I seek your help in maintaining at all times the bond of peace.

June 9th

KEY WORD: **Keep**

KEY VERSE: **Ephesians 4 : 3**

Make every effort to keep the unity of the Spirit through the bond of peace.

As we saw yesterday, hard work is required in keeping the spirit of unity within the Church. The word that Paul used was the word that spoke of diligence and effort. Paul also went on in this key verse to speak of the duty of maintaining and 'keeping' this unity of the Spirit.

Paul had in mind a very interesting concept when he used the Greek word '*tereo*'. This word is translated as 'keep' within this key verse today, but a better and far more correct translation is 'to watch over' or 'to preserve'. The word was used in the context of a watchman who presided over a tower or a house in order to keep guard. We have this concept in our English understanding when we speak of a tower in a castle where people could be safely placed during a battle. We call this safe place a 'keep'. This concept of safety and preservation is the same as the Greek word '*tereo*'.

In Paul's mind was the sense of preservation concerning the spirit of unity. Not only was hard work involved but there was also the concept of preserving something that was very special.

It is also interesting to note that Paul said that we are to 'keep' the unity of the Spirit. He did not say that we should 'bring' the spirit of unity and nor did he say that we were to 'find' the spirit of unity. The vital message that Paul was conveying was that we already have this unity, it is already within the body. Our job is not to find it or even seek it, but to seek to 'keep' it at all costs. The preservation of unity and peace is the most vital thing that the Church is involved in apart from the reaching out to a lost world. Within the Church, unity is vital and we must make every effort to keep it. This requires hard work and effort and it also requires us to preserve this Spirit at all costs because it was bequeathed to us at an even greater cost, even Calvary itself.

My Journal

KEY PRAYER

Heavenly Father, I bless you today for the spirit of unity that you have given to the Church by your sacrifice of Jesus on the cross. I pledge today that I shall seek to maintain this unity at all costs and that I shall seek to preserve this great gift.

June 10th

KEY WORD: **Unity**

KEY VERSE: **Ephesians 4 : 3**

Make every effort to keep the unity of the Spirit through the bond of peace.

Over the past two days we have studied the concept of preserving and maintaining the unity of the Spirit, and we have seen that this requires great effort and diligence on our part. But what are we seeking to maintain?

In the key verse today Paul stated that 'unity' is what we are striving to maintain and that it is this aspect of unity that is easily lost when our efforts begin to grow weak. The Greek word used for 'unity' is the word *'henotes'* which means 'to be at one'. The interesting fact however, is that this vital word is only used twice within the New Testament and both uses are within this same chapter. As I have mentioned before, there are times when God hides vital truth in just a few references or just a few mentions of a word. It is as if He is using certain words very sparingly so that we have to search for truth and then take notice. The word *'henotes'* appears also in verse 13 of the same chapter, when Paul is speaking of the fact that we are all seeking to come to unity of the faith. This is our goal: that we become mature and strong in God and that we all arrive at a place of unity.

That this vital subject is only mentioned twice in the whole of the New Testament is quite amazing because unity dominates our thinking and we struggle at times to maintain it. Jesus prayed, in John 17, that the church 'might be one', but the actual word 'unity' and the concept that Paul brought within this key verse is only found twice. *'Henotes'* literally means to be at one with each other, and we only have to take a brief look and a simple review of Church history to realise just how many times the

Church has lost the unity of the Spirit and has descended into strife and division.

God has hidden a vital truth within just two verses, however, now that we have discovered this urgent and vital truth, it is up to us to make every effort to maintain it and promote it at all costs.

To be at one with each other is one of the greatest assets that a church can have and it is one of its greatest gifts.

My Journal

KEY PRAYER

Heavenly Father, I bless you today for truth and I thank you for the truth of unity. Now that I have discovered its blessing I pledge today, once again, that I will seek to uphold the truth and promote its blessing within my church and within my life at all times.

June 11th

KEY WORD: **Spirit**

KEY VERSE: **Ephesians 4 : 3**

Make every effort to keep the unity of the Spirit through the bond of peace.

Paul urges us to maintain at all costs the unity of the Spirit and we have learned together that this requires great effort and diligence to maintain. We have also discovered that when we maintain unity, the Church is greatly blessed and is much stronger and far more effective than when it is plunged into division and strife.

What we are urged to maintain, however, is the unity of the Spirit, not merely a sense of unity or even the concept of being one with each other. We are charged to keep the unity of the Spirit. Paul uses the Greek word *'pneuma'* which is the usual word used in the New Testament for the word 'Spirit'. *'Pneuma'* means literally 'the wind' and it was used whenever the writers wanted to convey the concept of 'breath' and 'breeze', and even 'wind' and 'blowing'.

In using this word within the key verse, Paul is stating the fact that the Church has the spirit of unity and that this spirit is the wind of God that has been breathed upon the Church. The same word is used for the ministry and the dynamic of the Holy Spirit. So, the use of this word is vital in Paul's thinking. He is literally saying that God, by His Spirit, has breathed upon the Church in such a way that He has given and bequeathed His peace to us as a gift. It is therefore now up to us to maintain this gift and preserve this treasure because it is God's Spirit that is in question.

We have all been in meetings where something occurred that 'cut' across the atmosphere and something was lost within the meeting. The Holy Spirit of God was grieved by an action or by an act of fleshly conduct that hindered God from doing what He wanted to do, and He withdrew at that moment. The New Testament states that in one certain place Jesus could do no mighty works because of the lack of faith. It is very easy to hinder God's progress and to grieve the Holy Spirit. Sadly, some churches do it all the time!

What Paul sought was a Church that welcomes the '*pneuma*' of God in such a way that it places safeguards upon all practices. A Church that works hard to keep the unity, so that the wind of God is able to move and breathe at any time that He wants to, is a Church that is alive. This is why unity is so vital and this is why we must preserve the truth of being one with each other.

My Journal ____

KEY PRAYER

Heavenly Father, I need your wind to blow over my soul at all times. I need to know your breath upon me and I long for more of your Spirit. Please help me each and every day to preserve the concept of the unity of your Spirit, and help me to learn when and how to work for the unity of the Spirit.

June 12th

KEY WORD: **Bond**

KEY VERSE: **Ephesians 4 : 3**

Make every effort to keep the unity of the Spirit through the bond of peace.

As we have seen, the Church is required to work hard at maintaining the unity of the Spirit. The Church does not have to seek the unity of the Spirit that is already bequeathed, but has been charged to keep it at all costs.

We have also seen that the unity that we have been charged to keep is the unity of the Spirit, not just a sense of being one with each other, but a sense of Spirit-led unity. This unity, said Paul, was to be maintained through the bond of peace. It was as if Paul was saying that we shall only be able to maintain unity with each other through the aspect of spiritual bondage with each other. At this point within the key verse he described a very important aspect of truth by introducing a brand new word.

The English word 'bond' brings with it a sense of binding or constraint, but the Greek word used by Paul goes even further. He used the word '*sundemos*' which is a word that is made up by combining two words. The two words used are '*sun*' which means 'with' and '*demos*' which means 'to bind'. '*Demos*' was the word that was used when a prisoner was taken into captivity, and was bound with strong cords in order to prevent his escape. Paul brought this concept into play when he chose this particular word to convey just how this concept of maintaining unity could be achieved.

What Paul was actually stating was that the Church is required to keep the unity of the Spirit by allowing the strong bands and cords of peace to be tied around us. We are all 'tied' to each other within the Church. The Church is not a club nor is it a group of people that have no reference to one another, save that we worship together now and then. It is far more relational than that. We are actually bound to each other with strong cords that restrict our freedom to operate alone. We are one. That was the concept that Jesus was praying in John 17. We are bound to each other in such a way that peace is the outcome of our bondage.

When we understand this we rise into a new understanding of what we are actually involved in. This Church is a Church of 'love bondage' and the outworking of this is peace and the unity of the Spirit. I need you and you need me, and together we really make things happen. Our enemy knows this and seeks to untie the bonds at every opportunity, which is why Paul brought his challenge of maintaining the unity of the Spirit at all costs.

My Journal

KEY PRAYER

Heavenly Father, I understand today just why Paul brought his challenge of keeping the unity of the Spirit and I pledge again today to work hard at this venture. Thank you for the cords that bind me to everyone else within the Church. Thank you for saints within the Church that I have not even met as yet. I am one with them even though I do not know them. Thank you for this great Church.

June 13th

KEY WORD: **Peace**

KEY VERSE: **Ephesians 4 : 3**

Make every effort to keep the unity of the Spirit through the bond of peace.

Several months ago – in March, actually – we studied together the concept of peace. We saw then that peace was a deep and meaningful aspect of harmony. As one church notice board once stated: 'Peace is not the absence of war, but the presence of God.'

In this final word within this key verse, Paul was seeking to convey that the bond of peace was vital if the Church was going to keep the unity of the Spirit. As we read yesterday, the Church is bound together by strong cords that unite us at all times, and these are cords of peace and love.

Paul used the usual word for peace which is the Greek word '*eirene*', meaning 'harmony' and 'wholeness' and 'concord'. In using this usual word for peace, Paul was bringing to the Ephesian church the thought that keeping the unity of the Spirit would only be achieved by understanding that the church was bound together by strong cords, and that these cords produce a sense of harmony with one another. It is no wonder then, that the enemy of our souls would seek to disrupt this harmony by planting seeds of division and discord. His overwhelming passion is the disruption of the Church, and the breaking down of the concord and harmony that we have been bequeathed by the God of peace. This is the very reason why Paul urged the church to work hard at the maintenance of the unity of the Spirit.

We see something of Paul's heart within this key verse because his desire was for the prayer of Jesus, in John 17, to be fulfilled in every local church. His heart beat with a passion for unity and harmony and his words to the Ephesian church need to be read over and over again, so that the full truth might be revealed to us.

For the past week we have spent our time considering this verse. My prayer is that it might fill our minds for the rest of this year, so that unity becomes our very life and that the local church might prosper.

My Journal ______________________________

KEY PRAYER

Heavenly Father, at the end of this week of studies I praise you once again for the Church that you have brought me into. I thank you for everyone within my local church and I pray for them all, that you would bring them into the full understanding of peace and unity. I bless you for these truths and I will seek to work for the good of my church at all times.

June 14th

KEY WORD: **Worship**

KEY VERSE: **John 4 : 24**

"God is spirit, and His worshippers must worship in spirit and in truth."

Those of us who have been in the Church for years will have noticed that styles of worship have undergone a major change within the last ten to fifteen years. Those of us too, who have been around for many years within church life, will also know that patterns and styles of worship undergo changes in each and every generation. Church history reveals that worship patterns are part and parcel of the changing and developing aspect of the Church.

However, it is interesting that within the changing and developing patterns of worship that have taken place within each generation, there is no real difference in what happens in the church service at any time or even in any place. What we call our 'worship time' may differ, with its different kinds of songs, but most changes only reflect a differing mode of worship. Some churches confine themselves to structured hymns and the worship hardly changes from year to year. Other churches have removed the hymn book altogether and sing only praise songs. There are other churches that stand to sing all their songs – often for quite a long period of time – while others sit for lengthy periods of structured singing or periods of silence.

Some churches seek to combine new songs and old songs and new structures and old structures. However, within all the changes it is very hard to produce anything that is absolutely new as there is nothing new under the sun. All the changes that take place from generation to generation only reflect new styles. The church has often simply changed from one style to another and from one mode of music to another. And yet the worship service has been kept to the same length of time with a similar structure year after year. But we should not be thinking about what we like to do, or even what our style preferences might be. We should be asking ourselves: What does God require?

In today's key verse John wrote that God seeks those who will worship Him 'in Spirit and in truth'. John used a very lovely word when he sought to convey God's requirement for 'worship' in Spirit and truth. He used the Greek word '*proskuneo*' which means 'to do reverence'. This word was formed from a combination of two Greek words. The words are '*pros*', meaning 'towards' and '*kuneo*', which means 'to kiss'. The truth that John was conveying was that our worship should be like someone who turns towards God and seeks to embrace Him with a kiss. Whether we use new songs or old songs, new styles or old styles is not important. We should ask ourselves: Do we kiss God each time we turn to Him?

Tomorrow we will look at just how we should kiss God.

My Journal

KEY PRAYER

Heavenly Father, thank you that you have brought me into a Church that enjoys worshipping you. Thank you too, that each time I come before you I have the unique opportunity to embrace you with my songs and with my singing. Help me to do this in each and every song that I sing, whether the songs are old or new.

June 15th

KEY WORD: **Worship**

KEY VERSE: **John 4 : 24**

"God is spirit, and His worshippers must worship in spirit and in truth."

Over the past few years, church life has seen an increased emphasis on what we have come to know as 'worship leaders'. This emphasis upon the worship leader is one of the newest forms of change seen in the Church for many generations. We have always had song leaders or service leaders, and we have always had song services and worship services led by someone. These people were called 'choirmasters' or the 'leader of the meeting'. However, in recent years the 'worship leader' has acquired a ministry all of its own.

As with all ministries, there are good worship leaders and there are bad worship leaders. There are those who bring the congregation into the presence of God with great ease and a sense of awesomeness, and there are those who only draw attention to themselves. For these people the leadership of a song service is only a means to an end. This 'end' is usually the fulfilment of themselves.

There were worship leaders in both Old Testament and New Testament times. These people were called minstrels. In Old Testament times they were the leaders of songs and singing. In King David's time they were vital to the flowing of worship within the life of the children of Israel. These song leaders and worship leaders were normally found to be from the Tribe of Levi. In New Testament times worship leaders were also important to the life of the temple worship and temple songs.

In many versions of the Bible we find musicians or minstrels mentioned, and the Greek word used is normally '*mousikos*'. It is not difficult to see that we derive our English word 'music' from this Greek word. Normally this word was used when someone was playing an instrument or bringing music to accompany singers, and it was only given to those who were 'devoted to music' or to those who were 'skilled in music'.

In Church life today we need those who will lead songs or lead worship, but also we need those who are skilled at bringing a congregation into God's presence. Worship leaders who lift a congregation into new dimensions of praise are those who will please God, because He seeks those who will worship Him in Spirit and truth.

My Journal ____

KEY PRAYER

Heavenly Father, I pray for all those who lead worship within the Church. I pray that they will be men and women of God whose ministry will bring great blessing to the Church and great praise to you. I pray too, that each time that I worship with others, that I will sense the awesomeness of your presence and rise within my worship to embrace you.

June 16th

KEY WORD: **Sing**

KEY VERSE: **Colossians 3 : 16**

Let the word of Christ dwell in you richly as you teach and admonish one another with all wisdom, and as you sing psalms, hymns and spiritual songs with gratitude in your hearts to God.

It is quite obvious from New Testament teaching that we are to sing. We are to sing to ourselves and we are to sing to one another. In other words, we are to sing on our own and we are to sing collectively as a corporate congregation. The New Testament in fact places great emphasis upon corporate singing and it gives various illustrations where this actually happened, including the Passover meal, when, following the singing of a hymn, Jesus and His disciples went out into the Garden of Gethsemane.

In the key verse today Paul wrote to the church in Colosse and urged them to sing psalms and hymns and spiritual songs, because he said that the singing of them would actually bring admonishment and teaching to one another.

Paul used the Greek word '*ado*' when he was writing this verse. '*Ado*' is translates as 'to bring an ode' and it is always used within the context of bringing this 'ode' unto the Lord. In other words it was never used in the New Testament for the singing of ordinary songs, it was confined to the singing of godly songs to the Lord.

This word is used only five times in the New Testament and on each occasion its use brings strength to the vital aspect of saints singing together in worship. Twice it is used when the Church was engaged in worship and three times it is used when the heavenly throng are singing praises to the Lord. So you could say that the Church on earth used singing as a form of practice for when the heavenly Church commences its eternal form of worship.

What matters is that we are commanded to sing. We are urged to sing whether we feel good or bad, whether we feel happy or glad, because to sing is the greatest form of praise that we can bring and it delights the Lord. He has chosen to fill heaven with the sound of many voices.

My Journal

KEY PRAYER

Heavenly Father, I take great delight in bringing praise to you and I raise my voice to you today as I sing my praises to you. Help me to remember to do this at all times, even when I do not feel like singing. Help me to remember that I build myself up with the singing of praise songs to you.

June 17th

KEY WORD: **Kneel**

KEY VERSE: **Luke 22 : 41**

Jesus withdrew about a stone's throw beyond them, knelt down and prayed.

Some churches stand for long periods of worship while other churches use the posture of sitting for long periods of worship. There are congregations who actually seek to combine those practices so that the worship has a mixed sense of posture. There are some denominations who still hold to the practice of kneeling down for certain aspects of praise and prayer, while other denominations never use this posture of praise.

Those congregations who never kneel to pray are missing something that is quite essential within the concept of New Testament worship. This concept is the act of reverence that kneeling to pray actually brings.

In the key verse today, Jesus left and withdrew Himself from His disciples and knelt before His Heavenly Father to pray. This act of kneeling brings with it, not just the sense of reverence, but of humility. The one who kneels down is stating that they are allowing themselves to be subjected to humility as they come before One who was so much greater. This is what Jesus was doing in the Garden of Gethsemane.

The word 'kneel' or 'knelt' in the New Testament is the Greek word '*gonupeteo*' and once again it is a word that is formed by the combination of two Greek words. The words are '*gonu*' which means 'to kneel' and '*pipto*' which means to 'fall prostrate'. The combining of these two words brings the sense of falling down. However, people often fell down for other reasons. Sometimes it was a form of address or greeting. The actual emphasis of falling down upon the knees before God in worship is strengthened by adding another two words from the New Testament to that of *'gonupeteo'*. The word *'tithemi'* combined with *'gonata'*, which meant 'to put', is the word that is used within the key verse today. Jesus did not just kneel down in a greeting or an address – He 'put down' His knees in an attitude of prayer that brought Him low before God.

This act of stooping low and of bending the knees is a posture that we still need to adopt today. It is a shame that some congregations never kneel down during their services. They never show God just how great they think He is and just how small they really are, which is something that needs to be considered. As we pray today it would be good to kneel down in an act of humility as we seek God's face in prayer.

My Journal

KEY PRAYER

Heavenly Father, I bow down before you today as I seek your face. I fall upon my knees so that I might make myself small and so that I might make you big. I magnify your name and I exalt you as Lord, and in my posture today I seek to bring you glory and honour.

June 18th

KEY WORD: **Silent**

KEY VERSE: **Acts 15 : 12**

The whole assembly became silent as they listened to the miraculous signs and wonders God had done among the Gentiles through them.

Some churches sing for long periods of worship while other churches use the mode of silence for long periods of worship. There are congregations who seek to combine those practices so that the worship has a mixed sense of noise and peace.

It is interesting that in the key verse today, when Paul and Barnabas were rehearsing the signs and wonders that God had done before the church in Jerusalem, the whole assembly fell quiet before God and before each other, because this was not the time for noise but for silence.

Some churches fear the absence of sound as if silence is threatening and embarrassing, so they avoid such feelings and their services are filled with as much music and praise, noise and activity as is humanly possible. However, aspects of silence and silent praise can be both beneficial and therapeutic.

The New Testament word for silent is the Greek word '*sigao*', which means to 'hold one's peace', and it was used when it was right at a particular moment to keep quiet. Within most of what we call our worship time, periods of silence are never requested. We never seem to know when to keep quiet. I have been in meetings where a holy sense of God has been felt and the meeting has descended into a period of awesome quiet; except for one person, who possibly felt embarrassed by the quietness or even threatened by it, and commenced to sing a praise song. The singing of the song at that moment was not right, and even a lovely song of praise did not fit the moment. Rather than being embarrassed by the silence, the congregation were more embarrassed by the inappropriate singing of a song. We need to learn when to speak and when not to speak, when to sing and when not to sing. To spend a period of silent meditation before the Lord is one of the most rewarding ways to worship and we should learn to cultivate such moments of blessing.

This kind of worship is called being sensitive, and we need to learn this aspect of ministry before the Lord.

My Journal

KEY PRAYER

Heavenly Father, please teach me how to be more sensitive in every aspect of my prayer and praise. I long to be in your presence and I long to treat you in the right way. Please forgive me when I have been silent when I should have been shouting, and forgive me too, when I have been shouting when I should have been silent. Help me at all times to praise you in the right way.

June 19th

KEY WORD: **Loud voice**

KEY VERSE: **Revelation 5 : 12**

In a loud voice they sang: "Worthy is the Lamb, who was slain."

Heaven is full of noise and praise and it sounds like the rushing of many mighty waters, as if thunder were echoing across eternity. Heaven is a very noisy place. The angels and the multitudes in heaven raise their voices and sing as loud as they can. Heaven is full of the sound of thanksgiving.

Loud rapturous praise is part of worship, and I wonder when was the last time that you lifted up your voice in a shout of praise unto the Lord. As I commented a few days ago, worship should not just fit our preferences, we should stretch ourselves from time to time with differing aspects of praise.

The most important lesson to learn in all our times of praise and worship is that continuous noise is wrong, just as continuous silence is wrong. We should not use just one or the other, but both together. Both aspects of praise are right before God but we need to learn when to energise our loud rapturous praise and when to refrain from noise and enter into a period of meditation. Some churches prefer to 'be quiet before the Lord' – which is fine – but God requires more than silence. Some churches never seem to slow down and relax into meditation. God requires worshippers to worship Him in Spirit and truth and we must learn when and how to do this, during each and every one of our gatherings together.

If your preference is quiet, reflective worship, then you will be quite out of place in heaven. In heaven there are moments of silence and stillness, but over all heaven is a very noisy place. In the key verse today angels sang with a loud voice, and there were thousands upon thousands, and ten thousand times ten thousand angels (Revelation 5 : 11). That is a lot of angels, and it is also a lot of noise. The Greek word used for 'loud' is the word '*megas*' which means 'to give force to the voice with intensity.' Whichever way you look at it, the angels shouted with a great shout and the force of their voices reached from one end of heaven to the other.

Reach out to God in your praise and worship and express yourself before Him. In your private times of worship why not learn to shout before Him. Doing this privately might help when it comes to times of shouting in a corporate gathering. Whichever way you prefer to worship, don't forget that God requires all aspects of praise to be raised to Him.

My Journal

KEY PRAYER

Heavenly Father, please help me to be more expressive in my worship. Help me to learn how to shout before you and teach me how to worship you in ways that I have not learnt as yet. I long to worship you in the right way and I pray today for your help.

June 20th

KEY WORD: **Sacrifice**

KEY VERSE: **Hebrews 13 : 15**

Through Jesus, therefore, let us continually offer to God a sacrifice of praise – the fruit of lips that confess His name.

Over the past few days we have been considering the whole aspect of praise and worship and we have learned that there are many different ways to offer praise. The most important aspect of praise and worship however, is the fact that God requires us to worship Him in Spirit and truth. The mode of praise may be varied but Spirit-led worship is vital.

The writer to the Hebrews brings another slant to the offering of worship when he writes that we should offer the fruit of our lips in a continual offering of sacrificial worship. The fact that he uses the word 'sacrifice' brings a new and fresh light on this subject. Most of us have grown up understanding that worship is not a sacrifice but a joy and that in bringing praise, we are not bringing a costly sacrifice, but an offering of pure joy and ease. The word 'sacrifice' seems to conjure up the aspect of a costly and hurtful experience – until of course we study the actual word that is used. The writer used the Greek word '*thusia*' which has often been translated as 'sacrifice', however, the meaning of '*thusia*' denotes 'the act of bringing an offering'. The English notion of enthusiasm springs from part of this word, and it is this very idea that the writer is seeking to convey. We are not only bringing an offering and a sacrifice but we are bringing an act of thanksgiving with such a sense of intense eagerness that fervency and passion are seen, and this is the root of '*thusia*'. In other words, I am to bring forth my offering of praise and worship with great joy and I should be very enthusiastic about it.

There are times when praise is easy to bring before the Lord and we feel good and quite at ease about bringing worship. However, there are times when we do not feel quite so at ease about things, and at these times, the last thing that we feel like doing is worshipping the Lord. We might feel like praying and we would probably feel like being counselled by someone; but it is at these very times that we are commanded to bring praise. Praise is not optional and it should be brought to the Lord at all times – whether we feel like it or not.

When we feel particularly poor in spirit or down in the dumps, the praise that we bring is a sacrifice, because it is costly and difficult. But the breakthroughs that we receive at times like these are immense and they teach us each time that praise and worship through tears is the most blessed of all. As we come with enthusiasm God meets with us, and as we come with our sacrifice God accepts the gift and blesses the giver.

My Journal

KEY PRAYER

Heavenly Father, I bless you today with my praise and with my worship. You deserve all of my worship and I gladly bring it as an offering before you. I glorify you with enthusiasm and I seek to bring my sacrifice of praise which is the fruit of my lips.

June 21st

KEY WORD: **Fruit**

KEY VERSE: **Hebrews 13 : 15**

Through Jesus, therefore, let us continually offer to God a sacrifice of praise – the fruit of lips that confess His name.

We are using the same key verse today as we did yesterday because within the verse there is a very important and descriptive word. The writer to the Hebrews spoke of the way that we bring our praise and worship, and as we studied yesterday, this praise is to be brought before God at all times, even when praising the Lord means we have to make a sacrifice.

As we sacrifice praise the writer stated that we are actually bringing the fruit of our lips, which is a very descriptive way to state what we are doing. The Greek word used for 'fruit' is the word '*karpos*' which means 'the fruit of the trees or field'. It is the word that is used for the inherent energy of a living organism that grows and produces something worth tasting and enjoying. What a perfect description of our worship!

When we praise God the inherent energy of our praise produces a living organic fruit that is so pleasing to God and is something that He enjoys so much that He wants to taste it again and again. So when you praise Him today, remember that you may be enjoying your worship time, but not half as much as He is enjoying the taste of the fruit that that you are producing when your lips praise His name.

The word '*karpos*' also refers to the fruitfulness of abundance similar to the gathering of a harvest of fruit. So my praise is not a one-off, one time piece of fruit that is offered. When my praise and my worship is brought before the Lord it is like a bountiful harvest of fruit.

The word '*karpos*' can also be associated with righteousness, and so the term 'fruits of righteousness' is used widely. '*Karpos*' is also used to mean the 'fruit of the Spirit', which was used by Paul in Galations 5 : 22 to indicate an abundance of fruitfulness. And Jesus used this word during the Sermon on the Mount, when He was seeking to show that there are good fruits and bad fruits.

So this word is used throughout the New Testament and it speaks of a fullness and abundance of fruit. As we praise the Lord therefore, we produce a harvest of thanksgiving that is pleasing and acceptable to God.

My Journal

KEY PRAYER

Heavenly Father, my lips shall praise you; and the fruit of my lips is an offering of abundance before you. Help me to praise you at all times and please help me to bring my fruit before you so that my thanksgiving is an offering of acceptance before you.

June 22nd

KEY WORD: **Lips**

KEY VERSE: **Hebrews 13 : 15**

Through Jesus, therefore, let us continually offer to God a sacrifice of praise – the fruit of lips that confess His name.

Today we will conclude our studies of this key verse. We have learned that praise and worship is a wonderful sacrifice of thanksgiving which delights God. This praise is fruitfulness that blesses God and which brings to Him a harvest that is pleasing and acceptable in His sight.

The praise that we bring is the fruit of our lips. This phrase is a very interesting one because it could be quite acceptable to say that praise is the fruit of our lives, or even of our hearts. However, the Hebrew writer quite categorically stated that the praise that we bring is the fruit of our lips.

The reason that he chose to use the concept of our lips as the organ that produces fruit goes back a very long way in Bible terms. There was, and still is, a Jewish custom whereby the worshipper would wear a woollen scarf called a tallith, which was wound around the head and neck during times of prayer. This tallith had a tassel hanging from it, and during prayer the worshipper would place this tassel against the lips. This act signified a sign of acceptance of the Law from the heart.

The reason it was placed upon the lips was the fact that the mouth and the lips were the organs of honour and speech. Jesus used the expression, in Matthew 15 : 8, that the people "honour me with their lips, but their hearts are far from me." The lips were the organ of speech and thereby the organ of honouring or dishonouring. So, when the Hebrew writer spoke of the fruit of our lips, he was recalling the tallith way of honouring God with the kiss of our lips.

The Greek word used for lips was '*cheilos*' which is translated quite simply as 'lips', and it was used only six times within the New Testament.

We should make quite sure that as we bring our praise and worship before the Lord, our lips are pure, so that we might bring to Him the kiss of our lips and the honour of our mouths. Because to do anything else is unacceptable to God.

My Journal

KEY PRAYER

Heavenly Father, I want to honour you with the fruit of my lips. So today I carefully bring my praise so that my lips might be pure and clean. My mouth praises you and my lips bring the pure honour of worship before you; for you are the Lord, and beside you there is none else.

June 23rd

KEY WORD: **Lion**

KEY VERSE: **Revelation 4 : 7**

The first living creature was like a lion, the second was like an ox, the third had a face like a man, the fourth was like a flying eagle.

As we draw towards the close of this month, we are going to spend a few days considering the four beasts that surround the throne of God in heaven. When John saw these four beasts he was filled with a sense of divine awe, because he was looking at the very throne of God with its guards. The beasts were standing around the throne and they uttered the words: "Holy, holy, holy is the Lord God Almighty, who was, and is, and is to come." These words were uttered all day and all night and it seemed as if these four beasts led the worship of heaven.

The first beast, the New Testament says, was like a lion and this beast had the qualities and nature of a lion. The Greek word used here is the word *'leon'* and it is simply translated as 'lion'.

There were two lions mentioned within the New Testament. There was the description of Satan, who was 'like a roaring lion', and there was the Lion of the tribe of Judah, which is a symbolic reference to Jesus Christ.

It is interesting to note that one of the descriptions of Satan was 'like a roaring lion' (1 Peter 5 : 8). There is only one true lion and that is Jesus; everything else is but a shadow or a substitute. Satan might think that he is a lion, but he is only a pale shadow. The lion of heaven depicted standing around the throne is a symbol of kingship, because the lion is regarded as the king of all animals. This symbol showed the watching multitudes of heaven that the throne of God was being guarded by one of the greatest and most kingly of all animals.

The four beasts around the throne are often described as symbols, and they have a correlating relationship to the four gospels. The Gospel of Matthew is quite often referred to as the 'King of all Gospels', as it describes Jesus as the King and has much to say about His rule and reign.

The lion has three main strengths of character which stand out above all others. The features of a lion are its majesty, its strength and its courage. It is no wonder therefore that John saw a lion at the throne of God, and it was guarding the true Lion of Judah who was seated upon it.

My Journal

KEY PRAYER

Heavenly Father, thank you for Jesus who is the Lion of the tribe of Judah, and I thank you too that a lion stands at the throne of God in heaven. I praise you today for the majesty of Jesus and for the symbol of majesty that guards the throne.

June 24th

KEY WORD: **Ox**

KEY VERSE: **Revelation 4 : 7**

The first living creature was like a lion, the second was like an ox, the third had a face like a man, the fourth was like a flying eagle.

We are spending a few days considering the four beasts that surround the throne of God in heaven. When John saw these four beasts he was filled with a sense of divine awe, because he was looking at the very throne of God with its guards. The beasts were standing around the throne and they uttered the words: "Holy, holy, holy is the Lord God Almighty, who was, and is, and is to come." These words were uttered all day and all night and it seemed as if these four beasts led the worship of heaven.

The second creature was like an ox. If the symbol of the first creature was the symbol of majesty and power – the lion – then the second creature symbolised the beast of the field or the working animal of the farm. The Greek word used here is an interesting one, because it is not the usual translation for 'ox'. The Greek word for 'ox' is usually '*tauros*'. However, John used the word '*moschos*' in this key verse, which is usually translated as 'young calf' or 'young heifer'. This flexible word was used to denote the fact that around the throne of God the symbol of power and workmanship was also being seen. But the symbol not only denoted work or workmanship, but that the creature was a youngster, capable of long periods of work and great stamina. This denoted the fact that God was guarded by a strong figure capable of much stamina and long periods of effort and strength.

The second Gospel – the Gospel of Mark – is often referred to as the 'Gospel of the ox', because it dwells mainly on the fact that Jesus came as the one who would work for us as the strong man – the one who would overcome evil and the enemy.

The throne of God is guarded by the lion's strength of courage and the ox's strength of stamina, which means that the guards of heaven are quite capable of overseeing the throne for long periods of time with majesty and stamina.

My Journal

KEY PRAYER

Heavenly Father, I praise you today for the young ox that stands guard at your throne in heaven. I thank you that the ox symbolises work and stamina, and I praise you that Jesus came to work with great strength at seeking and saving those that are lost.

June 25th

KEY WORD: ***Man***

KEY VERSE: ***Revelation 4 : 7***

The first living creature was like a lion, the second was like an ox, the third had a face like a man, the fourth was like a flying eagle.

When John saw these four beasts he was filled with a sense of divine awe, because he was looking at the very throne of God with its guards. The beasts were standing around the throne and they uttered the words: "Holy, holy, holy is the Lord God Almighty, who was, and is, and is to come." These words were uttered all day and all night and it seemed as if these four beasts led the worship of heaven.

The third creature that stood around the throne of God was like unto a man, or at least with the face of a man.

As we have seen, the throne of God was guarded by the majesty of a lion and the strength of an ox. The third symbol was that of a man standing guard. The word used in this key verse for 'man' was the Greek word '*anthropos*', and we derive our English word 'anthropology' – meaning the study of man – from this word. At the throne of God, there is a creature that symbolises the strength of a man and this is vital as we know that man was made a little lower than the angels but was still crowned with glory and strength. Man was the greatest of all of God's creations and man was given the authority over all of the earth and its animals.

God has chosen to surround Himself with the kingly strength of the lion. God has also chosen to surround Himself with the earthly strength of the ox of the field. Also, in having one of the heavenly creatures appearing as a man, God has chosen to surround Himself with the king of all of His creation.

The third Gospel, which is the Gospel of Luke, is quite often referred to as the 'Gospel of man', because Luke features Jesus as the Son of Man and his descriptions of Jesus often cover His earthly needs and His earthly passion.

The throne of God is guarded by the lion's strength of courage and the ox's strength of stamina, which means that the guards of heaven are quite capable of overseeing the throne for long periods of time with majesty and stamina. Also, the throne is guarded by a creature that appeared to be that of a man, and this means that there is kingly authority at the throne of God as well.

My Journal

KEY PRAYER

Heavenly Father, thank you that the whole of heaven has at its centre your throne, and that around your throne there is kingly strength, kingly stamina and kingly authority. All these symbols feature pictures of Jesus, who is Lord and King over all things. With this thought in mind, I praise you today.

June 26th

KEY WORD: ***Eagle***

KEY VERSE: ***Revelation 4 : 7***

The first living creature was like a lion, the second was like an ox, the third had a face like a man, the fourth was like a flying eagle.

When John saw these four beasts he was filled with a sense of divine awe, because he was looking at the very throne of God with its guards. The beasts were standing around the throne and they uttered the words: "Holy, holy, holy is the Lord God Almighty, who was, and is, and is to come." These words were uttered all day and all night and it seemed as if these four beasts led the worship of heaven.

The fourth creature seen standing at the throne of God was like unto a flying eagle. As we have seen, the throne of God is guarded by the king of the animals, the king of the beasts of the field, the king of God's creation. And lastly, it is guarded by the king of the air. The flying eagle denotes the symbol of the greatest flying bird to be created, that of the majestic eagle.

In placing an eagle at His throne, God was symbolising the fact that the throne was being guarded by one who was greatest within the heavenly realm of the skies. The eagle symbolised the domination of all things above us. Whenever we find the eagle mentioned in the Scriptures it always denoted great power and great kingdoms. Egypt was represented by an eagle, as was Babylon; and there were other nations which also featured the eagle as an emblem of strength and power.

The Greek word used for 'eagle' is the word '*aetos*' which means not just the bird of the air but carries with it the thought of 'connected with the wind' or 'blowing like the wind'. This translation paints an image of the king of the air swooping in from a distance with great authority and using the air thermals as a passage for its power and strength.

The fourth Gospel – the Gospel of John – is often referred to as the 'Gospel of the eagle', because it brings a sense of divine majesty from the start of its verses, when it speaks of the Word being as from the beginning. John seems to majestically fly back to the beginning of all things to speak of Jesus as the living Word, who is from the beginning. Matthew and Luke feature the birth and nativity of Jesus, whereas John features the divine Jesus as being before all things.

The throne of God is guarded by the lion's strength of courage and the ox's strength of stamina, which means that the guards of heaven are quite capable of overseeing the throne for long periods of time with majesty and stamina. Also the throne is guarded by a creature that appeared to be that of a man, which means that there is kingly authority at the throne of God as well. However, in using the eagle as well as the other three creatures, God has completed the picture of the throne of God being guarded by the king of the air, whose strength and majesty is awesome.

My Journal ________________________________

KEY PRAYER

Heavenly Father, thank you for the symbols of heaven which all speak of kingship and authority, and I praise you for the fact that God has hidden truth within the symbols of heaven. I praise you too, for the fact that I can also raise my voice with the creatures of heaven and say: "Holy, holy, holy."

June 27th

KEY WORD: **Humble**

KEY VERSE: **1 Peter 5 : 6**

Humble yourselves, therefore, under God's mighty hand, that He may lift you up in due time.

We are going to close this month of June with its last few days, by considering this key verse and its many facets of truth. Peter was not an eloquent and learned writer, like the apostle Paul, but he could still state truth with great power and clarity. In this key verse he set out four important truths which are vital that we understand.

Firstly he set out the truth of being 'humble before God', and he commanded us to 'humble ourselves' under God's hand. Many sincere Christians believe that it is God who should humble us, but Peter made it quite clear that it is our responsibility to humble ourselves. I have often heard people pray, 'Please Lord, humble me,' or even, 'Please Lord, teach me to be humble.' Peter started from a quite different position. He taught that we must take the route of humbling ourselves and that we must learn how to do it.

Peter used a very interesting Greek word that was translated in the passage above as 'humble'. The word used was '*tapeinos*' which means 'low lying' or even 'low degree'. The word conveys the thought of being brought down to the lowest place, and it has its roots in the description of contoured hills and valleys, where the lowest place could be seen – a valley that rested between two hills.

The thought that Peter was seeking to convey here was that, in order to be exalted in due time, each of us has to take the lowest path. This thought is the opposite concept to that of the modern world. In today's world, finding the way to the top of a profession or a career is like finding the quickest path up a mountain – because you want to climb as fast as possible. But Peter said, and the Word of God confirms, that the fastest way upwards is to take a lowly path of servanthood and service. When we humble ourselves, God takes notice and in His own time He will raise us up. We should not be looking for exaltation, but we should walk humbly with our God.

My Journal ______________________________

KEY PRAYER

Heavenly Father, thank you today for this word of truth: that I am to walk humbly before you and that this walk of humbleness is my responsibility. Help me to discover each day the path of humility, and help me to tread its paths wisely and with great care.

June 28th

KEY WORD: **Hand**

KEY VERSE: **1 Peter 5 : 6**

Humble yourselves, therefore, under God's mighty hand, that He may lift you up in due time.

The second truth that Peter sought to convey within this key verse is the truth of 'God's mighty hand'. We are not just seeking to humble ourselves within a vacuum, as if humbling ourselves in isolation could produce something. We are not seeking to be humble for humility's sake. We are, however, seeking to humble ourselves under God's hand for our own spiritual sake.

The phrase 'the hand of God' appears many times throughout the Bible in both the Old and New Testaments. 'The hand of God' was a well known phrase and a well known concept. Peter was stating something that his readers would readily understand when this epistle was read out to them. Therefore the truth is not that humility should be sought as an advantage, but that humility should be sought so that we might be nearer to the hand of God, and that we might feel His presence closely.

Peter used the Greek word '*cheir*', which in its ordinary sense means simply 'the hand'. However, when it is linked to the word 'God', or '*theos*', it has a more powerful statement to make. There are human hands and there is 'God's hand', and it is God's hand that makes a difference. Peter is bringing to us a metaphor – a word picture that conveys a truth. The metaphor here is that '*cheir*' is an ordinary hand that is used for ordinary business, but when it is linked to '*theos*', the word becomes an extraordinary hand with far more power and authority.

The '*cheir*' of '*theos*' is something that we all seek to have upon us and we would all long to be touched by God's mighty hand. Peter has given us the route for this blessing to happen. It is the route of humility before God and the lowering of ourselves under His hand. It is vital that we learn this lesson and that we learn it quickly.

My Journal

KEY PRAYER

Heavenly Father, I would want to be included today within those who say that the hand of God is upon them. Please help me to learn these vital lessons quickly so that I might see you working within my life. I will take steps today to lower myself before you so that your mighty hand might be felt within my life.

KEY WORD: **Lift you up**

KEY VERSE: **1 Peter 5 : 6**

Humble yourselves, therefore, under God's mighty hand, that He may lift you up in due time.

The third truth that Peter was seeking to convey within this key verse was exaltation, or the raising and 'lifting up' of someone. Peter stated that if we took a lowly path of humility there would be a time when the hand of God would lift us up. I would repeat here again, that the path of humility should not be used only for you to be raised up, but we should be low before God in a sense of spiritual posture. If God lifts us up, so be it; but if He does not lift us up, then we should still praise Him and give Him all the glory He requires. We should learn to wait for God's time and season for blessing us.

God will exalt us in a time of His choosing, and this 'lifting up' will be His way of bringing us blessing and growth. However, He will only do this if we have learned how to cope with the exaltation, and we learn this through our lowly walk with God.

Peter used the Greek word '*hupsoo*' which means 'to bring to height' – literally meaning to lift someone up to a new height. This word was used when Jesus was raised upon the cross; He was 'lifted up'. It was also the word that was used when someone was raised to a new position of dignity and privilege, as in the case of Mary's song, in Luke 1 : 52, when she sang that rulers and thrones have been brought down, but God has lifted up the humble.

God will bring new blessing and privilege in due time when we have shown that we are able to cope with the learning that takes place within humility. Most of us struggle with God's time agenda and we think that we deserve to be raised up far sooner than we actually are. Some people even seek to raise themselves before God is ready to trust them with greater responsibility. The fall of these people is often quite great! When God is ready and we have learned the lesson that spiritual progress is a matter of lowly walking with God, His agenda and timescale bring us to greater blessing.

When we have learned to rejoice when others are exalted before us and when we have learned to praise God for their successes, we will be almost ready for God to raise us up to a new path of responsibility in Him.

My Journal ______________________________

KEY PRAYER

Heavenly Father, I want to walk with you whether it means being raised to new blessing or not. I want to learn the path of true humility before you. I will rejoice when others are exalted before me, and I will praise you for their successes. Help me to wait patiently for your time and season.

June 30th

KEY WORD: **Due time**

KEY VERSE: **1 Peter 5 : 6**

Humble yourselves, therefore, under God's mighty hand, that He may lift you up in due time.

The last truth contained within this key verse is the truth of God's timing. His appointed time for blessing us and raising us up is all part of the times and seasons of God. We learned this lesson way back in April, when we studied together the times and the seasons that God has planned for our lives.

However, it is good to remind ourselves that everything is on God's agenda and not on our timescale. God has everything appointed and He will not rush and do things before the time that He has appointed. We saw in April that there are moments of 'time and space'. When time means the chronology of things, the Greek word used is *'chronos'*. We saw that there are times and seasons that have their measure in periods of the characteristics of certain times, such as spring and summer, autumn and winter. The Greeks used the word *'kairos'* for these times.

In learning about these times and seasons of God, it is good to know that God has all things under control. The times and seasons may not be our time plans or our timescale, but God is God and He will do what He wants to do at the time that He wants to do it.

If we take the lowly path of humility and we learn to walk with God with patience and care, the season will come when He will take the decision to lift us into a new path of blessing and responsibility. The timescale of this new pathway rests entirely with us. If we rush the lowly, humble walk, then God will delay our possible exaltation. If we seek to promote ourselves, the path will lead to failure. It just depends upon what we want and when we want it, and God has it all in hand anyway!

My Journal

KEY PRAYER

Heavenly Father, the times and seasons of my life are in your hands and I rejoice in that truth. I seek your face today to ask for nothing more than your plan and purpose in my life. I rest in your timescale and I trust in your agenda and I praise you for all things. Thank you for truth, and thank you that I am learning little by little to walk the lowly path with you.

July 1st

KEY WORD: **Counsellor**

KEY VERSE: **John 14 : 16**

"I will ask the Father and He will give you another Counsellor to be with you for ever."

The disciples were beside themselves with fear, misapprehension and discouragement, because Jesus had just told them that He was going to leave them. They could not imagine being without Him. After three years, He was the centre of everything within their world. They had forsaken everything for Him, and now they felt that they were being forsaken themselves. However, the message that they received was that although Jesus would be leaving, another Comforter/Counsellor would be taking His place.

The disciples had only heard part of the message and that was the part that grieved them. If they did hear the second part of the message they did not want to receive it, or they did not understand it at all.

The word that is used for counsellor has undergone various translations within the different Bible versions. The Old King James Bible translates to the word that was used as comforter. However, the Greek word that was used is *'parakletos'*. Bible scholars all over the world have come to love this word because its most common translation means 'called to one side', and it is this wonderfully descriptive word that accompanies the ministry of the Holy Spirit. The Holy Spirit is the divine *'paraklete'* – the one who comes alongside. *'Paraklete'* is one of the most beautiful words in the New Testament because it introduces us to the ministry of the third Person of the Godhead.

The word is usually understood as the 'one who gives aid', and it was used when a person was in a court of justice. The court always had a legal assistant who would act as a means of defence or an advocate. This advocate would come alongside during a court case to give help, advice, comfort and sustaining strength. When New Testament writers were seeking to convey the truth of the Holy Spirit's ministry, they used this word because it gave the best description of what the Holy Spirit was seeking to do for the Church as a whole, and for each believer.

Jesus told His disciples that He might be leaving them but that another Counsellor would take His place, and that this Counsellor would be with them forever as their friend, sustainer, comforter and guide.

My Journal

KEY PRAYER

Heavenly Father, thank you for the ministry of the Holy Spirit who is always with me, and walks alongside me. I praise you today for His ministry within my life, even when I do not appreciate His presence. Help me each day to rely upon Him and to sense His wonderful presence.

July 2nd

KEY WORD: **Guide**

KEY VERSE: **John 16 : 13**

But when He, the Spirit of truth, comes, He will guide you into all truth.

Jesus had told His disciples that He would be leaving and as we saw in yesterday's key verse, they did not understand this message and they could not comprehend the truth of another Comforter. However, Jesus continued His teaching with the key verse today, when He showed His disciples the possibility of the awesome fact that when this new Comforter had come, that He would guide them into all truth.

One of the Holy Spirit's great attributes is that He is our guide, and that His guidance, when given and received, will bring all believers into the fullness of truth. The words of Jesus to His disciples were not spoken for them alone, but for the Church of all ages. So when we need guidance into truth, the Holy Spirit is always available.

The Greek word that John used for 'guidance' is *'hodegeo'*, and it is the word that was used to convey the sense of being led somewhere, because it means 'to lead the way'. The word was always used when someone sought to describe the actions of a leader who knew the way and who knew what he was doing. The Greek word is constructed by combining two words together. The first is *'hodos'* which means 'the way', and the second word was *'hegeomai'* which means 'to lead'.

When seeking to describe the ministry of the Holy Spirit, the New Testament combined these two words to beautifully describe just what the third Person of the Godhead was seeking to do for all of us.

The Holy Spirit is not just leading the way, He is The Way

and when we follow Him we are taken into all truth. Problems arise when we think that we know the way, or we think that we know all truth. At times like this the Church has suffered its greatest defeats; however, it is when we submit to the guidance of the Holy Spirit that the Church has had its greatest successes and blessings.

If you want to know the way that you should go, follow the Holy Spirit because He will lead you into all truth.

My Journal

KEY PRAYER

Heavenly Father, I thank you today for the beautiful and powerful ministry of the Holy Spirit, thank you that you have given Him to us as our Comforter and guide. Please help me at all times to follow His guidance, and help me too, to realise that without Him I will have my greatest defeats.

July 3rd

KEY WORD: **Convict**

KEY VERSE: **John 16 : 8**

When He comes, He will convict the world of guilt in regard to sin and righteousness and judgement.

Jesus told His disciples that He would be leaving, and as we saw, they did not understand this message and they could not comprehend the truth of another Comforter. However, Jesus continued His teaching and in the key verse today, He showed His disciples that another aspect of the Holy Spirit's ministry involved the convicting power of sin and righteousness.

Jesus said that when the Comforter came, His ministry to the Church would be that of guidance into all truth and sustenance to all believers. However, the ministry of the Comforter to the world would be completely different. The world would see, through the Holy Spirit's ministry, just how far it had fallen away from righteousness, and just how far it had to go to return to righteousness and forgiveness. This convicting ministry would be part of the ongoing ministry of the Holy Spirit throughout all ages.

The Greek word used for 'convict' is '*elencho*', and it can be translated to mean 'to confute' and 'to refute,'. The word was always used in the sense of putting someone to shame when that person was at fault. It was used when someone had transgressed the Law of God, and it was used when someone had committed an act that brought them before justice.

The act of putting a person to shame seems to be a very harsh act. However, we must understand that when the Holy Spirit puts someone to shame, it is for the purpose of showing that person that there is no way out other than to seek mercy. When someone has been convicted of sin and seeks mercy, then the ministry of the Holy Spirit will draw that person into all truth and the circle is complete. But to put someone to shame is not the desired end result. The conclusion should be that people will be drawn into truth and come to know the Lord.

When you think about it, that is exactly what happened to you!

My Journal

KEY PRAYER

Heavenly Father, I rejoice today because you found me and you sent the Holy Spirit to convict me, and then the Comforter brought me into all truth and I came to know you as Lord and Saviour. Thank you for this wonderful ministry that the Comforter always brings to us.

KEY WORD: **Reclining**

KEY VERSE: **John 13 : 23**

One of them, the disciple whom Jesus loved, was reclining next to Him.

A wonderful moment was being described within the key verse today. Jesus was eating the Passover meal with His disciples when John, the disciple that Jesus loved, leaned into His breast and rested himself upon the Lord. The NIV translates this phrase as 'reclining', and the Old King James Version translates it as 'resting'. Whichever way you look at it, it was a most beautiful moment.

In some parts of the world today a sense of 'independence' is being celebrated and Independence Day is a day of great rejoicing for some nations. The Greek word that was used in the key verse today speaks very strongly of total dependence upon the Lord. We can not rejoice in a sense of independence as we need to rely upon the One who has saved us and the One who is keeping us.

The Greek word used for 'reclining' is '*anakeimai*' and it means 'to be laid up', which is why John used it to describe what he did during the Passover meal. He laid himself upon Jesus, or he leaned upon Him. The word was used when someone was seeking to convey the thought of totally resting oneself in order to be at ease. The root of the word is in the sense of resting at a table during a meal – you would become inactive apart from eating. The very fact that you had sat down to eat a meal meant that you were no longer active in any other way, and that you were resting yourself in order to concentrate upon a meal.

John used this word in order to convey the thought of resting and reclining. This idea is the very one that we must cultivate if we want to develop our total dependence upon God. We are not independent in the sense of being allowed to go our own way and do whatever we feel is right. We belong to God and, as we have seen many times during the year, He has a plan and a purpose for our lives. We can not go our own way and expect Him to bless us, and we can not live according to the passion and dictates of our own heart. He is our Master and Lord, and our sense of independence has long gone. We can not celebrate an Independence Day in the sense of being selfishly independent, because we are totally dependent upon Him.

My Journal

KEY PRAYER

Heavenly Father, many nations rejoice today in their independence, but I thank you that I have found the pathway to the greatest blessing and peace of all – that of being dependent upon you. Help me to rest and recline in your arms at all times and help me to understand that there is only one way to real joy, and that is resting in you.

July 5th

KEY WORD: **Worshipping**

KEY VERSE: **Acts 13 : 2**

While they were worshipping the Lord and fasting, the Holy Spirit said, "Set apart for me Barnabas and Saul for the work to which I have called them."

This key verse is a very interesting one and we shall take a few days to study it closely together. It is found in the section of the Acts of the Apostles where we are being introduced to the brand new church in Antioch. This church had been planted by the believers who had been scattered abroad during the fierce persecutions that had fallen upon the church in Jerusalem.

The new church had both grown well and quite quickly and had Barnabas and Saul as its main leaders. It was during a prayer and worship time that God dramatically broke into the life of this new church and brought a word of guidance and challenge to all who were worshipping together at that time.

The church leaders were told that Barnabas and Saul were to be released into a new ministry that God had called them for, and that they were to leave the church for this purpose. The wording in the key verse needs examining as it brings fresh insight into New Testament truth and practice.

The NIV records that the leaders of the church were 'worshipping' together, however, the KJV puts it a little differently and says that the church leaders were 'ministering' before the Lord. Whichever way you read the phrase, it forms a lovely concept – that leaders were together in worship and ministry. However, the Greek word that was used gives a different impression altogether. The word that was used is '*leitourgeo*' and it was a classical Greek term that signified the 'rendering of public service to the state', which can be construed as 'giving service for the greater good'. It was also used by the Greeks to mean worship and service to their own gods. The New Testament takes this word and cleanses it by using it to convey the highest form of worship and ministry. The word is used to describe the Antioch church and its form of ministry before the Lord.

The leaders in Antioch were serving the Lord in worship and prayer – their highest form of service. They may have been appointed to serve the church and its people but their greatest and highest form of service and ministry was to the Lord.

Local leaders often forget this and spend so much time with agendas and business that they do not have time to seek the Lord. It is good that this new church had its priorities right, in that even in the church's brief history its leaders gave priority to seeking God and ministering before Him.

We would do well to remind ourselves of this priority and to seek to obey the traditions of the church in Antioch.

My Journal

KEY PRAYER

Heavenly Father, I thank you for lessons that we learn from the Scriptures and I thank you that here is another valuable lesson from this young church in Antioch. Help me to ever remember that my highest and greatest form of service is not to others but unto you. I must serve others but I must serve you first.

July 6th

KEY WORD: **Fasting**

KEY VERSE: **Acts 13 : 2**

While they were worshipping the Lord and fasting, the Holy Spirit said, "Set apart for me Barnabas and Saul for the work to which I have called them."

As we saw yesterday, the new church in Antioch was following the principle of its leaders by making their service before God one of the most vital aspects of their ministry. They gave themselves to seeking God, and it was during one of these times of seeking that God broke in amongst them to give a directional word to the church.

Part of the ministry of the leaders was to fast, as well as to pray and worship. It is clear that the New Testament Church used this aspect of ministry many times as Jesus taught it and practised it, and the New Testament writers also featured it quite often within their writings. It is important that we understand fasting because it can often be used incorrectly in a way that is not helpful. The Jews of the Old Testament fasted frequently and held many 'national fasts', as well as their own personal ones. The New Testament Church developed and continued this practice, and fasting has been practised throughout Church history.

The Greek word for 'fast' is '*nesteuo*' and, as with many Greek words that conveyed new and fresh truth, it was a combination of two well-known words, used in order to form fresh truth with impact. The two words used were '*ne*', which means a negative 'no', and '*esthio*', which means 'to eat'. The combination of these two words describes how the believers would 'voluntarily not eat food for a period'. For just how long the leaders at Antioch were abstaining from food is open to question. It could have been just one meal, or it could have been a night of prayer and fasting. Then again, it could have been a prolonged period of seeking God with fasting.

It does seem that two distinct types of fasting were taking place at times within the Church. Firstly, there were the regular prayer times that were coupled with fasting as a kind of spiritual discipline, and then secondly there was the 'calling of a fast' or the determination to fast, due to a major crisis or as a response to some calamity that might have befallen the Church. It does seem that within the key verse today there was no major need to fast at this time, so it could have been that the leaders at Antioch had established fasting as a regular spiritual discipline within their times of seeking God.

We should seek to do both forms of New Testament fasting within our spiritual walk with God. Firstly, we should seek to discipline ourselves so that we spend time with God, possibly forsaking a meal or two, so that we can energise our spiritual appetite in order to concentrate upon God. Secondly, we should use fasting as a spiritual weapon whenever we feel we are battling or in a fierce spiritual fight.

God takes special notice when we express a keen desire in deciding not to eat but to do business with God. His attention is gained when we engage in such activity.

My Journal

KEY PRAYER

Heavenly Father, I thank you today for spiritual weapons and I praise you that you have revealed just how important fasting can be in the whole aspect of ministry and spiritual warfare. Help me to engage in fasting as a spiritual discipline so that when a battle rages I am more equipped to face the trial and overcome it.

KEY WORD: **Called**

KEY VERSE: **Acts 13 : 2**

While they were worshipping the Lord and fasting, the Holy Spirit said, "Set apart for me Barnabas and Saul for the work to which I have called them."

As the leaders in the Antioch church were seeking God and fasting the Holy Spirit broke into their midst and brought a word that gave guidance and direction, not just to the church in Antioch, but to the whole Church worldwide. The word from God was that the two main leaders, Barnabas and Saul, were to be directed into world mission rather than staying in local church work and service. This word from God was to change things in Antioch and was also to change things within the world scene.

God said, "I have called them", therefore they were to be 'set apart'.

There are at least 15 Greek words that translate into the English word 'call'. There are words that mean a child is 'called' a specific name, and there are words that mean 'to call out' to someone. Each Greek word has a specific meaning with certain nuances that our English language does not have, so translators have settled in this case for the simple translation of 'called'. However, it is not as easy as that, because God was not only saying that these men were 'called'. The Greek word that was used was '*proskaleo*' which means 'bidden to come' or 'bidden to go'. The emphasis within this meaning was on 'bidden'. God was not saying that they were called in the sense of being released to preach or minister – every believer is 'called' to do that. What this word conveys is that these two men were bidden by God directly to something more than preaching; they had been touched by God for something bigger and greater. These men were to bring the gospel beyond boundaries and barriers, and they were destined for spiritual breakthroughs that most people would never see.

God has called all of us to minister and He has set every one of us apart for service because that is His plan for each of us. However, God also has a personal plan for our lives: some may be 'called' into full-time service, some will be 'called' to leave their home country and serve God within a mission programme. Others will be 'called' to some form of service that is quite distinctive, and yet others will be 'called' to stay at home in the local church and serve in a way that is quite different. This is called God's personal will for our lives. We are all called to serve, that is God's collective will for the church, but there are those who are also 'called' in a different and personal way to serve God.

My Journal

KEY PRAYER

Heavenly Father, as I come before you today it is with a sense of wonder that you have chosen me for your service. I will seek to follow your plan for my life, understanding that I am to serve you with gladness and singleness of heart. Wherever you lead me, I will follow and wherever you call me, I will go.

July 8th

KEY WORD: **Barnabas**

KEY VERSE: **Acts 13 : 2**

While they were worshipping the Lord and fasting, the Holy Spirit said, "Set apart for me Barnabas and Saul for the work to which I have called them."

As we draw towards the conclusion of our studies within this key verse there are a few more things that we need to consider. We have seen that God broke into a time of prayer which the leaders were conducting in the church at Antioch. This time of prayer included worship and ministry, prayer and fasting. The word from God was to dramatically change the way that this church was operating and the direction that the gospel would take throughout the world. The men who were being called into wider service were Barnabas and Saul. Saul, who would later be called Paul, we know a great deal about, but who was Barnabas? A quick look at his life is quite revealing, and tomorrow we will start to take a look at the church itself.

It is interesting to note that in the account concerning the involvement of Barnabas and Saul within the Antioch church, the passage always reads Barnabas and Saul. Much later it would become Saul (Paul) and Barnabas, but at this point in Church history, Barnabas came first. This is because he was sent by the church in Jerusalem to investigate this new church in Antioch, and having conducted his appraisal, he decided to bring Saul to the church for teaching and ministry. Barnabas was, in a sense, in the driving seat at this point in the history of Antioch.

Barnabas is mentioned 29 times within the New Testament, and 24 of those times are references in the Acts of the Apostles. He himself is called an apostle and his name means 'son of consolation'. He was a good man and full of faith, and in every reference he was described in a very positive way. Even later, in his disagreement with Paul over John Mark and his involvement in a missionary journey, Barnabas acted with strength and grace and with courage and care. He was later found to be correct in his decision concerning John Mark, and Paul even admitted this when he wrote to Timothy and said that John Mark was 'useful within the ministry'.

Barnabas was an outstanding New Testament character and within his life there is much to commend and much to learn from. His ministry was always conducted with faithfulness and with spiritual integrity. He was a very great man within the Church.

My Journal

KEY PRAYER

Heavenly Father, I thank you for the men and women of the Scriptures who teach us many things, and I thank you for the lessons that we learn from their lives. Help me to remember the lessons that I learn, and help me each day to be more like Jesus.

July 9th

KEY WORD: **Antioch**

KEY VERSE: **Acts 13 : 2**

While they were worshipping the Lord and fasting, the Holy Spirit said, "Set apart for me Barnabas and Saul for the work to which I have called them."

We are going to take a few days to look at the this new church in Antioch because there is much within God's plan for this church that we need to learn.

The amazing church in the city of Antioch is first introduced to us in Acts 11. The birth and foundation of the church took place as the migration of Christian people moved further and further away from Jerusalem – most of them journeying to far away places in Asia and Europe.

The people were seeking to remove themselves from the persecutions suffered by the Early Church at the hands of the Romans in occupied Judea. They were 'scattered abroad' as Peter termed them, in 1 Peter 1 : 1. A little later these scattered people would become known as the strangers of the 'Diaspora' – the 'scattered ones'. As this exile took place many people moved northwards, and some of the 'scattered ones' arrived in the city of Antioch which was 300 miles from Jerusalem.

Before the lessons concerning the Church are learned, it is worth noting that Antioch was a very strategic city in the eternal plan of God for His Church.

The city was known as Antioch on the Orontes. It was founded in 300BC by Seleucus I Nicator, who also founded fifteen other Antiochs. This city on the Orontes river was, however, the most famous of them all.

The city fell to Pompey in 64BC and it became a free city. Subsequently it became the capital of the Roman province of

Syria and was the third largest city in the Roman Empire.

It was inhabited by a mixed population of Seleucids, Jews, Romans and Greeks. The New Bible Dictionary records that, 'The city gained a reputation for energy, insolence and instability, which manifested itself in a series of revolts against Roman rule.' There was a high level of sexual sin within this city, which cloaked itself under the guise of religion, and its moral tone was in serious decline by the time that the 'believers', or 'scattered ones', arrived from Jerusalem. With such a history and such a sinful decline it is no wonder that, in the plan of God, Antioch was earmarked as a prime city for the expansion of the gospel. The city had a mixed race of people, a navigable river with a fine seaport and a hungry people searching for the meaning of life. And above all it had a concise network of streets, a large forum, theatres and amphitheatres, and an energy of lifestyle that would be the rock-bed of the new zeal for Jesus and His work.

The eternal preparations were complete – preparations that in earthly terms had taken hundreds of years – so that, as the gospel came and believers filled the city, the New Testament Church was ready to receive a new thrust that would touch the known world.

My Journal ______________________________

____

____

____

____

____

KEY PRAYER

Heavenly Father, I thank you today for the fact that you have a plan for every church and every city. Help me to understand your plan for my church and city so that I might be able to minister more effectively for you and so that I might bless others that are around me.

July 10th

KEY WORD: **Antioch**

KEY VERSE: **Acts 13 : 2**

While they were worshipping the Lord and fasting, the Holy Spirit said, "Set apart for me Barnabas and Saul for the work to which I have called them."

God was about to bring immense changes to the city of Antioch, and yet they would be noticeable at first in small ways. For instance, Acts 11 : 26 says, 'The disciples were called Christians first at Antioch.' This was a change of position and status that would be very far reaching. The change was also noticeable in larger ways, such as how this church would take on the role of the primary church in the New Testament, and, as such, many missions would emanate from this city and seaport to the ends of the earth.

Acts 11 : 20 records that believers spread the gospel to the Greeks and that 'A great number believed and turned to the Lord' (verse 21). In this short and concise verse the amazing plan of God leaps into action from the unseen and unheralded divine manoeuvres of history. The whole plan is put into perspective in the introduction to the same verse, through the words: 'The Lord's hand was with them.' This was the divine hand of history and purpose.

One of the major lessons to learn from the church in Antioch is, therefore, that we all need to understand the plan of God for our city, town or community – because God has a plan for every town and city. He has been working to complete His plan and we need to tune in to His wavelength.

If the city of Antioch can teach us anything, it is that God prepared a city before He prepared the people. After this He simply brought them together.

God does not suddenly start to move, as if He were reacting to circumstances beyond His control, nor does He suddenly sweep into an area, bringing revival and blessing. He is always working to a preordained plan that was nurtured in eternity. In fact, I don't believe that there is such a thing as an instantaneous healing or a sudden move of God. Behind every act that seems to us to be sudden – as we earthly beings view it with our misty understanding – is the rule and reign of a sovereign God. He can be moved by faith, but He is 'setting up kingdoms and putting down kingdoms' (Daniel 4 : 25) and working to His own majestic plan.

Behind every revival is a praying group of people who have been holding on in prayer, sometimes for years. Behind every miracle is the operation of someone's faith, or the prayers of faithful people, or the sovereignty of God, because the healing leads to the salvation of the person, the family or the area. Careful study of Old and New Testament history, along with the studies of Church history, teach us that the hand of God which moves silently and powerfully, is always visible in pre-arranged ways and we often call them sudden invasions of His power.

The time had arrived for God to begin to build a new church with a new vision and a new future. However, this beginning was not a new idea He had just devised. God was not reacting to the problem of persecution in Jerusalem because the beginning had been planned in the counsels of eternity. Persecution did not suddenly come to Jerusalem, nor did people suddenly arrive in Antioch. God was fulfilling His purposes right on time.

KEY PRAYER

Heavenly Father, I thank you today for your divine purposes within the world and within your Church, I thank you too for your divine purposes within my life. Thank you too that I have learned today that you never suddenly move as if you were reacting, you move according to your pre-arranged plan and purpose and all is well.

July 11th

KEY WORD: **Antioch**

KEY VERSE: **Acts 13 : 2**

While they were worshipping the Lord and fasting, the Holy Spirit said, "Set apart for me Barnabas and Saul for the work to which I have called them."

God's plan had been set in motion to build a great church in Antioch and His plan and purposes were right on time. In our last study today within this city and church we see that Paul and Barnabas set out to follow their divine call into God's plan for their lives.

The city was now prepared; the roads and highways had been built; the theatres and forums were in place; and the seaport was now established. The people were prepared for the gospel. All was ready and now it was time for the new Church.

Antioch was about to be invaded by God and His purpose and the city would never be the same again. The city was about to take its place in Early Church history and would be remembered long after its walls were in ruin and its foundations laid waste. God had a plan to build a model church that would be an example for all churches, of all ages and all cultures. Lessons would be learned within this church that would become the ethos for all churches to follow.

We need to understand the plan of God for us and our church and our cities, because He does have a plan and He is working to accomplish it. Then, having heard God's agenda from heaven, we need to release God to do whatever He wants to do; and then, having released Him, to follow that plan with clear direction and vision to its ultimate end within our lifetime. Bear in mind that He was working before you arrived on the scene and by His grace, He will go on working long after your departure.

This sobering thought tends to put things into perspective, because the Church is not mine, it is His; they are not my plans, but His will and purpose.

The city, therefore, was ready and the believing people had arrived. The church in Antioch was ready to commence its ministry. And what a ministry it would have! The happenings within the Antioch church were going to change the world.

It is so often the little, seemingly insignificant, things that make the greatest changes. Who would have thought that a scrawny child, that joined a Sunday school class one hot Sunday afternoon, would have become the greatest evangelist that this world has ever known. If only Billy Graham's Sunday school teacher could have foreseen the future. But he taught the child with unsuspecting faithfulness, not knowing what he had in his hands.

Who would have anticipated that a Jewish zealot, who persecuted the Church and who consented to the death of a young Christian, and who passionately sought to destroy the Church, would be changed on a journey of destruction. Paul would become the greatest leader that the Church would have, and his impact on the Antioch church was immense.

The journey of destruction that was taking Paul towards Damascus became the journey of discovery. It is often the little, seemingly insignificant, things that change the world. In Antioch it was a leader's prayer meeting that changed the world. A simple time of prayer and fasting that was part of the church's ethos. God was waiting to speak to a team of leaders within a church that was situated within the city that He had taken time and care to produce over hundreds of years of earthly history.

KEY PRAYER

Heavenly Father, thank you today for the little things that take place within my life that seem to be insignificant, but turn out to be your plan and initiative within my life. I praise you for the little things and I ask you to help me see what you are doing all around me.

July 12th

KEY WORD: **Will**

KEY VERSE: **Colossians 1 : 1**

Paul, an apostle of Christ Jesus by the will of God

We have spent the last seven days considering the church in the city of Antioch, and we have learnt that this church and this city were impacted by God according to His divine plan and purpose. In fact, God's will was in action when the city was founded and God's will was also in action when the church was planted.

We can not move on from this church and this city without considering the vital importance of the will of God. Again and again we hear the words 'God's will' referred to when we speak of God's plan and purpose for our lives. It was God's will that Paul and Barnabas were involved in the Antioch church. It was also God's will for them both to move on into greater ministry within the scope of the worldwide Church.

When we refer to God's will, we are normally talking about God's plan for our lives, or His plan for a church or even the world. We know that God has a plan for each one of us and we also know that God has a plan for each church and even for the world. However, what we often do not appreciate is that God's will is a definite and defined action of His ways and purposes, and that this will was ordained in the counsels of eternity long before we were ever born.

The Greek word for 'will', when fully understood, will help us to grasp this immense thought. The word that is used is '*thelema*' which translates to 'that which is willed', or even more pointedly 'that which is wished'. Our English language cannot fully grasp this truth because there have been word changes over the centuries, and our word 'wish' has completely lost its impact.

To wish for something today means to long for something that might not happen. However, to wish for something centuries ago meant that it would take place, because it was within your gift to grant it. Using this form of understanding we conclude that God can grant anything that He wishes for, because it is within His gift to grant it.

God wished that Paul should be an apostle, so He granted it. He wished that the Antioch church should be in blessing, so He granted it. And within our limited understanding, He wished that we should be in some form of ministry, so He willed it to happen.

'*Thelema*' was used in the New Testament to convey the truth of God doing whatever He wants to do. It is a dramatic word that brings a sense of power and authority to what God wants. It also reveals just how mighty God is and just how weak and human we really are. Even the greatest monarch or president, with all his might and power, can not do everything that he wants to do, but God, with His divine authority, can do anything that He wishes, and when He acts, He does so according to His will. It is His will that we should be saved and it is His will that we should be blessed. So He wished it and He planned it and He brought it into being by His will.

My Journal ____

____

____

____

____

KEY PRAYER

Heavenly Father, thank you today for your plan and purpose within my life, I understand that you wish me to be blessed so therefore you decree it and you bring it into being by your will. I understand too, that you have willed that my life is an anthem of praise, so, you bring all things into being so that I am directed towards you and that I seek your face.

July 13th

KEY WORD: **Manifold**

KEY VERSE: **Ephesians 3 : 10-11**

His intent was that now, through the church, the manifold wisdom of God should be made known to the rulers and authorities in the heavenly realms, according to His eternal purpose which He accomplished in Christ Jesus our Lord.

We are going to spend a few days considering this key verse because it is one of the most vital verses in the Scriptures. It is as if God put all of His main purpose towards this world in this one text and it is key to everything that we know about Him and His purposes.

Since there is so much contained within this verse we shall study the key words one by one, in order to gain as much light and truth as we can from this lovely Scripture. God has a plan – we all know that – but this plan has an ultimate end and a direction that we all need to constantly rediscover. God's intention for His Church is that, through us, His manifold wisdom is made known to the rulers and authorities in the heavenly realm. The Greek word that is used for our English word 'manifold' is, as is so often the case, derived from two words. The word is '*polupoikilos*'. It is made up by combining the two words '*poikilos*' which means 'varied', and '*polus*' which means 'much'. The result is a word that is difficult to translate, because it can literally mean 'much-varied' or 'multi-varied'. In trying hard to bring this truth to the church, it was as if Paul was struggling to convey just how varied and great God's wisdom really is. Paul's human wisdom could not find the eloquence to describe just how wonderful and spacious God's wisdom is, so he combined two words that sought to convey the richness and the diversity of God's wisdom.

One translator described the concept of God's 'manifold' wisdom, as a 'multi-faceted, all-encompassing, richly diverse and highly-illuminated insight into what God thinks about us – His Church'. We could never grasp just how varied and wonderful God's thoughts really are about us. Even in our moments of greatest faith we could not reach the heights of just how majestic God's thoughts and plans really are.

God's wisdom outstretches man's wisdom by light years and His ways of dealing with problems and circumstances are so much more diverse than ours, and yet He brings His word and revelation to us in ways that are easy to understand. When He speaks to us He makes Himself so clear that even the most spiritually weak of us can understand Him. Yet He lives in majestic splendour and in eternal richness. It is as if we see things in black and white, while God sees things in the most dazzling of colours. Our poor, sepia understanding is in stark contrast to the multi-coloured display of His spectacular wisdom.

As we pray today we should ask God to allow us to see more and more of His ways so that His colours may reach our blindness.

My Journal

KEY PRAYER

Heavenly Father, please help me to see more and more of your wisdom and ways. Please help the colour-blindness of my faith to be impacted by the brightness and richness of your colourful wisdom towards us. Help me to grasp the full measure of your thoughts concerning the Church so that I might impart a little of your glory to others.

July 14th

KEY WORD: **Wisdom**

KEY VERSE: **Ephesians 3 : 10-11**

His intent was that now, through the church, the manifold wisdom of God should be made known to the rulers and authorities in the heavenly realms, according to His eternal purpose which He accomplished in Christ Jesus our Lord.

If God's ways are higher than our ways and His thoughts higher than our thoughts, it would be very difficult to fully understand what God is seeking to do. However, in this key verse God outlines His plans through the Church. His intention is that His manifold wisdom should be displayed through the Church and that the Church should display His creative and wonderful ways. One commentator describes this divine desire as the Church being a 'theatre of the wonderful ways of God's wisdom being displayed to a watching universe'.

If God's ways are a multi-coloured spectacle of glory, then His wisdom is the true understanding of all things. The Greek word used for 'wisdom' is '*sophia*' which translated means 'insight into the true nature of things'.

God sees all things, He knows all things and He understands all things. There is nothing that is beyond His comprehension. Therefore, His grasp upon the past, the present and the future is absolute and He can plan accordingly.

When Paul sought to convey the truth of God's greatness and His desire to use the Church as a theatre of activity for His glory and grace, he used the Greek word that conveyed the most powerful sense of 'wisdom'. If he was seeking to convey the natural sense of wisdom, he would have used a different word, and if he sought to convey the human form of wise understanding he would have taken yet another Greek word that conveyed philosophy or intellectualism. However, the only word that was available to him when seeking to convey the highest and purest forms of wisdom was '*sophia*'. This word was used when people were trying to understand the difference between the lowest form of human understanding and the highest form of divine comprehension.

Paul took this word and applied it to God's perfect will and His desire to use the Church for His glory. The message is loud and clear: God has a multifaceted plan to show His awesome wisdom, grace and divine direction to a watching universe through His greatest creation – the Church.

My Journal

KEY PRAYER

Heavenly Father, my human mind can not grasp the divine dimensions of your plans and purposes but I know that you desire to reveal your wisdom to those who seek your face. Therefore, I pray today that you would reveal to me your plan and purpose, and that, through the Church, I might see your wisdom displayed to all who seek you.

July 15th

KEY WORD: **Rulers and Authorities**

KEY VERSE: **Ephesians 3 : 10-11**

His intent was that now, through the church, the manifold wisdom of God should be made known to the rulers and authorities in the heavenly realms, according to His eternal purpose which He accomplished in Christ Jesus our Lord.

Over the past two days we have understood that God has revealed Himself through the Church and that His wisdom is being declared to a watching universe. The revelation that God is seeking to bring is the fact of His awesome wisdom in the whole area of His divine plan and purpose. Paul revealed to us that those who are watching are called the rulers and authorities in the heavenly realm.

The King James Version names those who watch God's revelation being unfolded as 'principalities' and 'powers'. The NIV, however, uses the words 'rulers' and 'authorities'. To understand just who these beings are, we have to return to the original Greek language and seek to uncover the truth. The Greek words that are used are '*arche*' and '*exousia*' and they are correctly translated as 'government' and 'unrestricted authority'. These words have their origins in human government and administration but Paul took them and used them as the basis of his teaching concerning spiritual powers and spiritual principalities. When he used them, he always linked them with the words 'in heavenly realms' or in 'high places'.

Paul was speaking of angels and spiritual authorities when he taught that the Church was being watched and scrutinised. He also sought to teach us that the Church, which is the theatre of divine activity, is seen as the platform for God to reveal His purposes to all beings everywhere.

The actual words *'arche'* and *'exousia'* convey the concept of governmental rule within the heavenly realm and they are the words that were used when someone spoke of the power of the angels and the power of the rulers of spiritual authority. What Paul was seeking to convey was the truth of the Church being the vehicle for God's plans and purposes, and that the whole of heaven is transfixed by the revelation that constantly emanates from you and me.

This truth brings us to the startling thought that if the whole of heaven is watching the Church, which is made up by people just like you and me, then we need to be constantly on our guard in our thoughts and in our actions and deeds, and in the way that we react. Heaven is watching us all the time.

My Journal ______________________________

KEY PRAYER

Heavenly Father, I have learned today that I am being watched all the time and that angelic powers are monitoring my life. Help me, therefore, to live my life as an open book so that your plans and purposes are not hindered in any way by my lifestyle and my testimony before man and before angels.

July 16th

KEY WORD: **Accomplished**

KEY VERSE: **Ephesians 3 : 10-11**

His intent was that now, through the church, the manifold wisdom of God should be made known to the rulers and authorities in the heavenly realms, according to His eternal purpose which He accomplished in Christ Jesus our Lord.

In the last of our studies within this key verse we look today at the finality of these sentences, which lead to the thought that God has completed or accomplished His plan. His will is that the Church should show forth His glory and grace and that the watching universe should be made aware of His purposes through the multicoloured and awesome varieties of His wisdom.

The fact that this has been completed is another awesome truth. We are but the instruments of God's purpose and we are but the servants that God uses in the outworking of His divine plans.

The past 2000 years are the revelation of the Church in the world, and in the spiritual heights of the heavenly realms. If Jesus should tarry for another thousand years, the Church will go on revealing God's wisdom and glory.

This plan and this purpose has been completed and there is nothing that heaven or hell can do to hinder the plan. It has been accomplished. The Greek word that Paul used was the word *'poieo'*, which translated means 'definite conclusion', as in 'doing something' or 'completing something'. The word was used by those who wished to convey the thought of finality or completeness and when Paul wanted to bring the full impact of this key verse to its ultimate end, he could think of no better word.

The fact that God is in control and that He has the final word about His plan is so releasing and so reassuring that we can learn to rest in His finished work. Satan and his resources can do nothing against the finality of God's purpose. The heavenly beings in the heavenly realms watch the unfolding spectacle with great amazement, and we within the Church stand in awe of the One who planned it all and who completed it all. And we bring all our praise and worship to the One who has done all things well!

My Journal

KEY PRAYER

Heavenly Father, I bless you today for the wonder of your completed plan and I rest in the assurance that all is well, for you have completed your purpose. The Church awaits its redemption and its call to join you in heaven, and, until then, we can go on serving you in the full knowledge that all is well.

KEY WORD: **Kiss**

KEY VERSE: **Romans 16 : 16**

Greet one another with a holy kiss.

Having spent several days studying the whole concept of God's plan for the Church, it would be good if we spent several days considering those within the Church – the people of God.

We all know that the members of God's Church are called Christians and that this name was first given to the people of God in the city of Antioch. The title 'Christian' has unfortunately been stolen by all types of people, and we now find people calling themselves 'Christian' if they were born in a certain country, or if they do good works. This title is also given to those who simply attend church, believe certain facts and follow certain doctrines. However, you can only be truly Christian if you have received the Lord Jesus Christ as Saviour and are trusting Him for salvation.

These true Christians are called to be 'salt and light' in their communities and they are to bring care and concern to those who suffer. They are also called to be worshippers of the Lord and to love Him with all their hearts, with all their minds and with all their strength. They are also called to bless one another and to love one another and there are many verses in the Bible that express these actions of love. In the key verse today, Paul charges the Roman Christians to greet each other with a kiss. The Greek word that is used to mean 'kiss' is '*philema*', and the word means a 'token of brotherhood'. The Christian kiss was a form of greeting or a form of farewell and it was often linked with the word 'holy'. It was often called the 'kiss of the Lord' and these added words brought the full impact of the embrace. Paul was not talking about a sensual kiss, nor was he talking about an embrace between lovers, but he was talking about an affectionate and holy form of love embrace between those who were members of His Church.

The holy kiss was practised within the New Testament Church, and was continued within the Church for centuries; and it is still practised in many churches today. God wanted a freedom within the Church from class distinctions and social standing, so the kiss was a form of love-greeting that was practised between slaves and their masters and between the rich and the poor. This love-greeting brought people together and allowed them to express the fact that, in Christ, everyone is equal. There were no slaves or masters, there were no rich or poor, and there were no racial distinctions and no hypocrisy.

There was only one aspect of a kind of Church rule towards this holy kiss and this was the custom of the kiss being between members of the same sex. So you would find men kissing men and women kissing women. This was not thought to be wrong. In fact it became a very precious form of love greeting. Even in some apostolic writings from the fourth century, you would find that the Church rule expressed the fact that men sat on one side of the church and women sat on the other side of the church during acts of worship. Fortunately, freedom from this rule has now found its way back into the church and it is no longer the case that we find this distinction. However, the kiss should be treated with the greatest respect and should be used with care and grace.

The book of Psalms also commands us to 'kiss the Son', which is an expression of love towards God. We should, therefore, not just practise this highest form of endearment towards each other, but we should learn how to embrace God within our worship.

KEY PRAYER

Heavenly Father, as I approach you today it is with great concern that I do all things in the right manner. I want to be right in every practice within the Church. Please help my motives to be pure and my actions to be righteous when I spend time with those who love the Lord just like me. Help me, too, to love you in such a way that I embrace you with tender affection.

July 18th

KEY WORD: **Greet**

KEY VERSE: **Romans 16 : 16**

Greet one another with a holy kiss.

We continue today by looking at aspects of our attitude to one another within the Church, and the different forms of expression that we should manifest to one another.

When Paul commanded the early Christians in Rome to greet one another he was simply extending the form of love greeting to all believers everywhere. This embrace or greeting was a form of love-expression, with or without a holy kiss. To embrace each other was a wonderful form of expressing togetherness when, at the time, life was very difficult. Persecution was a fact of life and many Christians lost their lives for the sake of the Church, and for their love of the Lord. So, when they came together, the embrace was a form of closeness and affection.

In Romans 16, the word 'greet' is actually used 21 times by Paul. The constant use of this word is worth noting. Paul was not using the word 'greet' as we would use it today when we quickly and formally shake hands or we speak a word of greeting to each other. Paul was talking about an affectionate embrace that was warm and endearing. The Greek word used to mean 'greet' is the word '*aspazomai*', and it is more correctly translated as 'drawing to yourself' or even 'holding to yourself'. It is this action that Paul is commending when he instructs those in the Roman church to 'greet one another'. He had in mind an affectionate and warm embrace that brought the receiver of the greeting into a close and tender moment of bodily contact. This action of drawing one to yourself showed to those around that the Church was one in a time of separation and persecution.

This embrace was used at first greeting and at final departure, and was often used within the act of worship when worshippers would impart to each other the peace of God and the act of greeting within a moment of worship. This action is worth remembering within times of worship today, when we actually speak to each other and embrace each other in love.

The members of the Anglican Communion today will often be called by the leader of worship to 'bring the greeting to each other'. At this moment the worshippers will leave their pews and embrace one another. It is an interesting thought that, within the freedom of the Non-Conformist church, there are some things we do not do that are thought of by others as a measure of worship, embrace and blessing. Maybe we should seek to return to our roots and begin again to greet one another properly in real New Testament terms.

My Journal

KEY PRAYER

Heavenly Father, thank you for truth that is constantly reaffirmed throughout the Scriptures. Thank you for teaching me today about the actions of love. Help me to greet those with whom I worship so that we can express our love for each other in a practical and loving way.

July 19th

KEY WORD: **Warn**

KEY VERSE: **1 Thessalonians 5 : 14**

And we urge you, brothers, warn those who are idle, encourage the timid, help the weak, be patient with everyone.

Within this verse there is much to learn concerning the attitudes that we should express to one another. In fact there are four concepts that Paul urges the Thessalonian church to follow: they are 'warn', 'encourage', 'help' and 'be patient with' each other.

We will look at each one in turn, starting with 'warn' so that that we can learn as much as possible about New Testament attitudes.

Paul urged the believers to 'warn' those who seem to act in an idle manner. The Greek word for 'warn' is '*noutheteo*' and it was used for the concept of admonishing and setting things straight. The Old King James Version translates this word as 'admonish' whereas the newer versions use the word 'warn'. The concept was one of 'bringing things to mind', which is the nearest translation that we can achieve today, and it deals with the whole concept of bringing people into line, in the sense of acting in the right manner.

The word is a kin word to the concept of teaching; however, teaching is a positive action whereas 'warning' has a more negative connotation attached to it. When teaching is given, its main emphasis is to build up and to instruct. However, when a warning is given within this context, it brings a sense of discipline to those who seem to be walking in a way that contradicts the lifestyle of the Christian and who seem to be bringing a sense of disrepute to the Church.

In the key verse today, Paul stated that the warning should be given to those who seem to be acting in an idle manner. The

Greek word for 'idle' is the word '*argos*', which translated means 'to be inactive and unfruitful'. It would seem that Paul was anxious that each and every believer should be active in the sense of participation within the meetings and within the church, and that their lives were producing fruit. Inactivity and barrenness were, in Paul's eyes, something to be warned about so that the Church might not fall into the trap of resting in its work and witness.

It seems that this warning was given by the brothers, as mentioned in 1 Thessalonians 5 : 12. Paul did not ask the elders to bring the warning, nor did he ask the apostles or prophets to warn those who were acting in an idle way. It seems that the church disciplined itself in the sense that each member watched out for the others and watched over each other's lives. The warning was given from people within the fellowship so that each believer was entitled to care for each other. Maybe we should seek to return to the place where we can watch out for each other and learn to receive from each other, so that the Church might function in a stronger and healthier way.

My Journal ____

KEY PRAYER

Heavenly Father, help me to care for others and keep watch over their lives, and help me too, to receive from those around me so that the Church might be stronger and more disciplined. I praise you for those who love me enough to speak into my life concerning my strengths and my weaknesses.

July 20th

KEY WORD: ***Encourage***

KEY VERSE: **1 Thessalonians 5 : 14**

And we urge you, brothers, warn those who are idle, encourage the timid, help the weak, be patient with everyone.

Paul urged the church to be on its guard concerning those within the Church who were not quite as bold or as strong as most believers. As the Church was growing and becoming numerically stronger, it was obvious that Paul taught that each believer was responsible for those around them. It was not just the apostles or prophets, or the elders and deacons that assumed responsibility, but it was the job of each believer to care for one another.

The second concept that Paul dealt with within this key verse was to encourage those who were timid, and we have to understand what Paul describes as timidity before we can understand the concept of encouragement. The Greek term for the English word 'timid' that is used within this verse is '*oligopsuchos*' which translated means 'small souled' or 'despondent'. It is translated in different versions of the Bible as 'feebleminded' or even 'fainthearted'. The word is connected to the concept of being without strength. There were those in the Church who were growing stronger and more mature each and every day, but there were also those people who were struggling to grow and failing to mature. It was not so much weakness or lack of maturity that concerned Paul but the thought that there were those who were failing to grow spiritually.

Paul urged the Church to care for these people by encouraging them in their Christian growth. The Greek word for 'encouragement' is one of the most descriptive words that the New Testament used. It is the word '*paramutheomi*' and this word is translated as 'drawing alongside with comfort'. As with many New Testament words, this one is derived from two other words: '*para*' which means 'alongside' or 'by the side of', and '*muthos*' which means to 'bring counsel and advice'. This brings the concept of believers caring for each other in the sense of coming to the aid of those who were failing to grow – the 'smaller-souled' people within the Church who found it hard to grasp the truth and who were not spiritually maturing.

'Encourage' is a positive word and not a negative one. This form of drawing alongside to bring counsel and advice was not heavy in the sense of admonishing or discipline. It describes gentle comfort and care, and walking alongside those who found the way difficult. In church life today we are quite often impatient with those who seem to lack spiritual growth and we tend to dismiss quite easily those who take time to find their spiritual maturity. Maybe there are lessons we could learn from the Early Church in the way that each believer took the time to care for one another and took the time to walk alongside brothers who found the way more difficult.

My Journal ______________________________

KEY PRAYER

Heavenly Father, as I come before you today it is with a measure of concern about the way that I may have treated others within the Church. Please forgive me for leaving the growth of the Church and other people's lives simply to those in leadership. Please help me to watch out for those who might be struggling and help me to draw alongside to care for them.

July 21st

KEY WORD: **Help**

KEY VERSE: **1 Thessalonians 5 : 14**

And we urge you, brothers, warn those who are idle, encourage the timid, help the weak, be patient with everyone.

Paul urged the church to be on its guard concerning those within the church who were not quite as bold or as strong as most believers. As the church was growing and becoming numerically stronger it was obvious that Paul's teachings meant that each believer was responsible for those around them. It was not just the apostles or prophets, or the elders and deacons that assumed responsibility, but it was the job of each believer to care for each other.

The third concept that Paul was concerned about within this key verse was the concept of helping and enabling those who were found to be weak. Again, we have to understand the concept of weakness before we can understand the help that was given to those who found themselves in this position.

The Greek word for 'weak' was the word *'asthenes'* which has two possible translations. Firstly it means 'physical weakness', which was seen in illness or bodily weakness, and secondly, it means 'spiritual weakness', which was seen in the whole sense of both lack of spiritual growth and dependency upon others. Paul urged the believers to care for those who found themselves in either bodily weakness or spiritual weakness and he used a very important word for this kind of ministry.

Paul said, "help the weak", and the Greek word for 'help' that he used was the word *'antilepsis'*, which translated means 'to support' or 'to lay hold of'. The concept of this word is in the area of structure and support, and it was used in the area of building. A building, in order to be built, needs a framework placed around it. Paul used this concept when he was seeking to care for those who were in greatest need. He was actually asking the church to build a framework of supporting care around those who were at the point of greatest concern and greatest need.

There was another meaning to the word '*antilepsis*' which is also vital in our understanding of the framework of support that is needed. The word can also be translated as 'exchanging something'. In this translation Paul may have had in mind the whole concept of exchanging strength for weakness. If we accept both meanings then we will be well on the way to understanding the New Testament concept of caring for one another.

Those who find themselves wallowing in weakness need a structure of support and a helping hand given by those who are stronger and spiritually fitter. Therefore strength can be imparted to those who are weak and we can exchange our strength for someone else's weakness.

Because the word 'help' is such a rich word with many facets of truth to discover we shall return to it in a few days time, once our studies in this key verse have been completed.

My Journal

KEY PRAYER

Heavenly Father, I long to support those who are weak, because I can remember being supported myself in the earlier days of my spiritual growth. Help me to draw alongside those who need care and help me to be instrumental in building a structure of love and care.

July 22nd

KEY WORD: ***Patient***

KEY VERSE: **1 Thessalonians 5 : 14**

And we urge you, brothers, warn those who are idle, encourage the timid, help the weak, be patient with everyone.

Here is a key word today that needs to be implemented within each and every church. So often in Church life today we become impatient with people and with their actions, and in many ways our trust and loyalty can be greatly tested. Paul urged the believers to be patient with each another so that the whole Church might move forward in a careful and caring way.

The word 'patient' is an interesting word. The Greek word used was the word '*makrothumeo*' and we actually studied this several months ago, in March. However, since it appears again in this key verse it is worth further consideration because it falls within a new context: the context of the believers caring for one another.

The translation of this Greek word means 'to be long tempered' or to be 'longsuffering', and several Bible versions actually use the word 'longsuffering' in their attempt to bring the true meaning to light. Longsuffering is a Bible virtue and it is often the case that we are short-tempered with one another and we do not act in a patient manner with one another. Our likes and dislikes and our prejudices and our traditions lead us to be quite impatient with one another, therefore, knowing this trait of human character, Paul urged a different lifestyle on the church.

Two great theologians, Hogg and Vine, give a very clear exposition of patience and longsuffering that is worthy of our consideration. They say that: "Longsuffering is that quality of self-restraint in the face of provocation which does not hastily retaliate or promptly punish; it is the opposite of anger and it is associated with mercy, and it is used quite rightly of God."

God does not treat us with retaliation for our sins but He treats us with patience and love, and this attribute of God is one that we should seek to emulate within the Church, so that the believers are covered with a sense of care, patience and longsuffering. If this attribute were to be seen within each church then the true picture of loving kindness and tender mercy would appear. After all, Jesus said that you would know His disciples "by their love for one another". It is not by miracles or power that we shall be known but by our patient care one for another.

As we conclude our studies within this key verse today, it is with the great desire that we should seek to minister to one another in a New Testament way and not with the lifestyle that we see around us within the world.

Over the next few days we shall return to the New Testament concept of 'help' and we shall continue to learn what it means to minister to one another.

My Journal

KEY PRAYER

Heavenly Father, I cry out to you today to make me worthy of my high calling in Christ Jesus. Father, I long to be a mirror image of you in the way that you are patient and kind to your children. Help me each day to practise loving care to those who are around me.

July 23rd

KEY WORD: **Help**

KEY VERSE: **Hebrews 4 : 16**

Let us then approach the throne of grace with confidence, so that we may receive mercy and find grace to help us in our time of need.

There are at least ten different Greek words that are used for our English word 'help', and each one of the ten different words conveys a slightly different meaning to the English word and to the concept of helping one another. In the key verse of the past few days we examined the concept of helping one another and we saw that the Church needed every believer to take the responsibility of caring for one another.

This caring was manifested in the form of helping one another and because this concept of helping care is so vital, we shall spend a few days studying some of the ten Greek words that are used for this concept. However, in an attempt to find out how we should treat each other it is important to find out just how God treats us. If we can understand this, we will then understand helping each other in a better manner.

In the key verse today, the writer to the Hebrews sought to convey the thought that there is a is throne of grace that is awaiting our attendance, and that this throne is one of total acceptance and confidence. We can approach this throne with boldness and openness and we will always find grace to help in time of need. This 'help' through grace is an interesting concept. The writer uses the Greek word '*boetheia*' and it has been translated as 'help' in most versions of the Bible. However, the true and more correct translation is 'succour', which conveys more than just simply a measure of help. The word is constructed from two others: '*boe*' which means 'to shout', and '*theo*' which means 'to run'.

If we take these two different words and place them together the concept is far different than the simple understanding of helping someone or being helped. What the writer was trying to convey was the thought of boldness and confidence. We do not need to approach the throne of grace with reticence or fear; we can actually come before God with a sense of a shout of triumph and we can also run to Him in time of need.

This fuller understanding of the word brings us to a place of total acceptance in God with the thought that, when we have a need, it is not with a sense of trepidation that we approach God but with a sense that He is just waiting and wanting to help us. Therefore our approach to Him is one of triumphant shouting and pleasure and one of confident acceptance, so that we can run to Him.

My Journal

KEY PRAYER

Heavenly Father, thank you for an open throne of acceptance where I can come boldly before you. Thank you too that you do not reward me for my sin but that you reward me through grace. I can approach you at any time of need and you always furnish me with grace and mercy.

KEY WORD: **Help**

KEY VERSE: **Acts 18 : 27**

When Apollos wanted to go to Achaia, the brothers encouraged him and wrote to the disciples there to welcome him. On arriving he was a great help to those who by grace had believed.

Having noticed already that there are at least ten different words in the Greek language that are translated as our English word 'help', it is already understood that the richness of Greek causes differing variations within words so that word meanings can become stronger and far more pronounced. Our word 'help' normally conveys the thought of coming to someone's aid or the assistance given at a time of need. However, the Greek language is deeper and far more pronounced.

When Apollos wanted to go to Achaia the brothers encouraged him and wrote letters of support, which were received by the Achaian disciples. The key verse today makes it quite clear that Apollos had help and support. But when he arrived in Achaia he gave a quite different form of help to the people there.

The Greek word for the form of 'help' that he gave is the word '*sumballo*' which translated means 'to throw together'. Again, it is a word that has been formed by using two different words, '*sun*' which means 'with', and '*ballo*' which means 'throw'. This form of help was not merely the assistance in time of need and nor was it simply aid in a crisis. Apollos literally threw himself into the work of God in Achaia and gave himself in a literal way to those he sought to serve.

The word was used at a time of great activity when someone would give themselves completely to helping and serving. This was not grudging service given without enthusiasm nor was it help that was ordered by someone else and carried out without much desire. Apollos gave his help willingly, tempered with an overwhelming desire to serve God and others. So upon his arrival, once the formalities were completed, he threw himself into the work of God and served with great enthusiasm.

The Church today needs more and more people to serve in an Apollos way so that momentum is gained and direction is followed, with a sense of wholehearted and total commitment. There is no place for half-heartedness and lack of resolve. We have too much to do to be faint-hearted and lacking in passion. Apollos gave himself with energy and zeal to the people in Achaia and threw himself into ministry. An important lesson to learn today!

My Journal

KEY PRAYER

Heavenly Father, help me to serve you with a willing heart and a ready mind. Help me to abandon myself to ministry so that, with all my heart and with all my mind and with all my strength, I might serve you and the Church with passion.

July 25th

KEY WORD: **Help**

KEY VERSE: **2 Corinthians 1 : 11**

...as you help us with your prayers. Then many will give thanks on our behalf for the gracious favour granted us in answer to the prayers of many.

Here, once again, the richness of Greek exceeds the English language and we have a word that is simply translated as 'help', even though it fails to fully convey the richness of meaning.

Paul was conveying his thanks to the church for prayers that were being prayed on his behalf. He saw it as a great form of ministry and help to those who were travelling in ministry. This help was spiritual as well as practically supportive and Paul saw it as a very vital part of 'back-up' ministry. He used a word that was rich in its meaning and the church in Corinth would understand when they read his letter, just how much their prayers meant to this apostle.

The Greek word used was the word '*sunupourgeo*'. We have noticed many times that certain words were word pictures that were formed by the joining of certain words together. In order to convey the depth of meaning that prayer support meant to Paul, he joined together three different words in order to give full expression to the kind of help that he was receiving.

The three words were '*sun*' which means 'with', '*hupo*' which means 'under' and '*ergon*' which means 'work'. So the word picture that Paul built here was the fact that the Church was combining together to pray for those who were travelling in ministry, and that this prayer ministry was with great feeling and that those who were praying were undergirding the work of God.

Today, there are often superstars of ministry within the Church – people who seemingly have no need of anyone else and who seemingly can do all things themselves without reference to anyone else. This word picture, built by Paul, conveys the truth of the fact that we all need each other. The truth is that there are no real superstars within the New Testament Church, because we are all in submission to each other and all of us need the value of supportive prayer and ministry at all times.

The church in Corinth was of great value to Paul. The church members were not travelling with him. They were not part of the ministry of outreach or church planting, but their prayers were undergirding the apostolic ministry of those who were on the road for the gospel's sake. Paul was weaker without their prayers and the Church was weaker without Paul. They needed each other and they had learnt to support and help each other. Holding each other up in the Lord is a vital component of ministry.

My Journal

KEY PRAYER

Heavenly Father, thank you for those who hold me up in prayer. I praise you today for all who have been a help and a support to me over the years. I fully understand that I am where I am today because of their undergirding ministry. Help me to remember to hold others up in prayer too.

July 26th

KEY WORD: **Help**

KEY VERSE: **Luke 10 : 40**

But Martha was distracted by all the preparations that had to be made. She came to Jesus and asked, "Lord, don't you care that my sister has left me to do all the work by myself? Tell her to help me!"

Once again we find that an English translation fails to convey the depth of meaning that someone was searching for. In the key verse, Martha was moaning to Jesus about the fact that she had been left to do all the work while her sister Mary was sitting at the feet of Jesus enjoying moments of blessing and grace.

Martha asked the question: Why do you not "tell her to help me"? Martha was not simply saying that she could do with another pair of hands, nor was she saying that it was time for someone else to come and help her in the sense of assistance. Her cry was much deeper and far more searching than the simple request for help.

The Greek word used was '*sunantilambano*' and once again it was a word picture drawn up from two other words. The meaning was 'to take hold of' or 'take a share in'. The two words that were used were '*sun*' which means 'with' and '*antilambano*' which means 'to take a turn' or 'to give support to'. This cry from Martha with the word picture in place simply meant: Tell Mary to come and work with me so that I might have some support at a time like this.

Martha was being overwhelmed by the task at hand and she was looking for a measure of support from those who were closest to her. She felt let down and very much on her own when the task was at its greatest moment. A very biblical word can be drawn from this account and the word has its roots in the word picture that was being conveyed. The word is 'partake', and Martha was looking for someone who would partake of her need and be with her at her moment of greatest need.

Partaking is a very strong word within the Bible. It is a ministry word and it conveys the depth of feeling when someone comes alongside you and gives help and support. 'Partaking' is feeling what you feel and joining in; it is understanding how you must feel and immediately responding. Martha was looking for someone near to her to reach out and feel her pain.

In Church life today we must learn to feel and to sense when those around us are hurting, so that we can immediately respond by caring and helping. It is not enough to use words of support and it is not enough just to pray. We must be ready to share in the need by taking our turn to support.

My Journal

KEY PRAYER

Heavenly Father, forgive me when I have not noticed someone's need; when I have selfishly been concerned with only my own needs. Help me to draw alongside those in need so that I might share in their pain and be a support. Thank you today for those who have given help to me in time of need – I bless you for their help.

July 27th

KEY WORD: **Help**

KEY VERSE: **Acts 26 : 22**

But I have had God's help to this very day, and so I stand here and testify to small and great alike.

In this key verse today Paul was standing to testify before King Agrippa and his court. Within his testimony of saving grace and protection, he stated that God had granted him help in all things and that this is the reason why he was able to stand in the court.

The word that he used for the English word translated as 'help', once again does not fully convey the impact of the Greek word. Paul's choice of words was important in the conveying of truth. Paul was not just saying that God helped him, as we might say someone gave us a hand. The Greek word that he used was the word '*epikouria*' which means 'an ally' or 'an aid', and it was the term that was used in circles where a person called an '*epikouros*' was needed. This person was someone who stood in line simply waiting to serve. We use a similar expression today when we talk of a waiter who stands by a table waiting to serve. The amazing fact is that this word was used by Paul of the service that God had granted to him.

It was not that Paul was saying that God was like a waiter, simply standing by, waiting at Paul's beck and call. The truth that Paul was seeking to convey was that God was always ready whenever Paul had a need, and that this readiness was translated into glorious action whenever Paul cried unto Him. God does not act like a waiter and we should not treat Him as such. However, like a waiter, He is always there and, like a waiter, He is always ready to grant assistance. We have an ally in heaven who waits for us to call upon Him, and who is always ready to come to our aid.

And we have an even greater truth than this. The fact is that even when we do not call, our Heavenly Father seeks to help. Even before we call He is there, ready to grant us aid.

Paul testified before King Agrippa that God had given him divine aid constantly during the years of his salvation and that it was only God's grace and provision that had brought him through. This testimony brought a sudden and fierce response from Festus, the Roman Governor, who actually shouted and behaved badly. King Agrippa's response, however, was entirely different. Having listened to Paul's testimony and having heard of the help that he had received from God, he spoke at length, stating that he had almost been persuaded to become a Christian

We need to remember that when we give a testimony concerning the goodness of God we must always remember to depend upon His help and His divine aid. The response to our testimony is not dependent upon us, it is always dependent upon the listener's position before God. What matters most is that God receives the glory for His grace that helps in time of need.

My Journal ______________________________

KEY PRAYER

Heavenly Father, I bless you today for your constant goodness and your grace and your mercy which has been granted to me over the years. Even before I call you are ready and waiting to bless me. Thank you for your provision and your willingness to be there all the time as my ally and aid.

July 28th

KEY WORD: **Help**

KEY VERSE: **1 Corinthians 16 : 16**

Submit to such as these and to everyone who joins in the work, and labours at it [that helps with the work].

In our final look at the word 'help' we turn today to a word that is only used four times in the New Testament. In the Old King James Version the word is translated as 'help', however, in the NIV, it is translated as 'joins in the work'. The Greek word is '*sunergeo*' which means 'to co-operate' or 'to be a co-worker'.

The word is a used when someone joins you in a form of work in which help is needed and which without them it could not be accomplished. Paul used this word to convey the truth of partnership and co-workers. It is only found once in the New Testament but it is a most powerful word.

At this point in his ministry, Paul was finding the work quite difficult and he needed refreshment due to the fact that no one had given him support. He actually stated, in Corinthians 16 : 17, that his need was not being met by those in the church at Corinth, and that he had to wait for those who were arriving from Achaia before his need of refreshment was granted.

Three men arrived from Achaia: Stephanas, Fortunatus and Achaicus, and Paul noted the fact that upon their arrival they immediately sought to minister to him. Maybe it was his demeanour or maybe it was his lack of zeal that troubled them, but they instantly sought to bless him and to minister to him. Paul's testimony concerning this action was that they refreshed his spirit. He found this ministry to be just what he needed at that time, and he therefore stated that these men helped him and that they had joined in the work and become co-workers with him and that they were in co-operation with him at a time of great need.

One of the things that we have learned together over the past few days instudying the word 'help' is that we are in great need of each other all the time. There is no place in the Church for the 'lone ranger' or the isolated figure at the helm of some great ministry. We are one in spirit and in fellowship and we need each other.

If Paul found the need to be refreshed then I am convinced that there will be times in our lives when the need to be refreshed will become acute. It is at times like this that the Church body needs to minister and it is at times like this that we need to learn to receive.

We all need help from time to time and we all need to be helpers.

My Journal

KEY PRAYER

Heavenly Father, I thank you today that you have planted me within a family and that within this family we are one. Help me to be a helper and help me to also learn to receive help. Thank you for teaching me the truths of partnership in the work of God and I bless you for all the support that I have received.

July 29th

KEY WORD: ***Suffering***

KEY VERSE: **2 Corinthians 1 : 5**

For just as the sufferings of Christ flow over into our lives, so also through Christ our comfort overflows.

The word 'suffering' and the word 'afflictions' are used in different translations of the Bible but are used concerning the same thing: the troubles and trials of our flesh. Each one of us goes through suffering and affliction throughout our entire walk with God. Suffering and affliction are part of life and are part of spiritual growth and development.

There are several words used in the New Testament for suffering and they all convey something a little different from each other. We find words that teach hardship as a form of suffering. There is a word that conveys the thought of torment as a form of suffering and there are several others. The word, however, that conveys the thought of spiritual development through suffering and affliction is the Greek word '*pathema*'. From this we derive our English words 'pathos' and 'passion' because it conveys the sense of suffering through pain and the understanding of sympathy.

The word '*pathema*' teaches the fact that even though we may suffer and even though our afflictions may be severe, the whole process is one of sympathetic understanding from a God who is in overall control of all things and who is leading us by the hand through pain into a place of greater spiritual growth and blessing.

Many of the New Testament writers saw the principal of suffering as a means of growth and they wrote about this frequently. We find numerous passages relating to the fact of affliction and pain producing blessing. However, we have several problems relating to affliction and suffering because we find it hard to see clearly when we are going through a period of suffering, and we also find it hard to understand the purposes of God at that time. One of our problems is that we often fail to grasp the fact that all things work together for good. We tend to see periods of suffering as isolated events within our lives when the reality is that God is in control of all things, and that what we go through is not a series of isolated events but a lifetime of spiritual growth and development.

Also, we often fail to see the good in our sufferings and this is displayed in questions such as: Where is God now? Or: Why am I going through this kind of pain? God is always in control and nothing is outside of His care and understanding. Our pathway may be through suffering and affliction at the moment but it is only that we might be brought through into a place of greater understanding of God's ways and deeper realisation of His Presence.

When we pass through periods of '*pathema*' we should learn to rejoice because, the greater the pain is, the greater is the blessing, and the harder the path is, the greater are the rewards. As the key verse stated at the beginning of our reading, "As we suffer, so are we comforted".

My Journal

KEY PRAYER

Heavenly Father, help me to understand the problem of pain and suffering and teach me each day to rejoice in my afflictions so that I might rest in you. Forgive me when I misunderstand your plan and purpose in my life and help me to trust you fully through all of my experiences. I rejoice today that, no matter what I go through, you are walking with me through each and every trial, and your comfort overflows.

July 30th

KEY WORD: **Good**

KEY VERSE: **Matthew 19 : 17**

"Why do you ask me about what is good," Jesus replied. "There is only One who is good. If you want to enter life, obey the commandments."

In our study yesterday we looked at the problem of suffering, and we considered the fact that all things worked together for good. In the New Testament there are two main words for the English word 'good', so at the close of this month we shall consider both of them. The first one today and the second tomorrow.

In the key verse today Jesus is being confronted by the Rich Young Ruler who asks the question: What good thing must I do in order to obtain eternal life? Jesus replied, "There is only One who is good", and that One is God.

The Greek word used here for the English word 'good' is '*agathos*' which means that which is 'beneficial in its effect', and it was used of things that were physically good and things that were morally good. In the moral sense Matthew uses the word concerning God, and he said that only One is good, and that is God. This meaning, in the moral sense, is that everything else and everyone else has the pollution of badness, only God remains free of any pollution and only God is essentially good.

The word '*agathos*' can really only be applied to those things that have their origins in God or that are connected with Him. For example, now that we have become born again Christians, the word 'good' can be applied to us in the sense of doing good works or living a good life. Those who are outside of Christ might do good things but they are not and can not be essentially 'good'.

'Good' can also be applied to blessings both temporal and spiritual when it is recognised that they come from God. He is the giver of all things good and every good gift comes from Him. We should give thanks every day for the good things that He gives to us, as we take so much for granted.

'Good' can also be applied to everything that stems from God in the spiritual realm. For instance heaven is good, Calvary is good, eternity is good and the gospel is good – in fact it is so good, it is called Good News. So we find a realm in which God dwells, and from His grace emanates all goodness and all good things.

'Agathos' is the word that has roots in the divine world and it can only be applied to those things that have their origins and their future in God. God is good and He alone knows goodness. In fact, He is the author of good and goodness, and even when things don't work out exactly as we plan, He still makes all things work together for good, because He is 'good'.

My Journal

KEY PRAYER

Heavenly Father, I thank you today for your goodness and for the overwhelming and wonderful fact that you are good. I praise you for this great truth and I bless your name for the fact that you dispense goodness wherever you please. Thank you today for the fact that you have touched my life with your goodness.

July 31st

KEY WORD: **Good**

KEY VERSE: **Galatians 6 : 9**

Let us not become weary in doing good, for at the proper time we will reap a harvest if we do not give up.

The second word in the New Testament that is translated as 'good' is the Greek word '*kalos*', which means 'those things that are intrinsically good'. This word is applied to such things in the New Testament as good fruit, good trees, good ground, good works and good testimony. It was the word that was used when the Greeks were seeking to describe something that was pleasing, so they used this word in order to convey the thought of beauty and fairness.

Christians are urged to do good works. Only God is good and whatever He touches can become good, but our works are good in the sense that those that benefit from our works receive a beautiful thing. When we serve others the fragrance is a beautiful offering unto the Lord.

In the key verse today, Paul was seeking to convey the truth that when we feel like giving up due to spiritual or even physical weakness, if we keep on doing good things, we shall reap a harvest in the end. So the urgency is to keep on doing those things that are good.

Paul could say this out of his own experience because there were many times when he felt like giving up, and many times when the easiest thing would have been to leave the Church planting and the work of the ministry to someone else much younger and the work of overseeing the Church to other mature leaders. But his desire was to reap a harvest, so he kept on doing these good things in the knowledge that he would finally receive the accolade 'well done, good and faithful servant'.

God is good, as we saw yesterday, this is essential goodness and is beneficial in its effects. However, our works and the beauty around us are intrinsically good and these things are honourable, pleasant and right.

It is a good thing to give praise unto the Lord. As we consider just how good God is, we should praise Him, for this is a good thing to do. As we conclude another month of studies it would be good to consider the fact that He has brought us safely this far and He has been very good to us. It would also be a good thing to consider the fact that, throughout the remaining months of the year, He will still be very good to us, so our desire should be to bring Him honour and praise so that our voice is raised in good and honourable thanksgiving.

My Journal

KEY PRAYER

Heavenly Father, I do bless you today. I thank you for the past few months – months that you have filled with good things. I will also give thanks for the good things that are yet to come. I lift my voice and I lift my praise unto One who is so good.

August 1st

KEY WORD: **Truth**

KEY VERSE: **Galatians 2 : 5**

We did not give into them for a moment, so that the truth of the gospel might remain with you.

As we commence a brand new month of our studies we shall consider an absolute: the matter of truth. It is an interesting fact that almost all false doctrines and almost all heresies begin with a measure of truth. In other words, people who are caught up in false doctrines and those who propagate heresy normally are people who have started in truth and moved away into error.

To hold onto truth and to continue in truth is absolutely vital in a fast changing world. Jesus said 'that the truth shall set you free,' and to remain free is one of the most important facets of the journey that we are all on. The word 'truth' appears many times in the New Testament and it always has its origins in either 'God' or 'the Word'. The key verse today speaks of the fact that Paul was determined not to waver from the absolute of remaining in truth so that the Galatian Christians might stand upon the truth of the gospel. There were many false teachers at that time and a vast number of false doctrines, so Paul's determination was greatly commendable in the sense that he was standing firm in truth.

The Greek word that he used for the word 'truth' was '*aletheia*' which means 'the manifested essence of a matter', and it really was a word that could only be applied to Christian truth. It was a word in the Greek language that could only be described as 'the bottom line' or the 'basis of something'. The reason that Paul used this word, and he used it several times in his writings, was show that Christian doctrine was the basis of faith and that there was no other.

In a world of changing values where 'new' things constantly keep appearing, it is good to know that one thing remains the same and always will do, truth stands firm. So, we need to stand firm too and remain in truth.

The word *'aletheia'* can also be used to describe a person's character, so that if a person has a good character with integrity and honesty, then we would say that he is a truthful person who always acts in a right way. The opposite of this would of course be someone who lacks integrity and is dishonest, we would say that this person could not be trusted. Therefore, it is the same with Christian truth, it can be trusted because it has as its basic foundation the essence of integrity. Truth stands alone and truth stands forever.

Jesus was the Word so, therefore, He was the truth. This is why He stated that He was 'the Way, the Truth and the Life'. Jesus was not saying that He was simply 'one way' or even 'one aspect of truth' but His statement embodied the whole basis of truth, that He was the absolute, the full truth and the only truth.

We must at all costs hold on to what we believe. Many teachers will come with persuasive words and many attacks will be made on truth, but the Word of the Lord remains forever, therefore hold on to truth.

My Journal ______________________________

____

____

____

____

____

KEY PRAYER

Heavenly Father, at the beginning of a new month I will set out to pledge before you that I shall remain in truth. Thank you for the fullness of truth that you have granted to me and thank you, too, for the light that I have received thus far. Help me to ever walk in the light of your Word, so that truth might remain.

August 2nd

KEY WORD: **Sects (heresy)**

KEY VERSE: **Acts 26 : 5**

They have known me for a long time and can testify, if they are willing, that according to the strictest sect of our religion, I lived as a Pharisee.

Yesterday we studied together the concept of truth and the absolute necessity to remain in truth at all costs. Today we shall consider the opposite of truth, which is of course error.

The New Testament is full of strong appeals to remain in truth because error is all around us. Most false doctrines begin their lives in a measure of truth and quickly fall into error as soon as strong opinions are added to truth. These strong opinions are the inventions of man, and as soon as man places his hands upon truth we begin to be in great danger. There is a very interesting New Testament word for the opinion of man and it has several meanings.

The Greek word for 'heresy' or 'sects' is the word *'hairesis'* and it is best understood as the 'choosing or choice'. It was always used when someone was seeking to exert a 'strong self-willed opinion upon a chosen line'. In other words, when a teacher began to exercise a strong opinion and asserted that this was the right path and the right way, then this was called *'hairesis'*. The strong opinion by this teacher would then lead to error and the teacher would become a false teacher. This word is translated as both 'heresy' and 'sect' in differing Bible versions, but it always meant the same thing, the departure from truth and the entering of error.

In the New Testament, Peter calls this kind of departure from truth 'destructive' and Paul sought throughout his ministry to teach the avoidance of men's doctrines and false doctrines. All heresy leads to the departure from truth into the formation of sects and more and more divisions. This word was only used nine times in the New Testament but on each occasion it carries a strong plea for men to avoid error.

It is an interesting fact that in the key verse today, in the eyes of the Pharisees, Christian truth was 'a sect and a heresy'. Evil men had decided that Christian truth ought to be destroyed because they were blinded within their own error and filled with strong opinions so that they could not see the light of truth.

So the question might be asked by some: How do we know that we are speaking the truth if others strongly believe that they are right? The only answer to this question is really to pose another question: Where does what you believe lead you? If the answer is 'away from Jesus Christ', then the answer is, you are in error, but if what you believe leads you towards Him, then you are in truth.

All truth is centered in Him and has its focus upon Him and Jesus is the essence of all truth; anything that leads us away from Him is an error that must be avoided. All error leads to division and division leads to sects and heresies, and these in turn lead to destruction.

My Journal

KEY PRAYER

Heavenly Father, I thank you today for the promise that, as I walk with you, the Holy Spirit will lead me into all truth. Help me to ever walk in the light so that I might never be in error or danger. I bless you for your guidance and thank you for your truth.

August 3rd

KEY WORD: **Error**

KEY VERSE: **James 5 : 20**

Remember this: Whoever turns a sinner from the error of his way will save him from death and cover over a multitude of sins.

Having considered truth and that which is false, at the beginning of this month, it would be good if we understood just what error is and just what error can do. There is no better verse in the New Testament that depicts error than the one that is our key verse today. James spoke of the error that leads to sin and death and he dealt with this in a very graphic manner. If we manage to 'turn a sinner away from error we save him from death and cover over a multitude of sins'.

James used an interesting word to describe just what error is, he used the Greek word *'plane'* which translated means 'a wandering away from the right path'. This word only appears ten times in the New Testament, seven times it is translated as 'error' and the other three times it appears as 'deceit' or 'delusion' or 'deceiving'. It is a very powerful word as its strength comes from the fact that it was used by the Greeks as the word for those who would be morally corrupted. In other words James was saying that to live in error is like being corrupted with impure morals in such a way that you leave the right path and wander down a wrong path.

Truth is our plumb line and if we stray away from truth we lose our sense of balance and rightness and the danger is that we shall be led into paths that lead to destruction and danger. The word *'plane'* was used in two ways within the New Testament. Firstly, it was applied to those who were immoral as in 2 Peter 2 : 18. Peter was speaking of those who were living according to the 'fleshly lustful desires of human nature', he called those people, 'people of error'. This kind of lustful error appears a few times in New Testament writings. Secondly, the word was used of those who had departed from Christian truth and who were following false teachings. Peter again used the word when he was warning about evil teachings that could lead us away from our secure position in Christ (2 Peter 3 : 17).

W E Vine has a very important quote concerning this word when he states that 'errors in doctrine are not infrequently the effect of relaxed morality and vice versa'.

Our calling is to hold on to truth and to allow this truth to constantly set us free because the revealing of new truth will help us to grow and mature in Christ, remembering all the time that real truth will always lead us to Jesus whereas error takes us away from Him into paths of destruction.

My Journal ______________________________

KEY PRAYER

Heavenly Father, help me each day to walk with you in such a way that I shall discover new and fresh truths concerning Jesus. Help me to continually grow in Him so that I shall become stronger and more mature in my understanding of doctrine and Christian practice. Thank you for your Word that is a light unto my path.

August 4th

KEY WORD: **Escape**

KEY VERSE: **2 Peter 1 : 4**

Through these He has given us His very great and precious promises, so that through them you may participate in the divine nature and escape the corruption in the world caused by evil desires.

In the New Testament the English word 'escape' appears many, many times. However, as usual with the translations from Greek into English much of the richness disappears. There are several Greek words that are used for the one English word 'escape', and over the next few days we shall seek to discover the truth of some of them.

In the key verse today Peter was seeking to convey the truth of the fact that through the precious promises of God we can escape the pollution of this present world, a world that is infested with evil desires. The truth that we can escape this infestation of evil is to be found in the word that is translated as our word 'escape'. Peter used the Greek word '*apopheugo*' which means to 'flee away from'. The normal Greek word that is used for our word 'escape' is '*pheugo*' and we derive our word 'fugitive' from this root word. When other descriptive words are added to this basic word, a word picture appears which gives a very clear definition to what the New Testament writers were trying to convey.

'*Apopheugo*' literally means 'to flee away from', which gives the key verse an added impact. Sin is always present and has been since Adam fell in the Garden of Eden. Sin is strong in its temptations and strong in its entanglements. However, through the precious promises of God it is possible to flee away from the temptations of sin with its evil desires and pollution.

We shall never escape the presence of sin until we reach eternity and the presence of God, however, the power of sin with its strong urges and desires can be thwarted by the use of this word.

By adding the word *'apo'* to *'pheugo'* Peter added a dimension of power to the concept of fleeing, *'apo'* means 'from' and *'pheugo'* means 'to gain flight'. So Peter was not just saying 'run away from sin and temptation' his command has much more urgency than that, he was commanding his readers to literally take flight from sin as quickly and as strongly as they possibly can. You see so often we play with temptation and we flirt with sin and then we wonder why we become ensnared with evil desires and sinful pollution. Peter's emphasis is placed upon the fact we should 'take flight' at the first hint of temptation.

If we took heed of his words, through the precious promises of God, we should be able to remain free of sin.

My Journal

KEY PRAYER

Heavenly Father, I thank you today that you have provided a way of escape from sin and temptation. I praise you that through the precious promises of God I can remain free from sin. Help me each day to take flight from temptation so that my life remains pure.

August 5th

KEY WORD: **Escape**

KEY VERSE: **Luke 21 : 36**

Be always on the watch, and pray that you may be able to escape all that is about to happen, and that you may be able to stand before the Son of Man.

In the New Testament the English word 'escape' appears many, many times. However, as usual, with the translations from Greek into English, much of the richness disappears. There are several Greek words that are used for the one English word 'escape', and over the next few days we shall seek to discover the truth of some of them.

In the key verse today Jesus is talking to His disciples about the Signs of the Times and the End of the Age. He urges them to be on guard against casual living and the temptation to relax their spiritual guard. He also urged them to watch and pray about the Signs of the Times so that they might escape the impending calamities that will be the backdrop to the end of all things.

Luke uses a word in his writings that produced an urgency in his hearers when he added the Greek word '*ek*' which means 'out of' to the normal Greek word '*pheugo*'. '*Pheugo*' means to 'gain flight' as we saw yesterday, and by adding the dimension of '*ek*' to the word, Peter literally urges the Church to 'gain flight out of the situation'. Peter's words would have brought a very clear picture to the hearers and the readers of his gospel, as the word '*ekpheugo*' was the word that was used to describe the action of escaping prisoners from jail. If men and women, who had been committed to prison had found a way of escaping, this was the word that would have described their urgent run from the gates and from the cells that had imprisoned them.

Peter used this word picture to describe the action of the Church, when during the last days the Signs of the Times began to point to the near return of Jesus. He urged the Church to watch and pray, and to be ready for the flight into eternity. This flight would be like that of prisoners escaping from jail, only this time it would be believers escaping the clutches of sin and the presence of evil.

The same word is used in the book of Acts, when Sceva's sons escaped the clutches of the demoniac man, when the one with demons jumped upon them and beat them in such a way that they had to run for their very lives.

This is quite a graphic picture of the End Times, when we literally have to escape the evilness of this present world. Keep watch and pray at all times, so that we might escape.

My Journal ______________________________

KEY PRAYER

Heavenly Father, thank you for the warning that has been given by Luke, I take heed of it today and I will watch and pray so that I might escape the calamities that are about to befall this present world. Thank you for the fact that Jesus has become my escape route.

August 6th

KEY WORD: **Escape**

KEY VERSE: **1 Corinthians 10 : 13**

No temptation has seized you except what is common to man. And God is faithful; He will not let you be tempted beyond what you can bear. But when you are tempted, He will also provide a way out (a way of escape) so that you can stand up under it.

In the New Testament the English word 'escape' appears many, many times. However, as usual with the translations from Greek into English much of the richness disappears. There are several Greek words that are used for the one English word 'escape', over the past few days we have been seeking to discover the truth of some of them. We conclude our thoughts in the word 'escape' with possibly the most descriptive word of them all.

In the key verse today Paul was seeking to convey the truth that God has always provided us with a way of escape when temptation has come. He also stated that God does not allow us to be tempted more than we are able to stand, which is a very comforting thought in itself. This provision of an escape route is an interesting one. The Greek word that he uses here is the word '*ekbasis*' and, once again, it is a word that has been formed by the joining of two words together. The first word is '*ek*' which we have seen before means 'out of' and the second word is '*baino*' which means 'to go'. The formation of these two words means that when temptation has come God has provided an escape route that allows us to 'go out of' the power of the temptation and the clutches of sin.

The 'going out of' the power of temptation means that when we are tested and tempted we do not have to stay within the boundaries of the testing, we can escape by the simple route of 'going out of' the way. In other words, if we are doing something that is not right, we should stop doing it and move out of the way. If we are seeing something that we should not see, we should look away and move out of its range. If we are joining in with something that we should not be involved in, we should look for the escape route and take it immediately. It is pointless to say that we can not help falling into sin, or that we could not help ourselves at the moment of temptation because God has provided the route that will 'take us out' of the power of the temptation.

As we conclude our studies within this whole area the lessons learned are not just ones that affect our theological understanding alone they should also affect us practically, so that we should now be able to say that the Lord has taught us to flee from sin and cleave to that which is good. It is one thing to know this as a concept, but it is another thing to put the concept into practice.

My Journal

KEY PRAYER

Heavenly Father, please help me today to look for the route of escape at the moment of each and every temptation, help me to be ready to escape through the provided way whenever sin comes to deceive. Thank you for this route of escape and thank you, too, that it is always a welcoming way.

August 7th

KEY WORD: **Submit**

KEY VERSE: **James 4 : 7**

Submit yourselves, then, to God. Resist the devil and he will flee from you.

Within this key verse there are two words that are immensely challenging and very, very pointed, they are the words 'submit' and 'resist'. We shall take one of the words today and the second one tomorrow.

James was writing to the Church that was scattered abroad – the 'diaspora' or the scattered ones – and in his writings he constantly sought to reaffirm those who were being persecuted and mistreated. His encouragement to his brothers in Christ was very effective, and in this key verse, he is insisting that the only way to overcome the enemy was in the submitting to God and in the resisting of the devil. James used a very interesting Greek word for the English word that has been translated in most Bible versions as the word 'submit.' It is the Greek word *'hupotasso'* and as with many Greek words it is a word that is made up by the joining of two words together.

'Hupotasso' means 'to set in array' and the two Greek words that are joined together to form this word are the words *'hupo'* which means 'under' and the word *'tasso'* which means 'to arrange'. Because James chose to use these two words together he drew a military picture in the minds of the scattered Church. These two words literally conveyed the concept of the submission of rank by junior officers to senior officers in charge. The concept therefore in James' mind to the overcoming of the enemy was complete allegiance to God and the submission to His ways.

Most of the Bible versions translate this word as 'submit' which is not entirely correct as the word 'submit' does not fully convey the depth and force of this word. In military terms the senior officers have total and absolute control over those who are 'under' them, they can command them to do whatever their will may be. If the junior officers were commanded to go, they had to go, there was no discussion and disobedience was not tolerated.

James was not saying that God expects blind acceptance as a dictator would, but he was seeking to convey the concept that God is over all, in all, and through all things, and that the only way to true spiritual success was in total obedience to Him.

Unless the Church learns this lesson we will always have a problem with temptation and sin. Sin and temptation can be overcome, but they can only be overcome by the total submission of our will to God's and by the acceptance that He is Lord of all.

If we can accept the action of submission, then we are halfway to overcoming the devil, then if we can couple the resisting of the devil to the submission to God, we ought to be well on the way to a successful Christian experience and Christian life. We will consider the action of resisting the devil tomorrow.

My Journal

KEY PRAYER

Heavenly Father, I thank you today for the twin agencies of submission and resisting that you have given to the Church and pledge today, like a soldier, to submit myself unto you, so that I might learn again and again that you are Lord.

August 8th

KEY WORD: **Resist**

KEY VERSE: **James 4 : 7**

Submit yourselves, then, to God. Resist the devil and he will flee from you.

In yesterday's studies we learned that in order to be successful in overcoming the enemy we have to learn to submit to God, yet as James pointed out in the key verse today, submission is only one aspect of overcoming the devil. We must also learn how to resist the devil so that he might flee from us.

James uses a very powerful word that has been translated as the English word 'resist', it is the Greek word *'anthistemi'* which means to 'set against'. As with many Greek words it is once again the combination of two different words that brings the force of the word 'resist'. The two Greek words that are used are the words *'anti'* which means 'against,' and the word *'histemi'* which means 'to cause to stand'. The combining of these two words drew the picture of total opposition against a force, so James could think of no better word than this to convey the thought of totally opposing the devil, with all his schemes and tactics.

It does not need much imagination to recognise the fact that we derive our word antihistamine from this Greek word. The antihistamine is the force that 'stands against' an allergy and causes it to cease from its power. This is the same concept, if we can learn to stand against the enemy and if we can learn to set ourselves against him, we are well on the way to overcoming sin and temptation.

When Jesus was attacked by the devil in the wilderness, He faced a whole 40 days and 40 nights of the enemy's actions. However, only three of the temptations are actually recorded by the gospel writers. During each and every one of these temptations

Jesus chose to withstand the attack by quoting Scripture. He resisted each attack by standing against the devil and He did not discuss the matter, He did not provoke the enemy, and He did not argue the fact that the devil had no real power against Him, He simply chose the method of resisting each attack by quoting Scripture and by resisting the onslaught by standing firm in the faith.

If we can learn to do this and if we can couple this by submitting more and more to the Lordship of Christ, we will be far more successful in overcoming sin and temptation.

It should be our prayer today that God will teach more about His Lordship and more about the snares and traps of the enemy, because even when we feel that we might have learned how to cope with his attacks, his devices are such that when we feel strong we are proved to be quite weak. When he comes, resistance is the only way and as he comes we can hide ourselves in the Lordship of Christ.

My Journal

KEY PRAYER

Heavenly Father, I have learned through years of experience that the only way to overcome everything that I face is by your Word and by the resisting of the devil. Help me each day to live in your strength and not mine, and help me each day to submit to you in such a way that I find shelter in your presence.

August 9th

KEY WORD: **Scattered**

KEY VERSE: **James 1 : 1**

James, a servant of God and of the Lord Jesus Christ, to the twelve tribes scattered among the nations, greetings.

The epistle of James was written to those people who were 'scattered abroad'. The people that were scattered were the Children of God who had fled from Jerusalem and Israel due to intense persecution. He wrote to encourage them and he also wrote to in order to teach them that through their sufferings they would find peace and patience.

He commanded them to submit to God and resist the devil – as we have seen over the past two days – however, in order to understand just how important these words are, we need to understand just what these people were going through. James wrote to the twelve tribes which were scattered among the nations and he addressed these people with a very important title. The Greek word that he used for these 'scattered people' was the word '*diaspora*' which literally means 'the dispersed' or the 'ones sent away'. This collective term was the Greek way of describing a people that were without a home, without a nation and without hope.

Due to intense persecution by the Romans, the Jews had fled from Israel and were now dispersed among the nations of the world. They felt like a people without hope and both Peter and James had written to them in order to lift them up from their suffering and to seek to give them hope. Both epistles were filled with messages of encouragement and teaching concerning suffering, and in a very prophetic sense both epistles saw the day when the Jews would return home and would once again be a people within their own land. Over the years since these two epistles were written there has been a kind of 'coming and going' to the land of Israel by the people of God. However, it is only in our generation that we have actually seen a 'returning home' by the Jews of Israel. During the Second World War there was another intense persecution of the Jews and millions of them perished in terrible ways. At the end of this war the land of Israel had virtually given up hope that there would ever be a nation of Israel again. However, God had other plans, in three short years within the United Nations Congress, the vote had been taken that Israel, although divided, would once again be the land of the Jews, and once this vote was taken an amazing scene took place.

It was as if the *'diaspora'* was turned upside down and reversed, because Jews from every nation began to return home to claim their inheritance. Since 1948 and this UN vote, the nation of Israel has increased numerically by ways that were thought impossible at the end of the war in 1945. Also the nation of Israel has hardly been out of the news ever since, as it makes headlines every day.

It was as if God dispersed His people throughout the nations in order that they might learn to trust Him more, and then it was as if He brought them home in order to turn the attention upon the 'prophetic clock' that would begin to announce the return of Jesus to this world.

My Journal ______________________________

____

____

____

KEY PRAYER

Heavenly Father, I see today that God has always had a plan for His people and that this plan is right on time. Please forgive me when I often think that you have forgotten me and that you have overlooked me, the 'diaspora' teaches me once again that you are in total control.

August 10th

KEY WORD: **Carpenter**

KEY VERSE: **Mark 6 : 3**

"Isn't this the carpenter? Isn't this Mary's son and the brother of James, Joseph, Judas and Simon? Aren't his sisters here with us?" And they took offence at him.

In this key verse today several pointed questions were being posed by the congregation in the synagogue in Nazareth. Jesus had visited the synagogue on the Sabbath day and had taught there, and the Scripture says that 'many were amazed at Him and His teaching'. The accusation was that how could such an ordinary person, a carpenter, preach like this and, what was even worse, this preacher was a 'child of the village'. All his brothers and sisters were there and those that heard him could not believe that such a thing could be possible.

The congregation at the synagogue that morning had received the most amazing teaching and the deepest teaching that they had ever heard, and their minds could not accept that this was an ordinary lad who had been brought up in a carpenter's workshop within this small village in Galilee. We of course know that 'no man ever spoke like this man', but for the attenders on the Sabbath Day this was amazing.

What was also interesting was that they could not believe that an ordinary workman like a carpenter could speak in such a way, it was not just that Jesus was from this town but that he was a 'simple carpenter'.

The Greek word for 'carpenter' reveals a great deal about Jesus and His upbringing. The word used is *'tekton'* which literally means 'a worker in wood', it can be applied to any craftsman, but it generally meant a woodworker. We derive our English word 'technical' from this word, and the meaning for us is simply someone who is gifted or is technical with his hands.

There is not much mentioned about the childhood of Jesus except for a few passages of Scripture. A veil seems to be drawn over His childhood and little is known. However, the few passages that we have suggest that Jesus was drawn to those who taught in the synagogues and the Temple. He seems to have enjoyed a full family life with many brothers and sisters, and it is possible that His father, Joseph, died early, as it is only His mother Mary who is mentioned often.

He was also obviously gifted with His hands as He took on the trade of His father and worked as a carpenter. He must have been gifted in this area as the crowd that day called him 'a carpenter', He was obviously well known within the village as one who was technical with His hands.

As we look back and review our spiritual lives it is very obvious to us that Jesus has never failed us and has never let us down. All through our spiritual journey He has been our strength and our guide. This carpenter from Nazareth is Lord of all. He may have been a simple village worker two thousand years ago in His earthly life as the Son of Man, but as Jesus the Son of God He is now both Lord and Saviour. His earthly life may have reflected His natural gifts, but the Gift of God to the world, this Saviour and Lord, now reflects His greater gifts as one who never fails. The congregation was amazed at Him, we simply praise Him.

KEY PRAYER

Heavenly Father, thank you for sending Jesus to this world and thank you Jesus that you came. The congregation in Nazareth was amazed. We today bring our offering of praise. I praise you today for the greatest gift ever given, my Lord and my Saviour.

August 11th

KEY WORD: **Double-minded**

KEY VERSE: **James 1 : 8**

He is a double-minded man, unstable in all that he does.

When James wrote to those who were scattered among the nations his primary goal was to bless them and encourage them in the Lord, and as we have seen over the past two days, his heart was very much with them in their sufferings. As he developed his epistle however, his teaching also brought instruction and guidance in holy living. Very early on in his writings he brought the message that doubt and fear would lead to instability and that any one who was coming before God in prayer must not doubt but must trust and believe.

He stated that the man who is gripped with doubting is like the waves of the sea, tossed about by the wind. As he developed this thought James stated that this man would not receive anything from God because of his doubting, and he actually states that this man is double-minded and unstable.

James used a very interesting word in order to convey his message, the Greek word that he used was the word *'dipsuchos'* and, as with many Greek words that we have been studying, it is a word that is made up by the joining of two words together. The word picture that is created by the joining of the two words conveys a very startling picture. James used the word *'dis'* which means 'twice' and the word *'psuche'* which means 'soul'. So the concept being set out by James is that an unstable man is 'two-souled' in his outlook in life and in his spiritual capabilities.

The thought behind this key verse is that a man who is unstable due to his doubts being stronger than his faith is struggling with the whole realm of spiritual growth and spiritual perception. The battle between the 'Spirit' and 'flesh' is such that this man feels that a war is being conducted within him. He is unstable due to the demands of the flesh and the desires of the spirit, so James urged him to do a number of important things. Firstly, James said that he must humble himself before God so that God can eventually exalt him. Secondly, James said that he must come before God in prayer with total belief and faith in the One who will answer prayer and bring deliverance. Thirdly, James said that this unstable man must ask God for wisdom in his dealing with the war that is going on within him.

If these lessons are learned and if these instructions are obeyed, the unstable man will become stable and the warring battle between the flesh and the Spirit will be lessened, as the double-minded man will become single-minded and much stronger.

The book of James must not be considered as just a book to those who were scattered among the nations 2000 years ago. God has seen fit to include this book among the books of the New Testament in order that we might have help, due to the fact that the battle between the flesh and Spirit is still raging today. James' words to the scattered Church are still pointed and true to the gathered Church of today.

We would do well to take heed!

My Journal

KEY PRAYER

Heavenly Father, please help me each day to be faithful and true to your Word so that I might learn how to control the demands of the flesh and submit to the desires of the Spirit. I thank you today that you have provided teaching through your Word so that I can learn these spiritual lessons and I thank you too, that you have provided the way of true blessing, the way of trust and faith.

August 12th

KEY WORD: **Double**

KEY VERSE: **1 Timothy 5 : 17**

The elders who direct the affairs of the church well are worthy of double honour, especially those whose work is preaching and teaching.

As we learned yesterday in the teaching of James, the double-minded man is an unstable man and the concept that James was teaching was that of double-thinking and double trouble!

It is an interesting exercise to trace where the word 'double' originates from within the Greek as it has a very powerful meaning. The word that is used for our English word 'double' is the word '*diplous*' and this word means 'two-fold' or 'twice' and the interesting thing is that this word only appears three times in the New Testament. It is a word that is taken from the area of giving and receiving and it was applied to those who had received a gift or who had given a gift.

If a Greek person was to receive a gift or even if they had given a gift the word was applied to the spirit of the action. This is why Timothy used the word in the key verse today for the ministry of elders in that if they ministered well they should receive a gift and in fact they should receive a double gift or double honour.

It is an important thing to note that God gives gifts unto men and that He expects us to use the gift well. The whole concept of excellence comes into play when we consider the gifts of God and His expectancies. God wants us to excel in our gifting, and when we do excel He grants greater blessing and we receive even more. It is a concept of giving and receiving and blessing and even greater blessing.

Timothy used this concept for eldership, especially to those elders who were preaching and teaching elders. If they excelled in their gifting then God would grant them double honour and double blessing.

We do not serve God for what we would get or receive from Him, we serve Him because we love Him. However, when we serve well and our hearts are single-minded in the sense of truth and integrity, then God rewards us with greater and greater blessing. His measure is pressed down, shaken together and running over, such is His measure towards us. Double blessing and double rewards.

If we honour Him, then He honours us.

My Journal ____

____

____

____

____

____

____

____

____

____

____

____

____

____

KEY PRAYER

Heavenly Father, I bless you today for your goodness and mercy and I praise you for the fact that you are a giving God. As I serve you with a faithful heart of integrity, then you pour blessing back into my life. It is with a grateful heart, filled with your blessing, that I praise you today.

August 13th

KEY WORD: **Christian**

KEY VERSE: **1 Peter 4 : 16**

However, if you suffer as a Christian do not be ashamed, but praise God that you bear that name.

Everybody knows that the name 'Christian' means 'Christ's men' and that it was applied to those who followed Christ and who were members of His Church. However, what most people do not know is that it was a Roman word coined by those who were against the Church and against the Lord.

The believers did not called themselves by this name, the adoption of this name by believers took place a little later in Church history. This name 'Christian' was a derogatory name used in spite and in anger at the growth and the blessing of the Church. To us now – in the latter days of the Church – it has come to signify the name by which we are known and by which we like to be known, yet it had its roots and origins in misuse and disgust.

The word in New Testament Greek is '*christianos*' and it literally meant 'those who were called' or 'those who adhered to Jesus'. It was applied to the Antioch believers by the Gentiles of the town when they saw that the Church was prospering and growing. The believers did not call themselves Christians nor did they seem to enjoy the name, however, it came to be linked with those who loved the Lord. Tacitus, a leading Roman near the end of the first century said that 'the vulgar call themselves Christians'. It also seems that King Agrippa used the term to Paul in a kind of scornful way when he said that 'did Paul think that he could be persuaded to become a Christian'.

In the key verse today, Peter states that when this name is used in a scornful way we should 'not be ashamed' as we are being identified with the Lord. He also said that we were to 'praise God that we bear that name', as it was a form of closeness with the Lord.

During the second century it is obvious from the early Church writings that the believers began to enjoy being addressed by this name, it came to be seen as a form of honour and a form of joy to be called by such a name. The interesting thing about this name is that it is only found three times in the entire New Testament, once in Peter's writings and twice in the book of Acts. The fact that this name is now used as the title of those who love and follow The Lord is amazing, seeing how it had its roots and origins in scorn and shame and that it was only used three times in early Church history.

It seems that God has chosen this name and preserved this name as the title of those who follow His Son and that this name is precious to Him. It is also amazing that today 'The Christian Fellowship' or 'The Christian Centre' is very much in use, as more and more churches and denominations are using this name to identify themselves within their towns and cities.

My Journal ______________________________

KEY PRAYER

Heavenly Father, thank you for this wonderful name that links me with Jesus. I thank you that you have chosen to preserve this name even though it began as a scornful term. Thank you too, that I belong to you and that you belong to me.

August 14th

KEY WORD: **False Christs**

KEY VERSE: **Mark 13 : 22**

For false Christs and false prophets will appear and perform signs and miracles to deceive the elect – if that were possible.

As we saw yesterday the title Christian was applied to those who loved and followed the Lord, it was a title bestowed by the world upon the believers. However, another word found its way into New Testament use, the word 'false Christs'. This word was used to describe those who were not real Christians and who did not follow the Lord but who seemed to preach a similar kind of gospel.

The term 'Christian' was the word '*christianos*' which meant 'adherents of Christ' whereas 'false Christs' were known as '*pseudochristos*' which meant 'one who falsely laid claim to the name of the Lord'.

In two Gospels, Matthew and Mark, the writers spoke of the need to be aware of the fact that false prophets and false Christs would come and that these men would lay claim to authority but they would not be true believers but false ones. They would seek to lead people away from truth into error and they would seek to undermine the authority of Jesus with 'another gospel'. In the key verse today Mark seeks to warn the Church about these men, saying that they were deceivers. He suggests that they would produce signs and miracles in an attempt to give authority and credence to their claim of truth, but that their goal is deception and error and the destroying of the Church.

The word '*pseudochristos*' is only used twice in the entire New Testament but it has become the name of those who conduct themselves in error throughout the Church and throughout the world.

Part of the word has also found its way into the English language and it has come to be known and used for anything that speaks of falseness, the word *'pseudo'* now stands for the 'counterfeit' and the 'abnormal' according to the American Dictionary. This is exactly what the New Testament writers are seeking to convey, the counterfeit gospel and the abnormal truth of men who would seek to destroy.

We should be ever watchful for those who come in the name of the Lord because not all who seem to do His will are true apostles or true prophets, some are in fact false Christs. If there is a prayer that should unite the Church, it should be: 'Lord help us to see the false amongst the truth, and help us to gain more and more perception so that we might understand what is right and what is wrong.'

My Journal ____

KEY PRAYER

Heavenly Father, I pray today that you would give to me true discernment so that I might know the difference between the true and the false. Help me to beware of those who would seek to destroy the Church so that I might be ready to guard the Church and fight the good fight.

August 15th

KEY WORD: **Elect**

KEY VERSE: **Mark 13 : 22**

For false Christs and false prophets will appear and perform signs and miracles to deceive the elect – if that were possible.

Over the past few days we having been considering the concepts of 'double-mindedness' and 'falsehoods' and in the key verse of yesterday and today the writer Mark sought to show that if we are not careful even the elect of God might be deceived by false Christs. This would obviously pose a few questions: Who are the elect? And also: What is the elect?

Mark used a very powerful word to describe the Church, he called the Church 'the elect' the Greek word is '*eklektos*' which means 'picked out ones' or even 'gathered chosen ones'. As we have often seen, the Greek words that are used in the New Testament are frequently 'joined up words', two or three words added together to form one word or even a new word. '*Eklektos*' is formed by the joining together of the word '*ek*' which means 'from' and '*lego*' which means 'picked out'.

The truth that Mark was seeking to convey is that God has a group of people picked out and chosen to become His Church. The word is used of Jesus, who was God's chosen vehicle of salvation. The word was also used of angels, who are God's chosen agents of messages and administration. The word is also used of the Jews as they are God's chosen people and God's chosen race. However, the word really comes into its fullest use when it is applied to the Church.

The Church of Jesus Christ – which means all true and real believers – are 'God's chosen people,' and, as the New Testament teaches, these chosen people were chosen before the foundation of the world. In God's mind the Church was formed before the world was formed. God chose His people and predestined them to 'be with Him' long before sin came into the world and long before the world was created. The source of election is God's grace, human will plays a part in the destiny of man, as man can choose to follow The Lord or reject Him. However, God knows who will follow Him and who will reject Him as He is omniscient – all knowing.

Even a casual reading of the Bible reveals a God who knows the end from the beginning, He is never 'caught out' by circumstances, he is never surprised by events, He knows all things and controls all things.

This truth is so important to the Church that we need to understand it carefully. W E Vine in his 'Expository Dictionary of New Testament Words' says that 'Christ's death was sufficient for all men and is effective in the case of the elect, yet men are treated as responsible, being capable of the will and power to choose'. What he is saying is, that man has a free will to choose or reject God's offer of salvation, yet grace, when it touches man, brings him to the place that God has already destined him for.

God knows us, God chose us and God will take us safely home.

My Journal

KEY PRAYER

Heavenly Father, I bring my offering of thanksgiving to you today with a grateful heart of praise for the fact that you chose me before the foundation of the world to 'be with you'. Help me each day to live worthy of my high calling in Christ Jesus and help me to be worthy of your love.

August 16th

KEY WORD: **Tithes**

KEY VERSE: **Matthew 23 : 23**

"Woe to you, teachers of the law and Pharisees, you hypocrites! You give a tenth of your spices – mint, dill and cummin. But you have neglected the more important matters of the law – justice, mercy and faithfulness. You should have practised the latter without neglecting the former."

In this key verse today Jesus was harsh in His criticism and rebuking of the teachers and Pharisees. He spoke very directly about their need to not just fulfil the law but to deal with the matters of the heart. The Pharisees were incredibly strict concerning their obedience to the law of God but their hearts were far from God in matters of justice, mercy, grace and faithfulness.

Jesus dealt in this verse with the concept of the 'ten percent' of tithing. Tithing was very much a part of Old Testament teaching and practice, there is very little in the New Testament about the giving of the tithe, in fact the word only appears eight times in the New Testament and most of those are direct quotes from the Old Testament. In the New Testament there is much more emphasis upon cheerful giving and a generous spirit and heart. However, if the Old Testament saints were commanded to give ten percent of their income and substance without a Saviour and without redemption, how much more should we give seeing that we have a Saviour and the blessing of an eternal destiny. We should be giving much more than the strict ten percent of the law because all our substance belongs to the Lord. Our blessing is to give, therefore we should give at least ten percent plus offerings.

The Greek word used for 'tithing' is the word *'apodekatoo'* and it is a word once again made up by the combining of two words: *'apo'* which means 'from' and *'dekatos'* which means 'a tenth'. The exact meaning therefore is 'a tenth paid from my income'. However, the word is not a legal kind of word in the sense that having given a tithe 'I am alright.' This was the sin of the Pharisees, for they paid their tithes, quite often very publicly, so they thought that having done this they had pleased God. However, Jesus pointed out, very strongly, that their hearts were not right with God. *'Apodekatoo'* is a 'spirit' word not a 'Law' word. The word is derived from the joy of giving or the spirit of blessing.

We give unto the Lord not because we are commanded to or because of expectation, we give unto the Lord because it is the right thing to do within the area of joy and blessing. We have learned that the more we give, the more we receive and that God gives without measure.

If Old Testament saints 'had' to give, we as New Testament saints 'need' to give. If we want the blessing of God upon our home, our family, our substance and future, we have to give because not to give is robbing God and to give is to receive His blessing.

Our prayer today should be: 'Lord teach me to give unto you more and more so that I might delight in your blessing.'

My Journal

KEY PRAYER

Heavenly Father, thank you for the fact that I can never out-give you. As I give to you, you give to me and as I bless you with all that I have I find favour and joy in your presence. Thank you that all that I have belongs to you and that all I have I give to you.

August 17th

KEY WORD: ***Jot and tittle***

KEY VERSE: **Matthew 5 : 18**

I tell you the truth, until heaven and earth disappear, not the smallest letter, not the least stroke of a pen, will by any means disappear from the Law until everything is accomplished.

In the key verse of yesterday we considered the concept of Jesus and the hypocrites and their insistance on keeping the law of God while their hearts were far from Him. We noticed too the fact that the giving of our tithes and offerings is a pathway to blessing. In the key verse today Jesus is also dealing with the hypocritical Pharisees and their insistance on the keeping of each and every smallest stroke of the Law. They would teach and preach that even the smallest letter of the Law should be kept and that even the least stroke of the pen was vital. These smallest issues commanded much attention while their hearts were filled with jealously and pride.

Jesus used a word picture to convey to these hypocrites just how far they were from the Kingdom of God. In the King James Version of the Bible the translation uses the words 'jot and tittle' which means the 'smallest letter and the least stroke of the pen'. The two Greek words that convey this meaning are the words '*iota*' which means 'smallest word' and '*keraia*' which means 'a little horn.' This was the word that was used to convey the thought of a small stroke of the pen, in the midst of Hebrew writings. The teachers of the Law, the Rabbis, attached great importance to the 'smallest letters' and the 'little horns' of Hebrew script. They taught that these tiny script marks were vital to salvation and that in the keeping of even the '*iotas*' they would receive God's blessing upon them.

Jesus, however, taught something quite different to this, He majored on the heart and not the Law. Jesus said that while the Pharisees kept the most scrupulous reverence to the Law of God, their hearts and spirit violated the things of God because they were filled with the sin of pride.

God does not look at the outward appearance concerning the things that we do He looks at the heart and He searches for those who 'have a spirit like His spirit and a heart like His heart'.

So in the key verse today the word picture being formed by Jesus is that God will not cause one thing to disappear until His ways and His will have been accomplished. The Pharisees may depend upon the jot and tittle but God will cause His Word to be fulfilled, and His ways to be completed, before even the smallest letter and the least of all strokes of a pen are removed. The message was quite clear: stop depending upon the insistance on the law and the scrupulous reverence for the minute brushes of a pen upon parchment, but rather depend upon the Lord to bring all things to the conclusion of His plan and purpose.

There is a time and season to all things and nothing will disappear before God says so!

My Journal

KEY PRAYER

Heavenly Father, I have learned again today that you are Lord of all things, and that nothing will pass away until you have completed your plan and purpose. Thank you for the total assurance and stability that this brings to my future and my destiny, I can rest in you because 'it is well with my soul'.

August 18th

KEY WORD: ***Whitewashed tombs***

KEY VERSE: ***Matthew 23 : 27***

"Woe to you, teachers of the law and Pharisees, you hypocrites! You are whitewashed tombs, which look beautiful on the outside but on the inside are full of dead men's bones and everything unclean."

Having considered for several days the sins of the Pharisees that Jesus took a great deal of time to deal with, we shall begin to draw to a conclusion our studies in this area by looking at the way that Jesus saw them in their sins.

Jesus was quite devastating in His remarks concerning their dependence upon even the smallest letter of the Law, and even the least of the strokes of Hebrew script. He called them, in the key verse today, whitewashed tombs. The word picture could not have been more vivid, outwardly these Pharisees looked good, their appearance was clean and beautiful, but inwardly their hearts and lives were dirty and unclean. The use of the sense of 'uncleanness' was very, very graphic, for the Pharisees prided themselves upon being clean vessels, unlike the Gentiles who were regarded as being unclean vessels.

The Greek words for 'whitewashed tombs' are the words '*koniao*' which means 'lime-clean' or 'whitened' and '*taphos*' which means 'sepulchre' or 'place of burial'.

Jesus was stating a startling truth to these hypocrites with their pride of cleanliness and abstinence of anything deemed to be unclean, even the avoidance of death and things pertaining to death. Jesus was actually saying that their lives and religious practices were nothing but stinking graves and that their inward spirit was nothing more than death.

We would totally agree with the words of Jesus, but we

would do well to remember that there are times when we would seek to please man before we seek to please God, and that there are times when our outward appearance is far different to that which lurks beneath the flesh. God sees all things and knows all things and nothing can be hidden from Him. It is important to remember this when we come before Him in prayer and worship, He knows our hearts and He knows how we really feel.

There is little point in trying to please God, and please others, and present ourselves as 'limestone tombs' when deep within there is nothing but death. God searches our spirit and He knows what we are really like so it is vain and pointless to seek to prove otherwise. We should live our lives before men as we live our lives before God, because He knows!

My Journal

KEY PRAYER

Heavenly Father , I bless you today for the amazing fact that you really know me, I can not fool you and I can not deceive you, you really know me. Help me to remember this when I pray, and when I worship, help me, too, to keep my life clean inwardly as well as clean outwardly.

August 19th

KEY WORD: **Stiff-necked**

KEY VERSE: **Acts 7 : 51**

"You stiff-necked people, with uncircumcised hearts and ears, you are just like your fathers: You always resist the Holy Spirit."

Jesus had a lot to say about the hypocritical nature of the Pharisees and teachers of the Law. In fact, as we have seen over the past few days, He was quite devastating in His remarks about them. The most scathing term that He used concerning them was 'whitewashed tombs' which was a startling remark in His generation.

However, the New Testament writers also used graphic language in order the describe these people. We shall look at a few of the names that they used when they dealt with the Pharisees and their particular sin of pride and rebellion.

In the key verse today, Stephen – who was the first Christian martyr in the New Testament and in fact the first martyr within the early Church – used a phrase, concerning the Pharisees that were members of the Sanhedrin, that was a very graphic one. He called them 'stiff-necked' due to their inability to understand and accept the fact that Jesus was the Messiah. This term 'stiff-necked; came from a word that was used when people were seeking to describe a stubborn trait in someone's character. As with many Greek words the word is made up by the combining of two words. The word is *'sklerotrachelos'* and the two words that were used are firstly, *'skleros'* which means 'hard' or 'harsh' and secondly, *'trachelos'* which means 'a neck'. Our translation is 'stiff-necked,' however, the more literal translation should be 'one who has a harsh and hard neck'.

The symbol was of a person who stubbornly refused to accept something and, in the manifestation of the stubbornness, the neck would be kept rigid in the form of refusal to bend.

Stephen, just before he was stoned to death, turned to the Sanhedrin and called them stiff-necked due to the fact that he had just spent considerable time teaching from the Scriptures that Jesus was Lord and that He was in fact the long awaited Messiah. From the attitude of the Pharisees it was obvious to Stephen that he had failed to convince them of this truth and that his end was nigh. The title given to them by Stephen would live with the Pharisees for many years to come. It was only used once in the New Testament, yet it came to be accepted as a kind of descriptive title for those who would not bend to accept new truth.

There are many today who stubbornly hold on to things that are not right and there are also those within the Church who resist change and development, although to called these people stiff-necked would probably be quite unfair and harsh. Yet the spirit of stiff-necked stubbornness needs to be removed if we are to see progress and change within the Church of today. God wants to lead us all on to greater blessing, and the refusal to change and the stubborn lack of acceptance of new things can lead to a rebuke from God concerning our ways. We should not be those who are deemed to be stiff-necked people, but we should always aim to be called those who are pliable of spirit and soft of heart.

My Journal

KEY PRAYER

Heavenly Father, I do not want to be someone who stands in the way of change and someone who resists your Spirit. Please help me to be a gentle spirit and a soft hearted child of God. I long for the moving of your Spirit, so please help me to see the Holy Spirit when He comes and help me to embrace Him when He moves.

August 20th

KEY WORD: **Uncircumcised**

KEY VERSE: **Acts 7 : 51**

"You stiff-necked people, with uncircumcised hearts and ears, you are just like your fathers: You always resist the Holy Spirit."

In the key verse that we looked at yesterday and which we are still considering today, Stephen did not moderate his language at all when he was dealing with the Pharisees and their hard-heartedness. He called them stiff-necked people with uncircumcised hearts. He could not have called them a worse name, however, he could not have described them in a better way.

The circumcision was practised by the Jewish people for hygienic reasons and for spiritual reasons. This cutting of the flesh brought a sign to the people that they had entered into a covenant with God. The cutting of flesh also showed that they were a different people and that they belonged to God. This rite also had a moral significance in that the people who had accepted circumcision were to be a people that belonged to God, not just in the sense of a nation, but also in the sense of righteousness. The Greek word for circumcision is *'peritome'* and it was applied only to Jews. Those people who were not circumcised were considered to be outsiders, and it came to be used in a derogatory way concerning the Gentile people.

In the New Testament circumcision became not a literal cutting of the flesh but a symbolic cutting of the heart, so that the New Testament believers and the New Testament Church was a people who had allowed God to work upon the flesh thus creating a new covenant. This new covenant was with the heart and not the flesh.

The uncircumcised of the New Testament were those who

were outside of the Church. They may have been people who had followed the strict code of the cutting of the flesh, but if their hearts had not been touched by grace, then they were called the 'uncircumcised'. The Greek word for 'uncircumcision' is '*akrobustia*' which literally means 'no cut' or 'not cutting around'. This term meant that those who had refused to allow the heart-change of grace were still those who allowed the corrupt desires of the flesh to operate within them. So, for Stephen to call the Pharisees – who still practise the rite of the fleshly cut – 'the uncircumcised' was one of the worst things that he could have said, although it was the most pointed of truths.

God wants us today to have a circumcised heart, a heart touched by grace and a heart open to the moving of the Spirit. The act of fleshly circumcision may have passed as a rite and ritual of religion, but the act of spiritual circumcision should still be practised, as God longs for a people that come to Him with willing hearts of thanksgiving. The flesh is no longer important, it is the spirit that takes the foremost place within the Church and within the New Testament covenant of grace.

My Journal

KEY PRAYER

Heavenly Father, I praise you and thank you today for the glorious fact that my sins have been forgiven and that I am on my way to heaven. No longer do I have to trust in the ways of the flesh and the ways of the Law. I am now free to enjoy the work of the Spirit within my life. Help me today to appreciate just how free I am.

August 21st

KEY WORD: **Strengthened**

KEY VERSE: **Acts 9 : 31**

Then the church throughout Judea, Galilee and Samaria enjoyed a time of peace. It was strengthened; and encouraged by the Holy Spirit, it grew in numbers, living in the fear of the Lord.

Following Stephen's devastating remarks concerning the Pharisees – as we saw yesterday – and his subsequent death, the Church moved into a period of tremendous blessing. The opponent of the Church, Saul of Tarsus, had been encountered by the Lord and had been soundly saved and called into ministry. The Church was growing and developing as a mighty force within the land and everything was going well.

In the key verse today there are some important lessons to be learned concerning growth and development and we shall take a few days to consider them.

Luke wrote that the Church was being strengthened. The word 'strengthened' is an NIV word, the Old King James Version uses the word 'edified'. The actual Greek word that was used was '*oikodomeo*' which translated means 'to build a house' or 'the building of a house' It was the word that was used when someone had drawn up plans and presented the blueprint to the builders and then the builders had started work. It was not the word simply for the building of walls and ceilings, it was the word that was used when a builder was following the plans that had been presented.

If we accept this word, it means that neither the NIV or the Old King James really has translated the word correctly. The Church was not just strengthened nor was it simply edified, it was entering a period that God had destined and designed for it, a period of peace and stability. The translators could not find an English word that fully conveyed the truth of *'oikodomeo'* so they settled for the nearest word that would fit. However, it does not fully convey exactly what was happening.

God has a plan for the Church, and He has done for the past two thousand years, and He still has, until the Church is raptured and taken home. After several years of persecution and threat, God now had destined that the Church should move into a period of peace and stability and growth and prosperity. God was following the blueprint for the Church, a blueprint that had been prepared before the foundations of the world. God was bringing to the Church a period of tranquillity and rest, this was all part of the plan.

God always has a plan, whatever is going on around you at present within the local church, it is all part of God's plan and purpose. We can rest in Him because all is well.

My Journal ______________________________

KEY PRAYER

Heavenly Father, I praise you today because you are building your Church, and the gates of hell can not prevail against it. You have a plan and purpose for your Church and you have not finished yet. Help me to rest in you and watch the unveiling of your plan.

August 22nd

KEY WORD: **Encouraged**

KEY VERSE: **Acts 9 : 31**

Then the church throughout Judea, Galilee and Samaria enjoyed a time of peace. It was strengthened; and encouraged by the Holy Spirit, it grew in numbers, living in the fear of the Lord.

As we saw yesterday the translators of the New Testament often settled for the nearest English word when they sought to convey the truth of the Scriptures, and in the key verse today, they have done this again. The NIV translates the word as 'encouraged' whereas the Old King James uses the word 'comfort'. In order to discover exactly what was going on within the Church at this time we have to consider what was actually written.

The Church was in a period of growth and stability and God was blessing the Church in such a way that it felt good at this time. The Greek word that Luke used for the word 'encouraged' or 'comfort' was the word '*paraklesis*' which meant 'a calling to one side'. It was a word that was formed by the combining of two words, firstly, '*para*' meaning 'beside' and secondly, '*kaleo*' meaning 'to call'. So the truth that God was seeking to convey at this time to the Church was that He was 'calling them to one side' so that He could embrace them and minister to them.

The Church had suffered a tremendous persecution and many believers had lost their lives, and a great deal of tension had been within the Church. Yet now, following this intense period, God was drawing the Church to one side in order to bless it and nourish it. The fact that the translators had used words like 'encouraged' and 'comfort' was not wrong, as this was part of what was going on. And these words do convey something of the truth, yet they do not convey the fullest sense of what God was seeking to achieve within His Church and amongst His people.

'Paraklesis' is one of the words that is used for the ministry of the Holy Spirit. He is our 'paraklete' the one who 'draws alongside'. The ministry that the Church was receiving at this point within its history was a gentle comforting and caring touch of the Spirit. It was as if the Holy Spirit was touching the Church at its point of hurt and bringing healing and strength when it was at its lowest point.

God often does this to His Church. There are times when the local church goes through a period of hurt and strain and arrives at a place where it desperately needs to be loved and cared for. All the programmes in the world cannot soothe the hurt of a wounded church. All the best preachers, chosen from the best conferences in the world, will not preach the church into comfort and blessing. All these remedies can help to a point, but what the church needs following a period of hurt and trouble is the ministry of the One 'who draws alongside'. Only the Holy Spirit can bring the kind of care that the church needs when it has been touched by trouble.

Our greatest need within the Church is twofold. Firstly, to recognise the times and seasons when it is only the ministry of the Spirit that we need, and secondly, to be sensitive and bold enough to stop the programmes and scrap the systems so that God is allowed to do what He wants to do.

My Journal

KEY PRAYER

Heavenly Father, please teach me your ways and help me to be sensitive to your touch so that I might know what to do at the right times and seasons. Thank you that you are Lord of your Church and that you always do what is right, when you are allowed to do it.

August 23rd

KEY WORD: **Numbers**

KEY VERSE: **Acts 9 : 31**

Then the church throughout Judea, Galilee and Samaria enjoyed a time of peace. It was strengthened; and encouraged by the Holy Spirit, it grew in numbers, living in the fear of the Lord.

When the New Testament Church was enjoying this period of rest from persecution and trouble, and as the Holy Spirit was tenderly ministering to a bruised and hurting people, the Church grew in numbers and multiplied. When Luke was seeking to describe this period he wrote that the 'church grew in numbers and lived in the fear of God'.

He used a very interesting word when he was seeking to convey the truth of numerical growth. He used the Greek word '*plethuno*' which means 'to increase', we actually derive our English word plethora from this Greek word, and the word plethora means 'abundance' or 'much'. Luke was conveying the fact that the Church was increasing numerically at this time due to its period of intense ministry by the Holy Spirit. However, to only see a numerical increase is not what this word actually means. '*Plethuno*' conveys more than simply numbers and statistical growth. The word means 'to increase' and it was applied to the Church in many senses. Yes, there certainly was numerical growth, but there was much more to the 'increase' than simply numbers.

The Church was growing and increasing in influence within the towns and cities where churches had been planted, and this influence was being seen in the way that it was touching every stratum in society. Jews and Gentiles were being saved and added to the Church and they were actually worshipping together.

The Church was growing and increasing in prosperity and favour in the sense that the members of the Church were reaching out financially and materially to each other and to those who were deemed to be poor. The widows were being cared for and family needs were being met and it would not be long before offerings would be taken that would bless churches and areas where there was hardship.

The Church was also increasing in the sense of governmental structure: elders and deacons were being appointed, evangelists and other New Testament gifts were being recognised and used within the Church, and growth was being seen in the whole area of stability and strength.

The Church was also growing in the sense of morale and confidence. During the persecutions life was very difficult for the new Church, and the believers were being scattered around many towns and cities. However, now, during the period of peace the Church was rising in morale and 'good feeling'.

The Church was on the move and God was blessing. Numbers were increasing, other churches were being blessed, elders and deacons were being appointed and financial increase was abounding. There was a sense of abundance within the Church which was a launch pad for even greater success that was just around the corner.

My Journal ______________________________

____

____

____

____

KEY PRAYER

Heavenly Father, thank you for the way that you have blessed your Church and prospered your Church throughout the ages. Thank you for the way that you draw alongside to care and nourish, I bless you for the increase that we see even today as the Church marches on towards its 'welcome home'.

August 24th

KEY WORD: **Fear of God**

KEY VERSE: **Acts 9 : 31**

Then the church throughout Judea, Galilee and Samaria enjoyed a time of peace. It was strengthened; and encouraged by the Holy Spirit, it grew in numbers, living in the fear of the Lord.

As we draw to a conclusion within this key verse that we have been studying for the past few days we have to conclude with the fact that the Church, although in its best period since the day of Pentecost, walked in the fear of God and lived in the light of openness to the Lord

In the month of May we spent several days considering many aspects of fear but the truth concerning the fear of God is so important that we have to return to it as we conclude this key verse.

Luke used the Greek word '*phobos*' which means 'causing to flight'. This word had a positive aspect to it and a negative aspect to it. In the negative sense, someone could be fearful and have a dread of something that would cause them to flee away from whatever it was that caused the fear. In the positive aspect of fear, someone could flee towards an object due to a sense of awesome respect and reverence. This was the aspect of the word that was being used here in the key verse today. The Church was moving closer to the Lord out of a genuine sense of reverence and submission to Him.

Negative fear was all around the New Testament Church. Many believers had lost their lives due to persecution and many had lost their homes and had been scattered to other towns and cities and many were now in unfamiliar situations without friends and families. Yet, as God moved, the positive reverential fear of a holy loving God drew them closer to the Lord and in fact closer to each other.

We do not fear God any longer due to sin and guilt, and we do not fear what judgement and punishment may befall us. Grace has saved us and Calvary has covered it all, our past with its sin and shame is no longer dominant. However, we do fear God because He is holy and He is righteous. This fear is not a negative fear that drives us away from Him, but it is a positive fear that draws us closer to Him.

Our desire should always be that we should be drawn closer to the Lord, and that we should be driven into His arms so that we might shelter in the place that is the safest of havens, the arms of Jesus.

My Journal

KEY PRAYER

Heavenly Father, as I have studied the New Testament Church again, and as I have seen its days of blessing and growth, I long for a greater sense of godly fear so that I might shelter closer to you. Help me to draw near to you because, as I do that, you draw near to me.

August 25th

KEY WORD: **Helps**

KEY VERSE: **1 Corinthians 12 : 28**

And in the church God has appointed first of all apostles, second prophets, third teachers, then workers of miracles, also those having gifts of healing, those able to help others, those with gifts of administration and those speaking in different kinds of tongues.

Paul wrote to the church in Corinth and listed in the key verse today the New Testament ministry gifts that he thought were appropriate to bring to the attention of this particular church. The fact that the order and type of gifts is different to the ones that he listed to the Ephesian church matters not a bit. What Paul was seeking to do was to set out the gifts that were important to the church in Corinth at that particular time. There is no contradiction to the list in the Ephesian epistle and there is no contradiction in Paul's mind, it is just a matter of importance at this particular time and in this particular church.

In the list we have several gifts that are very well known, and in the list there are a couple of gifts that are not so well known, and, in fact, they only appear once in the New Testament in this key verse. So we shall consider these two lesser known gifts over the next two days.

One of the gifts that Paul said is vital to the church is the gift of 'helps', he said that 'those who are able to help others' are a very special gift to the church. Paul was not talking about the general kind of help that many people exercise around the church such as hymn book collection following a service, or the clearing up of a building before the lights go out. This kind of help is very important and without it the church could not function. However, he is talking about something far more vital than that.

The Greek word that he uses for the English word 'helps' is '*antilepsis*' and last month we studied this word in the sense of seeking to understand all the shades of meaning that the New Testament has when it uses the word 'help'. This Greek word in the key verse means 'laying hold of' or even 'exchanging' and it has its roots in the whole concept of exchanging strength for weakness. So it is a spiritual word for ministry rather than a practical word for general help around the church.

The word is formed by the combining of two Greek words, '*anti*' which means 'in exchange' and '*lambano*' which means 'support,' so, the concept is, 'one who exchanges his strength for someone else's weakness'.

The ministry of strength for weakness is a vital ministry within the Church. Our eyes are often upon the major roles of the apostle and prophet, however, people who are willing to come alongside and to seek to exchange their strengths for other people's weaknesses also have a major role to play within the Church. Helpful assistance given during periods of hurt and pain are so important that it can hardly be expressed in simple words. The vital ministries of the support of the weak, or the caring for the widows, two matters that the New Testament Church saw as foundational ministries, are beyond words. Paul himself benefited from this ministry of helps when he was served and encouraged by the arrival of Stephanas and his two friends. Paul was encouraged and greatly blessed by the help that he received.

Maybe our churches would be so much better if we devoted ourselves to serving one another and seeking to exchange strength for weakness. Maybe you could become a helper within the church if you are not serving already in this valuable New Testament ministry.

KEY PRAYER

Heavenly Father, help me to serve in the capacity of a New Testament helper and help me to seek out those who need my strength for their weakness,. Help me, too, to receive this ministry at the times of my own weakness.

August 26th

KEY WORD: ***Administration***

KEY VERSE: **1 Corinthians 12 : 28**

And in the church God has appointed first of all apostles, second prophets, third teachers, then workers of miracles, also those having gifts of healing, those able to help others, those with gifts of administration and those speaking in different kinds of tongues.

Paul wrote to the church in Corinth and listed in the key verse today the New Testament ministry gifts that he thought were appropriate to bring to the attention of this particular church. The fact that the order and type of gifts is different to the ones that he listed to the Ephesian church matters not a bit. What Paul was seeking to do was to set out the gifts that were important to the church in Corinth at that particular time. There is no contradiction to the list in the Ephesian epistle and there is no contradiction in Paul's mind, it is just a matter of importance at this particular time and in this particular church.

In the list we have several gifts that are very well known, and in the list, there are a couple of gifts that are not so well known, and in fact only appear once in the New Testament in this key verse. One of these gifts is the ministry of administration. There are times when we are very 'heavenly-minded' and we think of ministry only in terms of 'platform gifts' or 'public demonstrations' of ministry. However, Paul, in this key verse, brings another ministry into the public arena: that of the gift of administration. We need those who will give structure to the clear thinking of others. Some people are greatly gifted in the area of dreams and visions, but often they do not know how to implement these visions and dreams. They can inspire a congregation with the possibilities of the future, but they cannot 'lay out' the plans and administer them. So Paul stated that the ministry of the administrator is just as vital.

The Greek word used here for this gift of administration is the word '*kubernesis*' which means 'to guide' as in the steering of a ship or the piloting of a vessel. The whole concept here is not so much one of administering in the sense of 'paperwork' or 'office procedure', but it is the guidance given when other gifts express vision or prophecy. The 'guide' gives structure and direction to the concepts being expressed. The Old King James Version translates this word as 'governments' as it seeks to bring the concept of the gift piloting the church as it grows and develops.

This gift is vital within the Church as too often we have dreams and visions without direction and structure. We often have concepts and presentation without the thoughtfulness of a 'pilot-like' figure giving expression to their gift in the guidance of these dreams towards fulfilment. Many congregations are disillusioned and dispirited due to the continual announcement of new plans and dreams without any thought being given to their conclusion or structured direction. Many churches have blueprints scattered in the dust and unfinished, when the only thing missing was the thoughtfulness of the gift of administrations that would have allowed for direction and structure and the pathway towards completion. Could this be the gift that you are seeking God for because it is often missing in today's Church?

My Journal ______________________________

____

____

____

KEY PRAYER

Heavenly Father, I long to be used by you in the whole area of New Testament gifts, as I seek you today I am aware of the need for wise counsel and guidance within the church. I offer myself afresh to you for use within this area of often 'missing' gifts.

August 27th

KEY WORD: **Sackcloth**

KEY VERSE: **Matthew 11 : 21**

"Woe to you Korazin! Woe to you, Bethsaida! If the miracles that were performed in you had been performed in Tyre and Sidon, they would have repented long ago in sackcloth and ashes."

As we draw towards the close of another month we shall consider over the next few days the whole concept of New Testament repentance and declaration. The key verse today expresses how much repentance should take place, and be seen to take place as well. Jesus was quite direct to two towns, Korazin and Bethsaida, for their lack of repentance and their lack of public demonstration of repentance.

We have been considering over the past two days a few of the New Testament gifts that Paul placed emphasis upon; it is also interesting to note that Jesus placed great emphasis upon New Testament repentance. Gifts are vital within the Church and of course it is important to place emphasis upon them. However, Jesus insisted upon a demonstration of repentance that would be the pathway towards salvation and new life and the commencement of a journey that would lead eventually to the receiving of New Testament gifts.

One of the outward demonstrations of repentance was an Old Testament form of public demonstration, the wearing of sackcloth and ashes. We shall consider the first aspect of this today.

Sackcloth was a material made from the hair of a black goat from Cilicia. If this sort of material was hard to find then the sackcloth of a camel was acceptable. The Old Testament saints would adorn themselves with this material as a sign of the outward confession of repentance. These garments were worn in order to express just how much someone was repentant for their sins, and just how much they were penitent for what they done.

The Greek word for sackcloth was *'sakkos'* and it literally meant 'the hair of the goat'. The Old Testament recorded the fact that this garment was worn by individuals at the time of great repentance. It also recorded the times when the Nation of Israel was in collective repentance, and when this garment was worn by a multitude. The *'sakkos'* featured very highly in the thinking of Jesus when He compared the lack of repentance in Korazin and Bethsaida to the swift and meaningful repentance of Tyre and Sidon. Jesus expected towns and cities as well as individuals to express themselves with a demonstration of public repentance. The *'sakkos'* was also worn at times by prophets when they were seeking to bring a powerful message of national repentance to the nation.

We may not express ourselves in such a way today. However, the Lord still expects that there will be a repentance at the time of wrongdoing and that this repentance should manifest itself in a public manner, such as the turning away from all wrongdoing.

My Journal ______________________________

KEY PRAYER

Heavenly Father, I confess before you today the things that I have recently done wrong, I repent of all my sin and I turn away from evil. Help me always to walk before you in a way that pleases you and help me always to confess my sin when I fall into temptation.

August 28th

KEY WORD: **Ashes**

KEY VERSE: **Matthew 11 : 21**

"Woe to you Korazin! Woe to you, Bethsaida! If the miracles that were performed in you had been performed in Tyre and Sidon, they would have repented long ago in sackcloth and ashes."

We are considering over these few days the whole concept of New Testament repentance and declaration. The key verse of yesterday and today expresses how much repentance should take place, and be seen to take place as well. Jesus was quite direct to two towns, Korazin and Bethsaida, for their lack of repentance and their lack of demonstration.

One of the outward demonstrations of repentance was an Old Testament form of public demonstration: the wearing of sackcloth and ashes. As we saw yesterday, the sackcloth was a public form of repentance when it was worn. However, the sackcloth was not worn on its own, ashes always accompanied the garment. These ashes were taken from the altar of sacrifice, following the roasting of a bull or a lamb for the sins of the people, and then the ashes were either thrown into the air with loud weeping, or they were placed upon the heads of those who were repenting.

The Greek word for ashes was '*spodos*' which meant simply 'the ash' and it was very much part of an Old Testament form of repentance. The word is only found three times in the New Testament, twice it is found associated with sackcloth and repentance, and once it is found in connection with animal sacrifice as mentioned by the writer to the Hebrews when he spoke of the sacrifice of the Old Testament as compared to the New Testament and the greater sacrifice of our High Priest, Jesus.

The ashes speak of the dirt of sin and shame and outward

manifestation of the defilement of sin, and, in the sprinkling of the ashes over the head, it drew the picture of someone who was not just inwardly sorry for their sin but also outwardly sorry for their sin. It showed to the world the act of repentance and shame.

We may not express ourselves in such a way today. However, the Lord still expects that there will be a repentance at the time of wrongdoing and that this repentance should reveal itself in a public manner, such as the turning away from all wrongdoing. Sackcloth and ashes may have passed into history, but repentance is still needed in the future if we are to progress towards greater and greater levels of blessing.

My Journal

KEY PRAYER

Heavenly Father, I confess my sins before you and I seek to be made clean. Wash me again in the precious blood of the Lamb and purify me afresh. I confess my sin and I seek to live a righteous and blameless life before you.

August 29th

KEY WORD: **Repented**

KEY VERSE: **Matthew 11 : 21**

"Woe to you Korazin! Woe to you, Bethsaida! If the miracles that were performed in you had been performed in Tyre and Sidon, they would have repented long ago in sackcloth and ashes."

We are considering over these few days the whole concept of New Testament repentance and declaration. The key verse of yesterday and today expresses how much repentance should take place, and be seen to take place as well. Jesus was quite direct to two towns, Korazin and Bethsaida, for their lack of repentance and their lack of demonstration.

We have noted that Jesus called for not just repentance but an outward manifestation of Korazin's and Bethsaida's repentance by the use of sackcloth and ashes. And as we have seen these outward manifestations brought about inward change. Jesus used a very interesting word for the word 'repent' in this key verse, the word used was *'metanoeo'* which means 'to perceive afterwards' it was a word that was formed by the joining of two words together. Firstly, the word *'meta'* which means 'change' and secondly, the word *'noeo'* which means 'the mind'. The meaning was quite simple, repentance was a changing of the mind after the perception of guilt.

Jesus was seeking fundamental change in people's thinking and actions following His ministry. It is not just enough to say 'I will change my ways' or 'I will seek to do better', repentance is a complete change of mind and habits once guilt has been understood.

The word *'metanoeo'* is found 31 times in the New Testament, and it was the foundational message of the gospel and the basic teaching of Jesus and His apostles whenever they preached the good news. The whole concept of repentance was one of the changing of your ways and the turning away from sin; the New Testament teaches very clearly that you can not stay in sin. Not only must you be sorry for the sins committed but you must also turn away from them and change your mind concerning them and live a new life.

There is no salvation without repentance. This is the 'bottom line' of the gospel; to simply preach 'come to Jesus' does not change lives. Many people have 'come to Jesus' and have gone on to become members of a local church without the repenting of sin and the changing of their lifestyle. There cannot be regeneration until there has been '*metanoeo*', a complete and full repentance.

My Journal

KEY PRAYER

Heavenly Father, I so long to become more and more like you and yet I find at times that sin and temptation are ever with me. Help me to live so close to you that I may find that sin and temptation lose their grip upon me. Help me to always live in an attitude of repentance so that my desires concerning you are fulfilled.

August 30th

KEY WORD: **Rend**

KEY VERSE: **Matthew 26 : 65**

Then the high priest tore his clothes and said, "He has spoken blasphemy! Why do we need any more witnesses? Look, now you have heard the blasphemy. What do you think?"

Along with the outward manifestation of repentance, the wearing of sackcloth and ashes quite often accompanied those who sought to show just how repentant they felt, and they would also tear their clothes, or as the Old Testament Scriptures might say, they would 'rend their garments'.

This tearing of clothes was a symbol of just how they felt when sin was tearing at their lives and they wanted to be free from the associated guilt. In the key verse today, the high priest when he confronted Jesus was so angered by the words from the lips of Jesus that he actually tore his clothes in a demonstration of just how he felt.

The Greek word for 'rend' or 'tear' is the word '*diarrhesso*' which means 'to break asunder,' and it was a word that was only associated with the tearing of clothes. There were other Greek words for the various meanings of the word 'tear', but only this word could fully convey the desperate tearing of clothes in anger, the demonstration of guilt and the act of repentance.

The word conveys more than just the action of the tearing of clothes, even the action of desperation and repentance; it seeks to convey the thought of 'bursting through clothes'. It was not that someone simply tore at their clothes but that they 'burst out of them' with a great ferociousness that showed, to those who might be around them, that this matter was serious enough to be treated with great demonstration and severe action.

The high priest considered Jesus to be guilty of blasphemy,

obviously quite wrongly, but his actions showed the degree to which his considered opinion had taken him. He tore his clothes in a fit of total and uncontrolled anger and his expression left a lasting impression upon those who witnessed the event.

The Old Testament saints who 'rent their garments' would also leave behind them a very vivid picture of anger, guilt, remorse and repentance. God would see their hearts as they sought to show Him just how they felt and He would forgive them for their sins time and time again. It just goes to show what a loving and patient God we have as He goes on forgiving us too, time after time. The rending of garments may not be practised today, but God still requires us to rend our hearts over sin and shame. We treat sin today far too casually, in fact the lessons from the Old Testament and the New Testament need to be seriously heeded.

My Journal ______________________________

KEY PRAYER

Heavenly Father, I have seen again the need to remove myself from sin and shame and to repent of all that is evil. Help me to rend my heart and not my garments over the actions that cause you pain.

August 31st

KEY WORD: **Weep**

KEY VERSE: **Mark 5 : 38–39**

When they came to the home of the synagogue ruler, Jesus saw a commotion, with people crying and wailing loudly. He went in and said to them, "Why all this commotion and wailing? The child is not dead but asleep."

Having arrived at the last day of another month, we also arrive at the last word that we shall study concerning repentance and the outward manifestation that goes along with it. In the key verse today, Jesus arrived at the home of Jairus whose little girl had just died following a period of sickness. Outside and inside the house the professional mourners had already gathered. These were people that had been engaged to manifest the corporate grief that a family or even a town would have when a person had died.

The act of weeping and wailing was not just an act of professional grief, it was a display of inner feelings at a moment of crisis. When a person or a family or even a town felt that they committed an act of sin or that God was against them for their acts of sin, they would weep and wail, as well the wearing sackcloth and ashes and the tearing of their clothes. The individual act of weeping and the corporate act of wailing were an outward sign of grief and repentance and of pain and hurt.

The Greek word used for 'weep' is the word *'klaio'* which means 'a loud expression of grief.' In fact the deeper that the pain was felt by the people then the louder the weeping and wailing became. It was an amazing corporate act of contrition and repentance when it was associated with an act of God when He chose to rebuke His people over their sins.

We would do well today to remember that the only way to

salvation is through the repentance of sin, and when accompanied by the weeping of emotion, it touches God's heart as well as our own hearts. In our desperation to 'get people saved' and in our earnestness to build the Church, we should remember that the only way to true salvation is through the preaching of the gospel and through the heart-changing of repentance. No easy methods and no simple presentations can ever take the place of the conviction of sin and the repentance of the human heart.

Jesus sought to show just how He felt about the corporate act of wailing when He arrived at the home of Jairus. The loud expressions of sadness did not touch His heart as He recognised that this was a contrived weeping and wailing and not a true expression of hurt and pain. We would do well to remember this, God does not just look at the outward expression, He also searches the inward parts of the heart to see if what is going on outside matches what is going on inside.

My Journal ______________________________

KEY PRAYER

Heavenly Father, I have learned again over these past few days that there is only one way to salvation, and that is through the way of repentance and through the forgiveness of sin. I pledge before you today that I will seek to always present before you the outward expression of my feelings that match the expression of my inward heart.

September 1st

KEY WORD: **Huge fish (whale)**

KEY VERSE: **Matthew 12 : 40**

For as Jonah was three days and three nights in the belly of a huge fish, so the Son of Man will be three days and three nights in the heart of the earth.

Mentioned only once in the entire New Testament, the huge fish or whale of Jonah's Old Testament experience, is something to seriously consider. In fact all the animals, birds and reptiles of the New Testament are interesting to consider, so at the beginning of this month we shall give time for a few days in order to study some of them.

Jesus used the huge fish or whale to illustrate the fact of His death and resurrection. He used the analogy of the whale's belly in order to convey the concept that He Himself would spend three days and nights in the 'heart of the earth'. The very fact that Jesus actually used this story and this fish is ample confirmation that Jonah's whale actually existed. There have been arguments and discussions for centuries as to whether or not a huge fish could actually swallow a man, and even when in recent history a fisherman actually lived following being swallowed by a creature from the sea, the discussions and arguments still did not cease.

Jesus used this story, which is good enough to confirm the incident that took place in the life and ministry of the Old Testament prophet, and the fact that Jesus actually used it as an illustration of His own death should silence the critics immediately.

The Greek word for 'huge fish' or 'whale' is '*ketos*' which means 'a sea monster.' The fact that the normal Greek word for fish: '*ichthus*' was not used suggests that this was not simply a large fish or even a huge fish. The word used suggests a kind of monster fish or sea creature and the only creature known to man to fit this description is a whale.

'Ketos' is the kind of word that was associated with 'something out of the ordinary', so, even if it was a whale, it was a very large whale indeed. Jonah was three days and nights in the whale's belly, without being consumed or drowned in the acidic nature of the creature's stomach. This would suggest a cavernous place suitable for the survival of a man, even without the supernatural power and intervention of God.

We can give thanks today that Jesus actually used this story as an illustration which proves the Old Testament event, but more than this, we can gives thanks for the fact that God is in control and can even speak to sea creatures and control supernatural events. If He can do that to huge fish, He can certainly take care of us!

My Journal

KEY PRAYER

Heavenly Father, I praise you at the beginning of a new month that you are on throne and that all is well. The story of the huge fish and Jonah's survival proves again that you can take care of your children. It is well with my soul.

September 2nd

KEY WORD: **Camel**

KEY VERSE: **Matthew 19 : 24**

"Again I tell you, it is easier for a camel to go through the eye of a needle than for a rich man to enter the kingdom of heaven."

The camel is mentioned just six times in the New Testament, which is strange seeing that it was very much an animal of the Middle East, and, at the time of Jesus and the New Testament Church, there would have been tens of thousands of them all around the Middle East. The interesting thing, too, about the fact that there are six references to camels, is that three of the references refer to the same incident. Firstly, the way that in the teaching of Jesus, He charges the Pharisees with 'straining at a gnat and swallowing a camel'. Secondly, the strange clothing of John the Baptist and his camel's hair tunic, and thirdly, the key verse today concerning the fact that a rich man would find it hard to enter the Kingdom of God but easier to enter the 'needle's eye'.

The Greek word for 'camel' is '*kamelos*' and it means 'a bearing carrier' and it was a word that was derived from a Hebrew word. It was applied to the camel as it was a beast capable of bearing great weights for long distances and it could carry someone day after day.

It is this very fact that Jesus was alluding to when He used His illustration of the 'eye of the needle'. The 'eye of the needle' was a small doorway in a much larger city wall door. A traveller arriving after sunset at the gate of a city would find the main, large doorway closed and bolted for the night. However, within the larger door would be this smaller door. The camel would have to be stripped down of all its weights and parcels, and then it would be pushed and pulled through the smaller doorway into the city streets beyond. Then, one by one, the parcels and weights would be carried through the 'eye of the needle' and re-attached to the camel. This was a difficult process that took a great deal of time, so Jesus used this as a picture of just how difficult it would be for a rich man to enter the Kingdom of God. It is much easier, even with the lengthy and difficult process of stripping down of the camel, to get it through the eye of the needle than it would be to get a rich man into the Kingdom of God.

This great beast of burden, with its ability to carry people day after day through desert lands, was an ideal picture of the kind of message that Jesus wanted to convey. We need to take heed to the message so that nothing hinders us in our progress towards heaven and the Kingdom of God. There are many things that might distract us and many paths to choose. We should keep a single eye to the will of God so that we do not miss the way, as He is the only door by which we can enter.

My Journal

KEY PRAYER

Heavenly Father, thank you for the truth of the way of the Lord. Help me to walk this way worthy of my high calling in Christ Jesus, thank you for the teaching of Jesus, help me each day to keep a single eye upon Him.

September 3rd

KEY WORD: **Fox**

KEY VERSE: **Luke 13 : 32**

"Go tell that fox, 'I will drive out demons and heal people today and tomorrow and on the third day I will reach my goal.'"

Jesus often used the animals of the field as graphic illustrations within His teaching. As we have seen the whale and the camel were all helpful in illustrating His messages. However, no animal was more helpful than the 'fox'. Jesus used this animal in a devastating way when He called King Herod a 'fox' following the news that 'Herod wanted to kill Him'.

The fox was a cunning and clever hunting animal. The Greek word that was used for the 'fox' was the word *'alopex'* and it summed up the animal completely as it had its roots in the Hebrew word which means 'jackal', and jackal means 'cunning worker'. To call someone a fox was to call them a cunning and devious kind of person, as a fox will use all kinds of devious tricks to reach its prey and make its kill.

However, when Jesus called Herod a 'fox', it was even more devastating than simply calling someone devious and cunning because the Greek reference in the key verse today is in the feminine gender which makes it a far more cutting and hurtful phrase. Jesus actually called Herod, a 'she fox', a phrase that would have summed up the cunning and devious king perfectly.

The 'fox' was also used when Jesus was alluding to the fact that He came into the world with nothing. He said that even the cunning and devious animals of the field have a home, but that He, the Son of Man, had nowhere to lay His head.

The nature of the fox is a perfect description of the cunningness of sin and corruption as Jesus went on to say, following His description of Herod, that He had come to minister to a world of suffering and that He was going to drive out demons and heal people, and that He would continue to meet people's needs while the old cunning king sat upon his throne. Jesus came to heal, seek and save and nothing was going to stop Him in His goal to reach Jerusalem and Calvary. We can thank God today that the mission of Jesus went on unhindered by Satan, demons, kings and any flesh. He came to seek and to save those who are lost and He did not waver, not even for a king!

My Journal

KEY PRAYER

Heavenly Father, I praise you today that you set your face as a flint towards Jerusalem and nothing hindered your progress to the cross, you went all the way because that was your mission and nothing else mattered. Thank you for saving me and thank you for Calvary.

September 4th

KEY WORD: **Horse**

KEY VERSE: **James 3 : 3**

When we put bits into the mouths of horses to make them obey us, we can turn the whole animal.

The horse is mentioned in the New Testament 18 times, but the interesting thing about this is that of the 18 references to horses and horsemen, 17 of them are in the book of Revelation. There is only one reference to a horse appearing in the New Testament apart from the book of Revelation and that is in the key verse today in the epistle of James.

To have such an animal as a horse hardly mentioned outside of the last book of the bible is quite strange as it is a valuable beast and an important animal in the development of the Church. It is almost certain that horses, and no doubt camels, would have carried the apostles on their journeys to and from the new churches. However, it is only James who makes mention of this animal and he uses the reference to the horse as a word picture that conveyed a message.

James was speaking about the 'tongue' being an unruly member of the body and that the tongue can be the source of great danger and trouble. He compares the tongue, with its capability of causing so much corruption, to the horse and the bridle of a horse. He says that, if the strong and well built animal like a horse can be tamed by the fitting of a bit and bridle, then we ought to be capable of taming the tongue and bringing it under control.

The Greek word for 'horse' is '*hippos*' which simply means 'the horse.' It has no complex meaning and it does not have any other oblique meaning, it is simply the word for horse.

This animal would almost certainly have been the main

method of transport, along with possibly the camel, that most of the New Testament travelling ministries would have used, although there is no confirmation of this. To travel the vast number of miles that the Apostles would have travelled would have been out of the question apart from the use of horses. The horse with its strength and speed would have been an ideal vehicle for this use.

The horse with its strength and speed was also a very good illustration to use within the book of Revelation when John saw horses and horsemen riding into victory. He also saw Jesus riding a white horse. The whole symbolic nature of this would have caused the readers of the final book of the New Testament to rejoice because the horse is a symbol of victory and overcoming. How many times has history portrayed its victorious conquerors as riding a horse into battle and statues and monuments have been erected throughout towns and cities across the world with victory portrayed as a horse and rider.

In the book of Revelation, Jesus rode a white horse which would have portrayed Him as 'more than a conqueror', white signifying the whole aspect of purity and power.

My Journal ______________________________

KEY PRAYER

Heavenly Father, thank you today for the vivid picture that the New Testament gives us of our Lord and Saviour riding a white horse into victory. He is more than a conqueror and I rejoice today in His finished and completed work. He comes riding on a horse as King of kings and Lord of all lords.

September 5th

KEY WORD: **Dragon**

KEY VERSE: **Revelation 20 : 2**

He seized the dragon, that ancient serpent, who is the devil, or Satan, and bound him for a thousand years.

The dragon is a key New Testament creature that appears twelve times in the book of Revelation, in fact this is the only book in the New Testament that features this creature. The reason that this creature features as a key aspect is the fact that Satan, the devil, is called a dragon, and that he is also featured very symbolically as 'The Dragon'.

Twelve times in Revelation the picture of a dragon is revealed as the sign of darkness and satanic power. The revelations that were granted to John as he wrote this book included the vision of a creature so awesome that, for all who would read this book throughout the ages of the Church, the full understanding of just what Satan is, would be revealed: he is a dragon.

The dragon mythically breathes fire, it is able to overcome most other creatures, and it has the ability to crush anything that stands before it, an awesome portrayal of our enemy and a picture that will last in the mind of the Church.

The Greek word for 'dragon' is simply '*drakon*' and it meant 'a large serpent' or 'mythical monster'. The word was created from the root word '*derk*' which means 'to see,' and the word was taken by the Greek people and used for this monstrous creature because it revealed the fact that here was a monster that seemed to be all-powerful, all-seeing and all-conquering.

The fact that it was used in the book of Revelation at the 'end times' is interesting because it reveals just how much people would fear the onslaught of the enemy when they regarded him as a dragon to be feared. What we must understand is that in the key verse today an 'ordinary' angel from heaven comes down and takes hold of this dragon and binds him for a thousand years and then throws him into the abyss. This angel was not an archangel or a mighty angel he was simply called 'an angel from heaven'. Then this angel locks and seals the chamber and denies him any more power and authority.

It only took an 'ordinary' angel to that, so why should a picture of a mythical monster have any power over us at all. We are free from the power of sin, Satan and the ravages of temptation. So we need to remember to read the last book of the Bible and to read its final verses whenever this dragon seeks to destroy, as we are more than conquerors over what is a defeated foe. This dragon may still breath fire at us at times, but Jesus is Lord.

My Journal ______________________________

KEY PRAYER

Heavenly Father, I see afresh today the limitations that the enemy has, I understand that he has no authority against me, and that I can overcome him with the blood of the Lamb and with the word of my testimony. Help me to keep this in perspective whenever the dragon rears its head within my life.

September 6th

KEY WORD: **Wolf**

KEY VERSE: **Acts 20 : 29**

I know that after I leave, savage wolves will come in among you and will not spare the flock.

One of the most graphic animals to appear within the New Testament is the wolf – a most savage and fearsome animal that frightened people whenever it appeared. It was taken by New Testament writers as a picture of those who would seek to destroy, and in the key verse today Paul's words echoed across the beach at Ephesus as he prayed that God would keep His hand upon this new church and guard it against the wolves.

The Greek word for 'wolf' is '*lukos*' and it simply means wolf. These animals could be heard baying in the night and striking fear into the hearers. They could be seen lurking in packs just waiting for an unsuspecting animal to stray near, then they would savagely attack leaving only a few bones of a dead and eaten prey.

It is no wonder that this animal was used by the writers of the New Testament when they sought to convey the threat of false teaching and the savagery of church splits and divisions. Paul prayed against the wolves and against the attacks that they would bring to the new churches that had been planted throughout the world.

The wolf was also known for its total focus upon a prey, it would see nothing else and it would fear nothing else as it bore down upon its helpless victims. Paul saw the wolves as a major threat to the new churches. He saw, firstly, the Pharisees as wolves as they set themselves against the Church, then secondly, he saw the Romans as wolves when they sought to destroy the Church through persecution, and then thirdly, he saw the false teachers and false apostles and prophets as wolves as they sought to ravage the Church with error and false teaching.

Paul saw the dangers of these wolves, so his method of counter-attack was, firstly, to appoint elders within the churches who would be those of spiritual standing and authority. Secondly, he commenced writing to the churches in order to bring teaching and instruction, and revelation and discipline to those who were younger in the faith. Thirdly, he commenced his journeys around the churches in order to strengthen them and inspire them to go on with God.

His writings also reveal a man that gave himself to prayer as he constantly understood the threat of the wolves among the churches. We should take heed today against those who would seek to destroy and we should be on our guard against all wolves.

My Journal

KEY PRAYER

Heavenly Father, I see why Paul was so anxious and so keen to guard the Church from those who seek to ravage it with false teaching and error. Help me to guard my local church from the wolves who would seek to destroy. Help me to hold on to truth against today's wolves and today's enemies of the Church.

September 7th

KEY WORD: ***Snake***

KEY VERSE: ***John 3 : 14***

"Just as Moses lifted up the snake in the desert, so the Son of Man must be lifted up."

The snake, although not an animal but a reptile, is worthy of consideration as a vital creature within New Testament thinking and practice. The snake or serpent is mentioned 14 times in the New Testament and its references range from the symbolic use for the devil, the old serpent, to the name that Jesus used for the Pharisees and Sadducees in a times of rebuke and chastisement.

The serpent also appears when Jesus was giving authority to His Church. Whenever they would find themselves in difficulty Jesus said that, 'they would be able to pick up deadly serpents and find no harm in them'. His words were proved true when Paul, following his shipwreck when finding himself on an island and being bitten by a viper, he felt no ill effects of any kind.

The most important reference to the snake was in the key verse today, when Jesus was quoting from the Old Testament history of Moses raising up a bronze serpent upon a stick so that all who looked upon the bronze serpent would find health and healing. Jesus said, that 'as Moses raised up the snake in the desert, even so the Son of Man would be lifted up'.

The Greek word for snake was '*ophis*' and it meant simply 'snake' or 'serpent'. The reason why this reptile was often used as a New Testament illustration was quite simple. The snake was a sly and venomous creature capable of great destruction and harm. This was a perfect illustration of the devil and his work and was a graphic way of using a word picture to great effect. People would understand just how venomous Satan was when the picture of a snake was portrayed for them.

The bronze serpent was quite different in that this picture was a symbol of salvation and healing, the living serpent was capable of death and a deadly effect; however the bronze form of a snake was portrayed for them in a special way.

The bronze serpent was quite different in that this picture was a symbol of salvation and healing. The living serpent was capable of death and a deadly effect; however the bronze serpent was a picture of the curse of sin being borne away. The bronze metal being figurative of purity and righteousness.

To be called a snake is still regarded today as a rebuke and as a derogatory term. When Jesus used this term for the Pharisees He was regarded as being devastating with His remarks. We can rejoice today in that the serpent and snake no longer hold any power over us as the Son of Man has been lifted up and we are free.

My Journal ______________________________

KEY PRAYER

Heavenly Father, I thank you today for the freedom from sin that I enjoy through the cross and through Jesus. The old serpent, the devil, no longer holds any power over me because Jesus paid the price for my salvation. I rejoice that He has become my bronze serpent, who was raised up to new life.

September 8th

KEY WORD: **Eagle**

KEY VERSE: **Revelation 4 : 7**

The first living creature was like a lion, the second was like an ox, the third had a face like man, and the fourth was like a flying eagle.

Over the next few days we are going to turn our attention away from animals to some of the birds that are mentioned within the New Testament. We will find as we study them that birds were used greatly by New Testament writers as symbols and signs. None more so than this first bird, the eagle.

There are only four actual references to eagles in the New Testament although on a couple of other occasions vultures feature within the same translations. The Greek word for 'eagle' is '*aetos*' and its meaning is slightly vague, it can mean 'to blow' or it can mean 'of the wind.' The words were taken for the incredible ability of the eagle to glide through the wind with effortless ease. The eagle is a most powerful bird and was regarded as the 'king of the air.' Because of this powerful position and because it had the ability to reign over all things that were above the ground, the eagle was used as the symbol of great strength and commanding presence. Egypt and Babylon in the Old Testament used the eagle as their symbol of power as did many other nations. God often used the picture of the power of the eagle to punish Israel when they had rebelled against God and had spent much time being unfaithful to their Lord.

However, the eagle was also used by God to describe just how much He loved Israel, as He describes Israel as being borne on eagles wings unto Himself.

In the New Testament the eagle takes on the symbolic nature of power and authority. In the key verse today, the four creatures that surround the throne of God in the heaven symbolise each 'kingly' beast of the earth. The lion as the king of all ground beasts, the ox as the king of the beasts of the domestic field, the man as the king of God's creation, and the eagle as the king of all that is above the earth. These beasts guard the throne of God day and night and symbolise strength and honour, glory and power.

So the eagle is a contradictory bird. On the one hand it symbolises judgement and destruction, and on the other hand it symbolises strength, majesty and power. It is no wonder that the New Testament writers, even though they used the eagle only a few times within their writings, used this bird as a graphic illustration of a kingly nature

In New Testament Palestine there were eight diffcrent species of eagles and they reigned supreme in the skies of their day.

My Journal ____________________

KEY PRAYER

Heavenly Father, thank you for the picture of the eagle and its strength which reminds us of the Lord and His strength and power and that you still bear us each day upon your wings as you minister to us. I praise you for this wonderful picture of love and power.

September 9th

KEY WORD: **Hen**

KEY VERSE: **Luke 13 : 34**

"O Jerusalem, Jerusalem, you who kill the prophets and stone those sent to you, how often I have longed to gather your children together, as a hen gathers her chicks under her wings, but you were not willing!"

The hen is a bird that has a wonderful symbolism attached to it as the bird that Jesus referred to when He sought to teach Israel, and Jerusalem in particular, just how much He cared for them. So the fact that this bird is only mentioned twice in the New Testament is quite amazing. It is even more amazing when you discover that the two references, one in Matthew and the key verse today in Luke, both refer to the same event. So the actual bird is only referred to once and yet it carries such an amazing place in the history of the nation of Israel.

The Greek word for 'hen' is the word '*ornis*' which actually means 'fowl', and the word was used for both the male and female varieties of the bird. There was another word that was also used for hen in the Greek language, and this word was '*nossia*' which means 'to brood' or 'to form a nest'. In the key verse Jesus actually uses both words in order to convey the strength of His feeling towards Jerusalem. What He actually stated was 'how often would I have built a nest with you like a hen when it gathers its chicks around her'.

God longed to have an intimate relationship with Israel and with Jerusalem but they had continually rejected Him. They had killed the prophets and stoned those who were sent to them, and they had rejected each and every advance of God's love. When Jesus spoke these words over the City of Jerusalem, He knew it would only be a few short days until these rebellious people would finally reject Him too and crucify Him, so you can almost hear the anguish in His voice.

The hen was a beautiful picture of love and caring concern, at the first hint of danger the hen would raise its wings in order that the chicks might run for shelter; other birds would take flight in an expression of their own fear, but the hen would stay and give protection.

This graphic picture was given by Jesus as a love picture to His people. He cares and He protects and He gives us covering at each and every moment of the day, just like a hen and her chicks.

My Journal ______________________________

KEY PRAYER

Heavenly Father, I bless you today for this lovely picture of care and concern, and of love and protection. Thank you that I can rest in the shadow of your wings and that in this place of safety there is abiding shelter.

September 10th

KEY WORD: **Dove**

KEY VERSE: **Matthew 3 : 16**

As soon as Jesus was baptised, He went up out of the water. At that moment heaven was opened to Him, and He saw the Spirit of God descending like a dove and lighting on Him.

We could not possibly leave our studies in the symbols of New Testament birds without considering the dove. The dove was regarded as the gentlest and the most tender of all birds and it came to symbolise the most beautiful things in the New Testament.

The dove is mentioned only nine times in the New Testament, which is amazing seeing that it features so dramatically within the teaching of Jesus and His apostles. It is even more amazing when you discover that of the nine references, four of them refer to the same event as all the gospel writers record the baptism of Jesus. Matthew, Mark, Luke and John, all record that fact that a dove sat upon Jesus at the moment of His baptism and that it was regarded by all as a symbol of anointing and confirmation of the Father.

Because the dove was used at this moment of baptism and the Father's confirmation, it came to be recognised as the symbol of the Holy Spirit and the anointing of God,

The Greek word for the bird called the 'dove' is the word '*peristera*'. The word meant 'a dove' or 'a pigeon', and it symbolised perfectly the action and nature of the bird rather than the bird itself. The dove is a harmless bird and a sensitive bird. The dove could not possibly cause harm or cause injury to anything around it, it is not within its nature to attack or cause harm, it would be quite beyond its ability to do anything that could be regarded as hostile.

The dove also is a very sensitive bird in that the slightest movement, threat, or noise and the bird will instantly take flight, only returning when it is certain that there is no further threat to its safety.

What greater picture could there be of the Holy Spirit whose work and ministry only brings healing and care, there is nothing hostile about the work and ministry of the Holy Spirit. He is a gentle Spirit and a caring Person with only the greatest desire to bless.

The Holy Spirit is also a sensitive spirit, He will not linger where there are fleshly actions and hard-heartedness. His ministry is gentle and soothing and any threat to that will cause the Spirit of God to remove Himself. It is no wonder that the New Testament writers chose such a beautiful, sensitive bird as the dove in order to symbolise the ministry of the third Person of the Godhead.

My Journal

KEY PRAYER

Heavenly Father, I have learned afresh today that the nature of the Holy Spirit is gentleness, I ask you to help me to always be as sensitive as He is, so that we can flow together in love and grace. Please help me to always be aware of His presence so that He might minister to me without threat.

September 11th

KEY WORD: **Dog**

KEY VERSE: ***Matthew 7 : 6***

"Do not give dogs what is sacred; do not throw your pearls to pigs. If you do they may trample them under their feet, and turn and tear you to pieces."

As we draw near to a conclusion of our studies in New Testament animals, birds and reptiles we shall return to two final animals that are mentioned in one verse together, the key verse of today and tomorrow.

The first animal in this key verse is the 'dog', one of the most popular animals in the world today and the favourite family pet. However, in both Old Testament and New Testament settings, this was not so at all. Dogs were regarded as dirty beasts and as 'outsiders' and the very name came to be linked with those who were without the blessing of God. Gentiles were regarded by the Jews as 'dogs' and they were not even to be associated with, as they were regarded as being outside of the covenant that God had made with Israel. This is why, in the key verse, Jesus said 'do not give sacred things to dogs', and in His mind was the whole Gentile world who were not yet part of the ministry of grace. This ministry of grace would not commence towards the 'Gentile dogs' until the beginning of the day of grace, at Calvary.

Dogs are mentioned nine times in the New Testament and there are two Greek words that are ascribed to them and they both have differing features. The first word is *'kuon'* which means 'a natural hound' and the second word is *'kunarion'* which means 'little dogs, ' we would say today young dogs or 'puppies'.

The symbolical sense of 'the dog' was regarded as the ceremonial sense of impurity, and it was regarded by the Jews as quite acceptable to treat the other nations of the world and all who were not Jewish as 'dogs'. It was also acceptable to treat all people that were outside of the covenant of the law as 'dogs', and the fact that Jesus actually stated this within the Sermon on the Mount reinforced this message and thinking.

On one occasion a woman came to Jesus seeking blessing and she was ignored by Him. Finally, in an act of desperation to be heard, she stated that even the dogs eat crumbs from the table, and this statement proved to be the very entrance for her to the blessing of God. Even dogs, Gentile dogs, could feed from the crumbs of grace. This showed the real heart of Jesus towards all who are lost, even the 'dogs' of a lost covenant.

Uncleanness to the Jews was something to be abhorred and something to be avoided. We can only rest in the amazement of grace to find that we, who are considered to be but 'dogs', can not only sit at the table of grace but are accepted in the Beloved.

My Journal

KEY PRAYER

Heavenly Father, thank you today for grace, and thank you that you have welcomed me to your table and that you have furnished before me a table of plenty. I bless you that God's love is upon me and the banner over me is love and I have been welcomed in to the covenant of grace.

September 12th

KEY WORD: **Pig**

KEY VERSE: **Matthew 7 : 6**

"Do not give dogs what is sacred; do not throw your pearls to pigs. If you do they may trample them under their feet, and turn and tear you to pieces."

Yesterday we were studying the symbolic nature of the dog, and we saw just how much Israel regarded the dog as a dirty beast and how they related this dirty beast to that of the nations of the world, especially the Gentiles. However, if we thought that the dog was regarded as a dirty beast then the second animal mentioned in the key verse today is even worse.

The pig was regarded as being the lowest of the low and the dirtiest of the dirty, and a most amazing feature takes place regarding this animal. As it was treated as the lowest form of life and totally unclean, the individual 'pig' is not even mentioned once in the New Testament. The only time that it does appear, it appears in a collective form as 'pigs' or swine. In this form it is mentioned 14 times and eleven of these references are to the same event, the demons leaving the 'mad man of Gadara' and entering a herd of swine, and two other references refer to the food that the Prodigal Son was eating.

The pig was so unclean that it was regarded as almost unmentionable in Jewish thinking. The Greek word for 'pig' or 'swine' is the word '*choiros*' and it meant 'hogs' and 'pigs'. There was another word that was linked to '*choiros*' and this was the word '*hus*' which meant a 'boar' or a 'sow', this word was used for both a female boar or a male boar.

The whole nature of the pig was one that allowed itself to be linked with all the worst in nature, and the Jews loved to consider everyone else as 'swine' and 'pigs'.

The Jews would not eat of the meat from a pig nor would they allow themselves to touch this animal. The whole nature of this beast brought about the avoidance of it by every true Jew.

Therefore today we can thank God that, although we had been regarded as Gentile dogs and Gentile pigs, the worst of the worst and the lowest of the low, God lowered Himself even further to the cross so that He might become our Saviour. Because of this God has highly exalted Him and He is now enthroned in splendour.

My Journal

KEY PRAYER

Heavenly Father, how I love you today when I realise afresh just how low you came to bring me up. I bless you for your sacrifice and I praise you that you have made even a dog sit with you in high places and become accepted in the Beloved.

September 13th

KEY WORD: ***Fig tree***

KEY VERSE: ***Matthew 21 : 19***

Seeing a fig tree by the road, He went up to it but found nothing on it except leaves. Then He said to it, "May you never bear fruit again!" Immediately the tree withered.

For several days we have been studying the concepts of animals, birds and reptiles within the New Testament. Before we leave this whole area of nature and creation we are going to look at some of the trees of the New Testament that featured in the ministry of Jesus and within the ministry of the New Testament Church.

The fig tree is one of the most familiar trees within the pages of the New Testament books. It is well known as the emblem of Israel, and many prophecies feature the blossoming of the fig tree as a major sign of Israel's renewed strength and prosperity. The fig tree appears several times in the Scriptures as a tree of great substance and fruit, and in its season it was a bountiful provider of beautiful fruit.

In the key verse today Jesus cursed this particular fig tree because it was not doing what it should be doing, providing fruit for passers by. When Jesus cursed the tree it died almost immediately and withered into the ground. Jesus was not just angered that there was no fruit, but He used the occasion to teach His disciples lessons of faith.

The word used in the New Testament for fig tree is '*suke*' or even '*sukea*' and the words mean quite simply 'a tree of figs'. This is one of the reasons that Jesus cursed the tree because it was not a tree of figs, but just a tree of leaves.

There was no sign of any fruit when Jesus passed by, many leaves should have indicated that fruit lay within the deepest part of the tree, underneath the leaves. However, there was no sign of any fruit, not even young and unripe figs, it was just a barren tree. The disciples would have learned two lessons, firstly, the faith lesson, because Jesus said you can have power over all things if you have faith, even barren fig trees, and secondly, that fruitfulness is vital. We are expected to produce fruit. No fruit is a sign of barrenness and this was unacceptable, so Jesus cursed the unprofitable tree. We should also learn this lesson of fruitfulness and barrenness, as we are expected to produce fruit, and lots of it, at all times.

My Journal

KEY PRAYER

Heavenly Father, there is much to learn from the fig tree and its barrenness. Please help me to learn as much as I can so that I might produce fruit for you in season and out of season. Thank you for the lessons that I have learned today and thank you too for your patience with me because you have not treated me as you treated the unfruitful tree .

September 14th

KEY WORD: **Sycamore tree**

KEY VERSE: **Luke 19 : 4**

So he ran ahead and climbed a sycamore-fig tree to see Him, since Jesus was coming that way.

The sycamore tree has gone down in history as the tree that Zacchaeus climbed when he wanted to see Jesus. Every Sunday School curriculum has featured this Bible story throughout the ages. The sycamore was a fig tree, although it was a different variety of fig to the one that Jesus cursed in the key verse of yesterday.

This fig tree was very different, it had leaves like a mulberry tree and thicker fruit figs than an ordinary fig tree. It would grow in a different way too. It would spread its leaves and branches widely, to almost 60 to 80 feet in diameter according to W E Vine, and these trees were often planted by the side of the road so that shelter was obtained by those who were passing by. This tree was ideal for Zacchaeus as its branches were low, it was easy to climb and its thick strong leaves, of wide diameter, were ideal to hide in. Zacchaeus thought that he was quite safe and out of view, until Jesus stopped right beneath him and encountered him in such a way that salvation came to his house that very day.

The Greek word for 'sycamore' is '*sukomorea*' which means 'mulberry tree.' There is also another word in the Greek language for mulberry tree, which is '*sukaminos*'.

This sycamore tree, although world-famous through its Sunday School attention throughout the years, is only mentioned once in the entire New Testament and its fame is down to the signal fact that Jesus passed by. This one-time mention of this tree has far exceeded its place within the New Testament, it is not that this tree is important, however, it is the fact that Jesus passed by, and that He stopped, and that He knew exactly who was in this sycamore tree and, what is even more important, He knew exactly what was going on.

The lesson learned today is not that the sycamore tree was important, but that Jesus knows us, He knows where we are and He knows all about us, we cannot hide from Him, He knows!

My Journal

KEY PRAYER

Heavenly Father, I bless you today for the fact that you know all about me and like Zacchaeus I can not hide from you. You have searched me out and you know my every need. Thank you for caring enough about me to look in my direction,

September 15th

KEY WORD: **Olive tree**

KEY VERSE: **Matthew 21 : 1**

As they approached Jerusalem and came to Bethphage on the Mount of Olives, Jesus sent two disciples.

The olive tree is probably the best known tree in the whole of the New Testament. It is certainly one of the trees that has the most references attached to it as it is mentioned nineteen times. olive trees were planted all over Israel and it was a tree that featured in abundance, especially on the Mount of Olives where there were olive trees covering the whole hill. The Mount of Olives drew its name and fame from this tree.

Olives were used to produce oil and of course oil was a type of the Holy Spirit and anointing. All the kings and priests of Old Testament Israel were anointed with olive oil in their preparation for service and ministry. So the tree and its oil had a significant place in the life and times of this nation.

Jesus was a frequent visitor to the Mount of Olives and this Mount, having featured greatly in His earthly ministry, will also feature greatly once again when Jesus returns to earth at His Second Coming. The Mount of Olives is the designated place of His actual physical return. Maybe it is the association with the oil of the olive that Jesus enjoyed so much or the thought that the oil of anointing was so rich. Whatever it was, it is quite obvious that He richly enjoyed the atmosphere and ambience of the Mount of Olives.

The normal Greek word for olive tree was the word *'elaia'* which meant simply 'olives' or 'berries.' However, there were also two other important Greek words attached to the olive tree.

The first word was used when you were seeking to convey the aspect of order and beauty of a well-ordered olive garden, for this you would use the word *'kallielaios'* which meant 'olives of beauty'. This word was only used when someone had 'laid out' a garden of olive trees and had tended them with great care.

The second word that was used was *'agrielaios'* which meant 'wild olive.' This word was only used when the tree was found growing wild having received no attention and no care.

It would be an obvious thing to the olive growers that the best fruit and therefore the best oil would be obtained from the olive trees that had received the best attention. This is very much like our lives. If we are left to our own devices we do not prosper, but, when the heavenly gardener cares for us, at times with careful pruning and cutting, we then grow to become more and more effective and beautiful for Him. Under His care we prosper the best and produce the best results.

The olive tree in the New Testament was also a symbol of the End Times as it was featured in the book of Revelation with the connection to the 'two witnesses' of chapter eleven. It is also the tree that is used by Paul in Romans when he speaks of the Gentiles being grafted into the Jewish olive tree and becoming accepted as the beloved of God. Paul uses the beautiful word-play of the two extra Greek words for the olive tree. What he literally says is that the Gentiles were 'wild olives' but they have now become 'olives of beauty'. He uses the two Greek words *'agrielaios'* and *'kallielaios'* to bring strong emphasis to this teaching. Having been wild olives we can rejoice today that we are now olives of beauty unto the Lord.

KEY PRAYER

Heavenly Father, I rejoice today in the tender care of your loving concern for my life, I praise you that you have taken what was the wild olive of my life and that you have produced an olive of beauty. Only you could do that, for, out of the brokenness of my sin you produced order and form that now bring you praise and glory.

September 16th

KEY WORD: **Palm tree**

KEY VERSE: **John 12 : 13**

They took palm branches and went out to meet Him, shouting, "Hosanna!" "Blessed is He who comes in the name of the Lord!" "Blessed is the King of Israel!"

Of all the trees mentioned in the New Testament, you would have thought that the palm tree would have the most prominent one. The amazing fact is that the palm tree is only mentioned twice in all the books of the New Testament.

This tree has a very special place in the Old Testament where there are 34 references. The earliest is the one where the Israelites in their wilderness wanderings came to an oasis, where there were 70 palm trees and twelve wells of water, which they named Elim, which meant to them 'a place of refreshment and palm trees'. This symbolical picture stayed in the minds of the people of God throughout their history and the palm tree featured often.

In the key verse today, John records the fact that when Jesus rode into Jerusalem on a donkey, the multitude cut down branches from the palm tree and threw them under the donkey's feet as a way of expressing royalty and splendour. This journey into Jerusalem is recorded by all four Gospel writers, but it is only John who recognised the fact that the branches were from the palm tree. Two other writers, Matthew and Mark, only said that 'branches were cut down,' and Luke ignores the fact that there were any branches at all. So, we owe it to John that Palm Sunday has a special place in the history of the New Testament Church and in the Church today.

The Greek word for palm tree was *'phoinix'* which means 'date palm,' and it was the affectionate name for this particular tree. The tree also has a place in history for another reason. Two important cities, Phoenicia and Phoenix in Crete, are named after the palm tree, as these two cities had an abundance of these trees. Jericho was also called the 'City of Palms' as there were many palm trees within the area.

The branches of the palm tree were thick and luxurious and would have been ideal for the royal pathway of a king. Any branches from any tree could have been cut down as a kind of pathway for Jesus on Palm Sunday, but it was this thick, leafy branch that the people chose as their covering for the ground when Jesus passed by. The people chose the best branches from the best tree, as their expression of worship towards the Lord on Palm Sunday.

Jesus is our Saviour and Lord and only the best is good enough for Him. We should remember that, when we serve Him and when we worship Him, only our best is good enough for the Lord.

As we draw towards a conclusion in our studies of New Testament trees, we shall turn to one tomorrow that has the most vital place of all trees.

My Journal ________________________________

KEY PRAYER

Heavenly Father, it is with great joy that I remember Palm Sunday and the entrance into Jerusalem of Jesus. I can hear the joy of the multitude, and I can see the abundant entrance of Jesus as He makes His way through the streets that are covered with palms. Help me to ever keep this picture in mind as it reminds me that only my best is good enough for Him.

September 17th

KEY WORD: ***Vine***

KEY VERSE: ***Matthew 26 : 29***

"I tell you, I will not drink of this fruit of the vine from now on until that day when I drink it anew with you in my Father's Kingdom."

Of all the trees that are featured within the New Testament this tree has the most outstanding place and the most significant place. The vine tree, or the vineyard tree, was the tree that had the closest place in the hearts of the Jewish people, as it stood for the harvest time and the gathering time of plenty and abundance. The fruit of the vine was enjoyed by the people of God as a symbol of richness and joy. It was used by Jesus, in the key verse today, when He instituted the Lord's Supper. Every Jew would have the fruit of the vine in use at the Passover feast when they remembered that their forefathers had escaped the clutches of Egypt and death. The wine would flow when they celebrated this feast, however, Jesus used the same feast and the same emblem for the time when He changed the law into grace and the old covenant into the new covenant.

The vine and the vineyard are featured within the New Testament 42 times, making it the New Testament's most featured tree. It appears at the time of feasting, it appears when Jesus was seeking to teach the truth of the Church abiding in the Father, and He used the vine as a symbol of the Church and the Father abiding within each other.

The Greek word for 'vine' and 'vineyard' is interchangeable and there are several words that are used. Firstly, there is the word for 'vine' which is *'ampelos'* and it means 'vine fruit'. Secondly, there is the word for 'vineyard' which is *'ampelon'* which means 'a gathering of vine fruit'. There was also a word for the worker in a vineyard, this word was '*ampelourgos*'. This word is formed by the joining of two words together, firstly, the word '*ampelos*' which means 'vine fruit', and secondly, the word '*ergon*' which means 'worker'. The joining of these two words brought out the truth of what was happening when the fruit of the vine was being tended for harvest. An expert dresser of the fruit of the vine would apply his expertise to the tending of the fruit in order that the best wine would be produced.

It is no wonder then that this is exactly the word that was used by John when he wanted to convey the truth that the Father is the vine-dresser, and that Jesus was the vine, and that the Church are the branches that spring forth within the vine. The best fruit is produced when we abide within the vine, and when we allow the heavenly Vine-Dresser to prune us as well, and when we allow Him to have His way within our lives.

New Testament trees were not just trees that were featured as pleasing aspects to the eye, each one of them was used in some way to bring teaching and illustration to truth.

My Journal ____________________

KEY PRAYER

Heavenly Father, I thank you and praise you today for all that I have learned over these past few days concerning the symbolical nature of trees. Thank you that you use even trees to convey just how much you love us and just how much you care. I praise you that you are the Vine-Dresser and that when I allow you to have your way in my life, then my life is so much better, help me to abide in the vine.

September 18th

KEY WORD: **Diligent**

KEY VERSE: **1 Timothy 4 : 15**

Be diligent in these matters; give yourself wholly to them, so that everyone may see your progress.

The aged apostle Paul was writing to the young and inexperienced Timothy who was pastoring a church at the time, and who was finding the going very difficult indeed. In an effort to bring wise words of instruction and helpful words of encouragement, Paul wrote not once but twice to this young man in ministry.

The key verse today is full of rich advice and constructive teaching, and we shall take each keyword separately so that we do not miss anything of value within the instruction of this wise apostle.

Paul said that Timothy should be diligent in his attention to all the matters that he had set out in the three previous chapters: matters that concerned worship, and the appointment of elders and deacons, and also matters that concerned teaching and prophecy. Timothy was encouraged to dwell on these things and to give careful thought to just how he would implement these matters within his own ministry.

Paul used a very interesting word when he urged Timothy to be 'diligent'. The Greek word that he chose to use was the word '*meletao*', this Greek word was used when someone wanted to convey the thought of urgency for it meant 'to care for' or to 'meditate upon'. The Old King James Version actually translates this word in its version as 'meditate'. The 'urgency' of this word, however, conveyed more than a simple instruction to 'think upon something' and it was stronger than the simple advice to 'give consideration to something'. Paul was actually saying to Timothy, that, within all the advice, guidance and counsel that he had given, there was truth that needed careful and urgent thought so that from these words would spring forth an impact within his life.

Over the past months this is the very aspect of what we have been doing. We have been considering New Testament words and their rich meaning, and we have been giving serious thought and meditation to the truths that have been presented. It is not enough to simply read God's Word as if it was just another book. God's Word requires the urgency of careful thought and deep meditation if it is to be understood and applied to our lives.

Paul's words to Timothy were meant to be the springboard to deeper truth that would inspire him to preach better and minister more effectively.

We may not all be preachers, and we may not all be in the full-time aspect of ministry, but we all need to meditate upon the Word of God so that we might grow into the full stature of Christ and become mature in the Lord.

My Journal

KEY PRAYER

Heavenly Father, please forgive me when I have treated your Word casually and when I have not allowed the Word to dwell in my heart. Please help me to give more time to the meditation upon the Word so that I might grow deeper in the Word of God. Your Word is a lamp unto my feet and a light unto my path, therefore cause me to take the time to receive it.

September 19th

KEY WORD: **Wholly**

KEY VERSE: **1 Timothy 4 : 15**

Be diligent in these matters; give yourself wholly to them, so that everyone may see your progress.

Paul wrote to Timothy in order to encourage him at the beginning of his ministry. Paul was now nearing the conclusion of his ministry, and he had much to 'leave behind' as a memorial to this younger man who was not only younger in age but also younger in ministry and experience.

Paul urged Timothy to meditate upon the matters that he had shared with him so that he might grow and become mature. However, Paul said that it was not just meditation that was needed but also a sense of total dedication. 'Give yourself wholly to these things' was the injunction of Paul to this younger man. The Greek word that Paul used here was the word *'holoteles'* which meant 'through and through' or 'to be in these things'. It was a word that was formed by the combining of two Greek words together. Firstly, the word *'holos'* which means 'whole' and secondly, the word *'telos'* which means 'an end'. So the impact that Paul was seeking to have on Timothy's growth and development was one of complete commitment to the task of the ministry. Paul was requiring that Timothy 'be completely in these things' and not simply be a kind of casual worker for the Lord and the gospel.

This same dedication is required of each one of us, although we may not all be in the full-time aspect of ministry, and although we may not all be called to serve as an apostle or prophet, we are all called to be 'wholly' available to God and fully involved and committed unto the Lord. There is no room for a passenger in the service of the Lord. As Timothy was commanded to be 'wholly given over to these things' so we are commanded to be ready for action and completely available.

Not only was this word *'holoteles'* translated as being 'into these things' but it also extended itself into the area of the personal life; commitment and dedication could be outwardly seen, but this word also had a more personal aspect to it. Wholly meant to give an inward sense of dedication as well as the outward sense of dedication. Paul was not just dealing with Timothy's public life of ministry but he was also dealing with Timothy's personal walk with God. Paul was calling Timothy to a life of personal holiness and personal sanctification. God requires us to be inwardly righteous, as well as outwardly professing righteousness. It is very easy for any of us to say and do one thing while living privately a different form of lifestyle altogether.

God wants us to be just as holy and just as righteous before Him as we appear to be before men.

My Journal ______________________________________

KEY PRAYER

Heavenly Father, your word today is a salutary reminder that you require holiness unto the Lord. Please help my inward life to mirror my outward life and help me to also live before you as I live before men. Thank you for the challenge of your Word, today I renew my vows before you so that I might be openly and inwardly righteous and holy.

September 20th

KEY WORD: **Progress**

KEY VERSE: **1 Timothy 4 : 15**

Be diligent in these matters; give yourself wholly to them, so that everyone may see your progress.

The Greek word for the English word 'progress' is *'prokope'*, and the translators have made a very poor job in seeking to convey the true impact and the real meaning behind this word.

Most versions of the Bible have translated this word as 'progress' or 'profit', both of which are poor translations.

Our understanding of progress is either one of two things: firstly, we think of progress as gaining ground and getting ahead, or secondly, we think of it as increasing in a certain area. These two understandings come from an English perspective which is not the one that Paul was seeking to convey to young and inexperienced Timothy.

Paul said to Timothy that he should be diligent and totally committed to the work of God, and that he should seek to meditate upon the Word of God in such a way that he would be totally immersed in the ministry. In this way, said Paul, people would be able to see his progress within ministry.

The word that Paul used, *'prokope'*, is the word that was used by a pioneer when he was cutting through forests and thick undergrowth seeking to forge a new pathway into unknown territory . The concept was one of new ground and trailblazing in such a way that those who would come later would benefit from those who 'went before'. The word was formed by the combining of two Greek words. Firstly, the word *'pro'* which means 'forward' and secondly, the word *'kopto'* which means 'to cut' or 'to strike'. Within these two words the whole concept of what was in Paul's mind concerning 'progress' appears. He wanted Timothy to strike out and go forward in such a way that he would leave a trail behind for other people to follow.

In a very real sense Timothy was a follower. He was a follower of Paul and he was a follower of other apostles and he did not have a very high opinion of himself, but Paul said that he was to become a trailblazer and a leader. This spiritual progress would be seen if he gave himself diligently to study and meditation and the whole concept of ministry.

What Paul charged Timothy to become we all must become whether we are in full-time ministry or whether we are simply members of the local church. We should all leave a trail for others to follow, and we should all seek to become leaders and not just followers whether we are in full-time service or not.

My Journal ______________________________

KEY PRAYER

Heavenly Father, as I have seen today, I need to become a leader and not just a follower. Help me to live my life so that anyone who is watching might glorify God for the progress and impact that I am achieving. Help me to be a Paul and not a Timothy.

September 21st

KEY WORD: **Hell**

KEY VERSE: **Matthew 5 : 30**

"And if your right hand causes you to sin, cut it off and throw it away. It is better for you to lose one part of your body than for your whole body to go into hell."

We are going to turn our attention over the next couple of days to a subject that causes controversy in the Church today, the subject of hell and its associated words and themes. There are many in the Church today that deny the existence of a literal hell and there would be those who would seek to persuade us that hell is no longer a relevant matter for the Church to discuss or believe. However, the fact is that Jesus spoke about a literal hell, and He also referred to a literal hell more than He did to heaven. The English word 'hell' is used twelve times in the New Testament and eleven of these times the word was actually uttered by Jesus Himself.

The Greek word for 'hell' is '*geenna*' or '*gehenna*' and it referred to a literal place called the Valley of Tophet or the Valley of Hinnom. This valley was the rubbish dump near to Jerusalem where the city placed its waste, the waste rubbish would be set on fire, and, as there was so much waste issuing from Jerusalem and the surrounding towns and cities that needed to be consumed, it was said that the fire would 'never die'. It was this literal burning valley that Jesus referred to over and over again when He sought to describe hell.

This valley had a dreadful history as the place where Israel, when they were filled with idolatry generations previously, had burned their own children when they sought to appease the god Molech. It was said that the smell of burning flesh could be smelt on the wind miles and miles away. The fact that Israel could descend so low as to commit these dreadful acts reinforced the fact that Jesus used this descriptive valley as the picture of hell, with its literal consequences.

For the hearers of Jesus to be shown the literal Valley of Gehenna and told that hell would be like this, would have brought back the memories of darkness that had haunted their history. To be told also that religion and religious practices would not save them, and that being pharisaical in their approach to the law would not keep them out of hell, would have produced in them a sense of anger and despair. However, Jesus came to seek and to save all that were lost, not just the poor in spirit but the Pharisee with his religion and his pride. The gospel message that 'all have sinned and come short of God's glory' is very apt when confronted by the burning waste tip of Gehenna and its kinship to hell and a lost eternity.

The fact that Jesus talked more about hell than He did about heaven should serve as a warning to each and everyone of us.

My Journal

KEY PRAYER

Heavenly Father, I thank you today that you have provided a way of escape from a lost eternity, through the Cross of Calvary, and that Jesus came willingly to seek and to save all who were lost. I praise you today that you found me and that I found you and that I have escaped the penalty of sin and hell.

September 22nd

KEY WORD: **Abraham's side**

KEY VERSE: **Luke 16 : 22**

"The time came when the beggar died and the angels carried him to Abraham's side. The rich man also died and was buried."

In our studies in the words that are used concerning hell and its associated meanings, a word has been very wrongly translated in many versions of the Bible. For ease of use and for ease of translation, the translators caused almost every word that spoke of hell to be translated as 'hell' and sadly many of these words did not refer to hell at all.

In the key verse today Jesus was telling a story about a rich man and a beggar who both died. The rich man was buried and was transported to 'hell' – '*Gehenna*' and the poor beggar at his death was transported by angels to 'Abraham's side' which was often referred to as 'Abraham's bosom'. This place in many versions was also translated as 'hell', which is a very wrong and a very poor translation.

The Greek word for 'Abraham's side' is '*hades*' and this word meant something far different. '*Hades*' means ' all receiving' or 'resting place' it could even be referred to as the 'hollow place,' as the Greek word has a kind of 'spin off' meaning to the literal translations. These difficulties with the Greek meanings were the reasons for translators wrongly choosing the word 'hell' rather than the word 'resting place'. This resting place was regarded as the place where souls, who were in Christ, would reside until the resurrection. The fact that Jesus used this as His reference point to a chamber for those in Christ who had died, gave authority to this fact.

'*Hades*' is also the kin word to the Hebrew word '*sheol*' which in the Old Testament meant 'the unseen state'. This place was the intermediate place between earth and heaven. It is not a permanent place nor is it purgatory, it is a chamber for those who have died righteously in Christ but who are awaiting their resurrection and their acceptance into heaven.

The feature of 'Abraham's side' was that it was a good place to be. The rich man in hell, in the story of Jesus, saw the beggar in a place of comfort and in a place that was unobtainable to him. The beggar, after receiving nothing but pain and sorrow throughout his life, was now in a place of rest and beauty, while the rich man, who had received nothing but riches and fame throughout his life, was now in a place of anguish and loss.

Jesus used this word 'hades' on four occasions in the gospels, and He always used it in connection with those in Christ. In the book of Revelation it is referred to as the place where Jesus had total authority, as He had the 'keys of death and hell' which should be translated as 'the keys of death and *hades*'.

We can thank God today that we have a place that is reserved for us and that Jesus paid the price for our rescue from sin, death and hell.

My Journal

KEY PRAYER

Heavenly Father, I do praise you again today for the glorious fact that I am free from sin and the penalty of death and hell. You have made it possible for me to be with you forever, and I rejoice in my privileged place of grace and glory.

September 23rd

KEY WORD: **Heaven**

KEY VERSE: **Matthew 5 : 16**

"In the same way, let your light shine before men, that they may see your good deeds and praise your Father in heaven."

Having considered hell and its associated words over the past couple of days, we now turn our attention to a far better place, the place that the Bible calls 'heaven'. If hell is a literal place according to the Scriptures, then heaven is also just as literal and just as real. The Bible speaks much about the place called heaven, however, the Greek word that is used has a variety of meanings and we will consider some of them over the next few days.

The normal Greek word for 'heaven' is the word '*ouranos*', and it means 'to lift up' and it always speaks of a 'high place' or a place that 'is above'. The fact that the word can mean 'high above' or 'lifted up' allows it to be used in quite different ways throughout the New Testament .

The first meaning that we shall consider is the 'dwelling place of God'. '*Ouranos*' is used in the key verse today for the place where God dwells. Jesus used this phrase when He gave His Sermon on the Mount and spoke of the Father receiving praise in heaven.

God dwells in total and complete splendour and glory and, if we use the Greek word correctly, He is 'high and lifted up' far above all heavens. This place of regal splendour is the place where the throne of God is seated, and it is where Jesus is seated at the right-hand side of the throne. From this very throne Jesus will return to earth in what is called His Second Coming.

The fact of heaven is very real, and the fact that Jesus spoke about it and visibly returned to it in Acts 1 reveals that heaven exists and that it is a place to be greatly enjoyed.

The word *'ouranos'* is used frequently for different aspects of heaven, and it is because of this that a measure of confusion reigns. There are some who teach that there are sections of heaven that are reserved for certain levels of authority in the Church. They believe that certain 'church leaders' will go to certain sections of heaven and that they will have a greater degree of glory and position. Some believe that certain sections of heaven are reserved for a company of people from certain religions. Although the word can be translated as meaning differing sections of heaven, it is very hard to argue that certain sections are reserved as the Bible does not teach this nor does it support such beliefs.

What the Bible does teach, however, is that God dwells at the central point of this 'high and lifted up' place, and that everything in eternity and in time focuses itself upon His throne and upon the Lamb of God.

We can praise God today that He is on the throne and that He is Lord of heaven and earth, and that He has a place prepared for us where shall be with Him forever. It is not a place where we shall receive honour, glory or authority, it is the place where only Jesus and the Father receive the praise.

My Journal ______________________________

____

____

____

____

____

____

KEY PRAYER

Heavenly Father, I do praise you for the fact that heaven is real, and that you are seated upon your throne and that you are in control of all things. I give you praise and I seek to live my life in such a way that men will see my good works and therefore praise you in heaven.

September 24th

KEY WORD: ***Heaven***

KEY VERSE: ***James 5 : 18***

Again he prayed, and the heavens gave rain, and the earth produced its crops.

The Bible speaks much about the place called heaven. However, the Greek word that is used has a variety of meanings and we are considering some of them over the next few days.

The normal Greek word for 'heaven' is the word *'ouranos'*, and it means 'to lift up' and it always speaks of a 'high place' or a place that 'is above'. The fact that the word can mean 'high above' or 'lifted up' allows it to be used in quite different ways.

In the key verse today, James reminds us that there is another aspect to the word *'ouranos'*, he brings to remembrance the time when Elijah was praying on Mount Carmel for rain. The story, taken from the history of Israel, was very much a feature of blessing for the people of God. Elijah prayed and prayed until he saw the cloud the size of a man's hand. Having witnessed the cloud appearing, he then runs before the king's chariot as there was the sound of abundance of rain.

James says that the heavens gave forth rain and the earth therefore produced its crops. The fact that the same word *'ouranos'* is used signifies that heaven has many aspects to it. Yesterday we saw that heaven was the place where God dwells and that Jesus will return from this 'high and lifted up' place. Today we notice that the same word is used by James but that he uses it in a different way.

James is speaking of the 'heavens of the air' this aspect of heaven is the aerial heavens of the birds and of the wind. It is from this aspect of heaven that rain is produced and it is from this aspect of heaven that we see the beauty of God's creation.

We see stars and planets, we see birds and living creatures flying in the skies of the heavens with such joy and freedom, and it is from this aspect of heaven that we receive our winter rainfall and our summer heat.

God dwells in the aspect of heaven that is 'high and lifted up', and which is in another dimension altogether; however, He displays His glory in the heavens of creation. You only have to look up during the daytime to see the visible works of His hands, and the wonder of cloud systems and the spectacle of sunshine with its rays of light and glory. Then you only have to look up during the night-time to see the spectacular aspect of the moon and stars and the planets in their orbits.

God dwells in the aspect of heaven that is the 'high and lifted up' place of glory, but He displays His glory in the 'heavens of the air' and His presence fills all things.

My Journal

KEY PRAYER

Heavenly Father, I glorify you today for the wonders of your creative works. I see the sun, moon and stars and I bow in wonder and thanksgiving. Thank you that you have created such a spectacle of glory for me to enjoy and help me to be forever grateful for your actions of love .

September 25th

KEY WORD: **Heaven**

KEY VERSE: **2 Corinthians 12 : 2**

I know a man in Christ who 14 years ago was caught up to the third heaven. Whether it was in the body or out of the body I do not know – God knows.

The Bible speaks much about the place called heaven. However, the Greek word that is used has a variety of meanings and we are considering some of them in our studies together.

The Greek word for 'heaven' is the word *'ouranos'*, and it means 'to lift up' and it always speaks of a 'high place' or a place that 'is above'. The fact that the word can mean 'high above' or 'lifted up' allows it to be used in quite different ways.

Paul speaks in the key verse today about being caught up into heaven and, in fact, the third heaven. This phrase was only used by Paul on one occasion, yet it has become the basis for some very erroneous teaching concerning the aspects of heaven for levels of authority and blessing. As Paul does not claim to be special and he expressly says that he cannot boast about such a place or the fact that he was even there. Teaching concerning special places in heaven for special types of people is completely wrong. The only special thing about heaven is the fact that Jesus the Son and God the Father are there.

Two verses after the key verse today, Paul also calls this place 'paradise' and this word might explain this aspect of heaven a little better and shed some light on where Paul might have actually been during this translation into heaven. The Greek word for 'paradise' is *'paradeisos'* and the word meant 'a walled park'. The word was taken from the oriental background of Persia where certain parkland was reserved for kings and nobles, no one else was allowed to roam there. The Greek word was formed by the combining of two separate words, firstly, the word *'peri'* which means 'around' and secondly, the word *'teichos'* which means 'a wall', so you have the fuller meaning of 'a wall around'.

In Paul's mind, when he was caught up into this place and received visions and understandings, was that it was a special place, not reserved for anyone special but a place that allowed him to receive things from God. The fact that he wrote most of the New Testament is testimony to the fact that in this special place he received special things from God.

This place was obviously beyond the natural heavens of creation and beauty and yet it was obviously not the place where God dwells in a 'high and lifted up place'.

We should not be looking to go to a special place for divine revelation, that was a one-time action that allowed a one-time vision for only one man. We should, however, be looking to receive from God at all times, because He is always with us at all times.

My Journal ________________________________

KEY PRAYER

Heavenly Father, I bless you today for Paul who was treated to visions and revelations and who then wrote of these revelations in order to give guidance and direction to the Church. Help me not to seek to go to special places but to simply walk with you each and every day.

September 26th

KEY WORD: **Heaven**

KEY VERSE: **Philippians 3 : 20**

But our citizenship is in heaven. And we eagerly await a Saviour from there, the Lord Jesus Christ.

The Bible speaks much about the place called heaven. However, the Greek word that is used has a variety of meanings and we have been considering some of them over the past few days.

The Greek word for 'heaven' is the word *'ouranos'*, and it means 'to lift up' and it always speaks of a 'high place' or a place that 'is above'. The fact that the word can mean 'high above' or 'lifted up' allows it to be used in quite different ways.

In the key verse today, Paul uses the same word to convey a different aspect of heaven altogether, he speaks of our citizenship as being 'in heaven' and as being heavenly. He is not speaking here of the 'high and lifted up' heaven where God dwells, nor is he speaking of the 'heavens of the air' and he is not even speaking of the 'third heaven' of paradise.

Paul is using the word *'ouranos'* quite correctly when he is seeking to convey the fact that we do not belong here as citizens of earth, but that we belong to a spiritual place that is very different to that of earth. We belong to 'heaven', a place that is a spiritual concept for a new territory and a different dimension altogether.

This place is figurative for a dwelling place beyond the natural. At the end of time God is going to create a new heaven and a new earth, and all true believers will then dwell with Him forever and ever. This new heaven will be another creation that has yet to be seen by man. Only one man was caught up in the spirit to the place called paradise; no earthly being has ever entered the 'high and lifted up' heaven where God dwells and no one has ever been allowed to dwell in heaven, except Jesus. Some men have entered into the 'heavens of the air' and have travelled as far as the moon and dwelt in this special place designed to reveal the glory of God. But all believers have entered into the special spiritual place called the 'heavens' of our citizenship.

We do not belong here on earth and our citizenship is not an earthly one. We belong to a different realm and our future destiny has already been decided by a God who has chosen to take us to be with Him forever. Until then, we walk with God on earth, with the knowledge that we dwell in a different dimension to those around us. We have present glory and a future blessing which is a wonderful thought as we conclude our studies in the word 'heaven'.

My Journal

KEY PRAYER

Heavenly Father, it is so hard for me to fully grasp that I do not belong here. Everything I see and feel seems to tell me that I am a very earthly person. However, your Word tells me that I belong to you and that I belong to heaven. Help me to understand this and to enjoy the privilege.

September 27th

KEY WORD: **Keep**

KEY VERSE: **Jude 24**

To Him who is able to keep you from falling and to present you before His glorious presence without fault and with great joy.

We are drawing towards the conclusion to yet another month and we often wonder just where the time seems to go. The days just seem to fly by and a month is gone before we realise it. As this month comes to an end we are going to look at a verse of Scripture that concludes the last but one book of the Bible, the epistle of Jude.

The verse that we shall study together is called the doxology, and it is often quoted in church services at the conclusion of a gathering or a meeting. Jude was writing to the Church and brought teaching concerning purity of lifestyle and the need for holiness. He also called the Church to persevere in spite of scoffers and mockers and, as he came to the conclusion of his writings, it was as if he suddenly rose into a different dimension, as he lifted his thoughts above Church problems. It is this doxology that we shall consider over the next few days.

He stated that God was able to keep us from falling. The word that he used for 'keep' was a word that brought to his readers a very interesting concept. The Greek word used was '*phulasso*' which meant 'keeping guard' or 'keeping watch' and it was the word that was used when someone was entrusted to keep guard over another person's property. A guard would be set so that the property was kept intact and so that no harm or danger might befall it.

Jude uses this word to convey the thought that God is able to 'keep' us. His teaching was that God, who has saved us and set us on a new direction and who has created a new destiny in our lives, is the same God that will bring His protection to us during our earthly walk through the battles of life and through the temptations of the flesh.

God has set a guard around and about us so that He might protect us from all danger. Even when we seem to fall into great difficulty, God is there and He is guiding our lives in such a way that nothing ultimately will go wrong. He is our protector and He is our keeper.

Jude deliberately chose to close his epistle with these words because he had spent quite some time dealing with the godless aspect of man and the sinful nature of the world. Having dwelt upon these things Jude then turned his attention to the conclusion of his epistle and the conclusion of time as we know it.

As we get nearer to the end of all things, it is good to be reminded again that we are loved and that we are protected and that God is our keeper at all times. He is our guard and He is keeping watch over us.

My Journal ______________________________

KEY PRAYER

Heavenly Father, as I study this lovely doxology please help me to understand the truth of your Word, that you are my guard and keeper. I praise you today for all the protection that you have given to me and for all the protection that I shall receive during the rest of my earthly life.

September 28th

KEY WORD: ***Falling***

KEY VERSE: ***Jude 24***

To Him who is able to keep you from falling and to present you before His glorious presence without fault and with great joy.

In the month of May we took the time to consider seven Greek words that are to be found within the New Testament that have all been translated as 'fall', there are many more than seven words we just looked at a few of them. One of the words that we did not consider in the month of May was the word that Jude used when he was seeking to convey the truth of God guarding our lives so that we might not fall down. Jude says that God 'is able to keep us from falling'.

The Greek word that Jude uses is the word *'aptaistos'* which means 'without stumbling' and it can also mean to be 'sure footed'. Some Bible versions actually use the words 'keep us from stumbling', the concept is one of 'sure-footedness' in the midst of temptation.

Jude is wanting the Church to understand that God has provided us with protection from all the things that disturb us and that God has also provided us with 'sure-footedness' in the midst of everything around us.

The word *'aptaistos'* is formed by the combining of two words so that truth might be imparted, the first word is 'a' which means 'negative' and the second word is *'ptaio'* which means 'to stumble'. The concept that Jude was explaining to the Church was that God has given to us a measure of understanding in that, having learned afresh that worldliness and carnality were wrong and that sinful desires would lead to entrapment and danger, we should not negatively stumble into sin and temptation. The concept, to Jude, is a very clear one, in order to remain free from falling into sin and temptation we should always keep our eyes upon the Lord who is our keeper and guard and in that way our walk with God will be sure-footed and not negative stumbling.

If we could learn that lesson over and over again and not just learn it but apply it in our walk with God, then we would be much stronger and our ability to become much more mature would increase.

Our daily walk with God is vital, it needs to be positive and not negative, if we analysis the preaching and teaching that we so often hear, it is normally quite negative. We hear that we should 'not do this' and that we should 'not go there,' and that we should 'not touch this'. This aspect of preaching, although not wrong, is quite negative. Jude reminds us to be positive in our walk with God as God is able to keep us sure-footed in our daily walk. He also reminds us that He keeps us from stumbling.

My Journal

KEY PRAYER

Heavenly Father, how I thank you today for the truth of your Word, you have set before me a pathway of blessing and a life of purity. I recognise today that the only time that I fall is when I take my eyes off you and when I negatively stumble. Help me to watch for your guidance as you watch over my life.

September 29th

KEY WORD: **Present**

KEY VERSE: **Jude 24**

To Him who is able to keep you from falling and to present you before His glorious presence without fault and with great joy.

Jude's theme, as he draws his epistle to a close, is one of thanksgiving and triumph. He states that God is able to keep us from falling and that He is also able to present us to the Father in a faultless condition. To state this truth in such a way shows that Jude has understood the whole concept of God's protecting care. Jude appreciated that God watches over our lives and that He makes us very sure-footed in our walk.

This sure-footedness would lead us to the place where we would be able to be presented to the Father with a sense of faultlessness. James rose to the occasion when he stated this and you can almost feel the passion of his joy, which is why this section of his epistle is called the doxology.

The Greek word that he used for the English word 'present' is the word *'histemi'* which means 'to cause to stand,' or it could even be translated as 'station'. The meaning behind this word is one of position or rank as in someone who rose to a certain 'station in life'.

What Jude was seeking to convey was the whole aspect of arriving at place where acceptance and position had been agreed and where God was pleased to accept the gift that was being presented to Him. We are a gift unto the Lord from a loving and willing Saviour who gave His all that we might be a sweet offering unto His Father. It will be with great joy that He takes us and presents us before the Father.

There will be a day when all the travails and pain will be over, and when sin and sickness will have passed away, and when we shall be complete before God. On this day, Jesus will escort us into the throne room of heaven and, before the massed ranks of angels and heavenly beings, He will stand before His Father, and He will bring us before God in our station and He will cause us to stand and, with great and exceeding joy, He will present us as a faultless gift to His Father.

In the words of a great old hymn of the Church: 'What a day that will be'. Heaven will stand still and the angels will acclaim The Lord as the One who has done all things well.

We shall stand on that day and no accusation will be levelled against us because we will have arrived at the place of 'standing,' and we will take up our 'station' before the Lord.

My Journal

KEY PRAYER

Heavenly Father, I rejoice when I think of the day that has been planned when I shall stand before you and when Jesus will present me before you. I long for the day of your coming, and I long for the day of your power. Help me to remain faithful unto that day.

September 30th

KEY WORD: **Faultless**

KEY VERSE: **Jude 24**

To Him who is able to keep you from falling and to present you before His glorious presence without fault and with great joy.

Jude's doxology brings a great epistle to a triumphant conclusion. His understanding of the 'end times' and his portrayal of a victorious Church with a triumphant Saviour is a wonderful theme.

'God is going to keep us' said Jude, and He is going to protect us, and He is going to keep us sure-footed in our walk with God and, what is more, He is going to present us at the final day to His Father with great joy. We shall have arrived at our appointed destiny, and we shall take up our designated station, and we shall be forever with the Lord.

This presentation will take place before God who is righteous and pure, and the fact that we can actually stand before Him in a faultless way is a truth that we really need to grasp and understand. The Old Testament psalm sent out a challenge when it stated 'who can stand before the Lord, only those who have clean hands and a pure heart'. No unclean thing can come before God and certainly no unclean thing could be presented to Him. So Jude is seeking to convey a truth here that we really must examine.

Jude uses a word that is one of the most wonderful of words that were ever used by New Testament writers. The English word 'faultless' conveys a little of the impact and power of the word. However, the Greek word is much more powerful. Jude uses the word '*amomos*' which means 'without blemish' and it is the same word that is used when writers sought to describe the Lamb of God who was without blemish. In other words, Jude was saying we are going to appear before God in the same way that Jesus appeared before Him after the Cross and after the sacrifice of Calvary, without spot or stain. That we can actually come before God is a miracle but that we can come before Him in the same way that Jesus came before Him is almost breathtaking in its dimensions.

The fact that God protects us and provides us with a sure-footed walk and brings us to a destined place of acceptance is a wonderful aspect of truth, but that He also receives us as He received His Son, is so overwhelming that it is almost too great to conceive.

This momentous truth should inspire us to hold on to truth and to keep ourselves in the pathway of holiness so that, when that day comes, we shall be found worthy of our high calling in Christ Jesus.

My Journal

KEY PRAYER

Heavenly Father, this truth that I have learned today is almost too great for me to understand, but I praise you for the way that you plan to welcome me home. I pledge before you today that I shall set my face to serve you and love you, and that I shall always seek to do only the things that please you, so that I might be found worthy before you.

October 1st

KEY WORD: ***Saints***

KEY VERSE: **Philippians 1 : 1**

Paul and Timothy, servants of Christ Jesus. To all the saints in Christ Jesus at Philippi, together with the overseers and deacons...

As we commence a brand new month we shall also commence a brand new theme, and we shall consider it for a few days. This new theme is the 'Church of Jesus Christ'.

There are many and varied names that the New Testament gives to the people of God who are normally referred to as 'The Church.' Each name or title is a distinct and unique way of describing us as the New Testament seeks to reveal 'just who we are'. The studying of these names and titles always undergirds truth and always brings insight into what God requires of the Church and what He expects of His Church.

In the key verse today, Paul and Timothy write to the church at Philippi, and they introduce themselves as servants and they address the corporate church in Philippi as 'saints'. The title or reference to 'saints' was not unique to the people in Philippi, it was a name that the collective New Testament Church was addressed by. In fact, the word was used over 60 times by differing New Testament writers and was used to refer to eight different churches and congregations.

Today, the word 'saint' has a variety of very extreme interpretations, ranging, on one hand, to someone who has been dead for hundreds of years and who has been canonised by a section of religious people, to those, on the other hand, who do good deeds and who are idolised. Because of the extreme views concerning this word, it is therefore vital that we know what the New Testament writers were seeking to convey when they used this term in their epistles concerning the 'Church'.

The Greek word that they used which is translated as 'saints' is the word *'hagios'*, and it is the root word for the translation of the New Testament concept of holiness. The word literally means 'set apart ones' and it was used as a collective term for the people who were born again into the family of God and who were part of the Church.

This word was designated to those who were not exceptionally holy as we probably understand holiness today, nor did it refer to those who had died, it was simply applied to those who were members of the Church, and who had tasted and seen that the Lord was good. The root word for holiness was *'hagiasmos'* and, as we saw in the month of March, this word means 'separating unto God', and it refers to the process of bringing something nearer that was afar off. The word *'hagios'* was part of this process in that those who were far away from God had now been brought nearer to Him and were now very close to Him and part of the structure of His body.

The saints were very ordinary people from very ordinary backgrounds, and were at times those who had been called the enemies of the Church, but whose lives had been touched by grace, and whose lives had been fundamentally changed. They had become saints. It is possible to become a 'saint' in a second, as grace can change a life in the twinkling of an eye. Certain religions state that to become a recognised saint you would have to wait hundreds of years and that sainthood can only be granted if certain requirements have been fulfilled. Whereas New Testament sainthood is not based upon what you have done but upon what God has done. New Testament sainthood is based upon a work of grace and not upon works achieved.

We are all 'saints' if we have trusted God for our salvation and if we are part of His Church.

KEY PRAYER

Heavenly Father, I depend upon you at all times for my salvation. It is not what I have done but what you have done that counts, and I praise you today for my sainthood which has been granted to me by a loving and faithful Saviour.

October 2nd

KEY WORD: **Family**

KEY VERSE: **Ephesians 3 : 15**

From whom His whole family in heaven and on earth derives its name.

As we are considering in the early days of this new month the names that the New Testament gives to the members of the Church, we shall look today at probably the most precious name of all names that is designated to the Church.

When Paul wrote to the church at Ephesus he called them the 'Family' of God', and this gentle and intimate expression has found its way into Church life right around the world. We enjoy being known as the 'family' and we rejoice in this unique role that the New Testament brings to us. However, this name and this precious truth is quite remarkable as the word 'family' is only used once in this form within the entire New Testament. The fact that it has been preserved to this day and is used so widely, is an amazing fact. I often hear people referring to themselves as being part of the 'family of God' and we hear preachers using this term all the time. In fact I have even sung it, as many songs carry this theme.

There are two Greek words that are used for 'family' in the New Testament, one denotes the 'ordinary' family of mother and father and the children and it can also mean 'household' or even 'home'. This word is '*oikos*' and it means 'a dwelling' or 'a house' and it links itself to people and not to a building made with bricks. So 'the dwelling' in Greek is a group of people or a family and not bricks and mortar.

The second word that is used for family is the word that is linked with the Church, it is the word '*patria*' which means 'tribes' or even 'related people'. The relationship that it speaks of is not the 'dwelling' of a personal family but the relationship of ancestry or lineage. The word is derived from the Latin word 'pater' meaning 'father' and it was linked to the 'family of God' by the fact that God is our Father and that we are related to Him and that we belong to Him.

God is the author of the spiritual relationship that exists between Him and His children, and between what happens to each one of us when we become part of the Church. We may never have met one another before and we may have worshipped in a different church in a different country miles and miles away, but we are one in Christ and members of His family. When preaching in other nations and not knowing one word of the language, I find that the barriers are non-existent as spirit touches spirit and as fellowship is enjoyed.

We are all saints and we are all members of one body and we are 'family' in the Lord.

My Journal ____

KEY PRAYER

Heavenly Father, I praise you today for this special and unique family that you have brought me into, I praise you for the fact that in Christ we are all one. Thank you for saving me and making me part of such a wonderful body that stretches right around the world.

October 3rd

KEY WORD: **Body**

KEY VERSE: **Colossians 1 : 18**

He is the head of the body, the church; He is the beginning and the firstborn from among the dead, so that in everything He might have the supremacy.

As we have seen so far in our studies concerning the names that were given to the Church of Jesus Christ some of these names were very special and very precious indeed. Today we look at a name that described the Church rather than a name that was special and rare.

The Church was described by Paul in the key verse today as a 'body'. This was a term that he used quite often as it described to the people within the Church just how and where they fitted within this body. Paul used a very common word in the Greek language for his description of the body, and in the use of this word everyone would know and understand the truth that he was seeking to convey.

The word that he used was the normal and common word for 'body' which was '*soma*'. This word meant 'the instrument of life' or it could be translated as 'a living body'. This term embraced everything within the Greek language that conveyed the aspect of life. The word was used to express the living body of a man or woman and it also expressed the body of corn in a cornfield and the body of water that comprised a sea or an ocean.

It also referred to the physical nature of man and a corpse that was lying dead. Every time '*soma*' was used it was fully understood what was being conveyed, so when Paul used this word to describe the Church the people who heard this word would have understood the concept.

The concept was that a living '*soma*', a living body, had a frame and a structure. So did the Church, and in the same way that a living body has many differing parts to it, so does the Church with differing gifts and differing functions. As a living body requires food and water and daily sustenance, so does the Church with its need of input concerning spiritual food. The whole nature of the body lent itself perfectly as a description of the Church, so that Paul felt quite confident of using the word concerning the body to bring to his readers and hearers the truth of what the Church really is. We are all members of a body, the Body of Christ.

My Journal

KEY PRAYER

Heavenly Father, I thank you today that you have allowed the truth of the natural body to become the illustration of the Church. I praise you that in the normal things of life you have hidden truth which when it is revealed displays just what the Church really is. Thank you for making me part of your Body and thank you too, for caring for your people.

October 4th

KEY WORD: **Bride**

KEY VERSE: **John 3 : 29**

The bride belongs to the bridegroom. The friend who attends the bridegroom waits and listens for him, and is full of joy when he hears the bridegroom's voice. That joy is mine, and it is now complete.

There is a wonderful descriptive word that is used as a picture of the Church within the New Testament and it is the picture of a bride. On five occasions this word is used to describe either the Church or the new heavenly Jerusalem, and it is a word that fully conveys just what the Church is and just what God longs for the Church to be.

In the key verse today John the Baptist is speaking concerning Jesus and the future Church. He testified of Him saying that 'Jesus was the greater and that he himself was the lesser'. He pointed to the One who was to come as being the bridegroom of the Church and that the Church was the bride.

This word picture was most profound because it taught the people that there was going to be a wonderful marriage of a bride and groom, and that the Church would be a beautiful bride prepared for a marvellous groom because that is a exactly what the Greek word for bride conveys.

The Greek word that John uses in this key verse for the word bride is '*numphe*' which means 'young wife' and we derive our English word 'nymph' from this root word. The normal understanding of bride in the western sense is anyone who is getting married, in other words, any female person on the wedding day is simply called a bride.

However, in the Greek language the word '*numphe*' conveyed something far deeper than simply someone being married. The word was used in a way that conveyed the absolute 'specialness' of the unique occasion of the union of marriage. The word came from the Latin word *'nubo'* which meant 'to veil' and it was a very special word indeed. At the wedding ceremony the *'numphe'* was adorned with embroidery and a vast number of jewels. She was led, by the bridegroom from the family home to the ceremony with great pomp and procession, and she was veiled until the moment of acceptance into the bridegroom's home. This was no ordinary ceremony and this was no ordinary occurrence. This activity was the finest moment of a woman's life when she became a *'numphe'*. The western wedding has lost its significance completely when compared with the eastern spectacle of the greatest moment of all.

Is it any wonder then that when this word is used for the Church it causes such delight and joy to the bridegroom Jesus and to the universal Church. God is preparing a wonderful bride that is being bedecked with jewels of grace and garments of righteousness, so that when the wedding ceremony finally takes place the bride will be at her very best. What a word to describe the Church, and what a blessing that we belong to this Church, the bride of Christ.

My Journal ____

KEY PRAYER

Heavenly Father, I bless you today for the fact that your Bride is being prepared and that right now the wedding ceremony is approaching. Help me to live for you in purity and righteousness so that I might be a true and faithful member of your Body and your bride.

October 5th

KEY WORD: **Flock**

KEY VERSE: **Acts 20 : 29**

I know that after I leave, savage wolves will come in among you and will not spare the flock.

Today we shall consider a very descriptive word that the New Testament uses for the Church. We have seen over the past few days just how the New Testament writers sought to convey the truth of the Church when they used words like, 'body', 'bride', 'family' and 'saints'. When Paul spoke to the elders at Ephesus he used another very clear term for the Church when he called the Church, the 'flock'.

Last month, in September, we looked at the thought of savage wolves entering into the Church and causing great damage. Paul calls it 'not sparing the flock' and we saw just how savage wolves could be. Several months ago, in April, we looked at the concept of sheep and we saw then just how gentle and careless sheep could be. When you put savage wolves into the same area as gentle sheep you have a recipe for disaster, which is why Paul gave his warning in this key verse.

A group of sheep is called 'a flock' and this term normally conveys the group that eats together and wanders around together . Paul used the Greek word *'poimnion'* when he sought to convey the truth that the Church is a flock of sheep. The true meaning of *'poimnion'* is 'the herd' or 'the group of sheep'. The Greek word for 'sheep' is *'probaton'* which means to 'go forward' and it was used by the Greeks when they spoke of small animals, and in the New Testament it was only used of actual sheep. So the reference would be a *'poimnion'* of *'probaton'* or 'a flock of small animals'.

Paul used this word to convey just what a threat evil was to the new Church, and just how vulnerable the Church was to the threat of wolves. Paul wanted the elders and the whole flock to know just how much he cared for them and just what he wanted them to be careful of.

This descriptive word is so clear, we are not just a body and a bride, and a family and saints, we are also a flock of sheep and, therefore, very vulnerable when it comes to the enemy's attacks and the enemy's tactics.

We must make sure that we are on our guard at all times and that we keep our eyes upon the Lord. Only in walking with Him and in listening to His voice will we find guidance from the Great Shepherd. If we allow Him to lead and guide us then the 'flock of God' will safely graze.

My Journal

KEY PRAYER

Heavenly Father, please help me to hear your voice at all times so that I might not stray and that I might not wander into wrong paths. Help me, too, to stay close to you so that if a wolf might draw near I shall be safe under your care.

October 6th

KEY WORD: **Ark**

KEY VERSE: **Matthew 24 : 38**

For in the days before the flood, people were eating and drinking, marrying and giving in marriage up to the day that Noah entered the ark.

As we draw to a conclusion in our studies concerning the names and descriptive titles of the Church we shall close with a name, that, although it does not address the Church, it certainly is a type of the Church.

In the key verse today Jesus was addressing His disciples and talking about the 'signs of the times'. This is a term that collectively describes the actions and signs that will be seen within the world as the Church gets nearer and nearer to its Rapture and its marriage to the bridegroom, and also its triumphant entrance into heaven and eternity. Jesus said that one of the signs would be the appearance of a similar type of day to that of the day of Noah who found that the only way to save himself and his family was to prepare an ark. God had warned him of judgement and had guided him to the building of the ark, and had destined that the animal kingdom as well as the family of Noah would be saved.

Jesus likened Noah's Ark and its method of salvation to that of the Church, and two New Testament writers took up the same theme. Peter wrote in his epistle that the Ark was a symbol of salvation and that all who hearken to the words of safety and salvation will be saved.

The writer to the Hebrews also took this theme when he stated that Noah was moved by fear to save his family, and that he became the heir of righteousness because of his faithfulness to God's Word and because of his willingness to obey God.

In both of these epistles Noah's Ark is used as a kind of symbolic picture of the Church and the message is clear, if you are in the ark, or in the Church, you will be saved. This obviously does not just mean that you become a 'church member' but that you become a saint within the family of God, and that you have undergone a transforming work of grace.

The Greek word that is used for the word 'ark' is *'kibtos'* and it means a 'wooden box' or a 'wooden chest'. This word was used within the New Testament for any box made out of wood, but it had its fullest use when it referred to three things. Firstly, the 'Ark of the Covenant', secondly, the 'Ark of the heavenly vision' in the book of Revelation, and lastly the 'Ark' that belonged to Noah and his family and the animal kingdom.

If the Ark is a picture and type of the Church, we should take careful note of the signs that are around us, because it appears that the days in which we live are very much like the days in which Noah lived. God showed him a way out through the building of an ark. We can thank God today that we have found our way of escape through the blood of the Lamb and through the body of Christ, the Church.

My Journal ______________________________

KEY PRAYER

Heavenly Father, thank you for the types and symbols of the Church within the New Testament. I thank you today for the fact that you have provided a perfect way of escape and I praise you for the Church. Help me to be ever worthy of my place within the ark of salvation and within your family.

October 7th

KEY WORD: **Head**

KEY VERSE: **Ephesians 1 : 22**

And God placed all things under His feet and appointed Him to be the head over everything for the Church.

When we were studying the names and types of the Church over the past few days, we looked at the name and title that referred to the Church as 'the body' and we saw that the Greek word '*soma*' meant the natural body and that it could easily be understood as the body of Christ. What we did not consider, and we shall correct this over the next few days, is the way in which each part of the body relates to each other and just how each part has an important role and function.

We shall commence to consider some parts of the body by looking at the 'head' and its role and function within the body and within the Church. The Greek word for 'head' is '*kephale*' and it means, very simply, the 'head' or the 'top'. It refers quite naturally to the top of the body and it designates the place of headship or authority. The body cannot function without the head as it commands the place of thinking and of actions and it also houses the brain. There are various parts of the body that you can live without but the head is vital and nothing else will function if the head is removed.

Within the New Testament the head is regarded in several ways. Within the Church, Jesus is regarded as the Head and in the key verse today, Paul states that everything has been placed under the feet of Jesus because He is Lord and because He is the Head of the Church.

Within each local expression of the body, the local church, the 'heads' are regarded as those who lead with authority and direction; this can be a Leadership Team or a Church Board. This local headship is often comprised of pastors and elders and it can also have deacons within it. This local headship is appointed to serve as the head of the local church serving the Head of the Church – Jesus.

Within marriage the New Testament teaches that the husband is the head of the home and the head of the marriage. However, this does not mean that he takes the final aspect of authority as if he is a dictator. The whole point of New Testament teaching concerning headship is that it is a service not a rulership. Jesus came as a servant to save us and He serves now as our Lord with grace and mercy. Local church leaders should also see their role as one of serving the rest of the local body in the same way. In marriage too, the husband should serve his wife and love his wife as Christ loves the Church.

Headship is authority in love and rulership through service, this is the pattern for the universal Church and the pattern for the local church too. If we understood this and practised it fully, we would have a much better and a much stronger Church.

My Journal

KEY PRAYER

Heavenly Father, as I look at the New Testament, I see a serving Saviour and a headship of grace. Help me to be like Jesus within my local church and within my home and within my family. Keep me right within every aspect of my life.

October 8th

KEY WORD: **Arm**

KEY VERSE: **Luke 1 : 51**

He has performed mighty deeds with His arm, He has scattered those who are proud in their inmost thoughts.

In the New Testament the arm is a very interesting part of the body, and it features in many different ways. Within the natural body too it is a feature of action and strength. It is not too difficult to think of ways that, in the spiritual body, the arm reaches out and ministers.

There are two main Greek words in the New Testament for the English word 'arm.' Firstly, there is the word *'ankale'* which means 'the curve' or the 'angle' and in fact our English word angle is actually derived from this word. The second word that is used in the New Testament for arm is *'brachion'*, and this word means 'short arm' and it relates to the short part of the arm that reaches from the shoulder to the elbow.

The first word for 'arm' which is *'ankale'* is the word that is always used for the embrace, when the curved part of the arm reaches out in love and embraces others. It is used when Jesus reached out to children and took them in His arms. The curved part of the Saviour's arm would have closed around them in an embrace that would have been both secure and warm. This is the part of the body that cares and has the action of caring. In the local church, the Body of Christ, the arm of love and care ought to reach out to others more than it does, as at times the Church can be very introspective and can appear to be uncaring. The arm of love ought to be extended far much more.

When the old priest Simeon saw Jesus at His dedication in the Temple, Luke says that he took Jesus in his arms and praised God. The love action of the curved arm was very much in evidence that day.

The second word for 'arm' which is *'brachion'* is the word that denotes strength and power. It is the part of the arm that stretches itself and flexes itself and produces muscle and action. It is always used in the New Testament for the 'power of God' when He 'stretched forth His mighty arm'. In the key verse today, Luke is taking a direct quote from the Old Testament book of Psalms and he speaks of God performing mighty deeds 'with His arm'.

The strength of God is always a feature of the Psalms and within this poetic book there is ample evidence of God extending His arm, not just in love and not to show the curved part of the arm as an embrace. But He extends His mighty arm in power against His enemies and He defeats them with His actions of righteousness.

The *'brachion'* part of the arm is mentioned only three times in the New Testament and it is always used for the strength or the power of God's action. If we should extend the curved part of our arm in love and outreach, we should also extend the action part of the arm, as we should always be engaged, very much, in the taking of our cities and in the 'taking back' of all the things that the enemy has stolen from us.

My Journal ______________________________

____

____

____

____

KEY PRAYER

Heavenly Father, please help me today to extend my arm in love to those who are in need, and help me, too, to extend my arm in powerful spiritual warfare so that I might take my city for God and redeem the things that the enemy has stolen from me. I bless you for your power and strength and I bless you too, for your love and grace.

October 9th

KEY WORD: **Hand**

KEY VERSE: **Acts 13 : 11**

"Now the hand of the Lord is against you. You are going to be blind, and for a time you will be unable to see the light of the sun." Immediately mist and darkness came over him, and he groped about, seeking someone to lead him by the hand.

Within the New Testament, and in fact within the Old Testament too, the 'hand' is featured strongly as the weapon of warfare and the body-part of most action. The description 'the hand of God' is very frequently quoted by Bible writers, especially the prophets. The prophets saw the hand of God as an instrument of judgement and divine action, and they prophesied this over and over again quite strongly.

Within the New Testament the hand of God in judgement and action appears much less frequently. In fact, the word 'hand' in connection with God, appears much more in the New Testament to bless than to judge, although judgement is also featured.

In the key verse today, Luke is writing about the time when Paul, who at the time was called Saul, was confronted by God during his mission to destroy the Church. Having been encountered by God on the road to Damascus, he is first knocked to the ground and then blinded. Upon hearing the voice of God he accepts Jesus Christ as Saviour and Lord, and the apostle to the Gentiles was born. As he is later giving his testimony in Acts 13, he states the hand of the Lord was against him.

The Greek word for 'hand' is a very complicated word indeed, the word is '*cheiragogos*' and it means 'hand-leader'. As with many Greek words that seek to convey a message, it is formed by the combining together of two other words. The first word to be used is the word '*cheir*' which simply means '*hand*',

and the second word to be used is the word *'ago'* which means 'to lead'. This combined word was the word that was always used when the Greeks wanted to describe the 'action' of the hand rather than just the physical aspect of the four fingers and thumb. The hand was therefore regarded as a kind of 'leader' in the action of the body; it gave signals, it could be animated and it could show forth the outward expression of inner thoughts. In speaking of the hand the Greek language would say, 'it was the leader of the body'.

Is it any wonder then that both the Old and New Testaments, when considering the 'hand of God,' would say that they were led by His hand, or that the hand of God was against them?

Within the body of Christ we need to extend our hands as a form of ministry agency to the world and to each other. We need to give expression to our feelings by 'hand action' as well as words. Words are easy and words can be cheap, however, the action of the hand goes deeper and further. 'Hand action' can include the ministry of relief, as in help towards the poor and the needy, in a physical sense. Other actions could include the spiritual ministries of building one another up in God and the spiritual maintenance of encouragement, and it also includes the laying on of hands during periods of ministry and prayer.

My Journal

KEY PRAYER

Heavenly Father, I have seen your 'hand' extended so many times over the years into my life and I bless you for the way that you have led me. Help me to be a ministering agency to others not just by the words of my lips but also by the actions of my hands.

KEY WORD: **Finger**

KEY VERSE: **Luke 11 : 20**

But if I drive out demons by the finger of God, then the kingdom of God has come to you.

Within the New Testament the finger is seen as an instrument of God and as a part of judgement and divine action. If the hand is seen as a body part of action, as we studied yesterday, then the finger is the pointed part of the action. When this part of the body is mentioned within the New Testament its main effect is to give a metaphorical sense of the power of God.

The Greek word for 'finger' is the word *'daktulos'* and the word means simply 'the finger'. This word is used eight times in the New Testament writings and all the references are within the four Gospels and all four gospel writers use this word at least once.

Of the eight references only three of them refer to Jesus and the 'power of God', yet these references are the ones that produce the greatest effect; of the other five references, all refer to the natural finger. It is vitally important that we understand just how the power of God is seen in the three references where the word *'daktulos'* is used in connection with the ministry of Jesus. So we shall consider each one separately.

In the key verse today, Jesus was demonstrating that He had the power to drive out demons with the 'finger of God' and that within this demonstration of power the onlookers would see that the Kingdom of God had come. The word used in this context proved to His disciples that the 'finger of God' was a powerful and present force within their lives and within their ministries.

In Mark 7 : 33, Jesus placed His fingers in the ears and His spittle on the tongue of a deaf and dumb man, and the result of this symbolic act was the healing of the dumbness of the tongue and the deafness of the ears. Once again the strange actions produced a sense of power and enabling, within those who saw this act, and it was again a demonstration of the power of God.

The last reference to the 'finger of Jesus' being used is John 8 : 6, when He wrote on the ground with His finger at the time when a woman, who was caught in the act of adultery, was brought before Jesus for punishment and judgement. Jesus stooped down and used His finger to write in the dust of the ground. Having completed this action, those who brought this woman for judgement left the scene. This action proved more than a symbol of power, it showed on this occasion the authority of God as well as His power.

If the finger is a symbol of power and authority then the Church should be exercising this small member of the body in similar actions to the actions of Jesus. At times, if the Church seems powerless to help and feeble in its actions of ministry, we should seek to extend our finger into the lives of those in need. This pointed action ought to bring power and authority and it ought to demonstrate the same things that were seen in the ministry of Jesus: actions of love and actions of power and actions of pointed authority and influence.

My Journal ______________________________

____

____

____

KEY PRAYER

Heavenly Father, at times I seem so powerless to do anything of significance in ministry and I long to be more effective for you. Help me today to exercise my finger of power of authority so that I might make a difference. I recognise that the finger is a small member of the body but I have seen too, today, that this small member is the pointed symbol of power and authority. Help me to be more willing to extend my finger into the lives of those in need.

October 11th

KEY WORD: **Feet**

KEY VERSE: **1 Corinthians 15 : 25**

For He must reign until He has put all His enemies under His feet.

The final part of the body that we shall consider together is the part of the body that causes us to stand, the feet. Without feet it would be impossible to stand up or to keep our balance, therefore it is one of the most vital parts of the body. Within the New Testament this vital body part features quite a lot because as well as its literal meaning it also stands for the symbol of motion and humility.

The Greek word for 'feet' is the word *'pous'* and it means simply the 'foot' or the 'feet', and of the body parts that are mentioned within the New Testament writings it has the most references. This word is used 85 times and it appears in eleven of the books of the New Testament.

Most of the 85 references use this word to speak quite literally of the feet and we find instances where Jesus washed His disciples 'feet' and where New Testament offerings were brought into the church and laid at the 'feet' of the apostles. These references and many others have no symbolic meanings and no hidden meanings, the word simply means the literal foot or feet. However, within some of the references there are huge symbolic meanings such as in the key verse today.

When Paul was seeking to convey just how powerful and majestic Jesus is, he used the symbolic wording of the authority of kingship. He stated that Jesus would reign until all His enemies were 'under His feet'. This symbolic use of the word *'pous'* was a feature of the abject surrender of an enemy and the absolute power of the conquering king. The conquered enemy would be brought before the victorious king and he would be thrown down upon the ground. Then the victorious king, in a symbol of power and victory, would place his foot upon the head of the defeated enemy and victory was assured. In fact, victory was not just accomplished, it was seen to be accomplished, and it was total and complete by this symbolic action.

Paul used this metaphorical picture to describe just what would happen to the enemies of Jesus, as Jesus was placed in the kingdom of God as King of kings and as Lord of all lords. All enemies will be placed under His feet and He will reign forever and forever.

This use of the word '*pous*' in this form is seen as surrender and subjection, however it is also used for the actions of worship and the actions of humility. When a woman once approached Jesus she broke open a container of ointment and anointed Him with it and washed His feet with her tears. This action of worship and thanksgiving was commended by Jesus and used as symbol of just how we should always come before Him. The word is also used in the sense of humility when Jesus washed His disciples feet when they neglected to wash each other's feet. In our Church life today we should learn the lessons of the New Testament when it portrays the feet as the symbols of worship and humility, and we should seek the right way to worship, and we should seek to humble ourselves to meet the needs of others.

My Journal ______________________________

____

____

____

KEY PRAYER

Heavenly Father, as we conclude our studies in the parts of the body that are featured within the New Testament, I ask today that I might learn the lessons that they have sought to teach me. I long to worship you with the right spirit and I long to serve others with the right spirit. Help me each day to bring my worship to you and my service to others with the Spirit of Jesus.

October 12th

KEY WORD: **Conform**

KEY VERSE: **Romans 12 : 2**

Do not conform any longer to the pattern of this world, but be transformed by the renewing of your mind. Then you will be able to test and approve what God's will is – His good, pleasing and perfect will.

This key verse is one of the most well known verses in the New Testament and it is one of Paul's strongest and most challenging directions to the Church. Within this verse he uses some of the most far reaching and descriptive words in all of his writings and over the next few days we shall seek to discover the deeper meanings of his teaching to the Roman Church

We all know this verse and we have probably heard countless sermons preached upon it and it has impacted many lives throughout the ages of the Church. Yet this verse has some deep and profound lessons that we must learn and obey in order to grow and develop our spiritual lives.

The first word that we shall study is the word 'conform'. Paul said that we, as the Church, must not 'conform' any longer to the patterns of this world, but that we should be transformed by the renewing of our minds. He used a word that is very, very powerful for his message to the Church concerning just how the Church should live and conduct itself. The Greek word for the English word 'conform' is the word '*suschematizo*', this word was used by the Greeks when they wanted to convey the thought of a substance being fashioned into shape. The meaning of the word is 'to shape one thing to the image of another'. It was used by potters when they were seeking to copy another vessel, the clay would be moulded and fashioned until it formed itself into an exact replica of another vessel.

Paul took this powerful and strong word to describe what was happening when the children of God allow themselves to be moulded into the shape of the world. They would be seen to be exact replicas of the world and they would lose their distinctiveness as spiritual beings. Paul wanted the Church to be different and to be seen to be different to the world and to those within the world. Paul was not of course talking about the world of creation, this is a beautiful world with God's love and creative design shining all through it. Paul is talking about the world of immorality and the spirit of the world that is anti-Christ and anti-God. His desire is that the Church, having been called out of the spirit of the ages, should now walk in a different path to those who are still within the spirit of the world.

The Church should not fashion itself after the dictates of the spirit of this age but should be different in every aspect to those around them.

My Journal ______________________________

____

____

____

____

____

____

____

____

____

KEY PRAYER

Heavenly Father, I know it hurts your heart when the Church is seen to conform itself to the spirit of this age and the spirit of this world, and I know that I should not allow myself to be fashioned after the pattern of this world. Help me today to allow you to fashion me after your ways and after your design.

October 13th

KEY WORD: ***Transformed***

KEY VERSE: **Romans 12 : 2**

Do not conform any longer to the pattern of this world, but be transformed by the renewing of your mind. Then you will be able to test and approve what God's will is – His good, pleasing and perfect will.

Within the key verse today Paul's words brought urgency and direction to the Church in Rome. He urged them not to allow themselves to be fashioned according to the dictates of this world but to be transformed by the renewing of their minds. He did not want the Church to be conformed to the anti-Christ spirit that was prevalent within the world but he wanted a different spirit within the Church.

He used a lovely word to describe just what he required from the Church regarding this different spirit, he urged them to be 'transformed'. The Greek word that he used for the English word 'transformed' is the word *'metamorphoo'* which means 'to change into another form'. This word is formed by the combining of two Greek words, firstly the word *'meta'* which means 'to change' and secondly, the word *'morphe'* which means 'form'. The meaning therefore was quite easy to understand, Paul was seeking to urge the Church to allow themselves to undergo a reforming change within their minds.

If the Church was not to allow the conforming of themselves to the pattern of this world, they should therefore allow themselves to be transformed into a different fashion, the fashion of renewal and reform.

The word *'metamorphoo'* is a lovely word as it conveys the change between the caterpillar and the butterfly. The caterpillar forms itself into a chrysalis and a reforming and renewing takes place. It undergoes a metamorphosis and the butterfly emerges from the chrysalis and flies into the heavens. The change from an earth-bound creature of ugliness to a heaven-bound creature of beauty is just what Paul was seeking to convey to the Church. The Church was no longer an earth-bound and fleshly product of nature, it was now a heaven-bound product of beauty and joy. So, therefore, a renewal of thinking and acting should take place. The Church becomes powerless and ineffective when it seeks to continue in an unchanged state, the aspect of power and authority takes place when the Church no longer conforms to the old state but allows the new state its rightful place.

This same word can also be translated as 'transfigured' and it is indeed this word that is used when Jesus was transfigured on the mountain. His earthly nature took on the form of a heavenly nature at this moment of transfiguration, and Paul deliberately uses the same word to convey to the Church what he is seeking for. He does not want us to shine, as Jesus shone on the mountain, because we are not divine. What happened there was just for that moment, the divinity outshone the humanity of the Saviour. However, what Paul does want is the nature of glory to be resident within the Church so that we are constantly renewed and reformed into a state of usefulness to God and effectiveness within the world.

It is not so much an outward change that Paul is seeking for, although there ought to be outward change, it is the inward change of renewal that this word carries with great force. We are different so we should act differently.

KEY PRAYER

Heavenly Father, thank you today for the change that has taken place within my life, thank you for the renewing and reforming that has developed within me. Help me to always remember that I am no longer an ugly earth-bound creature but a heaven-bound creature of beauty and help me to always remember that I need to renew my mind each and every day.

October 14th

KEY WORD: ***Renewing***

KEY VERSE: **Romans 12 : 2**

Do not conform any longer to the pattern of this world, but be transformed by the renewing of your mind. Then you will be able to test and approve what God's will is – His good, pleasing and perfect will.

The actions of renewing are an important aspect in the life and ministry of each and every Christian. Paul sets out in this key verse to show just how vital it is that we allow the transforming work of the Holy Spirit to take place so that we are no longer conformed to a dark and savage world of sin and evil.

Paul set out the pathway of change when he urged the Church to release itself from the chains of worldliness and earth-bound poverty, and to allow itself to take on the nature of a heaven-bound, beautiful body of people. This change of nature and change of lifestyle however could only be undertaken if there was a renewal taking place within the mind of each and every member of the church. This renewal was more than a change of thinking and more than a change of heart, it was a radical and fundamental change that Paul was seeking. In order to convey the depth and power of this change, Paul used a word that could almost be called a 'new word'. The Greek word that he used was the word '*anakainosis*' which meant 'to make new' and this word was formed by the combination of two very interesting words.

The two words that Paul brought together were the words '*ana*' which meant 'back' or 'again' and the word '*kainos*' which meant 'new' or 'different'. In the forming of these two words Paul was almost coining a brand new word, the spirit of this word literally meant that the Church, having been released from the earth-bound spirit of poverty and weakness, was now released to be a heaven-bound body of beauty. Therefore, the Church should allow itself to be radically and completely brought back again and again to a place of reforming and renewal. The power of this word lay in the fact of 'the different' spirit, this word was not talking about the same spirit or even a similar spirit, this word gained its strength and power from the fact that it stressed that this was a new spirit or a completely different spirit to the one that was seen before.

One Bible commentator has suggested that this word speaks about the Church's 'adjustment of moral and spiritual vision and thinking to that of the mind of God', which is an awesome aspect to consider. No longer are we shackled to the ways of the world but now we have the glorious possibility of being chained to the mind of God and to His ways and His Spirit.

This key verse also stresses the continual process that the Church should willingly express in its response to the Spirit of God. We should not expect to change our minds and lifestyle just once, but we should continuously adjust ourselves to the renewing of our minds so that we might ever be in the place of effective usefulness to God.

My Journal

KEY PRAYER

Heavenly Father, I praise you today for the change that has already taken place within my life, but I long today for more and more of you and I recognise that this will only take place as I adjust myself to your ways and to your will. Help me to continuously renew my mind and help me to no longer be conformed to this world.

October 15th

KEY WORD: ***God's will***

KEY VERSE: **Romans 12 : 2**

Do not conform any longer to the pattern of this world, but be transformed by the renewing of your mind. Then you will be able to test and approve what God's will is – His good, pleasing and perfect will.

The reason that Paul lays so much stress upon the renewing of our minds is that, through this renewal process, we shall be able to test and prove what God's will is for our lives. The renewing of our minds is not a process that simply stands alone, the whole process is a means to an end, and the end result is the pure and simple understanding of God's will for our lives and for the Church.

The Greek words that comprise the thought of 'God's will' are '*theos*' which means 'God' or 'deity' and '*thelema*' which means 'to be willed.' We studied this word in the month of July.

The thought that Paul is seeking to convey when he uses the words '*theos thelema*' is the process that the Church has to go through in order to understand the perfect and pleasing will of God for us all.

The will of God is twofold and these two Greek words express them perfectly. Firstly, there is the collective 'will of God' for the Church, this is expressed in Paul's desire that the Church is no longer conformed to the ways and patterns of this world. Paul longs that the Church is set free from the fashions of this world in order to be transformed into the perfect will of God. This godly desire is seen when Paul sets his mind to the expressing of the fact that God wants His Church to be pure and holy and He wants His Church to express a completely different lifestyle to that of the world. When Paul conceived this thought in his mind he was expressing the heartbeat of God towards His Church. God's will is that we should become a collective holy people whose lifestyle is godly and pure, this is the pleasing and perfect will of God for us collectively

Secondly, the will of God is also personal, this is expressed in the way in which He calls some to be apostles and some to be prophets. Some people in the Church enter full-time ministry as pastors and teachers and other assume the role and function of evangelists. For many the will of God is to leave their home and family in order to travel the length and breadth of their own land or the lands across the sea. For others it will be the call to remain within possibly their own home town and local church all their lives but to live for God in ways that express His will for them.

Whichever part of God's will it is for us, either personal or collective, we can only test and prove God's will by the renewing of our minds and by the submission to the transformation that takes place when we are no longer willing to be conformed to a world that is anti-God and anti-Christ in its whole ethos.

My Journal

KEY PRAYER

Heavenly Father, I rejoice today in the fact that my mind has been renewed and that my spirit is tuned in to your Spirit. Help me each day to live with the reality of a spirit-filled pure lifestyle that reflects your will for my life. Help me too, to discover your perfect will for my life whatever the cost.

October 16th

KEY WORD: **Pleasing**

KEY VERSE: **Romans 12 : 2**

Do not conform any longer to the pattern of this world, but be transformed by the renewing of your mind. Then you will be able to test and approve what God's will is – His good, pleasing and perfect will.

As we conclude our studies within this key verse we do so with a very fascinating word indeed, this word is translated in the NIV as 'pleasing' and it is translated in the Old King James Version of the Bible as 'acceptable'. The NIV gets a little closer to the real meaning when it uses the word 'pleasing'.

If we are no longer conformed to an alien world, and if our minds have been renewed by the transforming power of the Holy Spirit, then we shall begin to discover the will of God for our lives. When we discover this perfect will we shall be, firstly, pleasing God and, secondly, we shall be pleasing ourselves because the will of God is the best way to live and the best way to enjoy ourselves. If we have all the money in the world and if we have everything that our heart desires but are living outside of the perfect will of God, we shall have a sense of frustration and emptiness because we are not doing what God wants us to do.

Paul uses a word that was not familiar to the Church when he phrased himself in such a way concerning the pleasing will of God. The Greek word that he used was the word '*euarestos*' which means 'to please well' or 'to be pleasingly acceptable'. It is a word that is formed by the combining of two words, firstly, '*eu*' which means 'well' and secondly, '*arestos*' which means 'acceptable'.

This forming of words is not easy to understand as it does not mean what it appears to mean. For instance, it could be 'acceptable' in some countries to take the life of another if there were no means of recovery or a return to health. It could be acceptable to practise this but it does not make it right, it could be acceptable but it is not pleasing. This word's power comes from the whole area of prayer. The Greek word for prayer is '*euchomai*' and we studied this word earlier in the year, in the month of January. Prayer is pleasing to God and is acceptable to Him, for when we spend time in prayer we are giving attention to the aspect of service and worship. However, it would be acceptable to pray and spend long hours telling God what we need, but it would not be pleasing to Him. What pleases God is when we spend time in prayer listening to His voice and seeking His face as well as the bringing of our requests.

God requires us to discover His will for our lives, both the personal will of God and the collective will of God. In the discovery of His perfect will we will both please Him and please ourselves, because it is good to live this way.

My Journal ______________________________

____

____

____

____

____

____

____

____

KEY PRAYER

Heavenly Father, at the conclusion of this key verse I have come to the knowledge that I must please you and not just do the things that may be acceptable. Help me today to always please you and to always spend my life in the attitude of prayer and service. I long to be effective in my life so I set myself today to discover your perfect and pleasing will for my life.

October 17th

KEY WORD: ***Same***

KEY VERSE: ***Hebrews 13 : 8***

Jesus Christ is the same yesterday and today and forever.

This wonderful key verse is one of the most revealing and deeply truthful verses in the entire Bible. It reveals that Jesus Christ, our Lord and Saviour is always the same that He never ever changes and that His unchanging nature will always be. Heaven and earth may pass away but Jesus never changes.

However, even though this verse is complete within itself and full of truth there are deeper truths just waiting to be uncovered. So we shall spend a few days searching the Scriptures for more of its meaning.

The writer to the Hebrews has spent a long time in the previous chapters dealing with the fact that the high priest of the Old Testament was a mediator between God and man, and that this high priest held a most sacred and privileged position. However, the writer then goes to great lengths to explain that even though this position was sacred and mediatorial, our High Priest, Jesus, is even greater. The high priest of the Old Testament was but a shadow and a forerunner of a greater High Priest and Saviour.

Jesus never changes. High priests may come and go but Jesus remains the same, yesterday, today and forever. As a young boy in church I remember reading this text over and over again as it was painted on the wall over the pulpit. The sermons have been forgotten but the vivid writing of this key verse has remained in my mind, Jesus never changes.

The writer used ordinary words to convey this truth, but they were words with deeper meanings. The writer states that Christ Jesus is the 'same' at all times. The Greek word that was used for the word 'same' is the word *'autos'* and it literally means 'the same,' but it is a word that is only linked with 'substances' and not with personal things. If you wanted to describe a personal thing that was remaining the same you would use the Greek word *'houtos'*. *'Autos'*, however, described substances like 'trouble' and 'days' and being 'like-minded' with someone. You would literally say, 'people are going through the 'same' kind of trouble, or we are going out on the 'same' day'. This word lacked any form of personal feeling, it only dealt with an impersonal substance.

So the writer was therefore not talking about Jesus personally when he used this word, he was talking about the substance of an unchanging nature. It is impossible for Jesus to change, He is unchangeable. Nothing can make Him change or cause Him to alter.

The substance of water can change, it can become ice, or it can become steam and it can evaporate altogether, but nothing that you can do and nothing that heaven and earth can do can affect the Saviour at all, His unchangeableness is a substance that remains forever.

What a comforting thought when we are going through the most stretching times of trouble and trial. We might be changing all the time but Jesus can not and will not change, whatever takes place around Him and around us.

My Journal ________________________________

____

____

____

KEY PRAYER

Heavenly Father, I praise you today for the truth that Jesus never changes, because of this great truth I know that Jesus cannot fail and that He cannot let me down. I also know that I can change all the time, sometimes I am strong and sometimes I am weak but I praise you today that in a changing world the only constant thing is your unchanging love.

October 18th

KEY WORD: **Yesterday**

KEY VERSE: **Hebrews 13 : 8**

Jesus Christ is the same yesterday and today and forever.

Jesus Christ remains always the same, He never changes and He never will. For Him to change would be impossible.

This truth is hard for us to understand and very hard for us to grasp as we are in the midst of change all the time. Change goes on at all times around and about us and also within us. We are not the same as we were twenty years ago, and we are not even the same as we were twenty minutes ago, we change all the time.

This truth is hard to understand because of its eternal nature. So, the writer to the Hebrews does a very strange thing indeed, in order to try to express this eternal truth he uses the measurement of time. He states that Jesus is the same yesterday and today and forever, which is a strange way of trying to express unchangeableness because, if something is eternal and always the same and if something is eternally unchangeable, then yesterday and today do not exist. Eternity is outside of time and time ceases to exist. However, in order to convey this eternal truth to mortal man some kind of measurement has to be created, so a kind of contradiction is created in order for us to understand and grasp eternal truth.

The writer uses two Greek words to explain 'in' time what is 'outside' of time, he uses the measurement of yesterday and today to explain that Jesus never changes. The first word is '*echthes*' or '*chthes*' which means 'yesterday night' and the second word is '*semeron*' which means 'this day'.

The first word is almost unpronounceable and it only appears in the New Testament three times and it always refers to the measurement of time that existed the 'day before this day'

The second word appears in the New Testament 17 times and it always refers to the measurement of time that is a literal day.

This 'time-frame' that the writer refers to is seeking to give a kind of point of reference to the fact that Jesus remains unchanging. We can never understand eternity and eternal concepts this side of heaven, so in order to help us grasp this truth the writer refers to a point of reference that we can grasp and that we can understand. He says that this eternal Jesus remains unchanging in our time-frame of yesterday and today, and that, for as long as this time-frame remains, He will not and can not change.

My Journal

KEY PRAYER

Heavenly Father, thank you for truth and thank you for those who help us to understand truth. I praise you today for the fact of an unchanging Saviour who remains constant and true in an ever changing world. In the midst of a fluctuating and turbulent period of time, I have an eternal anchor.

October 19th

KEY WORD: **Forever**

KEY VERSE: **Hebrews 13 : 8**

Jesus Christ is the same yesterday and today and forever.

Jesus Christ is the same yesterday and today and forever. This eternal truth has been unfolded in a deeper way over the past few days as a result of understanding what the writer was seeking to convey. He used the measurement of time to describe what was outside of time and gave us an understanding of eternal things by using the time-frame of our natural understanding.

In concluding this truth he goes on to say that, although Jesus cannot and will not change and although we can now understand that in our past, 'yesterday', and in our present, 'today', He did not alter once, we can now seek to understand what is in our future.

The writer says that Jesus will remain the same forever, and He uses a unique phrase to describe the fact of 'forever'. There is not a word in the Greek that describes this truth, so he had to use a phrase in order to convey the truth. The phrase is *'eis tous aionas'* which is very hard to explain, the nearest meaning is 'unto the ages'. The Greek word for 'eternal' is *'aionios'* which means 'ever' or 'everlasting,' but this word does not fully explain the facet of truth that the writer seeks to convey. So, in order to convey the thought of future timelessness, the writer has to grasp for a phrase that would adequately convey the truth of the fact that Jesus would not change and could not change for the future time-frame of forever.

This phrase is used about eight times in the New Testament and it always speaks of the ages to come and it was a favourite phrase of Paul who used it five times in his epistles to the Romans and the Corinthians. He always used it to convey the truth of God who is eternal and who reigns forever in total splendour and majesty.

The phrase also lends itself to the truth of the fact that God is unending and unbroken in His rulership and reign, and that Jesus has the same uniqueness attached to His rulership and reign. It is so hard for us to understand this as we constantly change in our thoughts and our opinions and in our ways and in our attitudes. Yet, Jesus never changes and in the ages that are yet to come, He will remain forever the same.

As we conclude this verse we should thank God today that, in the 'yesterdays' of our history, and in the present moments of our 'today' and in the extending future of the ages that are yet to come, Jesus Christ remains forever the same. We could say, He remains the same day after day, but that is only our time frame and our point of reference. In eternity there is no beginning and no end, just an eternal Saviour and just an eternal God.

My Journal ______________________________

KEY PRAYER

Heavenly Father, I do praise you for the fact again today that Jesus is forever the same. I cannot fully understand it and I cannot fully appreciate it but I praise you for the truth of an unchanging Saviour. Help me in the midst of a changing world to hold on to the anchor that always remains.

October 20th

KEY WORD: **Treasure**

KEY VERSE: **Matthew 19 : 21**

Jesus answered, "If you want to be perfect, go, sell your possessions and give to the poor, and you will have treasure in heaven. Then come, follow me."

In the key verse today we are introduced to a truth that we often miss and that we often do not even consider.

Jesus was addressing the person that we have come to know as the Rich Young Ruler. This young man was desiring eternal life and had been quite diligent in his seeking of righteousness. In fact he says that he had kept all the commandments, and that he had always sought to be righteous and circumspect in all his dealings. History records for us that he went away from Jesus very sorrowful and sad because Jesus required more than the keeping of the law and the commandments. He required a change of heart and a change of lifestyle. The Rich Young Ruler was required to sell all of his goods, he was required to give all the money raised to the poor, and he was required to follow Jesus. He could not accept this directional truth into his life as the Bible says he had great wealth.

If he had followed the directional word that Jesus had given to him, his life would have changed, he may have had less down here, but he would have stored up treasure in heaven.

This lovely phrase 'treasure in heaven' is a phrase that is well worth studying today as it has great depth and meaning.

Matthew uses a beautiful word to convey the thought of 'treasure' in heaven, when he uses the Greek word '*thesauros*' which means several things in different contexts. It can mean 'a casket', and it can mean 'a place of safe keeping' and it can also mean a 'storehouse'.

When Matthew uses this word he has all three meanings in mind as the context of the verse gives itself to all three meanings. The Rich Young Ruler was required to place his treasure in a different place to the one that he was using at present. He was using his own storehouse for his own pleasure but God was now requiring him to place his riches in another storehouse, heaven.

Jesus was also requesting this young man to place his treasure in a safe place where it could be used for others rather than being frittered away in the pursuit of happiness. Jesus also required this young man to die to self and to live for Him, so that his treasure might be buried in a casket and forgotten, so that he might 'come and follow me'.

The richness of the word '*thesauros*' has been taken by our day and age and it is used for the treasury of language as a dictionary often referred to as a 'thesaurus', the word being derived from the Greek word. The use of this word actually means a place of great wealth, it can be a dictionary, a compendium of great wealth and learning, and it can mean a depository or museum where an encyclopaedic wealth of treasure is kept.

Our storehouse is heaven where all our good works and good deeds are remembered and stored like treasure in heaven. This depository of good deeds will remain until we are called home to our eternal reward where we receive the accolade, 'Well done, good and faithful servant'. We are not saved by our works, we are saved by grace alone, but our works 'do follow us' and they are reserved for our eternal future. 'Therefore store up for yourselves treasure in heaven where moth and rust cannot corrupt.'

KEY PRAYER

Heavenly Father, I thank you today for grace that saved me and for grace that keeps me every day. I praise you, too, for the fact that each day my good works are seen by heaven and are being stored up for me and will be remembered on that 'great day' when I finally arrive home.

October 21st

KEY WORD: **Treasury**

KEY VERSE: **Mark 12 : 41**

Jesus sat down opposite the place where the offerings were put and watched the crowd putting their money into the temple treasury. Many rich people threw in large amounts.

The key verse today recalls an incident in the ministry of Jesus when He observed what has come to be known as the 'widow's mite'. Mark recounts this incident and refers to the widow when she placed all that she had into the temple treasury following the rich people's large offerings being thrown into the treasury in large amounts.

The teaching that followed from Jesus dealt with the fact that the rich receive nothing but that the poor receive much when they seek to give all that they have.

The temple treasury was the place where tithes and offerings were received by the temple priests, and it was the place of great wealth. It was said that gold and silver bullion was kept there, and it was the place where Israel drew its strength from. It was near to this treasury that Jesus drove out the money changers because they had made 'His Father's house a den of thieves'.

This treasury was a very unique place where there were thirteen chests, six of them were for general gifts and the other seven were kept for distinct purposes and designated giving. The chests were shaped like a ram's horn or a trumpet shape and they were guarded by temple guards who remained at their posts at all times. The name 'treasury' was derived from a Greek word that was a very interesting word, and it was from this word that we derive the thought of the heart being a treasure deposit or treasury. The Greek word used by Mark is the word *'gazophulakion'* which means 'place of treasure'. It is a word that is formed by the combining of two different words, '*gaza*' which means 'treasure' and '*phulake*' which means 'a guard'

These two words together produced the thought of placing a guard upon something of great wealth, and, although there is not a direct link, it is quite in order to use the thought that we ought to place a guard upon the treasury of our heart as, from the heart, can emanate all the worst of sin and all the best of righteousness. Once we have had our nature changed by grace, we have a new heart and we need to keep ourselves pure and clean. Only those with clean hands and a pure heart can come before God in prayer and praise, so we need to guard our hearts just like the guarding of the temple treasury.

Jesus sat by this place of temple treasure and He watched the worshippers giving their offerings, some of the things that He saw did not please Him, but the widow found acceptance in her gift. We should always be aware that the eyes of the Lord are ever watchful over our lives and we should only seek to do what pleases Him.

My Journal

KEY PRAYER

Heavenly Father, out of the treasure of my heart I bring you praise today. Help me to keep a guard upon my heart and upon my life so that I might have clean hands and a pure heart to come before you. I want a heart that is a treasury of praise unto you today.

October 22nd

KEY WORD: **Temple**

KEY VERSE: **Mark 11 : 11**

Jesus entered the Jerusalem and went to the temple. He looked around at everything, but since it was already late, He went out to Bethany with the Twelve.

Over the past two days we have been considering the aspect of treasure and the treasury, and we have seen that Jesus took great interest in this whole aspect of the giving and the receiving of money. He also took great interest in the whole aspect of the temple and temple worship, in fact He was a regular temple visitor since the age of twelve. Over and over again in the gospels we read that He went to the temple and it is obvious that He loved His Father's house.

There were two Greek words that were used by New Testament writers for the temple. The first word was the word '*hieron*' which means 'sacred place' and this word was used for everything within what we now know as 'the temple'. It was the word that was used for all temples including The Temple of Diana in the book of Acts. This word for 'temple' denoted the outer courts and the precincts and included all buildings and activities.

Everyone was allowed to visit the '*hieron*' and Jesus taught from the outer courts because anyone and everyone was allowed to enter these courts and everyone was welcome.

There was another place within the temple where only priests could lawfully enter and we shall consider this place tomorrow.

The temple was the seat of Jewish worship and was also the place where they felt their national distinctiveness was truly seen. The temple in Jerusalem, that the key verse speaks about today, was commenced by Herod in BC 20 and it was destroyed by the

Romans in AD 70.

The temple features highly in Jewish worship and Jewish nationalism. It was the place where many prophets in the Old Testament would prophesy, and it was the place that had the greatest significance, when, following the destruction of Jerusalem, the national revival would have its greatest effect. Nehemiah would spend his whole time, both day and night, overseeing the reconstruction of the temple following the return home of the Jews from Babylonian captivity.

This place was called by Jesus 'my Father's house' and it held a very special place in His heart. Following His entrance into Jerusalem, He cleansed His Father's house and brought purification and holiness back into His hearts desire, His Father's house.

Jesus was a frequent temple attender and His obvious desire to be in His Father's house should encourage us to attend our place of worship as often as we can.

My Journal ____

KEY PRAYER

Heavenly Father, thank you for the place of prayer and worship that you have called the Church and which hymn-writers have chosen to call 'The House of Prayer'. As you so obviously loved the house of God, help me to be always ready to attend my local church as often as I can so that I might encourage others in their act of worship.

October 23rd

KEY WORD: **Temple**

KEY VERSE: **Mark 11 : 11**

Jesus entered Jerusalem and went to the temple. He looked around at everything, but since it was already late, He went out to Bethany with the Twelve.

Over the past few days we have been considering the aspect of treasure and the treasury and we have featured the place that we now call the temple of God. We have also seen that Jesus took great interest in this whole aspect of the giving and the receiving of money. We have also seen that He took a great interest in the whole aspect of the temple and temple worship. In fact Jesus was a regular temple visitor since the age of twelve and over and over again in the gospels we read that He went to the temple and it is obvious that He loved His Father's house.

There were two Greek words that were used by New Testament writers for the temple. The first word was the word '*hieron*' which means 'sacred place' and this word was used for everything within what we now know as 'the temple'. This word for 'temple' denoted the outer courts and the precincts and included all buildings and activities.

The second Greek word in the New Testament for 'temple' was the word '*naos*' which means 'sanctuary' and it was the word that was used to denote the place where only priests could go. It was not the holy of holies where only the high priest could venture once a year, but it was the inner court of worship where sacrifices and prayers were offered. Jesus did not visit this area although He was our Great High Priest, but in Jewish law He was of the tribe of Judah and therefore barred from this 'holy court'. His ministry was conducted in the temple from the outer courts where everyone was welcome.

The word *'naos'* came to be used quite frequently by New Testament writers when they sought to describe the fact that following the resurrection of Jesus and the birth of the Church, all believers are now 'temples of the living God'. *'Naos'* was the word that Paul used when he described the individual believer, in 1 Corinthians 6 : 19, as the 'Temple of the Holy Spirit'. The individual believer is now part of God's holy building, the living body of Christ, and the Holy Spirit dwells within us.

Jesus also used this word when He described Himself as 'a temple.' He stated that if 'this temple was destroyed it would be built again in three days'. Most of the people who heard these words did not understand as they thought that He was talking about the literal temple within Jerusalem.

The inner courts of the literal temple were regardcd as being a 'holy place' and were kept sacred for priests and were not allowed to be desecrated. We should remember this when we think of our own bodies which are now God's own temple and in which the Holy Spirit dwells. We should at all times seek to remain pure and holy so that the temple of God is not desecrated.

My Journal

KEY PRAYER

Heavenly Father, I bless you today for the fact that my body is a temple to the living God and that the Holy Spirit dwells within me. Help me to be ever watchful over my life so that I keep my body holy and acceptable to you so that I might at all times be a holy place for you to dwell in.

October 24th

KEY WORD: **The poor**

KEY VERSE: **Luke 4 : 18**

The Spirit of the Lord is on me, because He has anointed me to preach good news to the poor. He has sent me to proclaim freedom for the prisoners and recovery of sight for the blind, to release the oppressed and to proclaim the year of the Lord's favour.

This key verse is often called the 'Manifesto of Jesus' as it sets out very clearly and very distinctly the reasons why He came from heaven to earth. This Scripture is a direct quote from the Old Testament where Isaiah was prophesying the 'Coming of Jesus' and His message.

The setting for the reading of this 'Manifesto' was the small town of Nazareth when Jesus visited the synagogue on the sabbath day and began to read from the scroll, the prophecy of Isaiah. Luke says that every eye was upon Him when, following the reading, Jesus stated that: 'Today this Scripture is fulfilled in your hearing'. The crowds were amazed at Him, and everyone spoke well of Him, and it could be said that from this day on the 'Manifesto' was put into divine action.

The 'Manifesto' was set out in order to help and reach four types of people, the poor, the prisoners, the blind and the oppressed. The whole ministry of Jesus can be expressed in these words as: 'He came to seek and to save those who were lost'.

As the four areas of great need are expressed in this way and cover such a wide aspect of ministry, we shall consider each one of them in turn and take a few days to study them together.

Firstly the 'Manifesto' expresses that Jesus came to 'preach good news to the poor'. There are two Greek words that are used for the word 'poor' they are the words *'ptochos'* and *'penichros'* and they are both very expressive words. *'Ptochos'* means literally 'the poor,' and it was the word that was used when the Greeks were seeking to express 'abject poverty'. This word was applied to those who had literally nothing in the sense of money or substance, and it was used to describe not just the absence of money but the feeling that this absence of money would create. The New Testament uses this word 34 times and in each use it does not just refer to those who have nothing but it also refers to those who are 'poor of spirit.' The word also carries with it a sense of 'trembling' as it often refers to the 'poor people' coming before the Lord, with fear and trepidation and with trembling.

If we use this sense of the word then even rich people who do not know the Lord are considered to be 'poor'. The sense of abject poverty brought about, in some people, the feeling of being inferior and brought with it the sense of trembling and the feeling of being 'absolutely nothing' in a world that bases success upon greed and finance. Jesus came for such a people as this, which includes each and everyone of us and no one is exempt. If anyone is 'outside of Christ' they are poor, they might have great wealth but they are poor of spirit.

The second word that is used is *'penichros'* which is a word that is only used once in the New Testament and it was used to describe the woman in Luke 21 : 2, the woman that we saw a few days ago being called 'the widow' by Jesus. She came to the treasury and gave her 'mite' unto the Lord'. This word describes total and complete destitution and it was used for this woman alone. However, if we understand the 'Manifesto' of Jesus correctly, it is to this kind of person that Jesus came.

We are all destitute without Him and as Isaiah prophesied and as Jesus stated: 'He came to preach good news to the poor and needy', and we can rejoice in this.

KEY PRAYER

Heavenly Father, I do praise you today for the fact that you came to preach good news to the poor, and that through this means you have changed poverty to riches and you have changed poor people into saints. Thank you Jesus that you came and thank you too for the message of hope.

October 25th

KEY WORD: **The prisoners**

KEY VERSE: **Luke 4 : 18**

The Spirit of the Lord is on me, because He has anointed me to preach good news to the poor. He has sent me to proclaim freedom for the prisoners and recovery of sight for the blind, to release the oppressed and to proclaim the year of the Lord's favour.

This key verse is often called the 'Manifesto of Jesus' as it sets out very clearly and very distinctly the reasons why He came from heaven to earth. This Scripture is a direct quote from the Old Testament where Isaiah was prophesying the 'Coming of Jesus' and His message.

The setting for the reading of this 'Manifesto' was the small town of Nazareth when Jesus visited the synagogue on the sabbath day and began to read from the scroll, the prophecy of Isaiah. Luke says that every eye was upon Him when, following the reading, Jesus stated that: 'Today this Scripture is fulfilled in your hearing'. The crowds were amazed at Him, and everyone spoke well of Him, and it could be said that from this day on the 'Manifesto' was put into divine action.

The 'Manifesto' was set out in order to help and reach four types of people, the poor, the prisoners, the blind and the oppressed. The whole ministry of Jesus can be expressed in these words as: 'He came to seek and to save those who were lost'.

As the four areas of great need are expressed in this way and cover such a wide aspect of ministry, we shall consider each one of them in turn and take a few days to study them together.

The second part of the 'Manifesto' was that Jesus had come to proclaim freedom for the prisoners. The Greek word that is used here for the word 'prisoners' within this key verse, is the word '*aichmalotos*' which literally means 'one taken with a spear'. The word is formed by the combining of two different Greek words, firstly, the word '*aichme*' which means 'a spear' and secondly, the word '*halotos*' which means 'to be captured.' So, the Old King James Version is actually a little more correct when it states that Jesus came to set the 'captive' free. The word is taken from a military background when an enemy was taken prisoner and was held captive by a warrior who was armed with a spear. The picture being presented is one of total captivity with no way out and Jesus used this word, along with Isaiah's prophecy, to describe just what He was about to do. He had come to bring total and complete freedom for those who were being held captive and His mission was to release all who would turn to Him.

Anyone who is outside of Christ can quite rightly be regarded as being captive to a greater enemy than anything that this world can offer, kings and kingdoms do not measure up to the power of our enemy, Satan. Satan has taken prisoner all who do not follow the Lord, and they have become imprisoned to him and his devices. There is no way out and no other way of escape than the grace of God and Calvary's cross. We can thank God today that Jesus came and that He came to proclaim freedom for the captive.

My Journal ____

____

____

____

____

____

____

KEY PRAYER

Heavenly Father, how I praise you for the glorious fact that I have been set free, once I was in chains of darkness but now I have been set free. Thank you for your 'Manifesto' and thank you too for coming to release me.

October 26th

KEY WORD: **The blind**

KEY VERSE: **Luke 4 : 18**

The Spirit of the Lord is on me, because He has anointed me to preach good news to the poor. He has sent me to proclaim freedom for the prisoners and recovery of sight for the blind, to release the oppressed and to proclaim the year of the Lord's favour.

This key verse is often called the 'Manifesto of Jesus' as it sets out very clearly and very distinctly the reasons why He came from heaven to earth. This Scripture is a direct quote from the Old Testament where Isaiah was prophesying the 'Coming of Jesus' and His message.

The setting for the reading of this 'Manifesto' was the small town of Nazareth when Jesus visited the synagogue on the sabbath day and began to read from the scroll, the prophecy of Isaiah. Luke says that every eye was upon Him when, following the reading, Jesus stated that: 'Today this Scripture is fulfilled in your hearing'. The crowds were amazed at Him, and everyone spoke well of Him, and it could be said that from this day on the 'Manifesto' was put into divine action.

The 'Manifesto' was set out in order to help and reach four types of people, the poor, the prisoners, the blind and the oppressed. The whole ministry of Jesus can be expressed in these words as: 'He came to seek and to save those who were lost'.

As the four areas of great need are expressed in this way and cover such a wide aspect of ministry, we shall consider each one of them in turn as we have done over the past few days.

The third part of the 'Manifesto' of Jesus was that He had come to give recovery of sight to the blind. The Greek word that is used here for the word 'blind' is a very strange word it is the word *'tuphlos'* which means 'to blind'. It is this word that brings the strangeness to the whole concept of the word *'tuphlos'*. The root of this word is the first part of the word 'tuph' which means 'to burn and smoke' and it was used for the sense of someone who was blinded by the natural means of smoke within the eyes. It could be used, and indeed it was at times, for the fact that someone was born blind, however, its greatest use was in the metaphoric sense of a word picture.

If we take this literally, Jesus had come to recover the sight of those who had been blinded by smoke in their eyes as if someone had deliberately sought to blind them. We know of course that the god of this world has deliberately blinded the eyes of the people who are outside of Christ. Jesus recognised that He had to do battle with not just the physical blindness that had scarred some people but with the spiritual blindness of those who had got smoke in their eyes. The Rich Young Ruler that we studied several days ago was not blind in the physical sense but he certainly was in the spiritual sense, as money and possessions had brought smoke to his eyes.

We can rejoice today that the smoke has cleared and that we can now see the glory of God all because Jesus came to seek and to save those who were lost.

My Journal

KEY PRAYER

Heavenly Father, once I was lost but now I am found and once I was blind but now I can see, thank you for removing the 'smoke from my eyes' and allowing me to see clearly. I praise you for good and clear spiritual eyesight today.

October 27th

KEY WORD: **The oppressed**

KEY VERSE: **Luke 4 : 18**

The Spirit of the Lord is on me, because He has anointed me to preach good news to the poor. He has sent me to proclaim freedom for the prisoners and recovery of sight for the blind, to release the oppressed and to proclaim the year of the Lord's favour.

This key verse is often called the 'Manifesto of Jesus' as it sets out very clearly and very distinctly the reasons why He came from heaven to earth. This Scripture is a direct quote from the Old Testament where Isaiah was prophesying the 'Coming of Jesus' and His message.

The setting for the reading of this 'Manifesto' was the small town of Nazareth when Jesus visited the synagogue on the sabbath day and began to read from the scroll, the prophecy of Isaiah. Luke says that every eye was upon Him when, following the reading, Jesus stated that: 'Today this Scripture is fulfilled in your hearing'. The crowds were amazed at Him, and everyone spoke well of Him, and it could be said that from this day on the 'Manifesto' was put into divine action.

The 'Manifesto' was set out in order to help and reach four types of people, the poor, the prisoners, the blind and the oppressed. The whole ministry of Jesus can be expressed in these words as: 'He came to seek and to save those who were lost'.

As the four areas of great need are expressed in this way and cover such a wide aspect of ministry, we shall consider each one of them in turn and we have reached the final part of this 'Manifesto'.

The last part of the 'Manifesto' of Jesus was the releasing of the oppressed. The Greek word that is used here for the word 'oppressed' is the word *'thrauo'*. This word is only used once in the entire New Testament and it gives itself perfectly to the ministry of Jesus. *'Thrauo'* is a very difficult word to translate which is why there are several translations which differ quite significantly. The Old King James Version translates this word as 'bruised' whereas the NIV translates it as 'oppressed'. The actual word means 'to smite' or 'to shatter' so both of the translations in the Old King James and the NIV are both fairly wide of the mark. It can be understood that both of them seek to convey the fact that outside of Christ people are bruised and shattered but it still does not fully convey what Jesus was seeking to do.

People who do not know the Lord are completely spiritually shattered and smitten by sin, they are not just simply bruised by sin and shame nor are they simply oppressed. They are completely and utterly shattered by Satan and his ways, and Jesus came to give them hope and a future and a destiny.

The probable reason why this word is only used once in the New Testament is because the ministry of Jesus was so unique that it set out the fact that He had come to do what no one else could do, to release those who were so broken by sin and so shattered by their experiences of shame, that no other ministry, up until this time, had been able to help them.

What a Saviour and what great salvation!

My Journal ______________________________

____

____

____

____

KEY PRAYER

Heavenly Father, as I have studied the words of the great 'Manifesto' in Luke's Gospel I have come to the conclusion once again, that there is no one just like Jesus. He can do what no other can do and I praise Him again and again. 'My sin not in part but the whole' has been dealt with by a Saviour who cares and understands.

October 28th

KEY WORD: **The year of favour**

KEY VERSE: **Luke 4 : 18**

The Spirit of the Lord is on me, because He has anointed me to preach good news to the poor. He has sent me to proclaim freedom for the prisoners and recovery of sight for the blind, to release the oppressed and to proclaim the year of the Lord's favour.

The closing part of the 'Manifesto' of Jesus, following His declaration to deal with the four areas of greatest need, was to preach and proclaim the year of the favour of God.

This phrase the 'favour of God' was a phrase that would be readily understood by hearers as it was a phrase that was drawn from the pages of the Old Testament and Israel's history. In fact it concluded the prophecy of Isaiah when he prophesied concerning Jesus. The page of the scroll from which Jesus was reading, in the key verse, came from Isaiah's lips and the phrase was a very precious one.

The Greek word that was used for the 'year of favour' was the word '*dektos*' and, as with many Greek words, its translations prove to be a little difficult. This is why, once again, the Old King James and the NIV differ in their understanding of this word. The literal meaning of '*dektos*' is 'to be regarded favourably' which is why the NIV uses this translation 'the year of favour'. However, the Old King James Version uses the words 'acceptable year of the Lord' because the word '*dektos*' carries with it the sense of great acceptance. The word is only used five times within the New Testament and on each occasion the Old King James Version translates the word as 'acceptable' because it places the emphasis upon the fact that this period of time or a particular person was acceptable in the sense of being received well.

The NIV however, always translates this word as 'favour' as this version places the emphasis upon the fact that this period of time or a particular person had found a measure of favour.

Whichever way you look at it, Jesus had come to preach about a new kingdom and a new age of grace, and the key verse goes on to say that in Nazareth that day the people were amazed at Him and all spoke well of Him. This is because the words struck their hearts like no other words had ever done, and it was not just the words, because they would have read these words from Isaiah many times. It was the power of the words and the graciousness which emanated from His lips that touched their hearts.

It also goes on to say that the mother of Jesus, Mary, treasured these things in her heart as she pondered upon them later in the day.

These words spoken by Jesus signalled the beginning of His ministry and the commencement of a new age of grace. No one had ever spoken like this, and no year had ever been so favourable and so acceptable. This 'year' was not a literal year, of course, as the favour of God is still within the Church and still among His people.

My Journal ______________________________

KEY PRAYER

Heavenly Father, I bless you today for the fact that the favour of God still rests upon the Church and upon us today. It began in a small town in Galilee having been prophesied hundreds of years before, and it has reached around the world, and still goes on today. Thank you for your favour and the fact that I have been accepted in the Beloved.

October 29th

KEY WORD: **Synagogue**

KEY VERSE: **Luke 4 : 20**

Then He rolled up the scroll, gave it back to the attendant and sat down. The eyes of everyone in the synagogue were fastened on Him.

Over the past few days we have been considering the 'Manifesto' of Jesus that was announced in the synagogue within the home town of Jesus, in Nazareth. Jesus was handed the scroll of the prophet Isaiah and He read from the part that had announced the coming of the Messiah and His ministry. Following the reading, the key verse today states that, the 'eyes of everyone were upon Him'. In a few minutes time they would be amazed at Him as He would state that 'today this Scripture is fulfilled'.

Jesus was announcing that His earthly ministry was commencing and that a new age of grace was beginning.

The setting of this announcement was in a synagogue in the home town of Jesus on the sabbath day. Jesus did not read these words and make His announcement in the temple at Jerusalem, He chose the rural setting of His home town to make this dramatic proclamation. We shall spend the last few days of this month considering the three aspects of this setting, the synagogue, the Sabbath Day and Nazareth.

Jesus went to the synagogue in Nazareth on a sabbath day to make this announcement and He shook up a quiet rural scene.

The first aspect that we shall consider is the aspect of the actual setting, 'the synagogue'. This setting was chosen by Jesus as the synagogue held a very unique place in the life and times of the Jewish people. The Greek word that the New Testament uses for the word synagogue is '*sunagoge*' and it means 'a bringing together,' and as with many Greek words it was formed by the combining of two different words. The first word that was used is the word *'sun'* which means 'together' and the second word was the word *'ago'* which means 'to bring'. The thought that was produced by the forming of these two words was the concept of a 'gathering'. The word meant the 'gathering together of things', 'a collection' of certain items, and the 'coming together of people'. It was this last meaning that brought the word into its greatest use.

The New Testament uses this word to describe the Jewish gathering of people together in worship, and it also used the word to describe the way in which the New Testament believers would also assemble themselves together.

The word has its roots within the Old Testament when the Jews were held captive in Babylon. During this exile, their custom of worship and gathering together continued. Normally the Jews would meet in the temple to conduct their worship, however, without their temple they would simply meet together, probably in the open air, to conduct their act of worship and their times of prayer. The word *'sunagoge'* springs from this period of their history when the people of God would gather together.

However, the word is used frequently within the New Testament to mean 'the place where the Jews met'. In other words, the synagogue came to be the 'place of meeting' rather than the 'act of gathering'. Jesus loved the house of God and He also loved the meeting place of Jewish people, the synagogue, and it was in this kind of place that He chose to announce His 'Manifesto'.

The word was also used later in the New Testament to describe the meeting place of Christian Jews and it held a special place in the hearts of the early believers as it came to be known as the meeting place of Christians. They loved their meeting place, which is a lesson for us today in that we should not neglect the place of meeting, but attend our local church as often as we can.

KEY PRAYER

Heavenly Father, I have learned afresh today that the New Testament believers loved to meet together within their local synagogues and that they met together as often as they could. Help me to remember this and to seek to attend my local church as often as possible so that I might enjoy fellowship with others and fellowship with you.

October 30th

KEY WORD: **Sabbath Day**

KEY VERSE: **Luke 4 : 20**

Then He rolled up the scroll, gave it back to the attendant and sat down. The eyes of everyone in the synagogue were fastened on Him.

This key verse concerning Jesus and His 'Manifesto' took place, as we have seen over the past few days, in a synagogue on the sabbath day in Nazareth. Jesus chose this rural setting, within His home town, to bring the amazing message that His ministry was now commencing.

The fact that He chose the sabbath day was a very interesting feature of this amazing announcement. Jesus used this day not just to make His announcement concerning the new age of grace, but He chose it because He wanted to place emphasis upon the fact that the age of the law was now at an end and that the age of grace had dawned.

The sabbath day was very much part of the age of the law as it stood for the 'day of rest' and 'the day of God'. The word 'sabbath' comes from an Aramaic root and it came to be known as a day of extreme laws and oppression. The word 'sabbath' comes from the word '*sabbaton*' and it means 'to intercept' or 'to interrupt', and because there are two b's within the word it carries greater impact. The whole concept of an 'interrupted' day or a 'intercepted day' came from the fact God rested on the seventh day of creation. He interrupted His creative work to rest to show His people that this day was a day of rest and that all peoples should observe this day as a day of worship.

The problem arose, however, when the priests and the Pharisees began to place legalism upon this day and began to invent systems of oppression that would, in fact, be opposite to the design of God and the purpose of this day. Old Testament regulations were developed and imposed that became an absurd restriction to the people of God. This day was created for rest and the whole idea was one of cessation from activity and an interruption from the normal activities of life, yet the sabbath day became a day that was dominated by laws and restrictions that became a great effort to uphold.

Jesus and His disciples were in trouble with the authorities for 'plucking the ears of corn' on the sabbath day. They had broken the law by plucking, which was deemed to be reaping, and for rubbing the ears of corn to eat, which was deemed to be threshing'. The imposition of laws and regulations changed the concept of this day from one of rest and gladness to one of heavy domination of legalism.

Jesus chose this very day to announce that He had come to release people from the shackles of law and regulation and to give them freedom to enjoy His Father's blessings. The choosing of this day was not an accident nor was it a coincidence, Jesus knew exactly what He was doing in choosing this day, He was setting out to show that for all time He was changing law into grace and the day of regulations into a day of greater and greater freedom and blessing. We no longer keep the sabbath day which is the seventh day, Saturday, as our day of rest. We now worship on the Lord's day which is Sunday, the first day of the week, and we observe this day as our day of the Lord.

My Journal ______________________________

____

____

____

KEY PRAYER

Heavenly Father, I long to worship you in spirit and truth and not with man-made regulations and impositions. Help me to always keep my spirit free from the restrictions of law and to rejoice in grace and grace alone. Thank you for the freedom that the Lord's day has brought to us and help me to keep it precious.

October 31st

KEY WORD: **Nazareth**

KEY VERSE: **Luke 4 : 20**

Then He rolled up the scroll, gave it back to the attendant and sat down. The eyes of everyone in the synagogue were fastened on Him.

On the final day of the month of October and on the final day of our studies in the 'Manifesto' of Jesus we shall consider the place where Jesus announced the commencement of His earthly ministry.

Jesus had read from the prophet Isaiah and had announced that the day of the Lord's favour was now commencing, and in fact He had announced that He was the 'long awaited one' the Messiah. The people in the synagogue that day were firstly amazed at Him and had spoken well of Him, but their amazement quickly turned to anger and they would have killed Him if He had not departed from them. Jesus used this setting to announce His ministry for a very good reason. He chose a synagogue on a sabbath day in Nazareth to make His proclamation so that it had the greatest impact. The sabbath day was chosen to show that the law, with its restrictions and legalism, was now at an end. He also chose Nazareth, to show that even in the worst town, God's gracious favour could be demonstrated.

In the month of May we studied the town of Nazareth as Jesus was always called 'Jesus of Nazareth'. It was as if this town above all towns was the identifiable place of Jesus' origins.

A phrase was often used in and around the neighbourhood of Nazareth and beyond, 'Can any good thing come out of Nazareth?' It was felt that this town was inferior and of no use. The fact that Jesus allowed Himself to be linked and identified with this 'inferior' town showed that this place had a special place in His heart

Jesus was brought up in Nazareth as a carpenter and was always linked with it and always identified with it. The town was set high in the hills that surrounded Galilee and it had a poor reputation. The town was synonymous with a crude sounding dialect that was totally different to any other form of speech. It also had a reputation for sin and crime and heavy religious practices, including strong synagogue attendance and sabbath day worship. Nazareth was also regarded as being 'out of the way' as it was set high in the hills, and therefore with its background of crime and sin and its religious fervour and the strange dialect, it was noted for the fact that 'nothing good could come from this town'.

Jesus chose this place rather than Jerusalem to make His announcement as it was the kind of 'last place on earth' to begin a major impact on society. This was in keeping with the whole of New Testament truth, that God always takes the weak things to confound the mighty, and that God always takes the poor in spirit and makes them become the inheritors of the kingdom of heaven.

We can thank God at the end of this month and at the end of our studies concerning the 'Manifesto' of Jesus, that God takes the least and makes them the greatest. He did this on a sabbath day in a synagogue in Nazareth to announce His earthly ministry of release and freedom, and He has continued to do this throughout the age of grace.

My Journal

KEY PRAYER

Heavenly Father, I do rejoice in the fact that you take the weak things and cause them to become mighty, and that you take the foolish things of this world in order to confound the wise. I worship you today for your goodness and love, thank you that you came to save me and thank you that you have used even me for your glory.

November 1st

KEY WORD: ***Signs***

KEY VERSE: ***Matthew 24 : 3***

As Jesus was sitting on the Mount of Olives, the disciples came to Him privately. "Tell us," they said, "when will this happen, and what will be the sign of your coming and of the end of the age?"

As we commence a brand new month we are going to consider for a few days the whole question of the Second Coming of Jesus and the Signs of the Times. The disciples came to Jesus when He was sitting on the Mount of Olives and asked Him the question that appears in the key verse today. This question was prompted by something that Jesus had just said privately to them. He was speaking about the temple being destroyed and His disciples felt a sense of shock and uncertainty and they responded with the question, 'tell us about the Signs of the Times?'

In several of the New Testament books there are certain 'clues' or signs that point to the fact that the Second Coming of Jesus is drawing nearer and nearer. These signs were given so that the Church might expect His coming, and be prepared for this final event of the ages. Jesus spoke at considerable length about these signs and, in order for us to grasp just how close we are to this final event of history, we shall take a few days to consider some of them.

Firstly, however, we need to consider the term 'Signs of the Times', as this phrase occurs frequently within New Testament philosophy and Church teaching. We need to understand what is meant by this term before we can understand what each sign means, and what each sign relates to.

The word 'sign' is normally regarded as a kind of 'pointer' or directional aid, we have signs all around us that give direction on motorways and highways, they point us in the right direction, and they help us to navigate our way from one place to another. We see other signs around us that advertise certain products, and these signs give us help in distinguishing one item from another, and one product from another. Signs help us to understand and signs give us direction.

The Greek word for 'sign' is the word '*semeion*' which is normally translated as meaning a 'mark' or a 'token' and it can also be understood as an 'indication'. The word appears frequently within the New Testament and is readily understood as the word that gives a warning or an indication of something.

In the key verse today, the word '*semeion*' is used as a kind of token of future events, the disciples were asking for an indication or a token of impending events that would happen before Jesus would return again to this world. When this phrase is linked with the word 'times', so that you have Signs of the Times, it takes on a greater significance as we shall see tomorrow. For now, it is good to know that God has arranged for certain events to take place so that we might know when the Second Coming is drawing near.

My Journal

KEY PRAYER

Heavenly Father, I know that I am not supposed to know the day or the hour of your coming, as not even the angels in heaven know that, but thank you that you have arranged events to take place that will give us a sign of the approaching day. Help me to understand these signs and to be prepared.

November 2nd

KEY WORD: **Times**

KEY VERSE: **Matthew 24 : 3**

As Jesus was sitting on the Mount of Olives, the disciples came to Him privately. "Tell us," they said, "when will this happen, and what will be the sign of your coming and of the end of the age?"

The Greek word for the English word 'sign' is the word '*semeion*' which means an 'indication' or a 'token', and, as we saw yesterday, this kind of indication gives us an understanding that the Second Coming of Jesus is drawing near.

When the word 'sign' is linked with the word 'times' it brings extra urgency and greater impact to the Church. The usual word in the New Testament for 'time' or 'times' is the word '*chronos*' which means a 'space of time' or a 'period of time'. However, when it comes to times and seasons and the Signs of the Times, the New Testament uses the word '*kairos*' which means a 'measurement of time' or a 'season of times'. We studied both of these words in the month of April when we were looking at the times and the seasons of earth.

Jesus Himself, and also all the New Testament writers used the words 'Signs of the Times' to convey the period that will take place between the Ascension of Jesus and His Second Coming, and the kind of events that will take place during this period. The words '*semeion kairos*' would indicate to those who received these words, the 'token of the season' and it would clearly mean to them that, during this coming season, there would be tokens and reminders that Jesus would return.

Over the next few days we are going to consider several of these signs and we will be reminded again and again that the Second Coming of Jesus is drawing nearer and nearer, and that we should be ready for this final event of history.

It has been said that there are over 350 clear signs of the Second Coming in the Bible, and that they appear within three distinct fields. Firstly, the Old Testament declares that Jesus will come again, and gives clear signs of this event. Secondly, Jesus Himself gave indications of His coming and gave clear signs of future events and happenings. Thirdly, the New Testament writers wrote much about the event called the Second Coming, and they also gave clear signals as to what would happen before Jesus came.

Within the Church today there are many interpreters of these signs, and each one of them professes to 'read' these signs with great authority and they expound their theories and their conclusions. Many have been forced to admit that they were wrong, when they predicted that the sign had come to pass, and that Jesus was about to return immediately, then, sadly, the Second Coming did not take place, to the great embarrassment of the predictor. We are not told to look for the signs but we are told to look for His coming, it is not for us to know the day and the hour but to be prepared, as this final event could happen at any time.

My Journal

KEY PRAYER

Heavenly Father, I long for your coming and I eagerly await your return, help me to be faithful unto that day and help me to be ready to meet you. As we study the Signs of the Times over the next few days help me to understand more and more about your return, and more and more about the need to prepare myself.

November 3rd

KEY WORD: **Deception**

KEY VERSE: **Matthew 24 : 5**

For many will come in my name, claiming, 'I am the Christ,' and will deceive many.

When Jesus answered the question of His disciples concerning the Signs of the Times, He began to give them portents and tokens of the things that would take place before His return.

He told them of many things that would come to pass, and He gave them signs to watch for. One of the first signs that He gave them was the sign of deception, He said that many would come in His name and declare that they were the Christ. Last August we studied together the fact that there were 'false Christs', and that they were deceiving many people. We said then that the Greek word for 'false Christs' was *'pseudochristos'* which meant 'one who falsely lays claim to being the Messiah'. We also said that the English word 'pseudo' was derived from this word, and that 'pseudo' means false or counterfeit.

Jesus was literally saying to His disciples that, in the time between His Ascension and His Second Coming, there would be those who would claim to be the Messiah, and that they would deceive many. However, these false Christs would only be a counterfeit of the real thing, and they would be totally and completely false.

However, Jesus said that they would look like the real thing, and, because of this, they would deceive many. He told His disciples in the previous verse to the key verse today, to 'watch out', so that they might be on their guard against being deceived and falling into deception.

In order to understand exactly what Jesus was seeking to convey we have to go as usual to the Greek language for the full truth. There are many Greek words for our word 'deception', the most common word is the word *'apate'* which means 'to cheat' or 'to beguile,' this is the word that is mostly used in the New Testament for deception. There are over nine other words for deception that are used, and they range from the word for 'a bait', to the word for 'a lure'. The least-used word for 'deceive' is the one that Matthew uses in the key verse today, in fact it is only used a few times in the New Testament. It is the word *'planao'* which means to 'go astray,' and our English word 'planet' is derived from this word. The word was used when the Greeks were seeking to describe someone who had been seduced from one pathway into another that, then, led to the loss of direction. This is why the word was translated as 'going astray'. What Jesus therefore was seeking to convey to His disciples was that, in the time between His departure and His Second Coming, there would be those who would seek to lay claim to being 'Christs'. These false Christs would deceive many into a pathway that was not designed for them. This pathway, Jesus said, would lead to a loss of direction, and they would go astray.

As a Church we need to be ready to stand for truth whenever falsehood and deception rears its head, so that we might not be deceived into a wrong path, but keep on walking the straight and narrow path to everlasting life. Jesus gave the warning, and we must take heed.

My Journal ____

____

____

____

KEY PRAYER

Heavenly Father, help me each day to live my life in such a way that I am ready, whenever falsehood arises, and whenever those who lay claim to truth, but who are wolves in sheep's clothing, appear. Thank you for truth and thank you for the gifts of the Holy Spirit that are given as aids to truth and weapons against deception.

November 4th

KEY WORD: **War**

KEY VERSE: **Matthew 24 : 6**

You will hear of wars and rumours of wars, but see to it that you are not alarmed. Such things must happen, but the end is still to come.

One of the main Signs of the Times that Jesus gave to His disciples was the sign of 'wars and rumours of wars'. Jesus said this in response to the question concerning the end of the age and His Second Coming, His disciples said 'tell us what it will be like' before you come again.

Jesus gave them directions and tokens of things that would take place before He would return. In the key verse today, Jesus sets out the fact that conflict would take place and that it would be a key element within the world before His Second Coming. Jesus went even further than just simply talking about conflict, He stated that 'nations would rise against nations and kingdoms would rise against kingdoms'. This seems to indicate that there would not simply be a few wars scattered across history, but there would be a constant and a continual rise of warring among the nations on earth, that would be a devastating sign of unrest and unease.

Since Jesus uttered these words almost two thousand years have come and gone, and, if we add up the period of peace and the absence of war, it only adds up to around 200 years in total; nine-tenths of the time has been spent in fighting and war. Our world has only seen a period of less than 200 years without war and fighting. Scholars also tell us today that there are over 40 wars being conducted at this very moment within the world, and that another 20 areas are under such tension; wars could break out at any time.

The period between the Ascension of Jesus and His Second Coming is, therefore, a period marked by human tension and war. The word that is used within the key verse for 'war' is the Greek word *'polemos'*, and it is translated in different ways by different versions of the Bible. For instance the Old King James Version translates this word as 'battle' while the NIV translates it as 'war'. The Revised Version translates it as 'fight' and other versions use the words 'quarrel' or 'conflict', in order to convey the truth of the word. The word is probably best translated as 'to make war,' as it has a sense of continual activity rather than simply 'one war' or a single fight. What Jesus was seeking to convey in this Sign of the Times, was that continual and constant unrest would characterise the age between His Ascension and His return and that nations would rise against nations because of this period of unease.

The most devastating sign of this unrest is of course the two world wars that have taken place during the recent period of our history. In the last hundred years, the world has seen the dreadful and terrible state of nations pitched together in war on two occasions, that brought total and complete upheaval to the whole world. This was not just a single nation rising against another nation, but a conflagration that was total and complete in bringing together all nations into battle.

We can rejoice today in the fact that, when Jesus comes, He will bring peace on earth, and there will be an absence of the Signs of the Times called *'polemos'*, as Jesus will cause all nations to bow before Him and peace will reign.

KEY PRAYER

Heavenly Father, I praise you today for the glorious possibility of world peace and endless rest, I recognise the fact that nations will never be at peace until you, the Prince of Peace, are allowed to take your rightful place. I pray today that peace will be in my heart even though peace is absent in the world.

November 5th

KEY WORD: **Famine**

KEY VERSE: **Matthew 24 : 7**

There will be famines and earthquakes in various places.

As we are studying the Signs of the Times as forecast by Jesus, it is interesting to note that His description of these signs was not confined to one location upon earth, but was widespread in their definition. Jesus was talking to His disciples about the signs that would take place between His Ascension and His Second Coming, and He spoke of a world in crisis and a world paralysed by conflict and greed.

Jesus recognised the fact that, during the period when He had returned to heaven to await His return to earth, the earth would suffer the birth pangs of pain and anguish, because it was a world that was living in the rejection of a Saviour and the loss of true love. Therefore humanity, being what it is, would act in such a manner as would reduce its self into the basest of forms, and the saddest of actions.

Jesus said that one of the Signs of the Times was the outbreak of famine that would affect the world, and one of the saddest facts is that many of the famines that we have faced within the world have been 'man made' famines that have been caused by the greed of others and the immoral politics of some leaders.

The Greek word that is used within this key verse for the word 'famine' is the word '*limos*', which is normally translated as meaning 'hunger' or 'dearth'. This word only occurs twelve times within the New Testament, and it has three main translations. Three times it is translated as 'hunger,' and then twice it occurs as 'dearth,' and the other seven times it appears as simply 'famine'. However, even in these three different translations it fails to fully convey just what Jesus was seeking to say to His disciples. The Sign of the Times called 'famine' that Jesus was speaking about, was the total and complete destruction of food and harvest. What He had in mind was not the loss of one harvest and not the failure of a few crops that would produce a local kind of loss. This word *'limos'* conveys total dearth and full hunger that a continent-wide loss of several harvests would produce.

We only have to look at the pictures upon our television screens to see exactly what Jesus was seeking to convey: the human tragedy of a whole continent of people without food, not just for the loss of one harvest, but the total loss of food and grain for many harvests. There have always been famines, even in Old Testament times, but it just seems that, as we get nearer and nearer to the end of the ages, that this Sign of the Times increasingly points to the return of Jesus. Famines have become more widespread, and far more devastating than ever before, producing a global problem that taxes the rich nations as well as the poorer ones.

In our plenty we can thank God for His provision, but we should never forget those who are in the pain of famine and despair, and we should also cause our minds to reflect upon the fact, that the coming of the Lord draws near.

My Journal

KEY PRAYER

Heavenly Father, I do pray today for those who have nothing at all, and for those who have no idea where their next meal is coming from. I recognise that this is a Sign of the Times, but I also recognise my responsibility to care, and to pray, and to give. I praise you for my provision, help me to give, out of my abundance.

November 6th

KEY WORD: **Earthquakes**

KEY VERSE: **Matthew 24 : 7**

There will be famines and earthquakes in various places.

Jesus was talking to His disciples in the key verse today about the Signs of the Times, and we have been considering some of them over the past few days. He spoke of one such sign which has been translated in the NIV as 'earthquake'. However, the word that is used does not just relate to a physical earthquake that shakes and convulses the earth, it is much deeper than that.

The Old King James Bible uses the word 'pestilence' in its translation of the words of Jesus, so, in order to fully understand what Jesus was saying to His disciples, we must go to the original text to uncover the truth.

Jesus said that there would be certain signs taking place on earth between His Ascension and His Second Coming, and that these signs would produce a picture that would convey to the watching world, and the watching Church, that His return was drawing near.

The Greek word that was used for the translation 'earthquake' is the word '*seismos*', which means a 'shaking' or a 'shock'. It is obvious that we derive our English word 'seismic' from this word, and 'seismology' is now recognised as the word for the study of earthquakes. The word '*seismos*' has its roots in the first part of the word '*seio*', which means to 'move to and fro', and it conveyed the thought of a concussion. This is why some versions of the Bible only translate the word as a concussion of earth, a simple earthquake. However, the word can be applied to more things than simply the earth 'shaking' in the shock of an earthquake.

The word can be applied to the sea as well as the earth, and it is found earlier in Matthew's Gospel when, in Matthew 8, Jesus calmed the tempest on Lake Galilee, this was a 'shaking' of the sea. This word can also be applied to the 'shaking' that a calamity can bring, as well as the physical shaking of an earthquake. Plagues can be '*seismos*', as they can shake a nation and even the world, the devastating plague of AIDS is an earth-shaking pestilence of gigantic proportions. The world has been shaken by this plague, and it has ravaged some nations far more than a physical shaking ever could.

If we total up the vast number of diseases that are savaging nations upon this planet right now, and then if we add to them the floods and the ravages of storms and tidal changes, not to mention 'global warming' and its effects. We have pestilences that go far beyond the simple earthquakes of the NIV, these are Signs of the Times.

My Journal

KEY PRAYER

Heavenly Father, within all the disease and rampant plagues that are affecting the earth upon which we live, I give you thanks that you are my great physician, and that you keep me from all harm. I pray today for all those who are affected by calamity and pain and I ask that you would reveal yourself to them. Keep my eyes ever watchful as your coming draws near.

November 7th

KEY WORD: **Earthquakes**

KEY VERSE: **Matthew 24 : 7**

There will be famines and earthquakes in various places.

Jesus was talking to His disciples in the key verse today, about the Signs of the Times, and we have been considering some of them over the past few days. He spoke of one such sign which has been translated in the NIV as 'earthquake'. However, the word that is used does not just relate to a physical earthquake that shakes and convulses the earth, it is far deeper than that.

The Old King James Bible uses the word 'pestilence' in its translation of the words of Jesus, so, in order to fully understand what Jesus was saying to His disciples we must go to the original text to uncover the truth. The word for earthquake, as we saw yesterday, is the word *'seismos'* which means a 'shaking' or a 'shock'. It is obvious that we derive our English word 'seismic' from this word, and 'seismology' is now the recognised word for the study of earthquakes. The word *'seismos'* has its roots in the first part of the word *'seio'* which means to 'move to and fro' and it conveyed the thought of a concussion.

Jesus used this word to convey the thought of this planet being 'concussed' by a shaking and a shock. The word was used, as we saw yesterday, for all kinds of pestilence such as plagues and calamities, and it was translated this way in the Old King James Version. However, the NIV stays with the most natural translation, that of earthquakes.

The world has always seen earthquakes, and probably always will, until the return of Jesus. However, Jesus was seeking to convey something to His disciples that went beyond the natural force of the occasional earthquake. Jesus said, in the key verse today, that there would be earthquakes in various places, and the clue to what He was saying was not in the wording of earthquakes, but in the wording of 'various places'. The Greek word for 'various' is the word *'poikilos'*, which means 'manifold' or 'multicoloured,' and it was used by Matthew in His translation to describe the literal words of Jesus, when He stated that earthquakes would become more and more widespread and more and more manifold in their number and strength.

Jesus could not have been describing any clearer the fact that earthquakes would increase and become more widespread around the world. This picture of a world shaking in shock, following multitudes of seismic concussions, could not be clearer, Jesus was describing the End Times that would occur just before His return. This word *'seismos'* occurs 14 times in the New Testament, and always appears when the description is at its blackest. Whether the word is used for plague or calamity, or whether it is used as the word for seismic shocks, it is always with a warning that we are to watch very carefully, as these are but the signs of the end.

My Journal

KEY PRAYER

Heavenly Father, I set my heart to watch very carefully the Signs of the Times, as it is very obvious that we are getting nearer and nearer to the end of the age. I look up with great expectancy as the coming of the Lord draws near, please help me to be faithful and true, as the day approaches.

November 8th

KEY WORD: **Earthquakes**

KEY VERSE: **Matthew 24 : 7**

There will be famines and earthquakes in various places.

Jesus was talking to His disciples in the key verse today, about the Signs of the Times, and we have been considering some of them over the past few days. He spoke of one such sign which has been translated in the NIV as 'earthquake.' However, the word that is used does not just relate to a physical earthquake that shakes and convulses the earth.

The Old King James Bible uses the word 'pestilence' in its translation of the words of Jesus, so in order to fully understand what Jesus was saying to His disciples, we must go to the original text to uncover the truth. The word for earthquake as we saw yesterday, is the word '*seismos*', which means a 'shaking' or a 'shock.' It is obvious that we derive our English word 'seismic' from this word and 'seismology' is the study of earthquakes. The word '*seismos*' has its roots in the first part of the word '*seio*' which means to 'move to and fro' and it conveyed the thought of a concussion.

The reason that the different versions of the Bible translate the word '*seismos*' differently, is because of the confusion that this word brings. It can fully mean a physical earthquake with its 'concussion' effects upon the earth, and it can fully mean a pestilence like Aids, and calamities like famine and plagues. However, Jesus was not just talking about these things, the clue to the depth of teaching that Jesus was seeking to bring lies in the root part of the word '*seismos*'. The first part of the word '*seio*', which means, as we have seen, to 'move to and fro,' actually relates to far more than a one-time effect of a localised earthquake. Of course, plagues can 'move to and fro' across a country, and

AIDS has 'moved to and fro' across continents. However, Jesus was conveying much more than simply this.

The root word *'seis'* speaks of a gigantic movement of disturbance across the earth which is exactly what Jesus was seeking to convey. Matthew noticed this and conveyed the same substantial thought when he used this very deep Greek word. We are not talking hear about the increasing effects of physical earthquakes or the rampant spread of plagues and famine. We are talking about a greater calamity and pestilence than this.

Jesus was saying that the End Times, with their signs and tokens of direction, would begin to see a colossal disturbance across the face of our planet that has not been seen before. We only have to listen to the news broadcasts or watch the 'global picture' being presented to us on our nightly television news shows, to know that globally we are being 'moved to and fro'.

A localised earthquake in one continent can have devastating effects upon another continent hundreds and thousands of miles away. Tidal waves are created that 'move to and fro' across oceans with unbelievable effects, and ground movement, as the earth's plates shift, creates volcanic disturbance far across the world. This world is being shaken apart and shocked by *'seismos'* more than at any time of its history. The age is coming to a close and Jesus will soon return.

My Journal

KEY PRAYER

Heavenly Father, I recognise today that Jesus was speaking about more than the simple earthquake and pestilence that I have previously considered, I now realise that this planet is under serious threat, thank you for your protecting hand upon the Church. Thank you too, that the times and seasons are in your hand and that all is well because you are fully in control.

November 9th

KEY WORD: ***Fearful***

KEY VERSE: **Luke 21 : 11**

There will be great earthquakes, famines and pestilences in various places, and fearful events and great signs from heaven.

Over the past few days we have been considering the whole question of the Signs of the Times and the tokens and directions that they bring to us. We have been looking at a variety of them as described by the Gospel writer Matthew. Today we are going one step further and we are going to commence looking at some of the Signs of the Times as described by Luke.

Luke heard the very same question being answered by Jesus. The question was: When shall the end of the age come? Jesus gave His answer by listing some of the signs that would take place. Matthew gave his description of them and Luke gave his description, the signs are almost the same except for one or two. Maybe Luke was a little more perceptive than Matthew or maybe he heard a little more than Matthew heard. Whichever it way it was, Luke covers a few more signs than Mathew did.

Following the list of signs such as earthquakes and pestilences, Luke mentions two more, he speaks of 'fearful events' and 'great signs from heaven'.

When Luke wrote about 'fearful events' he used a most strange and descriptive Greek word, and, in fact, it was only used on this one occasion and it does not appear again in the entire New Testament. Because of the nature of the word the English translators were quite at a loss as to how to bring the truth of this word to English readers, so they wrote and translated the word as 'fearful events', or as the Old King James Version puts it, 'fearful sights'. The word is '*phobetron*' which has the incredible meaning of 'terrible' or 'dreadful' or 'terrific appearance'. The translators could not just say that 'there would be terrible', as it would not make sense, nor could they say that 'there would be dreadful', as again it is not good English. So, to help us understand the context and the word, they produced two words, 'fearful events'. This makes a little more sense and a little better English, but it still does not produce the truth of the word.

The word *'phobetron'* is taken from the root word *'phobos'*, and we saw in May, when we studied five words that are translated as 'fear', it means 'causing flight' or 'being scared'. Jesus added another dimension however, when He extended the word to mean something akin to this but far more terrible and dreadful. Luke and the translators struggled to convey this thought and came up with the word *'phobetron'*. What Jesus was describing was total and complete terror and abject fear caused by things that were not natural. For instance, earthquakes would cause fear, but not like this. Dreadful events like plagues and famines would cause fear, but again, not on this scale and not at all like this.

Jesus was talking about something that was great in dimension and much stronger in its effects and something that would produce more than the normal kind of fear.

We only have to look at world events and the command structure of terrorist units around the world, to discover the real meaning of this word. Bombs placed in city streets that detonate without warning, aeroplanes that are used as 'flying bombs' and the abject terror that is caused by the indiscriminate terror activity of a relatively small group of fanatics. The sad thing is that most countries in the world are affected by this kind of terror and instruments of dread, and they are increasing, and they are filling hearts with a total and complete feeling of helplessness and fear. The end is surely near!

KEY PRAYER

Heavenly Father, I recognise in this Sign of the Times that the end is very near, never have we had such signs before and never has there been such overwhelming fear as there is today.
I thank you that perfect love casts out all fear and that I can rest in you. Cause me each day to trust you more and cause me to lean upon you in such a world of fear.

November 10th

KEY WORD: ***Great signs from heaven***

KEY VERSE: **Luke 21 : 11**

There will be great earthquakes, famines and pestilences in various places, and fearful events and great signs from heaven.

Luke, in his description of the Signs of the Times described certain events taking place that could only be translated as 'great signs from heaven'. He was at pains to portray these events as being Signs of the Times and he went to great lengths, as we saw yesterday, to convey the right words in the right place and at the right time, to fully describe the truth that he was bringing to the Church.

Luke actually uses a Greek phrase in this portrayal of 'great signs from heaven' which is literally almost a sentence, he stated '*megas semeion ouranous*', which literally translated means an even fuller sentence. Luke's words literally translated mean that ' huge marks and great degrees of intensity would abound from the aerial skies above us'.

This phrase and its subsequent translation can be applied to two main things. Firstly, the strange natural phenomena that can take place in the heavens above us, and, secondly, the huge events that have their origins in God's heaven alone. If we examine these two applications of the phrase we shall discover that, during the time between the Ascension of Jesus and His Second Coming, both of these applications have been taking place.

There have always been strange and natural phenomena taking place above us, such as 'shooting stars' and 'comets,' with their long and fascinating tails, that stretch for thousands and thousands of miles. We have read about the incredible balls of light and the deep black holes that abound in deep space, and we have also been amazed as giant telescopes, like 'Hubble' and other deep space probes, have beamed back pictures from the edge of our galaxy. We have watched in wonder as pictures of utter clarity have shown our world from tens of thousands of miles away, as spacemen have orbited the planet in their rockets and shuttles. Amazing natural sights have been shown to us in our day and generation that no other generation ever saw or could see.

The second application of this phrase can be applied to the huge events that have their origins in God alone. They are not natural events nor are they natural wonders, but they can only emanate from God's creative work and God's heaven . These are things like the 'Star of Bethlehem,' that guided the Wise Men to Jesus, this was not a natural star but a supernatural and intense indication from heaven. Other signs like this would be the 'voice of God' being heard audibly from heaven by Paul on the road to Damascus, and the appearance of a 'dove-like' being from heaven at the baptism of Jesus. The 'open heavens' of John's Revelation concerning the last times is another of these supernatural signs. There have also been accounts throughout Church history, when people have recounted the times when visions appeared in the heavens, and times when the audible voice of God was heard echoing across the heavens.

'Megas semeion ouranous' speaks of huge and intense moments of wonder in the heavens both natural and supernatural, in our day and age we can look up as the coming of the Lord draws even nearer.

KEY PRAYER

Heavenly Father, as we have studied these Signs of the Times over the past few days I have noticed more and more that everything seems to be coming to a head in our day and generation. I praise you for the fact that I am alive in this age and that I am a watcher of these spectacles. Help me to be worthy of my high calling and of my place in history.

November 11th

KEY WORD: **Terrible times**

KEY VERSE: **2 Timothy 3 : 1**

But mark this: There will be terrible times in the last days.

Over the past ten days we have been considering together some of the amazing Signs of the Times that Jesus and some of the New Testament writers described to us. Today our thoughts in these signs reach a new level of depravity and savageness, with possibly one of the strangest and most far-reaching of all the signs that are mentioned. We are going to study this one today and a few others of depravity over the next few days. Paul wrote to his prodigy Timothy, using a description that would clarify for him the kind of times that could be expected before Jesus would return again.

Paul uses a word that is a very unique one, in fact it only appears twice within the entire New Testament, and it has a very awkward meaning to try and explain.

The Greek word that is used for the word 'terrible times' is the word '*chalepos*', and this word is difficult to translate, which is why it appears in different forms in different versions. The NIV has the word translated as 'terrible times,' whereas the Old King James Version uses the word 'perilous'. The Revised Version uses the word 'grievous' and other versions use their own words to try and explain the meaning. The literal meaning of '*chalepos*' is 'hard to deal with', and it signifies the aspect of something that is fierce or desperately difficult. The word appears twice in the New Testament, here, in the key verse today, when Paul was outlining the Signs of the Times that would characterise the last days and the End Times.

The only other time that this word appears in the New Testament is in Matthew 8 : 28, when Jesus confronted the two 'mad men of Gadara', who were so demonised and so violent that no one would pass that way due to their '*chalepos*'.

The use of the word to describe the demonised men and the use of the word to describe the character of the End Times, gives us an insight into the character of the last moments of history.

The Greek word with its literal meaning of 'days that are hard to deal with', and its counterpart for the description of the mad men, reveals that the last days would be days of violence and demonic power which would create a sense of helplessness within mankind.

Having set out the kind of character of the End Times, Paul then lists a catalogue of the types of things that this word '*chalepos*' brings. Paul said that men would 'love pleasure more than God', and that they would be 'without love' and 'unholy'. There are several other descriptions of the kind of lifestyle that people would be living in some of the verses that follow the key verse. The word 'brutal' appears, as does the word 'disobedient', which tends to paint a picture of great danger. The whole scenario painted for us by Paul is a time when there would be an outbreak of great demonic power that would produce fear and helplessness within people, and where the whole day would be difficult to deal with. No one would have an answer, and no one would be able to cope with the kind of things that would be taking place.

As we look at the day in which we live we can only say that these 'terrible times' seem to have arrived among us. We can thank God that there is an answer in Jesus, and that we have found the way out of these terrible times.

KEY PRAYER

Heavenly Father, I praise you that Jesus is the answer to the terrible times that afflict us at this present moment, and I praise you too that you have brought me to the place where I can see clearly that there is no other name under heaven that can bring a release from the suffering of these terrible times. Thank you for saving me and thank you for keeping me.

November 12th

KEY WORD: **Brutal**

KEY VERSE: **2 Timothy 3 : 1**

But mark this: There will be terrible times in the last days.

Yesterday we studied together the kind of character of the age that appears, during what we call the 'last days', and we saw that the days were filled with violence and fear and a sense of demonic helplessness. Paul wrote to Timothy in order to describe what would take place before Jesus comes again.

A little later in verse three of the same chapter, Paul outlines not just the character of the day but he also describes some of the types of men that would populate the planet during these times of '*chalepos*', which literally means 'times that are hard to bear.'

Paul speaks of men who would be 'brutal' as the NIV calls these men, the Old King James Version refers to them as 'brutal men'. The Greek word that is used is the word '*anemeros*' which means 'not tame' and it is a word that is taken from the aspect of savage wild beasts.

This word is formed by the combining of two words. Firstly, the word '*a*' which is a negative word meaning 'not', and, secondly, the word '*hemeros*' which means 'gentle'. So this word was combined to form a word picture of a kind of person that was 'not gentle'. Moulton and Milligan, two great Greek scholars say of this word that its formation produces a sense of 'wild and savage beasts resembling the lion', in order to describe people who left God out of their lives, and who had turned and abandoned themselves to sin.

If the character of the day produces a sense of helplessness and awesome fear, then the day is further characterised by people who had abandoned themselves to outright wickedness.

This day would then be best described as a savage day of wicked and degenerate activity by men who had given themselves over to reckless sin and shame. If we look at the day in which we live, and if we see just how these kinds of activities have escalated between the time of the Ascension of Jesus and the day in which we live, we can only draw the conclusion that we are indeed in terrible times, and that the end is fast approaching.

We can give thanks again today that God has had mercy and grace upon us, and that He has saved us from sin and shame and has given us hope in a hopeless world.

My Journal

KEY PRAYER

Heavenly Father, thank you for the hope that lies within me, and that, in spite of the abounding wickedness all around me you have shown me loving kindness and tender mercy, and that you have saved me from sin. Thank you for hope in a hopeless world.

November 13th

KEY WORD: ***Depraved mind***

KEY VERSE: **Romans 1 : 28**

Furthermore, since they did not think it worth while to retain the knowledge of God, He gave them over to a depraved mind, to do what ought not to be done.

Over the past twelve days we have extensively studied some of the Signs of the Times that the New Testament describes to us and we are drawing near to the concluding of our studies in these signs. Over the next two days we are going to look at one of the most difficult signs to talk about, the sign of the 'depraved mind'.

Paul wrote to the church in Rome and described the kind of attitude of mind that would characterise the last days. He used a very descriptive word to classify these days as being filled by people whose minds were depraved because God had 'given them over' to the state of mind where they were beyond all common sense, and beyond all natural judgement.

The word that is used to describe this kind of attitude is a very interesting one, however, it brings a slight confusion to our English 'westernised' minds. The NIV translates the word as 'depraved' whereas the Old King James Version uses the word 'reprobate'. The Greek word that was used is the word *'adokimos'* which means 'not standing the test'. The word is formed by the combining of two words. Firstly, the word *'a'* which means a negative 'not', and secondly the word *'dokimos'* which means 'approved'. So, we have a word picture formed for us of a people whose mind is 'not approved by God'.

This attitude of mind, Paul says, will characterise the last days on earth. It describes people that God does not approve of, so He has given them over to minds that are devoid of understanding. Two questions immediately force themselves to be addressed. Firstly: What caused God to give them over to such a state of mind? Secondly: What is the outcome of such a mind? We shall attempt to answer the first question today and then attempt to answer the second one tomorrow.

What caused God to give people over to a mind that was devoid of understanding? The answer to this is a difficult one because to answer it runs the risk of being misunderstood. The answer is found in the preceding verses, where Paul describes the natural affections of love between men and women being given up for the unnatural affection of lust between men and men and between women and women. This unnatural affection God says is totally wrong and needs to be rejected, and, because men and women refuse to listen to God, and refuse to forsake this unnatural lifestyle, God has therefore given them over to the unnatural state of mind where they are devoid of natural understanding.

The morality of men and women is now so clouded by this unnatural affection that they go about and practise their lifestyle to such an extent that they are beyond shame. They promote their lifestyle with the feeling of utter 'rightness', that is breathtaking to those who seek to follow God and who seek to follow His ways. Their mind and their judgement is beyond understanding and Paul says that God has allowed them to execute this style of behaviour, but that the end result is utter judgement and punishment. Our prayer should be as a result of what we see around us, 'even so come Lord Jesus'.

KEY PRAYER

Heavenly Father, I look at this rotten world of sin and desperate wickedness and I cry out to you to save those who are lost in a depraved state of mind, and I ask that you would have mercy upon them, and I also pray today with the writer of the book of Revelation, 'even so come Lord Jesus'.

November 14th

KEY WORD: **Depraved mind**

KEY VERSE: **Romans 1 : 28**

Furthermore, since they did not think it worth while to retain the knowledge of God, He gave them over to a depraved mind, to do what ought not to be done.

Paul wrote to the church in Rome and described the kind of attitude of mind that would characterise the last days and that would appear upon earth. He used a very descriptive word to classify these days as being filled by people, whose minds were depraved because God had 'given them over' to the state of mind where they were beyond all common sense and beyond all natural judgement.

The word that is used to describe this kind of attitude is a very interesting one, however, it brings a slight confusion to our English 'westernised' minds. The NIV translates the word as 'depraved' whereas the Old King James Version uses the word 'reprobate'. The Greek word that was used is the word '*adokimos*', which means 'not standing the test'. The word is formed by the combining of two words. Firstly, the word '*a*' which means a negative 'not', and secondly, the word '*dokimos*' which means 'approved'. So we have a word picture formed for us of a people whose mind is 'not approved by God'.

This attitude of mind, Paul says, will characterise the last days on earth, it describes people that God does not approve of, so He has given them over to minds that are devoid of understanding. Yesterday we said that two questions immediately forced themselves to be addressed. Firstly, What caused God to give them over to such a state of mind? Secondly, What is the outcome of such a mind? We attempted to answer the first question yesterday, and today we shall attempt to answer the second one.

The first question concerning 'What caused God to give these people over to a mind devoid of understanding?' produced the clear answer that the lifestyle of those who had left God out of their lives was so unacceptable to Him. These people had forsaken the natural force of love and had turned to lust and the unnatural behaviour of men with men and women with women. The answer to the second question concerning 'What is the outcome of such a mind that is devoid of understanding?' is equally as clear, in that God cannot approve of this lifestyle, so He has given people over to minds that cannot register good and evil. A mind that is devoid of understanding is a mind that finds it impossible to clearly grasp truth and the difference between right and wrong. This outcome is seen in society today.

How many times has it been said that 'punishment seems to be weighed against the innocent,' and that 'the guilty never seem to be punished correctly'? It seems as if we find it impossible to care any more and we find it impossible to act with integrity. This is the clear outcome of a mind that is devoid of natural understanding, caused by a rejection of God, and the abandonment to unnatural behaviour. This kind of thing will get much worse as we get nearer and nearer to the end of the age. The result of this will be that justice will be forsaken and punishment will be forgotten. We should not be surprised at this, as the world is run by people with depraved minds that are devoid of understanding.

As we get nearer to the end of the age this kind of depravity will only get worse. If we think it is bad at present, then we should remember that Jesus said that one of the descriptions of this age would be like the 'days of Sodom and Gomorra'. These days were disgustingly bad, so we can only expect the worst as we get nearer to the end. However, as we shall see tomorrow, things on one hand will get worse, but on the other hand, will get better!

KEY PRAYER

Heavenly Father, I thank you today for the fact that you have granted protection to those who turn to you from depravity. You have promised a mind of perfect peace in contrast to the mind devoid of understanding. Thank you for such great love and thank you for such great mercy.

November 15th

KEY WORD: **Times of refreshing**

KEY VERSE: **Acts 3 : 19-21**

Repent, then, and turn to God, so that your sins may be wiped out, that times of refreshing may come from the Lord, and that He may send the Christ, who has been appointed for you – even Jesus. He must remain in heaven until the time comes for God to restore everything, as He promised long ago through His holy prophets.

Over the next few days we shall begin to conclude our studies in the Signs of the Times. We commenced this study at the beginning of the month, some fourteen days ago. As we conclude we shall look at some of the more positive signs concerning the coming of the Lord.

All of the signs that we have considered so far have been the signs that produce trouble and fear, and hurt and sorrow. Over the next two days we shall consider the signs that produce revival and restoration, and we will see that there will be an amazing contradiction taking place on our planet over the days that remain, and in fact it has already commenced. On one hand the world will get worse and worse and yet on the other hand the Church will get better and better. The days in which we live will get blacker and darker, and yet the last days will also get brighter and clearer. The contradiction is best seen in the comment that 'many shall fall away and yet many shall be gathered.'

Peter was preaching in the key verse today, and He prophetically ministered that God would send 'times of refreshing' before He would send Jesus back to earth. Jesus has to remain in heaven before everything has been restored that needs to be restored. We shall look at the sign that is called 'times of refreshing' today, and we shall conclude the Signs of the Times, by looking at the sign of 'restoration' tomorrow.

Peter said that 'times of refreshing' would come, the Greek phrase for this is *'kairos anapsuxis'*, which means 'a fixed period of cool relief'. What Peter was describing was a period of time when the Holy Spirit would come and bring to the Church, and to the world, a time of cool breezes and refreshment, and that this period would last until Jesus returned from heaven.

These times of refreshing commenced at the day of Pentecost when Peter said that the outpouring of the Holy Spirit, which was prophesied by Joel, was a direct fulfilment of his prophecy that said that 'in the last days God would pour out His Spirit upon all flesh'.

From then, until now, we are seeing this time of refreshing within the world, with almost every nation seeing a unique sense of visitation from God. The outcome of this refreshing is being seen in growth and blessing within the Church, and a visitation of the miraculous.

On one hand it is getting decidedly worse and worse but within the Church things are getting better and better.

My Journal ______________________________

KEY PRAYER

Heavenly Father, I praise you today for the fact that you are visiting your Church afresh and that things are getting better and better. I see a world that is decaying all around me, and I see an age that is getting darker and darker. Yet I also see a time of great blessing and refreshment and I praise you for this amazing contrast of light and darkness.

November 16th

KEY WORD: **Times of refreshing**

KEY VERSE: **Acts 3 : 19-21**

Repent, then, and turn to God, so that your sins may be wiped out, that times of refreshing may come from the Lord, and that He may send the Christ, who has been appointed for you – even Jesus. He must remain in heaven until the time comes for God to restore everything, as He promised long ago through His holy prophets.

Most of the signs that we have considered so far have been the signs that produce trouble and fear, and hurt and sorrow. We are now considering the signs that produce revival and restoration. There will be an amazing contradiction taking place on our planet over the days that remain, and in fact it has already commenced. On one hand the world will get worse and worse and yet, on the other hand, the Church will get better and better. The days in which we live will get blacker and darker, and yet the last days will also get brighter and clearer. Many shall fall away and yet many shall be gathered.

Peter was preaching in the key verse today, and He prophetically ministered that God would send 'times of refreshing' before He would send Jesus back to earth. Jesus has to remain in heaven before everything has been restored that needs to be restored. We looked at the sign that is called the 'times of refreshing' yesterday, and we shall conclude the Signs of the Times, by looking at the sign of 'restoration' today.

Peter said that God was going to 'restore' everything as He promised and he linked this with the promise of the return of Jesus to this world.

The Greek word for 'restore' is the word '*apokatastasis*', which is a very precious word indeed. It means 'putting down again,' and it was taken from the area of finance and accounts, where the bottom line of the financial account would have to balance, and the total would need to be put right. The word is formed by the combination of two words. Firstly, the word *'apo'*, which means to 'go back' or 'again', and, secondly, the word *'kathistemi'*, which means to 'set in order'. The accounting term therefore would literally mean 'balances set in order so that they would not need to be put down again'.

This was a wonderful word and a wonderful concept for Peter to use. He was stating in the key verse that God was going to set everything in order before Jesus would return. He also said that God would create a climate where everything was put right, and where the balance of spiritual accounts would be totalled up to His satisfaction.

Over the past 2000 years the Church has been going through this preparation period, and there is still work to do on the complete restoration of everything that God wants to do. In spite of a world of darkness, where it seems that everything has gone wrong, God is working according to His plan and everything is working according to His time-frame. The world might seem to be 'out of gear' but God is in total control and all is well.

We can thank God today that heaven must contain Jesus until all the 'sums' are right and all the 'totals' are complete. God is producing His accounts and the 'balances' are perfect.

My Journal ______________________________

____

____

____

KEY PRAYER

Heavenly Father, how I praise you today that all things are well with the Church. The world may be in desperate need, and the wicked might seem to prosper, but you are working all things out according to your plan and purpose, and the 'books will balance' in favour of a healthy spiritual profit.

November 17th

KEY WORD: **Pearls**

KEY VERSE: **Matthew 7 : 6**

Do not give dogs what is sacred; do not throw your pearls to pigs.

This key verse today is taken from what is normally known as the Sermon on the Mount and in order to understand what Jesus is saying and doing we have to understand this sermon.

The sermon commenced in Matthew 5, and it says that when Jesus saw the crowds He went up to the top of a mountain and sat down. When He was set in position on the mountain, His disciples came unto Him and He began to teach them. This aspect of just who Jesus was addressing is key to understanding this verse today. Jesus was bringing spiritual truth to the Church, His disciples. He was not teaching the world because the crowds had been left behind at the foot of the mountain.

Spiritual truth therefore is not to be presented to the world but to believers and this verse puts this into perspective by saying that the presentation of spiritual truth to unbelievers is like 'throwing your pearls before pigs'. The Old King James Version puts it even more poetically; it is like 'casting your pearls before swine.'

The Greek word for 'pearls' is the word *'margarites'*, and this word brings even sharper force to the fact that the world cannot receive the truth of God. The word means 'precious gem' or 'pearl of worth', and this word has been passed down to us within the name 'Margaret', which is a very popular name for a female child.

'Precious gem' is what spiritual truth really is, and if it is presented to unbelievers, who are deemed to be 'pigs' within this context, it is unacceptable to them due to the fact that it cannot be understood nor received. I remember walking through Trafalgar Square in London many years ago and being offered a 'gospel tract' which I received with joy, as I thought that the gesture of someone out in the square witnessing like this was a great blessing. I then opened the tract to find that it was an exaltation to be 'filled with the Spirit'. My joy quickly evaporated as I recognised the fact that someone was acting without discernment, and was actually 'throwing pearls before pigs'.

Pigs cannot distinguish between good things and bad, everything is trampled under their feet. As it is with pigs, so it is with the unbeliever. The child of the world cannot receive the things of the Spirit, so to seek to present truth to them is like the casting of a precious gem before a herd of swine.

Even to receive the truth of the gospel an unbeliever has to undergo a work of the Spirit so that conviction of sin might come, and the acceptance of truth might dawn upon them.

Jesus called His disciples away from the crowds so that He might teach them privately. We should therefore spend time with Him alone so that spiritual truth might be learned and applied.

My Journal ____

KEY PRAYER

Heavenly Father, how I praise you today for truth and for spiritual knowledge. I bless you for the fact that I can now receive truth, as you have changed my life from the wallowing in the mire of sin to the soaring in the Spirit of a new life. I praise you for this wonderful change and I bless you for truth received.

November 18th

KEY WORD: **Precious**

KEY VERSE: **2 Peter 1 : 1**

Simon Peter, a servant and apostle of Jesus Christ,
To those who through the righteousness of our God and Saviour Jesus Christ have received a faith as precious as ours...

Yesterday we spent some time considering the whole aspect of casting pearls before swine and we saw and understood that the natural man cannot receive the things of God because they are foreign to him. It is like precious gems being ground underfoot by pigs.

There are many things in the New Testament that are called precious and they have a very important place in the whole concept of the Church.

Peter wrote to the Church concerning precious faith in the key verse today, and he raised the whole concept and level of faith by calling it 'precious'. The Greek word used here for the word 'precious' is the word *'isotimos'*, which means 'of equal honour,' and it is a word that is formed by the combining of two different words. Firstly, the word *'isos'*, which means 'equal' and secondly, the word *'time'*, which means 'costly'. Therefore, the picture being drawn by the combination of these two words is a faith that is 'highly costly and of equal value to the most precious of gems and jewels.'

Peter regarded faith as a highly sought-after commodity and very precious thing, and he sought to raise the whole concept of faith to higher place and a higher realm, by calling it 'very precious'.

There are many words in the Greek language that speak of 'preciousness'. There is a word that means 'very expensive', and it was this word that was used concerning the ointment that a woman brought before Jesus. She poured it over His head and then washed His feet with her tears. Another use of the word 'precious', is the word that depicts the blood of Jesus which means 'very costly and very precious'.

However, the highest and best word for precious is the word concerning our faith. Our faith is more precious than the most costly ointment used for perfume and anointing, and our faith is equally as precious as the blood of Jesus.

The faith that has been nurtured and grown in our lives is something to thank God for each and every day, as it is a most precious and a most wonderful treasure.

My Journal

KEY PRAYER

Heavenly Father, as I think about the faith that has been imparted to my life and the faith that has grown in maturity over the years, I give thanks with a grateful heart and I praise you for faith granted and faith grown, and for faith that is yet to be gained. Help me each day to overcome my feeling of a lack of faith and help me to trust you more.

November 19th

KEY WORD: **Flaming arrows**

KEY VERSE: **Ephesians 6 : 16**

In addition to all this, take up the shield of faith, with which you can extinguish all the flaming arrows of the evil one.

In this key verse today, Paul writes with a very strong and sober warning to the church at Ephesus concerning the fact that they need to be aware of the enemy's plans at all times, and that they need to wear the 'whole armour of God'. This 'armour' is the defensive clothing that God has given to us in order for us to overcome the 'evil one' and his attacks upon us.

Over the next few days we shall study some of the aspects of this armour, and we shall seek to understand just what this armour is and just what it can do.

We shall commence to study this armour by firstly taking a look at what the enemy's attacks look like and, once we have done that, we shall be in a better position to understand the protective armour.

Paul uses a very strong and persistent word when he describes the 'flaming arrows' of the enemy, and it is a word that is only used once in this form in the whole of the New Testament. The Greek word for 'flaming arrows' is the word '*puroomai*', and it means 'to set on fire' or 'to burn up'. The word comes from the root word '*pur*', which means 'fire', and its use here, with the added '*oomai*', gives it a forcefulness that is very strong and very persistent.

The translation ought to be more correctly in English, 'the arrows, the flaming arrows'. The use of the repetition, is because the word is such a strong and forceful one. The Old King James Version uses the words 'fiery darts' in its translation but it still misses the force of the word. What the word seeks to convey is the utter devastation that the enemy can bring, when he fires one of his 'flaming arrows', for they are not just arrows but 'flaming arrows'.

The truth is taken from some of the enemies of the Roman empire who would often attack using arrows dipped in pitch or tar, which would then be set on fire and aimed at the Roman armies and the Roman strongholds. Many attacks would cause utter ruin because the arrows with burning tar or pitch would rain down in their hundreds, and cause fires to breakout with accompanying death and destruction. Paul likened this to the attacks of our enemy who comes against us, quite often, with a whole range of fiery arrows. His determination to cause destruction and ruin is often quite successful, due to the fact that we are not on guard and because we are not carrying the equipment that God has given to us.

Over the next few days we shall see just how vital it is to wear our armour and just how vital it is to be on our guard against the enemy at all times.

My Journal ______________________________

KEY PRAYER

Heavenly Father, I recognise today just how vital it is to be ready at all times, as the enemy's attacks are not always when I expect them. I recognise, too, that I need to watch for these attacks, as they can bring devastation to my life and home and my family. Help me to watch and pray and be prepared for his attacks at all times. Thank you for the armour and the protection that you have given to me so that I can be an overcomer.

November 20th

KEY WORD: **Flaming arrows**

KEY VERSE: **Ephesians 6 : 16**

In addition to all this, take up the shield of faith, with which you can extinguish all the flaming arrows of the evil one.

Yesterday we commenced to study the 'whole armour of God' with its protection and its value for helping us to become overcomers in the battle that rages against us. Our enemy 'Satan' comes with great force against us and uses the weapons that can only be described as 'flaming arrows' of destruction. We can stand against these weapons with our God-given armour and by watching at all times for these attacks.

Paul uses the analogy of the Roman army for his description of the weapons that God has given to us, and there is none more descriptive than the 'shield of faith'. The Greek word that is used here for 'shield of faith' is the phrase '*thureos pistis*', which means literally, 'faith shield'. The word '*thureos*' is an interesting word as it had two meanings: it firstly meant 'a stone for closing a cave', and then it had a second meaning which was 'a large oblong piece of metal'. This second meaning came to be the main meaning. The Romans used the 'large oblong piece of metal' for the way in which they formed their shields. The shields were interlocked at the sides and curved at the top and were at least seven or eight feet high. This shield would grant full and complete protection against the 'flaming arrows' of the enemy. The Roman soldiers would march in formation with the '*thureos*' locked together at the sides and curved over the top. The enemy would see them coming like a huge metal wall advancing towards them.

Paul used the second word '*pistis*' as well, which means 'faith', which gave the full truth of this shield as a 'shield of faith'.

This phrase conveyed to the Church the fact that we need to block the enemy's attacks by using the shield of faith as a kind of 'faith wall'. This shield is enough for our own protection and, when we link it together with the faith of others, the Church becomes stronger and our faith rises higher. Whichever way you use this word, whether it is used for the 'stone against the cave', or the 'large oblong piece of metal', the force of the word is fully conveyed. It means 'full protection'.

When we carry this shield with us, and when we stand on guard at all times, we have a sense of full protection from anything that the enemy would aim at us. It is when we lower our guard and become careless that the 'flaming arrows' have an opportunity to find their target. Keeping the shield up at all times affords protection, and when we link it with the shields of those around us, we protect each other.

There was one other very important aspect of this shield with its accompanying armour, there was no armour given for the back of the Roman soldier. All the armour was given as a 'frontal' protection, and the shield then added its protection too. The soldier's armour was only to protect the front of him, there was nothing given for his back, which meant that a Roman soldier could never retreat or turn round. The battle that we are in is one of victory and advance, there is no turning back and no retreat. With the armour on and with the shield in place, we press on to final victory.

KEY PRAYER

Heavenly Father, I praise you today for the fact that final victory is assured for us, we may lose a few battles here and there along the way, but we will not lose the war. Thank you for the shield that you have a granted to me and thank you for the shields of others. Help me at all times to raise my shield high and to press forward and onward and upward.

November 21st

KEY WORD: **Helmet of salvation**

KEY VERSE: **Ephesians 6 : 14, 15, 17**

Stand firm then, with the belt of truth buckled round your waist, with the breastplate of righteousness in place, and with your feet fitted with the readiness that comes from the gospel of peace. Take the helmet of salvation and the sword of the Spirit, which is the Word of God.

Today we commence to study the actual 'armour of God' having looked so far at the 'flaming arrows' of the enemy, and the protection that we are granted when we use the 'shield of faith'. There are four main parts to the body armour that the Roman soldiers would use and they would also carry with them their shield and sword. Paul likens the spiritual armour to the physical armour of Rome, which would carry a mental picture to the Church, as everyone knew exactly the kind of armour that the Roman soldier would use.

We shall look at the four parts of the body armour from the top to the bottom, which is a different order to the one that Paul gives us in the key verse today.

Paul challenged the Church to wear the first part of the armour when he said to them that they were to 'put on the helmet of salvation'. This phrase was a very unique one as it brought to the Church a very clear understanding of what was required of each and every church member. The Greek phrase was '*perikephalaia soteria*', which meant 'salvation around the head'.

The word '*perikephalaia*', is a word that is formed by the combining of two Greek words, firstly the word '*peri*', which means 'around', and secondly '*kephale*', which means 'the head'. The combination of these two words brought about the picture of 'the head being protected'. With the use of the word '*soteria*' being added to it, the full truth and meaning of Paul's words came into focus, it conveyed the truth of 'the head being protected by salvation'.

The Roman helmet was a heavy and protective piece of armour, it covered the head and the face and it afforded to the soldier the total protection of his head. This helmet was used by Paul to convey the thought that our 'spiritual heads' need to be protected at all times. Our mind is a very active one and can lead us into trouble if we are not prepared. The helmet, a figurative term for spiritual guard, must be worn constantly so that when thoughts and imaginations rise within our minds we would have our 'head protected by salvation'. The washing of God's Word and the cleansing of our minds by the Spirit will grant to us the possibility of being clean in thought and deed, if we wear the helmet.

The 'flaming arrows' of the enemy will find a resting place in the fertile soil of the imagination of our minds, if the helmet is discarded, or casually left aside. Paul's words are not optional words, they carry with them an 'imperative'. We must wear the armour and we must wear the helmet.

My Journal

KEY PRAYER

Heavenly Father, I praise you today for the total possibility of victory in our minds, because as we wear the helmet that you have provided for us, we have the fertile soil of our minds under guard. Thank you for the helmet that you have provided for us and thank you too for its protection.

November 22nd

KEY WORD: **Breastplate of righteousness**

KEY VERSE: **Ephesians 6 : 14, 15, 17**

Stand firm then, with the belt of truth buckled round your waist, with the breastplate of righteousness in place, and with your feet fitted with the readiness that comes from the gospel of peace. Take the helmet of salvation and the sword of the Spirit, which is the Word of God.

A few days ago we commenced our studies in the actual 'Armour of God' and we have looked so far at the 'flaming arrows' of the enemy, and the protection that we are granted when we use the 'shield of faith', and we have also considered the 'helmet of salvation'. There are four main parts to the body armour that the Roman soldiers would use and they would also carry with them their sword as well as their shield. Paul likens the spiritual armour to the physical armour of Rome, which would carry a mental picture to the Church, as everyone knew exactly the kind of armour that the Roman soldier would use.

The second part of the armour that Paul urged the Church to wear is the 'breastplate of righteousness' for the protection for the front of the body and in particular 'the heart'. The Greek phrase that he used was a very clear and descriptive one, he wrote that the Church must wear the '*thorax dikaiosune*', which meant the 'the corset of righteousness'. It is obvious that we derive our word 'thorax' from this Greek word, and we use it to describe the throat and the front part of the upper torso. Paul linked the word with '*dikaiosune*', which means 'righteousness', to describe the fact that our heart and other vital organs and upper torso must be protected by truth and wholeness.

The breastplate would cover the aspect of throat and shoulders and would reach right down to the waist; this protection would mean that the heart, above all, was covered. Linking it with truth and righteousness, Paul stated that the heart should be protected with truth.

The Greek word '*thorax*' literally meant 'the corset', and it was a piece of metal that consisted of two parts, it covered the front and the sides of the upper torso and it was often referred to as the 'coat of mail'. This term was used for the full protection of the body and it found its way into medieval use, as armour wearers would often be referred to as wearing a 'coat of mail'.

Paul urged the Church to wear this part of the armour, as the heart is considered to be the main organ of the natural body, and the main organ of the spiritual body. The heart is also the 'seat' of man and it is from the heart that, before salvation, sin and wickedness would emanate. Following salvation, the heart would be considered as the dwelling place of the Lord, although nowhere in Scriptures do we find the words that we are to 'ask Jesus into our heart'. This has become a Church phrase that is rather sentimental and not entirely Scriptural, as we do not 'ask Jesus into our heart', but we ask Him to become Lord of our lives. However, the heart is still regarded as the 'seat of the body'.

Paul's words are urgent and true, we must put on the breastplate of righteousness every day of our lives or else our heart becomes vulnerable and exposed.

My Journal ________________________________

____

____

____

KEY PRAYER

Heavenly Father, how I praise you today for the fact that you have made it possible for me to be fully protected against the enemy, and that you have given to me everything necessary for my protection. Thank you Lord for your goodness and grace, and your desire to see me grow into a strong soldier and become mature in the battle of the Lord.

November 23rd

KEY WORD: **Belt of truth**

KEY VERSE: **Ephesians 6 : 14, 15, 17**

Stand firm then, with the belt of truth buckled round your waist, with the breastplate of righteousness in place, and with your feet fitted with the readiness that comes from the gospel of peace. Take the helmet of salvation and the sword of the Spirit, which is the Word of God.

Several days ago we commenced our studies in the actual 'armour of God' and we have looked so far at the 'flaming arrows' of the enemy, and the protection that we are granted when we use the 'shield of faith'. We have also considered the 'helmet of salvation' and the 'breastplate of righteousness'. There are four main parts to the body armour that the Roman soldiers would use and they would also carry with them a sword as well as their shield. Paul likens the spiritual armour to the physical armour of Rome, which would carry a mental picture to the Church, as everyone knew exactly the kind of armour that the Roman soldier would use.

The third part of the body armour that Paul urged the Church to wear was the 'belt of truth', and once again he used an interesting Greek phrase to convey the kind of armour that the Roman soldiers would be wearing. The words that he used were '*osphus perizonnumi aletheia*'. The phrase was translated in the following way. Firstly, for this 'belt of truth', Paul used the word '*osphus*' which meant 'the seat of generative power'. Secondly, he used the word '*perizonnumi*', which meant to 'gird yourself for service', and lastly, he used the word '*aletheia*', which meant 'manifested matter.' The full meaning that Paul was seeking to convey was quite a mouthful, in that the soldier was to 'prepare himself for service by holding on to the full manifested truth of God, so that his seat of generative power was fully protected'. This was quite a full sentence to convey, but he did it using the clearest Greek words that he could.

The 'belt of truth' was hung around the waist and on this belt hung the sword and the dagger, and the pouch in which personal belongings could be stored. Paul used this phrase 'belt of truth' as the phrase for full protection of the loins, the Old King James Version actually uses the term 'loins girt about with truth'. The loins were regarded as the 'seat of generative power' and regarded as needing protection, therefore Paul brought this injunction to guard the loins and to protect them, so that the future might be assured. The belt was also regarded at the custodian of the weapons, as they hung from it, therefore Paul urged that the belt should be worn at all times so that a kind of 'readiness for action' was ensured.

The Church should therefore hold itself ready for action and advance at all times, and it should also guard itself for the destiny for which God had prepared it.

The loins were also regarded by the Greeks as the stability of power, or the seat of power. The waist and the upper legs were the symbols of balance and of bracing oneself. Without the stability of the upper legs the whole body would become vulnerable, and it would lose its sense of balance and its sense of bracing. Therefore Paul uses this analogy as well, to teach the importance of truth as a symbol of balance and bracing, so that the Church might stand firm.

KEY PRAYER

Heavenly Father, today I praise you for truth that has kept me firm in the faith, and for the fact that truth braces my life. Thank you for the belt of truth that houses the weapons of my warfare. Help me at all times to wear it with care, so that I might be ready to advance in your kingdom and to be ready for action at all times.

November 24th

KEY WORD: **The gospel of peace**

KEY VERSE: **Ephesians 6 : 14, 15, 17**

Stand firm then, with the belt of truth buckled round your waist, with the breastplate of righteousness in place, and with your feet fitted with the readiness that comes from the gospel of peace. Take the helmet of salvation and the sword of the Spirit, which is the Word of God.

Several days ago we commenced our studies in the actual 'armour of God' and we have having looked so far at the 'flaming arrows' of the enemy and the protection that we are granted when we use the 'shield of faith' and we have also considered three parts of the armour. There are four main parts to the body armour that the Roman soldiers would use and then they would also carry with them their shield and their sword. Paul likens the spiritual armour to the physical armour of Rome, which would carry a mental picture to the Church, as everyone knew exactly the kind of armour that the Roman soldier would use.

Paul urged each soldier in the Church to make sure that their 'feet were fitted with the gospel of peace', which is the last part of the armour, and in the use of this phrase he brought a very creative lesson to the people of God, as he described this final piece of the 'armour of God'.

The Greek phrase that he used was the phrase '*pous hupodeo euangelion eirene*'. These words were linked together to form a beautiful phrase that was very clear and very descriptive. The four words were understood in this way. Firstly, '*pous*', which meant 'in motion', and it was the word that was used to describe the action of the foot. Secondly, the word '*hupodeo*', which meant the 'binding underneath', and it was the word that was used for the binding of sandals. Thirdly, the word '*euangelion*', which was the word that was used for the 'good tidings of the gospel message' and lastly, the word '*eirene*', which was regarded in the New Testament as the natural word for 'harmony and peace'. If we link the four words together with their natural meanings, you would form the sentence 'feet in action, bound underneath with the good tidings of harmony'.

Paul used this lovely phrase to describe the protection of the soldiers' feet in battle, and the possibility that the soldier would have of advancing in combat, bringing the victory for his Empire, and the message that this victory would convey to a watching world.

Another place in the Bible states that the 'feet that bring good news' are considered to be 'beautiful', so we have the thought that the gospel is a message of hope and peace being borne on beautiful feet of action. We also have the thought conveyed to us that the feet of soldiers in action are undergirded by a strong binding, that affords protection to the wearer. Therefore the gospel message is not just conveyed as peace and harmony but it is also a protecting force against harm and danger.

If we wear the sandals of protection in our march towards victory we will be assured of protection against anything that might threaten our march forward. Our battle cry ought to be 'onward and upward' towards victory.

My Journal

KEY PRAYER

Heavenly Father, as I have read about the final piece of armour I praise you again for the provision that you have made for us on our journey through life. We are in a battle each day and you have granted to us final victory with clothing to protect us in this fight. Help me each day to wear my armour so that the flaming arrows of the enemy will not halt my progress.

November 25th

KEY WORD: **Sword of the Spirit**

KEY VERSE: **Ephesians 6 : 14, 15, 17**

Stand firm then, with the belt of truth buckled round your waist, with the breastplate of righteousness in place, and with your feet fitted with the readiness that comes from the gospel of peace. Take the helmet of salvation and the sword of the Spirit, which is the Word of God.

Several days ago we commenced our studies in the actual 'armour of God' and we have looked so far at the 'flaming arrows' of the enemy and the protection that we are granted with the 'shield of faith' and several other parts of the armour. There were four main parts to the body armour that the Roman soldiers would use and they also carried with them their sword and their shield. We have studied each and every part of the armour and we have noticed that Paul likens the spiritual armour to the physical armour of Rome. This comparison would carry a mental picture to the Church, as everyone knew exactly the kind of armour that the Roman soldier would use.

As we conclude our studies within the 'armour of God' we shall consider the only 'attack weapon' that was carried, the sword. Every other part of the body armour was regarded as being protective, the helmet, the breastplate, the belt, the sandals and, of course, there was the shield. All of these were used for covering and protection in the battle. The sword, however, was not for protection nor was it simply a weapon for defence, although it had excellent defensive capabilities, it was the only part of the armour that was given for outright attack and forward use.

The Greek phrase that Paul used to describe this weapon was '*machaira pneuma*', and the literal meaning of these two words was quite simple and readily understood. Firstly, he used the word *'machaira'*, which meant 'short dagger' or 'short sword', and it conveyed the thought of the Roman sword, which was very short and razor sharp, and had two edges rather than the normal type of short dagger which had only one sharp edge. The second word was *'pneuma'*, which was the usual New Testament word for 'breath' or 'wind' and it denoted the 'Spirit of God'.

The Roman sword was not a 'swashbuckling' type of instrument as portrayed by French swordsmen and medieval fencers of long ago. The Roman sword was for hand-to-hand combat which would take place in the thickest of the battle, and at the hottest part of the action. Paul used this weapon to describe just what the action would be in the spiritual warfare of our lives. We need the 'sword of the Spirit' in order to cut through the attacks of the enemy, and to advance in the kingdom when the battle is at its worst. Two edges are needed in the cut and thrust of battle, as attacks can come from all sides, and we need on one hand to defend ourselves from temptation, and on the other hand to advance through the enemy's lines with great haste.

The Spirit of God is with us and aids us at all times, He is our defender and He is our victory. In Him we have the perfect weapon to overcome the enemy and to take ground.

Paul also had in mind when he wrote concerning the 'sword of the Spirit', what we now call today our 'Bible' or the 'Word of God'. As we use the Scriptures against the enemy, the power of the Word blunts his attacks and gives us the ability to move forward in the power of the Spirit.

KEY PRAYER

Heavenly Father, as we have come to the end of our studies in the 'armour of God', I praise you for all that you have done and for all that you have given to me to make my walk with you a walk of victory and a walk of joy. I praise you for the battles that I have already come through and even for the ones that I have yet to fight, as I know that with you and the armour I am an overcomer.

November 26th

KEY WORD: **Prayers and requests**

KEY VERSE: **Ephesians 6 : 18**

And pray in the Spirit on all occasions with all kinds of prayers and requests. With this in mind, be alert and always keep praying for all the saints.

Yesterday we concluded our studies in the whole 'armour of God' and we have looked at each part of the armour and its various meanings and uses. As Paul drew towards the conclusion of his writings to the Ephesian church, he gave a few warnings about praying and prayer ministry that are vital for us to understand. We can wear the whole 'armour of God' and we can carry our swords and shields and still not be ready for action and still not be prepared for warfare. Paul stated that the 'armour of God' ought to be worn, but that we should also 'pray in the Spirit' so that we are in a constant state of readiness and a constant state of preparedness for action.

Paul said that we were to 'pray in the Spirit' with all kinds of 'prayer and requests', the NIV uses this particular translation to try and help us understand what Paul is seeking to convey. However, in its attempt to help us to understand, it has caused a little confusion. Paul is not talking about 'prayer requests', as you would have in a normal kind of prayer meeting when the leader asks 'are there any requests for prayer?' When the leader says this, he is meaning, 'what are the prayer items' or 'who has requested special prayer?' The Old King James Version tries even harder to help us understand what Paul is seeking to convey, when it translates this key verse as 'prayer and supplication', which actually gets a little closer to the truth.

The two Greek words that Paul used in the key verse today are the words '*proseuche*' and '*deesis*'. The words mean firstly, 'fervent prayer' or 'the place of prayer', and secondly, 'entreating' or 'a great need'. The force of the words is in the fact that Paul used them together as opposed to using them separately. If they were used on their own or separately the force would not be there, but linking them together in this way, it is like a 'hammer blow'.

Paul was literally saying that now the Church is wearing its armour, it must 'pray with fervency and force and must stay in the place of prayer'. At the beginning of the year, in January, we studied just how vital prayer is, and just how vital prayer was, to the Church, and to each believer. Now Paul is saying even more that prayer must be sustained with great force at all times.

Sadly, in Church life today the 'prayer meeting' is often the weakest meeting of the week and the least attended of all meetings. Sadly, too, it is often the weakest meeting due the lack of fervency and passion. It is one thing to wear the armour but it is another thing altogether to sustain prayer and to keep on praying. Paul's urgency must be felt and his warning must be obeyed.

My Journal

KEY PRAYER

Heavenly Father, I have been praising you for the whole 'armour of God', but now I ask your forgiveness for my prayerlessness and my lack of urgency in the whole area of prayer and supplication. Help me to begin today to pray more, and help me to pray without ceasing.

November 27th

KEY WORD: **Alert**

KEY VERSE: **Ephesians 6 : 18**

And pray in the Spirit on all occasions with all kinds of prayers and requests. With this in mind, be alert and always keep praying for all the saints.

Today is our final look at this key verse, with its forcefulness upon praying and continuing to pray. Paul has listed for us the weapons and the protective aspects of the whole 'armour of God', and he has brought the injunction to us to keep on praying.

The final aspect of his words are that we are to 'stay alert' at all times, even when we are wearing the whole 'armour of God', and even when we are experiencing victories. Wearing the armour is not enough nor is the aspect of praying without ceasing. It is the armour, plus prayer, plus alertness, that will bring final and complete victory.

The Greek word that Paul uses to convey the thought of alertness is the word '*agrupneo*', which is a very interesting word. The usual word for being watchful or alert is the word '*phulake*', which means setting 'a guard', but Paul ignored this usual word and wrote to the Ephesian church that they were to '*agrupneo*' which means 'to be sleepless' or 'to chase'.

The word is formed by the combining of two Greek words, firstly, the word '*agreuo*', which means 'to chase', and secondly, the word '*hupnos*', which means 'to sleep'. So the meaning becomes in this context, 'to not allow sleep to come, but to chase it away so that you can pray.'

Two things always happen when you set yourself to pray. Firstly, your mind starts to wander to all the things that you have not done, and to all the things that you need to do. Secondly, you begin to feel weary and you begin to need some sleep, this happened to the disciples in the Garden of Gethsemane, and Jesus had to rebuke them by saying, 'could you not watch with me for one hour?'

Paul's use of this word was to introduce the theme of physical action in the 'chasing away' of sleep so that the believers might stay at prayer and continue to pray. Prayer is not always easy, and probably none of us finds it simple, it is a battle and it needs concentration. It also needs direct action in the whole area of discipline so that, when sleep wants to assert itself, we actually force sleep out of our minds.

This word occurs four times in this form in the New Testament and on each occasion it is used in the context of being watchful and staying awake, and being intent upon what you are doing. Therefore, the teaching is very clear and unmistakeable, stay awake, concentrate upon prayer and dismiss the whole idea of resting and sleeping until you have broken through and claimed your victory.

My Journal

KEY PRAYER

Heavenly Father, I praise you for the Word of God today that urges me to pray, I receive this Word and I seek to apply it to the spiritual actions of warfare. Help me to learn how to pray and help me, too, to set my mind to pray without ceasing.

November 28th

KEY WORD: **War**

KEY VERSE: **2 Corinthians 10 : 3–4**

For though we live in the world we do not wage war as the world does. The weapons we fight with are not the weapons of the world. On the contrary they have divine power to demolish strongholds.

Yesterday we concluded our studies in the whole 'armour of God' and having spent about nine days in total considering them, we are now well acquainted with each aspect of the body armour that Paul described. Paul cleverly described and detailed the Roman armour and used it as a comparison in his attempt to acquaint the Church with its spiritual armour. The Roman force and Roman soldiers populated Israel at the time of the birth of the Church, and their armour and their ways were very well known.

Rome had conquered every known country and nation and had become the 'world empire' of its day and generation. The Roman force had control over every aspect of daily life and therefore they were an obvious illustration for Paul to use, in order to describe much about armour and warfare, and the whole aspect of conquering and being an overcomer.

The Greek words for war and warfare that are used in the New Testament, are very descriptive words and very clear words, and they produce a picture in our minds that is easy to understand. The Greek word that is used in the key verse today is the word *'strateuo'*, which means 'to make war', and it is formed by the root word *'stratos'*, which means 'an encamped army'. We derive our English word 'strategy' from this root word and our word means more about the plans and tactics of war and warfare than the actual battle itself, which is exactly what *'stratos'* meant. The army would be 'encamped' and would be making itself ready for war, the commanders would be detailing the plans and the tactics to the foot soldiers and each battalion would have its own strategy.

No army went to war without planning and thought, and no army would risk fighting without clear strategies. The Romans were very clever at planning warfare, which is why they became the 'world empire'. This was not achieved without clear plans. Paul used the physical concepts of their body armour to teach about spiritual protection and he used the whole picture of physical plans and tactics to teach about spiritual strategies.

The Church is engaged in a spiritual battle at all times and therefore it needs its body armour and its protective help, and it also needs the help of plans and strategies for the possibility of overcoming the enemy.

Paul said in the key verse that we do not fight with earthly weapons, and that our weapons have great potential because they have their origins in divine agencies. He also stated that our weapons have the incredible potential of the demolishing of strongholds. As we draw to an end in this month's studies we shall consider what a stronghold really is, so that we understand just what Paul is seeking to convey. However, for now, it is good enough to know that there is no power that can stand against us and that we are overcomers.

We are a conquering army and we are a force that can bring down strongholds.

KEY PRAYER

Heavenly Father, I praise you today for the amazing fact that I am part of an army that is victorious and that is marching on. Thank you for the plans and strategies that you have granted to us for the pulling down of strongholds and for the truth that the battle is the Lord's.

November 29th

KEY WORD: **Strongholds**

KEY VERSE: **2 Corinthians 10 : 3-4**

For though we live in the world, we do not wage war as the world does. The weapons we fight with are not the weapons of the world. On the contrary, they have divine power to demolish strongholds.

Yesterday we studied together the amazing fact that we are overcomers in the Lord and that there are plans and tactics granted to the Church for victory. God has set in the Church the strategies for total victory, all that we have to do is implement them.

There are four Greek words for 'war' that are detailed within the New Testament and they all relate to a different aspect of war and warfare. We saw yesterday that one of the words related to the whole question of plans and tactics, which are vital in the whole question of the battle.

The main Greek word for the fighting aspect of war is the word *'polemeo'*, which means 'to fight', and it was the word that was used for the actual hand-to-hand combat, and the struggle that ensues when an army is seeking to overcome an enemy. Our fight is not against flesh and blood, and the weapons that we have are not the weapons of this world. Our fight is a spiritual one and our weapons are therefore spiritual weapons.

The reason for our battle is quite clear, in that Paul states that the intention of our fight is to demolish strongholds, and to release the Church and this world from the oppression of the enemy. Paul used the Greek word *'ochuroma'* to describe the kind of fierce battle that we face against these strongholds, as he was seeking to convey the fact that we do not face an ordinary enemy. Our enemy has set up strongholds that need to be demolished before we can gain ground and overcome. The word that he used brings this truth into sharp focus as it means 'fortress' or 'strong place', as the word has its roots in the Greek word *'ochuroo'*, which means 'to make firm'.

The Old Testament concept of a stronghold was the fortified city of an enemy which were normally constructed upon high ground or hills. There was usually immense walls built around these cities that were erected upon hills, and they were very difficult to penetrate and extremely difficult to overcome. Medieval castles were constructed in the same way and in the same locations. You can see this when you visit an ancient site or city, as some of the immense walls still stand unto this day. In order to achieve victory you would need clear strategies and you would need strong men that were skilled in fighting to overcome a stronghold. Paul says that with the right weapons and the right plans, and with divine power, the Church is capable of clear victory even to the demolishing of the biggest and greatest stronghold that the enemy has.

My Journal ____

____

____

____

____

____

____

____

____

KEY PRAYER

Heavenly Father, thank you for victory and the possibility of outright success in the demolishing of Satan's strongholds. I praise you for the fact that you have granted to us the weapons of warfare, and the plans that we need to face any spiritual obstacle that stands in our way. The Church is a victorious army and it is marching on to war.

November 30th

KEY WORD: **Soldier**

KEY VERSE: **2 Timothy 2 : 3**

Endure hardship with us like a good soldier of Christ Jesus.

On this last day of the month we shall consider one last aspect of armour and warfare, that of being a soldier in the army of the Lord. We have spent the last eleven days thinking and praying about being in a battle, and we have considered the armour and the battle and we have considered the whole question of our weapons and strongholds. On this last day of the month we shall conclude these studies by considering the aspect of our place in the army of the Lord.

Each one of us is a soldier in the army of the Lord, we often sing about this in hymns and praise songs, but it is more important that we understand our place in the army than it is to sing about it. Paul wrote to Timothy in the key verse today calling him a 'good soldier'.

Paul used the Greek word '*strateuo*' in order to convey what he was thinking regarding Timothy, and what he was thinking about the Church. A few days ago we looked at a 'near relative' to this word when we were seeking to understand the concept of warfare and the plans and strategies that are needed for success. The word '*strateuo*' means 'men who war' and it has roots in the concept of not just the fighting of a battle but it has its concept in the whole area of understanding what we are doing.

Foot soldiers normally do not know the plans and tactics, they are just sent out to fight. They normally know that the 'ridge' in front of them needs to be 'won', and they know that holding a particular bridge is vital in the overall plan of the war campaign. What they do not know is that the ridge that they are seeking to win, or the bridge that they are seeking to hold, is part of a bigger plan or a wider picture. Troop reinforcements and supplies are waiting to be brought over the bridge, or a major initiative is planned, once the 'ridge' is taken. This is part of the bigger picture that is known to the commanders and the leaders of the war. The foot soldiers just obey orders, and the leaders have to lead. The word that is used for the word 'soldier' is not the word for a simple 'foot soldier', who does not know the bigger picture. It is the word that is used for the concept of the 'Church soldier' fighting a battle that it knows it will win, because God is on our side and the final book of the Bible reveals victory. The New Testament soldier is not fighting blindly, but is fighting with a clear insight into final and complete victory.

The word is also used for the fight and the service that the soldier undertakes during his period of service. This is the word that is normally used for the whole aspect of going to war as a true soldier, this is why Paul said to Timothy that the service may at times be hard. However he was encouraged by Paul to endure this as a 'good soldier'. We are promised victory but we are not promised an easy path. We have been called to endure to the end and we have been called to be faithful. We will win and we will overcome because God has said so, and the book of Revelation reveals a triumphant Church.

My Journal ____

KEY PRAYER

Heavenly Father, as I come to the end of another month and another series of studies, I recognise the fact that you have called me to be a soldier in the greatest army of all time, the army of the Lord. Help me to be a good soldier and a faithful soldier even to the end, so that I might glorify your name.

December 1st

KEY WORD: ***Agreement***

KEY VERSE: ***Matthew 18 : 19***

I tell you that if two of you on earth agree about anything you ask for, it will be done for you by my Father in heaven.

On this first day of the last month of the year, what better way of commencing could there be than to remind ourselves that unity is the greatest asset that we have within the Church. Unless there is agreement and accord, the Church does not function in power and unity, or, to put it another way, division is the enemy's greatest weapon. If he can sow seeds of division the Church becomes powerless.

We are introduced to a very beautiful thought in Matthew 18, that of full agreement. Jesus was teaching on relationships in this chapter and sought to explain to His Church that unity is the greatest asset. Matthew 18 opens with the thought that we must enter childlike into the kingdom, as the kingdom is only granted to those who humble themselves in this way.

Following this teaching, Jesus talks about the lost sheep, with the major message that all are vital in the kingdom, and that a major search will be conducted, even for one that is lost.

Following the words of Jesus concerning the lost sheep, He commences to talk about unity. Unity is discussed in this chapter by the introducing of just how Church discipline should be handled, bringing us to the place of power in prayer and fellowship. Jesus used the word 'agreement', which at first sight almost suggests that if we get two or three people who agree on an issue to pray, then anything can happen and prayer will be answered. If this is the case why are there seemingly unanswered prayers, and why are people not healed immediately if only two or three people need to agree 'on anything'? Either this message is not true or we fail to understand the depth of meaning of the word 'agree'. The Greek word used in this key verse is the word '*sumphoneo*', which literally translated means 'to sound together', and is primarily used of musical instruments. We derive our word 'symphony' from this Greek word.

Jesus was not talking about agreement on an issue but agreement in relationship.

Relationships should be like an orchestra, everyone in unity, all playing from the same sheet of music, all in the same key producing a wonderful sound of harmony, beauty and symphony – music to the ears. An 'out of tune' orchestra can only produce a sound of division and pain.

It is not just a question of finding two or three people who might agree with you on an issue, but it's a question of finding two or three people who will have a heart with you, and who will walk with you through pain and who will agree with you in relationship. The Billy Graham organisation caught the impact of harmony and beauty when they introduced 'prayer triplets' into their system of forward crusade planning. This concept was one of finding three people who would meet, not just to pray over an agreed issue, but that these three people would meet together, pray together and cultivate an harmonious relationship. The success of this venture has passed the test of time, prayer triplets work.

As God walks with us and we walk with Him there is the sound of agreement, a symphony of sweet sound. Then, as we walk with others in relationship, the same symphonic sounds are created. On this first day of the last month of an old year we should make a resolve to be part of a new orchestra playing a new sound of praise.

KEY PRAYER

Heavenly Father, please help me today and throughout this last month of the year to produce a sound of harmony in my relationships. Please allow me to become a sweet sound of symphony with those around me and allow me to cultivate my relationships in such a way that pleases you, and brings delight to others and that produces power within the Church.

December 2nd

KEY WORD: **Open**

KEY VERSE: **Matthew 3 : 16-17**

As soon as Jesus was baptised, He went up out of the water. At that moment heaven was opened, and He saw the Spirit of God descending like a dove and lighting on Him. And a voice from heaven said, "This is my Son, whom I love; with Him I am well pleased."

The baptism of Jesus was an extraordinary event, and was actually recorded by three of the Gospel writers, and then mentioned by the fourth. John writes about it as a major fact of the ministry of Jesus, but Matthew, Mark and Luke record the whole scene as it took place.

There are, however, slight differences in their approach and language, as they seek to convey what was happening. As this is important, we shall spend a few days considering several aspects of the scene of the baptism. We know that Jesus was fully and completely immersed in the waters of the Jordan as the Greek word for 'baptism' is '*baptizo*', which means 'to dip' or 'to dye', and we studied this word in June. The root of this word conveys the fact that something, a piece of cloth or a garment, had to be immersed in a dye, in order for it to receive a new colour.

Once Jesus had been baptised in the waters of Jordan's river, He made His way back to the riverbank and then saw heaven 'opened' unto Him. Matthew, Mark and Luke all agree on the fact that heaven became open, but they do not agree on the way in which it was opened. Matthew and Luke use the Greek word '*anoigo*' to describe this event, while Mark chooses the Greek word '*schizo*', to describe the opening of heaven.

The two different words produce something that is slightly different in the way that this event was perceived. Matthew and

Luke say that 'heaven was opened up like a door', as the word *'anoigo'* means to 'open like a door'. It was the word that was used when someone was opening a door or a gate or even a grave. It was the word that was used when the sepulchre was opened up, following the resurrection of Jesus. It produced the feeling of openness and freedom, where once there was a closed door. This is how Matthew and Luke viewed the scene. Their awareness was such that, as they saw Jesus come out of the water, their attention was drawn to the heavens, and the spectacular sight of a doorway opening in the sky to reveal the dove-like form of the Holy Spirit.

Mark however, saw something far more dramatic, he used the word *'schizo'* to describe this event. This word meant 'to tear' or 'to split', and was translated in his gospel with the great force of the word 'torn' being added to the fact that 'heaven was opened'. Mark felt that the action of the open heaven was far greater than simply a door being opened, he felt as if he was watching the tearing open of heaven, or the splitting of the skies. Maybe Mark was more sensitive in his viewing of the event, or maybe he was more attuned in the Spirit at that moment. Whatever it was, this event was viewed by him as being much more dramatic than a simple opening up of a doorway into the sky.

There are times when people can sit in the same congregation and feel differently about the same event. The moving of God's Spirit can be seen as a dramatic event by some people, and a fairly ordinary event by others. It all can depend upon perception and upon 'where you are in God' at that moment. It is so easy to be 'in the Spirit' at one moment and 'in the flesh' the next. It is also quite natural for some people to see something as dramatic, while others witness the same event and become far less impacted by it.

However, the important lesson to learn is that we see what we are supposed to see, because it is vital that we do not miss the moving of God, and it is vital that we are 'in the Spirit' at all times.

KEY PRAYER

Heavenly Father, I bless you today for the fact that you have made it possible for me to be 'in the Spirit'. Help me not to miss the event whenever you move upon a congregation, and help me always to be aware of what is happening around me.

December 3rd

KEY WORD: **Descending**

KEY VERSE: **Matthew 3 : 16-17**

As soon as Jesus was baptised, He went up out of the water. At that moment heaven was opened, and He saw the Spirit of God descending like a dove and lighting on Him. And a voice from heaven said, "This is my Son, whom I love; with Him I am well pleased."

A very beautiful word is used within this key verse for the actual way in which the Spirit of God came down upon Jesus. The actual event was seen as a dove-like form, 'descending' from heaven and resting upon Jesus. The word 'descending' is a translation of the Greek word *'katabaino'*, which means 'to go down', which in itself does not seem to be very important. However, the word is derived from the combination of two root words. The two root words are firstly the word *'kata'* which means 'to go down', and secondly the word *'baino'* which means 'to go'. As this particular word was used, it adds a force to the scene which literally means that this dove-like form was sent from heaven in a way that was viewed as being 'sent down and down'. In other words, there was a very strong compulsion by the dove to go down.

Most doves would fly around and around, they are gentle and caring birds, and they would not fly compulsively in a straight line downwards. You only have to watch a dove to notice that it flies in gentle arcs, and at times allows the thermal airwaves to lift it up. This dove-like form however, came 'down and down'. It flew in a straight path, directly from the heavens, on to the physical form of Jesus.

It was as if nothing could, or would, stop the descent of this bird. There was a compulsion that drew this bird from heaven, to Jesus. The Holy Spirit is always seeking to rest upon people, it is as if He looks for a resting place, in order to bring an anointing upon people. The Holy Spirit is attracted to people who walk in obedience, and who seek to act in integrity in everything that they do.

Jesus had been obedient in His decision to be baptised, John the Baptist had tried to deter Him, but Jesus had said that it was 'the right thing to do'. Not only was there obedience in this, but Jesus was also acting with integrity, as He stated that it was right according to the law, in order 'to fulfil all righteousness'.

Once these statements had been made, and once the baptism had taken place, it was as if God could do nothing else but be pleased with His Son, and it was as if the Holy Spirit could do nothing else other than to 'come down and down'. The Spirit of God is attracted to obedience and to integrity and longs to bless the one who acts in this way.

Our prayer today should be: 'Lord help me to act in a way that draws your presence and your anointing down and down upon my life.'

My Journal

KEY PRAYER

Heavenly Father, I do pray today for your anointing and your presence. Help me to walk in obedience and integrity, so that your Spirit is drawn upon my life. Thank you today for the truth that you come down upon a life that is separated unto you by a different lifestyle.

December 4th

KEY WORD: **Lighting**

KEY VERSE: **Matthew 3 : 16-17**

As soon as Jesus was baptised, He went up out of the water. At that moment heaven was opened, and He saw the Spirit of God descending like a dove and lighting on Him. And a voice from heaven said, "This is my Son, whom I love; with Him I am well pleased."

The Holy Spirit came down upon Jesus and rested upon Him in a dove-like form, once He had been baptised. This lovely and dramatic scene had been witnessed by John the Baptist, and he had spoken of it as being the key testimony to the fact that Jesus was the Son of God.

Heaven had been opened and the dove had come down and down to finally rest upon Jesus, and the key verse today states that it had 'lighted' upon Him. The Greek word that was used here was the word '*erchomai*', which meant 'to come', however, there were dozens of Greek words that were translated as 'come'. There were words that would seek to convey the thought of 'coming' as a kind of visitor, and there were words that conveyed the thoughts of 'coming in' and 'coming and going'. There were words that had the thought of 'coming back' and 'coming again'. Over and over again, different words were used that were all translated as the single word, 'come'.

This word '*erchomai*' means 'to come' but it carries with it a much stronger force. It was the word that was used when someone had arrived and was being announced as having arrived. Its literal force should be 'I have come and I have arrived'.

If we use this sense for the particular scene in the River Jordan, we have a greater impact than just a dove-like figure resting upon Jesus.

If we accept that the dove came down and down, and was drawn upon Jesus because of His holy and submissive act of obedience and integrity, then if we add the force of the word 'I have arrived' to the scene, we have a mighty scene to describe.

It was as if the Holy Spirit had signalled a major change in the way that He had been working and anointing. Throughout the Old Testament the Holy Spirit had come down upon prophets, kings and priests, and upon ordinary people at various times. He had come down but He had always withdrawn. It was as if He came upon people for a season or for a reason, and then had withdrawn, in order to come again and again.

At the baptism of Jesus the Holy Spirit was announcing the fact that He had arrived. The symbolic use of the dove and urgency of the word 'erchomai' meant that the Spirit of God had come to rest upon Jesus, and that He was here to stay.

What a beautiful thought to convey, God was so pleased with His Son, that He sent the Holy Spirit to stay and remain upon Him, so that He might carry the anointing throughout His ministry. We can rejoice in that today, and we can rejoice also in the fact that the Spirit of God is still here, having been poured out at Pentecost, He has never left us. He is our constant comforter.

My Journal

KEY PRAYER

Heavenly Father, I thank you today that the Holy Spirit came and that He still remains with us. Help me to appreciate Him more and more, and help me too, to adjust my life of obedience and integrity in such a way that He is pleased to rest upon me and my ministry.

December 5th

KEY WORD: **Pleased**

KEY VERSE: **Matthew 3 : 16-17**

As soon as Jesus was baptised, He went up out of the water. At that moment heaven was opened, and He saw the Spirit of God descending like a dove and lighting on Him. And a voice from heaven said, "This is my Son, whom I love; with Him I am well pleased."

The baptism of Jesus was a very dramatic event with some very significant moments attached to it, as we have seen. The fact that the heavens were torn open to reveal a dove-like form coming down and down upon Jesus was striking. The fact that this dove rested upon Jesus in such a way as to announce the arrival of the Holy Spirit was again quite striking. However, nothing that took place was greater than the next part of the revelation.

Once the symbol of the Spirit had taken residence upon Jesus, there was a voice from heaven saying, 'I am well pleased with my Son'. The fact that the translators had to add the word 'well' to the phrase 'I am pleased' should signal the fact that God was not just pleased, in the sense of being happy or glad. The fact that 'well' had to be added to give it a little impact ought to be noticed and noted.

The Greek word that was used in the key verse today was the word '*eudokeo*', and this word means 'to be highly pleased' or 'to think well of'. The word was formed by the combining of two other words, firstly, the word '*eu*', which means 'well', and secondly, the word '*dokeo*', which means 'to seem good'. When these two words are combined, the force of the feeling of pleasure is conveyed.

God was actually watching from heaven as an event of great magnitude was taking place. His Son was submitting in obedience and integrity to the law of righteousness, and this made His Father's heart so glad. His natural response was one of pleasure and He could nothing else but signal this by the arrival of the dove, and an audible voice from heaven.

God actually stated that He was well-satisfied and found great pleasure in His Son. His statement from heaven revealed the fact that He was exercising the right to express this pleasure, and to stress His resolve to do so.

The same word is used when Jesus speaks about the Church, and about us as individuals. When He speaks about His little flock, He states in Luke 12 : 32 that it is the 'Father's good pleasure to give you the Kingdom'. So we have God saying that He takes pleasure in His Son, and we have God also saying that He takes pleasure in giving His kingdom to His very own flock.

The word *'eudokeo'* was a word that was often found in legal documents. Just before they were accepted and probably stamped with a seal, the bearers or the receivers would express satisfaction or acceptance of the contents. They would also use the word to state that they found pleasure in the contents of the document and that they were satisfied.

The fact that God expresses this kind of pleasure and satisfaction about His Son and about us should cause us great pleasure too, as it with great joy that we rest in this acceptance, and it is with great joy that we are able to come before Him. He delights in us and we delight in Him.

My Journal ______________________________

KEY PRAYER

Heavenly Father, thank you for expressing your pleasure in Jesus and thank you, too, for expressing your pleasure in me. Help me today to be worthy of such an expression and help me, too, to live in such a way that your pleasure always rests upon me.

December 6th

KEY WORD: **Temptation**

KEY VERSE: **Luke 4 : 1-2**

Jesus, full of the Holy Spirit, returned from the Jordan and was led by the Spirit in the desert, where for forty days He was tempted by the devil.

Following the baptism of Jesus we have quite an extraordinary event. For 40 days and 40 nights Jesus was driven into the desert and was tempted by the devil. We often make the mistake of thinking that He only received three temptations during this time. It is true that three temptations were recorded: firstly, the temptation to turn stones into bread during a period of intense hunger, secondly, the temptation to bow down and worship the devil himself, and, lastly, the temptation for Jesus to throw Himself down from a high place so that angels might care for Him.

Today's key verse records the fact that Jesus was tempted for the full period of 40 days and 40 nights. Only three of the actual temptations are recorded for us, but this period was one of intense trauma and continual bombardment from the enemy.

There are three different Greek words that are used by Luke to describe these actions of the devil against Jesus during this desert experience. Each one of them has been translated as 'temptation', which is not wrong, but each one of the words has a slightly different meaning, and it is important for us to understand the difference. If we can understand the difference, then we might understand what temptation really is. We shall study the first one today and then we shall consider the rest over the next two days.

The first word that Luke uses for the word 'temptation' is the Greek word *'peirazo'*, which means 'a test' or 'a proving', and it was the word that was used by the Greeks when they wanted to process an examination or a test. The word meant a full and complete testing of someone, in order to gain an insight into their ability by means of a test or an examination.

This word was applied by Luke when he sought to convey just what was happening when Jesus was forty days and nights under the severest of tests and examinations by the devil.

It is an interesting thing to note that this severe test followed immediately after the baptism of Jesus and the approval of His Father, and the audible voice from heaven. Temptation quite often follows a similar path, just when we feel particularly strong, or we have had a spiritual 'success', the enemy will often attack. We should always remember this, because quite often a failure can take place following a blessing, and a fall into temptation can come following a major spiritual breakthrough.

The 40 days and nights of temptation of Jesus should show us that, when we are similarly tempted, our victory can also be the same. It is recorded that Jesus followed the Spirit into the desert, and that He overcame each and every one of the tests and examinations and He returned from the desert in the 'power of the Spirit'.

Our temptations might follow the same pattern, but victory can also be achieved if we do exactly what Jesus did during His temptations. He overcame by quoting the Scriptures on each occasion when the enemy came. There is power and victory when we speak out the Word of God, we will never simply overcome temptation by clever methods and easy tactics. The only way to succeed, when the testing time comes, is to cling to the Word of God, and quote it on each occasion.

Jesus passed His test, and His '*peirazo*' was successful because He relied on the Word of God and its ability to strike at the heart of each temptation. This is the lesson of '*peirazo*', and this is the lesson that we need to learn every day.

KEY PRAYER

Heavenly Father, thank you for the fact that Jesus was an overcomer, and that you provided Him with the weapon of the Word of God. Thank you, too, that this weapon is also my weapon, and that I can pass the test using the same method. I praise you today for the fact that, following the temptations, Jesus returned in the power of the Spirit. Help me too, to suceed when the enemy comes.

December 7th

KEY WORD: **Temptation**

KEY VERSE: **Luke 4 : 12**

Jesus answered, "It says: Do not put the Lord your God to the test."

During the 40 days and the 40 nights of the temptations of Jesus, He used quotations from the Scriptures as His weapon of warfare, and we noticed yesterday that He was always successful in overcoming.

Each time a temptation came, and there are only three actually recorded, but it is clear that He was tempted for the full period of the forty days and nights, Jesus overcame by the use of the weapon of Scripture. In the key verse today, Jesus said, 'it is written' or 'it says'. He quoted the Word of God and this was more than enough to send the devil away, however, the devil kept coming back again and again. This is a lesson for us, that even when we have been successful in the overcoming of a temptation, we should still remain on guard, because there will be many more temptations just waiting to catch us out.

Luke used a different Greek word this time for the word 'temptation', in the NIV it is translated as 'test', but in the Old King James Version the word is translated as 'temptation'. The Greek word that is used is the word '*ekpeirazo*'; this word is a kin word to the word that we studied yesterday. Yesterday's key word was '*peirazo*', which meant 'the test' or 'the proving', and, as we saw, it was applied to the actual test or examination. The word '*ekpeirazo*' means 'intense test', and it was applied to not just the test, but also the effects of the test. In other words, it was a 'feeling' word for the actual effects of pressure and testing.

The word was used for pressure and intensity, the same word was used by Luke in Luke 10, when he recorded the fact that an expert in the law sought to trap Him with a very clever question. The use of this word on this occasion showed that this was no ordinary question, and that this was no ordinary person asking it. The verse states that 'an expert in the law stood up to test Jesus'. The actual event in Luke 10 was a test of the most pressurised kind, Jesus however, once again, passed the test by saying, 'it is written'. The quoting of the Word of God brought victory.

If this was the word that was used, and it was, it showed just how much pressure Jesus was under during the 40 days and 40 nights in the desert. This word only appears four times in the New Testament, and on three of these occasions it refers to the intense pressure that Jesus was under during the desert experience, and when the expert in the Law confronted Him.

If Jesus found His temptations to be a pressurising experience, then we should take careful note, because the same pressure will be applied to us when temptation comes. We should never be cavalier about temptations, and we should never treat them lightly. Temptations are powerful and many, and we should always be on our guard against them. However, Jesus overcame each one, and gave us the same Spirit and the same methods of success.

My Journal ____

____

____

____

____

____

KEY PRAYER

Heavenly Father, please help me each day to recognise that temptation will come my way, and that the experience will often be quite pressurising. Teach me to follow the ways of the Lord, so that I might be as successful at overcoming as He was. I bless you today for victory, and I praise you for breakthroughs.

December 8th

KEY WORD: **Temptation**

KEY VERSE: **Luke 4 : 13**

When the devil had finished all this tempting, he left Him until an opportune time.

Over the past few days we have been studying the baptism of Jesus and in particular, the effects of the following 40 days and 40 nights that Jesus endured when He was tempted in the desert. We have seen that there were several uses in the New Testament for our word 'temptation', and that they all had a slightly different meaning. We are looking today at the third word that was used when the writers tried to convey just what Jesus was experiencing.

The first word that we looked at that was translated as 'temptation' was the word '*peirazo*', which meant the 'the test' or 'the proving'. The second word that was used was the word '*ekpeirazo*', and this word was used to convey the kind of 'pressure' that was created by continual temptation. The last word that was used, was the word in the key verse today that was also translated as temptation. It was a kin word to the others, but it conveyed something a little different. The word was '*peirasmos*', this word meant 'trial' or 'proof', and it was the word that was used when you wanted to convey the fact that a trial had been undergone, and that it had been 'beneficial in its effects'.

The previous words for temptation had dwelt upon the testing and the pressure of a test and trial, this word was now introduced in order to reveal something fresh.

This word proved something to Jesus and proved something to the devil. The devil had finished his testing and tempting and was about to leave Jesus alone for the present. The reason that the devil was withdrawing was in the fact that Jesus had not only overcome each temptation, but what had been taking place was proving to make Jesus stronger and stronger. The devil tried to make Jesus weaker and weaker with this bombardment of testing, but it only had a beneficial effect upon Him. He was now stronger and fitter after 40 days and nights than He was at the beginning, which is why it declares that, following this period of intense pressure, Jesus returned in the 'power of the Spirit'.

Our temptations, although intense and pressurising at times, ought to have the same kind of effect upon us. Instead of 'going under' when temptation comes, we should be rising above each onslaught of the enemy, and we should be able to gain ground and strength from each situation just like Jesus did.

The fact that the devil withdrew from tempting and testing Jesus proves the fact that He was more than a match for anything that may have been thrown at Him during this period. This situation that is revealed to us in the New Testament, with its three key words, ought to greatly encourage us in our walk with God. As what happened to Jesus could happen to us, His ministry and His daily life grew better and stronger as a result of the forty days and nights, and what took place was greatly beneficial to Him. Not only did He overcome but He grew in spiritual stature and maturity as a direct result of the onslaught of the enemy.

We should not grow weak in temptation but we should be growing stronger.

My Journal ______________________________

____

____

____

KEY PRAYER

Heavenly Father, how I praise you for the record that this situation presents us with: Jesus grew stronger as a result of His temptations, and He was still in the Spirit at the end of them. Help me to learn these lessons so that I might grow too, and help me to grow stronger as a result of what I go through as well.

December 9th

KEY WORD: **News**

KEY VERSE: **Luke 4 : 14**

Jesus returned to Galilee in the power of the Spirit, and news about Him spread through the whole countryside.

Following the baptism of Jesus and His intense period of temptations, Luke records the fact that Jesus was still in the Spirit, and that He returned from this period in great strength and blessing. It is interesting, too, to notice what took place following this period of testing and trial.

The key verse today records the fact that Jesus went to Galilee, and that 'news of Him spread around'. The word that was used for our translation 'news' is one of great interest, as it teaches us something that we may not have considered before. The Old King James Version translates the word as 'fame', and it states that 'His fame went throughout the region'. The Greek word that was used was the word '*pheme*', and the more correct translation is not 'news' or 'fame', but 'a saying' or a 'report'. The word is actually taken from the root word '*phemi*', which means 'to shine', and it was the word that was used when you wanted to convey the thought of 'a clear shining voice'. This word was actually used when the translators wanted to convey the thought of God speaking, and it denoted a 'divine voice'. It was such a unique word as it only appears in the New Testament on two occasions, and on both occasions it refers to Jesus.

It appears in the key verse today as the word for what was happening following the return of Jesus from the desert, and from His temptation experience. News of Him, or the fame of Him, spread around the region in a dramatic manner. It was as if a bright and shining light had rested upon Him, and He drew the crowds, and they listened to Him as if God was speaking to them.

The word appears again in Matthew 9, when, following the raising of a ruler's daughter from the dead, it states that the 'news of this spread through the region'. The same reaction was taking place in Matthew's Gospel; the fame of Jesus was spreading around.

A Latin word was derived from the Greek word *'pheme'*, this was the word *'fama'*, and it is from this word that we derive our English word 'fame'. The interesting thing about this root translation is that our word fame actually has roots of its own, and it can be traced back in English history, and its meaning has changed a little. We now use this word to convey the sense of reputation or renown. However, the old meaning was close to the original translations from the Greek and Latin. The word 'fame' used to be used to convey the thought of 'eminence' or 'glory', and even 'honour'.

If we trace these roots back far enough we arrive at the origin of the word, which is the one that was used in the New Testament for what was happening to Jesus. His fame, or His shining honour and His clear voice, was echoing around the region, and He was attractive to the crowds in such a way that they crowded to hear Him.

Following our tests and trials there should be a sense in which we ought to shine, having overcome temptation and having grown in God as a result of the beneficial effects of beating the enemy.

KEY PRAYER

Heavenly Father, thank you for the truths that these lovely New Testament words bring to us as we uncover their meanings. I praise you today for the glorious possibility that we have. of shining through our trials and tests, and for the fact that we can grow in God in such a way that we actually show forth the glory of God as result of temptation.

December 10th

KEY WORD: **Weary**

KEY VERSE: **Matthew 11 : 28**

"Come to me, all you who are weary and burdened, and I will give you rest."

In the key verse today there is a word that we need to consider following the teaching of the past few days. In the past few days we have considered the fact that Jesus was triumphant over temptation, and that He shone with fame following His victory over the devil. We also said that we should overcome in the same manner, and that we have the potential to shine, too, as a result of our victories over the enemy. However, we need to set things into balance a little, or we might be seen to be a little cavalier or casual over our tests and trials.

What we have learned is that it is gloriously possible to be triumphant over temptation in the same way that Jesus was triumphant. This means that, when temptation comes, we need not fall into sin but rise above it. This is possible for all believers at all times. However, it is still a strong test, and there are at times moments of great weariness and tiredness. It says of Jesus that He sat at Jacob's Well, because 'He was tired' on one occasion. It also states that Jesus recognised that the weariness of the flesh could be an obstacle to us, when He spoke in the key verse today of 'coming to Him in order to find rest'.

Jesus taught that spiritually we can grow stronger, but yet physically there might be a drain upon us following ministry and service. Matthew translated the words of Jesus in the key verse and used the Greek word *'kopiao'* in order to convey this aspect of weariness and tiredness.

This word *'kopiao'* means 'to grow weary' or 'to be beaten out'. This word was taken from a root word *'kopos'*, which meant 'a beating', and it was the word that was used for an actual physical beating. Jesus used this word to convey the thought that when tests and trials come it can have the effect of a physical-like beating upon the flesh, even though our spirit might grow stronger. Because Jesus recognised this, we should be greatly encouraged. He taught His disciples to 'come to Him' when this kind of symptom appeared, as He had the ability to bring rest unto our souls.

The whole ministry of Jesus can be summed up in these words, as He came to bring rest and comfort, and He came to bring strength to the weary. The Old King James Version uses the word 'labour' in its translation of this word and concept, which is a very good word to use, even though it misses the point a little. As we labour in service and ministry it is possible to grow weary, so Jesus has provided us with a remedy. As we come to Him for rest from our labours, there is sufficient comfort and strength provided that enables us to continue in our ministry for Him. It is not so much the labour of 'toiling on, toiling on' of the old hymn that we need to consider, as He provides rest for us. It is much more the 'victory in Jesus' hymn that provides the truth of this word.

Our flesh may grow weary, but He has rest for us. However, our spirit grows stronger, as we press on to victory through the blood of the Lamb.

My Journal

KEY PRAYER

Heavenly Father, I thank you today for the fact that I have victory in Jesus, and that, even when I grow weary, you have provided rest for my soul and for my flesh. Help me always to recognise the fact that in my weariness you have provided me with rest and comfort, so help me always to 'come to you' at the right time.

December 11th

KEY WORD: **Bethlehem**

KEY VERSE: **Luke 2 : 3-4**

And everyone went to his own town to register. So Joseph also went up from the town of Nazareth in Galilee to Judea, to Bethlehem the town of David.

It is only two weeks to Christmas Day and therefore it is time to turn our attention to what has become known throughout the world as the Christmas story. Only two Gospel writers actually record the Christmas story, they are Matthew and Luke. Mark and John commence their Gospels with the baptism of Jesus and the creation account respectively. They both completely ignore the Christmas story.

It is left to only two writers to capture the extraordinary story of the birth of Jesus. Over the next two weeks we shall be looking at some of the key words that go towards making this story the greatest story ever told.

We shall commence our studies by looking at the place of the birth of Jesus, the city of Bethlehem. This town features throughout the Old Testament and the New Testament as the city of King David, and, as the Christmas carol reminds us, this all happened 'Once in Royal David's City'.

The name 'Bethlehem' is a Hebrew word, and it was used in the New Testament in its Hebrew form. This word means 'food house' or 'place of food', or even more literally 'house of bread'. It was first mentioned in the Bible as far back as the book of Genesis, when it was called Ephrath, and it was the burial place of Rachel. This first mention was in BC 1729, however, Bethlehem really came to fame in BC 1083, when David was born there and made it his very own city.

Bethlehem had its position about six miles south of the City of Jerusalem, and, because Jesus was born there, it has now lost its title of 'David's city', and is now recognised by pilgrims as the 'city of Jesus', and it is celebrated as the place of His birth. This is a lovely play on words, as the 'House of Bread', was the place where the 'Bread of Life' commenced to feed the world.

Jesus was born there, due to the fact that that an edict had been sent out by Caesar Augustus that all the world should be 'counted', and we will consider this tomorrow. This edict was sent out by the 'world leader' at that time, who obviously thought that he was in total control and demanded a census of all 'his' people. However, there was a greater power behind all of this, as God was preparing to bring His Saviour into the world, and this Saviour was going to be born into the 'prophesied' city. Micah, hundreds of years before the Christmas story would ever commence, prophesied that Jesus would be born in this city and that this would be the beginning of salvation. Mary and Joseph lived in Nazareth and were no where near the vicinity of the prophecy, so God raised up a Caesar, who would 'decide' to 'count the world', which in turn would bring Joseph and Mary to the right place, at the right time, in the right way.

God is God, and there is none else. He alone rules the affairs of heaven and earth, and 'Royal David's City' proves the point completely.

My Journal ______________________________

____

____

____

____

KEY PRAYER

Heavenly Father, thank you once again for the amazing truth that you alone rule and reign. Other kings might think that they rule and reign, but Bethlehem and the Christmas story once again show us that you are the only true King of kings and Lord of lords.

December 12th

KEY WORD: **Register**

KEY VERSE: **Luke 2 : 3-4**

And everyone went to his own town to register. So Joseph also went up from the town of Nazareth in Galilee to Judea, to Bethlehem the town of David.

All the world should be counted, decreed Caesar Augustus, and therefore Mary and Joseph went to Bethlehem, the city of David, so that the prophecy from Micah might be fulfilled.

The decree declared that a census should be taken of the whole world, and that everyone should register themself for this census in the city of their birth. Joseph was born in Bethlehem, and was of the house of David, so he had to travel to the city of David in order to register himself. There was a major mass movement of people at this time all over the Roman world, as people migrated back to their birthplaces.

The Greek word that is used for this census is the word '*apographo*', which means to 'write out' or to 'enrol'. The Old King James Version has this word translated as 'taxed', and a very sentimental and poetic version of this actual happening has been stored in our minds because of it. We think that poetically 'all the world should be taxed', and we have grown up with this poetic thought since childhood. However, it is a false thought, as the word does not convey at all the thought of taxation or a monetary situation. Caesar Augustus simply wanted to count the population of the world, probably as a matter of pride, and he therefore decreed that 'all the world should be counted'. The registration of this count would have to be taken in the 'city of birth', so the whole world had to move, in order to '*apographo*' – to register.

This census, was confirmed in history by several historians, and they confirm the fact, too, that the whole Roman Empire went on the move, in order that everyone could go to their own town of origin. A little bit of history is interesting in that this census, when concluded, was drawn up into a kind of Roman Domesday Book, where the whole world was listed. This book was called the Rationarium, and it was formed by 20 commissioners, who took years to complete their findings. The final book was called the Breviarium, and it was a massive exercise in the counting of the entire known world.

The interesting thing about this is the fact that, while 20 commissioners and all the world was focusing upon this world Breviarium, God brought His Son from heaven to become the Saviour of all the world, and only a handful of people noticed.

It is just like God that, when the people were preoccupied in their own false sense of power and pride, grace and mercy should be made available, and those who saw it, the shepherds, the Wise Men, Joseph and Mary, all found grace to help in time of need.

My Journal ______________________________

KEY PRAYER

Heavenly Father, thank you grace abounds, even when it is not noticed. Thank you, too, that Jesus came into a world that was taken up with its search for pride and power, and that even now, with the same pride and power still being searched for, Jesus is Lord of all.

December 13th

KEY WORD: **Birth**

KEY VERSE: **Matthew 1 : 21–23**

"She will give birth to a son, and you are to give Him the name Jesus, because He will save His people from their sins." All this took place to fulfil what the Lord had said through the prophet: "The virgin will be with child, and will give birth to a son, and they will call Him Immanuel" – which means, "God with us."

The Old King James Bible poetically says that 'the birth of Jesus was on this wise', and this beautiful phrase has found its way into the Christmas story forever. The NIV states it a little more 'matter of fact', when it says 'this is how the birth of Jesus came about'.

The birth of this baby boy in Bethlehem was not 'a' birth, nor was it a 'major' birth, it was 'the' birth. The birth of all births, and the beginning of all things new.

The Greek word for 'birth' is the word '*gennesis*', which translated means literally 'the beginning' or 'the begetting'. This is why the first book of the Bible is called the book of Genesis, because it records the 'birth of the world'. The Greek word has its roots in the Hebrew word '*gennesis*', and no better word could have been chosen in order to describe the commencement of life than this word.

Jesus had His genesis in the ancient city of Bethlehem, due to the plan of God. Prophets had spoken of it and the world had waited for it, and almost everyone missed it when it happened. Only a handful of people knew what had happened, and only a few people had been present at the birth. Normally when a king was born it was a matter of great fanfare and importance. However, in a humble manger, in a tiny city, Jesus, the Saviour of the world, came to birth.

The genesis of His life was totally supernatural from beginning to end, and the story has thrilled and yet puzzled people ever since. There was a supernatural star, and an angelic visitation, there was a visit from the Wise Men, and a visit from frightened shepherds. There was an attempt to halt this genesis by Herod the king, who would order that every baby should be killed. And there was the flight into Egypt, and the supernatural preservation of the Saviour. Above all this there was the supernatural implantation of the seed of the Spirit into Mary's womb, so that her conception could be correctly seen, as it was prophesied that 'a virgin would conceive'.

No other birth was like this birth, and no other birth of any generation would measure up to this genesis, this was the 'birth of all births'.

Jesus was born to be our Saviour and He will forever be our Immanuel, God with us. We shall consider this amazing concept tomorrow.

My Journal

KEY PRAYER

Heavenly Father, over and over again during this year I have thanked you for sending Jesus to be my Saviour. Yet once again I find myself praising you for the fact that Jesus came. Thank you for His sinless birth and His wonderful arrival. I bless you today for the fact that He is not just the Saviour of the world, but that He is also my Saviour, and my very own friend.

December 14th

KEY WORD: ***Immanuel***

KEY VERSE: ***Matthew 1 : 21–23***

"She will give birth to a son, and you are to give Him the name Jesus, because He will save His people from their sins." All this took place to fulfil what the Lord had said through the prophet: "The virgin will be with child, and will give birth to a son, and they will call Him Immanuel" – which means, "God with us."

Jesus was called 'Immanuel', or 'Emmanuel', which we all accept means 'God with us'. However, a little later on we shall discover an even greater truth concerning this name. This name, given to Jesus, conveyed something very special indeed, as the name was taken from rich symbolism. However, before we consider the actual name, we must firstly consider something else.

The name has been recorded by hymn writers and composers over the years, and has been used in some of the most well known poetry of all time. It has been sung by choirs and congregations throughout the world, and it has been used by all of us at some time or another, especially at Christmas, to denote the fact that God is with us. All of this is quite amazing seeing that this name only appeared three times in the entire Bible: once in Matthew, in the key verse today, and twice in the Old Testament, in the book of Isaiah. In Isaiah it appears in its Hebrew form of 'Immanuel', and in Matthew it appeared in its Greek form of 'Emmanuel'.

This total focus of song and hymn over the past 2,000 years is quite extraordinary, as its appearance in the Bible is very limited. Yet this name has become one of the most well known names for Jesus, and one of the most loved names of Jesus, in all the world.

The name was derived from a symbol meaning deliverance, and its first use, in Isaiah, was when King Ahaz needed to pronounce deliverance for his people. He declared that an 'Immanuel' would come who would be a deliverer, and that, when he appeared, the people would know that deliverance was on its way. The people waited and waited for this fulfilment, and they waited until the Bethlehem scene was accomplished. The promise of the long awaited Immanuel was also coupled with the fact that this deliverance would be completed by this 'Immanuel' being born to a virgin.

The name means, as translated, 'God with us', or even more literally, 'with us God'. *'El'*, being the name of God, was placed at the conclusion of the name. *'Immanu'*, meaning 'with us', was placed at the commencement of the name. The concept was therefore not that 'God was with us', but that 'with us would be God'.

God has declared such love for us that He has come in the form of flesh to be our Saviour. This love gift is Jesus, who is our 'Emmanuel', and for all time, and for all people, He is now with us. And in an even greater sense, 'with us is now our God', who will never leave us nor forsake us.

My Journal

KEY PRAYER

Heavenly Father, you are forever with me, and you will never leave me. As Christmas approaches, what a wonderful anthem to bring, that Jesus belongs to me and I belong to Him, not just for time but for eternity. Help me to understand it and help me to take it in.

December 15th

KEY WORD: **Inn**

KEY VERSE: **Luke 2 : 7**

She gave birth to her firstborn, a son. She wrapped Him in cloths and placed Him in a manger, because there was no room for them in the inn.

If ever there was a verse that summed up an event so perfectly, it is this one verse. If we had no other verses to convey the Christmas story, this one verse would do. Mary gives birth to her first son, then she wrapped him in cloths, or as the Old King James Bible records it, 'she wrapped Him in swaddling clothes'. Then she laid him in the manger for His first rest outside of her womb.

The Christmas carols record this event for us, and many other songs and anthems record the fact that there 'was no room in the inn'.

Luke writes about this event and he does a very strange thing, he ignores the usual Greek word for 'inn' and he uses a word that is not often associated with a lodging place or resting place. The usual Greek word in the New Testament for 'inn' is the word '*pandocheion*', which means 'a place of reception'. This word was formed by the combination of two different words, firstly, the word '*pas*', which means 'all', and secondly, the word '*dechomai*', which means 'to receive'. The word therefore denoted the place where 'all people could rest, and where all strangers could be received for a night'.

This usual word for 'inn' was ignored when Luke was seeking to convey what was taking place that night in Bethlehem. He used a word on this occasion which produced a word picture, and which conveyed something completely different. Luke uses the word '*kataluma*' to describe the place where Mary and Joseph stayed for the night. This word meant 'a guest chamber' rather than an 'inn'. This word was also formed by the combining of two different words, firstly, the word '*kata*', which means 'down', and secondly, the word '*luo*', which means 'to loose'. The combination of these two words formed a word picture that conveyed the thought of 'loosing your baggage and your animals, and then laying down to rest'. It conveyed more than the simple thought of Mary and Joseph looking for a place of rest, it conveyed the thought that these two travellers were desperate to lie down, and desperate to loosen their burden.

The mass movement of people across Israel, due to the registration order by Caesar, meant, however, that there was no accommodation in any inn or guest house in Bethlehem. Mary's heavy pregnancy meant that she was near to birth and desperate to rest, but there was no room in a '*kataluma*', a 'place of rest from a burden'.

Jesus once said that the 'foxes had holes, and the birds had nests, but the Son of Man had nowhere to lay His head'. He came as the world's Saviour but we could not even give Him a guest chamber or a lodging place. Jesus was the Lord of heaven but not even a guest on earth. As we reflect in prayer today we should thank God that He not only sent His Son, but that He allowed Him to stay among us, even when we had treated Him so badly. The Saviour of the world was not even given the courtesy of a room in a resting place.

My Journal

KEY PRAYER

Heavenly Father, I do rejoice today that Jesus came, but more than that, I marvel at the fact that you allowed Him to stay, when He was treated with such contempt. We did not even recognise the Lord of glory and we refused Him room in an inn. The Lord of heaven was not even treated as a guest. Thank you Father, for your great love for us.

December 16th

KEY WORD: **Manger**

KEY VERSE: **Luke 2 : 7**

She gave birth to her firstborn, a son. She wrapped Him in cloths and placed Him in a manger, because there was no room for them in the inn.

Jesus was placed in a manger for His first rest outside of Mary's womb, and the Christmas cards and the films portray something of a sanitised view of this amazing event. We have pictures with almost a halo of glory surrounding what was termed 'the manger', and we have Christmas cards that portray the scene with an air of almost 'wonderment', as the Lord of glory takes His very first rest in cloths and this manger.

Our western minds cannot fathom exactly what a manger is, and so we have allowed the romanticism of the film makers to teach us. However, the film makers have lost the plot completely and they have missed the point. The manger was not a clean and sanitised eating place full of straw for animals, it was very different to that. The Greek word for 'manger' is the word '*phatne*', which means 'a stall' or 'an animal resting place'. It denoted the place where animals would rest and where they would feed, give birth, and generally live during the night and during harsh winters. All types of animals would be there, and it would not be unusual to find goats and camels, as well as sheep and oxen. Travellers' horses would also be bedded down for the night in a '*phatne*'.

Mary and Joseph had travelled all the way from Nazareth and were desperate to find a place of rest, but, due to the mass movement of Caesar's census, there was no room in an inn. So they would have been offered a place in either a small cave or a large hut, outside and to the rear of an inn, where the animals would have been resting. This was not a clean place and it certainly was not sanitised for giving birth, but it was the only place that remained in the entire city of Bethlehem.

This *'phatne'* would have been an area that would probably be marked out by wooden rails, and where all types of animals would have rested. Some animals would almost certainly have been moved, in order to find extra space for the pregnant Mary and her husband. The smell would have been pungent, and the atmosphere far from conducive to labour and birth, but there was no room in the inn.

As we sing our carols this year and as we celebrate Christmas, it would be good to look beyond the romantic pictures of the hay and the straw, and beyond the remembrances of the animals quietly lying down, so that Mary might give birth in peace. This sentimental 'mind picture' that we have is far removed from the animal stench and the dirt and squalor of the real manger and the real stable.

Jesus came from the heights of glory and the splendour of heaven to the dirt and squalor of a world of sin and shame, and no picture portrays this better than the first moments of His birth. The manger and the stable, and the exclusion from the normal type of birthplace to that of an animal's bed, are eloquent testimony of His submission to His Father's will.

My Journal

KEY PRAYER

Heavenly Father, as I celebrate Christmas this year, I pray that I might see beyond the sentimental story and pictures, to see the real event in its starkness and its emptiness. Thank you that Jesus was willing to come and to submit Himself to such squalor as to be born in a manger. Help me to understand it and help me to take it in.

December 17th

KEY WORD: **Cloths**

KEY VERSE: **Luke 2 : 7**

She gave birth to her firstborn, a son. She wrapped Him in cloths and placed Him in a manger, because there was no room for them in the inn.

Mary wrapped Jesus in cloths and laid Him in a manger. The way that this key verse today describes the way that Mary bound Jesus in these cloths, does not do justice at all to this amazing event. The Old King James Bible portrays this event in slightly more picturesque language when it says that 'Jesus was wrapped in swaddling clothes'.

This binding of a new infant child was a usual event in the Middle East at the time of Jesus and in fact is still practised in certain parts of the world today. The action and use of these pieces of cloth is one of the most graphic parts of the Christmas story, and it allows for poetic language to be used. One Christmas carol uses this part of the story for a very unique line indeed, when it states that, as Jesus came to the manger, He came 'from regal robes to swaddling clothes'. This action provides poets and writers with a whole lot of poetic licence.

The Greek word that was used by Luke in order to describe this event is the word '*sparganoo*', and this word is translated as 'cloths' by the NIV, and 'swaddling clothes', by the Old King James Bible.

The actual meaning of the word is 'to swathe', which is why the Old King James translators used the words 'swaddling clothes'. The NIV used a more modern word to describe this custom because it felt that 'swaddling clothes' would not be understood. The concept of this action was quite simple: in order to make a newly born child feel as if it was totally secure, like the womb from which it had just come, the baby would be bound up, quite tightly, in strips of linen cloth. This binding would take place from just below the chin, to cover each part of the body, right down to the feet. The arms and hands would be bound into the cloth, and the warmth and the security that this would bring would suggest to the tiny helpless form, that 'all was well', just like the womb-like experience of pre-birth.

This event was part of the angelic announcement that came to the shepherds in the fields, as the angels announced that they would find the child lying in a manger, and that this child would be 'wrapped in cloths'.

The picture of our eternal Saviour, who had unlimited power and glory, and who was seated at the right-hand of God in heaven, now wrapped helplessly in linen cloths, is a graphic portrayal of just how far Jesus came, and just what He had to suffer, in order to reach us with His love.

My Journal ______________________________

KEY PRAYER

Heavenly Father, I bless you today for your great love and your great sacrifice. It must have caused you great pain to see your only Son born into the bundle of tiny flesh and then bound tightly in linen bands. Thank you that the one who inhabited eternity was made flesh for me.

December 18th

KEY WORD: **The Son of the Most High**

KEY VERSE: **Luke 1 : 32**

He will be great and will be called the Son of the Most High.

The event and fact of the birth of Jesus is not denied, and cannot be denied by anyone at all. Historians agree that He was born, as do theologians and philosophers. The fact of His birth is undeniable. The argument and debate that rages is over the significance of His birth. The whole event, of course, is now treated by the western world as an excuse for feasting and drinking, and for the giving and receiving of presents. The greatest present of all is of course God's love gift to us, His Son Jesus.

The angels announced this love gift by calling Jesus the 'Son of the Most High'. This announcement, and in fact this command to Mary concerning His name and His title, were both prophetic and a revelation. This announcement, too, was one of great magnitude.

The phrase 'the Son of the Most High', which was conferred upon Jesus, was both a title and a name. It referred to the might and magnificence of God, and it contained words that would have frightened Mary as well as blessed her. The actual phrase in Greek was '*huios ek hupsistos*', which meant 'son of the highest degree'. There could be no other way of describing Jesus, and no other person could rightly have this description conferred upon them.

Jesus was God's Son, and, as such, He was the 'Son of the highest degree', as the word '*hupsistos*' meant a superlative degree of greatness.

Caesar Augustus thought that by counting the population of the world, and by conducting this census by ordering everyone one to their home towns and cities, he was in fact the greatest monarch of all time. Little did he realise that he was just a pawn in the power of prophecy. Prophecy decreed that Joseph had to reach Bethlehem, and that Mary had to conceive in a manger, and that Jesus had to be wrapped in swaddling bands. All this had to be completed in order that prophecy might be fulfilled, and in order that the whole of the Old Testament might be completed. So the 'Most High' God ordered the tiny little Caesar in Rome to have a census conducted, so that the whole of history and the whole of prophetic announcement might pivot upon the fact that Jesus was born in 'Royal David's City'.

The 'Most High' God brought Jesus, the Son of the Highest, to Bethlehem, so that the world might be saved, and so that the prophetic calendar might be completed.

How great is our God, and how small is mankind?

My Journal

KEY PRAYER

Heavenly Father, I have seen again today just how great you really are, and just how small mankind really is. Caesar thought that he was in total control, and he sat in his palace with great contentment, yet you rule heaven and earth, and with one breath you can change things and order things around. I worship you today, O Most High God.

December 19th

KEY WORD: **Wise Men**

KEY VERSE: **Matthew 2 : 1-2**

After Jesus was born in Bethlehem in Judea, during the time of King Herod, Magi from the east came to Jerusalem and asked, "Where is the one who has been born King of the Jews? We saw His star in the east and have come to worship Him."

Wise men from the east came to seek Jesus, who was born the King of the Jews, because they had seen 'His star in the east'.

These wise men are very strange men indeed, and they have been the cause of quite a lot of discussion over the centuries. First of all we need to remove the Christmas sentiment from our minds concerning these men. They were not 'three Kings from Orient'. They may have travelled far, but they were not 'kings'. There were not three of them – this numerical expression stems only from the fact that they presented three gifts, there could have been in fact 20 or 120. The Bible does not state their number, therefore we cannot, and we should not, speculate upon their number.

We also need to deal with the fact that they had 'come to worship Him'. This was not a kind of 'spiritual pilgrimage' that resulted in worship in the spirit and worship in truth. These men were eastern mystics and philosophers and were probably magicians, steeped in arts and astronomy. The fact that they followed a star ought to give us a clue as to their true nature.

The Old King James Bible calls these men 'wise men', while the NIV calls them 'the Magi'. The Greek word that is used for these travellers from the east is a word that is only used four times in the New Testament, and, on each of the four occasions that it is used, it is confined to this actual event, which is only recorded by Matthew. In fact, this amazing event is only recorded in Matthew's gospel. The word that is used is '*Magian*', and it meant 'astronomer' or 'priest'. The NIV gains its word 'magi' from this word, and the nearest English translation of this word, could only be 'wise men'. The ordinary words for 'wise men' in the New Testament would normally be '*sophos anthropos*'.

These 'magi' were probably from Persia and were probably eastern mystics of great magical arts, and, having seen a star that was most unusual, set off to follow it, not knowing where it would lead them. Their journey could well have taken them weeks or months, or even longer. Yet, so great was their desire to interpret the stars' meaning that they followed it to Jerusalem. It is obvious however that God was using them and was guiding them, as, following their presentation of the three gifts, God warned them in a dream that there was great danger from King Herod, and they went back to their land 'another way'.

Once again we see God in total control of the events, and we see God using whoever He wants to use, whenever He wants to use them, because God is God.

They may not have been 'wise men' in the truest sense of what we have been led to believe, but in the words of a church notice board seen over the Christmas period, 'Wise Men Still Seek Him'.

My Journal

KEY PRAYER

Heavenly Father, I praise you for all those who were involved in the story of Christmas, and for all those that you gathered together when Jesus came. Thank you that you have also been gathering people unto Him since that day, and thank you, too, that I am numbered among them.

December 20th

KEY WORD: **The east**

KEY VERSE: **Matthew 2 : 1-2**

After Jesus was born in Bethlehem in Judea, during the time of King Herod, Magi from the east came to Jerusalem and asked, "Where is the one who has been born King of the Jews? We saw His star in the east and have come to worship Him."

The Wise Men who followed the star came, as the Bible announces it, from the east, and there is great significance in the fact that they came from this direction.

It is not just a poetic phrase that 'wise men came from the east'. It would however lose its value and poetic flow if it was stated that 'wise men came from the west', or even 'the north'. There is something that is of true Christmas sentiment when we sing about these strange men from the east. The direction of their travel is however not just Christmas poetry, but it has a significant meaning.

The east is always regarded in the Bible as the rising of the sun, and therefore a major place within the compass points. The Greek word for 'east' is '*anatole*', which means literally 'the rising' or 'to rise', and it was used whenever the translators wanted to convey the direction of the east or the rising of the sun.

This same word is used of Jesus when He was being described as the 'dayspring that would come to us'. The east is always the place where it is said that the return of Jesus would focus, as He would arrive on the east of Jerusalem, on the 'Mount of Olives', and would pass through the eastern gate. Many hymns and spiritual songs have focussed upon the east, as they sought to interpret this spiritual direction. However it is quite possible that spiritual licence has been taken, as the east has probably been altered out of all proportion.

Yet these men travelled from their eastern home to seek Jesus, and to present Him with gifts as their act of homage and worship.

It is an interesting fact that these men were not put off from any danger on their journey, nor were they discouraged by the fact that the star kept on moving until it came to rest over the place where Jesus was born. These men were also not halted in their progress by the manipulations of King Herod and his men; they had come to worship, and they were going to worship, come what may.

We ought to learn a lesson from them today. We are often discouraged by events around us and we lose our spiritual momentum at times. We are often put off by our feelings, and we fail to worship Him at times due to our circumstances. These strange men from the east were not going to worship in spirit and truth, and they probably had no conception of how to worship a Saviour and Lord, yet they still came. We should learn that lesson, and we should seek to worship Him in whatsoever condition we find ourselves.

My Journal

KEY PRAYER

Heavenly Father, I have learned afresh today that you seek those who will worship you, and I pledge myself to be a worshipper at all times. Forgive me for the times when I have allowed myself to be affected by my circumstances, and when my praise has ceased. I will bless you at all times and your praise shall continually be in my mouth.

December 21st

KEY WORD: **His star**

KEY VERSE: **Matthew 2 : 1-2**

After Jesus was born in Bethlehem in Judea, during the time of King Herod, Magi from the east came to Jerusalem and asked, "Where is the one who has been born King of the Jews? We saw His star in the east and have come to worship Him."

The wise men came from the east to worship Jesus, guided by a star, and they presented their gifts when the star came to rest over the place where Jesus was born.

The focus of this star, and the meaning of this star, have given astronomers and astrologers much to consider over the centuries. Papers have been written about this star and much conjecture has taken place as to its function and form. Was it a comet, or a planet? Was it a true star or a fake star?'

I cannot add much to the debate as I believe that no one really knows the star's origin or its future course, and no one really knows whether it was a planet or a star. However, what we do know is that it was no ordinary star, as the Bible makes it quite clear that this was 'His star'. Tthis was not 'a star', nor even 'the star', but it was 'His star'. The wise magicians from the east had followed what they called 'His star', and it had led them right to the place where Jesus lay.

The ordinary Greek word for 'star' was *'aster'*, and it meant quite simply 'a star', and it was used whenever the New Testament wanted to convey the thought of stars in the heavens, and stars of light. It was also used whenever the New Testament writers wanted to convey the thought of a particular star, such as the 'star of the morning', or the 'star of Bethlehem'.

The word *'aster'* is used in the key verse today for the simple word 'star', even though this was no ordinary star. This star had moved slowly across the night sky, and it had moved so slowly across the sky that these men were able to track it and follow it. We know that meteors move across the sky at an amazing rate of knots, and that sometimes it is hard to track them, let alone follow them. We call them at times 'shooting stars', as that is just how they appear, as they shoot across our vision into the inky darkness of the night sky.

Yet, this seemingly ordinary star moved slowly and with great precision until it had completed its mission, and until it had brought these wise men to the conclusion of their journey.

God will use ordinary things and ordinary events to confound the mighty and the intellectual, and He will do just whatever He wants to do with His world and with His people.

If He wants to use a star, He will use a star, and if He wants to bring men from the east, He will bring men from the east. God is God, and the Christmas story constantly reminds us of this fact.

My Journal

KEY PRAYER

Heavenly Father, help me to constantly remember just how great you really are, and help me to remember that you are sovereign. You set up kingdoms and you put down kingdoms, you raise up nations and you put down nations, you are God. Help me to remember this the next time that I am in trouble. There is none like you.

December 22nd

KEY WORD: **Child**

KEY VERSE: **Matthew 2 : 11**

On coming to the house, they saw the child with His mother Mary, and they bowed down and worshipped Him. Then they opened their treasures and presented Him with gifts of gold and of incense and of myrrh.

The Wise Men with their gifts finally arrived at the place where Joseph and Mary were staying, and the key verse today states that, once they had arrived, they lost no time in worshipping Jesus, and presenting to Him their three treasured gifts.

When Matthew was writing about this particular event he sought to emphases just what was happening to Jesus by using a very creative word. The English translations simply say that the wise men 'saw the child', and the wording that was used does not fully convey the depth of passion and the scope of their worship.

There are nine different Greek words for the simple English word 'child'. There is a word that means 'to bear a child', and there is a word that means 'tiny or diminutive child', this word is used by a teacher to his pupils. This word is used by John in his epistle when he refers to his flock as 'little children'.

There is a word that is used for a 'son child', and another word that relates to 'a child relation'. All these words are used in the New Testament, and they all have relevance. However, Matthew takes another word for 'child' and uses it with great care, and with great passion. When the wise men saw 'the child' they worshipped. The reason for their worship was because what they saw amazed them. Matthew used the Greek word '*paidion*', which means 'young child', and it was the word that was used for a newly born infant.

These Wise Men had travelled hundreds and possibly even thousands of miles to meet with a king. They had gone straight to the palace of King Herod in Jerusalem, because that was where kings would automatically be born. Their frustration in not finding the new born king in the palace turned to amazement when they actually found a helpless, tiny newborn baby being cradled in the arms of His mother – in a stable, of all places. There were no regal robes or thrones of splendour; there were no musicians quietly playing in the throne room, and there was certainly no pomp or ceremony. There was just a tiny infant, helplessly dependent upon His mother, when they were expecting 'one who was born King of the Jews'. They had travelled from the east because they had 'seen His star', and now all they had for their trouble and sacrifice was a newly born *'paidion'*, a tiny little child.

Yet their instincts told them that this was the one that they had been seeking, and they bowed down towards Him, and they open their treasures and presented their gifts.

As we are drawing nearer and nearer to the day that we celebrate His birth, we should bring our offering of praise and the treasure of our worship, because He alone is worthy. The King of Heaven had left the glory and had come to earth, in the tiny form of an infant. His life would be short, and His rejection would be acute, but He still came, and He still sacrificed His life, because of the Father's love for His people.

My Journal ______________________________

KEY PRAYER

Heavenly Father, how I praise you as we draw closer to Christmas for the amazing fact that you allowed Jesus to enter human flesh and become a man. Thank you for this great sacrifice, and thank you, too, for the amazing gift of love.

December 23rd

KEY WORD: **Gold**

KEY VERSE: **Matthew 2 : 11**

On coming to the house, they saw the child with His mother Mary, and they bowed down and worshipped Him. Then they opened their treasures and presented Him with gifts of gold and of incense and of myrrh.

The Wise Men opened their treasures, and there for all to see were three amazing gifts. These three gifts had been borne on their horses and camels, probably for thousands of miles, in order that their presentation to the newborn king might be precious.

The three gifts were expressed in the Old King James Bible as gold, frankincense and myrrh, the NIV however expresses it slightly differently, in that it translates the gift of frankincense, as 'incense'. As these gifts are very expressive in their nature, we are going to consider each one in turn, starting with gold today and the others over the next two days.

The first gift that was presented was 'gold'. The Greek word that is used here in the key verse is the word *'chrusos'*, which means 'precious metal'. The word would normally have been used for a golden ornament or a golden coin. There was a similar word used when the gold was in the form of a small precious object, this word was *'chrusion'*. However, Matthew chooses to use the first word, which would suggest that the present was one of an elaborate image made of the finest gold.

Our western minds immediately draw the conclusion that gold meant a block of gold, similar to the ones that are seen in a bank reserve vault or a bullion reserve. However, in eastern minds 'gold' would represent a figurine, or an ornament, or even some coinage. This present was possibly an image or an ornament that would have been hand carved in the finest of gold, as only the finest gold was presented to a king. The Wise Men were expecting to be received by a king and queen in a royal palace, so only the best gold would have been acceptable.

Gold symbolised purity and completeness, and was the metal that was most costly at this time, and was always a 'kingly' gift.

Even though Jesus was born in an animal's manger and not a royal palace, He is still the King of kings, and as such deserves our very best. We may never present Him with gifts of costly gold, but we can present Him with our lives and with our destiny. The presentation of our lives to Him will be far more acceptable than pure gold, as it was for our lives that He came, and it was for our lives that He died.

My Journal ____

KEY PRAYER

Heavenly Father, I present my body before you today as a living sacrifice, which is far more precious than gold. As my Lord and King, I come before you with worship, and I seek your face today, and I bring my offering of thanksgiving.

December 24th

KEY WORD: **Incense**

KEY VERSE: **Matthew 2 : 11**

On coming to the house, they saw the child with His mother Mary, and they bowed down and worshipped Him. Then they opened their treasures and presented Him with gifts of gold and of incense and of myrrh.

The Wise Men opened their treasures and there for all to see were three amazing gifts. These three gifts had been borne on their horses and camels, probably for thousands of miles, in order that their presentation to the new born king might be precious.

The three gifts were expressed in the Old King James Bible as gold, frankincense and myrrh. The NIV expresses it slightly differently, in that it translates the gift of frankincense as 'incense'. As these gifts are very expressive in their nature, we are considering each one in turn. We started with gold yesterday, and now we are considering the second gift, incense, today.

The Old King James Bible uses the word 'frankincense', while the NIV stays with the word 'incense'. The actual Greek word that is used is the word '*libanos*', which meant 'white resin'. The word was taken from an old Semitic word that was used for the resin that was extracted from the bark of an incense tree: the 'arbor thuris'. The extraction took the form of a series of cuts into the bark of this tree until sap was found. This sap would then be allowed to drip into a container. This sap was very costly and was used for sacrificial purposes in worship; it was used for perfume and beauty treatments, and it was also used occasionally for burial and embalming.

The sap was white in colour, bitter and glistening, and was extremely fragrant. When it was poured out in quantity it would fill the house with its pungent perfume. It was used in the tabernacle of the Old Testament, and it was carried by the priests in a censer.

The purpose of its use by the wise men is uncertain. It obviously had a major purpose in their thinking, as they had treasured this gift and carried it safely on their long and arduous journey. We could be very spiritual and say that the gift was prophetic in the sense that it could have been presented for a symbol of His death, as the substance could have been used for the embalming of a corpse. However, it is also possible that the gift was given as a kind of worship act, as the incense would have spoken of offerings and sacrifice. However, it really is impossible to state the actual use that was in the minds of the wise men, except to say that this gift was extremely costly, and it was obviously felt that this was a right and proper gift for a king.

As Christmas Day draws even closer and dawns tomorrow, we should make a declaration that from now on, and into a brand new year, our desire would only be to give our very best unto the Lord, as He deserves and ought to receive – the best that we can bring.

My Journal ______________________________

KEY PRAYER

Heavenly Father, I come before you today with the desire that only my best will do. Help me to give you the best of my worship and the best of my praise. Help me, too, to give you the best of my time, the best of my talents and the best of my future.

December 25th

KEY WORD: **Myrrh**

KEY VERSE: **Matthew 2 : 11**

On coming to the house, they saw the child with His mother Mary, and they bowed down and worshipped Him. Then they opened their treasures and presented Him with gifts of gold and of incense and of myrrh.

The Wise Men opened their treasures, and there for all to see were three amazing gifts. These three gifts had been borne on their horses and camels, probably for thousands of miles, in order that their presentation to the newborn king might be precious.

The three gifts were expressed in the Old King James Bible as gold, frankincense and myrrh. However, the NIV expresses it in a slightly different way, in that it translates the gift of frankincense as 'incense', as we have seen. As all these gifts are very expressive in their nature, we are considering each one in turn. We started with gold, and yesterday we considered the second gift, incense or frankincense, and today, on this very special day of the year, we shall consider the final gift, myrrh.

The Greek word for 'myrrh' is the word '*smurna*', which literally means 'bitter resin', and it is formed from an original word in the Semitic language. This ancient language uses this root word to describe the resin from a 'shrubby tree'. This resin is the gum from the tree which grows in Yemen and certain parts of Africa.

The fruit from this tree is slightly larger than a pea and is edible to a few people. Most people however, would find it too bitter. The resin is also very bitter, and it varies from reddish-yellow to reddish-brown, and it can even appear at certain times within the year as bright red in colour. The gum would be tapped from the tree and used for several purposes; this gum or resin was used as an antiseptic on a cut or a wound, it would also be used for a kind of stimulant. This use would entail either the tasting of the substance, or its inhalation.

Another use of this resin was for perfume, and in this form it was mixed with other agents to form the anointing oil for kings and priests. It was also used during the time of purification for women, and its final use was for the embalming of the dead.

These many uses made this gum quite expensive, and very special. As this gum was so special, it is no wonder that the wise men brought it with them when they wanted to convey to Jesus just how special they thought that He was. This gift could have had prophetic elements attached to it, although this could be stretching the point a little. However, during the life and ministry of Jesus, this gum or resin featured twice: once at His birth, and secondly, at His death. It was as if these men had brought a gift that would minister to Him during the two most momentous moments of His time on earth.

The gift was presented at His birth, which would have conveyed the thought of perfume, both for worship and anointing, as they considered Him to be the King of the Jews. Secondly, the resin was featured at His death, as on the cross they offered Him a drink, which the Old King James Bible called 'gall', and the NIV called 'wine vinegar'. This mixture was myrrh and vinegar and wine, and it was used as a kind of drug to deaden pain.

The Wise Men probably had no conception of the beginning and ending of the life of Jesus. However, they conveyed more than the simple use of gifts when they presented to Him their three special packages.

KEY PRAYER

Heavenly Father on this very special day of the year, I bring you my special offering of praise and thanksgiving. I pray that, as the wise men brought their gifts that would have produced a sweet fragrance upon their opening, may my offering of praise, on this Christmas Day, produce before you a sweet fragrance of worship.

December 26th

KEY WORD: **Celebration**

KEY VERSE: **Leviticus 23 : 41**

Celebrate this as a festival to the Lord for seven days each year. This is to be a lasting ordinance for the generations to come; celebrate it in the seventh month.

The Greek word for 'celebration' does not actually appear in either the NIV or the King James version of the New Testament, and in fact the Hebrew word for 'celebration' only occurs three times in the whole Bible. However, as we reach the end of the Christmas period, with all its aspects of celebration, we ought to consider just what it means to celebrate.

Christmas is celebrated in a variety of different ways in the different countries of the world, as for instance in some countries the Christmas period is extremely hot, while in other countries it is very cold. The 'western' concept of Christmas is formed in our minds by history and by location, as the period usually has snow and ice attached to it. It is also framed in our minds as a time of feasting and enjoyment, with lights, trees, presents, turkeys and many other aspects of activity that go to form the western concept of a 'real' Christmas.

However, in the eastern aspect of Christmas, the fields of Bethlehem are full of carol singers and party-goers, and it would not be Christmas without the concept of parades and processions, and music with dancing. The southern aspect of Christmas would be barbeques on a beach, and water activities, all very, very different aspects of celebration.

The New Testament features aspects of celebration without actually using the word, it is obvious that the Wise Men celebrated once they found the One that they had sought, and when they presented their gifts. The shepherds also celebrated when the angelic anthem was sung above them in the skies.

The song of Mary was also a celebration when she raised her voice and said, 'My soul magnifies the Lord'.

The aspect of celebration was clearly seen in the New Testament, although the word is not found. The only use of the word 'celebrate' or 'celebration' is three times in the Old Testament where its uses are confined to the book of Leviticus, where it appears twice, and the book of Isaiah, where it appears only once. On each of the three appearances three different Hebrew words are used. Firstly, there is the word '*halal*', which means to 'give praise', secondly, there is the word '*chagag*', which means to 'keep a festival', which is the one that appears in the key verse today. Thirdly, there is the word '*shabath*', which means 'to keep a sabbath'.

All three words are used for the concept of celebration and celebrating, although they each convey a different aspect of celebration. However, each word does convey the thought of great joy and great festival and great occasion.

Christmas in the whole world ought to have each aspect of these three Hebrew words within the differing forms of celebration. It might be cold and icy in some Christmas celebrations, or it could be hot and filled with beach activity. Yet, we should be ready to 'give praise', we should be ready to 'keep the festival', and we ought to be filled with the sense of 'keeping a Sabbath', in the sense that Christmas is holy and special.

My Journal ______________________________

____

____

____

____

KEY PRAYER

Heavenly Father, in my celebrating during this period of the year, help me to remember that this time is a special time, and that this time should be a great festival of thanksgiving and praise. Help me to keep this perspective during the whole period of Christmas.

December 27th

KEY WORD: **Leave**

KEY VERSE: **Hebrews 13 : 5**

Keep your lives free from the love of money and be content with what you have, because God has said, "Never will I leave you; never will I forsake you."

As we leave Christmas behind us, and as we journey towards the end of the year, we are going to spend the last few days of the old year reminding ourselves of some of the precious promises of God.

In the key verse today the promise is certainly very precious, as it makes two quite different statements. The Hebrew writer is quoting one of God's promises to Israel, and he is using it now in the context of the Church, that 'God will never leave us nor forsake us'.

The promise is twofold. On one hand God says that He will never 'leave' us, and on the other hand He says that He will never 'forsake' us. As the two concepts are quite different in their meaning, and in their application, we will consider one today, and the other tomorrow.

The writer of Hebrews reminds us that God will not leave us for one moment during our earthly walk with Him. The word that he chooses to use for this concept is a very interesting word. The Greek word for 'leave' is the word '*aniemi*', and it means 'to loose'. The word is formed by the combination of two different words, firstly the word '*ana*', which means 'back', and secondly the word '*hiemi*', which means 'to send'. The combining of these two words therefore produces the concept, that throughout our lives, God will never 'cause us to go back or to be loosened'.

However, this promise is conditional on the fact that we do not choose to be bound by the love of money, and that we are content with what we have. We cannot take a conditional promise and try to make it unconditional, we have to obey the conditions in order to receive the promise. I remember years ago hearing a very well known preacher preaching on the promises of God, and he commenced reading from verse two of a certain chapter, and he concluded his reading at verse nine. He then preached powerfully on the wonderful promises that were granted to us within these verses. However, the verse before the one that he commenced preaching from, and the verse following the one that he was preaching from, contained two vitally important conditions. He sought to claim and preach the promises, without fulfilling the conditions of the promises. In fact, he totally ignored the conditions.

We only get the promises if we obey the conditions. Therefore, in this key verse, we must not be bound with the love of money, and we must seek to be content with what we have, in order to receive the promise that 'He will never leave us'. The concept is that God will not 'loose us to go back', in the sense that now we have come to Him, and found Him to be our salvation, we are tied to Him in the same way that a slave is tied to his master. The slave is not free to leave, nor can he go back to his old way of life, as he is now bound to his new master. The promise is the same in love and new relationship. God has purchased us at great price, and we now belong to Him. He will not allow us to go free. As long as we remain contented in Him, we are bound to Him, and we belong to Him, and we are no longer free.

As we pray today we should remember to thank God for the precious promises that work for us, when we fulfil the conditions.

KEY PRAYER

Heavenly Father, I praise you today for your promises that are faithful and true as long as I abide in you. Help me to be just as faithful and just as true, so that I may receive and enjoy all the precious promises that you have bestowed upon me.

December 28th

KEY WORD: **Forsake**

KEY VERSE: **Hebrews 13 : 5**

Keep your lives free from the love of money and be content with what you have, because God has said, "Never will I leave you; never will I forsake you."

As we leave Christmas behind us, and as we journey on towards the end of the year, we are spending the last few days of the old year reminding ourselves of some of the precious promises of God.

We saw yesterday that God has promised never to allow us to go back to our old way of life, or never to allow Himself to leave us, if we content ourselves in Him. Today we are looking at the second word that appears in this key verse, the word 'forsake'. God will never forsake us if we fulfil the conditions of the promise. And they are that we do not allow ourselves to be bound by the love of money, and that we find contentment in Him alone.

The Greek word for 'forsake' is a very graphic word indeed, and it brings to us a new element of truth. The word used is the word '*enkataleipo*', which means 'abandoned' or 'helpless'. The thought therefore being conveyed by this word, is the thought of God never abandoning us or leaving us helpless. The word is once again formed by the combination of two different words, firstly, the word '*en*', which means 'in', and secondly, the word '*kataleipo*', which means 'leave behind in straits'. The amazing promise is therefore, that God will not, and cannot, leave us behind to be helplessly abandoned.

The full thought is that God is always moving on, and always moving forward, in such a way that if we do not keep in step with Him, we will be left behind. However, God cares so much for us that He will not allow us to be left helplessly abandoned, He will always carry us when we cannot carry ourselves.

This wonderful promise was made firstly to Israel, and this promise was kept to the very letter, as God never did allow Himself to leave Israel or to abandon His people. However, the sad thing was that the people of Israel did not keep their side of the bargain, and they failed God many, many times. The Hebrew writer took God's promise to Israel, and brought it into the New Testament, stating that God has made the very same promise to the Church. God will always keep His side of the bargain, if we keep our side of the bargain.

Paul uses the very same word, '*enkataleipo*', when he wrote to his first epistle to the church in Corinth. He stated in chapter four and verse nine that, during his life and ministry, he had on many occasions been 'perplexed, but not in despair, persecuted but not "abandoned", and struck down but not destroyed'.

His testimony was that God had brought him through every trial and every test, and that God had never failed him once. As we draw near to the end of this old year, and as we claim the precious promises of God, we will find that, as God did not fail us this year, so He will not fail us next year. We will also find that, as God fulfilled His promises to us this year, so He will fulfil His promises to us next year. This ought to bring us to a place of worship and a place of praise.

KEY PRAYER

Heavenly Father, as we draw to the end of this year, it is with grateful praise that I review the year, and find that you have never failed me once. Thank you for all the precious promises that you fulfilled for me during this year, and thank you for the promises that await me during next year. You have been so faithful this year, please forgive my unfaithfulness over the past twelve months, and help me to become more faithful and true during the next twelve months.

December 29th

KEY WORD: **Contentment**

KEY VERSE: **1 Timothy 6 : 6**

But godliness with contentment is great gain.

Over the past few days we having been considering the precious promises of God, that He would never leave us and never forsake us. We noticed, as we studied these promises, that they were conditional promises, in other words, if we fulfil the conditions, then God would fulfil His promises. The condition to the promise of God never leaving us and never forsaking us was that we must not allow the love of money to bind us, and that we should be content with what we have.

As we fulfil the conditions that are attached to the promises of God, then He fulfils His side of the bargain with His fulfilment of promises. In order to fully understand the conditions that are attached to the promise that we have studied over the last few days, we are going to consider two words, one today and the second one tomorrow.

The writer to the Hebrews said that we are to 'be content with what we have', in order to receive the promise. Paul wrote a similar thing to Timothy in the key verse today, stating that 'godliness with contentment is great gain'.

The Greek word for 'contentment' is '*autarkeia*', which is a difficult word to fully translate. The NIV settles for 'contentment', as does the Old King James Bible. However, the word actually means 'satisfaction' or 'self-sufficiency'. This word only appears in this form twice in the New Testament, and on both occasions it carries the same meaning, 'to be self-sufficient'.

The truth that Paul is seeking to convey to Timothy is that, if we rest in what we have, and do not strive for money or material things, God will provide for us, and we will come to a place of great peace and satisfaction.

The word is formed by the combination of two different words which, as we have seen, often happens in Greek when a truth needs to be conveyed fully. The two words are *'autos'*, which means 'self', and *'arkeo'*, which means 'sufficient', the truth is therefore, not that we must become self-sufficient in the sense of being able to live without God or anyone else, but that we ourselves become satisfied with whatever we have. Whenever we are striving for more, in the terms of money or materialism, we are never satisfied, and we are never at peace. But when we learn to rest in the fact that God will always supply our need, and that He will never leave us or forsake us, there is peace. Our job in life is to learn to be satisfied within ourselves.

This word touches everything in the Christian life, it reaches our finances and our materialism, it touches our food and our clothing, and it reaches to our ability in God and our gifting and ministries. We must learn to be content with what we have and what we are because, if we can reach this level of trust, we will be at peace. We may never have plenty, but we will always have enough. So the promise simply is that, when we have enough, and all our needs are met by a loving and generous God, 'there is great gain'.

My Journal ______________________________

KEY PRAYER

Heavenly Father, with only a few days to go before this year comes to an end, please help me to become more and more at peace with myself, so that I can learn to trust you for all my needs. Help me, too, to rest in you, so that I become contented with my life and my future, and my destiny.

December 30th

KEY WORD: ***Great gain***

KEY VERSE: **1 Timothy 6 : 6**

But godliness with contentment is great gain.

In order to fully understand what Paul was seeking to convey to Timothy within this key verse, we have to understand Paul's motives. Paul, throughout his life, was always content with what he had, he never once complained about his trials and persecutions, and he always rested in what he had. He once stated that he was content with whatever took place, sometimes he had much, and at other times he had very little, but he had learned to be content.

It was this kind of lifestyle that he was urging Timothy to adopt, and he did it with great care and yet with great sharpness. He used two Greek words to bring this truth home to Timothy with a great deal of urgency. Paul said that 'godliness with contentment is great gain', and the two words that he used to convey this truth of 'great gain' were, '*megas porismos*'. The two words mean quite simply 'a measure of great intensity and procurement'. The meaning is quite simple. However, within the fairly simple translation, there is tremendous force with the word '*porismos*'. This word conveys the thought of something being granted with great emphasis, and in abundance.

The concept of this word is that God will pour out for us anything that we need during our daily walk with Him, and that during the entire duration of our lives here on earth God will provide for us, and bring to us, whatever our desires might be. He will not grant our 'wants' but He will always supply our needs, and this provision will be with great measure and great emphasis.

This old year is almost at an end, and with the end of the

year it is always good to review what has happened to us during the days, and the weeks, and the months that have just passed into history. During all this time we can truly say that God never once let us down and never once did He fail us. Throughout every day of this year His daily provision was such that we were daily loaded with benefits, and daily touched by grace and care. The only time that we struggled during the year would be when our contentment level had dropped, and when we would have sought for more and more.

When we learned to rest in Him, and when we were at peace with whatever came our way, then God fulfilled all His promises to us, with great abundance.

At the close of the year, we should remember these lessons and we should seek to correct the imbalances of this year. We should praise Him for all that is past, and, as a new year is about to commence, we should praise God for all that is yet to come.

My Journal

KEY PRAYER

Heavenly Father, thank you for your daily provision that has come to me this year with great abundance. I bless you for daily grace and for your constant favour. As I commence a new year, I do it with the intention of learning the lessons of the past, so that I do not make the same mistakes again.

December 31st

KEY WORD: **Amen**

KEY VERSE: **Revelation 22 : 21**

The Grace of the Lord Jesus be with God's people. Amen.

This is the final day of the year, and over the past twelve months we have considered hundreds of Greek words and sought to uncover the full truth of each one. We have studied these key words and learnt new lessons, we have prayed key prayers and sought to praise God each day for the lessons that we are seeking to put into practice. We have also written key thoughts into journal notes so that we might creatively understand what we have learned.

On this last day of an old year we are concluding all our studies with the very last word of the New Testament, the word 'Amen'.

This word is the same in both Old Testament Hebrew and New Testament Greek, and it is written the same in English, it is simply '*Amen*'. The word comes from the Hebrew and was translated into Greek and then into English in its same form, and the meaning has not been lost at all in these translations, it simply means two things.

The first meaning is when God utters 'Amen'. When God says 'Amen', it means 'it is and it shall be so'. The second meaning is when we, the Church, utter 'Amen'; when we state this word it means 'so let it be', or 'we agree'.

In the first instance, when God speaks this word, He is confirming His own actions, in the sense that, as the creator and sustainer of all things, He is speaking of finality and completeness. His 'Amen' is complete, and it is total, and nothing can be added to it or taken away from it.

When we, the Church, speak this word, we are only echoing what God has done, and we are expressing an agreement with Him. Our 'Amen' means 'so be it', or 'we agree', and we find completeness in His work.

In the Early Church 'Amen' was always expressed at the conclusion of prayers and worship, as it was felt that, having prayed or having worshipped, it was right to say 'so be it', when prayer and praise was finished. This kind of conclusion was a direct copying of the Old Testament pattern of worship when Israel would say an audible agreement at the conclusion of prayer and thanksgiving.

'Amen' was also a title of Jesus, and it appeared in this form when John was writing his Revelation. In chapter 3 and verse 14, he calls Jesus the 'Amen and the faithful and true'.

'Amen' also appears when the Church prayed together and everyone agreed with everyone else's prayers, this was another form of agreement.

In the key verse today, our very last verse of the year, the word expresses total agreement to the Second Coming of the Lord. John wrote 'even so come Lord Jesus', and the Church said 'Amen'. Then John stated that God's grace would always be manifested upon God's people until that great day, and the Church again said 'Amen'.

May God bless these thoughts to you, and all the key words that we have studied together. We should now say together 'Amen Lord Jesus, thank you for truth'.

My Journal

KEY PRAYER

Heavenly Father, I humbly bow in your presence to give you thanks for another year of blessing. I praise you for the good days, and I praise you for the difficult times that I have seen this year. I simply say at the end of the year, Amen; and Amen, for all that you have done, and for all that is yet to come.

Also by Geoff Feasey

Putting Things Into Perspective

From the Foreword, by Eric McComb
Superintendent of the Elim Pentecostal Churches, Ireland

A quick scan of the chapter headngs within this book motivates the inquiring mind to look further and to seek to assimilate the contents of this very enjoyable and stimulating book.

This book on leadership is not a heavy read, yet 'Putting Things Into Perspective' prepares the experienced and inexperienced leader. to carry the sometimes heavy burden of local church leadership. The author's easy to listen to preaching style of communication has found its way into every chapter of this book and Geoff has an ability to integrate a personal story of illustration into the fabric of the teaching material. This easy style of communication helps the reader to appreciate that this is not one of those 'how to books' by someone who has not experienced the 'pit face'. Rather the material and content is cut from the richness of personal encounter, which has more to do with practical advice based on participation than knowledge acquired within an academic institution. However, Geoff makes sure that personal testimony or the accounts of first-hand knowledge of the subject is never allowed to eclipse the teaching of Scripture.

Those taking the first steps in leadership and those who are experienced in leadership will find this book invaluable reading, especially when the blaze of enthusiasm has died out, caused by those who are less concerned and completely dispassionate to their goals and principles.

While the sacrificing of 'sacred cows' in church practice is often legitimate and justifiable this can be expedited in a more satisfactory manner if relationships within the local leadership are strong and healthy. Relationships of the right calibre and how to develop and maintain them should not be left to trial and error. There is instructive material here on how to avoid doing the right things in the wrong way, and how to take the one right step which avoids futile miles of lost time travelling in the wrong direction.

Holy Spirit leadership is of vital importance. This book clearly demonstrates the need for people to be motivated by Holy Spirit leaders who have gained and earned the trust and respect of their people through wise and careful use of their gifting.

Geoff allows himself to be a believer of his beliefs – beliefs that have been born and developed by his reading of the Scriptures and his personal experience through years of Christian leadership.

From the Introduction, by Goeff Feasey

One of the greatest assets that a Denomination or a Movement has is its local level of leadership, which is called in some instances, the church session or the church board or the leadership team. In general terms this overseeing board is formed by drawing together people from the ranks of the local church, which include the pastors, the elders, the deacons and the heads of departments, and could include anyone else within the church who could be 'appointed to serve'.

A great deal is required from those in leadership positions today. Many books have been written and many seminars conducted and many sermons preached covering the vast spectrum of leadership.

We expect, quite rightly, our national church leaders to be 'people of God'; they should be able to manifest wisdom and faith, they should be able to make important decisions with clarity and justice and to be constantly full of the Spirit, manifesting 'the Fruit of the Spirit' and 'the gifts of the Spirit', all of the time. High expectations indeed!

This constant high expectation is part and parcel of the pressure of national leadership and indeed all aspects of leadership.

If we have this kind of expectancy of our national leaders, is it wrong to expect the same kind of leadership gifting and attitude from our local level of leadership? It is vital that we have the right men and women with gifts and abilities at every level of leadership within the church.

The right people in the right place at the right time, both at national and local level.

Not wishing to add to the proliferation of leadership books just for the sake of it, the thoughts contained within this book deal with lessons from the Scriptures and from a wide aspect of Christian leadership that has been gleaned from almost 30 years of Christian ministry. I just felt that I wanted to put a few things into perspective' concerning leadership, which is why 'Putting things Into Perspective' came about.

They are lessons collated from sermons and seminars that I have given to churches and leaders throughout these years, and they have been reformed into short and concise chapters. These short and concise chapters will help leaders to imbibe the thoughts quickly and with ease.

They are simple, basic lessons that are aimed at leadership in a collective sense rather than at leaders as individuals. They are simple lessons that will teach, encourage, exhort, challenge and stimulate local leaders to 'better things'. They are lessons that will promote among us the charge that Paul gave to Timothy when he urged him to 'be an example to the believers', 1 Tim. 4:12.

1 Timothy 4 is a very important chapter for leaders. However, there are three other chapters in the New Testament that every leader should read on his or her knees before God. 1 Peter 5, 1 Timothy 3, and Titus 1.

Within these three chapters – important chapters from the pen of apostles – are contained the spiritual requirements of all church leaders. I firmly believe that every church session/church board, should set aside time to evaluate these chapters at regular intervals within the programme of its leadership meetings.

Our standards for leaders must be Scriptural standards; our leaders must be men and women of God, and our leaders must be 'God-appointed' for areas of service.

I feel that so often just to fill certain places on the leadership team we have tended at times to lower standards so that 'all the places might be filled'. Often they have been filled by good people, righteous people, people of great ability, but not necessarily the people with the right gifting for this particular ministry.

We must learn how to recognise each other's ministry and to be bold enough and brave enough to place ministries in the right place at the right time.

For instance, how do we find an elder? Is it through the vote of the church members? Is it through an appointment of the Church Board? Is it through the ballot box or the voting procedure? I would want to say that it is none of these. None of these measures can really produce an elder. It is God that raises up the gift of an elder within a local church, elders are birthed by the heartbeat of a giving God who delights to raise up ministries that bless and encourage His church.

Leadership teams/church boards should be seeking God on a regular basis, asking Him to raise up ministries within their local church, men and women after His own heart.

Leadership teams should be creating the space and the atmosphere for gifts to grow and blossom. As God raises them up and as space is created for them to grow, then the church members can recognise them by their voting procedures.

You cannot 'make a leader', and you cannot 'produce an elder', you can only recognise what God has produced.

Let's raise the standard high and keep it there, so that local leaders can prosper and minister in the best possible way. The thoughts that I offer aim to set a high standard and to place a high value on gifts and ministries within the local leadership team.

Lessons will be learned and focus will be placed upon excellence, so that leaders might be 'leaders'. There are many real life illustrations mentioned within the chapters of this book. I have deliberately changed the names of some of those mentioned, not necessarily 'to protect the innocent', but in order that those who are mentioned will not easily be offended by actions or feelings that were expressed in earlier times of their spiritual development.

Tom Marshall from New Zealand, in his excellent book 'Understanding Leadership', makes the comment that there is a 'crisis of leadership within American society' and that 'this lack of leadership is also within the American church and the church is being led by managers not leaders'. We could easily add to this comment that it is not only in America that this has been noticed.

If we get the right people, in the right place, at the right time, maybe we could correct this lack of leadership that seems to be within the Church at this time. The lessons within these writings may help the birth of leaders to take place and possibly help them to function better within the collective leadership teams of our churches.

My prayer is that we all function according to our various individual giftings and ministries, and that we also function collectively to the best of our abilities. The thoughts contained within this book are offered with the hope that we can all attain this goal.